RACHEL CARSON

Witness for Nature

RACHEL CARSON

Witness

for 

Nature

LINDA LEAR

HENRY HOLT AND COMPANY NEW YORK

Henry Holt and Company, Inc.
Publishers since 1866
115 West 18th Street
New York, New York 10011

Henry Holt ® is a registered trademark
of Henry Holt and Company, Inc.

Published in Canada by Fitzhenry & Whiteside Ltd.,
195 Allstate Parkway, Markham, Ontario L3R 4T8.

The author gratefully acknowledges permission to quote from the letters of Mary Scott Skinker (granted by Martha Skinker) and from the letters of Dorothy Thompson Seif and the letters of Mary Frye Llewelyn (each granted by the authors).

Frontispiece: Rachel Carson testifying before the U.S. Senate Government Operations Subcommittee Hearings on Environmental Hazards, June 4, 1963.

Library of Congress Cataloging-in-Publication Data
Lear, Linda J., date
Rachel Carson : witness for nature / Linda Lear. — 1st ed.
p. cm.
Includes bibliographical references and index.
ISBN 0-8050-3427-7 (alk. paper)
1. Carson, Rachel, 1907–1964. 2. Biologists—United States—Biography. 3. Environmentalists—United States—Biography. 4. Science writers—United States—Biography. I. Title.
QH31.C33L43 1997 97-8324
570'.92—dc21
[B]

Henry Holt books are available for special promotions and premiums. For details contact: Director, Special Markets.

First Edition 1997

Designed by Michelle McMillian

Printed in the United States of America
All first editions are printed on acid-free paper. ∞

1 3 5 7 9 10 8 6 4 2

To the loving memory of my father and mother,
James C. and Henrietta D. Lear

and for my son,
Ian Cole Lear-Nickum

Contents

Acknowledgments

My search for Rachel Carson has absorbed almost a decade. It has taken me full circle from my childhood home a few hills to the north of Carson's birthplace in Springdale to another Maryland suburb just west of her last home in Silver Spring. My exploration of her life has been long, often arduous, but never without generous companionship.

Writing Carson's life became a possibility through the intercession of four of Carson's closest friends: Paul Brooks, Carson's editor; Jeanne V. Davis, her administrative assistant; Shirley A. Briggs, Carson's colleague, a founder and executive director emerita of the Rachel Carson Council, and now the curator of the Council's Rachel Carson History Project; and Ruth Scott, a premier Pennsylvania naturalist. Without their personal friendship and advocacy this biography would never have been possible.

Since Carson's literary and professional papers were carefully screened by her literary executor prior to their deposit at the Beinecke Library, interviews with those who knew Carson or who were involved in one way or another with her life and work constitute a major source for this work. A list of those who graciously allowed me interviews is to be found in the bibliography. Helga Sandburg Crile, Frank Egler, the Reverend Duncan Howlett, Margaret Kieran, Martha Skinker, and Stewart Udall have also given me valuable material from their own collections.

I owe special debts in this regard to the family of Stanley Freeman, Jr. Stanley and Madeleine Freeman have shared letters, photographs, books, and diaries. They have patiently endured long visits and endless questions. Martha Freeman allowed me to have copies of the letters between her grandmother and Carson before they were published by Beacon Press and willingly shared her insights into people and relationships. I am particularly grateful for the Freeman family's permission to use and to quote from the unpublished letters in their possession.

I have enjoyed the direct support of three institutions. A Senior Postdoctoral Fellowship from the Smithsonian Institution enabled me to benefit from the enormous resources of scholarship, collection, and access available there as nowhere else. My fellowship committee, Pamela Henson, Patricia Gossel, Pete Daniel, and Jeffrey Stine, helped me find my way through a plethora of riches. My day-to-day debts are to the staff of the Office of the Smithsonian Institution Archives; its acting director, John Jamison; and its current director, Edie Hedlin. Pam Henson made it possible for me to continue my tenure as a Research Collaborator after the end of the fellowship. My immediate colleagues in the Joseph Henry Papers, Marc Rothenberg, editor, Kathleen Dorman, Deborah Jeffries, and Frank Millikan, have put up with me for the past four years of intense writing in residence among them. Their gifts of kindness and collegiality have been extraordinary. I am also grateful to Smithsonian librarians Polly Lasker and Valerie Wheat.

A Frederick Beinecke Fellowship for research at the Beinecke Rare Book and Manuscript Library at Yale University in 1994 allowed me several months' residence. For the first time I was able to immerse myself in the Carson papers there. I wish to thank Ralph Franklin, the Director of the Beinecke Library; Acting Director George Miles; and Archivist Diane Ducharme for the many courtesies each extended during that period. Patricia Willis, Curator of the Yale Collection of American Literature, was particularly generous in sharing her expertise. Stephen Jones and Dorothea Reading of Reader Services found ways to further my research and make a visiting fellow's life easier. The Carson Papers were first processed and described in 1990 by William K. Finley, now an archivist at the College of Charleston. His insights into various aspects of the correspondence were enormously helpful.

At George Washington University, Roderick S. French, until recently Vice President for Academic Affairs and Barbara Marshall, of the same office, both former colleagues and friends; John Logsdon, director of the Center for International Science and Technology Policy and Kim Lutz, administrative assistant; Edward Berkowitz, History Department Chair; and colleagues Robert Kenny, William Becker, and Quadir Amiryar of Gelman Library have all been instrumental in extending the privileges and resources of the university to me over the course of many years and especially helped this project along during hard times.

I have consulted numerous archives and collections in the course of my research and have accumulated debts to talented and informed curators, archivists, and librarians at each. I wish to acknowledge the contributions of John Cummins, Archivist, and Patricia Braeman of Chatham College; Gary Link, Allegheny County Records Center; James Stimpert, Ferdinand Hamburger, Jr., Archives, Johns Hopkins University; Richard Fyffe, Thomas J. Dodd Center for Research, University of Connecticut; Dianne Gutscher, Special Collections, Bowdoin College; Mary Ann Wallace, Special Collections, Westbrook College; Charles Huhn, Hood College; Rose Novil, National Louis University; Michael H. Nash, The Hagley Museum and Library; G. Thomas Tanselle, The Guggenheim Foundation Archives; Wayne Olson, National Library of Agriculture; Gary Weir, Historian, Contemporary History Branch, Naval History Center; Stephen Gegg, Woods Hole Oceanographic Institute Archives; Judy Ashmore, Woods Hole Marine Biological Laboratory Library; William Eigelsbach, University of Tennessee; John Glieber, Animal Welfare Institute; Gretchen Young-Weiner, Cranbrook Institute of Science Archives; Janice Goldblum, National Academy of Sciences Library; Carol Tomer, Cleveland Clinic Archives; Brian Rogers, Special Collections, Connecticut College; James Herring, Jimmy Carter Presidential Library; Herbert Pankratz, Dwight D. Eisenhower Presidential Library; Mary Wolfskill, Manuscript Division, Library of Congress; Jimmie Rush, National Archives and Records Administration; Matthew Perry, Patuxent Wildlife Research Center; Jonathan Shaw, Bok Tower Gardens Library and Archives; Roland Bauman, Oberlin College; Drexel Institute of Technology Archives; Montgomery County Records Center; The Martin Luther King, Jr., Library Photo Archives, Washington, D.C.; Emily Higgins, All Souls Unitarian Church Archives; Stephen M. Lott, Verger, and Richard Hewlett, Archives of the Washington National Cathedral.

I am especially grateful to Shirley Briggs, whose personal and professional archives, photographs, letters, diaries, and memory are without equal for material on Carson, and to my agent, Frances Collin, who made available the unique collection bequeathed to her as trustee for the estate of Rachel Carson. Her enthusiastic representation of this work and her advice and caring have been unfailingly generous.

I am grateful to the following newspaper archives, whose staff provided microfilm as well as reference assistance: *Boston Post* Archives, *Philadelphia Inquirer* Archives, *Baltimore Sun* Archives, *The Detroit News* Archives, and *The Boothbay Register* Archives.

Registrars at the following institutions provided crucial chronological data: Columbia Teacher's College, George Washington University, Northern Colorado University, Washington University, and National Louis University.

Two groups of scholars helped me as I struggled with the challenges of writing Carson's life. I owe particular debts to Marc Pachter, Special Counselor to the Secretary of the Smithsonian, who leads the Washington Biography Seminar. I have profited greatly from a decade of dialogue emanating from the monthly sessions of this group, but I am especially indebted to Marc.

Early in my research Neil Goodwin, founder and producer of Peace River Films, Cambridge, Massachusetts, asked me to be a consultant and to write the historical background for his production of "The Silent Spring of Rachel Carson" filmed for PBS's *The American Experience* in February 1993. I am grateful for the opportunity he gave me to work in his world. My colleagues on this project included the best and the brightest: William Cronon, University of Wisconsin; David Pimentel, Cornell University; Suzanne Smith, George Mason University; Margo Barnes Goodwin; and Sharon O'Brien. I am indebted to them for sharing their expertise and particular understanding of Carson's work.

Many individual scholars contributed to my understanding of the times in which Carson lived, and many others influenced my thinking about her life. Foremost among these is Clayton Koppes, whose friendship spans over two decades and whose thinking about environmental history has deeply influenced my own. I wish to thank Allida Black, Darlis Miller, Jennifer Logan, Ralph Lutts, Cheryll Glotfelty, Joseph B. C. White, Susan Hader, Samuel Hays, Carol Gartner, H. Patricia Hynes, Leo Ribuffo, Sharon Kingsland, Jane Maienshein, Edmund Russell III, John Perkins, Yaakov Garb, Jeffrey Ellis, Sara Jamison, Christine Orvavec, Craig Waddell, and Daria Martel, who have read, listened, conferred, and consoled for too many years but have never lost their interest in what I was trying to accomplish. Sandra Steingraber, biologist, writer, and cancer activist, gave me the perspective I needed to evaluate Carson's illness and her medical treatment. I owe other debts of a personal nature to Dr. Marc Bergman of Boca Raton, Florida, Dr. Bette Ann Weinstein of Bethesda, Maryland, and the Reverend Caroline Smith Pyle of Washington, D.C. Each of them has contributed to this work and to my well-being.

Few authors work very long without accumulating debts to those who save them from computer failure and irretrievable time trapped in assorted technological nightmares. Others named here have assisted in photographic reproduction, research, archiving, and indexing. I am grateful for the many talents of Michael Weeks, and to Linn Shapiro, Ph.D., Steven K. Allison, Ph.D., Lynn Wojcik, Terrica Gibson, Joan Mathys, Matthew Briggs, and David Schwartzman.

Cynthia Vartan, Editor-at-Large at Henry Holt, has guided this manuscript through the unforeseen travails that confronted and delayed its completion. For the lifetime of literary skills she brought to this work, and for her steadfastness, I am truly grateful.

Over the years I have come to count on the knowledge and advice of Roland C. Clement. He has willingly read parts of this manuscript, always to my advantage and edification. His friendship has been an unexpected gift.

Sandra Loving Linder, my dearest friend and esteemed literary critic, has read this manuscript several times. Her reading and editing saved me from assorted embarrassments and made this biography both richer and simpler.

My husband, John W. Nickum, Jr., has been faithful to this endeavor and has never wavered in his willingness to help me achieve it. For his sacrifices and his steady reassurance, I will always be grateful.

At the end of 1994, just as I was deep into my writing, I lost my best and truest muse, my mother, Henrietta DeHaven Lear. She was my touchstone, my keenest listener, and my best critic. With her death, I shared another sadder dimension of Carson's life. Twenty months later, my father, James C. Lear, died. He encouraged me to take this path and never questioned its course or successful outcome. These life events set this work back in different ways and at different points, but I'd like to hope that these losses were also enrichments to the process of writing a life of one for whom suffering was no stranger.

When I began this biography my son, Ian Cole Lear-Nickum, was ten years old. When it is published he will be a freshman in college. Growing up in the shadow of Rachel Carson, he has gained a perspective that I hope will enrich his life in the years ahead. He has willingly shared his time with Rachel and grown to understand my enthusiasm for the relevance of her witness to his generation. To honor his love, and for his support of his mother's creative life, this book is dedicated to him.

L. L.

Bethesda, Maryland
Spring 1997

Sources for Illustrations

1. Frontispiece. Photograph by Vincent A. Finnigan for *American Forests* magazine. Courtesy Vincent A. Finnigan.
2. Robert Warden Carson. Courtesy Rachel Carson History Project/Rachel Carson Council (RCHP/RCC).
3. Maria McLean. Courtesy RCHP/RCC.
4. Maria, Marian, Rachel, and Robert. Courtesy RCHP/RCC.
5. Rachel reading a story to her dog. Courtesy RCHP/RCC.
6. Rachel and her classmates. Courtesy RCHP/RCC.
7. Marian, Rachel, and Robert at the "beach." Courtesy RCHP/RCC.
8. Marian, Robert in uniform, and Rachel. Courtesy RCHP/RCC.
9. Rachel at the time of her high school graduation. Courtesy RCHP/RCC.
10. Robert Warden Carson and Maria Carson visit Rachel at Pennsylvania College for Women. Courtesy RCHP/RCC.
11. Grace Croff. Courtesy RCHP/RCC.
12. Mary Scott Skinker. Courtesy Martha Skinker.
13. Cora Helen Coolidge. Courtesy Chatham College Archives.
14. Margaret Stevenson. Courtesy Chatham College Archives.
15. Helen Myers. Courtesy Chatham College Archives.
16. Rachel Louise Carson. Courtesy Chatham College Archives.
17. Carson's entry photograph, Johns Hopkins University. Courtesy Ferdinand Hamburger, Jr. Archives.
18. Dorothy Hamilton Algire. Photograph by Glenn Algire. Courtesy Anne Algire Moretti.
19. Rachel at Woods Hole Biological Laboratory. Photograph by Mary Frye. Courtesy RCHP/RCC.
20. Elmer Higgins. Courtesy NOAA.
21. Clarence Cottam. Courtesy Office of Smithsonian Institution Archives.
22. Lionel "Bert" A. Walford. Courtesy Sarah Hollister.
23. Rachel Carson, author, editor, and aquatic biologist. Coutesy RCHP/RCC.
24. Kay Howe. Photograph by Shirley A. Briggs. Courtesy Kay H. Roberts.
25. Shirley Briggs. Photograph by Albert Linton. Courtesy Shirley A. Briggs.

RACHEL CARSON

Witness for Nature

Prologue

The prematurely white-haired junior senator from Connecticut peered over his fashionable reading glasses at the famous lead-off witness. It was the fourth day of hearings called by his special subcommittee on environmental hazards. Things had gone very smoothly so far; his staff had done well. But today was the big event.

An overflow crowd packed the small, windowless hearing room #102 on the ground floor corner of the New Senate Office Building. Television lights illuminated the walnut-paneled room, revealing stains on the maroon carpet and watermarks on the matching velvet drapes. Cameramen and equipment filled the aisles and cluttered the small space between the hearing table and the dais. Reporters checked their microphones and recording equipment.

The witness sat calmly but expectantly at the table, hands folded in her lap. Her carefully worded testimony, on large typewritten note cards, was arranged neatly in front of her. She seemed unaware of the commotion in the room or the anticipation of the crowd. She spoke to no one.

The room quieted when the senator cleared his throat and began his well-rehearsed paraphrase of Abraham Lincoln's remark on meeting Harriet Beecher Stowe. "Miss Carson . . . we welcome you here. You are the lady who started all this. Will you please proceed. . . ."

Rachel Carson was ready. She had thought about what she wanted to say in such a place long before she had finished writing *Silent Spring*. This was the moment she had hoped for: one final chance to translate her vision into policy, to make a difference, to change the way people looked at the natural world, to stop the warfare against it. Graciously thanking Senator Abraham Ribicoff for his invitation to present her views, she put on her thick black-framed glasses and began reading her testimony in her distinctive, low voice. The room hushed, all eyes on the attractive, middle-aged woman in the fashionable sage-green suit. She began: "The problem you have chosen to explore is one that must be solved in our time. I feel strongly that a beginning must be made on it now—in this session of Congress. . . ."

Her words marked an end and a beginning. As she spoke, Rachel Carson was dying of cancer. This appearance, and one two days later before the Senate Committee on Commerce, would be her last on Capitol Hill. Several present that sunny spring morning in June 1963 might have predicted that Carson's recommendations eventually would be translated into public policy, but probably no one could have guessed that as she spoke, her vision was already shaping a powerful social movement that would alter the course of American history.

Senator Ribicoff later observed that Rachel Carson's power came from the fact that she believed in her vision so strongly, had accepted her obligation to bear witness. The senator sensed that Carson was that rare person who was passionately committed when few others believed very much in anything. Hers was a singular vision encompassing nothing less than the mysteriously intricate living world whose workings she understood so deeply and described for others with such poetry.

Carson could not be silent. She had peered into the fairy caves and tide pools of her beloved Maine coast and had seen the fragility and tenacity with which even the smallest creatures struggled for life against the relentless ocean tides. Her flashlight had captured the unforgettable spectacle of the solitary crab on the rocky beach at midnight, vulnerable yet unassailably resilient. She could not stand idly by and say nothing when all that was in jeopardy, when human existence itself was endangered. That was the message that brought her to the Senate hearing room. That was what had sustained her for the past five difficult years.

Rachel Carson was an unlikely person to start any sort of popular movement. She treasured her solitude, defended her privacy, rarely joined any organization; but she meant to bear witness. She wrote a revolutionary book in terms that were acceptable to a middle class emerging from the lethargy of postwar affluence and woke them to their neglected responsibilities. It was a book in which she shared her vision of life one last time. In the sea and the bird's song she had discovered the wonder and mystery of life. Her witness for these, and the integrity of all life, would make a difference.

1

"*Wild Creatures Are My Friends*"

Most of all, it was her determination that set her apart. As a child, Rachel Louise Carson decided that she would be a writer. Literary talent, perhaps genius, and a hard-driving intelligence brought her that. But at the base of it, there was a ferocious will.[1]

Her literary career began innocently enough in the spring of 1918, when she was weeks shy of her eleventh birthday. Spring was always a season laden with meaning for her, and this one was no exception. Ever since she was quite little, she had been reading the stories written by other young people published in the children's section of *St. Nicholas Magazine*. Now Rachel was ready to enter her own story of 253 carefully counted words in the *St. Nicholas* League Contest #223 as described in the May issue.

Her mother endorsed the unlined coarse-grained tablet page in the upper right corner, certifying that "this story was written without assistance, by my little ten-year-old daughter, Rachel." The next day her father dropped it at the Springdale, Pennsylvania, post office on his way to the Butler Street train station. The little girl was confident this would be the beginning of her writing career, and she was right.[2]

When Rachel recalled that childhood time much later, she always linked this first *St. Nicholas* story with her love of nature and her mother's influence. "I can remember no time," she told a group of women in 1954, "even in earliest childhood, when I didn't assume I was going to be a writer. Also, I can remember no time when I wasn't interested in the out-of-doors and the whole world of nature. Those interests, I know, I inherited from my mother and have always shared with her." At other times when she spoke of her childhood, she would add that among her earliest conscious memories was a "feeling of absolute fascination for everything relating to the ocean."[3]

Springdale residents who remember Rachel as a young girl tell the story, perhaps true, perhaps apocryphal, that her romance with the ocean began one day when she found a large fossilized shell in the rocky outcroppings on the family's hillside property. It provoked questions that Rachel wanted answers to. She wondered where it had come from, what animal had made it and lived within it, where it had gone, and what happened to the sea that had nurtured it so long ago. Whether such a single event provoked her curiosity and drew her to the sea or not, the account is intriguing. Town children found and collected many fossilized shells on the Carson property as well as along the riverbanks. True or not, the story underscores the wisdom that "to understand the fashion of any life, one must know the land it is lived in."[4]

Rachel Carson was first of all a child of the Allegheny River, its woods and wetlands. Although she could not see the wide bend of the Allegheny from the front porch of the Carson homestead near the top of the hill just off Colfax Lane, she could look over the white pines that grew along the north bank and see the traffic on the road running parallel along the opposite shoreline. She could hear the horns of the riverboats and paddle-wheelers coming and going on the river. In the spring the fog would rise over the river, hiding the road and muffling all sound, allowing an imaginative little girl to wonder where the river had been long ago and what sorts of things it had carried in its swift current as it curved sharply at Springdale and headed down its last sixteen miles on its way to converge with the Monongahela at Pittsburgh.

Springdale was a promising Pennsylvania river community of 1,200 people when Rachel's parents, Robert and Maria Carson, settled on the western edge of town in 1900. In 1901 the *Pittsburgh Leader* focused on the more bucolic qualities of Springdale, noting "considerable acreage of woods and farm land, picturesque streets . . . and pretty little frame dwellings set amidst overhanging apple trees and maples."[5]

Such rural charm was even then being replaced by the relentless engines of industry, leaving scars on the land, pollution in the air, and debris in the river. Locks on the Allegheny enabled stern-wheelers to move iron and ore to Pittsburgh from the many furnaces that dotted the hills to the northwest. Oil moved down the river at accelerating rates after the Civil War, and the heavy logging of the Appalachians that began in the 1880s was soon reflected in both river traffic and shorelines awash in timber waste.

Until the panic of 1907, Springdale's economic prospects remained bright as new industries located upriver and workers and their families moved in. Rachel's father was counting on that growth continuing when he invested in real estate, but his gamble failed.

In the end, Rachel Carson remembered only how embarrassed she was by the foul smell of the glue factory that greeted disembarking passengers at the train station; how dreary and dirty the working-class town became when the West Penn Power Company and Duquesne Light Company squeezed it between their huge power stations at both ends, and how endlessly ugly Springdale was.[6]

Robert Carson's parents, James and Ellen, had come directly to Allegheny County from Ireland. They settled in Allegheny City, a bustling Scots-Irish working-class town on the north plain just across the river from downtown Pittsburgh. James Carson, a successful carpenter, provided adequately for his family. Robert, the eldest of their six children, was born in 1864 and may have finished high school, or come close to doing so. The family was active in the Fourth United Presbyterian Church of Allegheny City, where Robert sang in the choir and toured with the men's quartet.[7]

In the winter of 1893 Robert Carson's quartet participated in a choral social in Canonsburg, Pennsylvania, a prosperous sheep-farming community in Washington County, about eighteen miles southwest of Pittsburgh. Among the other groups performing in Canonsburg that evening was a local female group, the Washington Quintette Club, from nearby Washington, Pennsylvania, which featured alto soloist Maria Frazier McLean.

Maria was attracted to the quiet, debonair Carson, who at thirty must have appeared more mature than many of the young men she knew. Robert was a slender, pleasant-looking man of average height, with prematurely thinning dark hair and kindly blue eyes. He sported a thick, sweeping mustache in the grenadier's fashion that he waxed into perfect sharp tips. Robert courted Maria McLean, who agreed to marry him less than a year later in June 1894, even though his background was educationally and socially inferior to hers. Although Robert came from a proper United Presbyterian family, Maria's widowed mother, Rachel Andrews McLean, was probably not enthusiastic about the match.

The roots of the McLean family went even deeper into the western Pennsylvania soil than those of the Carsons. The McLeans were part of the first large Scots-Irish migration that settled in western Pennsylvania and eastern Ohio. Maria's father, Daniel M. B. McLean, was born on a farm in Wellsville, Ohio, in 1840. Coming from a family of some means, he graduated from Jefferson College in Canonsburg, Washington County, in 1859. He entered Allegheny United Presbyterian Theological Seminary immediately upon graduation, and was ordained and installed pastor of the Fourth United Presbyterian Church of Allegheny City, the same church that the Carsons attended, in 1863.[8]

The following year McLean married Rachel Andrews of Washington, Pennsylvania. The couple served in Allegheny City and for a time in Cleveland, Ohio. They had two daughters, Ida, born in Allegheny City in 1867, and Maria, born two years later in Cleveland. The climate of the lake region did not agree with the Reverend McLean, however. In November 1870 he answered the call from the Chartiers United Presbyterian Church in Canonsburg, Pennsylvania, and moved back to his college town with his wife and two small daughters. Three years later he nearly died of consumption. Thereafter he frequently was unable to fill his pulpit and was completely bedridden the year before he died of tuberculosis at age forty in 1880.

After his burial, Rachel McLean moved back to Washington to raise and educate her daughters, then fourteen and eleven. Intent on giving them the best education available, she enrolled Ida and Maria in the elite Washington Female Seminary there.[9]

The Washington Female Seminary, a strongly United Presbyterian institution situated on the edge of the Washington College campus, had a reputation for providing not just a finishing education for young women of good Christian standing but a rigorous, classical curriculum. Founded in 1836 with forty students, it grew to a school of over two hundred young women, many of whom boarded. It augmented its sizable female faculty with professors from Washington College who taught advanced classes.[10]

Both McLean daughters displayed intellectual curiosity and promise in their studies and graduated well prepared for civic responsibility and Christian motherhood. Ida graduated in 1885 and followed in her mother's footsteps, marrying the Reverend J. L. Vance, a leader in the western branch of the United Presbyterian Church, in 1891. They settled in Oak Grove, Illinois, a suburb of Rock Island, ten years later.[11]

Maria, the more studious of the Reverend McLean's two daughters, graduated with honors in Latin in 1887, taking advanced courses at Washington College. Maria was a becoming but not beautiful young woman with fine bones, a high forehead, deep-set eyes, curly light-brown hair, and a distinctive angular chin.

Maria's classmates remembered her for her uncommon musical ability, playing the piano, singing, and composing, and winning distinction in each. After her graduation in 1887, Maria McLean taught school in Washington County, was an enthusiastic member of the Washington Quintette, and offered piano lessons in her mother's home. Married women were not permitted to teach school in those days, so when the twenty-five-year-old Maria agreed to marry Robert Carson, she had no choice but to give up her career.[12]

The couple stayed in Canonsburg during the first few years of their marriage, probably living with Mrs. McLean, since Robert Carson, who was employed as a clerk of some kind, could not have afforded an independent home. In 1897 a daughter, Marian Frazier, was born, followed by a son, Robert McLean, barely two years later. In 1900 Robert and Maria Carson left Canonsburg to strike out on their own.

With their young family, the Carsons needed more room. On April 2 Carson signed a mortgage of $11,000 for a sixty-four-acre parcel in Springdale belonging to the estate of Samuel Pearce. Part of the tract included an orchard of forty apple and pear trees along the top of the hill behind the modest house. There was ample room for a few necessary farm animals—some sheep, a pig, chickens, and a horse.[13]

The Carson property was bounded by Colfax Lane, rising steeply on the west, and Ridge Road, on the north behind the orchards. Later Marion Avenue was laid out down the hill on the south, probably named for Carson's eldest daughter. A gable-roofed barn with matching garage, a springhouse, chicken coop, and two outhouses completed the original outbuildings.

The two-story, clapboard house with four small rooms had been built as a log cabin between 1867 and 1892. It faced south to the town and the river beyond. The house never had central heating or indoor plumbing during the twenty-nine years the Carsons lived there. There were fireplaces at both ends of the house and other rooms were heated by coal stoves, and the only electric light came from ceiling fixtures. The first-floor parlor and dining room were divided by the staircase that led up to two small bedrooms above. The kitchen was a one-story lean-to on the north end of the house with a wooden floor, one tall double-hung window, and a door opening onto a small stoop. At some point the Carsons added a gas stove.

A cellar, accessible only from outside steps, was used to store seasonal fruits and vegetables. Maria maintained a large kitchen garden behind the garage. A lilac bush softened the front of the house, while a small weeping mulberry and several maples traced down the front hillside. A vigorous honeysuckle curled itself up along the west end of the porch, lending color and scent in season. Sometime later Robert Carson laid out a rose garden, which he tended meticulously.

The hillside property remained rural while the town of Springdale spread industrially to the southwest. Another large farm, belonging to the Moyer family, bordered the Carsons' property on the east, and by crossing it, the Carson children could walk to the School Street School, about three-fifths of a mile away. Since the business district of Springdale was another mile east along both sides of Pittsburgh Street, the Carsons used horse and buggy for church and shopping. Otherwise it was a long walk to the post office and the Butler Street train station.[14]

Many of the Polish and Hungarian immigrants coming to Springdale after 1915 moved to the bottom of Colfax, with their homes spreading along the other side of Pittsburgh Street. There was a flag stop for the Conemaugh Railroad at Colfax. At one time or another nearly everyone in Springdale visited Carson's Grove, on the top of Colfax hill. The orchard was the site of many clandestine lovers' picnics and of festive town gatherings. On the latter such occasions Robert Carson often sold apples and showed off his real estate.

Robert Warden Carson remains an elusive figure. By most accounts he was a quiet, kindly man with a reserved but dignified manner. Thirty-six years old when he bought the Springdale farm, he listed himself as a self-employed traveling salesman for the Mercantile Company, a subsidiary of the Great American Insurance Company. He took little interest in developing the farm other than maintaining the house and outbuildings and keeping a few farm animals. A "city boy," he dreamed of being a developer. He subdivided the downhill sections of his property into large level lots and in 1910 began advertising them for sale for $300 each.[15]

Local bankers recall him as a reserved man who never defaulted on his loans but was often in arrears on payments. Carson was land poor and frequently had to borrow to make ends meet. But some other townspeople have less kindly memories of him, bitterly recalling the debts he left unpaid when the family moved somewhat abruptly to Baltimore in 1930.

In 1920 Carson was employed as an electrician at the Harwick Mine and was probably still selling commercial insurance for Great American on the side. Sometime later in the decade he worked part time for the West Penn Power Company. There is some suggestion that during these years he was frequently in poor health.

Although his many photographs of his children reflect his interest in them, Robert Carson was an affectionate but almost irrelevant parent. The Carsons were more often poor than of modest means, and this privation shaped Rachel's opportunities and her personality from the outset. Embarrassed by her circumstances but fiercely loyal, her personal reserve was, among other things, a necessary strategy of self-protection.[16]

Maria Carson had been raised in an exclusively female household. Her mother was a woman of strong opinion and independence, traits she passed on to both daughters. When Maria married Robert Carson, she exchanged narrower social and economic circumstances for the opportunity of marriage and family. The dominant personality within the family from the outset, she reproduced her own mothering in her unequal partnership and parenting.[17]

She energetically directed her children's social activities as well as their education, apparently with her husband's approval but certainly without his interference. Whether Maria was happy about leaving Washington County in 1900 or not, fervent letters indicate that she missed her mother and sister a great deal. Although she went to church regularly, her lack of means prevented much socializing. She made few friends in Springdale and kept herself and her family aloof. But she enjoyed the opportunities the large Carson property provided for out-of-door activities.

Maria was an avid reader and believed in using her leisure time to improve the quality of her children's lives as well as her own. One of her keenest interests was natural history. She was not alone in this passion, for botanizing, bird-watching, and nature study were interests avidly pursued by amateur naturalists all over the country at the turn of the century, particularly among middle-class, educated women.

Bird lore was popularized in women's books, literary magazines, and children's literature. It was touted as a special interest for young readers who would, through learning the habits of birds, come to love nature and make an emotional commitment to its protection. Beginning in 1875 and continuing until after World War I, talented female writers such as Olive Thorne Miller, Mabel Osgood Wright, and Florence Merriam Bailey turned out exceptional books and articles promoting an interest in all living creatures, particularly birds.[18]

The nature-study movement had its intellectual origins in natural history and theology, but it was popularized by the great botanist Liberty Hyde Bailey and his Cornell University colleague Anna Botsford Comstock about the time the Carsons' eldest child, Marian, entered public school.[19]

Nature-study advocates were not interested in botanizing, collecting, or bird-watching for the sake of taxonomy or mere scientific observation. Nor were they interested exclusively in pedagogical reform. Disturbed by the numbers of agricultural families leaving the land and by an increasing alienation of urban children from their agrarian roots, nature-study advocates like Bailey and Comstock wanted to put children in sympathy with nature.[20]

Important as Bailey was to the acceptance of the nature-study movement among the scientific community and agricultural leaders, it was Anna Comstock whose enormously popular published lessons and summer program for teachers at Cornell brought the movement into home and school.

Comstock's *Handbook of Nature Study* (1911) taught the methods by which every elementary-age child in the country could learn to love nature. Nature-study, according to Comstock, would cultivate the child's imagination, his perception of the truth, and his ability to express it. Most important, it would instill a "love of the beautiful," a "sense of companionship with life out-of-doors, and an abiding love of nature." Embracing the ideas of natural theology that by studying nature, the intricate design of the Creator would become visible, the nature-study movement taught that nature was holy. The implications for the individual were clear; conservation was, as Bailey said, "a divine obligation," and the conservation movement, a religious crusade.[21]

Maria Carson was the perfect nature-study teacher. She welcomed the Comstock readers that Marian and Robert brought home from school. Each one suggested outdoor lessons that parents could do with their children, and Maria Carson had a sixty-four-acre laboratory to work in. She and the children were outdoors every day when weather permitted, and she shared with them her knowledge of natural history, botany, and birds.

In the evenings, Maria played the piano, and she and the two children sang songs and read stories from the several children's magazines she subscribed to.[22]

Maria impressed her respect and love for wild creatures on all her children. When they returned from their woodland adventures with treasures to show her, Maria instructed the children to return them to where they had been found. This kind of care for the natural world had a spiritual dimension that at least her youngest daughter embraced and would practice all her life.

When Rachel Louise Carson came into the world in the early-morning hours of May 27, 1907, Springdale was still full of pristine possibility; the woods and hills behind the tiny house were wild and untouched. A proud thirty-eight-year-old Maria Carson named her infant daughter for her own mother. She described Rachel as a "dear, plump, little blue-eyed baby" of nine pounds who was "unusually pretty" and "very good."[23]

When Rachel was born, her father was forty-three years old and spent long periods away from home selling insurance. Marian was in the fifth grade at the School Street School, and young Robert had started first grade the fall before. Instead of being a lonely housewife with school-age children, searching for new interests and outlets, Maria Carson had a new baby daughter to care for and enjoy almost exclusively.

Symbolic of the delight she found in this child, Maria began keeping a "mother's diary" chronicling Rachel's babyhood. Three tiny, closely written pages of this diary remain, testifying to Maria's enchantment with her baby daughter's milestones of growth and documenting Maria's love of the outdoors and Rachel's early introduction to it.[24]

The Carsons had joined the Springdale United Presbyterian Church soon after they moved to Springdale. Robert was christened there, as was Rachel, who was presented just as she was recovering from influenza. Maria was thrilled with the baptism ceremony for her daughter, recounting in her diary that the Reverend Watson S. Boyce officiated but that the christening prayer was offered by the famous Reverend W. W. Orr of Charlotte, North Carolina, who was holding evangelistic meetings in Springdale at the time.

The Reverend Boyce left sometime in 1911 and the Carsons withdrew from the congregation the next year, apparently out of some dissatisfaction with the new minister. The family subsequently joined the Cheswick

Presbyterian Church on the other end of Springdale Township, where they remained members until they left the area. Rachel attended Mrs. Berz's Sunday School class and was confirmed on April 11, 1917.[25]

From the time Rachel was one year old, she and her mother spent increasing amounts of time outdoors, walking the woods and orchards, exploring the springs, and naming flowers, birds, and insects. With Marian and Robert gone all day, the two were left at home together doing chores, talking, reading, drawing, playing the piano, and singing "Mother Goose" rhymes, which Maria enjoyed setting to music. Some afternoons they would take one of their many dogs, cross the Moyer place on the eastern boundary of their property, and wait to walk the two older children home from school. They talked about what they saw in the woods and particularly watched for birds. The distinctive quality of their experience in the outdoors was shared delight. From the first Rachel responded emotionally to her mother's love of nature. Her acuity of observation and her eye for detail were shaped on these childhood outings.

Rachel remembered herself as a "solitary child" even if she was not an only child, for there were no other small children up on Colfax hill to play with. Resourceful and imaginative, she was always "happiest with wild birds and creatures as companions," and it would be so all her life.[26]

Like many little children, Rachel liked to draw. Two early efforts stand out. The first is a "night scene," so labeled in Maria's hand, of five clearly identifiable pine trees standing atop a hill with the moon coming out in the dark sky and large rocks in the foreground, a scene familiar to that part of western Pennsylvania, but an unusually observant rendering for a preschooler. The second is a childhood book of ten pages, carefully bound together with flour-and-water paste. It is the only known gift from young Rachel to her father.[27]

"The little book for Mr. R. W. Carson" begins, "This little book I've made for you my dear, I'll hope you'll like the pictures well; the animals that you'll find in here—About them all—I'll tell." The title page is illustrated with a fine drawing of an elephant. Although some of the laborious printing is Rachel's work, Maria obviously helped with the outlines of the nine animals and the picture of Mr. Lee, perhaps the owner of the Springdale laundry, who is the solitary human in the book. Rachel selected the animals, colored them in with crayon and colored pencil, not always neatly, and helped make up a verse to go with each drawing.[28]

The book is remarkable not for drawing or verse but for the obvious relationship that existed between the child author and the wild creatures pictured in her book. Mouse, frog, bunny, and owl are identified as woodland "friends" whom Rachel encountered in her walks. Dog, hen, canary, and fish are her farm animals and household pets. This charming present for "Papa" reveals her knowledge of the creatures she encountered in her woods and fields and reflected the influence of the nature-study movement in the Carson household.

Another of Rachel's earliest childhood memories was her love of books and reading. "I read a great deal almost from infancy," she recalled, "and I suppose I must have realized someone wrote the books, and thought it would be fun to make up stories too." At about age eight, she began a story in a controlled cursive entitled "The Little Brown House." The opening page is decorated with birdhouses in all four corners, similar in style to the illustrations accompanying the stories in *St. Nicholas Magazine*. Her story describes two wrens searching for an appropriate house and happily finding a "dear little brown house with a green roof." "Now that is just what we need," Mr. Wren exclaims happily to Jenny, his mate. In a longer version of the same story written a bit later, Rachel described the wren's nesting habits in her little green house, adding wonderful details.[29]

In fourth grade, Rachel wrote a story called "A Sleeping Rabbit." Her cover illustration shows a plump white rabbit sitting with eyes closed in a chair beside a small round table on which are placed a candle and a book entitled *Peter Rabbit*. These stories and drawings reflect not only Rachel's keen observation of bird and animal life but the kind of children's literature she was reading and being read. The stories she loved anthropomorphized animals so that they shared the same needs as humans for comfortable houses, domestic companionship, and good books.[30]

Rachel's favorites were the animal stories by Beatrix Potter with their wonderfully detailed drawings, which she painstakingly imitated. Like countless other children, she was captivated with the adventures of Toad and Mole and their friends in *Wind in the Willows*. Rachel imitated it in one of her most delightful college themes and returned to the animal adventure again and again as an adult.[31]

As an early independent reader, Rachel discovered the novels of Gene Stratton Porter, an apostle of the nature-study movement who believed that through nature a child was led to God. For Porter, studying wildlife was a source of moral virtue.[32]

Of equal if not greater influence on Rachel's romantic view of nature were the several children's magazines to which her mother subscribed, read stories from, and that Rachel studied intently long before she could read all the words for herself. By far Rachel's favorite magazine was *St. Nicholas*, which her mother loved and had subscribed to before Rachel was born. The magazine, founded in 1873, was edited by the creative Mary Mapes Dodge and was regarded by many as the best magazine ever published for children. Dodge intended it to be a "child's playground; where children could be delighted as well as be in charge." Beautifully illustrated and printed, it contained articles, stories, jingles, poems, and a "Letter Box" for readers. It featured some of the leading writers and illustrators of the day. Dodge wanted *St. Nicholas* to be full of "freshness, heartiness, life and joy." Generations of children, including Rachel Carson, found it so.[33]

The section children enjoyed most was the *St. Nicholas* League, established in 1899, which published work by children themselves and thereby gave them the privilege of membership. The League stood for intellectual achievement and high ideals. Each month it held contests for the best poems, stories, essays, drawings, puzzles, and puzzle solutions its readers could devise. It awarded gold badges for the winners, silver for the runners-up, and cash awards for "honor members"—those children who had won both gold and silver badges. In addition, the League printed as many other submissions as space allowed and listed the names of those whose good work could not be squeezed in. *St. Nicholas* League contests were open to any child under the age of eighteen, as long as a parent or guardian certified that the entry was the child's original work.[34]

No other juvenile magazine of the period adopted the values of the nature-study movement more completely than *St. Nicholas*. None glorified the virtues of a life lived happily at one with nature more enthusiastically. The League stood for "intelligent patriotism" and for "protection of the oppressed, whether human or dumb creatures." The editorial attitude toward animal welfare was further clarified in rules for photographic entries. All photographs of wild animals and birds were to be taken in their *native homes*, not even in large game preserves, and certainly not in zoos.[35]

When Rachel Carson sent off her first story, "A Battle in the Clouds," to the *St. Nicholas* League contest in May 1918, she joined a distinguished group of poets, novelists, essayists, artists, journalists, and scholars who first saw their work in print in the pages of the League. Between 1907 and 1917 League badge winners included such future luminaries as William Faulkner, F. Scott Fitzgerald, Edward Estlin Cummings, S. Eliot Morison,

Edna St. Vincent Millay, and S. V. Benet. In 1911 an eleven-year-old E. B. White won a silver badge for his essay "A Winter Walk," which recounted a boy's pleasure at being out with his dog where "every living creature seemed happy" and where nothing would harm "God's innocent little folk." It was a story Maria may well have read aloud to her four-year-old daughter.[36]

"A Battle in the Clouds" was a story about World War I and reflected the influence of Rachel's brother, Robert, who had enlisted in the Army Air Service in the fall of 1917. In one of his letters home, Robert told of the tragic death of a Canadian flying instructor who had been in combat in France. Rachel was so taken by his account of the bravery of the aviator that she retold the story in her own words for the *St. Nicholas* League.[37]

Rachel waited for the results of her first entry for five months. When the September 1918 issue of *St. Nicholas* arrived, she discovered not only that "A Battle in the Clouds" had been published by the League but that it had also been awarded a silver badge for excellence in prose. The Carsons were jubilant. Rachel, obviously delighted, was so excited by seeing her first story in the League that she entered the very next competition, #227, on the topic, "A Young Hero (or Heroine)."[38]

Clearly influenced by other war stories published in the magazine, Rachel wrote about a lone American soldier holding off a German patrol, killing several of the "Huns" before falling wounded and being rescued at the last moment by his comrades. Although not as dramatic as her first story, the setting in a shell crater is well drawn with dark clouds and flashes of lightning to heighten the suspense. This story appeared in the January 1919 League. A third story, "A Message to the Front," was published the following month, February 1919, and won Rachel a gold badge. The story describes the inspiration that America's entry into the war gave to a lonely group of French soldiers surviving the winter on the front. The plot is not unusual, but the clear, precise writing and the tension created in the brief dialogue are remarkable for an eleven-year-old.[39]

A fourth essay, "A Famous Sea-Fight," printed in the August 1919 issue, was written in April. It retold the story of Admiral Dewey's victory at Manila Bay in the Spanish-American War. Its appearance in the magazine gave Rachel the vaulted status of "Honor Member" of the League and ten dollars in cash. After four stories appeared in one year, Rachel was convinced she could become what she dreamed.[40]

Rachel's literary success also had an impact on her mother. Maria's intellectual frustration and disappointing marriage made it all the more important that her talented daughter have the opportunity to fulfill her promise. Maria knew that this child of her old age had exceptional gifts. It was also clear to Maria by 1917 that her older children, Marian and Robert, shared little of her interest in music, literature, or nature. Determined that Rachel's gifts would not be buried by domestic life in a small and increasingly ugly town, Maria Carson planned a different future for Rachel.[41]

By the summer of 1921 Rachel's writing had nearly outgrown the confines of the *St. Nicholas* League. Barely fourteen, she submitted a piece to the magazine for sale in June 1921. Assistant Editor Frances Marshal replied that while they could not buy her essay for *St. Nicholas*, they could use it for "publicity work" and paid her for it at the rate of a cent a word. When the check came Rachel was ecstatic. She scrawled across the envelope "first payment" and tucked it away.[42]

That same summer Rachel began sending her work to other magazines. In order to keep track of the disposition of her literary efforts, she designed and maintained a ledger. It shows that she submitted a story, "Just Dogs," of 4,000 words to at least three magazines: *St. Nicholas*, *Author's Press*, and *Our Animal Friends*. Although it was rejected by all three, apparently because of its ubiquitous subject matter, Rachel was undeterred.

The format of her ledger for "Just Dogs" is one she used all her life. Its categories included title, class, length, place submitted, dates sent and returned, postage cost, payment, and comments. Intensely conscious of her expenses, she noted that each story cost eight cents in postage to submit. In an unemotional and businesslike way, she recorded that the story was returned by the publishers three weeks later.[43]

Rachel's final League story, the first about nature, appeared a year later in July 1922. Entered in the category of "My Favorite Recreation," it tells of "going birds'-nesting" in the Pennsylvania hills with her dog for "a day of our favorite sport" armed with lunchbox, canteen, notebook, and camera. Rachel describes the trail and the birds she and her dog found together.[44]

As an adult, Carson liked to say she had become a professional writer at age eleven, confusing the sale of her publicity piece with her first *St. Nicholas* League publication. But her "determination that she would some day be a writer" was her most accurate memory, that and the amount of money she was paid.[45]

Rachel's recognition from the *St. Nicholas* League and her outstanding academic record did not surprise her teachers at School Street School any more than it had her mother. Rachel's report cards from elementary school were all As, with an occasional B in handwriting. From second through seventh grade, however, teachers noted extended absences. Although a few of these reflected genuine illnesses, more often when the winter weather was particularly harsh or when there were known outbreaks of diphtheria, whooping cough, or measles, Maria, like many protective mothers, elected to tutor Rachel at home. Her performance remained consistently superior. Maria's tutoring in fact was probably better than the instruction in the classroom.

Rachel used these occasions at home to read. It was during this time that she became keenly interested in authors who wrote stories and poems about the ocean and seafaring: Herman Melville, Joseph Conrad, and Robert Louis Stevenson. But her frequent and extended absences emphasized her singularity and kept her from making friends.

The Carsons lived not only on the top of Colfax hill but over two miles from the shops and businesses at the center of town. Neither the location of the farm nor Maria's attitude toward outsiders encouraged easy social interactions. Two friends who did come over to play remember that gaining the approval of the stern-looking Mrs. Carson was an achievement. Springdale had no high school, but tutorial classes for ninth and tenth graders were offered in two rooms at School Street. Most students entered high school somewhere else. Some went away to boarding school; others attended Peabody or Allegheny High School on the north side, commuting to and from class on the Conemaugh Railroad. The Carsons could not afford the train fare, so Rachel stayed at School Street for the first two years of high school.[46]

The source of Rachel's social isolation was not only economic and geographic but psychological as well. In 1921, when Rachel began ninth grade, her family already had weathered several economic and domestic crises. The initial source of the family's difficulties was Robert Carson's failure to find a position that paid him a salary rather than a commission. While the Carsons owned a great deal of valuable land and could borrow against it, Robert Carson sold only an occasional lot or two, and he could not support his family with such unpredictable income. As the economy retracted, the Carsons struggled to get by; at times they were unable to pay their milk and hay bills.

Sometime between 1922 and 1925, Robert Carson took a part-time position with West Penn Power Company, the huge utility sprawling along the riverfront on the eastern edge of Springdale. West Penn was fast becoming the largest employer in the area, and Carson found work at the Springdale switching station. For a time he was the night supervisor, but even this job did not pay enough to support the family. Never a robust man, his health seems to have prevented more vigorous work.[47]

Maria Carson supplemented the family income by offering piano lessons to Springdale's children, charging fifty cents a lesson, and also selling piano music. But the family's future was never financially secure, and they were forced to live spartanly. During their occupancy, the farmhouse was not modernized or remodeled.[48]

By the time Rachel entered her last two years of high school, her family's impecuniousness was a source of some embarrassment as well as community comment. This only added to Rachel's reticence about bringing friends home. In some ways, the Carsons' declining economic status made it easier for Rachel to be independent since she was under no pressure whatever to conform to the social values of her peers. By the time she entered high school, Rachel had embraced her mother's view that intellect and self-worth were far more important than material possessions or social recognition.

Maria's older two children, on the other hand, rebelled. Marian Frazier Carson, a strikingly good-looking young woman, had no desire to finish high school and went to work as a stenographer after completing tenth grade. When she was eighteen she began to date Lee Frank Frampton, age twenty-two, a student from New Kensington. The young couple decided quite precipitously to marry in November 1915. Robert Carson gave his permission for his underage daughter to marry. The minister of the Presbyterian Church of Cheswick performed the ceremony in the pink-and-white wallpapered parlor of the tiny Carson home.[49]

The newlywed Framptons had no money for rooms of their own, so they boarded in the already crowded family home. Although Frampton apparently expressed a preference to move in with his mother, the couple lived on Colfax Lane for four months. Then, on the evening of April 6, 1916, Lee Frampton disappeared.

After about three weeks, Marian found Lee at his mother's home and had him arrested for desertion and nonsupport. At hearings on those charges, Frampton agreed to pay Marian four dollars a week but disappeared completely at the end of that year, and she never heard from him again. In July 1918 Marian sued for divorce, which was awarded in May of the next year.[50]

After Frampton left her, Marian found work as a bookkeeper at West Penn Power. She married Burton P. Williams, a stenographer, in July 1920 in a civil ceremony by a justice of the peace of Allegheny County.[51]

Rachel was eight when Marian married Lee Frampton and the couple moved into the house; she was twelve when Marian's divorce was final. The house was so small that there could have been few secrets and little privacy for anyone. After Frampton deserted Marian, Rachel observed her sister's unhappiness and her mother's embarrassment. But she also saw how her mother ignored the fact that it would be difficult for a grown child to have a life and a marriage without the financial means to be independent. Rachel was thirteen when Marian married for the second time.

Like his older sister, Robert McLean Carson never went beyond the tenth grade in school. He worked in a radio repair shop for a short time and, in November 1917, volunteered for the Army Air Service and was sent to an air station in Texas. In the spring of 1918, Robert's squadron, the 1st Air Park, was sent to France and participated in the battles of Champaigne, St.-Mihiel, and Meuse-Argonne.[52]

Discharged in August 1919, Robert went back to Springdale quite cocky and full of himself. He found work at an electrical repair company in nearby Oakmont, Pennsylvania. Although he moved back home after he was discharged, he frequently stayed with friends during the week. The next year Robert joined his father and sister at West Penn Power, where he was an electrician's assistant. Robert was popular with the young women of Springdale and enjoyed an active social life. He was not only carefree but reportedly somewhat dissolute. A. W. Kennedy, one of his Springdale buddies, recalled that Robert was "the only man I knew who would steal chickens from his own mother."[53]

While Marian and Robert were going about their grown-up lives, Rachel immersed herself in books, the farm animals, her many dogs, and the outdoors. In 1923 her parents decided that she should attend high school for her last two years in Parnassus, a town two miles north across the river near New Kensington. Rachel commuted to school and back on the trolley, which was cheap but ran irregularly. At Parnassus she joined the class of 1925, composed of forty-four students, twenty-eight girls and sixteen boys. Despite meager facilities, students got individual attention from first-rate teachers and got to know one another well.[54]

Once again external circumstances made it difficult for Rachel to participate in much of the social or extracurricular activities of her classmates.

She could not stay after school or go to a friend's house very often because she had to catch the infrequent trolley home. Still, Rachel made friends and enjoyed herself. She liked basketball and field hockey, and played both sports tolerably. She always managed to get to pep rallies to cheer for the Parnassus football team. Her classmates discovered that Rachel, while quiet, had a mischievous sparkle and the ability to clown without being malicious.[55]

Rachel graduated from Parnassus in May 1925, just a few days before her eighteenth birthday. The yearbook's editors wrote a poem for each graduating senior. The poem that accompanied Rachel Louise Carson's class picture naturally commented on her academic skills and her perfectionism. She graduated first in her class. It read:

Rachel's like the mid-day sun
Always very bright
Never stops her studying
'til she gets it right.[56]

Students at Parnassus were required to write a senior thesis. Rachel's essay, entitled "Intellectual Dissipation," was a solemn and somewhat pedantic discourse in which she displayed an abhorrence of mental and moral sloth. It is noteworthy not only for its easy literary references but also for what it reveals about Rachel's formative attitudes toward education, friendship, mental discipline, and, most especially, intellectual independence.

Comparing intellectual dissipation to the "reckless squandering of natural resources," Rachel notes that while there was a new trend toward conservation of nature, "the God-given faculty for clear thinking and intelligent reasoning lies dormant and helpless from disuse." Introducing a theme that she would take up again in college, Rachel distinguishes between the development of true intelligence and the results of a college education, the former developed through reading great books, the cultivation of well-selected friends, and, most important, "the use of our own reasoning power."[57]

Rachel's high standards for both literature and friendship reflected her strict moral upbringing and a strong dose of Calvinistic responsibility and civic obligation. Her thesis, however self-righteous in tone, reveals an inner discipline and strong social conscience. Her childhood in Springdale had given her enough exposure to the superficial judgments and rash actions of others to induce a healthy skepticism about the world and a certain wariness. She was unshakably resolute in her independent pursuit of knowledge. By the summer of 1925 Rachel was ready for a wider world than Springdale could offer.

The only school Maria Carson ever considered for Rachel was Pennsylvania College for Women (PCW). Then as now, PCW (later Chatham College) was an elite private college in Pittsburgh. For Maria, the most important considerations were that it was a "Christian college," that it had an excellent academic reputation, and that it was a mere sixteen miles from Springdale.

Rachel won admission easily and was awarded an annual $100 tuition scholarship based on academic competition. She did not apply for a campus job to supplement her expenses because Maria insisted that Rachel's constitution was too frail and that she should devote all her free time to her studies.

In the spring of 1925 Rachel competed in the annual state scholarship examinations given by the State Department of Instruction. In June she was notified that she had won the $100 scholarship for the 40th Senatorial District.[58]

The Carsons planned to borrow money from the bank and sell off lots to help meet the $800 room-and-board fee. Maria laid out a plan to subdivide the property on three sides of the homestead, and Robert Carson planned to sell enough plots each year to meet Rachel's college expenses. But his asking price was too high and sales from these lots yielded only a small part of the total Rachel needed for tuition and expenses.[59]

At the same time Maria also increased her piano student roster and sold apples, chickens, and the family china. Even so, there was barely enough money to send Rachel to PCW properly dressed, with little extra for spending money. Like many other girls, Rachel's college wardrobe was handmade with an emphasis on serviceable clothes. Deeply aware of the sacrifice her family and particularly her mother were making to send her to college, Rachel deferred completely to her mother's wishes.

Rachel entered PCW already a serious student with well-defined goals and an unusual sense of purpose. Her childhood experiences had given her an acuity and an eye for detail, a recognition of the importance of the small, the commonplace, and the nearby that she would experiment with in her college themes. Rachel's love of the outdoors had about it the fresh delight of discovery. Her mother's companionship as teacher and partner brought with it an obligation to help others see and to share in the wonder. This love affair with nature also had become for Rachel Carson a substitute for the intimacy of the more conventional relationships of childhood and adolescence that she never had. Self-confident about her intellectual abilities and solitary by nature, Rachel had few social graces and little understanding of how to interact in a wider society. She was fiercely determined to become all that she could be for herself. She also had a vision, not yet articulated, an inchoate sense of some special calling that awaited her.

With a combination of excitement and foreboding, Rachel Carson said good-bye to her dogs and to her rocky woodland paths. She climbed into the Model T Ford her father had borrowed for the occasion and, with her parents, drove south to Pittsburgh and Pennsylvania College for Women, determined to become a writer, at the very least.

2

"The Vision Splendid"

Pittsburgh's reputation as the iron and steel capital of the world was earned at the cost of creating the worst air and water pollution in the country. Although PCW was located miles upriver from the Bessemer mills and the mountains of molten slag that illuminated the sky to the southwest by night, the campus was not immune from the fine soot that hung in the air, penetrating the crevices of every building, stinging the eyes, nose, and mouth, and making some people ill. During Rachel's four years at the college, Pittsburgh's air grew more foul, some days so thick with ash that the sun was nearly obliterated. Even on the clearest day, there was a telltale smell of ash.

The PCW campus was perched on ten and a half wooded acres on top of Murray Hill above Pittsburgh's mansion-lined Fifth Avenue in the east end enclave known as Shadyside. Chartered in 1869 as the nondenominational Pennsylvania Female College, it was founded by well-to-do Presbyterian congregations in Shadyside and East Liberty and guided by thirty trustees, two-thirds of whom were required to be Presbyterian communicants.

The campus and original building had once been the home of George A. Berry, a wealthy businessman, who sold the property and his three-story, red-brick, American Gothic–style mansion to the college. Berry Hall, as it became known, was reputed to be the largest private residence in Allegheny County. Its large reception rooms, living room, dining room, and several parlors on the first floor housed the president's offices, faculty quarters, and general classrooms. Dormitory rooms occupied the other two stories.

In 1889 Dilworth Hall was added to relieve crowded dormitories and classrooms and to house a large nondenominational chapel on the first floor. On the third floor of Dilworth were science laboratories and a skylighted art studio. The following year the college changed its name to Pennsylvania College for Women so as not to be confused with the Methodist-run Pittsburgh Female College and to increase its patronage. In 1909 Woodland Hall, another dormitory, and the president's house were added to the older buildings as enrollments increased. With its new tree-lined Woodland Road entrance, the hilltop campus became a serene yet impressive site of higher learning.[1]

When Rachel entered PCW, Cora Helen Coolidge was in the third year of her remarkable tenure as president. Miss Coolidge was a New Englander who had come to PCW in 1906 as its second dean from Cushing Academy in Ashburnham, Massachusetts. When President Henry Lindsay died suddenly in 1914, Coolidge was made acting president for one year. She continued as dean for three more years, resigning in 1917 to attend to personal and family business affairs.

Cora Coolidge came from a family of means and education. Her father had served as a congressman from Massachusetts. Coolidge had been raised debating the ideas of Emerson and Thoreau, politics, history, and theology. After graduating from Smith College with honors, she had traveled widely, taking courses at the universities of Chicago and Göttingen.

The Board of Trustees called her back to PCW as president in 1922. Deeply committed to women's education in the liberal arts, Coolidge needed to build a strong faculty and measurably increase the college's meager endowment. Well connected and admired by Pittsburgh's civic leaders, she was warmhearted and generally popular with the PCW student body.

Coolidge believed in the educational value of day-to-day living. She created a homelike atmosphere on the campus where "friendliness . . . courtesy and mutual helpfulness . . . was considered a fine art." A large, bosomy woman, with a strong patrician face, square jaw, and lively eyes emboldened by rimless glasses, Coolidge wore her silver-gray hair loosely twisted into a bun, making her look more matronly and austere than she was.

Coolidge considered good grooming essential to a woman's social code. She expected students to acquire proper social graces, and held afternoon teas and tea dances for the cultivation of such skills. She took a personal interest in each student's well-being. The door to her office in Berry Hall was always open. Only two things were guaranteed to make Cora Coolidge lose her temper: poor grades and smoking. Most PCW women recognized and appreciated the genuineness of Coolidge's concern. Many students thought of her as friend, mentor, and role model.[2]

In the early years of her presidency, Coolidge's attention was absorbed in raising money for the college's endowment so that it could compete more successfully in the world of women's education. Since she was frequently out of town, the day-to-day affairs of the college fell to the capable hands of college dean, the well-loved Mary Helen Marks.

Miss Marks, also a graduate of Smith College, had come to PCW in the spring of 1916 as field secretary to the president. She brought a respect for the traditions of the college instilled by her mother, who was a PCW graduate. After three years Marks was appointed college registrar and was elected dean in 1922. Coolidge and Marks were a remarkable team, inspiring the confidence of trustees, faculty, and students.

Academic life at PCW mirrored that of many private women's liberal arts institutions of the time. Students at PCW in the 1920s were required to take a year of English composition, science, contemporary history, sociology, two years of a modern language, and gym. Electives were allowed after the first year, and specific requirements in the predominant subject varied. Student affairs were governed by a faculty-student council and an honor system that applied to all aspects of social life and academic work.

Like the majority of female college students of the interwar years, PCW women envisioned their ultimate role as educated wives and mothers. In the interval between graduation and marriage, some found work in teaching, nursing, social service, or clerical fields. The few who came with plans for professional careers in law, medicine, science, or engineering were much the exception, although Coolidge professed to believe that women needed specific training for the new vocations they would someday enter.[3]

Rachel Carson came to President Coolidge's attention well before the two women ever met. Rachel's application for admission impressed Coolidge, as did the state scholarship she brought with her. Coolidge and Marks realized the Carsons needed additional financial assistance, and the president had friends who were happy to help a talented but needy student. Unofficially and very privately, the Carsons learned that the balance of Rachel's tuition for the year had been paid. Coolidge's risk was well taken, for Carson's freshman-year performance impressed her benefactors.[4]

Rachel arrived at Berry Hall in early September 1925 looking forward to meeting Dorothy Appleby, who had been assigned as her roommate. Dorothy came from a small town outside Harrisburg, Pennsylvania, where she had been raised by her grandparents after her mother's death. She attended public schools and the Presbyterian church. Lively, bright, and opinionated, Dorothy was eager to participate in campus life. About the only thing Dorothy and Rachel Carson shared was a determination to succeed academically.[5]

Rachel was never "one of the girls" at PCW, nor did she care to be. It was not just that she had homemade clothes, nor was it that she was impecunious. There were others on scholarship. But Rachel's values and attitudes were different. Her reserve, her inner self-confidence, and her independence were hard for other girls to read. These qualities, interpreted as arrogance or indifference by those who did not take the time to find out differently, isolated her, allowing her little opportunity to make friends.

When Rachel entered college her face, neck, and upper shoulders were severely broken out with acne, a problem that continued well into her senior year. Her thick, chin-length hair was so oily it required daily shampooing, which she often neglected. Rachel was outwardly indifferent to her problems, for her mother had never attached any importance to physical appearance, yet she surely suffered inwardly because of them and avoided social situations whenever she could.[6]

Her mother's frequent visits to campus also prevented Rachel from making friends. Maria came almost every weekend as soon as classes were over Saturday afternoon and stayed with Rachel until late in the evening. When Mrs. Carson did not visit, Rachel often took the train home for the weekend. Sometimes mother and daughter went to the library to read together, and sometimes Mrs. Carson typed Rachel's papers for her. At first, Dorothy Appleby and the other girls on Rachel's corridor thought she might be homesick and were compassionate. But when the maternal visits continued each weekend, they made fun of Rachel. Some girls wondered aloud if Mrs. Carson should pay tuition because she was around so much.

Dorothy Appleby remembers that Mrs. Carson was perfectly pleasant whenever she came but that she had time only for Rachel. Maria Carson would have been a formidable presence in any freshman dormitory. Older than most of the other girls' mothers, white-haired and stern-faced, usually dressed completely in black, Mrs. Carson made no small talk and had no interest in the lives or activities of any of the other girls. She always brought a basket of creams and astringents for Rachel's acne and a large box full of homemade cookies and bars. With some bitterness, Dorothy described mother and daughter sitting on Rachel's bed, eating cookies, without ever thinking to offer them to anyone else.[7]

If Rachel objected to her mother's frequent visits or to her exclusivity, she never showed any discomfort or resentment. Rather the opposite: Maria was not only Rachel's first mentor but her best friend as well. Certainly Rachel was deeply aware of the sacrifices her mother had made in order for her to come to college: the sale of McLean silver and china, the piano lessons, and the odd jobs. There was no reason in Rachel's mind why her mother ought not to share vicariously the pleasures of college life.

Maria Carson's visits to PCW allowed her to participate in an experience she had always wanted but that had been foreclosed to her. She could use the library, learn languages, and read along with Rachel. Visiting Rachel also gave Maria a physical and emotional respite from the stress at home. Both Marian and Robert continued to have serious personal problems, which even the resilient daughter of a Presbyterian minister never expected to confront.[8]

By 1925 Marian Carson Frampton Williams' second marriage was in disarray. Marian had given birth to a daughter, Marian Virginia, in 1924 and was still living with her husband, Burt Williams, in his mother's house on the North Side. Another daughter, Marjorie Louise, was born in late 1925. Although Marian pleaded with Williams to make a home for them, he refused to leave his mother.[9]

Robert's more recent marriage in May 1924 was turning ugly as well. Robert, his wife, Meredith Born, and their new baby, Frances, born the following year, had been living with the Carsons since their marriage. Robert spent long hours at his radio repair shop, but the business did poorly. The baby was sick frequently and needed constant attention. Meredith was lonely and upset by Robert's neglect as well as their lack of privacy. Maria Carson's weekend visits to PCW absented her from Marian's unhappiness and her son's domestic quarrels.[10]

Rachel adjusted quickly to life in Berry Hall. It was a luxurious existence for her. She embarked on her college classes with confidence and enthusiasm, registering for contemporary history, art history, sociology, spoken English, French, physical education, and, of course, English composition. Her first theme for English composition was an essay "Who I Am and Why I Came to PCW."

Describing herself as a "girl of eighteen years, a Presbyterian, Scotch-Irish by ancestry, and a graduate of a small, but first class high school," she enumerated the things she enjoyed, beginning with being "intensely fond of anything pertaining to the outdoors and athletics." But her real love, she confessed, was nature. "I love all the beautiful things of nature, and the wild creatures are my friends."[11]

She came to PCW, she said, because it was a "Christian college founded on ideals of service and honor." She wrote of her hope to have time to think, to "come to a fuller realization of myself" and responsibly play her "part on the stage of [life]." She was, she admitted, an "idealist," with an ephemeral but powerful vision of what she wanted for herself. "Sometimes I lose sight of my goal, then again it flashes into view, filling me with a new determination to keep the 'vision splendid' before my eyes. I may never come to a full realization of my dreams, but 'a man's reach must exceed his grasp or what's a heaven for?' "[12]

Since Rachel came to PCW intent on majoring in English and becoming a writer, the professor whose opinion of her work mattered the most was Miss Grace Croff, the new assistant professor who taught freshman composition. Croff was in her mid-thirties, but her vitality gave the impression of a much younger woman. She was the only member of the PCW faculty in 1925 with two degrees from Radcliffe College. A challenging professor, she had high standards and a lively imagination.[13]

By spring semester 1926, Croff had become Rachel's college mentor and friend. The two spent time chatting after class, having tea, talking about literature, writing, music, and art. When the weather turned warm, they often could be seen on one of the many wooden benches that dotted the shady woodland campus, engrossed in conversation. Croff was the adviser to the student newspaper, *The Arrow*, and to the occasional literary supplement, *The Englicode*. She encouraged Rachel to join both the following year.

As a freshman, Rachel's extracurricular activities centered on sports rather than literature. She worked her way up to goalkeeper on the so-called honorary field hockey team and played basketball as an enthusiastic substitute. Rachel was small, petite in stature, but quite scrappy and agile. Playing field hockey pleased her in spite of the required uniform of baggy blue serge bloomers, black silk stockings, and high white tennis shoes.[14]

Rachel always begged out of all the optional tea parties and dances at the elegant Schenley Hotel as well as the social functions arranged with boys from other schools, preferring to stay in her room and study. Instead of going to the required concerts at Carnegie Music Hall or the lectures at the Carnegie Institute on art appreciation, Rachel slipped out to the Carnegie Museum of Natural History to study the bird exhibits. She still managed an A in art history.[15]

The only requirement that met with Rachel's full approval and compliance was to attend church on Sunday. After the first few months at the imposing but rather stuffy East Liberty Presbyterian Church, Dorothy Appleby invited Rachel to come with her to Calvary Episcopal Church, a huge, gray-stone gothic structure. Calvary's architectural beauty impressed Rachel, and she went there frequently during her college years.[16]

Before the end of freshman year, Rachel and Dorothy Appleby had devised at least one ritual from which they took shared delight. Some Sunday mornings they prepared their own breakfast and ate in their room on the third floor of Berry Hall. Buying food for these repasts was the one luxury Rachel allowed herself. Most of their secret meals were cold ones, but every so often they managed to cook a steak in a chafing dish.[17]

By the end of freshman year, Rachel had produced three pieces that Croff considered unusually good. "Morning in the Woods" was a short theme that revealed her intimate knowledge of a woodland environment and her keen observation of woodland birds. Her description had an evocative lyric quality. The other two works were term papers: one a critical analysis of Dallas Lore Sharp, a late nineteenth-century essayist and nature writer, the other a short story set along the New England seacoast.[18]

"The Master of the Ship's Light" was Rachel's first college sea story. Her remarkably vivid setting of the seacoast and the ocean, even though she had never seen either, testifies to her years of reading the great literature of the sea. It was Rachel's first story selected for *The Englicode.*

Croff gave both term papers an A. But her comment on "The Master of the Ship's Light" captured for the first time the quality that would become a hallmark of Rachel's mature writing. "Your style," Croff wrote at the end of a long page of suggestions, "is so good because you have made what might be a relatively technical subject very intelligible to the reader. The use of incident and narrative is particularly good."[19]

As she packed up her room in Berry Hall that June, Rachel had reason to be proud of herself. She was one of ten freshmen selected for "freshman honors." She had a mentor who encouraged her writing and she was moving closer to her goal. She had enjoyed competitive sports and was recognized by her classmates as an enthusiastic teammate. Her summer, however, promised to be more difficult. There would be nine people living in the tiny Springdale house.

Robert, Meredith, and baby Frances were still there. To make matters worse, Marian had left Burton Williams and returned home with her two toddlers. When Rachel arrived from PCW later that month, Robert and his family had to move out of the house to make room for her. Since they could not afford rooms of their own, they pitched a large tent in the backyard of the Carson property. They took their meals with the rest of the family and used a hot plate Robert brought up from the radio shop for heat at night.[20]

Rachel spent the summer helping her mother and baby-sitting her three small nieces. The household was chaotic. Maria had never approved of Robert's marriage to Meredith, who was a Roman Catholic and refused to convert. She apparently treated Meredith with disdain and took no pains to hide her disapproval. Many nights Meredith and Robert quarreled loudly, especially when Robert stayed out late. Frances, who was just over a year old, was teething and fussy. Everyone was on edge. Marian, who was recovering from appendicitis, was especially miserable.[21]

Whenever she could, Rachel found solitude in the woods. She took long hikes up into the familiar hills above the Allegheny. She read and wrote poetry and made the best of the situation at home. At summer's end, Rachel looked forward to returning to PCW. She had registered for another class with Miss Croff and had decided to fulfill her science requirement taking biology rather than chemistry, which she had already taken in Parnassus High School.[22]

Rachel had a new room on the second floor of Berry Hall and a new roommate, Helen Myers, who had been recommended by some of Maria Carson's friends. Helen's family owned a successful dairy farm in Bentleyville, a rural community in Washington County. Helen was the youngest student in residence at PCW. In the fall of 1926 she was just sixteen, while Rachel and the others were at least three years older. Whether Maria Carson selected Helen as Rachel's roommate, or whether Helen and Rachel were matched up because no one else wanted to room with either of them, they were compatible enough to room together for the next three years.[23]

Helen was a petite young woman with dark, wavy hair, small dark eyes, and a porcelain complexion. She had a talent for languages and enjoyed singing in the glee club, but she was not a scholar. Helen was kind to Rachel although she thought her much too serious and a dependable friend even though they had little in common. Rachel was more like a big sister to Helen than a contemporary, never hesitating to give her advice and on more than one occasion chastising her for wasting time writing love letters.[24]

Rachel continued to play hockey for her class team. She joined *The Arrow* and *The Englicode* staff at Croff's invitation. In addition to biology, two English courses, and a second year of French, she took an elective class in psychology.

Her compositions during the fall of 1926 reflected her close observation of human behavior. Several themes were chosen each semester for publication in *The Englicode*. Croff commented marginally, "I have always felt that by using your imagination a little more you would limber your style." Increasingly, however, Rachel's intellectual energies were focused on the biology laboratory.[25]

Although PCW's catalog listed courses in chemistry, physics, geology, and astronomy, in actual practice course offerings in science depended on the instructor's interests and abilities. Most PCW students chose biology to fulfill their one-year science requirement. The beginning biology class, open to freshmen and sophomores, was a large lecture held in what had previously been the elegant wood-paneled drawing room of Berry Hall. Laboratory work was done in small groups that met in one of the two tiny labs on the drafty third floor of Dilworth Hall. Introductory biology was taught by Miss Mary Scott Skinker, a professor many PCW students avoided because of her high standards and rigorous requirements. But Miss Skinker changed Rachel Carson's life.

Much of Mary Scott Skinker's past is lost. She was born in Denver, Colorado, in 1891, the second youngest of a family of eleven children. Her father moved his family to St. Louis, Missouri, at the turn of the century, becoming a successful farmer. The Skinkers lived in the suburb of Kirkwood where Mary Scott graduated from high school in 1908. Skinker's mother died when she was young, so she and her younger brother, Thomas, were raised by their older sister, Anne.[26]

After high school, Mary Scott Skinker began teaching in St. Louis public schools. She specialized in English but, like all secondary teachers, actually taught a variety of subjects. She quickly moved up in the city's educational ranks, taking additional college courses each summer.

In the fall of 1920, after twelve years of teaching, Mary Scott Skinker returned to her family's western roots in Colorado. She earned a "ten-year certificate" in one academic year at what was then Colorado Teacher's College by transferring her previous college credits and her life experience in teaching. The following year Skinker moved back across the country to complete a bachelor's degree in science at Columbia Teacher's College in New York City in 1922 and was awarded a master's degree in zoology by Columbia University the following year. She was appointed to the PCW faculty in the fall of 1923 and moved to Pittsburgh. President Coolidge promoted her to acting head of the biology department in 1924. Mary Scott Skinker was then thirty-four years old.[27]

To the casual observer, Mary Scott Skinker was everything Rachel Carson was not: dynamic, energetic, and absolutely glamorous. Tall and slender, she had dark, dancing, deep-set eyes. Her chestnut hair was worn loosely coiled on the crown of her head. Elegant and graceful, her walk was quick and her speech softened by a hint of a southern accent. She was outgoing but at the same time properly professorial. When she listened to someone, she listened with her whole being. Her smile was genuine and she laughed easily.

Miss Skinker also loved clothes and wore them beautifully. Every night she dressed formally for dinner, a habit she continued all her life, no matter where she was. When she came to dinner on Saturday evenings, she always pinned a fresh flower to her waist or on her shoulder. The upper-class students knew the flower was part of a weekly gift Skinker received from an unknown, but obviously ardent, suitor.

PCW women regarded Skinker with a combination of awe and skepticism. Here was a beautiful woman who obviously could marry if she wished but who, for some unknown reason, chose to teach biology. Remembering Mary Scott Skinker years later, Mary Frye, one of her students, recalled, "I worshiped her; she was ethereal."[28]

Mary Scott Skinker had high standards for herself as well as for her students, but she warmly encouraged anyone who applied herself, even if the results were mixed. One of Rachel's classmates, Ruth Hunter, who was an art major, took biology at the same time Rachel did. She recalled that although she was not a very good science student, Skinker gave her high marks because she worked very hard on her laboratory notebooks, which were accurately drawn and beautifully illustrated.[29]

On the other hand, Skinker had no mercy for those who tried to glide through biology with charm rather than work. The most popular girl in the class of 1929 was also one of the wealthiest. Her family was outraged when Skinker gave their daughter a C in biology, a fair estimate of her effort and achievement, but a grade that kept her off the dean's list. Skinker was adamant about the fairness of the grade in spite of Miss Coolidge's personal intervention on the student's behalf.[30]

The incident was only one example of a growing schism between President Coolidge and Professor Skinker by 1926 over academic standards in general and the education of women in science in particular. The two women disagreed not just over appropriate academic standards for female college students but more fundamentally over whether women could or should be encouraged to study science. Earl Wallace, who later became head of the science department, was as adamant as Skinker that science was not too rigorous for women, but Coolidge never challenged his views. Skinker's position was more threatening to Cora Coolidge. Not only her outspoken views but her personal influence and popularity with the students disturbed Coolidge. The tension between president and professor was more than academic.[31]

Professor Skinker was immediately impressed by Rachel Carson's exceptional ability. It was not simply that she was always prepared for class or that her papers and laboratory work were meticulous. Skinker recognized in the unusual level of Rachel's classroom participation, the depth of her curiosity, and the breadth of her knowledge of natural history a categorical difference from the other students. Rachel's intelligence and delight were manifest when she stayed after class to ask more questions. Many of the other students in the large lecture were aware that the formal professor showed particular interest in Rachel. Some were irritated by the fact, but not many were surprised by the quiet English major's scientific competence: After all, Rachel was already established as the class intellect.[32]

One can only speculate about what Rachel thought of Mary Scott Skinker in the fall of 1926. But soon her attachment to the impassioned and brilliant Skinker was as transparent as her fascination with the subject matter. Rachel was awed by Skinker's knowledge and skills. She admired her personal dedication to science and her enthusiasm in teaching it. Rachel wanted to learn all that Skinker had to teach. Her inner vision had been sharpened and expanded by their encounter.

Much of what we know about Rachel's emotional and intellectual response to biology and to Mary Scott Skinker comes from Rachel's letters to two college friends, Mary Frye (Llewelyn) and Dorothy Thompson (Seif), who were both a class behind Rachel. Frye had entered as a biology major, Thompson, a history student. Rachel, Dorothy, and Mary did not become close friends until the fall of 1927, but they took Skinker's classes together.

Like some of the other girls, Dorothy Thompson recalls that she first thought Rachel Carson both unfriendly and unattractive. Her opinion began to change one day in the tiny lab on top of Dilworth Hall when Rachel gave the freshman some help with a slide she was having trouble getting in focus. Rachel's kindness surprised Dorothy. What she had perceived as unfriendliness was really reserve. Rachel observed more sympathetically than Dorothy had realized.[33]

Dorothy Thompson grew up on a farm in Bridgeville, Pennsylvania, a working-class community southwest of Pittsburgh. She was the oldest of four children. To meet her tuition costs, she waited on tables in the dining halls and typed other students' papers. Having little social experience as a young woman and being naturally rather blunt, Dorothy appreciated Miss Coolidge's tutoring in the social graces. In the activist college president she found a role model for herself.[34]

Dorothy Thompson was ambitious, smart, and assertive. She was inclined to be "bossy," but her energy and enthusiasm made her popular in spite of this. When Rachel understood that Dorothy was as taken by biology as she was, friendship between them was possible.[35]

Friendship with Mary Frye was a different matter. Her father was a successful ophthalmologist, and the family lived in the fashionable Dormont section of Pittsburgh's south hills. Before coming to PCW, Mary had traveled widely with her family, and had a certain worldliness and sophistication. She thought Miss Coolidge's lessons in manners and grace were silly and demeaning. But for all her advantages, Mary was not a snob. She was friendly, outgoing, and popular, certainly the most gregarious and openly affectionate of the three. Mary was also unique because she had entered PCW as a freshman with her heart set on going to medical school and becoming a doctor. It was Mary who first made friends with

Rachel and who insisted that they be lab partners for the second semester of biology.[36]

Mary Scott Skinker's biology class ignited Rachel Carson's mind. Biology revealed yet another way for Rachel to love nature. Her cognitive and observational skills were suited to it in the same way that her poetic skills enabled her to transcribe what she saw outdoors. Biology did not replace her love of observing nature or writing about it. Rather it reinforced her passion for the mystery and meaning of life, her "vision splendid." But the heady revelations of biology were hard to reconcile with her determination to be a writer.

Neither Croff nor Skinker seems ever to have suggested to Rachel that science and literature could be combined. What seems obvious now was then obscured at least in part by the chasm that existed in the 1920s in most liberal arts curricula between science and literature, a division enlarged by the issue of gender as well as the place of natural science in the lowest ranks of academic science. Rachel saw only the necessity of choosing between being a scientist and being a writer and the apparent incompatibility between the two disciplines. This was reinforced by the pressure to declare a major and accumulate the prescribed number of credits for graduation.

By the spring of 1927, Rachel admitted that her creative energies were focused on biology, not composition. Frustrated with her writing and what she considered her lack of imagination, Rachel lamented in a note to Croff written across a February theme, "I have gone dead! And have been since semesters!"

The truth is otherwise, however, for Rachel produced some of her best undergraduate writing in the spring of 1927, ending her sophomore year with As in English classes, biology, and psychology. One of her short stories, "Broken Lamps," won the coveted Omega literary prize awarded at Moving-Up Day in June. It was published in the *Englicode* on May 27, Rachel's twentieth birthday.[37]

"Broken Lamps" was written about the same time that Rachel experienced a defining moment. One winter night in Berry Hall, she was in her room alone reading Alfred, Lord Tennyson's poem "Locksley Hall" (1834), which Miss Croff had assigned for class that week. Outside a fierce thunderstorm was booming, rocking the rafters of the old Victorian mansion, the wind whistling and hissing through the iron-paned windows. Rachel read the lines

Cramming all the blast before it, in its breast a thunderbolt.
Let it fall on Locksley Hall, with rain or hail or fire or snow;
For the mighty wind arises, roaring seaward, and I go.

Something in the moment clarified her direction, telling her that the "vision splendid" she pursued lay with the sea.

Recalling that moment years later, Rachel wrote, "that line spoke to something within me, seeming to tell me that my own path led to the sea—which then I had never seen—and that my own destiny was somehow linked with the sea."[38]

Despite Rachel's harsh assessment of her literary abilities, what was different was not any lack of creativity but a change in its source. Her imagination was now stirred most by what she saw through her microscope, not what was fictioned by her experience. After searching conversations with both Croff and Skinker at the semester's close, Rachel struck a compromise; she would continue to major in English, but she would begin a minor in science.

The summer of 1927 proved to be another difficult one for the Carson family in general but particularly for Rachel, who once again had no time or place to herself. Marian and her daughters were still in the house. Robert and his family had nominally moved out, but Robert spent more nights at the Carson home than he did with his wife and daughter. In August Meredith and Frances moved to her father's house in Aspinwall, and Robert came back home permanently. So for part of the summer, there were five adults and two toddlers occupying the farmhouse. Apparently no one used the tent that summer.[39]

While Rachel was occupied with family matters, Mary Scott Skinker continued to work toward her doctorate in zoology. In the summer of 1925, Skinker had enrolled at Johns Hopkins University in Baltimore taking advanced embryology. The next summer she went to Cornell, completing courses in invertebrate zoology and comparative anatomy. In addition to earning advanced credits, Skinker was evaluating both institutions in order to decide where to enroll to complete her graduate degree.[40]

Skinker appraised her future at PCW realistically. Coolidge's appointment of Earl Wallace, who also had earned his degree at Columbia, as chair of the physics and chemistry department in 1925 had made it clear that Skinker had to complete her doctorate to advance in rank. Skinker got along well with Wallace, whom she may have known at Columbia, and they agreed on academic standards.

Wallace's promotion to the senior science position was part of a national trend by the end of the 1920s. He was the first of several male Ph.D.'s Coolidge hired. More and more women's colleges, especially those administered by a female, recruited men rather than women as department heads. Cora Coolidge defended her action on the basis of Wallace's degrees, but it was a thin disguise, as the other member of the chemistry and physics faculty was Katharina Tressler, an assistant professor, who had a Ph.D. from Cornell. For Skinker, Wallace's selection was further evidence of Coolidge's bias against women in science.[41]

In fairness to Coolidge, Wallace's appointment was in line with her goal of raising PCW's status and prestige. Like other college administrators of the period, female or male, Coolidge realized that male faculty upgraded the college's image. By 1929, when Rachel graduated, four of the nine departments at PCW were chaired by men.[42]

Rachel eagerly began the fall semester of her junior year with a course on the novel, composition with Miss Croff, and vertebrate biology and hygiene with Miss Skinker. She loved these classes but loathed her elective, an education course with a two-week practicum. Clearly secondary education was not her métier, and she thought herself fortunate to get a B minus in the course at the semester's end.[43]

In other endeavors Rachel was more successful that fall. She and Mary Frye were now good friends, and she was getting to like Dorothy Thompson. She continued to enjoy playing goalie on the hockey team. Although she never made the starting squad, she had the grades and the requisite practice times to be put in when her teammates failed to show up or were ineligible. She also was more active on the *Arrow* staff, and her byline appeared regularly in *The Englicode*. She had also found a close friend in her own class.[44]

Marjorie Stevenson, a bright day student from Pittsburgh who shared many of Rachel's interests and was herself a nonconformist, became Rachel's closest friend at PCW. Marj was a history major and excelled at ancient languages. Her father was a classicist at the University of Pittsburgh, and Marj grew up loving some of the same literature that Rachel did.

They met in French class freshman year, and both made the honor society, worked on the *Arrow* staff, and took German senior year. Stevenson was elegant, soft-spoken, fiercely independent, and uproariously funny when she wanted to be. As a day student, she had her own life at home and made little effort to involve herself in any campus activities except those she was expressly interested in. Like Rachel, Marj took her education seriously and was unabashedly scholarly.[45]

Both young women were frustrated by the embrace of materialism all around them and by academic requirements that sacrificed scholarship for the learning of numbing facts. Rachel was vocal in her dissatisfaction with the cultural and intellectual conformism she found at PCW. She believed a college education should provide a "sense of values—the ability to judge the good from the bad, the worthwhile from the unprofitable." She wanted education to be a "spiritual adventure" gained through the "undaunted efforts of an adventurous mind."[46]

By her junior year Rachel's intellectual frustrations were as honest as her idealism. While she was able to keep up her grades in other areas, biology absorbed her. Her excitement with the material was undiminished by her long hours of study.[47]

By the winter of 1927 Rachel was sincerely conflicted about her future course. In a mid-November writing slump, she complained "I want, above everything else in the world, to write, but that's the last job I can drive myself to do. I worship the idea of writing—yes, that's just the trouble." Yet during this period she produced some of her very best writing, including a difficult triolet of haunting beauty.[48]

Butterfly poised on a thistle's down.
Lend me your wings for a summer's day.
What care I for a kingly crown?
Butterfly poised on a thistle's down.
When I might wear your gossamer gown
And sit enthroned on an orchid spray.
Butterfly poised on a thistle's down.
Lend me your wings for a summer's day![49]

Croff read Rachel's verse to a silently admiring class. Afterward, the girls asked Rachel how she did it and where she got such a wonderful idea. Rachel replied that she knew a triolet was supposed to be a light, airy verse form, so she thought about the most beautiful, lightest things she knew: a butterfly and a thistle's down.[50]

About this same time Rachel, like the rest of the class of 1929, had her picture taken for *The Pennsylvanian*, the PCW yearbook. In order to save money, Coolidge had decided that the classes of 1928 and 1929 would share one yearbook. Pictures were taken in the early fall when Rachel was a junior. The class exchanged yearbooks and wrote in them in May 1928.[51]

Rachel's yearbook picture gives no hint of a young woman whose personal appearance might cause adverse comment. Rather, her portrait in black silk blouse with an organza rose on one shoulder stands out in the yearbook as one of the most attractive ones in her class. The poet in her is transparent in her face. There is little hint of the toughness or integrity that went along with the lyrical side of her personality.

Rachel's academic dilemma that fall was both philosophical and pragmatic. She was in college on a scholarship because she and her mother had planned that she would be a writer. Writing might lead to a professional life that did not require teaching. Moreover, writing was an accepted role for women. Coolidge and the faculty, especially Grace Croff, recognized Rachel's superior literary talent and encouraged her, sincerely believing that she could make a living that way. Coolidge did not believe that women had the intellect or the physical stamina for careers in science. Even if she was wrong, her objections were not frivolous. Her views reflected widely shared cultural norms and the real gender biases of the 1920s.

Comparatively few women succeeded in moving to the front ranks of science in the 1920s and 1930s, either in teaching or research. Most, like Mary Scott Skinker, found their way into teaching at women's colleges; fewer could support themselves in pure research or find jobs in business or government. Acutely aware of the financial implications of changing her major, Rachel knew that she also jeopardized her mother's dreams.[52]

But by 1928 Mary Scott Skinker had replaced Maria Carson and Grace Croff as Rachel's mentor. Skinker was a powerful role model. Her sober dedication and her infectious love of discovery unlocked possibilities of the same life for Rachel. Skinker showed her that through the life sciences she might understand, rather than merely observe, the natural world. Zoology, physiology, and bacteriology were addictive. A minor field in biology would not satisfy her. She wanted to immerse herself.

In January 1928 Rachel made up her mind. "I have something very exciting to tell you," she wrote Mary Frye who was on an extended trip with her family. "Get a big breath, Mary! I've changed my major. To what? Biology, of course. Miss Skinker hasn't recovered from the shock yet. She says after this nothing will ever surprise her. [I] broke the glad news to . . . [her] yesterday . . . and had a long talk with her last night. She certainly is a peach."[53]

She dropped her novel class and added chemistry and a required Bible course, in order to make up the necessary requirements for graduation. Rachel's relief at finally making a decision was palpable. Having no one else with whom to share her excitement, she urged Mary Frye to take embryology with her the following year. "You and I would have so much fun taking it with Miss Skinker. Isn't she a wonderful group advisor? I feel so 'safe' with my affairs in her hands now."[54]

Rachel's enthusiasm for what she was studying spilled over into other activities. The winter of 1928 was a particularly harsh one in Pittsburgh, but one evening proved memorable. A heavy snow had fallen over the weekend and the "house girls" in Woodland decided to have a coasting party. Rounding up two sleds and innumerable trays from the dining room, they went out coasting about eight-thirty one night and had "a perfectly glorious time."

Afterward the girls put on pajamas and bathrobes, built a fire in the drawing room, and feasted on "potato salad, olives, sandwiches and coffee." Then they turned off the lights and sat in the firelight singing songs until well after midnight. Rachel confessed that it "was one of the nicest times I've had since I came to college. I wouldn't have missed it for anything." It was one of the few times she felt perfectly comfortable.[55]

It might have been that same evening in front of the fire that someone asked Rachel how she ever got so interested in science in the first place. Rachel told them the story of finding the fossilized fish in the cliffs behind the Springdale farm and the questions it provoked for her. Rachel's classmates listened with a new appreciation after hearing this story.

In spite of the increased course load that majoring in science necessitated, Rachel had more fun that spring at PCW than at any other time. She played in all the basketball tournaments as a sub, and accepted a date for the junior prom. Rachel's roommate, Helen Myers, and her steady boyfriend fixed Rachel up with a fraternity brother. Rachel had a "glorious time" at the dance, she told Mary later. However, Rachel's letter to Mary told more about what Miss Skinker wore to the prom and how she looked than it did about her date.[56]

Helen Myers's recollection of the prom was less enthusiastic. Rachel, she said, seemed to enjoy getting all dressed up and being at the dance, but she was very quiet all evening. She thought the young man found making conversation with Rachel a challenge, but he asked Rachel out at least once more that spring. In late April 1928 he drove down from Westminster to PCW to see Rachel. There may have been other dates, but Rachel never mentions him again.[57]

By the spring of 1928, all Rachel's ambiguity about majoring in science had vanished. Instead she was already making plans for a career in science. Eager to have Mary come back to campus and share in the excitement, Rachel confided, "I think it's such fun to be majoring in Science! I don't see why I ever hesitated about it. Did I tell you that I'm hoping to go right on and get my Master's degree?"[58]

Skinker's oversight of Rachel's career fitted a well-regarded strategy among female scientists that had been going on since the late nineteenth century. Pioneering female scientists on the faculties of women's colleges guided the careers of their brightest students, ensuring their success and grooming their protégées to succeed them. Traditionally the teacher encouraged the student, becoming a mentor and close personal friend. Often the protégée joined the teacher on the same faculty, continuing the tradition. Skinker's relationship with Carson was typical.[59]

Mary Scott Skinker offered Rachel a vision of what she might become as well as a deep and enduring friendship. She quickened in Rachel a love of biology that they shared as long as Skinker lived. After Skinker's death, Rachel employed essentially the same process, although in abbreviated form, with Beverly Knecht, a talented young woman whose writing she guided for a time.

One of the very best things about being a biology major was going with Skinker on field trips. Rachel was in her element on these occasions, happiest outdoors, delighting both in finding a new specimen or recognizing an old friend. Skinker loved to take her classes out to a rural area called Wildwood in the north hills where rock quarries, pools, and creeks produced abundant specimens. Although Rachel and her mother had gone there often to find wildflowers and watch birds, with Skinker the experience was unforgettable.

Skinker had little training in botany or what would be considered ecology today. She was a keen naturalist and was sensitive to the preservation of rare species of plants and animals. Perhaps her experience in Colorado had added to her feeling for botanical conservation as well. For Rachel, who already had a deep understanding of wildflowers, birds, and animals, Skinker's passion for preservation was profoundly confirming. Skinker did not have to awaken an ecological consciousness in Rachel, she only had to broaden it.[60]

When Rachel returned after spring break, Mary Skinker stunned her with her news that she had decided to take a leave of absence from PCW the following year to work on her doctorate in zoology. Although she was not yet certain whether she would go to Cornell or Johns Hopkins, she planned to complete the course work in a year. Skinker fully appreciated how Rachel would feel about her departure and had agonized over being absent for her friend's senior year. But her position at PCW was increasingly tenuous and her dissatisfaction with the school's philosophy mounted each semester. Skinker had to think about her own career and, in doing so, influenced Rachel's career choices as well. President Coolidge was not enthusiastic about Skinker's leave, but she approved it.

Rachel's decision to switch majors had further eroded the relationship between president and professor. Coolidge resented Skinker's influence over Rachel and Dorothy Thompson, who had also switched her major from history to biology that spring. Coolidge could not help but be jealous of Skinker's personal popularity with these bright young women whose devotion was obvious. In the end, the issue of standards, gender, and science cost the college its most gifted female instructor in the biological sciences and the disaffection of its most celebrated alumna.

Rachel understood Skinker's decision to finish her doctorate. Her first response was not to mourn Skinker's departure from PCW but to leave PCW as well and follow her mentor, who had decided to enroll at Johns Hopkins. Confiding only in Mary Frye and Marjorie Stevenson, Rachel applied for graduate standing in zoology at Johns Hopkins University in April 1928.[61]

In her application, Rachel told the admissions committee that her specific interests were in genetics and comparative anatomy. She expected to complete her master's degree in two years. On May 8 Rachel was notified of her admission to graduate standing by H. S. Jennings, chairman of the Zoology Department.

Admission to Johns Hopkins was only half the battle. In order to go, Rachel had to have scholarship support. Students who did not enter with a bachelor's degree had to pay a hundred dollars more in tuition than "later-year" students. Rachel's scholarship application listed three references: Miss Skinker, O. W. Johnson, the principal of Parnassus High School, and Paul Stuart, her father's attorney, all of whom certified that she could not attend without financial assistance. In her letter, Skinker confided that Maria Carson, now fifty-nine years old, had applied to her for secretarial work to augment the family income so Rachel might be able to go.[62]

While Rachel waited to hear from the scholarship committee, she agonized about what to do. She wrote Mary Frye: "I still haven't any idea what I'm going to do next year. In lots of ways I'd hate not to graduate with my class. I wish I wasn't always having to make these awful decisions." She also told Mary that Coolidge had "let the cat out of the bag" in chapel, revealing that Skinker was taking a year's leave of absence. "I'll bet Miss Skinker could have choked her, for I know she didn't want to have it known."[63]

In the end, Rachel had no choice but to remain at PCW for her senior year. Although Johns Hopkins offered her a small stipend, the tuition amounted to several hundred dollars more than at PCW. She already owed the college over $1,500; further debt was out of the question. Rachel packed for the summer in Springdale with a heavy heart. Before she left campus, she and Mary gave Skinker a small going-away present of two carefully chosen books, including a collection of essays by Christopher Morley. Although Rachel was sad for herself, she was happy for Mary Skinker. That summer was calmer than the previous two had been. Rachel spent the early weeks reading and working on a bullfrog skeleton she had brought home. She tutored two high school students, one in Latin and English, the other in geometry. Both students passed their high school examinations, and Rachel earned seventy-five dollars toward her final year's tuition.

Rachel and Miss Skinker corresponded frequently that summer. Skinker was at the Marine Biology Laboratory, in Woods Hole, Massachusetts, on the extreme southwestern end of Cape Cod, where she had won a seat in protozoology. Skinker wrote enthusiastically about her days at MBL, as the laboratory was known. "To be engrossed in one's work is good form here and that's what I enjoy most. . . ." Rachel savored each letter, happily confiding to Mary that Miss Skinker "certainly knows how to write [a letter] that makes you feel as if you'd been talking to her."[64]

Skinker sent her protégée clippings from the Woods Hole newsletter to whet Rachel's appetite to study at the MBL someday herself. Rachel needed no coaxing. She had already decided that she and Mary should go there together the following summer. "It must be a biologist's paradise," she wrote Mary.[65]

Rachel and Mary spent time that summer refining their plan to organize a science club at PCW in the fall. Planning was meticulous and secretive. The club would be named Mu Sigma Sigma, which were Miss Skinker's initials in Greek. Mary Frye, ever the entrepreneur, had a Pittsburgh jeweler design and produce tiny jeweled pins with the Greek letters on them for the new club members. But Rachel anticipated trouble from the administration, which she believed would not be enthusiastic about their idea. "They would just as leave there weren't any science majors," Rachel told Mary.[66]

But Rachel's worries proved groundless; Coolidge did approve the club. Rachel became its first president, and Mary, vice president. An article in *The Arrow*, written by Rachel with her picture heading it, introduced Mu Sigma Sigma to the PCW student body as a society that "provides a place for scientific interests as part of the college activities."[67]

The summer held one last surprise. Rachel learned from Marjorie that Grace Croff was not returning to PCW either. Losing Croff at the same time as Skinker took Rachel aback. Croff had been popular with the class of 1929, who had dedicated their half of the yearbook to her. She had been Rachel's first mentor, and Rachel had been deprived of saying good-bye to her. They never found out exactly why Croff left, but Rachel speculated that it could not be to the college's credit. Rachel began the year feeling lonely and bereft of support.[68]

As it turned out, however, German instructor Brunhilde Fitz-Randolph became the one faculty member with whom Rachel enjoyed a warm friendship her senior year. Her high standards enabled both Rachel and Dorothy Thompson to pass their German language requirements in graduate school without difficulty. Fitz-Randolph and Mary Scott Skinker had been friends as well as colleagues. Fitz-Randolph's brother, an officer in the German air force, had been Skinker's suitor. Just before she left PCW in June 1928, Skinker ended the relationship. Her decision to pursue a doctorate was linked to her decision not to marry, a choice that Rachel understood and approved.[69]

Rachel's biggest difficulty her senior year was dealing with Skinker's temporary replacement, Dr. Anna Rachel Whiting, the wife of University of Pittsburgh geneticist Phineas Whiting. Skinker had concurred in Whiting's selection, a hasty action she later regretted. Anna Whiting was the first married woman Coolidge appointed to the faculty. A graduate of Smith College, she had a doctorate in eugenics from Iowa State University.

Anna Whiting offered a sharply different physical and intellectual image from the elegant and energetic Mary Scott Skinker. Whiting's style was plain, her speech broadly midwestern, and her manner laconic. Her academic training was also markedly different from Skinker's. The product of the science department of a state agricultural university, where she had worked in cattle breeding, Whiting had little training in laboratory life sciences and had no interest in field study. Eager to keep the position at PCW should Skinker fail to return, Whiting did everything she could to ingratiate herself with Coolidge. Whiting's ideas of how science should be taught to young women preparing for marriage and motherhood mirrored Coolidge's views.[70]

To her credit, Whiting had agreed to teach histology, embryology, and genetics to those students who needed such courses for graduate school. Rachel took histology and genetics from Whiting first semester, embryology and a seminar in scientific topics with Phineas Whiting at the University of Pittsburgh the second term. She also studied organic chemistry and qualitative analysis with Earl Wallace and a final semester of physics with Katharina Tressler.

Like many small women's colleges in the late 1920s, PCW was slow to drop outdated courses. The downturn in the economy, particularly in western Pennsylvania, combined with the lack of prospective employment for women in science, hardened Coolidge's resolve against offering advanced science courses to a handful of students. She allowed Whiting to offer these courses only for one year.

Unfortunately, it did not take the biology triumvirate, Rachel, Dorothy, and Mary, very long to find out that despite Whiting's doctorate in genetics, she was especially ill-prepared to teach the laboratory segments of histology and embryology. These classes were a farce as far as Rachel and her friends were concerned. Rachel became increasingly critical and bitter as the year progressed.

Rachel and Dorothy wrote Skinker regularly, apprehensive lest Whiting's courses leave them unprepared for graduate work. Skinker apologized for her part in bringing about Whiting's appointment. "You can never realize how sorry I am the way things have gone this year." Skinker admitted to Dorothy Thompson that she had been uneasy about Whiting's "high school" methodology.[71]

At the end of December 1928, Rachel reapplied to Johns Hopkins and was speedily admitted to zoology as a "higher student," scheduled to appear for the examination and degree in May 1931. In her application, she described her current research problem: a comparison of the anatomy of the brain and cranial nerves of the turtle (*Testudinata*) with those of other reptiles. She had made a beginning on this work, including laboratory dissection and extensive reading.

Her scholarship application this time was supported by Carl Doxsee, PCW English Department chairman, Anna Whiting, J. F. Mitchell, a family friend who was superintendent of the Pennsylvania State Employment Office, and H. Frank Hare, the principal of the School Street School. Anna Whiting's letter was brief but enthusiastic in its endorsement. "Rachel's training in the foundation courses," Whiting wrote, "has been thorough and her intense interest in research is most unusual in an undergraduate. She should become one of the few really exceptional graduate students."[72]

In her scholarship request, Rachel put the best face she could on her desperate financial situation, telling the committee: "My most serious handicap in undertaking my graduate work is a financial one. My undergraduate work has been a heavy strain, and my expenses next year will constitute a grave problem."[73]

In a separate letter, Skinker put it more bluntly. "She is undertaking graduate work at a great disadvantage financially, since she has been receiving assistance from the college and must at some time pay that obligation, though fortunately no interest accumulates on this and thus her burdens do not increase if she goes on with graduate work now." Reminding the committee that Rachel had been admitted the previous year but could not come because of her family's financial situation, Skinker added, "her qualifications are peculiarly high along other lines than scholarship, for she possesses discrimination and judgement of a person much more mature. . . . Her influence upon her fellow students is admirable."[74]

Skinker's letter had influence with the scholarship committee even though she was not then a doctoral candidate there herself, as she had planned. Skinker returned to the home of her older sister, Anne, in Washington, D.C., from her summer at the Woods Hole laboratory in poor health. Her doctors counseled against embarking on full-time graduate work. Skinker had to content herself with one advanced class at George Washington University. She never discussed her personal life or health with Rachel or the others, but kept up a cheerful correspondence with each of them through the fall.

President Coolidge asked Skinker for a status report at the end of the semester. When she learned that Skinker was not in graduate school full time, she was angry. Failing to extract more details from Rachel and Dorothy, Coolidge criticized Skinker, remarking publicly on her failure to carry out her program, implying a breech of ethics. In February Skinker submitted her resignation to Coolidge, stating simply that she would not be returning for the following academic year. Anna Whiting's appointment as acting head of biology was made permanent.[75]

In mid-April the news finally came. Johns Hopkins offered Carson a full tuition scholarship of two hundred dollars for her first year of graduate work. A proud Maria Carson made sure the local paper published the news. "The scholarship awarded by Johns Hopkins University is one of seven offered to applicants of high scholastic standing who have given evidence of their ability to carry on independent research. The honor of this award is seldom conferred upon women." Now the Carsons had to find a way to finance Rachel's living expenses in Baltimore.[76]

Robert Carson had never been able to sell more than a handful of his Springdale lots. With the Depression worsening, their value depreciated. After several meetings with Miss Coolidge in the fall of 1928, the Carsons deeded Rachel two large contiguous lots, which she in turn signed over to PCW as collateral against her obligation. If the Carsons could find no buyers for the lots, Rachel would begin making payment on her debt of $1,600 in the fall of 1930. Rachel and President Coolidge signed a legal agreement to this effect January 28, 1929.[77]

Rachel's undergraduate studies were nearing an end. In February she wrote a letter to her mother on her sixtieth birthday acknowledging her loneliness and her joy in her mother's companionship.

> Dearest Mama, . . . I only hope it may be in my power to help make the year you are starting today a happier and more comfortable one than you have known for many years. And your next birthday and many more to come, I hope I can spend with you—now this four year banishment or what ever you choose to call it is almost finished.
>
> You will never know—you are too modest and self-deprecating to know—what you mean to me and how thankful I am for each year we are spared to each other. I am glad that soon we can do more things together and share our experiences even more. All my love, Rachel.[78]

Perhaps the best news of all that spring came when Rachel learned she had won a seat at the Marine Biological Laboratory at Woods Hole for the summer, where she would be a "beginning investigator" for eight weeks. Mary Frye would go too, as a "student in invertebrate zoology." Skinker had nominated Rachel for the college's seat before her leave, and the PCW faculty had concurred. Rachel remembered the line from "Locksley Hall," "roaring seaward, and I go." At least for the summer of 1929, her destiny was linked with the sea.[79]

Commencement exercises at Pennsylvania College for Women took place on Monday, June 10, in the college chapel. It was a bright sunny morning when the seventy members of the class of 1929, all in black caps and gowns, followed Dean Helen Marks and President Cora Coolidge in solemn procession to their places in the front, each in alphabetical order. Eleven women graduated with honors, including Rachel's freshman roommate, Dorothy Appleby, and her best friend, Marjorie Stevenson. Rachel, two weeks past her twenty-second birthday, was one of only three to be awarded their degree magna cum laude.[80]

The entire Carson family attended, including Maria's older sister, Ida, who had come all the way from Illinois with her son, John. Maria's dreams for Rachel had come true in ways she had never imagined possible. Her daughter was the scholar she had always wanted to be. Now with honors and awards, Rachel was on her way to an independent life if she wanted, unfettered by the need to depend on a husband to support her. She was off to graduate school not to be a writer or a naturalist but to become a student of the life sciences. Maria Carson judged her sacrifices worthwhile.

For her family's sake, Rachel endured the congratulations and acclaim. But she winced especially whenever anyone said they were "not surprised" by her fine achievements. She always hated that particular remark. Writing to Dorothy Thompson exactly a year later, when Dorothy was awarded her degree with the same high honors, Rachel confessed, "I didn't care a rap myself about receiving the empty honors of PCW, but I knew those who were interested in me would have been disappointed if I hadn't gotten whatever glory was being handed out, and for that reason I was glad." Ever the pragmatist, she added "and then, since one has earned it, one might as well have that record to carry on to one's future Alma Mater."[81]

Mary Scott Skinker, responsible for so much of who and what Rachel was by 1929, was not present to see her protégée graduate. In the course of things Cora Helen Coolidge had maligned Skinker's reputation and personal integrity—an act Rachel Carson would never completely forgive. Yet she knew that Pennsylvania College for Women had set her on her course. She was not ungrateful.

That fine June afternoon as she packed up her belongings in the corner room of Woodland Hall that she and Helen had shared for three years, Rachel believed that she had forsaken the poetry in her heart for the vision in her head and the microscope's mysterious refractions. As she reread the notes her classmates had written in her yearbook, Marjorie Stevenson's words tugged at her. She would reread them often in the next couple years.

> Rachel, I want you to remember what I told you about a wild lady biologist. Remember I prophesy you'll be a famous author yet. Please don't take all the frogs and skeletons too seriously. . . .[82]

Thanks to Skinker, she was going "seaward." She had read about it, dreamed of it, even imagined the taste of it. The metaphors of her poems and the images in her stories had captured fragments of it. Her "vision splendid" had taken on a different aspect from what she had at first contemplated, yet it was only the medium that had changed, not the object at all. With the same unyielding determination she had brought to becoming a writer four years earlier, Rachel now turned to becoming a scientist.

3

"The Decision for Science"

Back in Springdale, neither the countryside nor the young woman was quite the same as either had been four years earlier. For the next month, Rachel took every opportunity to be outdoors, roaming the familiar woods and hills behind the house and following the streams that fed into the Allegheny River. It was a farewell gesture to her childhood and to the natural surroundings that nurtured her.

The woods were still there, but a large part of the Carson homestead had been cleared for lots. Unpaved streets intersected at right angles down the hill and off to the east. Several large trees had died in the apple orchard, and many of the rest looked tired. The honeysuckle bush at the end of the porch, however, was bigger than ever, and her father's prize rosebushes flourished in the front yard. The horse was gone as well as the other barn animals. A handful of chickens scratched about, happier with no dogs to harass them, and a family of cats lived in the old barn.[1]

The most dramatic changes that Rachel observed were not to the physical appearance of the farm or the house but to the river and the air. The glue factory and its stench were gone. In its place was the smell of sulfur, a by-product of the Harwick Coal and Coke Company, which supplied all the coal to Duquesne Light's new Colfax Power Station, now the Pittsburgh area's largest supplier of electrical power.

At the other end of Springdale was the newly enlarged West Penn Power Company. So now there were two plants generating power within two miles of each other, squeezing the town between them.[2]

The expanding utilities produced jobs, power, and pollution. Rachel's father still sometimes worked part-time as a night supervisor at the West Penn station, Marian had a stenographer's job there, and Robert worked as part-time repairman. The population of Springdale had increased and its schools and churches expanded. The school district bought several of Robert Carson's lots in 1925 for the new Colfax School.

It seemed that by 1929 the Duquesne Light and West Penn power plants competed to see which of them could disperse the most waste into the river. The fouling of the Allegheny River went on year round, but it was more obvious in the summer months. The river looked as dirty as it smelled.

Along the south side of Pittsburgh Street between the two power stations, new businesses and industries sprang up each year, each seemingly more environmentally damaging than the last. In the three decades since the Carsons had settled into the once wildly beautiful valley of the lower Allegheny, there was no doubt that industry had brought technological progress, higher income, and regular work, but it had also produced environmental blight. Springdale was not unique. All along the Allegheny, towns identical to Springdale were remarkable only by the degree of their ugliness.

When Rachel stood on the long front porch of the farmhouse that June, the horizon she looked out on was dominated not by the farms and fields of her childhood but by the tall smokestacks of the power generators. She felt little sadness about leaving Springdale. The memory of the defilement industrial pollution brought would remain.

By mid-July Rachel and her mother had finished hemming her dresses and settling what financial affairs they could at the bank so Rachel would have enough money for her summer travels. Rachel's departure for Woods Hole marked the first time she had ever left her mother to go farther than sixteen miles away. For the first time the two would be physically inaccessible to each other. With excitement and some small anxiety, at the end of the month Rachel boarded the eastbound train at the familiar Springdale station on Butler Street.

Rachel's first stop was not Woods Hole but Baltimore, Maryland. There she spent one very hot, muggy day finding a room for the fall and becoming better acquainted with the sprawling Homewood campus of Johns Hopkins University. She reserved a room at 216 Homewood Terrace, on the east side of campus within walking distance of Gilman Hall, where the zoology laboratory was located in cramped quarters on the ground level. As an urban and nearly exclusively graduate university, Johns Hopkins had only one dormitory, and it was not open to female students. Most everyone lived in a boardinghouse or found rooms around the perimeter of the rolling, wooded campus whose design had been guided by the sure hand of landscape architect Frederick Law Olmsted.

Rachel was not required to register until October 1, but she felt more comfortable knowing she had housing and knew her route to and from the laboratories. She took the trolley car back down North Charles Street, lined with its stately linden trees, to the bus station, where she boarded a bus for the short trip to Washington, D.C. This was the part of the journey that she looked forward to the most for at its end she would be reunited with Mary Scott Skinker.[3]

Skinker had not been idle since leaving PCW, in spite of her health problems. She took courses toward her doctorate in zoology at George Washington University at night and was employed at the zoological division of the U.S. Department of Agriculture as a researcher in parasitology. She lived with her older sister Anne Skinker.[4]

Mary Scott Skinker had gone ahead on vacation at the family cabin in Skyland, Virginia, just west of Luray on the eastern edge of the Shenandoah Valley. Rachel's bus from Baltimore arrived in Washington, D.C., in the early evening. Skinker had arranged for Rachel to spend that evening with Anne at their apartment and take the bus the next morning for Luray. Once she reached Luray, Rachel boarded a rattling old taxicab, which deposited her at the foot of the mountain. From there she continued up the nearly four-mile trail to Skyland on horseback.

Along the forest road Rachel was enchanted to see baby quail and even wild turkey scuttle off into the underbrush. Finally she reached the top of the mountain, an elevation of about 4,000 feet, and the sprinkling of cabins called Skyland. "I needn't tell you," she wrote Dorothy Thompson, "that the best part of the whole trip was when I saw Miss Skinker coming along the path to meet me!"

Mentor and protégée, now affectionate friends, spent the next three or four days together at Skyland. They rode horses on several occasions, hiked some of the nearby peaks for breathtaking views of the Shenandoah Valley below, and played a good deal of tennis.

Most of all, Rachel enjoyed sitting with Skinker in front of an open fire in the evenings, talking to the woman who not long before had seemed a distant idol but now had become the most important person in her intellectual and emotional life. There were no longer any boundaries between mentor and protégée. Both women were committed to the deepest well-being of the other.[5]

Mary Scott Skinker was Rachel's model, both of what a scientist was and what she herself might expect from a life spent in the practice of that discipline. Skinker's career also reflected the increasingly limited possibilities for women in the biological sciences in the 1920s and 1930s. Although she was a gifted teacher and had the respect of her colleagues in zoology both at Columbia University and the Marine Biological Laboratory at Woods Hole, Skinker was unable to support herself in full-time research or to advance academically because of a combination of impediments.

She had come to academic science after a distinguished career of fifteen years in elementary and secondary teaching, entering graduate study as an older student with the clear intention of teaching rather than research. Although she had been on the edges of the so-called Columbia gang, which included some of the leading students of marine biology during her two years of graduate work there, she had ended her studies with a master's degree. Without the advantages of a distinguished mentor and an advanced degree, Skinker's employment possibilities were limited to small third- or fourth-rank women's liberal arts colleges, such as PCW.

When she left Pittsburgh in 1928, Skinker had hoped that her teaching record combined with an advanced degree would lead to an academic appointment where science was taken more seriously than it was at PCW. But the depressed economy, the tightening professionalization of zoology, and her age, health, and gender were against her. In 1929 and nearing her fortieth birthday, Mary Scott Skinker was at a professional crossroads. The only way she could both support herself and gain the necessary academic credentials to move ahead was to find an interim position as a government scientist while finishing her graduate work in the evenings. Skinker's passion was teaching, communicating what she loved most to others, and inspiring them to learn for themselves. Science in general and biology in particular was her medium.

None of this had been wasted on Rachel Carson, whose enthusiasm for zoology was, in large measure, testament to Skinker's zest for the subject and her ability to inspire. Rachel would follow the main outlines of Mary Scott Skinker's career with only minor deviations until her literary success presented alternatives Skinker's more scholarly preferences and ill health never yielded. As single women in science, their choices were made for many of the same reasons. Rachel's dedication to research and her interest in educating the nonscientist reflected attitudes instilled by her mentor.[6]

At July's end, Rachel and Mary Scott left Skyland. They decided to walk rather than ride down the mountain. It was an arduous excursion, yielding something to look at and talk about at every turn, a walk each would remember. They rode the bus back to Washington together that evening. Skinker put Rachel on the train out of Washington bound for New York City at 1:25 A.M. Even at that hour, Rachel recalled that the heat was insufferable in the cavernous, copper-roofed Union Station, making it feel as if it were midday. Eight hours later she arrived in New York City for a day of sightseeing.

That evening Rachel collected her belongings and headed for the New York harbor and her tiny stateroom aboard the Colonial Line passenger boat, which would take her to New Bedford, Massachusetts, and from there to Woods Hole. The boat trip was longer but cheaper than the train and a much more exciting trip for Rachel, who finally found herself "at sea."[7]

Woods Hole was then, as now, a charming seaside resort of mainly small wood-framed houses. It was dominated by the rambling Victorian headquarters of the U.S. Fish Commission with its pillared porches, gabled roof, and distinguishing cupola. The Fish Commission laboratory next to it had windows across its entire length looking seaward. There were few reminders of the primitive industries that formerly had dotted the inner harbor of Woods Hole, including the guano factory, once the community's economic mainstay.

Spencer Baird, the assistant secretary of the Smithsonian Institution and the first U.S. Fish Commissioner, had chosen Woods Hole as the site of the commission's field laboratory in 1871. It had a pleasant climate, beautiful vistas, and access to a variety of marine habitats. These same virtues, in addition to its easy accessibility by train from Boston, led a larger group of scientists and teachers to join with Baird to locate the Marine Biological Laboratory (MBL) at Woods Hole in 1888 as an educational center for marine biological study.[8]

From the beginning of the MBL, its organizers decided that women would participate in the scientific community both as students and teachers. Such leading women scientists as Cornelia Clapp of Mount Holyoke College and Susan Hallowell of Wellesley College were founding participants. Women were members of the original board of trustees, although their role in the governing organization had been dramatically reduced by 1900. Even so, women continued to be welcomed and were well represented as students at various levels, less so as faculty, until World War II.[9]

Over the years aspects of research and institutional control changed, but the MBL was always characterized by its tightly interwoven network of scientists representing the leadership of American biology. Formal hierarchy of the laboratory was kept at a minimum; students and beginning investigators worked in the same laboratory as distinguished professors and Nobel laureates.

But the MBL was not just a scientific research community; it was also a social and academic elite whose members represented and maintained the core discipline and hammered out the implications of the latest theoretical and physical discoveries in an atmosphere of relaxed conviviality. The MBL was a "biologist's club" where scientists could relax in an environment free from university obligations and outside distractions. Many scientists brought their families to Woods Hole to vacation for the summer. The presence of wives and children enlivened the social activities and added to the resort atmosphere.[10]

The MBL offered six- and eight-week courses in the summertime. The basic course in elementary invertebrate zoology was distinguished by preselected and precollected marine materials and the experience of years of managing and culturing marine organisms. Embryology, general physiology, marine botany, and a popular course in protozoology offered by Columbia University professor Gary Calkins were standard curricula in the late 1920s.[11]

A particular advantage of research at the MBL was that participants could, if they preferred, study living organisms without having to tramp the wilds or brave the wilderness to find specimens. Living sea urchins, horseshoe crabs, limpets, and other mollusks offered live alternates to the standard fare of pickled specimens. In addition the MBL maintained its own collecting boat, the *Cayadella*, which daily supplied the latest population data as well as live material for identification and culture. If these sources should prove insufficient, then the Fish Commission with its aquaria and collecting tanks provided an even larger collection to sample.

When Rachel arrived in August 1929, the MBL consisted of approximately five buildings: Old Main, the newer L-shaped red-brick Crane and Lillie buildings, and the smaller supply and Candle Building. Rachel's seat was in one of the laboratories in Crane. There had never been a "woman's table" at the MBL as there was at the older Zoological Institute in Naples, Italy, upon which the MBL had been modeled. Female students and beginning investigators at MBL were assigned lab tables like everyone else on the basis of their research project. Rachel's "seat" cost one hundred dollars. PCW, as the subscribing institution, paid for it.[12]

The rest of Rachel's expenses for the six weeks were modest. Mary Frye, who had arrived several days earlier, had, at Skinker's direction, engaged a room for four dollars a week for the two of them in The Apartment House, conveniently across the street from Rachel's laboratory.

Rachel and Mary took their meals at the MBL Mess, which boasted linen tablecloths and formal white-coated waiters. Dinner started promptly at 6:00 P.M. Tables were assigned for the season and each table had a host. Everyone ate together, family style. Conversation was amiable but often intense. Information and ideas flew back and forth, and newcomers were drawn into the endless discussion of research. The mess cost less than seven dollars a week. Rachel was immediately enchanted with Woods Hole and the scientific lifestyle.[13]

"The town is much more attractive than I'd expected to find it," she enthusiastically wrote Dorothy Thompson. "One can't walk very far in any direction without running into water." The MBL library especially pleased her. Her first introduction to a large research library, it "seemed to have everything."[14]

Rachel discovered a bewildering array of scientific journals from around the world. Rare books and new books, each filled with widely scattered but rich information about the sea, provided a feast for her imagination and an endless source for her curiosity. She later recalled spending "long hours" in that "excellent library searching for the answers to questions that filled [her] mind." There is no doubt that the genesis of all Carson's sea books, but particularly *The Sea Around Us*, belongs to this first summer at Woods Hole. It was then that she "began storing away facts about the sea"—facts discovered in scientific literature cataloged in the MBL library, by dissection at the research table, in dialogue with others, and experienced with each walk along the Cape Cod shore.[15]

At Skinker's urging, Rachel had applied to the MBL as a "beginning investigator" in research. Rachel was one of seventy-one beginning investigators that summer, thirty-one of whom were women. It was a comfortable and compatible group including junior faculty, graduate students, and newly graduated students. As a beginning investigator, Rachel's task was to use the time to further define her research on the cranial nerves of reptiles that she had begun at PCW so that she would be further along on a project suitable for her master's thesis at Johns Hopkins.[16]

Rheinart P. (R. P.) Cowles, the marine biologist at Johns Hopkins with whom Rachel was to study, was also at the MBL for the summer. At his suggestion, Rachel spent a considerable amount of time in the library trying to narrow her research. She discovered that nothing had been done on the terminal nerve in any reptiles except the turtle, so she decided to compare its form and function in lizards, snakes, and perhaps crocodiles. Cowles encouraged her to do a comparative study. She also continued to refine the set of lab directions for the dissection of the cranial nerves of the turtle she had begun at PCW, which Cowles thought could be published. Rachel's biggest difficulty at the MBL was overcoming the lack of training she had experienced during her senior year in courses with Anna Whiting. Not only did she feel unprepared for the research she wanted to do, but she also lacked confidence that she had the skills to do it. With some bitterness Rachel advised Dorothy, who still had one more year at PCW, "You may be glad you aren't taking anymore courses from A.A.W. The less you can have to do with biology at PCW the better. (As if you didn't know that! Excuse me if I seem to indulge in aphorisms.)"[17]

Rachel did not spend all of her time at Woods Hole in the laboratory. She was delighted to discover the recreational opportunities the resort town afforded as well as the benefits of relaxed association with scientists who could give her advice about her career. There were impromptu beach parties, picnics, and collecting trips. Mary insisted on teaching Rachel how to swim the crawl, and the two frequently played tennis.

In her laboratory, at the Mess, and on the beach, Rachel also met scientists from the U.S. Bureau of Fisheries. She and Mary were invited to go out for a day on the *Albatross II*, the bureau's research ship, for a deep-sea collecting trip. During that trip and through association with the Fisheries' scientists, Rachel identified the bureau as a place with rich research potential.[18]

Rachel and Mary especially liked to walk along the shore at low tide, looking in the tide pools, finding new organisms among the rocks or clinging to the seaweed. Mary remembers that these excursions with Rachel had a "mystical quality" about them. Rachel would wander off by herself, silently watching the ocean, utterly captivated by the sounds, smells, and rhythm of the ocean as well as by the variety of the marine life all around her. She had dreamed about it for so long; now she was literally surrounded by it. When there was a full moon, Rachel and Mary went down to the fisheries' dock and observed the mating ritual of thousands of polychete worms, writhing just below the surface of the dark water. Watching it, Rachel felt united with an ancient time and rite. It was a breathtaking event, one she would watch again and again with utter fascination. Perhaps she shared some of her deeper feelings about this experience with Skinker; certainly she did with her mother; but her letters to Dorothy remained practical and descriptive.[19]

She urged Dorothy to apply for the "seat" next summer, telling her that all in all the MBL was "a delightful place to biologize." She now understood how people got in the habit of returning to Woods Hole and the MBL every summer. But ever the pragmatist, Rachel had already decided that a teaching position somewhere the following summer would be more valuable to her than returning to the MBL, much as she would like to do so. Rachel's six weeks at the MBL were both a rewarding intellectual experience and an intensely spiritual time. Comfortable working in a coeducational atmosphere where her research work was validated by her peers, she reaffirmed her decision for science. Although she had come to Woods Hole full of self-doubt about her skills, she left with a heightened sense of worth as a scientist, much more secure in her ability. Her silent walks along the shore at night, the explorations of the tide line, and her collecting experiences resonated with her spiritual apprehension of and wonder at nature's complexity. Her romantic, girlhood vision was given reality and her professional career concrete direction.

In mid-September, Rachel and Mary boarded a through train from Boston to Pittsburgh. Mary had only a few days left before she returned for her senior year at PCW. Classes began at Johns Hopkins two weeks later, and Rachel wanted to spend time with her mother.

At the end of September 1929, Rachel left Springdale to begin her graduate studies. She did not know then that it was the last time she would ever take leave from her childhood home and the grimy Allegheny River community that had once nurtured her sense of wonder and provided her earliest bonds with nature. In Baltimore, she quickly deposited her few possessions in her room on Homewood Terrace then once again set out for Washington.

Knowing of Rachel's growing interest in marine biology, Mary Scott Skinker probably made an appointment for Rachel to meet Elmer Higgins, the acting director of the U.S. Bureau of Fisheries, Division of Scientific Inquiry, then in the Department of Commerce. Skinker and

Higgins had met the previous summer when both of them had been at Woods Hole. They had colleagues in common in the intimate company of federal science.[20]

Although the economic downturn was beginning to affect jobs at every level of the government, Skinker thought that Elmer Higgins was a fair and intelligent man who could advise Rachel about employment possibilities in fishery biology. Higgins had navigated the pitfalls of federal science expertly in his brief career and had a broad view of the field of fisheries research. Once more Mary Scott Skinker's own experience shaped Rachel's choices. Skinker knew firsthand how difficult it was to find challenging academic employment. She realistically appraised the possibilities of a woman without either a doctorate or institutional affiliation to secure research funds. Considering her own and Rachel's similar financial limitations, Skinker thought Rachel should not rule out the possibilities offered by government science.

Elmer Higgins was an approachable, energetic bureau chief in his late thirties, who was an expert on shore fishes of the South Atlantic region. He was interested in Skinker's estimate of Rachel Carson's abilities and willing to meet her young protégée. Familiar with the employment barriers for women in biology, he thought government science a more likely option for Rachel than either teaching or museum work. The interview was brief but instructive. Neither participant could have predicted then that Higgins would play a critical role in Rachel's career as a scientist and writer. The business immediately at hand was for Rachel to complete a master's degree in zoology in the next two years.[21]

Biology at Johns Hopkins University at the end of the 1920s still bore the imprint of William Keith Brooks, the great American marine biologist and embryologist who, from 1876 until his death in 1908, directed the Chesapeake Zoological Laboratory, which anticipated Woods Hole by some years, and the Zoological Laboratory at the university during the period of its most impressive growth. Brooks was particularly interested in questions of vertebrate ancestry and the definitions of homologous structures. During his long tenure, he made Johns Hopkins famous as a center for the study of morphology, which deals with the identification of form and structure in plants and animals.

All zoology courses at Johns Hopkins emphasized laboratory training. Brooks believed that beginning graduate students should be left on their own to learn to work independently and become self-reliant. He also insisted that students be thoroughly conversant in the current scientific literature. Accordingly he instituted the Journal Club, composed of faculty and students who met weekly to read and discuss recent publications. He also established a Morphological Seminar on the German model that was organized around a central theme. During the course of the semester, students prepared and presented papers based on their readings in the current literature.[22]

Brooks's successor as director of the Zoological Laboratory in 1910 was the brilliant Herbert Spencer (H. S.) Jennings, who came to leadership as the direction of American biology was undergoing profound change. Jennings shared his mentor's broad philosophical understanding of biology but was an enthusiastic advocate of experimental biology, especially genetics.[23]

Complementing H. S. Jennings on the faculty of the zoological laboratory in the 1920s were S. O. Mast, in physiology, R. P. Cowles, a student of Brooks's, who concentrated on marine biology and hydrographic studies of the Chesapeake Bay, and E. A. Andrews, another one of Brooks's students, who spent his life studying tiny marine tube-dwelling ciliates. But it was Jennings who set the tone of the department. His emphasis on productive scholarship throughout the laboratory was legendary, as was his preference for graduate students who were clearly committed to careers in scholarly research.

By the end of World War I, Jennings had moved away from protozoology toward genetics, largely in response to the work of one of his own students, Raymond Pearl. In 1918 Pearl was appointed the first professor of biometry and vital statistics in the new Johns Hopkins School of Hygiene and Public Health.[24]

As a population ecologist, on the cutting edge of the biology of groups, Pearl was "iconoclastic, energetic and prodigiously productive." In 1925 he convinced the Rockefeller Foundation to fund a new Institute for Biological Research of which Pearl became the director. As part of his long-term study of the impact of various factors on the duration of human life, Pearl started two journals, including *Human Biology* in 1929. His research and daring conclusions focused on questions of hereditary and environmental factors, such as population density, starvation, temperature, and diet, all of which influenced longevity. Increasingly Pearl's institute overshadowed Jennings's Zoology Laboratory in competition for space, funds, and notoriety.[25]

Pearl's general philosophy that general biology and human biology go hand in hand influenced all his activities. He argued consistently that all biological research must tend toward the understanding of human life. It was a view that Rachel Carson would absorb unconsciously from Pearl and one that she ultimately expressed in *Silent Spring*.[26]

When Rachel became a candidate for a master's degree at Johns Hopkins in the fall of 1929, the ruling assumption of the Faculty of Philosophy was that most graduate students would continue on for the Ph.D. Between 1928 and 1931 the combined departments of zoology, botany, and plant physiology graduated approximately eighty-four students of which twenty-three were women. When Rachel entered she was one of thirteen female students, four or five of whom concentrated in zoology. Yet she seems to have made no personal connections with the other women in the laboratory that year. The intense atmosphere of the Zoological Laboratory was vastly different from that of the expansive, informal MBL, where research was informally shared and an easy camaraderie pervaded discussions. But Rachel's quiet seriousness and discipline inevitably impressed both her fellow students and her professors.[27]

She took four courses each semester during her first year. In spite of her fervent desire not to take organic chemistry at Hopkins, Professor Cowles, her adviser, insisted. Although it was her "chief agony" that first semester, the reality was less terrible than the prospect. She learned to be less meticulous than was her nature and was proud to see that soon she could "tear through the experiments as fast as the men" did. Rachel was one of two women and about seventy men in the class.

Professor Cowles reviewed Rachel's laboratory notebook from Skinker's course in comparative anatomy at PCW and realized that taking the same laboratory at Hopkins would be a waste of time. Rachel sat in on his lectures in "Comparative" as a way to review for her master's exams but found the material very familiar. It made her realize what an excellent course Skinker had given them.

The course on the "organization of plants," Botany 1, she found not "especially thrilling," but interesting because of the field trips. Rachel was pleased to be admitted into H. S. Jennings's genetics laboratory. She had to work very hard for him, but she liked Jennings very much. Unfortunately his laboratory requirements highlighted just how poorly prepared Anna Whiting's genetics class had left her. Rachel's enthusiasm for the material was dampened by her lack of preparation.

Her other classes were the mandatory weekly Seminar and Journal Club. There was only one other woman in the club that fall. Although she hoped to avoid becoming that "pitiable spectacle of a typical biologist," she quickly accepted the fact that "the lab is my world and is going to be my chief existence until I get my degree."[28]

In spite of the head start she had made on the dissection of cranial nerves of reptiles at Woods Hole, her research that first semester did not yield enough new material for a satisfactory thesis topic. Rachel spent long hours sectioning snake and lizard heads and making paraffin slides of the sections. By November both she and Cowles were still dissatisfied with the results. Cowles suggested, only partly in jest, that perhaps she should abandon the snake and the lizard and go to Florida to study the cranial nerves in loggerhead turtles. But it was a particularly unrealistic suggestion amid the economic uncertainty just a month after the stock market crash in October. Rachel doggedly continued on with her dissections.[29]

Life was not all drudgery in the lab for Rachel. She found she liked Baltimore, its people, and its climate very much. It was a far brighter clime than western Pennsylvania. "Most days," she told Dorothy Thompson, "are beautifully clear and sunny. Many roses are to be seen in bloom in the gardens and chrysanthemums everywhere. When it rains, it surely rains hard, because of the oceanic climate, I imagine."[30]

Rachel also noticed that business seemed to be in better shape in Baltimore than in Pittsburgh. Perhaps for that reason as much as anything, she had started hunting for a house to rent so that her mother and father could leave Springdale, combine their resources, and join her in Baltimore. Robert, Marian, and the two girls could live in the farmhouse until school was out or until Robert could find someone to rent it. Mr. Carson's business affairs had been in difficulty for some time and his health was declining, probably because of a heart condition. There seemed to be more promising possibilities for employment for everyone, especially for Rachel, in the Baltimore area than in Pittsburgh, so it made sense for the family to move.

There were other considerations as well. By the winter of 1929, Rachel and her mother had been separated for longer than they had ever been before. The family had no money for Rachel to travel back and forth from Baltimore to Springdale to visit, and even less for the luxury of long-distance telephone calls. She missed her mother's support and encouragement. Moreover, Rachel was never very interested in housekeeping. From a practical view, having her mother there to fix meals and keep house would leave more time for her studies. It was a pragmatic as well as an emotional arrangement she would choose again and again.

When she was finally reunited with her mother in Baltimore after not quite nine months apart, she fell back into an easy routine. It was the longest period mother and daughter would ever be separated during the course of both their lifetimes.[31]

Rachel found a house for rent in Stemmers Run, a rural community about thirteen miles northeast of the central city out on the Old Philadelphia Road. It was just two miles from the Chesapeake Bay. Regardless of its location and the longer bus or trolley ride to campus, Rachel fell in love with it. There was a "lovely woods at the very back door, a tennis court, a grove of oak trees," and inside, a "big open fireplace." Its natural attractions outweighed its rustic qualities.

The house itself was quite a bit larger than the one in Springdale and had indoor plumbing, a distinct improvement. It had no central heating, however, but neither had the farmhouse. Rachel hoped they could sign a lease by the end of the month and all move in by early January 1930. She optimistically invited Dorothy to come and visit, adding that "maybe Miss Skinker could come for a week at the same time."[32]

But the accelerating Depression complicated everyone's plans. It took longer for Mr. Carson to settle his affairs in Springdale. The senior Carsons did not move into the Stemmers Run house until spring. Marian and her daughters came in June, while Robert remained in Springdale trying to rent the house.[33]

In February Rachel received a newsy letter from Mary Frye, filled mostly with word of friends from Woods Hole. In her reply, the last extant letter to Mary Frye, Rachel told her how much she enjoyed being at Johns Hopkins. "I do like it tremendously—the professors are splendid to work with, and the students are a dandy crowd. I wish I could show you around the lab,—especially my own little corner of it."[34]

Her biggest news was that she had survived her final exams in organic chemistry. "I got an 85 in the course," she told Mary, "and I never was so proud of an 85 in my life!" Instead of going back to Woods Hole that summer, Rachel had gotten a teaching assistantship as she had planned, in one of the Hopkins undergraduate biology classes. She told Mary it would be "hard work, but wonderful experience, and of course I was thrilled to get the chance."[35]

At the end of her first year in graduate school, Rachel was moving closer to the possibility of a teaching career and planning to go straight on for a doctorate in zoology. Skinker was especially elated to hear that Rachel had done particularly well on Professor Mast's physiology final in

June. There were no grades in these courses, but Mast, "the terror of all aspirants at Hopkins," had written "very good" on Rachel's examination paper, which from him was a rare and coveted accolade.[36]

Skinker's pleasure in Rachel's achievement spilled over in a letter to Dorothy Thompson in June. Telling Dorothy that Rachel may be too modest to admit just how much it means, Skinker confessed that "*I'd* be walking in the clouds if *I* had such an achievement to my credit. She need do nothing more and yet she would remain the envy of many there. I'm so delighted with it that I'm actually a little envious."[37]

Rachel herself felt very satisfied with the outcome, particularly since she had stayed up until after 3:00 in the morning studying and had gone into the exam "all groggy and numb with weariness and terror." Although she tried to play down Skinker's appraisal, she confessed to Dorothy that she was "just materialistic enough to find my chief cause for joy in the fact that now he [Mast] can't very well say anything about my deficiencies in Chemistry."[38]

Summer school classes at Hopkins began the end of June, but Rachel worked the entire month collecting material for the biology laboratory and setting it up. She was assigned to assist Miss Grace Lippy, who had completed her master's degree in 1926 under Cowles and had since then been teaching the basic undergraduate zoology course while she continued her doctoral studies. When Rachel met Lippy she found a demanding but "very likeable sort of person" who promised to be "very easy to work with."

Grace E. Lippy came from circumstances not far different from Rachel's own. Six years older than Rachel, she was born in Snydersburg, Maryland, and moved to the equally rural town of Westminister, Maryland, just north and west of Baltimore, where she attended high school. For financial reasons, she had lived at home and attended the local Western Maryland College in Westminister for the first two years. She transferred to Wilson College, a small women's college, very much like PCW but with somewhat more academic standing, in Chambersburg, Pennsylvania, where she received her undergraduate degree in 1923.[39]

Lippy was admitted to the graduate zoology program at Hopkins in 1924 and completed a master's degree two years later, concentrating in physiology and comparative anatomy. Her work was of such quality that the department hired her to teach the undergraduate summer school zoology class that same year. She was the only woman appointed as instructor in zoology at Hopkins during these Depression years. In 1931

Lippy was offered a regular appointment as assistant professor of zoology at Hood College in Frederick, Maryland, and gave up her graduate work, but she continued to teach summer school at Hopkins to supplement her income.

Grace Lippy and Rachel Carson were a compatible and effective teaching team. Lippy was outgoing, volatile, and enthusiastic about the work of the lab. A short, large-boned young woman with intense blue eyes and indomitable energy, she was a contrast to Carson, who appeared reserved and almost lethargic by comparison. Lippy conducted the daily lectures, and Rachel designed and coordinated the laboratory experiments. Rachel admired Lippy's command of dissection techniques and her ability to give clear explanations. Lippy remembers Rachel's extraordinary patience with the students. When experiments failed or students got upset, Rachel calmly stepped in and took control of the situation. About once a week, after the lab was finished, Lippy went back to Stemmers Run with Rachel and had supper with the Carsons. The two women continued to teach summer school together for the next four years at Hopkins. Grace Lippy was the only person Rachel Carson made friends with during her three years in graduate school.[40]

The previous spring Rachel had reapplied for and received the $200 tuition scholarship that had supported her the first year. When the award letter came, Rachel naively thought a mistake had been made in the tuition charge for the following year. Instead of $250, it was $300. There was no mistake, of course, just a normal tuition increase, which meant that Rachel would have to pay an additional $100. Her summer school stipend went to pay the rent for the Stemmers Run house and to her debt at PCW. Her only alternative was to decline the scholarship, get a part-time job, and become a part-time student.[41]

Rachel flooded campus departments and the Johns Hopkins medical school with letters seeking half-time employment. Raymond Pearl's Institute for Biological Research in the School of Hygiene and Public Health was one of the first places she wrote. "By merest chance," Pearl was in need of inexpensive assistants in his laboratory, and on Jennings's recommendation, he hired Rachel on the spot.

Rachel's life took on a new aspect as her energies were diverted from her own corner of the zoology laboratory on the Homewood campus to Pearl's commodious laboratories downtown on East Madison Street in the medical school group. Rachel described Pearl's laboratories as "certainly the real thing" and found being there a "decidedly worth-while experience." She worked with Pearl's rat colony and with his genetic experiments on the fruitfly *Drosophila*.

With her assistantship at the institute, Rachel moved into a different world of science from that on the Homewood campus. In the 1920s and 1930s the medical school and the School of Hygiene and Public Health attracted a considerable number of talented female scientists. There were many more women on the staff of these schools than on the faculty of the university. Pearl's wife, Maud DeWitt Pearl, also a biologist, was the managing editor of the journal *Human Biology*. In the course of her work, Rachel must have met her as well as other female scientists living and working in Baltimore. Although her letters are silent on the matter, she could not help but have felt a certain psychological support for her work in association with the institute.[42]

At the same time, she struggled with two heavy laboratory courses that fall term, one on genetics and development with H. S. Jennings, the other, the advanced section of S. O. Mast's general physiology of animals. In whatever time remained, she "pretend[ed] to be carrying on [her] research . . ." but, she confessed to Dorothy, "it's a pretty up-hill business to do even the work for the courses," and the most she could do on her own research that spring was "a little reading at home." What Rachel did not tell Dorothy was that she still had no firm topic for her master's essay and that her experiments on a variety of reptiles had produced little of use. She did, however, confess to a certain frustration: "It's worse this year than ever before. I feel sometimes as though I'm not getting any where as far as the degree is concerned, but it's just that this business of doing two things at once doesn't work, at least unless you're an Amazon."[43]

Certainly Rachel Carson was not the only graduate student, male or female, in zoology at Johns Hopkins whose studies were altered by the Great Depression, but since there were comparatively fewer women in the program to begin with, her changed circumstances were more noticeable. Nor was she the only student whose research topic remained undefined; the two conditions in combination, however, created the impression in the minds of some of the faculty that Rachel was a difficult student. She needed special assistance, requiring administrative changes in program and financial aid. As she fell further and further behind in her program of study, her academic reputation and her future were increasingly jeopardized.

The grind of the fall semester 1930 was relieved by the promise of a visit from Dorothy Thompson during the Thanksgiving break. Dorothy, now in her first semester of graduate school in zoology at Bryn Mawr, wanted to see Rachel and to go to Washington to visit Miss Skinker. Accordingly she took the bus to Baltimore the day before Thanksgiving to spend the holiday with the Carsons in Stemmers Run.[44]

Rachel met Dorothy at the bus station and took her to lunch and then out to the Homewood campus, where she gave her a tour of the laboratory, including the corner where she was working on a case of pit vipers. Dorothy remembers Rachel had become interested in the function of the depression, or "pit," on either side of the snake's head. After working the rest of the afternoon in the lab, the two friends boarded a rickety old bus for the ride out to Stemmers Run where Mr. and Mrs. Carson, Marian, Virginia, and Marjorie were waiting.

Rachel had been eager to show Dorothy the beautiful woods surrounding the house and walk the two miles to the Chesapeake Bay, but rain spoiled her plans and Mrs. Carson insisted the young women stay inside by the fire. It was a less than satisfactory compromise for their private reminiscing. According to Dorothy, Marian's two little girls clung to Rachel, talking incessantly until she gave in and read them a story, after which they went off for a while to play. Dorothy thought Mr. Carson looked ill. She remembers that he sat with them by the fire listening but saying very little.

"Mrs. Carson," Dorothy later recalled, "was a kind woman, and I liked her, though some people didn't. She supported Rachel in every way. We got along because I understood that Rachel was her life." The next day Dorothy left Stemmers Run for what would be her last visit with Mary Scott Skinker.[45]

A month later Rachel spent part of her Christmas vacation with Skinker in Washington. Although her doctor had ordered her to rest for two hours each day, Skinker continued to work as a parasitologist at the Division of Zoology. Their conversation during this visit centered on the problems Rachel was having with her research. Skinker introduced Rachel to some of the invertebrate zoologists at the National Museum of Natural History, where Rachel looked at specimens and read during the mornings while Mary Scott worked.

By the end of the year, Rachel had given up the pit viper for the *Anomalurus*, a species of scaletail squirrel that resembles the flying squirrel but has a scaly tail used in climbing. In February 1931 she received permission from the Smithsonian Institution's Department of Zoology to dissect one of the two specimens of the rodent they had lent her to study. Her enthusiasm for this investigation was brief. Rachel explained some of the unanticipated problems to Dorothy. "The squirrels would not breed, and there was just nothing to do about it. No embryos, no problem, was the situation in a nutshell. Then my Texas dealer lost all his stock in a fire, so there was no more help from him. I have made so many false starts along lines which yielded no result," she complained, "but that, I am learning, is the fate of most people."[46]

Rachel's research quagmire severely undermined her economic stability because it delayed her degree and the possibility of employment, which was fragile at best. Brother Robert had rejoined the family in Stemmers Run early in 1931. He found work as a radio repair estimator in Baltimore, but like thousands of others in the Depression, he was not always paid in cash for his services. He contributed little to the family's budget. One evening he brought home a family of Persian cats—a mother and three kittens, a partial payment for a repair job. Rachel and her mother immediately took them in, dubbing two Buzzie and Kito. A particularly pretty shaded silver one became Timmy Tiptoes, or Tippy for short. Although Rachel had been partial to the company of dogs as a child on the farm, the Persians were a beginning of an important adult friendship with and preference for cats.[47]

Rachel was obligated to begin paying on her student loan from PCW in 1931. But in February, after making one payment, she had no choice but to inform the college that she could not make further payments. Although Mr. Carson continued to try to sell the two Springdale lots that Rachel had mortgaged to the college, the future of the real estate market was bleak.

At least by the summer of 1931, Rachel had completed all her course work while working in Pearl's laboratory. She looked forward to assisting Grace Lippy again with the summer school's zoology lab. This time their classes were smaller. Rachel recalled, "It was an exceptionally fine group of students, and I learned something of the delight that comes from working with alert minds with a real capacity for thought and originality." She enjoyed her teaching more than she had anticipated.[48]

Since Rachel's assistantship with Dr. Pearl had ended, she had to find another part-time position to pay her tuition for the following academic year when she would once again be a half-time student. For the fall, Rachel was required to enroll in "dissertation research" while she completed her master's thesis. Through Professor Cowles, she heard of an assistantship at the Dental and Pharmacy School of the University of Maryland, in College Park, Maryland, about thirty-five miles southwest of Baltimore. Cowles wrote recommending Rachel for the position.

Grace Lippy knew how vital this opportunity was for Rachel and telephoned the dean of the Pharmacy School, whom she knew personally, giving Rachel a glowing recommendation. Rachel got the job, becoming the only female biology instructor in the dental school. The assistantship, which paid slightly over $900, began at the end of September 1931. Rachel looked forward to this new teaching experience even though she would fall further behind in her own research. If she could find a research project that she could do quickly, she might finish the following May. Realizing that she was running out of time as well as money, Cowles suggested a topic he thought could be completed fairly rapidly.[49]

Cowles was involved in the organization of the new Chesapeake Biological Laboratory at Solomon's Island, Maryland, the successor to William Keith Brooks's Chesapeake Zoological Institute. He had prepared a plan for a biological survey of the water around Solomon's Island, and his attention was increasingly drawn to the marine life of Chesapeake Bay. Turning away from the research in comparative evolution to one in experimental marine biology, Cowles suggested that Rachel examine a facet of the evolution of the urinary system of fish.[50]

Rachel's thesis proposal called for an examination of the embryological development of the so-called head kidney, or pronephros, of fish. In 1931 biologists were uncertain of its function. In the early embryonic stages of fish, it helped to keep the free-swimming larva alive, but it lost that function, disappeared, and later reemerged with another function altogether. Rachel's examination was limited to a phase of embryonic development rather than to speculation on the ultimate changes in function.[51]

First Rachel reviewed the extensive and quite controversial literature on the function of the fish kidney. Next she had to dissect a series of fertilized embryos, stain them, and make camera lucida drawings under the microscope and photomicrographs of all the embryonic phases. From this evidence she would describe embryonic and larval development of the pronephros from the second through the eleventh day. Rachel finished the literature review and began dissecting thin sections of egg and larval embryos in late August 1931. But this project, like the others, soon developed unforeseen complications.

Getting a series of fertilized fish embryos proved more difficult than either she or Cowles had anticipated. Rachel "canvass[ed] the fish hatcheries of the nation" for material. Finally after several months of searching, she found one J. M. Murphree, superintendent of the State Fish Hatchery at Durant, Oklahoma, who could supply her with a complete embryological series of the catfish (*Ictalurus punctatus*). Murphree collected the embryos and larvae, preserved them, and shipped them to Rachel, who then embedded the material in paraffin, sectioned them transversely at a thickness of ten microns, and began the tedious process of dissection.[52]

In October Rachel bowed to the inevitable. Writing to the Board of University Studies, she requested a year's delay in standing for her degree.[53]

The next seven months flew by. By early spring Rachel was making slow, steady progress, renewed by the news that she had been named to one of the seats at the Johns Hopkins table at the MBL at Woods Hole for the summer. Grace Lippy, Rachel, and three other graduate students would go together as "investigators." This time Rachel also wanted to work at the Bureau of Fisheries laboratory.

Finally in April, her essay, "The Development of the Pronephros During the Embryonic and Early Larval Life of the Catfish (*Ictalurus punctatus*)," was finished. Rachel stood for her master's degree examination in early May 1932. R. P. Cowles and E. A. Andrews, who taught marine ecology, examined her on behalf of the zoology department. Their report to the Board of University Studies recommending Rachel for the degree of Master of Arts stated that she presented an "excellent review of the literature on the subject" and that the investigation was done with care as well as from an "exceptionally critical point of view." Although Cowles and Andrews found that there were "several points that needed further investigation," Rachel's essay made a "worthy contribution" to the knowledge of the urinary system of fishes. Rachel was awarded her degree at the commencement exercises on June 14.[54]

Like many other June graduates in 1932, Rachel had a degree but no prospect of full-time employment. She and Grace Lippy taught another session of summer school at Hopkins, and then left for six weeks of research at Woods Hole. Rachel and Grace roomed together, and Carson worked in the Fisheries lab, but exactly what she studied that summer, or what she did on Cape Cod, is lost. The evidence is clear that Rachel intended to continue on for her doctorate at Hopkins. She enrolled in

Zoology 6P, "Investigations," for the academic year 1932–1933, and she continued to teach at the Dental and Pharmacy School at the University of Maryland.[55]

In the late fall of 1932, still unable to make regular payments on her undergraduate debt, Rachel signed the mortgaged Springdale lots over to PCW, giving them the right to sell the land whenever they could get a price for it that would cover her obligations. Such a public admission of the extent of her family's financial plight must have been especially humiliating. She had been critical both of the PCW administration as well as members of the college's faculty and its science curriculum. Now she had to ask them to release her from further financial obligation.[56]

That fall Rachel also had a visit from Dorothy Thompson and her fiancé, attorney Charles Seif. Dorothy had just completed her master's degree at Bryn Mawr College with honors and had an offer of a teaching position in a fine private school for girls in Pittsburgh.

The two recent graduates spent the day after Thanksgiving in Rachel's laboratory in Gilman. Rachel had a corner in one large room where she was pursuing an experiment in protozoology as well as investigating the salt tolerance of eels. She was particularly eager to show Dorothy her enormous aquarium full of these mysterious creatures.[57]

Dorothy remembers that while Rachel changed the salinity of the aquarium and recorded the data, she told her how interesting she found the eels, their life cycle and their ability to migrate. Although Rachel never finished her academic research on the eels, she stored her understanding of these creatures away for later use.[58]

Over the next two years as the Depression tightened in the Baltimore area, the financial status of the Carson household continued to decline. Marian, who had become diabetic, was often too ill to work at even a part-time clerical position. Brother Robert's income remained sporadic, although he now lived on his own in downtown Baltimore. Rachel's father's health deteriorated as well. With her family's options so limited, Rachel had little choice but to end her graduate career. She dropped out of Johns Hopkins as a doctoral candidate in good standing before the start of the spring semester in early 1934. She continued teaching at Maryland while searching for a full-time academic position in general biology.

She set up a personnel file at the university's Bureau of Appointments, asking that they send her credentials for review by any school in the eastern states. Rachel listed her profession as "scientific research." In her dossier, she said she was qualified to teach any of the biological sciences in a four-year or junior college. Although she requested a starting salary of $2,400, she indicated she would accept half that.[59]

Rachel's credentials file contained seven confidential recommendations. Four were from Hopkins professors R. P. Cowles, S. O. Mast, H. S. Jennings, and Raymond Pearl. Letters from Grace Lippy, Guy P. Thompson, the senior assistant at the University of Maryland, and J. Ben Robinson, dean of the School of Dentistry, assessed her current employment. Those Hopkins professors who commented on her teaching ability rated it highly. But none of them, with the possible exception of Cowles, expressed any enthusiasm for Rachel's research or scientific promise. In fact, Jennings's recommendation was decidedly cool, reflecting, no doubt, his misgivings about the length of time and the difficulty Rachel had completing her research program. His letter also revealed the bias of a scientist who esteemed original research and dedication to scholarship above all other qualities. "Miss Carson," Jennings wrote, "is a thorough, hard-working person, not brilliant, but very capable, and with a good knowledge of biology. . . . She is thoroughly dependable and will continue to be a satisfactory teacher." His letter did little to promote Rachel's career in science or teaching.[60]

By contrast, letters from Rachel's colleagues at the University of Maryland Dental and Pharmacy School were enthusiastic in their praise of her academic promise. Grace Lippy wrote the strongest and the most detailed appraisal of her skills. Lippy, now a popular professor at Hood College, commented on Rachel's "unusual ability and exactness." She was impressed by the ease with which Carson carried out laboratory work and observed that Rachel was very kind, very patient, and that she was an "omnivorous reader" who had "much ready information" to share with students. She promised that anyone who secured Rachel Carson for their department "has a treasure." But despite such glowing appraisals of her teaching ability, Rachel's file was sent out only once, according to Bureau of Appointments records. Few teaching positions were available in the spring of 1935.[61]

Carson's credentials file listed "five partially dependent" family members. Only a few months away from her twenty-eighth birthday, she was five foot four inches tall and weighed a slight 115 pounds. A photograph attached to her dossier reflects a slim, very attractive young woman with a serious but direct demeanor. She still wore her curly, auburn brown hair at a becoming medium length, which set off her heart-shape face and small bones.

With no full-time employment at hand, economic necessity forced Rachel to return to writing as a potential source of income. Revising some of her best college works, poems and short stories, she sent them off to major magazines such as *Saturday Evening Post*, *Collier's*, *Poetry*, and *Reader's Digest*, magazines that paid well but were highly selective. Her efforts yielded the same rejection slips as they had in 1928, when she had last sent them out. But as she reworked this material, she was somewhat surprised to discover that the "old desire to write" began to "reassert itself." These rather casual efforts to find publishers for her college work and make some extra money ended abruptly one bright July morning in 1935.

According to Robert Carson's recollection of his mother's account of the event, their father came into the kitchen of the Stemmers Run house that morning complaining to Maria that he did not feel well. She suggested he go outside for some fresh air. Maria watched him walk into the backyard, pause, and suddenly pitch forward into the grass. Minutes later Robert Warden Carson died cradled in his wife's lap. Seventy-one years old, he had spent most of his life struggling ineffectually to find a place for himself.

Maria sent his body back to Canonsburg, Pennsylvania, where Robert Carson's three surviving sisters saw to his burial on July 9 in the McLean plot at the Oak Spring Cemetery. There was no money for the family to accompany the body. Rachel, who rarely spoke of her father when he was alive, mentioned him publicly only once some twenty-five years later during an interview for a Pittsburgh newspaper, dignifying him with business associations he never had. His death may have relieved her of a certain amount of false pretense. Since the family had always struggled, Robert Warden Carson's passing did not alter their real social status. Maria Carson experienced a certain domestic as well as personal freedom after her husband's death, and his youngest daughter may have as well.[62]

Whatever impact her father's death had on Rachel emotionally and psychologically, his sudden death marked the end of what little financial stability the Carson family had known. Although Robert McLean Carson was the obvious one to step into the void, he had never been particularly reliable and was not so now, although his mother continued to make excuses for him. Marian had only a part-time job, and she needed help to support her daughters Virginia and Marjorie. Inevitably, Rachel became the sole support of her mother and herself and the major benefactor of her sister Marian and her children. Without immediate prospect for a full-time job, Rachel turned again to Mary Scott Skinker.

Skinker's health had improved since 1928. In 1929 she was hired as a full-time research parasitologist in the Zoological Division of the Department of Agriculture's Bureau of Animal Industry. Rising from junior zoologist, Skinker distinguished herself as a government scientist, and she had completed her Ph.D. in zoology at George Washington University in 1933.[63]

Mary Scott and Rachel visited frequently while Rachel was in graduate school at Hopkins and living in Stemmers Run. Rachel often went to Washington to work at the National Museum and to see Skinker. Knowing the academic job market as she did, and happy as a government scientist doing meaningful work in a congenial group in the Division of Zoology, Skinker urged Rachel to prepare for the federal civil service examinations in several zoological areas. If a professional opening should become available, Rachel then would be eligible to apply for it.

After working with Skinker to prepare for the examinations, Rachel took the junior parasitologist exam in January 1935 and scored 76.5 points, her highest score. In May she completed the examinations for junior wildlife biologist and junior aquatic biologist, earning 61.0 and 75.0 ratings respectively. Skinker urged Rachel to pay another call on Elmer Higgins, especially since he was now the division chief. In early October Rachel called on him at his Commerce Department office in Washington.[64]

Elmer Higgins remembered his earlier interview with Rachel and was impressed with her new credentials and experience, but he had no professional openings. What he did have was a problem assignment from his superiors. The U.S. Bureau of Fisheries had agreed to produce a public education series of fifty-two short radio programs on marine life called "Romance Under the Waters." The scientists on Higgins's staff who had written the first couple of scripts for these seven-minute programs, which were known around the office as "seven-minute fish tales," understood fish biology but could not make the subject interesting to the public. A professional radio writer fared little better. As Carson remembered it, Higgins was desperately in need of "someone who could take over writing the scripts—someone who knew marine biology and who also could write." At the moment Higgins was writing the scripts himself.[65]

He asked Rachel if she would like to take a try at writing one or two and see if she could do any better. Rachel remembered Higgins saying "I've never seen a written word of yours, but I'm going to take a sporting chance." Later she realized that his offer was, "in its way, a turning point."

So two days a week for the next eight months, Rachel took the bus into downtown Washington to write radio scripts as a field aide in the cramped offices of the Bureau of Fisheries. She was paid $6.50 a day, which she accepted gratefully. With two part-time incomes, the Carsons' immediate financial crisis was temporarily relieved.[66]

Higgins liked what Rachel wrote. The weekly radio broadcasts were a success, and Higgins's superiors were delighted. When the program scripts were finished, Higgins asked Rachel to write a general introduction to marine life that would be suitable for a government brochure.[67]

Rachel began work on the essay she tentatively titled "World of Waters." But she also used her research for the radio scripts as a basis for several lengthy feature articles on various aspects of Chesapeake Bay marine life. In February 1936 she sent off her first article on the decline of shad fishery to the local newspaper, the *Baltimore Sun*. Sunday editor Mark Watson bought it and paid Rachel $20 for her densely researched, twelve-page article. It appeared as a special feature in the March 1 edition of the newspaper's Sunday magazine section, *Sunday Sun*, as "It'll Be Shad-Time Soon" under the byline R. L. Carson.[68]

Like all the subsequent articles Rachel wrote for the *Sunday Sun*, this one was concerned with the conservation of a resource, a respect for nature's intricate processes, and the effects of human intrusion on nature. But it also reflected the research of a thoroughly competent marine biologist familiar with the population and habitat studies of this mid-Atlantic fish. The decline of the shad population, she wrote, was "probably the result of destructive methods of fishing, the pollution of waters by industrial and civic wastes, and the development of streams for water power and navigation." She warned readers, "If this favorite of the Chesapeake Bay region is to hold its own against the forces of destruction, regulations must be imposed which consider the welfare of the fish as well as that of the fisherman."[69]

Rachel's initial success in using her fisheries research to write about the fish of the Chesapeake was addictive. Her research at the Bureau of Fisheries stimulated ideas for other articles. She haunted the bureau libraries and filled a notebook full of detailed notes.

In April Rachel went out to Johns Hopkins to update her credentials file. Still hopeful of finding a teaching position, she added to her employment history that she was currently employed part-time as a "feature writer of scientific subjects" with the U.S. Bureau of Fisheries in their "educational division." She increased her minimum salary requirements to $1,800, reflecting both her increased financial burdens as well as her successful employment as a science writer.[70]

Rachel's decision for science had been the right one, but it now appeared that it had not been as exclusive as she had first assumed. Instead of closing doors, it had opened new ones and provided opportunities Croff, Skinker, and Rachel could never have foreseen.

If her scientific career was not turning out to be the predictable academic one, her vision that the sea somehow held the clue to her life's purpose was still intact. Marine science had given her imagination and her intellect something rich and mysterious to feast upon. "I had given up writing forever, I thought," she recalled some years later. "It never occurred to me that I was merely getting something to write about."[71]

4

"Something to Write About"

Years later Carson still vividly remembered that spring encounter with Elmer Higgins. She had finished the eleven-page introduction to the fisheries brochure in early April 1936, which her mother typed neatly in the small elite typeface of her old black Smith Corona typewriter. Higgins had called a publications staff meeting to discuss the brochure and he needed the finished text. Higgins recalled that Rachel sat quietly in his crowded Washington office, his desk piled high with reports and papers, while he read her draft.

He was impressed with the eloquence of her essay, "The World of Waters." It was publishable certainly—but not in a government pamphlet on fish. No, this was a piece of literature. Acting more like a literary agent than an expert on the life history of fish, Higgins suggested that its quality would interest the top literary magazine of the day. Carson recalled their conversation: "My chief . . . handed it back with a twinkle in his eye. 'I don't think it will do,' he said. 'Better try again. But send this one to the *Atlantic*.' "[1]

Surprised and enormously pleased by his reaction, Rachel made some changes that he had suggested and put "The World of Waters" back in her desk drawer. Then she wrote another, simpler introduction for the brochure. While she answered the public inquiries on fish, which now constituted a large part of her job, she thought about what to do with her essay.

About a month later, following the same course she had with her childhood writing, Carson entered a slightly revised version in a prize competition sponsored by the *Reader's Digest*. The contest offered $1,000 for unpublished articles by new writers. She also sent Mark Watson at the *Baltimore Sun* another feature story. This one, on the increased mackerel population of the mid-Atlantic, appeared as "Numbering the Fish of the Sea" and earned her another twenty dollars. Although Carson checked the mail regularly for the next several months, she never received a response from *Reader's Digest*.[2]

Just as Higgins's enthusiastic appraisal of Carson's essay "The World of Waters" marked a new direction in her scientific writing about marine life, her appointment as a junior aquatic biologist with the Division of Scientific Inquiry in July signaled the beginning of a unique career as a government scientist. The Bureau of Fisheries had received approval for this position at entry level, P-1, earlier in the summer. Carson's Civil Service rating of 75.0 percent on the aquatic biologist examination placed her first on the women's register. She applied and was informed a month later that she had been recommended for the appointment. Although she was qualified for a higher-level appointment, federal agencies were fortunate to fill even entry-level positions during the Depression.[3]

On July 6, 1936, Acting Fisheries Commissioner Charles Jackson wrote a memorandum to the chief of the Appointment Division defending Carson's selection on the basis of her examination score and her "suitability by training and experience." Elmer Higgins had been waiting for a position to open and when it did, he requested that Carson be assigned to the Division of Scientific Inquiry, Baltimore field office. Her position had been created specifically to assist assistant bureau chief Robert Nesbit's study of the Chesapeake Bay fishes. Along with a team of scientists employed by the State of Maryland, the bureau was collecting large quantities of data for population studies and laboratory investigations, tasks that could be "effectively performed by a woman ashore."[4]

Rachel's new position guaranteed her a salary of $38.48 a week. Even better, she would soon be eligible for a small length-of-service increase. She took the oath of office as junior aquatic biologist on August 17, becoming a full-time government scientist and one of only two women then employed in the bureau at a professional level.[5]

Carson's assignments under Nesbit involved little more than an expansion of what she was already doing under Higgins, analyzing biological and statistical data of the region's fish, determining age and population variation, writing up reports and producing brochures for the public on fish conservation. Carson enjoyed her work and often was challenged by it.

Her research required her to locate and consult with experts in several fields of fishery biology. She visited bureau laboratories and field stations. Some reports required considerable library research in addition to routine laboratory study. Her duties employed both her scientific and literary skills. Her work reinforced her personal connections with nature, and deepened her understanding of the ecological tapestry of marine life.

As a testament to this widening vision, the list of topics on which she wanted to write expanded. Almost every other week she sent Mark Watson a synopsis for a new article. Although he vetoed one on ticks that he felt would alarm the public unnecessarily, Watson was impressed with Carson's ability to turn out interesting and scientifically accurate feature stories on a wide variety of Chesapeake marine life that appealed to the nonscientific reader. "I am glad to hear from you again," Watson wrote her, "particularly to know that you are going on with the writing which you do so well." Those features he could not buy for the *Sun*, he tried to place with its syndicated papers.[6]

Between January and June 1937 Carson published at least seven articles. Three were on oyster farming, in which she advocated privatization of the state's oyster beds as the best guarantee of renewal and stable productivity. Three others continued her investigation into the plight of the shad, and one was on the general economy of commercial fishing of the Chesapeake.[7]

It is hard to underestimate what Carson was learning as she researched and wrote these articles. Frequently she visited parts of the Chesapeake Bay she had never been to in order to write about a particular fish or to understand the economics driving the fish culture of an area. She talked to fishermen and to Chesapeake watermen and toured a variety of commercial plants and conservation facilities, most of the latter run by the Maryland Conservation Department, whose scientists she could depend on for information and access. These trips gave Carson valuable field experience. Always fascinated by shore life and shorebirds, she carried in her pocket a small spiral notebook, either black or brown, in which she jotted her observations of bird activity, weather, geographic peculiarities, geologic evidence, vegetation, the smells of a place, anything that caught her attention. Later she typed her notes on three-by-five cards, which she stored in a large wooden file box on her desk at home.

Carson had been an enthusiastic amateur ornithologist since she and her mother had first identified birds in the woodlands of Springdale. As a youngster, she began a life list of the birds she saw. Her trips around the Chesapeake added birds to her list and deepened her understanding of the interactions of shore and sea. Although her earliest feature articles were on fish, birds frequently appeared in her popular writing.

It was not long before Carson established a predictable rhythm between her professional research and her personal writing, the one leading easily into the other. By the end of 1936 her feature writing was producing a small but steady income. But another family tragedy soon made that inadequate for her family responsibilities.

In late January 1937 Rachel's older sister, Marian, succumbed to pneumonia a few days after her fortieth birthday. Virginia was now twelve, and Marjorie, eleven. Marian's ex-husband Burton Williams was alive, but he was unavailable for the children's nurture and for much of their support as well.[8]

Marian's death marked the end of any predictability for the household in general and the end of much of Rachel's independence. Maria Carson, almost seventy years old, took charge once again. The only thing to do was to raise her granddaughters herself. What other choice was there?

Robert Carson played no part in Maria's family restructuring, although he lived in the Baltimore area. Robert had been critical of Marian and her daughters and often of Rachel as well. He seems to have contributed his physical labor when his mother asked but offered nothing to relieve his younger sister of the financial or emotional burden.[9]

Months shy of her thirtieth birthday, Rachel faced a personal and professional crossroads. With Marian's death, she inherited not only increased financial obligations but also an altered domestic life that deprived her of privacy and drained her physical and emotional energy.

The roles Maria Carson chose for herself and her daughter were familiar ones; Maria was the housekeeper, Rachel was the breadwinner. If Rachel had any difficulty accepting her mother's decision to take in Virginia and Marjie or her financial responsibilities for them, she never expressed it. To every outward appearance, she joined in the decision. Resentment was an emotional luxury Carson did not allow herself.

Marian's life had been difficult. Much of her personal tragedy was brought on by impulsive decisions and a desire to be independent before she had the means to be so. Although Marian and Rachel were over a decade apart in age, Rachel had watched her sister struggle to find domestic happiness and saw that her decisions most often left her a victim of other people's behavior. Without a husband to support her children, Marian, once a beautiful, vivacious young woman, had no choice but to return to her family, where she grew more depressed and sickly. Like so many single mothers in the Depression era with few marketable skills, Marian had little to hope for. Her life held hard lessons that were not lost upon her younger sister. From Marian's heartbreak, Rachel observed the precarious nature of marriage and the outcome of failed choices.

Ever since her father's death the previous July, Rachel had been commuting by bus to her office in Baltimore and out to College Park to teach. Her new job required her to be more mobile, often traveling to the Washington headquarters for work in the departmental library or the facilities of the National Museum. Both the bus and the train were expensive. Living so far out in Baltimore County made these trips more time-consuming as well.

In late June Rachel had found a modest two-story red-brick house for rent at the corner of Highland Drive and Colesville Road in the Woodside Park section of Silver Spring, Maryland. The rent was higher than at Stemmers Run, but the promise of easier access to her various places of work overcame her reluctance. Silver Spring, then as now, was a flourishing commuter town between Washington and Baltimore, and only fifteen or twenty minutes from College Park. It had the advantage of good elementary and junior high schools close by for Virginia and Marjorie. Rachel sacrificed the forests and Chesapeake Bay that had lured her to Stemmers Run for the advantages of suburban access. It was the first of many such compromises to come. On the first of July, Mamma, Rachel, and the girls moved to Silver Spring.

Shortly after getting settled in their new house, Rachel drove what had been her father's car and was now hers into Washington one Saturday in July, perhaps to see Mary Scott Skinker or to do some research at the natural history museum. On the way back, her attention wandered and she was stopped by a policeman for speeding in a twenty-two-mile-an-hour zone. Chagrined, she had to appear in District of Columbia traffic court where she was fined five dollars, a fact she was compelled to report on her federal employment record for the next seven years.[10]

Given the changes in her personal life, it was no wonder that Carson was preoccupied. She needed to find other sources of income. After letting almost a year go by, she felt impelled to try to sell her essay "The World of Waters" as Higgins had suggested.

Unsatisfied with the way the essay began, Carson revised the opening paragraphs several times. The version she sent to the *Atlantic Monthly* editors in early June 1937 opened with an uncharacteristic flourish.

> The charting of the white wastes of Antarctica is accomplished; the conquest of Mt. Everest has passed into history. But although the flags of explorers have waved on the highest peaks of the world and fluttered on the frozen rims of the continents, a vast unknown remains, the world of waters. Even from those who have spent their lives in patient questioning, the sea knows how to guard its secrets well. To most it is, in very truth, a "mare incognita."[11]

Reading even the earliest drafts of "The World of Waters," it is easy to understand Higgins's enthusiasm. Rachel's essay is a narrative account of the myriad creatures of the undersea world and introduces two of Carson's enduring literary themes: the ecological relationships of ocean life that have endured for eons of time and the material immortality that involves even the smallest organism. Carson's uncommonly lyric description surveys the sea's ordinary and fantastic creatures much as one might discover them on a guided submarine tour to the deepest ocean floor. She conducts the tour from the immediate point of view of an underwater eye, describing each scene scientifically yet with such wonder and delight that the beauty and mystery of the underwater world she has discovered is accessible to the nonscientific reader.

She explains that:

> Every living thing of the ocean, plant and animal alike, returns to the water at the end of its own life span the materials which had been temporarily assembled to form its body. Thus, there descends into the depths a gentle, never-ending rain of the disintegrating particles of what once were living creatures of the sunlit waters, or of those twilight regions beneath. . . . Thus, individual elements are lost to view, only to reappear again and again in different incarnations in a kind of material immortality.[12]

On July 8 Edward Weeks, who was then acting as editor for retiring *Atlantic Monthly* owner/editor Ellery Sedgewick, responded to Carson's submission. "We have everyone of us been impressed by your uncommonly eloquent little essay, 'The World of Waters.' The findings of science you have illuminated in such a way as to fire the imagination of the layman."[13]

Weeks proposed to publish Carson's essay during the summer, when he thought readers would be particularly interested in the ocean. He had only two small suggestions: omitting the opening paragraph, "which seems . . . a trace too florid," and "substituting for your title the single word 'Undersea.' "[14]

Carson agreed to both suggestions. But, as would be her habit with all subsequent publications, she continued to polish the essay, rewriting until the last possible moment. She dropped the first two paragraphs completely. A new paragraph invited readers to "shed [their] human perceptions of length and breadth and time and place, and enter vicariously into a universe of all-pervading water. For to the sea's children nothing is so important as the fluidity of their world."[15]

Delighted by Carson's changes and her "friendly spirit," Weeks offered her one hundred dollars for the four-page essay, which would appear in the September number. All he needed was a short biographical introduction to "help me introduce you to our readers."[16]

On July 18 Carson proposed two further changes of personal pronouns and a complete recasting of another sentence, which, as she told Weeks, "expresses the thought more gracefully and at the same time more clearly." She included a one-paragraph biographical sketch but felt her signature, "R. L. Carson," required some explanation.

> From time to time in my work with the Bureau of Fisheries . . . I am called upon to prepare articles on commercial fisheries. Inasmuch as these articles deal largely with economic questions, the scientific basis of conservation measures, etc., we have felt that they would be more effective . . . if they were presumably written by a man. [F]or various reasons I prefer to use the same name in my personal writing.[17]

She did, however, allow Weeks to use her full name in the Contributors' Column, which told *Atlantic* readers, "Ever since Jules Verne's imagination went twenty thousand leagues deep, people have wondered what it would be like to walk on the ocean's floor. Rachel Carson . . . has a clear and accurate idea."[18]

On August 2 Carson happily received the *Atlantic*'s check.

"Undersea" appeared on newsstands a month later. It marked Carson's debut as a writer of critical interest. But it also established her unique voice, at once scientifically accurate and clear, yet with poetic insight and imagination, one that confidently captured the wonder of nature's eternal cycles, rhythms, and relationships. In the ecology of the sea, Carson had not only found something she loved to write about but the medium through which she could share her vision of nature's oneness. From those four remarkable *Atlantic* pages, Carson later admitted, "everything else followed."[19]

The critical response was immediate but did not necessarily take the form Carson expected. Quincy Howe, then the senior editor of the publishing house of Simon & Schuster in New York City, was the first to notice the quality of her writing. Telling Carson how much he enjoyed "Undersea," he wrote to inquire if she had plans for a book on the same general subject. Carson had "never seriously considered writing a book," but Howe's letter "put ideas in her head." She replied that she had no publishing commitments but would be happy to discuss her general ideas with him.[20]

The renowned journalist, cultural historian, and illustrator Hendrik Villem van Loon, one of Howe's authors, was equally impressed with Carson's essay. Rachel later recalled her initial reaction to van Loon's letter. "My mail had never contained anything so exciting as his first letter. It arrived in an envelope splashed with the green waves of a sea through which van Loon sharks and whales were poking inquiring snouts."[21]

Van Loon wanted to know what else Carson knew about what went on undersea. In his many voyages across the world's oceans, he had been "so impressed by its apparent lifeless aspect—'not a snout nor a spout did I see,' yet he knew that under the surface there was life in enormous numbers and variety and he felt an intense curiosity to know more about it." Van Loon thought Carson could tell him what he longed to know. In his illegible shorthand van Loon told her, "Maybe Jules Verne and his 20,000 leagues under the sea started me sixty years ago but I have always wanted to read something about that mysterious world and suddenly . . . in the *Atlantic*, most appropriately, . . . I found your article which shows that you are the woman . . . [who can help me.]"[22]

Van Loon and Howe discussed the possibility of Carson doing a book for Simon & Schuster. Seizing the moment, van Loon invited Carson to visit him and his wife in Old Greenwich, Connecticut, at which time he proposed to introduce her to "the firm." Few fledgling writers could have dreamed of better literary mentors than van Loon and Howe.[23]

"I had no idea that the publication of my 'Undersea' by the *Atlantic* would have consequences so interesting and pleasant as your very generous letter," Rachel told the historian. "It is good indeed to know that you liked my little picture of the ocean. I think I wrote it partly because I, too, had always wanted to read something of the sort, but never found it." As for his invitation to visit, Rachel wrote, "the opportunity to know you personally and to talk over my plans with you is so tempting that I cannot pass it by."[24]

A month later Rachel wrote to both men, enclosing a very rough book outline. "I hope very much that you will like my idea," she told van Loon, whose charm and avuncular manner set her at ease. "If you do, perhaps you can persuade Mr. Howe to like it, too." She left it to van Loon to arrange any further meetings.

Carson's letter was the beginning of a delightful correspondence with van Loon whose typing was nearly impossible to decipher and whose handwriting was worse. He often substituted pictures for words, charming pen sketches sometimes colored in, but always deliciously whimsical. His letters arrived in highly decorated envelopes featuring winsome pen-and-ink sea creatures, fabulous ships, or whatever struck his fancy. For Rachel he usually drew ferocious sharks and fanciful seahorses.[25]

Van Loon promised to ask "either Simon or Schuster for dinner" and to escort Rachel into New York the following day to visit "headquarters." After all, he told her "the better they do on other people's books the more they can afford to lose on mine." Underneath van Loon's persuasive chivalry was a keen critic. Perceiving that her talent was fresh and singular, he did not intend to let Rachel Carson slip away. "To make a discovery like you," van Loon wrote her, "is one of the few rare pleasures left to an [drawing of an old man] like myself. It's like finding a new sort of [drawing of a seahorse.]"[26]

The much-awaited meeting with the van Loons took place in the middle of January 1938. "To a young and very tentative" writer, she recalled later, "it was a stimulating and wonderful thing to have the interest of this great man, so overwhelming in his person and his personality, but whose heart was pure gold." Through him she caught her first glimpse of an "exciting and fabulous" world.[27]

True to his word, van Loon invited Quincy Howe and his wife to dinner in Greenwich where he introduced an inwardly nervous but outwardly composed Rachel Carson. The next day Carson met further with Howe in his offices at Simon & Schuster. Together they planned a book of about a dozen chapters arranged in groupings according to habitat. Howe thought "Undersea" would be a preface or a sort of introductory chapter. Rachel had sketched out part of a chapter on the migration of the eel based on her research at Hopkins, which Howe encouraged her to expand. To her great relief, he had no objections to her sale of any chapters to magazines such as the *Atlantic* or *Harpers* as she went along.[28]

Carson's initial conception of the book that would become *Under the Sea-Wind* was a narrative account of the daily life of several sea creatures, much in the manner of the great English naturalist Henry Williamson, whose popular *Salar the Salmon* (1935) she so admired. Carson had first discovered Williamson when she read *Tarka the Otter*, a book she found in the library about the time she entered graduate school. Williamson's prose style was an early model but her own perspective evolved somewhat differently from his.[29]

Rachel was determined to avoid the "human bias" of most popular books about the sea. "The ocean," she thought, was "too big and vast and its forces are too mighty to be much affected by human activity." She would tell the story as a "simple narrative of the lives of certain animals of the sea."[30] "The fish and other sea creatures must be the central characters and their world must be portrayed as it looks and feels to them—and the narrator must not come into the story or appear to express an opinion. Nor must any other human come into it except from the fishes' viewpoint as a predator and destroyer."[31]

The more she thought about the book's point of view, the more she realized, however, that the ocean itself was the central character. Carson recalled that "the smell of the sea's edge, the feeling of vast movements of water, the sound of waves, crept into every page, and over all was the ocean as the force dominating all its creatures."

To give the most complete picture of sea life, she decided to divide the book into three parts, or books, one for the life of the shore, one for the open sea, and one for the deep abyss. In each of these parts, she would tell the story of one particular animal. Taken together, the three narratives would weave a tapestry in which the ecology of the ocean and the interdependence of all its creatures would emerge.[32]

Henry Williamson had achieved his sense of identification with his animals by subtly anthropomorphizing them. Carson thought she could avoid this error by making the "sea and its life a vivid reality" and by more accurately re-creating the natural conditions sea creatures inhabit. Restricting herself to analogies to human conduct, she sometimes used words that suggested anthropomorphism, but was careful to distinguish them from scientifically accurate behaviors. She explained,

> I have spoken of a fish "fearing" his enemies . . . not because I suppose a fish experiences fear in the same way that we do, but because I think he *behaves as though he were frightened.* With the fish, the response is primarily physical; with us, primarily psychological. Yet if the behavior of the fish is to be understandable to us, we must describe it in the words that most properly belong to human psychological states.[33]

To be successful, Carson needed creative imagination, acute observation in the field, and a comprehensive scientific understanding of the sea and its inhabitants.[34]

To help her achieve this, Carson asked van Loon in February to introduce her to his friend William Beebe, the distinguished oceanographer and ornithologist, who, in 1938, was the director of tropical research for the New York Zoological Society. Carson explained that before the book was too far along she wanted to "go undersea" herself. A dive would give her the "feeling of the water as no amount of vicarious experience could do," and she dreamed of a trip to Bermuda or the Bahamas "to explore the ocean floor." Beebe could advise her on where to go and how to proceed.[35]

Carson's letter to van Loon is a thinly veiled plea for financial help. Perhaps van Loon could convince Quincy Howe to give her an advance. She told van Loon that Howe had "asked for a copy of the migration story when it is written together with an outline of the whole book, and I inferred that he will then be ready to talk business on the contract." Van Loon did introduce Carson and her work to William Beebe, but he could do little more about financial matters than continue his enthusiastic support of her project with Simon & Schuster.[36]

The tone of Carson's letter to *Atlantic Monthly* editor Edward Weeks, written the same day as the longer one to van Loon, reveals none of the desperation she must have been feeling. To Weeks, she was a confident professional writer adeptly manipulating the facts to serve her interests. "The Simon and Schuster situation seems to be working out very fortunately," she told him. "They appear to be anxious to have the book and propose signing a contract on the basis of an outline and a completed chapter or two." With studied casualness she mused to Weeks, "I am coming to the opinion that this migration subject might be most effectively covered by telling the story of the eel." Assuring him that such a story would be on "solid scientific ground," she wondered whether the *Atlantic* would be interested in it. It was not.[37]

Carson's next contribution to the *Atlantic* was only a book review, but it had unanticipated benefits. A. G. Ogden, the magazine's book review editor, asked her as "the *Atlantic*'s ranking expert on fishes," to review Lionel A. Walford's new book *Marine Game Fishes of the Pacific Coast*. The assignment earned her an easy fifteen dollars and introduced her to the work of Walford, then a biologist with the California Division of Fish and Game. She agreed to the review in exchange for Ogden's reluctant permission to let her review Henry Williamson's new autobiographical memoir *Goodbye West Country* as well. Out of necessity, however, she still had to focus on newspaper articles, which brought the most immediate and the most lucrative return. There was little time left to work on any book.[38]

For the next eighteen months Carson published at least one feature article a month. More of them were on other wildlife topics than fish. After the North American Wildlife Conference in Baltimore in February 1938, she wrote movingly on the activities of the General Wildlife Federation, then headed by conservationist and cartoonist Jay N. "Ding" Darling, the director of the U.S. Biological Survey. A month later the destruction of wildlife habitat again caught her attention. Introducing a theme that would appear often in her later writing, Carson gave an indication of her views on conservation: "The inescapable fact that the decline of wildlife is linked with human destinies is being driven home. For three centuries we have been busy upsetting the balance of nature by draining marshlands, cutting timber, plowing under the grasses that carpeted the prairies. Wildlife is being destroyed. But the home of wildlife is also our home."[39]

By fall, having exhausted all the topics she and Watson had previously agreed on, Carson suggested "an article on the much discussed starling." She had noticed that for all their complaining, people in Baltimore and Washington did not know much about the bird's general habits and their possible value. She thought she could rehabilitate the starling's reputation.

Her first effort was a feature, "Housing of Starlings Baltimore's Perennial Problem," which appeared in the *Sun Magazine* in early March 1939. Mail from the magazine's readers encouraged her to continue writing on the starling's behalf. She was able to sell her next effort, "How About Citizenship Papers for the Starling?," to *Nature Magazine*, which published it in the June/July 1939 issue.[40]

One of Carson's other suggestions to Mark Watson was an investigation of naturally occurring poisons in the soil, selenium and some of the fluorides. "It has been known for a good while," Carson told Watson, "that stock was being poisoned from this source and there is some recent work which indicates that people may not fare so well when their drinking water is polluted in this fashion. Also the cumulative effect on fish is rather startling."[41]

Watson never invited her to pursue this topic, just as he previously had ignored her interest in the tick, but both subjects reveal that, as early as 1938, Carson was already curious about ecological relationships between humans and the natural world and also interested in habitat pollution and environmental health.

For a fisheries' biologist, the breadth of Carson's understanding of natural processes perhaps was not unusual, but her response to the natural world, her sense of wonder and delight in it, distinguished her prose from the outset. Carson's work at the bureau, far from limiting her, continued to deepen and expand what was already part of her singular approach to nature. One of her most meaningful encounters with sea and land occurred on her first visit to the U.S. Fisheries Station in Beaufort, North Carolina.

In July 1938 she packed up her household for a ten-day vacation. The station at Beaufort was the largest fisheries research facility on the East Coast next to the one at Woods Hole. They rented a cottage on one of the outer banks nearby so Mamma, Virginia, and Marjorie could enjoy the seashore as well. On this, as on almost every subsequent trip, Maria Carson accompanied her daughter. It was a wonderful release from her normal housekeeping duties.

Rachel sought out the remotest sections of a beach. On that outer bank, she found a particularly lovely stretch of wild ocean beach that she would use as the background for the chapters in *Under the Sea-Wind* about the shorebirds. No matter how hard the wind might be blowing, Carson walked the beach at all hours, at high tides and low, watching the comings and goings of shorebirds, observing the smaller shore creatures, and collecting material. Sometimes she simply lay in the sandy dunes, flat on her back, arms behind her head, watching and listening to the birds as they circled and dived overhead.

She discovered the marsh pools and ponds in the flat sands where the dunes of the barrier island fell away to the ocean. There she would sit for hours, totally enraptured, watching wave after wave pour through the slough into the ponds where the high water released thousands of small fish that had been captive there perhaps since the last spring tide. Their race down the slough to the ocean moved her profoundly. Sometimes as she watched their leaping struggle, the tears streamed down her cheeks, tears produced by the awe she felt at the mystery of life.

Timing her visit to Beaufort for the tides and the full moon, Rachel especially loved to wander the beach at night. It was an adventure that became one of her favorite habits and one of the most meaningful for her personal appreciation of the natural world. Flashlight in hand, she watched the shore's nocturnal creatures come out of hidden homes, unseen to even the most careful observers during the daytime. Jotting down notes about the distinctive atmosphere of the shore at night when the smell and sound of the surf, the stillness of the ponds, the occasional call of a bird, and the scent of the pines behind her on the higher ground replaced the visual description of daylight, she gathered the images that would give her writing some of its most distinctive motifs.

Rachel fell in love with the barren dunes of the outer banks that summer and with the mysterious relationship between shore and sea. Although she returned to the Carolina banks spring and fall many times later, the wonder of that place as she first knew it in 1938 remained vividly in her memory.[42]

While her feature writing provided an outlet for Carson's widening interests in aquatic, wildlife, and environmental health issues, her scientific responsibilities for the Bureau of Fisheries were also expanding her scientific perspective. She had risen in grade several times, but in June 1939 Elmer Higgins recommended Carson for promotion in grade and for reassignment.

She was promoted to assistant aquatic biologist, grade P-2, at a salary of $2,600 a year, and once again Higgins recommended that the bureau create an entirely new position for Carson as well as transfer her from the Baltimore office to the field laboratory in College Park, Maryland. Higgins and Robert Nesbit, her immediate supervisor, justified their recommendation not only on the excellence of Carson's work but also on the fact that her wider research duties would release higher-grade biologists from preparing reports and compiling data.[43]

Rachel's new duties, however, were not those normally assigned to the position of assistant aquatic biologist in the Bureau of Fisheries. She performed no actual field investigations and only incidental laboratory work, functioning primarily as a research and reference assistant to Nesbit, who turned over to her all his laboratory and field reports, which Carson then verified, referenced, and rewrote. She researched biological material related to the overall studies of the laboratory, wrote excerpts and summaries, compiled bibliographies, and reviewed other investigators' field reports for comparative analyses. Her most important assignment was to produce descriptive and historical material for the public brochures that Higgins's division published in a series entitled "Our Aquatic Food Animals."[44]

Although the paperwork went forward for her relocation, the Commerce Department's director of personnel was uncomfortable with the promotion. Since there was a disparity between the duties usually performed by a person in the grade of assistant P-2, and since the entire Bureau of Fisheries was being transferred from the Department of Commerce to the Department of the Interior, he elected to defer Carson's promotion. Instead she was transferred to the College Park, Maryland, laboratory with only a two-hundred-dollar increase in pay and none in grade. Her promised promotion was another casualty of President Franklin Roosevelt's Governmental Reorganization Act of 1939.[45]

As part of a major bureaucratic reorganization of the Executive Branch and a streamlining of federal government departments, the Reorganization Act together with the President's Reorganization Plan #III created a new conservation agency in the Department of Interior, known as the U.S. Fish and Wildlife Service (FWS). Formed by combining the Bureau of Fisheries in Commerce with the U.S. Biological Survey in Agriculture, the Fish and Wildlife Service was part of the efforts of Interior Secretary Harold L. Ickes to make Interior the government's central conservation department.

A consummate political infighter, Ickes was an old-line progressive reformer, an early disciple of Theodore Roosevelt's conservation ideology, now in charge of a vast inland empire of natural resources. His most cherished mission was to wrest the Department of Interior from the influence of the big resource interests and to make it over into a Department of Conservation. Central to that plan was to get the U.S. Forest Service transferred to his department out of Agriculture. In the meantime Ickes raided Commerce and Agriculture of these smaller bureaus and centralized their functions in Interior. Although the Fish and Wildlife Service was officially created in July 1939, it took well over a year for the Biological Survey and the Bureau of Fisheries, both complex bureaucracies, to evolve into a single functioning agency under the skillful direction of wildlife expert Ira N. Gabrielson. But once accomplished, the wider mission of the new agency provided Rachel Carson increased responsibilities and the opportunity for much more satisfying field experience.[46]

Even without the title of assistant biologist, Carson's new work at the College Park laboratory was much more scientifically demanding than the Commerce Department's personnel office could have realized. She analyzed biological and statistical data of the fishes of the Middle Atlantic and drew very definite conclusions about their age and variations in population. She wrote countless scientific reports, interpreted research, and rewrote it in public documents, but even so she was not promoted to assistant aquatic biologist until May 1942.[47]

Ironically, as Carson's career as a government biologist was expanding and she was being promoted through the grades, Mary Scott Skinker's more traditional government career was coming to an unexpectedly tragic end.[48]

Skinker had come into the Division of Zoology with a master's degree and advanced quickly in grade after she completed her doctorate in 1933. She was the junior member of an unusual group composed largely of female parasitologists, none of whom was married and all of whom were extraordinarily fine scientists. Eloise B. Cram, the supervising division scientist, hand-picked her group, gave it cohesion, and was its stimulus. They worked primarily in helminthology, studying the parasites of poultry, producing "break through results." By all accounts, Cram, an outstanding parasitologist, was the first female in the field to make a scholarly reputation. Mary Scott Skinker, like the other women in the group, was devoted to Cram.[49]

At the end of 1936 Morris Hall, the head of the zoological division, was invited to bring a small group of his best associate scientists into the Hygienic Laboratory of the U.S. Public Health Service (later the

National Institutes of Health), which was expanding its research on epidemics of infectious diseases. Hall took Eloise Cram and two other members of her group. Skinker, who had the least seniority, was left behind in Agriculture.[50]

For the next year and a half, Skinker continued the projects bequeathed to her by Cram, but she received increasingly less support from Benjamin Schwartz, who replaced Hall as head of the division. Worse than Schwartz, who was generally regarded as merely disagreeable, was Dr. Emmett Price, who was promoted into Cram's place as supervising parasitologist. Price was a southerner of many prejudices and was deeply intolerant of female scientists. If, in fact, women were hired as scientists in the government—a policy he opposed—Price labored to ensure that they were not promoted quickly or easily.[51]

Emmett Price was an anathema to all the women in the division, especially to the lovely, dignified Skinker, whom he teased mercilessly about being an "old maid." She took it for eighteen months and then her health broke down. Without strong support from the division chief and left with a project that had no backing, she knew she had no future in the division.

In the fall of 1938 Skinker resigned from the Department of Agriculture and moved to New York City, where she became the director of a small private residence for women. She took advanced work in education administration at Columbia Teacher's College and began editing a textbook on parasitology.[52]

Skinker's experience as a female scientist in the federal government was not unusual. Job security and promotion depended heavily on unprejudiced supervisors, and most supervisors were male. The careers of most women in science proceeded at a snail's pace compared to their male counterparts. Carson, unlike Skinker, was able to avoid the worst of this inequity because, while she had a scientific classification, her work increasingly led her away from field and laboratory studies and into public information and editing, where women were more traditionally employed and accepted. Although she was not promoted as fast as she might have been, she made steady progress upward in rank and grade, being exceptionally lucky in supervisors who recognized her talents.[53]

Although there are no letters between Skinker and Carson, doubtless because they saw each other regularly and spoke often on the telephone, Carson witnessed Skinker's professional frustration and participated in her decision to leave government. Skinker's personal unhappiness, the loss of her talent to government science, and her departure from Washington saddened Rachel. Despite distance and infrequent visits, Rachel remained devoted to this exceptional woman who had been responsible for so much of her life's course.

By the summer of 1939, Carson finally was making real progress with her manuscript. She sent the first chapter, "Flood Tide," to Edward Weeks at the *Atlantic*, hoping that he would publish it as they had discussed nearly two years earlier. Editor Weeks rejected Carson's proposal, citing a new series of essays by the popular nature writer Donald Culross Peattie, which the magazine had committed to publish. Despite Carson's best efforts to convince Weeks that her work was not at all like Peattie's, the *Atlantic* never published a single chapter of *Under the Sea-Wind*.[54]

Without the promise of income from a magazine sale, Carson was in need of extra money to continue her research and to finance several weeks at the Fisheries Laboratory at Woods Hole later that summer. Unfamiliar with the financial arrangements of publishing, Carson turned again to van Loon for advice. Enclosing the first chapter and Howe's recent offer of an option to publish *Under the Sea-Wind*, she explained that a small cash advance would allow her to give all her spare time to the book.[55]

Trying to maximize her position, but worried about Simon & Schuster's commitment to marketing the book, Carson wondered whether accepting Howe's $250 option obligated her irrevocably. She told van Loon, "I should hate to let them do the book if those who would have the job of putting it over are going to be luke-warm about it." Van Loon assured her that when Simon & Schuster have a book "they really like, they perform miracles." But he promised to "make their life miserable until the book is out and is *paying*."[56]

Carson sent her outline to Howe at the end of June along with a letter pressing for an additional cash advance of $500, which, she told him, would allow her to return to Beaufort in the fall. Van Loon, who was also president of the Author's Guild, cautioned her not to have unrealistic expectations.

> Speaking *ex cathedra* . . . I would say that 250 dollars advance is on the whole much more than the average writer gets . . . remember that for book publication you are still new and a risk. What Howe offered you is entirely fair . . . if you have heard of other publishers who will do better . . . you are still a free agent but I doubt whether a reputable house would give you more.[57]

Only mildly chastened, Rachel accepted the $250 but extracted verbal agreement from Howe to an additional advance, once she produced 15,000 words.

In early August 1939 Carson headed north, without Mamma, for ten days of work at the Fisheries Station at Woods Hole. There she joined her colleague and friend Dorothy Hamilton, another research biologist, who had joined the bureau a year earlier. Dorothy had been at Woods Hole most of the summer working on a fisheries project.

The daughter of a remarkable artist, George Hamilton, Dorothy had spent a childhood that Rachel could only envy. She had grown up on a wild and desolate farm in the Berkshire Mountains on the Massachusetts border near Great Barrington. A naturalist from childhood, Dorothy had studied zoology with George Avery at Connecticut College and completed a master's degree at Western Reserve University. She loved biological research and shared many of Rachel's interests.[58]

Dorothy Hamilton knew that Rachel was at work on a book, but Rachel rarely talked about it and Dorothy was sensitive enough not to pry. Rachel moved in with Dorothy at the Fisheries Residence. Some days she worked in the library and the laboratory, but most often she walked the beaches along the harbor and sat on the Fisheries wharf making notes on the fish and watching the tides bring their treasure in and out of the Hole. In the early evening the two friends loved to visit the nearby Sipiwissit Marshes, with field glasses and notebooks, to watch the water birds.

With her head filled with new images and a greater understanding of the life of schooling fish and life "undersea," Carson returned to Maryland with Dorothy in mid-August to confront a very different environment. Anticipating her new job in College Park with the reorganized Bureau of Fisheries in the U.S. Fish and Wildlife Service, and feeling the need for some private space of her own where she could write undisturbed, Rachel moved her family again that fall. She found a quieter house on Flower Avenue in another section of Silver Spring, where her mother could enjoy a small garden. But its main attribute was a large bedroom occupying the entire second floor, where Rachel could work undisturbed. Mamma and the girls had their bedrooms on the first floor.

Once settled in, Rachel began the habit of working late in the evening or early in the morning when the house was quiet. Her creative process required solitude. She preferred silence and found herself distracted by even the normal household noises. Buzzie and Kito, her two Persians, kept her company during her solitary nighttime writing. "Buzzie . . . used to sleep on my writing table, on the litter of notes and manuscript sheets," she recalled. "On two of these pages I had made sketches, first of his little head drooping with sleepiness, then of him after he had settled down comfortably for a nap." She also doodled "October—November—December" on page three of the manuscript, reminding herself how little time remained until her December 31 deadline.[59]

Carson was a slow, painstaking writer, preferring to revise paragraph by paragraph, sometimes even sentence by sentence, before she went on to the next. One finds seven drafts of one page of the chapter "Spring Flight" among the preserved manuscripts of *Under the Sea-Wind*, and each chapter is heavily corrected. Conscious of the impact of alliteration and rhythm to create atmosphere, she read passages aloud to herself before she asked her mother to read them to her again. During the day Mrs. Carson typed what Rachel had revised after listening to it, so it would be on her desk when she returned at night. It was a pattern mother and daughter held to with every piece she wrote. Each draft was read aloud, over and over, until Rachel was satisfied with the way it sounded as well as the way it read to the eye.[60]

Carson sent Quincy Howe the five chapters that comprised Book 1, "The Edge of the Sea," in the early spring of 1940. It was more than enough on which to offer her a contract. Howe promised an answer within days, but it was over a month later when Rachel, nearly beside herself with anxiety, heard that the staff "liked it a lot." Still unable to commit himself, however, Howe told her he would have to wait until Max Schuster returned to town before making a definite offer.

Finally, in early June, Rachel received a contract for the book she titled *Under the Sea-Wind* and shortly thereafter an additional advance of $250. The completed manuscript was due December 31, 1940.

With a definite deadline, Carson went into high gear. She found that working under pressure was "not such a bad thing." One of her most urgent needs was to find an illustrator whose work she had confidence in but whom she could also afford, as she had to pay for all the illustrations. Mark Watson suggested that she talk to Howard Frech, an artist on the staff of the *Baltimore Sun*. Frech agreed to her price for a total of eight drawings, one to be used on the cover, and she convinced the publisher to accept the local artist. But taking no chances, she armed Frech with reference books to check the scientific accuracy of each drawing.[61]

The last week of July 1940 found Rachel back again at the Fisheries Station in Woods Hole. Dorothy Hamilton was back too, but this time with her new husband, Glenn Algire, a medical scientist from Baltimore whom she had met at Woods Hole the summer before. The three friends met for dinner and special field trips while Rachel was there.[62]

As a government employee, Carson had more opportunity to go out on the small Fisheries dredger, the *Phalathrop*, that daily steamed up and down Vineyard Sound or Buzzards Bay. When she had first beheld the dredger's treasure at Woods Hole in 1929, she had wondered where these creatures lived and how they survived. In the years since, she had let her "imagination go down through the water" piecing "together bits of scientific fact" until now she could see the "whole life of those creatures as they lived them in that strange world."[63]

Rachel spent hours on the Fisheries dock "watching the schools of young mackerel moving up and down along the stone breakwater, with squids and other predators often darting among them." She made a pretty picture, sitting on a large wharf pile, usually in a simple white cotton blouse and cotton slacks. At thirty-three she was a tiny-framed woman, with a very trim figure and, according to her friends, "exceptionally good legs." She wore her hair longer than she had in a while, but swept back off her face with combs holding her auburn curls in place. Her widow's peak was more pronounced than when she was younger, emphasizing the heart shape of her face and her angular features. Despite her petite stature, Rachel was very strong, physically fit, and well coordinated.[64]

The highlight of Rachel's two weeks at Woods Hole was the day she, Dorothy, and Glenn drove to Eastham, Massachusetts, determined to find the "outermost house" that Henry Beston had lived in while writing the book of the same name during his yearlong sojourn on that lonely seaside outpost. Next to Henry Williamson, Rachel most admired Henry Beston's nature writing. *The Outermost House* (1924) remained one of the works that she most loved. As chance would have it, Beston had been a Harvard classmate of Dorothy Hamilton's father, so Dorothy was just as eager as Rachel to discover the setting for his remarkable book. Glenn Algire happily went along to record their research with his camera.[65]

Coming upon the little house "and the surroundings with which [she] felt so familiar," Dorothy remembered that Rachel grew silent. She sat quietly, almost reverently for a long time on one of the dunes overlooking the site, lost in the place and her experience of the moment. She promised Dorothy she would write to Beston and tell him of their discovery, and while she truly meant to do so, it was years before she had the nerve to write him.[66]

This final trip to Woods Hole in the summer of 1940 helped Carson make those adjustments in her thinking and most of all "get the feel of a world that was entirely water." When she returned to Maryland, she had what she needed to finish the book.[67]

Although Carson was only vaguely aware of it at the time, she realized later that she was able to lose herself completely in her writing that fall. Her family obligations, difficult as they were, were manageable. She had quiet time for herself in the evenings. Mamma managed the household so efficiently that Rachel could give herself over to her creative endeavor. It was the last time she would have such luxury. She never recalled those months of 1940 without a pang of longing for that evanescent sense of total absorption in the creative process.[68]

Carson finished Book 3 in early November. She worked with Howard Frech on the illustrated glossary that identified more than a hundred of the sea creatures that populated her book. Maria Carson flawlessly typed the finished manuscript, and together they drove to the imposing U.S. Post Office in the District of Columbia on New Year's Eve to send it off to Simon & Schuster.[69]

With the manuscript out of Carson's hands, she returned to her reports and press releases at the Fish and Wildlife Service. But the book's progress was never far from her thoughts. In October 1941 she wrote van Loon, who had suffered a mild heart attack and was confined to his home, to tell him that the Scientific Book Club had bought it as its November selection. She fussed over the quality of the illustrations, dissatisfied with the reproductions of Frech's drawings, and worried about how the publisher was handling her advance sales.

Van Loon encouraged Carson to take the long view of her first book. "It seems to me," the venerable historian told her, "the older I grow, the more the whole damn business is but a gamble . . . what the public will swallow or not . . . who can tell . . . let us hope this time they prove to be fond of fish."[70]

Under the Sea-Wind was published November 1, 1941, and sold for $3.00 a copy. The cover, in a dull teal with beige lettering, was of two gulls in flight over a sandy dune along the shore. There was a sizable paragraph about Carson on the inside back cover flap but no photograph of the author.

Rachel gave the first copy off the press to her mother, who opened it and wept at the simple dedication, "To my mother." She gave the second copy to Elmer Higgins, inscribed: "To Mr. Higgins, who started it all. Rachel L. Carson. November 6, 1941." Then, as van Loon had suggested, she tried to wait patiently for the critics to react.[71]

While "Undersea" had given a submarine view of the ocean's floor, *Under the Sea-Wind* was, as she had hoped it would be, an intimate portrait of the sea and shore creatures whose world of air and water the reader enters. Although the three parts of the book focus on different protagonists—the first on sea birds, the second on "Scomber" the mackerel, and the last on "Anguilla" the eel—the whole is tied together by lives lived intimately with the sea.

The plot is formed by each creature's struggle to survive and reproduce. In the pattern of life held together by instinct and molded not by some fierce Darwinian determinism but by simple chance, survivors are merely those in the right place at the right time; others are just unlucky. Although danger lurks everywhere, Carson's narrative of sea life conveys an overall sense of calm. Everything is as it should be: the pattern of an ancient, sometimes violent, but endless cycle comforting in its certain repetitions. Yet what marks Carson's writing is not so much her interest in the impersonal forces of nature but her sympathetic identification with individual creatures with whom she feels a spiritual as well as a physical connection.[72]

Carson's stories of the sea creatures speak also to the larger problems of human existence. The ceaseless flow of life and death that she revealed "under the sea-wind" lent a certain optimism to the struggle of human existence.

As in "Undersea," Carson's awareness of "material immortality" pervades the narrative. The death of one creature contributes to the life of another in the endless chain of reincarnation. The very word "sea-wind" in the title underlines Carson's ecological vision of the unity of nature. The sea-wind binds equally within its breath the lives lived in air and those in the sea.

In this, her first book, as in all her subsequent writing, Carson was influenced by the romantic nature writing of Englishman Richard Jeffries. In *Under the Sea-Wind*, she draws particularly on his lyric *Pageant of Summer* (1905), in which Jeffries described how "the whole office of

Matter is to feed life." Jeffries's idea of the sea as both the real and spiritual source of life touched something essential in Carson's spirit. In later years, she always kept a copy of his poetry by her bedside to read from just before she turned out the light. The title for *Under the Sea-Wind* comes from one of her favorite passages in *The Pageant of Summer*: "As the wind, wandering over the sea, takes from each wave an invisible portion, and brings to those on shore the ethereal essence of ocean, so the air lingering among the woods and hedges—green waves and willows—full of fine atoms of summer."[73]

Carson confronts one of the central problems of all nature writing in *Under the Sea-Wind*: how to give the processes of nature metaphorical and spiritual meaning without compromising the scientific accuracy of the biological events, structures, or behaviors. The level of freshness that she brings to her account of the cycles of seasons and the struggle of each creature for survival mark *Sea-Wind* as in some ways her most successful work. Her voice is that of both scientist and poet, in love with the wonder in nature that she has discovered. The most moving passages of *Under the Sea-Wind*, not surprisingly, come from Carson's own experience.[74]

> To stand at the edge of the sea, to sense the ebb and the flow of the tides, to feel the breath of a mist moving over a great salt marsh, to watch the flight of shore birds that have swept up and down the surf lines of the continents for untold thousands of years, to see the running of the old eels and the young shad to the sea, is to have knowledge of things that are as nearly eternal as any earthly life can be.[75]

The Scientific Book Club Review established the tone of the critical notices. "Not since the publication of *Salar the Salmon* has there been a volume so replete with information about sealife. There is poetry here, but no false sentimentality. There is ruthlessness as well as beauty in nature." *The New York Times* daily critic found *Under the Sea-Wind* so "skillfully written as to read like fiction, but in fact a scientifically accurate account of life in the ocean and along the ocean shore." Critics for *The New York Times Book Review*, *The New York Herald Tribune*, *The New Yorker*, and *The Christian Science Monitor* all praised Carson's style and scientific understanding of the ocean.[76]

Pleased as she was by these accolades, Carson was more interested in the opinions of other scientists and naturalists like William Beebe, who reviewed *Under the Sea-Wind* for *The Saturday Review of Literature*, remarking on its lyrical beauty and its faultless science. In 1944 Beebe chose to include two chapters in his collection, *The Book of Naturalists: An Anthology of the Best Natural History*, which began with Aristotle and ended with Carson. Wildlife and wilderness expert Howard Zahniser also complimented Carson's writing in his review in *Nature Magazine*, describing the mackerel section as "a sketch that no reader of *Nature* would willingly miss." The best review, however, was not written until 1952, and Carson never knew about it until 1953, when a friend sent her a copy. Its author was Henry Beston.[77]

Most of Carson's colleagues at Fisheries, like Dorothy Algire, were delighted as well as surprised by the quality and beauty of her prose. Elmer Higgins, who was not at all surprised, gave it a superb review in *The Progressive Fish-Culturist*, which reached over 3,500 biologists, fishery administrators, and marine biologists. Carson was especially pleased by the warm reception these scientists gave *Under the Sea-Wind*, for they normally had little regard for popularizations of science.

Poised for the popular reception that she had every right to expect after such glowing evaluations, Carson's hopes were dashed by world events, which ultimately deprived her of commercial success. Barely a month after publication, Japanese war planes bombed Pearl Harbor on December 7, 1941, and world attention focused on preparations for U.S. entry into the world war. Carson later recalled her disappointment at the publication of *Under the Sea-Wind* with wry humor. "The world received the event with superb indifference." Sadly, the "rush to the book store that is the author's dream never materialized."[78]

Barely two thousand copies of *Under the Sea-Wind* were sold. When it went out of print in August 1946, Carson's royalties totaled $689.17. She bought the remaining copies and gave them away to friends as house presents over the years.[79]

Carson's association with Simon & Schuster, never truly comfortable, became more strained as the war went on and the publisher did little, in her estimation, to promote the book. Quincy Howe had turned the actual editing of *Sea-Wind* over to senior editor Maria Leiper. Carson and Leiper discovered they had much in common and a friendship flourished. Maria had grown up in Swickley, Pennsylvania, a prosperous river town west of Pittsburgh. She even knew some of Rachel's college classmates. Maria was a soft, gracious woman whose editorial skills were highly regarded in the publishing industry. Carson recognized and respected Leiper's talent and began to count on her judgment and advice.

Sonia "Sunnie" Bleeker, another talented and compassionate woman in Simon & Schuster's marketing department, also became an unexpected adviser. Bleeker was in charge of selling subsidiary rights for the firm's books. To Rachel, it seemed, she knew practically everyone in the business.

Sunnie was a person of energy, generosity, and patience. While Rachel understood in theory that her book could get only a fraction of the publisher's publicity budget, in practice she tried to direct her own publicity campaign. Bleeker credited Carson's editorial experience and tried to promote the book as she wanted, but it was not easy. Throughout the spring of 1942 Rachel bombarded Bleeker with suggestions and strategies for wider marketing. Rachel's need to be in control of the outcome of her published writing was nearly impossible to deflect, and only those who cared deeply about her could have endured her constant meddling. Maria Leiper and Sunnie Bleeker did so because they recognized Rachel's talent. Both women sympathized with the unyielding financial responsibilities that drove Rachel's efforts to find markets for her writing.

There was never any reticence in her directives to her editors and publishers, early and late. Always aware of prizes that carried a cash award, Carson unabashedly suggested that Simon & Schuster nominate *Sea-Wind* for a Pulitzer, but since it would have to be entered into the category of "history of the Atlantic shore," her hopes were "not too high." In the end, Rachel had to be content with critical praise alone. Frustrated with world events as well as publishers' budgets, Carson's government responsibilities also required more of her time and attention than before.[80]

With the outbreak of World War II, the federal bureaucracy mushroomed. New bureaucracies were organized and reorganized to wage the war and direct the domestic economy. Before the war there had not been enough office space in Washington, D.C., to accommodate all of Roosevelt's new creations. Now agencies like the Fish and Wildlife Service, whose wartime mandates affected only a few research laboratories and scientists, were pressed to relocate purely domestic personnel to free up office space for critical wartime support staff.

Rumors flew around the FWS that Fisheries would be moved out of town. The idea filled Rachel with dread. Her anxiety about the logistics of making such a move was heightened by her concerns over what to do about her mixed-generation household. In the middle of March 1942 the word came from Secretary Ickes that Fisheries would be relocated in Chicago for an indefinite period—just as soon as office space could be acquired and made ready. Rachel was depressed at the news but relieved that the decision was finally official.[81]

Carson's frustration with the indecisiveness of the federal bureaucracy made her long for some other kind of work where she felt her talents could be better employed in the war effort than "in boon-doggling, official Washington," she confided to Leiper. "Really, seeing the things that I do here in the government makes one very disheartened for the future." She qualified as an air raid warden and took a required course in first aid in the evenings. She commiserated with Mary Scott Skinker, a volunteer mail censor on Governor's Island, when she went to New York City in April to confer with Leiper and Bleeker, but there was little she could do to change the situation or feel more useful.[82]

For a short time in April, it looked as if the Chicago move might be delayed indefinitely. Fish and Wildlife personnel were to take over an apartment building on Lake Michigan, but first the tenants had to be relocated. Rachel was delighted with any possibility of reprieve.[83]

At the end of May, Carson finally received her promotion to assistant aquatic biologist along with reassignment to Fish and Wildlife Headquarters in the South Building of the Department of the Interior on C Street, N.W., just off Virginia Avenue. Her transfer came about when another biologist was suddenly moved to Puerto Rico.[84]

Carson's new position brought a much-needed $200 salary increase. Her formal responsibilities once again were primarily informational: writing memoranda, reports, and publications on the management, economics, and natural history of fish. She continued to assist Higgins in the review and editing of field reports and manuscripts, and became the editor of the *Progressive Fish-Culturist*. Before she left Washington, she and Higgins planned a new series of conservation bulletins entitled "Food from the Sea." Then, on August 7, 1942, Carson was given one week to report for duty with the service in Chicago.[85]

From the beginning, Rachel realized that Mamma would have to move out to Chicago with her, but she hoped Virginia and Marjorie would stay in Silver Spring with friends until she found out how long she would be gone. Marjorie had just graduated from high school, and Virginia was working as a stenographer. After leaving as much of their household goods as they could with Robert, Rachel and her mother drove to Chicago. There they found a small house in Evanston, an accessible suburb from which Rachel could commute into Chicago. Mamma set up the household as usual, and Rachel rejoined Elmer Higgins and assistant chief Edward Bailey in their new offices in the downtown Merchandise Mart.[86]

Carson's work involved more of the sort of mindless public information releases that took time to write but seemed purposeless. The early publication schedule of the "Food from the Sea" series saved her from the worst of the press release writing. Carson wrote four pamphlets, known officially as U.S. Government Conservation Bulletins, for the series.

Bulletin #33 concerned the fish and shellfish of New England and #34 described fish from the "home waters of the Middle West." Two others covered the fish of the South and the Middle Atlantic. The bulletins were substantial publications, each approximately seventy-five pages, specifically directed to the American housewife, who was urged to prepare seafood as a protein substitute for rationed meats and poultry. Carson's aim was not only to convince a public unused to eating freshwater fish to vary war-rationed meals with fish dishes but also to introduce readers to the fish of the inland waters. By educating the public about little-known fish, pressure would be taken off the more popular fish, which were overutilized.[87]

Each bulletin bore Carson's trademark of meticulous research and factual information presented in an interesting and engaging manner. In her profiles of a region's fish resources, Carson always endeavored to provide a sense of the delicate ecological balance that was necessary for reproduction and survival. The first two bulletins were ready to go to press by the spring of 1943.[88]

In late April 1943 a position finally opened in the Office of the Coordinator of Fisheries back in Washington for an associate aquatic biologist, P-3. Carson applied and was, of course, selected by Higgins. Her salary jumped $600 but her job description remained essentially the same. On May 1 she and Mamma moved back to Maryland.

With housing a scarce and expensive commodity in wartime Washington, Rachel was lucky to find a simple two-bedroom house that she could afford on Maple Avenue in Takoma Park, a booming suburb just east of

Silver Spring. Although the commute to the office was slightly longer than before, the improved bus service made up the difference. It did not matter much to Rachel where she lived; she was just grateful to be back in Maryland. Carson was also relieved to be closer to New York, where Sunnie Bleeker was looking out for her literary interests as best she could. A week later Rachel rejoined Elmer Higgins at the FWS offices in the cavernous new Department of Interior building.[89]

There Carson found an ever-changing group of new colleagues in the Fish and Wildlife Service as wartime assignments moved people around like so many Chinese checkers. Uncertain exactly what to do next, or how to move forward, Carson used the fall of 1943 to catch her breath. She had time to assess how the FWS was evolving in wartime and what her future there might be once the war was over.

At thirty-six, Carson was now a seasoned government bureaucrat, an associate aquatic biologist rising steadily through the government grades. As her government salary increased, her editorial responsibilities expanded, leaving less and less time for personal travel or writing. Carson was also a published and critically praised popular science writer, a respected feature writer, and a highly regarded government science writer and editor. Her writing had acquired new breadth and maturity since those first radio scripts for Elmer Higgins. No longer a novice in the world of publishing, she had friends, mentors, editors, and connections. Most of all, she was confident of how to combine her talents for science and literature.

Set against the momentous events of the end of the world war and the beginning of postwar recovery, Carson was restless in government, lacking purpose or the means to contribute something meaningful to the world. Some of the war work she was assigned at the FWS seemed trivial at a time when the whole world order was in turmoil. She ascribed part of her dissatisfaction to the nature and routine of government information services. But there was a deeper longing in her to remain faithful to the vision of her life's purpose. More and more that vision seemed to drive what few choices were hers to make. She was a "would-be writer who could not afford the time for creative work." But she was also a scientist who knew that her future was irrevocably entwined with the larger economic and technological changes that followed in the wake of the war machine. As Allied soldiers pushed toward victory in Europe and Japan to end the war in 1945, Carson sensed that her life and work were also in a period of recasting.[90]

5

"Just to Live by Writing"

Rachel Carson's office was in one of several suites occupied by the Fish and Wildlife Service on the third floor of Harold Ickes's expensive new granite Department of Interior. The enormous building itself covered a two-block area in the Foggy Bottom section of the city just north of the State Department cluster.

The seven-story complex was considered the state of the art in office buildings. Built off a north-south spine, the building featured six large wings on either side of the spine so that, in the spirit of democracy, every office had at least one large double window. The main lobby off "C" Street featured six great Tennessee marble obelisks, carved with motifs of ferocious thunderbirds holding up large alabaster bowls that lit the nineteen-foot ceilings with a mysterious indirect light.

Interior was the first government office building to have central air conditioning and both escalators and elevators. It also featured a museum, an art gallery, an Indian arts and crafts shop, a huge auditorium, an employee gymnasium in the basement, and a fully equipped radio station. Most significantly, Ickes's domain boasted the first integrated employee cafeteria in the nation's capital, where Rachel Carson and her staff often went for coffee.[1]

There were double windows in Carson's office as promised, but since the Office of the Coordinator of Fisheries occupied an inside position on one of the wings close to the building's "spine," they provided very little light. To see the sky at all, the occupant had to lean way out and crank the neck sharply to the right. But inside, her soundproofed space was a spacious rectangle, twelve feet by eighteen.

With her new job, Carson had been given more administrative responsibility for planning and preparing informational material. She still edited field reports and prepared press releases and technical bulletins for publication, including another conservation bulletin on the fish of the South Atlantic and an appendix on the nutritive value of fish and shellfish. But she was increasingly involved in policy planning for the Office of the Coordinator of Fisheries.[2]

Within six months, Carson was promoted to aquatic biologist, and shortly thereafter to information specialist in charge of "informational matters relating to the wartime fishery program." Although her salary had risen to $3,800 a year, it was still modest in light of her family obligations. She was too professional to complain about her increasing workload, but she acknowledged to Alice Mullen and Elizabeth Dickson, family friends, that she found the work sometimes tedious and that she had little time for herself. Maria Carson noticed the circles under her daughter's eyes and worried about her health.[3]

At least one supervisor during these war years noted in an otherwise exceptional performance review that Carson's health was "not robust." The strains of work revealed themselves in a variety of relatively minor health problems—colds, flu, and a chronic ear infection that caused severe dizziness. Carson had lost weight in Chicago and looked more frail than she was. Her nocturnal writing deprived her of sleep and probably contributed to her susceptibility to infection.[4]

The meager sales of *Under the Sea-Wind* had disillusioned Rachel, who vowed not to try to support herself by writing any more books. She decided to concentrate instead on magazine features. For advice, she turned to Sunnie Bleeker, at Simon & Schuster, who supplied her with a list of higher-paying magazines and patiently advised her on the best outlets. Bleeker's friendship and advice proved so valuable that Rachel wished she could pay her properly as the literary agent she had in fact become.[5]

Carson was already adept at turning government research into popular natural history features for the newspapers, but to be successful in selling to magazines, she would have to write simple informational pieces rather than the more poetic prose that had made *Under the Sea-Wind* and "Undersea" so memorable.

Her first endeavor in the early summer of 1944 struck a middle ground. The War Writer's Board, chaired by Clifton Fadiman, asked Carson to contribute an article on the oceanarium in Marineland, Florida. It would be published in *Transatlantic*, a magazine, as Carson put it, for "intelligent Brits about America" that promoted intercultural learning. She began research soon after she returned to Washington, working in the Main Reading Room at the Library of Congress after work and on weekends for well over a month. In the process, Carson added to her knowledge about marine life and ocean conditions.

The Marineland oceanarium, where thousands of marine creatures lived in conditions approximating their natural habitat, duplicated the known undersea landscape as closely as possible. Although the oceanarium was a tourist attraction as well as a research facility, Carson's article focused on what scientists had learned about predation and how the various large fish and mammals were able to live together in a small, contained habitat. Arthur McBride, curator of the oceanarium, supplied Carson with photographs as well as detailed answers to her questions. Gasoline shortages early in the war had forced Marine Studios, the owner of Marineland, to drain the oceanarium in 1942. After major renovations to the tank, McBride hoped it would be reopened as soon as the war ended. Carson's article, "Ocean Wonderland," appeared in *Transatlantic* in March 1944. With Bleeker's help, Carson sold the reprint rights to *This Month*, where it appeared as "Indoor Ocean" in June 1946, shortly after the oceanarium reopened.[6]

Her next literary effort was further afield and less successful. Using material she had collected for an earlier feature on oysters published in the *Baltimore Sun*, Carson wrote about some of the more curious aspects of the bivalve's behavior and sent it off to *Reader's Digest*. After holding the article for some time, the *Digest* finally turned it down. The experience reinforced Carson's frustration with having to write articles according to someone else's notion of "lively reading." As she told Bleeker, "while it is relatively easy to write about the oddities in nature, which we stressed in the oyster piece, my real interest is not in the believe it or not type of thing, but in developing a deeper appreciation of nature."[7]

Through the spring and summer of 1944, Carson continued to work on several other informational pieces, one on the properties of milkweed, the other describing the navigational system of bats, emphasizing little-known facts on modern radar that had become essential knowledge in war. These articles were the first ones based on classifed research reports just then beginning to cross her desk. Both illustrated how adroitly Carson adapted military science to popular natural history.

Reports from a variety of scientific groups discussed the alarming shortage of kapok because of the Japanese occupation of the Pacific islands, where ceiba trees flourished. Botanists proposed the substitution of milkweed floss for kapok in life preservers and sleeping bags, items vital to amphibious military operations. In June Carson polished off a quick article about the shortage and the government's milkweed pod collection program and sent it to *This Week*, where it was published in September.[8]

Her bat article offered more lucrative possibilities. Titled "He Invented Radar—Sixty Million Years Ago!," Carson explained how bats could successfully navigate in the dark, avoiding collisions with trees, cliffs, and buildings and even finding food on the wing using a sonic detection system similar to radar. Her 1,500-word article was based on the published research of two Harvard University scientists who employed some of the new sonic detection instruments developed for war to analyze the bat's ability for night flight. Carson added information on the bat's natural history and evolution and showed the similarities between the bat's sonic detection system and modern radar.[9]

She sent her article to *Collier's*, where it drew criticism from several editors who believed they had read a similar account in *Scientific American* and *Science Monthly*. When her research was challenged, Carson defended herself against *Collier's* thinly veiled charges of plagiarism, explaining the sources she had used. "I think it is worth while to point out," she wrote, "that none [of these articles] mention the parallel with radar, which is, of course the chief significance of my account. This is not surprising since they were written in 1941, when radar was still a closely guarded secret." She told the *Collier's* editor she was unaware that their policies "precluded a presentation from a fresh angle, and in more popular style, of basic material which has been mentioned in semi-technical publications." Satisfied with her explanation, *Collier's* published the article in November as "The Bat Knew It First."[10]

Publication in *Collier's* was central to Carson's further success in magazine publishing. Next she offered reprint rights for this feature to *Reader's Digest*. After another interminable wait, they agreed to buy it, publishing the article in August 1945. To make up for delay and a certain editorial confusion, *Digest* associate editor Harold Lynch insisted that Carson accept a total of five hundred dollars for the piece.[11]

The Navy Recruiting Office was also enthusiastic about Carson's article, calling it "one of the clearest expositions of radar yet made available for the public." The navy distributed it to all its recruiting stations and made it required reading for anyone interested in radar technology. A little later, the Office of War Information bought rights to distribute it to its news and radio stations in Europe.[12]

All of Carson's nature writing in 1944 was based on war research that came to her for editing. Besides reflecting her determination to write about scientific topics for the public, these articles were important predictors of her larger literary interests as well. All testified to her desire to make nature's wonderful processes understandable to the general reader.

At the FWS office, Carson spent most of her time editing reports on the migration patterns of the chimney swift. In November she and Charles Alldredge, another young information officer in the service, drafted a press release announcing "the solution of one of the few remaining mysteries of bird distribution—the location of the chimney swifts' winter home."[13]

Carson used the same material in "The Ace of Nature's Aviators" and offered it to *Reader's Digest*. Her article involved an extended discussion of what she termed the "remote and mysterious swift" and of the bird banding by amateur ornithologists, whose efforts had finally been rewarded when the swifts' winter home was discovered in Peru. Carson hoped the article would fit into the natural history articles the *Digest* ran nearly every month, few of which featured birds.[14]

Although they liked the piece a great deal, the *Digest* editors rejected the article because they were "more than well supplied with nature material" just then. So Carson sent it off to *Coronet*, whose editors responded with an immediate but disappointing offer of fifty-five dollars for a condensed version. After a five-day stint in the hospital for an appendectomy in February 1945, Rachel decided to let *Coronet* have it. Bleeker applauded her decision but took the occasion to offer a suggestion about her style: "One more thing Rachel, you may disagree entirely and it is merely my personal taste: you scientists are so impersonal about things and so unemotional. I would like to see more emotion in the piece and that personal touch because you do write a beautiful prose, Rachel."[15]

The condensed article, "Sky Dwellers," did not appear in *Coronet* until November. But by then Carson, working with the same material, had fashioned a larger feature on bird banding and the amateurs who had been responsible for discovering the swifts' migration patterns. A fragment of this included an introduction written more in the style Bleeker admired.

> I can see the meadow as clearly as though it had been yesterday, lying pale green under the grey sky. I can recall the smell of the freshly cut grass, a smell made sweeter and fresher by the rain that had fallen that morning and by the soft droplets no heavier than a mist.
>
> The rain fell so lightly that it did not deter the insects that rose in little swarming clouds from the fallen hay, as though shocked and infinitely confused by the cataclysm that had visited their world of green, swaying stems when the mowers passed, only that morning. It was because of the insects that the swifts were there.[16]

Carson could find no market for this kind of writing, however, and it was never published. For the time being the tension between the scientist/naturalist and the naturalist/poet remained unresolved.

Carson's financial responsibilities left her little choice but to continue to write natural history features in her spare time. Added to this frustration was a certain restlessness in her wartime information job. Not surprisingly, she began to think seriously about leaving government and finding a job where she could have more time for her own writing.

Rachel naturally turned to her first mentors for advice. Hendrik van Loon had passed away in March 1944, but Quincy Howe was still an editor at Simon & Schuster. Carson had noted a recent interest in the field of science by the *Reader's Digest* and thought a position might be available on the editorial staff there. She sent Quincy Howe a note asking if he knew any "ways and means of getting on the *Reader's Digest* staff?" Howe responded that Lincoln Schuster, the publisher, was on friendly terms with *Digest* owner DeWitt Wallace and would be happy to send a note to him on Carson's behalf if she would send him a letter outlining her experience.

Carson responded, "probably the most important single point to bring to the attention of the *Digest*, is the fact that I am that comparatively rare phenomenon, a scientist who is also a writer." After reviewing her education and government employment, she admitted "while no one is an expert in all branches of science, and I certainly make no claim to such extreme precocity, I think I can say with due modesty that my training at Hopkins, plus my subsequent experience with science and scientists, has given me a back ground and a perspective to judge the accuracy of manuscripts. . . ."[17]

In her letter to Howe, she further refines her relationship to popular science. "Because my free lance writing has been aimed at the general public, and most of the printed products of my Government position have been directed at the same audience, my relation to technical scientific writing has been that of one who understands the language, but does not use it."[18]

Carson told Howe she was in an ideal position to help the *Digest* take the lead in postwar popular science writing: "I feel very strongly that the reporting of the progress of science is going to assume even greater importance in the months and years to come. We are all aware that startling developments have come, or are on the way, that cannot be talked about at the present time. When the necessary restrictions are lifted some very important stories will be told the American public, and undoubtedly the *Digest* will take the lead in presenting them."[19]

Wallace was impressed with Carson's experience and credentials, but, as he told Lincoln Schuster, he had no editorial staff openings, though he promised to keep her in mind. As a consolation, he suggested that she submit an article.[20]

Ten months later, still in the mood to make a change, Carson tried to leave government service again. Her assignments for the wartime fisheries program were coming to an end, and she admitted that her writing and her creativity were circumscribed and she was "disinclined" to continue too much longer in a government agency. This time she wrote to oceanographer William Beebe, her early supporter at the New York Zoological Society, but her objective was still to write science for the general public. Telling Beebe she had read recent announcements that the society was expanding its activities in the field of public education in natural history and conservation, Carson hoped there might be an opening.[21]

Beebe told her that she "should have no trouble fulfilling every requirement if there is any opening anywhere" and forwarded her letter on to Fairfield Osborn, then the president of the society. Osborn thought there might be a lower-level position available, but Beebe told Carson in early November 1945 that what Osborn had in mind would not give her "the field and activity which is your measure."[22]

After consulting with Richard Pough, who had left the National Audubon Society staff and was now chairman of conservation and ecology at the American Museum of Natural History, Carson wrote to John H. Baker, president of the National Audubon Society, to inquire about a position as a staff writer on the magazine. This time Rachel emphasized her experience writing about natural history in general and about birds in particular. She sent Baker a copy of her article on bird banding and alluded to her interest in shorebirds in *Under the Sea-Wind*. Pough arranged an interview for Carson with Baker to discuss coming on as an editor, but Baker was unwilling to make her an offer.[23]

Rachel Carson was trying to leave government at the worst possible moment. Conservation and zoological organizations such as New York Zoological and National Audubon had been in the doldrums for years. First, their memberships plummeted during the Depression, and then their field staffs were decimated by the manpower drain of World War II. When the war ended with Japan's surrender in September 1945, hundreds of soldiers returned from both the European and Pacific theaters every month looking for civilian jobs. Carson's credentials suited her precisely for the kinds of writing jobs to which she applied but served her badly in the marketplace. None of those organizations had professional women on their staffs, and the *Digest* was nearly an impregnable all-male bastion.[24]

Carson was something of an anomaly for she was neither editor nor field scientist. Her expertise presented enormous difficulties for finding professional work outside a government conservation unit. To make matters worse, natural science and biology were low priorities in the halcyon days of 1945 after the successful use of the atomic bomb. High technology was the path to the future; biologists and other conservationists would do well to maintain themselves and their organizations in the immediate postwar. What few available jobs there might be would go to returning veterans.[25]

Carson made no further effort to leave the service after the negative response she received from National Audubon in November 1945. But her applications betrayed a subtle shift in self-definition. In her search for private employment she emphasized her abilities as a writer over her training and experience as a marine biologist. One explanation for her approach is, of course, a consideration of gender. Since her successful rise through FWS bureaucracy was based primarily on her writing skills, she may have thought her chances best as a writer. Or, observing the numbers of oceanographers and marine scientists returning to university and private positions once government funding of research began to decline with the end of the war, she may have correctly assumed that there would be even fewer jobs for female marine scientists.

More than likely it was a combination of these practical considerations and her personal preferences. By the end of the war, Rachel Carson's earlier conflict between her love of writing and her love of science had been resolved in favor of science writing. Nearly a decade of writing about scientific topics for the public had confirmed not only what she wanted to write about but also how her inner vision should be best directed. By 1945 Carson realized that the only way she could ever afford to leave government employment was to publish her way out.

That realization also forced her to examine the benefits of her current government position and directly influenced her choice of future subjects. For the past several years, Carson had been aware that military goals had drastically reshaped the science and technology of both oceanography and wildlife biology. The reports and research abstracts that she reviewed and edited every day only hinted at the extent to which naval technology, developed primarily for submarine warfare and amphibious landing, had contributed to what was now known about the physical properties of the ocean, its geology and geography, and consequently the behavior of marine life. The war produced tremendous changes in the science of oceanography as once-classified material slowly made its way into government reports.[26]

As an information specialist, Carson was in daily contact with wildlife biologists in those Fish and Wildlife divisions concerned with predator and pest control. They, along with the biologists at Patuxent Research Refuge in nearby Laurel, Maryland, were alarmed by some of the early test results of the new synthetic pesticide dichlorodiphenyltrichloroethane, known as DDT. Carson was particularly well informed on the progress of this research because her government mentor, friend, and former supervisor Elmer Higgins was collaborating with noted wildlife biologist Clarence Cottam on a series of research reports on the impact of DDT on fish and other wildlife. These reports came to Carson's desk for editing, and their conclusions were the subject of debate and discussion around the office.[27]

"And now here is a query for your consideration," Rachel wrote Harold Lynch at *Reader's Digest* on July 15, 1945.

> Practically at my backdoor here in Maryland, an experiment of more than ordinary interest and importance is going on. We have

> all heard a lot about what DDT will soon do for us by wiping out insect pests. The experiments at Patuxent have been planned to show what other effects DDT may have when it is applied to wide areas: what it will do to insects that are beneficial or even essential; how it may affect waterfowl, or birds that depend on insect food; whether it may upset the whole delicate balance of nature if unwisely used.[28]

She was, she explained, in a position to cover the progress of the Patuxtent DDT tests "first hand" and write a "timely story" about them if "the idea interests you." Enclosing a FWS press release on the Patuxent DDT tests that she had helped edit, Carson told the *Digest* editor, "it's something that really does affect everybody."

The *Digest*, however, found pesticides an unpalatable subject, and Rachel turned her attention to other research subjects. In retrospect, the *Digest*'s decision was fortunate, for when Carson returned to the subject of DDT, she did so as a private citizen without the restrictions imposed by federal employment with a conservation agency or previously published opinion on the subject.[29]

Carson's proposal for an article on the DDT tests reflected her currency in the earliest military research on the new pesticide. DDT had been used by the military against lice and insect-borne diseases during the war; its effectiveness as an insect repellent was well established by war's end, but chemical screening for its safety to humans had barely begun. Yet domestic chemical companies such as E. I. DuPont had such stockpiles of DDT that on August 31, 1945, without definitive tests concerning the chemical's chronic toxicity, the Department of Agriculture, with the U.S. Army's concurrence, agreed to release it for civilian use.[30]

Long before DDT was released to the domestic market, the popular press had been full of praise for the new "miracle" chemical and its success in the "war on insects." However, some scientists expressed alarm, believing that not enough was known about DDT's long-term effects to merit its immediate application in domestic agriculture.[31]

Edwin Way Teale, one of Carson's favorite nature writers, had written an article in *Nature Magazine* in March on the pesticide's possible ill effects on wildlife. Just four months before its release to the civilian market, *Time* magazine called DDT a "two-edged sword." Its science column on August 27, 1945, featured side-by-side articles on DDT, the "insect bomb," next to sequential declassified photographs of the first atom bomb explosion at Alamagordo, New Mexico, on July 16. But the link between DDT and the atomic bomb had already been made in the popular culture. Both promised an immediate and total end to enemy threat. *Popular Mechanics* in April 1944 had urged that our next world war be against insects with DDT as the exterminating technology, a position that the *Science News Letter* heartily endorsed in January 1945, extolling the benefits of a "total insect war." Such recommendations ran counter to what Carson read at Fish and Wildlife as research reports from Patuxent and elsewhere documented serious problems with the persistence of the new pesticide.[32]

By contrast, there was little controversy, and a great deal of excitement, about the new discoveries in oceanography stimulated by government-sponsored research during the war. In this area again, Carson's government position provided her access to material and association with experts in the field, and involved her peripherally in some of the earliest discussions about the discoveries concerning underwater sound and temperature patterns.

As a beginning investigator at Woods Hole in 1929, Carson had begun collecting information about the ocean. When years later she was asked what had led her to write about the ocean, she said that the genesis of *The Sea Around Us* belonged to that first summer "when I began storing away facts about the sea—facts discovered in scientific literature or by personal observation and experience."[33] But her later visits to the Fisheries Research Station at Woods Hole as a government fisheries scientist in the summer of 1939 and 1940, while working on *Under the Sea-Wind*, were probably even more critical to her decision, made sometime in late 1945 or early 1946, to focus her research on some kind of an extended essay on the ocean. Oceanographers at Woods Hole, such as Columbus O'Donnell Iselin and Maurice Ewing, with large U.S. Navy research contracts, attacked numerous problems that had military importance for submarine warfare and amphibious landing in particular. The scientific community of Woods Hole was tiny, and Carson would certainly have known about the experiments and been enormously interested in the discussions of ocean temperatures, currents, wave measurements, soils and sediments, and the new instruments being developed to try to measure them.[34]

Carson heard about the work of marine biologist Mary Sears, who was at Woods Hole during the summer of 1939. Later, as a naval reserve officer, Sears directed a new oceanographic office within the Navy Hydrographic Unit at the U.S. Hydrographic Office in Suitland, Maryland. Carson spent many hours poring over the "Sailing Directions" published by the Hydrographic Office, which described the coastlines and coastal waters of the world and the behavior and activity of waters outside U.S. shores. These and the "Coast Pilots" of the U.S. Coast and Geodetic Survey, which described the U.S. coastline and contained fascinating accounts of storms, icebergs, sea ice, and other weather conditions, were invaluable sources of information for her.[35]

These contacts from Woods Hole, plus her friendship with William Beebe, who had developed the bathysphere and was an expert on Arctic and deep-water oceanography, were all benefits of being a Fish and Wildlife biologist and editor. Due to her position, she had access to material that by 1948 would become the basis not of a magazine profile but of her next book.

In some ways the early postwar years were the most carefree years Rachel Carson would ever enjoy. Both her nieces, Virginia and Marjorie, were out of school and had at least part-time jobs, although they had moved back in with Rachel. Mamma was well enough to continue to cook and keep house. Rachel had a car for work and for weekend outings or for an evening with her Fish and Wildlife colleagues and their friends. She enjoyed the local Audubon Society excursions, joining them whenever she could. Although she had to be very careful of her expenses, she was free and unencumbered. Her time outside the office was her own; there just was not enough of it.

Before Rachel went to Chicago, her social circle was limited to somewhat older family friends. Alice Mullen, a married friend who later moved to New England with her husband, and Elizabeth Dickson, a nurse at Doctor's Hospital, were often invited to dinner or tea. Rachel still enjoyed the company of Dorothy Hamilton Algire, who lived with her husband in nearby Bethesda, Maryland. Rachel was godmother to Dorothy's first child, daughter Anne, born in 1942. Although Dorothy was busy with a young family and not free to join Rachel very often, she went out with her on bird forays and always invited Rachel and her mother to family celebrations and holiday events. Shortly after she returned from Chicago in May 1943, Rachel met Dr. Catherine "Kitty" Birch, and they too became good friends.

Kitty, a native of Washington who lived in the affluent section of Georgetown, was a successful ear, nose, and throat surgeon, one of the first women to be elected to the College of Surgeons in her field. Rachel probably met her when she began having terrible spells of dizziness caused by an inner ear disorder. Birch hospitalized Carson at least once at Doctor's Hospital, a private downtown Washington medical facility, and advised her on general health matters.

Kitty Birch was a beautiful, stylish woman who led an active social life but also loved the outdoors. She had a small sailboat, which she sailed on the Potomac River with friends. She introduced Rachel to sailing, and frequently accompanied Rachel on hikes around Rock Creek Park. They sometimes spent weekends together at Ocean City, where they both enjoyed the beach.[36]

By the summer of 1945 Rachel's social life was enlarged by the addition of three colleagues at Fish and Wildlife whose company she enjoyed in and out of the office. Lionel A. "Bert" Walford, Carson's immediate supervisor in the Information Division and the editor of all service publications, was in every way an exceptional wildlife biologist. Walford, whose book *Marine Game Fishes of the Pacific Coast* Rachel had favorably reviewed for the *Atlantic Monthly* in 1938, joined Fish and Wildlife as an aquatic biologist in California and was brought to Washington in 1944 as assistant chief of the service's information division.

Carson and Walford shared an office at Interior where Walford was primarily responsible for writing the so-called Bailey-Bland Report on fishery resources for Congress. An ichthyologist who got seasick on all his research trips, Walford was literate, witty, whimsical, and endowed with a cutting sense of humor. Walford, his wife, Lucille, and their three children lived in Old Town, Alexandria, Virginia, where they enjoyed an active social life. The Walfords frequently included Rachel and her mother in their activities.[37]

In the fall of 1944 Walford impetuously hired Katherine Howe, a talented and vivacious young artist, to help him illustrate *Fishery Resources of the United States*. Kay Howe was a breath of fresh air from upstate New York with a master's degree in art from the University of Iowa. An extrovert, she loved the outdoors and was daring, outspoken, full of fun, and usually juggling more than one suitor at the same time.

Kay had been bored teaching art at Wilson College in the small Pennsylvania town of Chambersburg and in 1943 found a job with the Glenn L. Martin Corporation in Middle River, Maryland, where she was an illustrator for military engineering manuals. Kay liked the job and invited her Iowa classmate Shirley Ann Briggs to join her in 1944. At the time Briggs was teaching art at North Dakota State. Briggs went to Martin and, at first, moved into the flat with Kay and her mother. Kay left Martin after a year and moved in with a friend in northern Virginia; thus she was in the unusual wartime position of having a place to live near Washington but no job. Thumbing through the telephone book one day looking for interesting places to work, she came upon the Fish and Wildlife Service. She inquired whether they needed an illustrator and Bert Walford hired her on the spot.[38]

A year later, in the fall of 1945, Howe persuaded Shirley Briggs to follow her to the Department of Interior, where Briggs was hired as an information specialist and illustrator in the Bureau of Commercial Fisheries. Shirley Ann Briggs was as different from Katherine Howe as anyone could be, but they shared interests in art, literature, travel, books, and human idiosyncrasies. Shirley was slender and sharp-featured with a dancer's body and agility. She had been a brilliant student at Iowa, and was curious, quick-witted, and a fine amateur ornithologist. Like Howe, Briggs was ready for almost any adventure, especially if it involved birds, botany, art, or natural history. In the fall of 1945, the two artist/illustrators were working on different projects but found themselves assigned to a Fish and Wildlife office next door to the one Rachel Carson shared with Bert Walford. Kay and Rachel had already met and liked each other. Shirley completed the triumvirate.[39]

Both Howe and Briggs were in their late twenties, over a decade younger than Carson, and somewhat older than Carson's nieces. While friendship, mutual admiration, and genuine affection developed between them, Rachel viewed Kay and Shirley as she might have two younger, irrepressible sisters. They were enjoyable colleagues and devoted friends. Kay proved an especially compatible travel companion and Shirley an excellent birding companion. After Carson left government, she and Briggs remained good friends by virtue of shared activities, interests, and proximity. Howe, who moved out West, was less frequently in touch with Carson.

Shirley's diary reveals an enthusiastic first impression of Rachel Carson:

> Aug. 4: Rachel Carson, who is the Aquatic Biologist, is a very good friend of Kay's and a very nice person. Might go on the trip to Fulton Market with Kay and me.
>
> Aug. 11: Rachel Carson is especially nice. We had lunch the other day, and found we are both hiking enthusiasts—and she is

> very interested in birds too. So we planned some expeditions for this fall.[40]

Along with Walford and other service biologists whom he invited to drop by for tea, Carson, Howe, and Briggs made light of the sometimes oppressive bureaucratic silliness that inflicted their work. Most days they gathered in Bert and Rachel's office at noon with their brown-bag lunches, brewing tea and Nescafé illegally on a hot plate in Rachel's closet. Shirley's diary records a typical get-together: "Our clandestine nescafe sessions break the monotony. Lock the door and huddle around furtively. Kay opened the door a crack to take something from the messenger and Walford thinks we should have a floozy wrapper to slip on at such times."[41]

During lunch Bert would read aloud from E. B. White's columns in *The New Yorker*, which they all admired. Other times the reading would come from a lesser literary publication or from some particularly hopeless report someone had to edit. There would be high hilarity as the group picked apart some atrocious syntax. Shirley recalls that "intransigent official ways, small stupidities, and inept pronouncements were changed from annoyances into sources of merriment. Nothing could pass the wry scrutiny of that gathering and still seem unsurmountable or too frustrating. . . ."[42]

Rachel, Kay, and Shirley often took morning and afternoon coffee breaks together down in the departmental cafeteria, where they planned their next naturalist outing or the weekend's social gathering. With the war and some of the more restrictive rationing over, government workers and their friends, many uprooted to wartime Washington, gathered at one another's homes to talk about their interests in music, art, literature, and, naturally, politics. The Walfords frequently dropped in and Rachel went as often as she could and always enjoyed the merriment and the conversation. Shirley remembers they attended "an astonishing number of parties."[43]

Outside the family, Rachel preferred to be called by the nickname Ray. It was a name she used exclusively with her government friends and with most other contemporaries for a number of years. Some weekends she invited Shirley and Kay to her house to play pinochle at which she was an acknowledged expert. Rachel and her household had moved back to Silver Spring again in 1945, this time renting a larger house on Sutherland Road. Shirley invited other groups of friends to her apartment on Tunlaw Road just north of Georgetown in Washington, where they played another favorite game, "Oh, Hell." Kay and her roommate, Mary Frances Howell, were often at these gatherings and sometimes entertained at their apartment. Sometimes Kitty Birch joined the group, and the others brought their roommates, friends, and visitors. To celebrate the end of a particularly onerous assignment or for special occasions, Walford and his colleagues would have lunch or dinner at the Watergate Restaurant at the far end of Virginia Avenue overlooking the Potomac, where they would plan future projects and dream of far-flung expeditions.[44]

In the office, however, Carson was a perfectionist and demanded the best from her associates. She was efficient and thoroughly organized. One colleague remembers he could always identify her by the purposeful, quick tap of her high heels down the corridor when she came and went. Carson was calm, polite, and deliberate in her official dealings with other scientists and writers no matter how incompetent she found their work privately. Mr. Ady, however, proved the exception.[45]

John Ady was the Government Printing Office liaison to the Department of Interior and as such had to approve the budget and specifications of all departmental publications. Ultimately he determined the quality of paper stock used for a publication, the number of illustrations, the process of their reproduction, and the typeface. As assistant editor of FWS publications, Carson had to meet with Ady and agree on the final form and budget of every report or pamphlet. He always wanted to do it the cheapest way possible. Carson, on the other hand, was trying to upgrade service publications both in terms of writing quality and appearance; consequently every meeting was a skirmish.

Kay and Shirley both remember Rachel bracing herself for her encounters with Ady. Stoically leaving the office with her forms in hand, she would announce she was ready to "go down and do battle with Ady." Sometimes she won, sometimes she and Ady compromised, and sometimes Ady won out simply by making so many mistakes in his directions to the Government Printing Office that the cost of corrections obliterated all Carson's effort to improve the quality or the appearance of the publication.[46]

In spite of such frustrations, Carson was considered a good manager by her staff. She knew how to make the system work. According to Kay Howe, Rachel could be "an immovable rock" when necessary, doggedly going after what she wanted knowing "when to push and when to wait."

But her delight in being a scientist was thwarted by duties that were increasingly administrative. Whenever she could, Carson joined forces with her friends for naturalist outings, which, of course, had the additional advantage of providing new ideas for magazine features.[47]

During the fall of 1945, Rachel and Shirley Briggs took a number of trips together. The first was probably to Ocean City, Maryland, organized when Rachel learned that Shirley, from landlocked Iowa, had never been to the seashore. The two drove over to Maryland's eastern shore late one Friday after work. Staying in a local rooming house, they got up very early the next morning to spend the day enjoying the shore and looking for birds.

On other occasions Shirley would sketch or take photographs. They might see marsh hawks, ospreys, horned larks, sandpipers, plovers, gulls, and several kinds of terns, depending on the time of year and the shore area. Whenever possible they cooked breakfast on the beach in the morning and watched the surf and the birds. When Shirley joined the D.C. Audubon Society, they signed up for the annual Christmas bird census in Rock Creek Park. But by far the most interesting expedition they took that fall was an Audubon outing to the Hawk Mountain Sanctuary in eastern Pennsylvania.[48]

Rachel drove her car, which allowed Shirley to crowd herself in along with Rachel's friend Alice Mullen. The Audubon Society organizers wished two other ladies into their party, one of whom, according to Shirley, "proved to be one of the most consistently obnoxious old granite-faced dames" the younger women had "ever had the misfortune to have to spend two days in the company of." But despite disagreeable and encumbering fellow travelers, Rachel, Shirley, and Alice enjoyed themselves. Scrambling up the mountain to a rocky promontory, they watched the hundreds of migrating hawks and eagles riding the air currents down through the narrow defile. Rachel thought they looked "like brown leaves drifting on the wind." By sitting on an outcropping near the summit, they could see a great number of all varieties of hawks at close range. But it was very windy and cold out there, sitting hour after hour wrapped in blankets and parkas.[49]

Shirley had her camera with her and kept active taking pictures. Rachel rationed her Thermos of coffee and sat, binoculars in one hand, taking notes with the other in a brown spiral notebook on the mountains, the mists drifting over the valley, and the "milling and tossing" of the hawks. Their second day was anticlimactic as far as the hawks were concerned, and when it began to rain, the group left early.[50]

They stopped at Rachel's house on the way back, where Shirley met Mrs. Carson and Rachel's nieces for the first time. Rachel immediately began planning their next outing to the bird refuges at Roanoke Island on Albemarle Sound in North Carolina. Shirley noted that there followed "much reading of maps and guide books and dickering with Walford for sleeping bags." The trip never materialized, however, because Rachel caught a bad cold and Kitty Birch insisted she stay home.[51]

But Carson and Briggs returned to Hawk Mountain the following October, this time in the agreeable company of Dorothy Algire, who was happy to take a break from her two young children and go on a bird outing. Rachel was working on an article about the fall migration of the hawks, and Shirley was assigned to take photographs for it. This time the weather was much more cooperative and the hawks numerous.[52]

Carson's obvious delight in these outings with her friends was reflected in her writing. The draft of her article on Hawk Mountain reveals not only her deep understanding of the ancient Appalachian Mountains she had explored in her youth but how consistently she related this, and most other naturalist experiences, to the sea.[53]

Sometimes her freelance writing not only allowed her to travel to new places but also introduced her to people who were experts in their fields, whose advice and unexpected friendship she valued. One such encounter began in the spring of 1945 when Carson tried to interest the *Saturday Evening Post* editor Robert Murphy in an article on terns, based on Fish and Wildlife research in long-range bird migration. At Sunnie Bleeker's urging, Carson decided to emphasize human activities focusing on the bird banding efforts of Dr. Oliver Austin whose sanctuary, Tern Island, off Cape Cod, Massachusetts, she had visited one summer when she was at Woods Hole. The *Saturday Evening Post* rejected her article, "Dr. Austin and the Cities of the Terns," finding it "not very spritely," a verdict shared by *The National Geographic Magazine* a few months later.[54]

Undaunted, Carson recast it as "Bird Banding Is Their Hobby," this time focusing on the activities of Austin and three other famous bird banders, one of whom was Mrs. Ada Govan of the Woodland Bird Sanctuary in Lexington, Massachusetts. In the course of corresponding about the article, Carson and Govan became friends. At the end of December Carson sent her article to *Holiday*, a new magazine owned by the Curtis

Publishing Company, which offered her five hundred dollars for it at the end of March 1946.[55]

Mrs. Govan was an amateur ornithologist, a dedicated bird bander, and the author of a successful autobiographical account of her work with birds, *Wings at My Window*. Carson's friendship with Govan, carried on almost exclusively by letter, was the most intense emotional connection she had made with another woman since Mary Scott Skinker. Their correspondence reveals Carson's longing for a relationship with someone who shared not only her love of nature but the struggle to make her way as a writer.

When Carson first wrote to her, Mrs. Govan was nearly sixty. Her sanctuary was besieged by ornithologists of all description and rank. Ordinarily she did not respond to such queries as Carson's, but she made an exception because she was impressed by Carson's desire to write an article to "interest more people in birds and their protection." In turn, Govan's personal courage and her love and dedication to birds moved Rachel deeply and made them instant soulmates despite a great difference in age, education, and experience.[56]

Ada Govan was a housewife with a young family when in 1930 she lost three infant children in succession and her ten-year-old son barely survived a prolonged illness. To regain her physical and mental health, she and her husband built a house in the Massachusetts woods. Shortly thereafter Govan suffered a terrible fall that reduced her to a housebound invalid. In great physical pain and deeply depressed, she looked out of her window during one terrible December blizzard to find a small chickadee clinging to her windowsill. She fed it, and the other birds that came, and soon found in their visits a reason to live.

Govan began writing articles about bird feeding and bird protection for "shut-ins," the housebound, and "young mothers who wanted to train their children to grow up loving birds" for *Nature Magazine* under a pseudonym. When her property and her birds were threatened by real estate development, she used the money that poured in from grateful readers to establish the Woodland Bird Sanctuary, where she and her family continued not only to feed an amazing number of bird species but began their bird banding work. Eventually Govan banded hundreds of birds and kept careful records of their returns, astonishing ornithological experts with her numbers. *Wings at My Window* was the story of Govan's backyard sanctuary and all that led to its establishment. In one chapter, "Children into Bird Lovers," Govan suggested ways to teach a child to learn to love and protect wild creatures. That chapter particularly impressed Carson, who absorbed many of Govan's ideas when she wrote on a similar subject a decade later.[57]

With her second letter to Govan, Carson enclosed a copy of *Under the Sea-Wind.* Govan's enthusiasm for Rachel's writing and her book allowed the friendship to turn from their mutual love of birds to the difficulties of trying to live by writing. Rachel told her, "Your feelings for birds and all wild things would make you especially sympathetic with what I tried to accomplish . . . even though it was not a profitable venture in the narrow sense, it was an extremely satisfying experience to be allowed to write what I wanted to write and to express what I really felt."[58]

Govan also noticed how much Carson's book reminded her of Henry Williamson's *Salar the Salmon*, which made Mrs. Govan all the more endearing. Rachel wrote her happily, "So you too, love Henry Williamson. He has influenced my writing more than anyone else, and to have you link my book with his is the greatest tribute you could possibly pay it."[59]

Rachel looked forward to meeting Ada Govan in the late spring of 1946 when she thought she would be at the Parker River Wildlife Refuge in Essex County, Massachusetts, about thirty miles north of Boston, as part of her field research for a new series of pamphlets she planned on the federal refuge system. But instead she was sent to the refuge in Chincoteague, Virginia, and so did not meet Govan until early June when she and her mother stopped in Lexington, en route to Maine for a month's vacation. Mrs. Govan, Mrs. Carson, and Rachel apparently enjoyed one another, but the visit was brief. When Carson finally visited Parker River later that fall, she spent at least one day with Govan at her sanctuary, but the details of that private visit are lost.

From Mrs. Govan's perspective, Rachel's life appeared "adventurous." Carson's work took her far afield allowing her to see whistling swans and Canada geese, which Ada Govan had not the "vaguest idea of." But Rachel thought Govan "underestimated the interest and importance of what goes on in your backyard."[60]

In one exchange of letters in February 1947, Govan revealed that she wanted to write a sequel to *Wings at My Window* even though she found it difficult to write even so much as a monthly article for the Massachusetts Audubon Society newsletter. "Writing anything now is hard work," Govan confessed. "It used to spatter down the page . . . I feel dead as a doornail at present, and I *know* what writing a book means, now. Before I could only guess. Your life seems to be well ordered, Rachel. You know where you are going."[61]

Govan's confession provoked a defensive outburst from Carson on the hard realities of writing books instead of magazine articles. "I'm going to sound very materialistic," she told the older woman, "but after all if one is to live even in part by writing he may as well look at the facts." Drawing from her own experience, Rachel advised Govan to stick to the magazine market, suggesting several ideas for articles drawn from material the older woman had at hand.[62]

In a rare glimpse of personal turmoil, Rachel confided to Ada Govan, "No, my life isn't at all well ordered and I don't know where I'm going! I know that if I could choose what seems to me the ideal existence, it would be just to live by writing. But I have done far too little to dare risk it. And all the while my job with the Service grows and demands more and more of me, leaving less time that I could put on my own writing. And as my salary increases little by little, it becomes even more impossible to give it up! That is my problem right now, and not knowing what to do about it, I do nothing."[63]

Carson admitted that her dilemma was made more complicated by the opportunities and assignments that were finally coming to her in the service. For the first time, the FWS was giving her the travel she had always wanted but could not afford on her own. Opportunities for fieldwork came with it, as well as the chance to publish a series of her own design. But all of these new assignments could be dashed at any moment by budget constraints and shifts in management. Bert Walford had applied for Elmer Higgins's job as head of Fishery Biology. Carson feared that if Walford was successful, she would be given his editorial responsibilities with even more administrative chores to tie her to her desk. Yet she was not unmindful that this same government position, while constraining, also provided access to the scientific experts and the wartime research in oceanography and wildlife biology that were dramatically changing her worldview.

Apologizing at the end of a very long letter in which she had been unusually candid, Carson confided to Govan wistfully, "I wish you did not live so far away. I think we would have a lot to say to each other, about many things, if we had a chance." But they never did.[64]

6

"Return to the Sea"

Like many professionals in and out of government, Rachel Carson was caught in a job that she was good at, that compensated her well enough, and that gave her certain critical advantages. At the same time, it was a job that increasingly prevented her from doing what she innately understood was her obligation, the real work of her life, and what she loved most. As her official responsibilities in the service's information division expanded after 1946, she had less and less time for her own writing, yet she enjoyed her work now more than ever.

In response to a federal questionnaire several years later entitled "Women in Government," she summarized her primary responsibilities as an information specialist.

> My job consists of the general direction of the publishing program of the Fish and Wildlife's information service—working with authors in planning and writing their manuscripts, reviewing manuscripts submitted, and overseeing the actual editing and preparation of the manuscript for the printer. I have a staff of six assistants who handle the various details of this sort including planning or executing illustrations, selecting appropriate type faces, planning general page layouts and design. It is really just the work of a small publishing house.[1]

She neglected to include other administrative duties, such as supervising the Fish and Wildlife Library and its staff, as well as a variety of special writing assignments she might be called on to do, including speeches for FWS officials or for department personnel who appeared at various public functions, and preparing congressional testimony for both. On these writing assignments she often worked with her friend Charles Alldredge, who was now on Secretary Ickes's staff and who often wrote speeches and congressional testimony for senior members of the department.

In March 1946 Albert M. Day became director of Fish and Wildlife, replacing the retiring Ira Gabrielson. Day and Frank Dufresne, chief of information, approved Carson's plan for a series of twelve booklets for the general public featuring the national wildlife refuge system. Carson hoped to use the new series, known as *Conservation in Action*, not only as guides to individual refuges but also as a model for service publications in style, illustration, and layout. Kay Howe designed the series and illustrated the four booklets Carson wrote. *Conservation in Action* provided Carson with just the kind of public education forum she had long hoped to introduce into the FWS, and she found it a challenging publishing project as well.[2]

After selecting the refuges to feature, Carson had to gather accurate background material for several that had been added recently or had been neglected during the war. She approached each one from a perspective that can only be described as ecological, even though that word had little common currency in wildlife science in the late 1940s. In one booklet Carson explained that the conservation philosophy behind the refuge system aimed at the "preservation of wildlife and wildlife habitat," which ultimately involved "the preservation of the basic resources of the earth, which man, as well as animals, must have in order to live. Wildlife, water, forests, grasslands, all are parts of man's essential environment; the conservation and effective use of one is impossible except as the others also are conserved." To do her research, Carson planned four site visits beginning in the spring of 1946, eventually traveling across the country in the fall of 1947.[3]

In mid-April 1946, Rachel and Shirley Briggs set out with quantities of strange-looking gear for Chincoteague, Virginia, and the waterfowl refuge at the southern end of Assateague Island. The Chincoteague refuge was then one of the nation's newest, coming into the FWS system in 1945. Part of a chain of sanctuaries along the Atlantic flyway, it was situated at a strategic point where several of the most heavily traveled lanes of waterfowl traffic converged. Chincoteague provided beaches, dunes, marshes, woodland, and protected waters for a great number of migrating species. The refuge was sited specifically to conserve the greater snow goose and the smaller American brant, which depended on abundant salt meadows and eelgrass for their winter feeding. Black duck, Canada geese, snow geese, even sea ducks and whistling swans appeared at Chincoteague. Unfortunately in late April, when Carson and Briggs visited, most of the waterfowl had left for their northern breeding grounds, but the shorebirds Rachel loved were still there in abundance: plovers, yellowlegs, sandpipers, nesting terns, laughing gulls, and black skimmers.[4]

Their mission was not only to gather background material and do sketches for the booklet but to take photographs of the thriving shellfish industry in oysters and clams in the waters surrounding the refuge. To understand the work of the refuge, they went about with refuge manager John A. Buckalew in an overgrown Jeep known in the service as a command reconnaissance (CR) car. In order to observe oyster seeding and clam harvesting, they traveled by boat often in the open sea. It provided a smoother ride than the CR car, but it frequently dropped them off some distance short of their ultimate destination, requiring them to wade across tidal streams or through shallow water along the beaches.[5]

As the two tromped through the lobby of the overpriced Channel Bass Hotel at the end of each day trailing their muddy gear, Shirley Briggs noted the astonished looks on the faces of the other guests: "We presented quite a spectacle on our return to the hotel of an evening . . . when we came lumbering through, wearing old tennis shoes, usually wet, sloppy and be-smudged pants, various layers of jackets, souwesters, and toting all manner of cameras, my magnificent tripod, and Ray's binoculars."[6]

It always bothered Shirley that Rachel never seemed to get as wet, muddy, or disheveled as she did and that no matter what the excursion, Rachel emerged looking neat and ladylike. After dinner, Rachel copied her notes out on three-by-five index cards, while Shirley checked film and equipment for the next day. Rachel tried to teach Shirley how to play pinochle, but most nights her pupil begged off as too sleepy to learn. When they finally checked out of the hotel after four days, the other guests appeared relieved. They brought back conch shells for their colleagues and enough oysters and clams for Shirley to host a shellfish party for their friends that weekend. Although Rachel had the text ready for "Chincoteague," number one in the series, by early summer, it was not published until nearly a year later because of particularly bitter battles with Mr. Ady and the Government Printing Office.[7]

On those occasions when she did not bring service work home with her at night, Carson read and collected material on the ocean for what, by the summer of 1946, she still thought of as an extended naturalist profile of the sea. The topic had the advantage of giving her both opportunity and excuse to visit other fishery research facilities on the nearby Virginia, Maryland, and New Jersey shores. But for the summer of 1946 Rachel planned a more elaborate trip. Celebrating ten years in federal service, she saved up a year's leave for a month's vacation in Boothbay Harbor, Maine, where she could visit the Fisheries' hatchery that was involved in a long-term study of lobster culture. Spending time on the coast of Maine had been one of her great ambitions.[8]

So at the end of June 1946 Rachel and her mother packed up the two cats, Kito and Tippy, and, much to the envy of her government colleagues, drove six hundred miles to the Sheepscot River just west of the town of Boothbay Harbor, Maine. Unwittingly, Carson had found a place to which she gave her heart, one that was to have a lasting influence on both her life and her writing.[9]

Knowing practically nothing of the area, Rachel had taken a chance and rented a cottage through Ethelyn Giles, who had recently opened a real estate agency in town, but, as Rachel told Shirley, it turned out to be "the one we would have chosen above all others." The cottage belonged to the Scotts, an elderly couple whose property was on the other side of the shore road from the tiny cottage Rachel and her mother occupied. From the road the cottage was invisible, nestled against a rocky hillside, surrounded by spruces and birches and literally on the very edge of the water. "If you jumped out of the windows on one side," Rachel explained to Shirley Briggs, "you would fall in, and in front there are only a few feet of grass to the water's edge. We are so secluded here because of the trees and the contour of the land, that we are not aware of human neighbors."[10]

The cottage consisted of a sitting room with bunk beds on the back wall and a small kitchen and eating area. A tiny atticlike loft with two beds and large windows on each end was accessible by ladder. Rachel and the cats went up there to read and watch the birds. There was also a narrow screened-in porch across the entire front of the cabin, with a small dock just beyond. Best of all, the cottage looked west "across the water to a long spruce-covered island—Indiantown," which, Rachel explained, "has only one house on it and that unoccupied. To the south of that is Little Island, which is only a tiny rocky reef at high tide and never much more, but the gulls love it, and the cormorants. Farther off in the distance are other islands, all of them beautifully wooded." Snuggled into the coast in glorious solitude, Rachel was thrilled that the only sounds were those of lapping water or the cries of the "gulls, herons, and ospreys, sometimes the tolling of a bell buoy, and—when the wind [was] right, the very distant sound of surf."[11]

Carson was thrilled, too, with the wonderful birds she found outside her door. A phoebe nested under the eaves of the cottage, and a song sparrow "who evidently regards this place as his, but generously lets us use it," gave them plenty of songs. But there were also black-throated warblers, chestnut-sided warblers, a male parula warblar, redstarts, cedar waxwings, cliff swallows, and, best of all, hermit thrushes that sang their evening song from the island. When the tide was low, the great blue herons and night herons flew over from Indiantown Island just for good measure. Mamma loved to feed the herring gulls, and they both watched seals sunning themselves on the island's near shore. In the evening, herring ran up the coves. Rachel told Dorothy Algire, "if the water is very still, we can hear a great splashing of the fish."[12]

Some days Rachel put on her bathing suit and lay on her back on the small dock looking at the birds overhead for hours on end. "On warm sunny days the gulls go so high," she told Shirley, "they look about the size of stars. Sometimes a dark star comes into sight, and that is an osprey."[13]

Rachel Carson was not the first or the last writer to fall in love with the raw beauty of Maine's rocky coasts and deep green forests of pine and spruce, but few others have been so aware of the nuances of land and sea, or have written of their textures with such artistry. On this her first trip, as on every other, she absorbed her surroundings, using all her senses.

To reach a rocky ocean shore, Rachel had to go five miles across to the western shore of Southport Island or about ten miles to Ocean Point, a wild and rocky point at the end of the peninsula that bounded Boothbay Harbor on the west and the Damariscotta River on the east. Ocean Point soon became one of her favorite haunts.

Waiting for an extreme low tide, when she could systematically explore the tide pools there, she discovered beautiful creatures hiding under seaweed or clinging to the underside of the rocks visible only at these times. Some of the more movable ones she took up to her mother who waited on the shore, enjoying the ocean view and watching the lobstermen.[14]

During their month in Maine, mother and daughter took several excursions. But most days they stayed close to the cottage, exploring the neighboring Squirrel Island with its colony of summer people and the woods and hills along the shore of the Sheepscot. Mamma, the cats, and Rachel all gained weight, so much that for the first time in her life, she told Maria Leiper, she had "to consider ways and means of getting rid of it."[15]

Rachel also loved the deep forests across the road, behind the Scotts' place. Particularly delighted by the "smell, taste and feel" of the reindeer moss, she noticed how it "crunched like snow that has a heavy crust on it" when it grew on sunny slopes, but in the deep shade of the pines, it was "soft and spongy and your feet sink into it soundlessly." A field beyond was bordered on three sides by dark spruces made "starry with daisies. Swallows swoop over it and warblers whisper in the evergreens around it. The wild strawberries are ripe in the grass," and there were "patches of moss big enough to lie down on."[16]

In a letter to Shirley Briggs, Carson summed up her feelings about Maine, hinting at how deeply moved she was by her time there: "From all this you will know that the only reason I will ever come back is that I don't have brains enough to figure out a way to stay here the rest of my life. At least I know now that my greatest ambition is to be able to buy a place here and then manage to spend a great deal of time in it—summers at least!"[17]

Rachel's notebooks were full of descriptions of what she had seen, heard, smelled, and felt, including four pages describing Kito and Tippy's feline reactions to Maine. On one page Carson noted three things she would remember vividly about her first visit there: "star shine on the water, northern lights, and dark water shot through with needles of light as fish disturb its surface and catch reflections of the sky." Rachel Carson had fallen hopelessly in love; Maine had won her completely.

Before her return to Silver Spring, Rachel wove her observations into an elegy to this first Maine summer, calling it simply "An Island I Remember." Although she probably thought of publishing parts of it someday, she allowed it to remain unfinished, its images to appear in other, later writing. But even when Carson was as absorbed in nature as she was in Maine, her financial insecurity was never far from her consciousness. In fact, now that she had found her heart's desire, she had an even greater incentive to become financially independent. Before she left Maine, Carson entered a competition sponsored by *Outdoor Life* magazine. Awards were offered for the best "Conservation Pledge" for young people. Entries were to be accompanied by a brief essay on the reasons for conserving natural resources.

Carson's four-page essay recounts the history of resource plunder of minerals, topsoil, and timber. The essay proves her a worthy follower of the progressive conservation tradition of which her boss, Harold Ickes, was but the most recent heir and champion. But as a child of the Pennsylvania hills, with the principles of ecology in her bones from childhood and firsthand knowledge of how human activities could foul nature, Carson's essay focused on habitat pollution rather than on wise resource use. Citing overfishing, unregulated hunting of waterfowl, and excessive damming of rivers where fish spawn, she acknowledged the negative impact of the culture of American abundance. "Because it is more comfortable to believe in pleasant things, most of us continue today to believe that in our country there will always be plenty. . . . This is the comfortable dream of the average American. But it is a fallacious dream. It is a dangerous dream. . . . Only so long as we are vigilant to cherish and safeguard [our resources] against waste, against over exploitation, and against destruction will our country continue strong and free."

Within this context she offered her "conservation pledge."

> *I pledge myself to preserve and protect*
> *America's fertile soils, her mighty forests*
> *and rivers, her wildlife and minerals,*
> *for on these her greatness was established*
> *and her strength depends.*[18]

In early October Carson received a reply from the editors of *Outdoor Life*, informing her that she was one of the three top prize winners and asking for biographical information and a photograph. In mid-December Rachel came in one day to morning coffee with the Walford gang and made a tantalizing remark about people in the service who won contests. After much questioning by Bert, Kay, and Shirley, she calmly announced that she had just won a thousand dollars—second prize—for a pledge for children to learn about conservation. There followed great jubilation, but when the group threatened to memorize and repeat the pledge in unison every morning, Rachel had a sudden lapse of memory and never provided them the text.[19]

For the next year and a half Carson had no time for contests or magazine features. Between the fall of 1946 and the winter of 1947, she did more traveling than she would ever do again as a federal employee or private citizen. With the enthusiastic support of the new assistant director of the service, wildlife biologist Clarence Cottam, plans for the publication of the *Conservation in Action* series went forward with dispatch.

Carson planned visits to two other waterfowl refuges on the East Coast Atlantic flyway, Parker River in coastal northern Massachusetts not far from the New Hampshire border in September 1946, and Mattamuskeet, Pea Island, and Swanquarter off Pamlico Sound, North Carolina, in February 1947. Then in the fall of 1947, she would spend a month visiting several western refuges, including Bear River near Salt Lake City, Utah, Red Rock Lakes and the National Bison Refuge in Montana, and the salmon fish hatcheries along the Columbia River for the most ambitious booklet in the series, *Guarding Our Wildlife Resources*. On these three trips Carson would be accompanied by series designer and illustrator Kay Howe.

One Sunday in late September the two friends and colleagues took the train to Newburyport, Massachusetts, where they were put up at a local inn, which provided comfortable rooms and a daily picnic lunch. They were met each morning by C. E. Addy, the refuge manager at Parker River, who took them about in his CR vehicle loaded down with Kay's heavy photographic equipment. Data on the numbers and species of birds at Parker River was scarce because of the wartime drain of refuge personnel. Populations of black duck in particular had been in decline for the past two years. Rachel asked many questions and took notes in a large notebook. She was particularly interested in the habitat the refuge provided and the successful efforts to increase the natural food supply and to provide more cover and nesting area.[20]

Their days at Parker River were strenuous, as Rachel wrote Shirley, "full of command cars, marshes, mud, sand dunes, mosquitoes, and Audubonites" which left them "sunburned, black-and-blue, mosquito-bitten and weary."[21]

Rachel, who had the fair skin of a redhead, was especially sensitive to sunburn and took extra precautions against it, including a hat she fabricated with a protective bandanna that hung down just below her eyes to shield her face. Picnic lunches shared with the mosquitoes and the mud left them famished, and ready for a bath and a steak dinner at day's end. Rachel and Kay spent most evenings in the refuge manager's office, where Rachel typed up her notes and Kay prepared her film.[22]

Most of the following week Rachel spent going over old records in the library of the Massachusetts Audubon Society searching for the data she needed on numbers and varieties of birds at Parker River in earlier periods. The Massachusetts Audubon asked her to contribute an article for their bulletin evaluating waterfowl conservation efforts at Parker River. But she also used the time to visit with Dr. Henry Bigelow, who in addition to being the former director of Woods Hole Oceanographic Laboratory was the oceanographic curator at the Museum of Comparative Zoology at Harvard University.[23]

Carson wanted to talk to Bigelow about his current research and to check her interpretations of recently published war material. Bigelow encouraged Rachel to proceed with her plan to write something on the new understanding of the ocean for the public. As a result of this meeting and Bigelow's enthusiasm, she began to think more seriously about a book on the ocean.[24]

Rachel's next adventure came at the beginning of February 1947, when she and Kay set out in a government car for four days at Mattamuskeet, the largest of three remote refuges on the easternmost coast of North Carolina that protected the endangered whistling swan and was used by a variety of other waterfowl. The lodge on the refuge had been converted by the Civilian Conservation Corps from an old pumping station built in the early 1930s. From the top of a circular staircase that had been built into the smokestack, Kay and Rachel had a panoramic view of the refuge and its surrounding countryside. Since they were visiting during the off season, they had the lodge, and its barely adequate dining room, mostly to themselves. Following the same pattern as at Chincoteague and Parker River, Carson and Howe drove around the refuge with the manager or hiked after him taking notes on what was being done to improve conditions.[25]

On their second morning there, Rachel got up before dawn to go birding out along the canal. Thrilled by what she heard, she described it in a letter to Ada Govan. "We heard them [the whistling swans], too, various conversational notes and—really a thrill—the high, thin note, almost a woodwind quality, that presumably gives them their name. . . . I still think the sound of a large flock of geese is one of the most thrilling in the world." She tried to reach the area where the flock was but, in unfamiliar terrain, could not find her way. Throughout the morning, she was aware of the "great undercurrent of goose voices sometimes rising to a great crescendo, then dying away again." As the geese flew off for the day's feeding, she told Govan, "they would pass over so close that I could hear the sound of their wings. In fact, I think it is the sounds of Mattamuskeet that impressed me more than anything else—the geese, the frogs at night, the sound of bird wings, the splashing of unseen deer in the swamps." Some of Carson's sensory impressions found their way into the finished text of the FWS booklet on Mattamuskeet, combining with her factual observations on refuge management and waterfowl behavior to make it one of the most successful of the series.[26]

At the same time as her official assignments were contributing to her wider naturalist experience and perspective, Carson's friends and colleagues were taking her to new places on a variety of naturalist outings. During the spring and summer of 1947, Rachel and Shirley Briggs went on several Audubon forays, including one extended camping trip to Cobb Island off the Virginia coast led by the D.C. Audubon Society president, Irston Barnes. Carson reveled in the opportunity such outings gave her to walk the beach, watch birds, take pictures, and explore island refuges.[27]

Rachel, her mother, and Shirley Briggs, often accompanied by Marjorie Williams, Dorothy Algire, or several other friends, frequently took bird walks on weekends or nice evenings. Favorite routes included Rock Creek Park or the towpath of the old Chesapeake and Ohio Canal, which stretched from downtown Washington out to rural Maryland, reaching as far as Cumberland. The canal towpath around Seneca, Maryland, was particularly beautiful, overlooking a wide stretch of the Potomac from high bluffs where it crossed over aqueduct bridges crafted of native red sandstone and meandered through remote stretches of woodlands. The Seneca lock on the canal was an unusually fine place for bluebirds, warblers, rough-winged swallows, vireos, and indigo buntings. Its naturalist treasures had recently been publicized in an account by local nature writer Louis Halle, who was, like Carson, a federal bureaucrat.

One morning in early May 1947 Rachel and Shirley decided to join the Audubon group's outing to Seneca, since they had enjoyed Halle's book *Spring in Washington*. Reaching the Seneca lock early, Rachel and Shirley set out by themselves. Along the lonely towpath, according to a letter Shirley wrote the next day, they came upon two men also "bedecked with binoculars and exchanged greetings. The gentlemen were watching a great swarm of swallows on the river" and called their attention to several rare species they had missed. As Rachel and Shirley proceeded on their way, Shirley remarked that one of the gentlemen looked like Louis Halle. Indeed it was Halle, and when they met the two again coming back the other way, "Rachel mustered her courage" and introduced herself, whereupon the four had a pleasant chat about the presence of pine siskins at Seneca.[28]

A literary opportunity presented itself during a visit from her friends Edwin Way Teale and his wife, Nellie, with whom she had been corresponding for a number of years. Carson had written Teale upon her return from Mattamuskeet, telling him where he could find young eels on the North Carolina coast and inviting them to stop for a meal with her on their way north. She expressed interest in meeting Louis Halle, and the Teales were happy to make the arrangements. Three weeks after their informal introduction at Seneca, Carson joined the Teales and Louis Halle for luncheon.[29]

Halle later remembered Carson as "quiet, diffident, neat, proper and without any affectation." She gave him the impression of being younger than her forty years, and had, he thought, "something about her of the nineteenth century. She had dignity; she was serious; and as with Lear's Cordelia, her voice was ever soft, gentle and low." Carson wanted this meeting with Halle ostensibly to talk about developing a literary style, and certainly the lunch with him and Teale, then one of the most accomplished of contemporary nature writers, provided her with advice. Rachel gave the gentlemen no indication that she was considering another book and, as Halle later recalled, "put herself in the role of a pupil," not a fellow craftsman. It was not until after *The Sea Around Us* was published that Louis Halle discovered to whom he had been giving stylistic advice and was much embarrassed.[30]

But the meeting was typical of Carson's unobtrusive method of finding the experts in a particular field, be they literary or scientific, and quietly and very unselfconsciously extracting the information or advice she needed. She had been doing it since she began to think seriously about being a writer and a scientist. Croff, Skinker, Watson, Higgins, Beebe, van Loon, and Howe had been experts whose counsel and experience she had sought. Teale and Halle, like Henry Bigelow and Ada Govan, were important to her decision to take on a project involving the mastery of an enormous amount of scientific literature, but presenting it in a literary style that was both comprehensible and interesting to a nonscientific reader. Meanwhile, as she pondered the information they had given, there was one last trip to make for the *Conservation in Action* series.

By the autumn of 1947 when Rachel and Kay Howe began their western tour, they were veteran traveling companions, sensitive to each other's moods and style. They had discovered what was essential for their happiness and well-being on these forays: an extra-long extension cord for rooms where there was only one electrical outlet, high-wattage light bulbs to read or draw by at night, and a flask of whiskey. Cheerful, outgoing, and energetic, Kay enjoyed talking to strangers particularly on the long train rides. Too reserved to initiate a conversation, Rachel would join in happily if it sounded interesting. Rachel was easygoing, as far as Kay was concerned, not at all bossy, and ready for adventure.

Unlike their visits to Parker River and Mattamuskeet, Kay took photographs but did little sketching. She enjoyed following Rachel around listening to the refuge manager's descriptions and snapping pictures. Kay loved the wild and beautiful western landscape and the birds and animals they saw. Rachel, on the other hand, had to get specific information about each refuge. Not only did she take copious notes, but she also asked detailed questions of the refuge personnel, local fishermen, hunters, and the locals.

Leaving her mother for nearly a month was difficult. Mamma was seventy-seven and had not been particularly well that year. It was hard on Maria Carson to have Rachel away. She worried about her daughter's health and wrote her voluminous letters, which she naively sent by special delivery to each stopover en route. But Rachel, engrossed by the opportunity to see a part of the county that she probably would never see again, took her mother's anxiety in stride.

The immediate purpose of the trip West was to get background information for pamphlet number five, *Guarding Our Wildlife Resources*. In it, Carson wanted to survey FWS activities to conserve migratory birds, big game mammals, endangered species, marine fisheries, and inland fishery resources, and to explain the latest agreements for international wildlife conservation. She also wanted to visit refuges that she hoped to include in later bulletins: Bear River Refuge in Utah, and the fish hatcheries along the Columbia River. It was a trip with a large agenda.[31]

On September 19, 1947, Kay and Rachel boarded a New York Central train to Chicago. From there they transferred to a Great Northern Pacific

Robert Warden Carson and Maria McLean, pictured sometime before their marriage in 1894.

Maria, Marian, Rachel (about 3), and Robert Carson.

Rachel, about 5, reading a story to her dog, Candy.

Rachel, far left, and her classmates at School Street Elementary School.

Marian, Rachel, and Robert enjoying an afternoon at the "beach" along the Allegheny River, ca. 1914.

Marian, Robert in Army Air Service uniform, and Rachel, ca. 1919.

Rachel at the time of her graduation from Parnassus High School in 1925.

Robert Warden Carson and Maria Carson visiting their daughter on the campus of Pennsylvania College for Women, 1926.

PCW English professor Grace Croff with one of her best students.

Mary Scott Skinker, mentor and friend, acting head of Biology Department, Pennsylvania College for Women, ca. 1925.

Cora Helen Coolidge, president of Pennsylvania College for Women, ca. 1925.

Margaret Stevenson, 1928, Carson's best friend at Pennsylvania College for Women.

Helen Myers, 1928, Carson's roommate.

Rachel Louise Carson, 1928.

Carson's entry photograph, Johns Hopkins University, 1929.

Dorothy Hamilton Algire, Woods Hole, 1940.

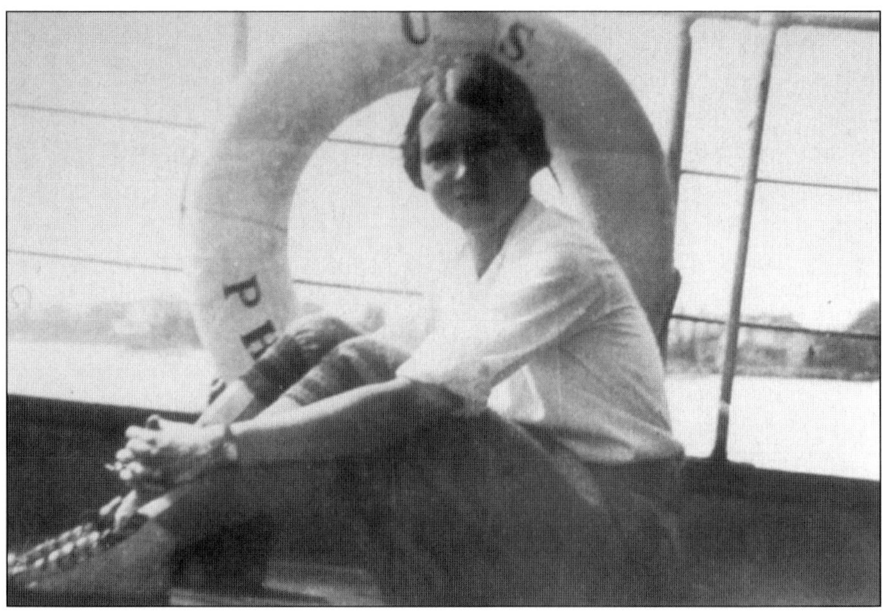
Rachel during her first summer at Woods Hole Biological Laboratory, 1929.

Elmer Higgins, Division Chief, Bureau of Fisheries, Department of Commerce, ca. 1935.

Clarence Cottam, Chief, Division of Fisheries, U.S. Fish and Wildlife Services, ca. 1948.

Lionel "Bert" A. Walford, Chief, Division of Information, U.S. Fish and Wildlife Service, ca. 1944.

Rachel Carson, author, editor, and aquatic biologist, U.S. Fish and Wildlife Service, ca. 1944.

Kay Howe, illustrator, U.S. Fish and Wildlife Service, ca. 1947.

Shirley Briggs, artist and naturalist, ca. 1947, on an outing of the D.C. Audubon Society.

Virginia and Marjorie Williams, Rachel's nieces, 1942.

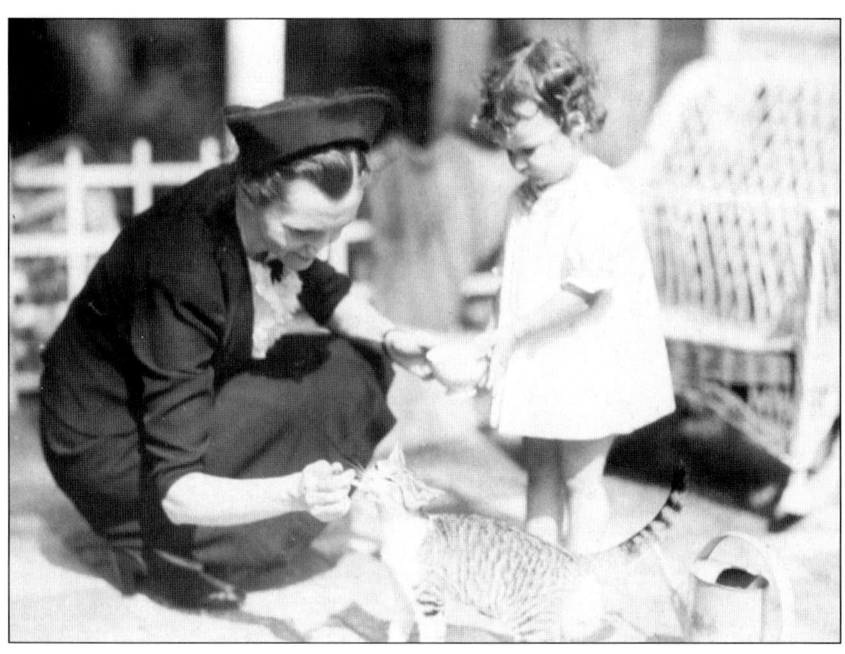

Carson with her goddaughter, Anne Algire, and cat, 1944.

Rachel and Shirley sneaking across the hotel lobby after a soggy excursion at Chincoteague Wildlife Refuge, 1946.

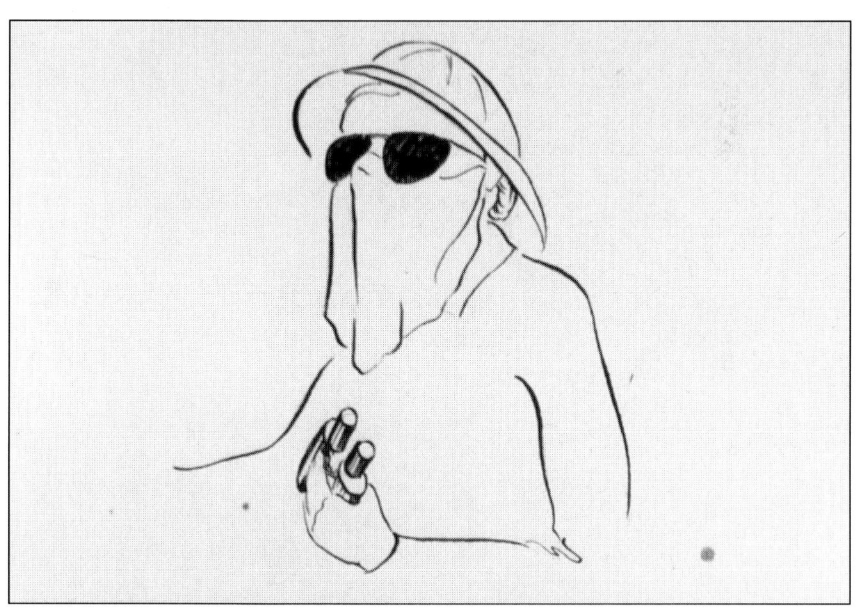

Rachel in her sun protection garb at Chincoteague.

Carson wading ashore at Chincoteague Wildlife Refuge.

Maria Carson and poet Archibald Rutledge after a visit to his home in Charleston, South Carolina, 1947.

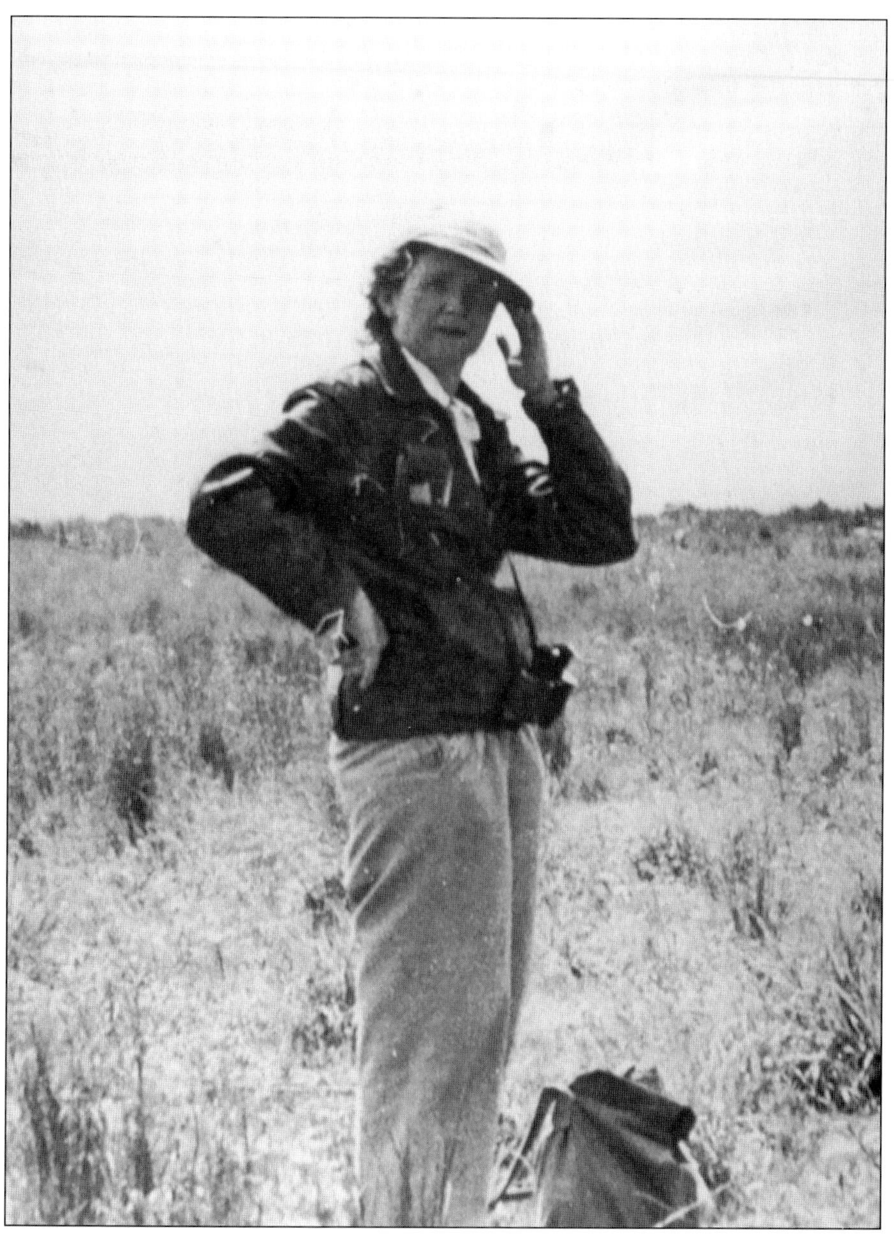

Carson at Cobb Island, Virginia, on an outing with the D.C. Audubon Society, 1947.

Rachel on the dock at Woods Hole, 1950.

train equipped with special a domed observation car for the trip West. These were the days of luxurious train travel. The two women had a stateroom with comfortable bunk beds, a private bath, and plenty of room to spread out books and papers. The food was delicious, the tables set with real silver, linen, crystal, and fresh flowers. An assigned waiter looked after them no matter where they sat, so they lingered in the dining car. They both loved sitting in the observation car watching the scenery. On the third morning, Kay woke up as they entered Montana to see snow on the ground and a pronghorn antelope poised on a little mound beside the track. During a layover in Butte, Montana, they saw their first cowboy in full regalia and received their change in silver dollars.[32]

Their first stop was Red Rock Lakes Refuge near the town of Monida on the border of Montana and Idaho, nearly in Yellowstone National Park's backyard. Looking for Monida in the atlas before they left, they learned it had a population of less than fifty, but when they got there, they were surprised to find the atlas had failed to mention that there were almost more bars than people. The refuge manager met them with his pickup truck, and together they bumped over dusty dirt roads for about two hours before reaching his comfortable log house in the wee hours of the morning. The refuge manager usually provided meals and sometimes several nights' lodging for which he was paid a set amount by FWS. When Rachel returned from a trip such as this, or visited someone, she always sent her hosts a copy of *Under the Sea-Wind* with a personal inscription as a thank-you gift, and she did so on this trip.

The mission of the remote Red Rock Lakes Refuge was the protection of the few remaining colonies of trumpeter swans, which could winter at the refuge because of its thermal lakes. The refuge supplied them with food, nesting cover, and protection. Although the stormy and snowy weather of the previous week had turned most of the roads to mud, Kay and Rachel awoke to fresh snow on the ground. Rachel was impressed with the moose in the willow swamps and the beauty of snow-clad peaks, dark fir and pine, and golden aspen. The group drove close enough to the swans to see their food supply and nesting areas. One evening Rachel also got her wish to see a yellow-haired porcupine, which the refuge manager cornered in the hollyhocks outside the cabin.[33]

On the way back down the now nearly impassable road to Monida two days later, Rachel and her party met the local mailman. The two pickups stopped in the middle of a huge flock of sheep, so the mailman could give

Rachel a special-delivery letter from her mother. It was the first special-delivery letter he had ever seen. Everyone had a good laugh at the absurdity of it.

From Monida it was back up to Butte and another train to Missoula, Montana. There the refuge manager, George Mushbach, of the National Bison Range took them to their lodgings, a room over a hardware store, next to the movie theater, in the tiny town of Ronan. The town consisted of a cluster of crude buildings with only two places to eat. Dinner the first night provided the most excitement of their trip. Two men entered the restaurant and got into such a violent argument, complete with threats and curses, that the women made plans to lie on the floor when the shooting started. Upon escaping back to their room, they discovered that their windows were nothing more than narrow slits near the ceiling, slits that opened into the movie theater. As Rachel wrote Shirley, "they were entertained by the sound effects of 'Bob, Son of Battle' and its unidentifiable co-feature, until midnight." The lodging was presided over by a woman they dubbed "the witch," whom Rachel described as a "gaunt, deep-voiced specimen," whose manner toward two government women from the East was less than hospitable.[34]

Mushback, on the other hand, was a jolly sort of person, and the trio enjoyed the rolling rangeland, with its clear streams and patches of snow. Mushback drove them out near the buffalo herds and showed them the pens where the animals were rounded up each year for shots, health checkups, and culling.

After this Rachel and Kay were ready for a social break. They spent the weekend on their own in Portland, Oregon, and drove down to Agate Beach. It was the first time either woman had seen the Pacific Ocean.[35]

On Monday they were met by a biologist with the FWS in Portland and his wife. They all drove up the Columbia River, stopping at a variety of fish hatcheries, the ancient Indian fishing grounds at Cello Falls, and on to Bonneville Dam, where they were given a tour and inspected the fish ladders around the spillways.

Rachel was particularly distressed by the pollution of the Willamette River at Oregon City, where paper mills and poorly constructed fishways made a spring fish run nearly impossible. Watching the salmon jumping up the steep ladders around the Columbia River dams, Carson "was struck by the incomprehensible nature of the destiny which requires all this of the salmon to return to their home, when for all we could see they could equally well fulfill themselves in the ocean from which they came." After crossing the Yakima Valley, they ended their tour at Grand Coulee Dam. Nearly a week later they got back to Portland, where they boarded the train for Ogden, Utah, and their last stop: the Bear River Migratory Bird Refuge on the edge of the Great Salt Lake.[36]

There they found the river and marshes so shallow that they traveled with the refuge manager in an airboat. Low water levels combined with the crowding of enormous numbers of waterfowl using the refuge had spread botulism. Every so often the manager would spot a sick-looking bird, grab it, inject it casually with something, and toss it into the boat. Rachel quietly seethed at his uncontrolled research methods. She considered the attempt to halt the spread of disease in such a haphazard manner not only cruel but a waste of time and money. The next day Kay and Rachel boarded an "interurban" train, which reminded Kay of a cigar with little round windows, that ran between Ogden and Salt Lake City. From Salt Lake City, it was a two-and-a-half-day trip back to Washington, which gave them a chance to sleep and relax after their monthlong sojourn.[37]

The *Conservation in Action* series was uniquely successful in part because of Carson's careful field research and in part because of the style in which the booklets were written. The five numbers that Carson authored or coauthored were considered among the best natural histories of the refuges that the service ever produced. Long after the data she presented was outdated, the booklets were read and regarded as examples of fine nature writing. They were remarkable most of all for the way in which Carson introduced the role ecology played in the cycles and rhythms of nature and the interaction between natural habitat and requirements of wildlife. Understanding the need to detail the history of the land and the uses of nature as well as the current mission of the FWS refuges, Carson was also sensitive to the political need to describe the multiple uses of each refuge.

Once again Carson commented forthrightly on humankind's generally adverse impact on the environment of a refuge: its habitat loss, habitat pollution, the effects of previously unmanaged market hunting, species extinction, and the spread of disease. *Chincoteague*, *Parker River*, and *Mattamuskeet* appeared in 1947, *Guarding Our Wildlife Resources* in 1948, and *Bear River*, coauthored with Vanez Wilson and illustrated by Bob

Hines, in 1950. Carson's ultimate purpose of getting people to recognize their personal connection with nature is never obscured by the other more practical, informational, requirements of a government publication.[38]

The two and a half years that Carson worked on the series were her happiest and most fulfilling time in the service. Certainly the trip to the western refuges was one of the highlights of her government career and added immeasurably to her overall ecological perspective.

Sandwiched in between traveling for the FWS series and her other responsibilities, Carson found time to keep abreast of the so-called red tide invasion of the Gulf of Florida. Rachel's old friend Paul Galtsoff, with whom she'd worked at College Park, Woods Hole, and Parker River, now the service's chief shellfish biologist stationed at Woods Hole, was assigned to direct an emergency survey of the Florida plague of microscopic sea creatures known as *Gymnodinium*. His survey began in the fall of 1946, after south Florida fishermen reported high fish mortality in areas where the water had turned red. By December 1947 millions of fish had died.

As information officer, Carson handled a flood of inquiries about the "red tide" phenomenon over the course of the year. Accounts of similar marine disturbances had been recorded in other parts of the world's oceans since 1844; she shared her research with Galtsoff and followed his fieldwork closely. Before she left on the western trip in the fall of 1947, Carson had completed a brief article on the "red tides" titled "Killer from the Sea" and wrote the summary FWS press release that reported Galtsoff's conclusions.[39]

Carson's article was published in *Field and Stream* magazine as "The Great Red Tide Mystery" in February 1948. Ironically, the photograph chosen to accompany her article depicted emergency crews spraying dead fish that littered the Florida beach with a mixture of DDT and deodorant to control flies. This article was a small but important part of Carson's broader oceanographic research that led her further into new areas of scientific inquiry.[40]

Carson was finding there were emotional and physical costs to having two simultaneous careers, a public one during the day and a private one at night, all the while functioning as daughter, sister, aunt, and head of household. Between February 1945 and June 1947, Carson was hospitalized three times: first for an appendectomy, then for the removal of a benign breast cyst, and finally, in July 1947, just before her trip West, for a hemorrhoidectomy. An emotionally as well as physically constrained person, Carson had little opportunity to relax other than that provided by occasional Audubon outings, the refuge trips, and an occasional summer sail.[41]

Her work as assistant editor in the Division of Information with a staff of six had the additional stresses of constant deadlines. Her difficulties with John Ady and the Government Printing Office (GPO) over the design and printing of the *Conservation in Action* series intensified after the printing office's first debacle on the Chincoteague number. Bert Walford discovered that Ady had deliberately changed the printing specifications he and Carson had agreed upon. Relations with GPO reached such an acrimonious level that Service Director Albert Day took the matter to the office of Secretary of Interior Julius Krug to be resolved. The anticipated postwar reductions in force kept Rachel in constant combat with department personnel to keep Kay Howe, Shirley Briggs, and other contract employees on staff.[42]

Illness and uncertainty increased Carson's stress at home as well. Just before Christmas 1946, Maria Carson had serious intestinal surgery. During her recuperation, Rachel had to care for her as well as take over domestic management of the household. Sometime later, both Rachel and her mother were saddened by the death of their beloved cat Kito and anxious about Rachel's brother, Robert, in Baltimore, who also had surgery.[43]

In January 1948 Rachel developed a serious case of shingles, a painful virus of the nervous system. Kay Howe, who had come back from their western jaunt to face an appendectomy, was of the opinion that "Ray wouldn't be so subject to these outbreaks if she lived properly and got enough exercise." Although Rachel recovered fairly rapidly, the illness put her further behind at the office and therefore further behind in her writing.

The next disruption occurred when Kay Howe quit her FWS job in July and moved to her aunt's home in Atlanta. Shortly thereafter she met Sam Roberts, an army officer teaching military science at Georgia Institute of Technology. Before she married Roberts in December 1950, Kay returned to Washington periodically to do freelance work and to visit with Rachel and her other friends.[44]

To replace Kay, Rachel hired Bob Hines, a veteran wildlife illustrator from the Ohio Division of Conservation, in August 1948. Over time he became one of her most loyal colleagues, a crucial professional collaborator, and a devoted friend. Rachel needed all the help and support she could get from her staff because Bert Walford's appointment as head of the Bureau of Fisheries came through, as anticipated, in the summer of 1949, and Rachel inherited his job as chief editor of all service publications.[45]

Yet during this same time, Rachel Carson was tediously but steadily organizing her research material and sketching an outline of a book on the natural history of the ocean that incorporated the latest oceanographic research. Shirley Briggs innocently recorded in her diary on March 3, 1948, that "Ray is concocting a fine scheme whereby she writes a Bestseller—Forever Amber theme—perhaps using an Audubon Society background, and so is wealthy and can retire and write natural history." Shirley and the others knew that Rachel was up to something more serious, but with the same general objective.

Ida Johnson, the reference librarian of the Interior Department Library, knew from Carson's wide-ranging requests for obscure articles and bibliographic searches that she was at work on a major project. Nearly every evening Carson picked up a batch of material Johnson had gathered and took it home with her, returning it the next morning. Bob Hines also was enlisted to pick up and return books from the Virginia public libraries near his home or from other specialty libraries in the area. His book runs for Rachel soon became a daily occurrence.[46]

Harry Ladd, the senior geologist at the U.S. Geological Survey, who was a specialist on the origin of coral reefs, and F. Raymond Fosberg, an expert in tropical botany at George Washington University and the National Museum, both talked to Carson at length about the geology of coral reefs and the complex formation of oceanic islands when she came to see them. They answered her questions, provided her with their latest research, and later Fosberg read a draft of her chapter on island formation. Charles Alldredge, however, knew more about what Carson was up to than anyone other than her mother.[47]

Alldredge and Carson had remained friends ever since they had first worked in the Division of Information. Early in 1948, Alldredge left Interior after serving ten years on the department's public relations and information staff, and established his own practice in Washington, where he wrote speeches for a variety of political clients.

Alldredge was a gentle, courtly southerner from Montgomery, Alabama, who had begun his career as a newspaperman. He loved to write, especially poetry, and because of his work in the Secretary of Interior's office, he knew just about everyone in town who was active in natural resource conservation. Occasionally Alldredge asked Rachel to write a speech for one of his congressional clients or for a lobbyist. Rachel took on the assignments willingly and wrote easily. Sometimes he and Rachel had dinner together or went to a movie or concert. Alldredge was impressed by Carson's writing and encouraged her to try another book in spite of her previous experience and initial reluctance.[48]

At Alldredge's urging, Carson had gotten a release from Simon & Schuster for the option on her next book. Relations had deteriorated between author and publisher since the publication of *Under the Sea-Wind*, not only because of the book's commercial failure but over such issues as subsidiary sales and remaindering. Alldredge supported Carson's desire to find a new publisher, but first he advised her to place her work with a literary agent, and he gave her the names of several.[49]

Although Carson initially was reluctant to follow Alldredge's advice, and particularly loath to share any royalties with an agent, she admitted by the spring of 1948 that she needed help with the editors of *Holiday* magazine, who had accepted her article on bird banding over a year before but had failed to schedule its publication.

Finally Rachel accepted Alldredge's suggestion. In April and May 1948 she interviewed several of the people on his list, including Marie Rodell, an editor and sometime mystery writer, who was a personal friend of Alldredge's. Rodell was just establishing her literary agency in New York. After several telephone conversations the two women met for lunch at the Algonquin Hotel in New York City. Rachel had a little black notebook with her, with the tentative chapter outline for a book titled *Return to the Sea*. Rodell was interested and Carson became one of her first clients. It marked the beginning of a remarkable partnership.[50]

Shirley Briggs also recorded in her diary that on November 30, 1948, Rachel was called to Chicago where a friend of hers was critically ill. The call, from a doctor at a hospital in Evanston, Illinois, brought the heartbreaking news that Mary Scott Skinker was dying of cancer.

Rachel borrowed the money for the plane trip to Chicago, perhaps from Alldredge, and made the sad journey to be with her dearest friend. Skinker and Carson's correspondence is gone, but it is clear that they had remained in touch and possibly saw each other in New York or Washington until 1946, when Skinker took a nonacademic staff position at the Hockaday School in Dallas, Texas. In September 1948 Skinker accepted a position on the faculty of the National College of Education in Evanston, Illinois, an institution designed to train elementary school teachers.[51]

Impressing the younger members of the faculty there with her warmth and graciousness, Mary Scott kept very much to herself. No one knew much about her. It was unusual to have a female scientist with a doctorate at National, but Skinker could not have been kinder to beginning science faculty nor more encouraging of their teaching. Still a dynamic, generous instructor, she communicated to others her love of teaching and of science. She taught only a little more than two months of the term when university officials found her one morning collapsed in her small apartment and took her to the hospital. She gave Rachel Carson's name as the person to be contacted.[52]

Carson stayed with Skinker as long as she was alert, then Skinker's brother Thomas and his wife arrived to take her back to St. Louis, where she died on December 19, 1948, at age fifty-seven. Rachel never talked about her trip to anyone at the office, but she did share some of her feelings with Marie Rodell, admitting, "I have been, and still am, pretty well shot to pieces emotionally by my friend's illness and the tragic circumstances connected with it, but I'm trying now to get my mind back to some of the things I'm supposed to be doing."[53]

Mary Scott Skinker molded Rachel Carson's ecological consciousness, nurtured her talent, supported her ambitions, set fire to her mind, and loved her unconditionally. Skinker was both mentor and intimate friend whom Carson loved more deeply than anyone ever guessed. Her death brought an important phase of Carson's own life to a close as well and left her with an emotional void.[54]

At forty-one, Rachel Carson was at another crossroads. In its own way, Mary Scott Skinker's influence on Carson's choices for herself was as strong as the example of marital limits and misery in her parents' and siblings' lives. Skinker placed a high value on the freedom and the wider opportunities that remaining single offered a female scientist of her generation. Her life, foreshortened and plagued by professional disappointments as it was, offered Carson an example of courage, independence, and achievement.

Intensely aware of the range of reasons behind Skinker's choices, Carson shared many of her intellectual mentor's values. Driven by her own ambition and her vision of her life's purpose, however inchoate it was at various times, Carson probably never considered that marriage, with its demands of personal denial and its implicit expectations of motherhood, had anything to offer her. She already had more family than she could manage, all without benefit of a partner's added economic resources or emotional support. What Rachel missed most was not a husband but an emotional intimacy with someone who understood the loneliness of her creative calling and could nurture and support her vision and her sense of mission. Mary Scott Skinker had given her that; for a time, Marie Rodell would also.

7

"Such a Comfort to Me"

It would have been difficult to find two more outwardly different women than Marie Fried Rodell and Rachel Carson. Five years younger than Carson, Marie Rodell was, by 1948, a world-wise, well-traveled, sophisticated New Yorker fluent in four languages who moved comfortably in many of New York's most elite literary and publishing circles.[1]

Rodell's parents, Isadore and Elizabeth Fried, had both immigrated to the United States from Russia. Her father began as a pharmacist in Manhattan, served in the U.S. Navy in the Spanish American War, and ended as an insurance executive, retiring modestly but comfortably in St. Petersburg, Florida. Her mother taught school on New York's Upper West Side, wrote plays and opera librettos, and dreamed of being a published playwright. The Frieds sent Marie and her younger sister to the Fieldston School and the School of Ethical Culture, after which Marie went on to excel at Vassar College, graduating in 1932. She spent her junior year at the Sorbonne in Paris and studied German at Middlebury College before finding a job as an assistant editor at the publishing firm of William Morrow & Company in New York City.

A member of MENSA, the society for people with extremely high IQs, Rodell spent her spare time writing mystery fiction and published three novels under the pseudonym Marion Randolph by 1941. She spent one year as fiction editor at Modern Age Books and then moved to Duell, Sloan and Pearce in 1939 as an editor and director of their mystery department. At the same time, she was active in the society of the Mystery Writers of America, where she served as secretary and was highly regarded for her intelligence and energy.

In 1943 Rodell produced a textbook on the theory and technique of mystery fiction, which went through several editions and translations and became the standard for many writers and students in the genre. She also wrote several short stories and articles, most published in women's magazines. But in 1948, postwar layoffs in the publishing business drove her out on her own as a literary agent. It turned out to be fortuitous, for although Rodell was an excellent editor, she was temperamentally suited to the intellectual and social skills required of an author's representative.

Along the way Marie was briefly married to John Rodell, a ne'er-do-well playwright of whom she rarely spoke kindly afterward. The likeness of Edgar Allan Poe on the Edgar statuette she received for her study of mystery fiction reminded her of Rodell. She kept both the award and the details of her marriage locked away in a closet that she seldom found the need to open.[2]

Marie Rodell was energetic, ambitious, naturally outgoing, and good company. Most of her clients soon became her friends. Rodell loved to cook and entertain, and surprised her friends with elaborate handmade dollhouses that she gave as presents to their daughters. She was also a chain smoker who played a fine hand of bezique and was equally adept at poker, which she enjoyed with several groups of mostly male friends. She had a quick wit and a hardy laugh and, although ultra-feminine in her person, could be pleasantly bawdy. Archaeology and anthropology were passions that took her traveling as often as she could afford.

Rodell was attractive, of average height, and of slightly stocky build, with a tendency to put on weight as she grew older. She had naturally curly auburn hair, which she wore fashionably upswept in the 1940s and 1950s. She liked stylish but not flamboyant clothes and occasionally indulged in strappy high-heeled shoes and decorative rings. Her literary taste as well as her grammar was impeccable; so were her ethics as a literary agent.

Colleagues in the publishing business found Rodell a woman of absolute integrity, whose word could be counted on. They considered her tough because she meant exactly what she said and stuck by it. Organized and efficient, she was a sharp negotiator who once wronged never forgot the injury or gave opportunity for a second.

What Marie Rodell and Rachel Carson had in common was less obvious but more important than their superficial differences. Both shared a moral commitment to the art of writing and the business of publishing, and a deep respect for each other's particular genius. Both women were keenly competitive, understood how to build and use a network of associates and friends, and were willing to take risks. They shared the same code of business and professional behavior. Both were devoted to their respective families, although they responded quite differently to familial demands. Independently, Rodell and Carson had gotten to where they were by 1948 by hard work, grit, and determination as well as by talent. Most of all they shared an understanding of the creative process, its unyielding demands, and the inevitable isolation of the writer.

Carson was drawn to Rodell's personal candor, her intelligence, and her obvious experience and business acumen. Rodell took Carson's measure as an artist and a person of singular talent, and their partnership was forged. It was an alliance that profoundly shaped the lives of both women.

In the spring of 1948 Rachel Carson was in a hurry to get on with her life's work. Defining herself more and more as a writer, she had an ambitious agenda. She described herself in a letter of introduction to tropical ornithologist Robert Cushman Murphy "as a marine biologist whose actual profession is writing rather than biology" and whose "consuming interest happens to be the ocean and its life." At forty-one Carson was well aware that she had to make the most of her creative years just ahead.[3]

Marie Rodell not only fit Carson's game plan perfectly but knew at once how to advance it. Initially their partnership had a number of strategic goals. The most immediate was a contract for the ocean book with a reputable house that would commit resources to its marketing and sales. Of equal necessity was a substantial fellowship that would allow Carson to take an unpaid leave of absence from the Fish and Wildlife Service to finish her research and have some uninterrupted time to write yet still meet her financial obligations. Crucial to a successful financial outcome of their partnership was the sale of chapters to magazines as Carson finished them to produce interim income. Likewise a scientific award or literary prize would bring extra money and at the same time advance Carson's name and reputation. The result would be a competitive market after the book was published for second serial sales, book club rights, and a more lucrative contract for her next book.[4]

Until *The Sea Around Us* was published, Rodell was most often the dominant partner in their literary enterprise as well as in the friendship, taking almost a maternal role with Carson, who struggled to fulfill her part of the commitment. As the book neared completion, however, their relationship shifted, and Carson more frequently controlled the literary and financial agenda. Rodell's patience, forbearance, and integrity won Carson's loyalty and affection. It is hard to imagine anyone else whom Carson would have trusted with her literary career. The chronicle of their first enterprise established the parameters of an equally exceptional friendship.

Rodell's first task was to sort out Carson's legal status with Simon & Schuster and to make sure that the copyrights to Carson's articles had been reassigned to her. Then she tackled *Holiday* magazine about the unpublished bird-banding story, finally getting them to admit that the story was definitely buried. In the course of business, Rodell passed along to Carson news of a publishing contest, fellowships that looked promising, and professional notes that might provide new opportunities for Carson, such as the oceanographic expedition of the *Atlantis* sailing out of Woods Hole, suggesting that Carson might want to participate in one of these cruises if she could get leave time. Rodell found Carson a "most satisfactorily business-like person to deal with" and was particularly impressed with the thoroughness of the records Carson turned over to her.[5]

Carson's job was to produce a suitable chapter and a detailed outline of *Return to the Sea* for Rodell to send out to prospective publishers. Throughout the summer she had been researching and writing the chapter on the formation of oceanic islands utilizing the expertise of tropical botanist Ray Fosberg and geologist Harry Ladd, who were close at hand in Washington. When she had a chance to discuss it briefly with Murphy in New York, he suggested that she contact Mary Sears and Maurice Ewing at Woods Hole Oceanographic for the latest research. She hoped to have the chapter ready to show Rodell in early September.[6]

"I can tell you are going to be a relentless slave-driver," Carson wrote Rodell. "What with Charles Alldredge prodding me by phone, I'm going to be a sorely beset author. My chief trouble about this islands chapter," she complained, "is that I keep finding so much terribly interesting stuff that I can't stop researching." By mid-August Carson decided that she and Rodell had been properly formal long enough. "Since we would presumably come to the point sooner or later," Carson told her, "shall we just use first names now? Most of my newer friends call me Ray, which I rather prefer, but I answer to either." After less than a month together Carson admitted "it is already proving to be a great comfort to have you."[7]

Rodell planned a trip to Washington in early September to discuss the islands chapter and book outline. But Carson wrote her on Labor Day weekend that while she had bought a ream of typewriter paper and gotten Alldredge's blessing on the outline she had sent up for Rodell's inspection, the island chapter would not be with it. In her opinion, the outline was sufficiently detailed that a publisher could tell whether he wanted the book or not.[8]

Rodell sent Carson's outline to Helen Taylor, an editor she knew well at William Sloan Associates, explaining

> Rachel Carson works for the US Department of Fisheries and, for my money, writes like an angel. In 1941 Simon and Schuster brought out *Under the Sea-Wind*, her first book. They did very little with it and it sold less than 3000 copies in spite of an ecstatic press. I am enclosing a copy. Now Miss Carson is at work on a new book, tentatively titled "Return to the Sea." I am giving you first crack.[9]

"This seems to be it," Carson wrote Rodell at the end of the month, enclosing a vastly altered islands chapter, "not much more left of the original than remained of Krakatoa after the blast." Rodell sent it on to Sloan's explaining that Carson wanted a commitment on the basis of the outline, the book, and the sample chapter.[10]

Marie thought Rachel would be anxious about the outcome, but her client was already thinking about future projects. Carson revealed for the first time that "among my remote literary projects is a book on the lives of shore animals, which Mr. Teale once asked me to write for his benefit." It is also clear from this letter that by 1948 Teale had taken Hendrik van Loon's place as avuncular mentor.[11]

At the same time as she sent Rodell the completed islands chapter, Carson queried her agent about an idea for a magazine article. It was the first of many such diverting proposals Carson would make over the next decade, each of which took a toll on her time and energy and invariably wreaked havoc with her book writing schedule. Such ideas sprang from both Carson's perennial need for money and her sincere interest in a particular area. Research on the islands chapter had taken her from the scientists at the Smithsonian to the offices of the Pacific Science Board, where she discovered fascinating new data on the flora and fauna of the Pacific Islands of Micronesia, which the United States inherited after World War II.

The islands of Oceania, as the area was called on prewar maps, became a trust territory of the United Nations under control of the United States in 1947. The Pacific Science Board grew out of a National Research Council conference held the previous year to plan resumption of scientific research in the Pacific, an area that had been closed to American scientists for thirty years. Beginning in 1947, the Pacific Science Board coordinated the largest biological and ecological field investigation ever undertaken. Carson was naturally excited about the biological survey reports produced by the board's scientists.[12]

She was convinced there was "a big magazine story in these Pacific islands and the conservation problems the United States has inherited along with them." A general book on the oceans, she explained to Marie, was not the place to write about the specific conservation problems presented by these islands, but a magazine was. Carson thought it worth taking time away from the book to write a magazine article, telling Rodell, "I am inclined to think there won't be many things quite as timely as this." Assuming Rodell thought well of her idea, Carson suggested that she query magazine editors.[13]

Carson's letter indicates that she was still not entirely comfortable leaving all her literary endeavors to someone else. Telling Rodell that she would send her a brief synopsis of the piece, Carson wondered if perhaps she should just write to the editor of the *Atlantic* herself since she had a previous relationship with him. "In making these suggestions," Carson somewhat sheepishly explained, "please don't think I'm proposing taking it out of your hands—that isn't the idea!"[14]

Rodell agreed with Carson's assessment of the importance of the Pacific Island conservation program and told her that she would query the *Saturday Evening Post* and a few other magazines. Meanwhile Carson should continue her writing.[15]

Carson's interest in the research of the Pacific Science Board was significant for other reasons as well. The board's long-range invertebrate survey was aimed at giving the navy specific advice about insect and pest control on these remote oceanic islands. Carson was fascinated by evidence of the various species that flourished there. A draft of her article in mid-November shows her keen understanding of the invasion of a species of wasp and the rather spectacular pest control work required by the navy to get rid of it, recalling her earlier interest in problems of insect control in 1948. In the case of the Pacific Science Board survey, the problem of insect transport fit in with her research on the ecology of coral atolls and on the extreme vulnerability of island faunas.[16]

In October Rodell received a negative response from William Sloan Associates. "I am sad and indignant at having to tell you that W. L. Sloan has returned our child," Marie wrote Rachel with some frustration, "on the grounds that they cannot reach a decision on so great an undertaking on the basis of the material submitted." Marie was unprepared for Rachel's pragmatic response.

"My rather absurd reaction to your news about Wm. Sloan," Carson replied, "was that I should try to console *you* about it, feeling that you were more disappointed than I. Of course I admit it would have been nice to have them clamoring for the book but somehow the news did not depress me." Ever the realist, she wondered at their description of the book as a "great undertaking," asking Marie if the outline suggested an extra-long book.[17]

> Perhaps the outline should be simplified; I guess it is a little staggering. Second, even though it annoyed you, their feeling that the chapter submitted wasn't enough for a decision is one I am rather in sympathy with. The island chapter seemed to me—as it developed—one of the least representative of the book as a whole. So perhaps we ought to wait for others.[18]

When Rodell concurred, Carson vowed to "retire into [her] sacred cave, emerging when [she had] a decent batch of manuscript finished." But Rodell and Carson would not have taken the Sloan rejection so sanguinely if they had known the truth. According to William Sloan's later version of events, he was out of the office when the Carson material arrived and a subordinate reviewed the synopsis and rejected it. Sloan considered the event the low point of his publishing career.[19]

Carson continued her research on the Pacific Science Board, telling her agent with some excitement a week later that she had an appointment with Harold Coolidge, Jr., the board's director, as well as someone in the Navy's Office of Island Governments who "is said to possess all sorts of treasured reports, and best of all, to be willing to let people read them."[20]

Carson's work was given a boost the following week, when Rodell received a cautious letter from Erd Brandt of the *Saturday Evening Post* expressing interest in seeing the island conservation piece. Rodell suggested sending an abbreviated version of the islands chapter along in order to offer them a two-part serial. Having failed to interest the *Post* in her work several times before, Rachel asked Marie to "instill a little confidence in my ability to do this in a way the *Post* will like. I'm afraid I suffer from some sort of complex about the peculiar tastes of *Post* editors."[21]

After three months together, the working relationship between author and agent had taken on many of the distinctive dimensions that would characterize it for the next decade. Rachel would send Marie drafts of chapters and articles, welcoming her reactions and revisions. Rarely did Marie offer suggestions about style or syntax. But she could be ruthless in cutting and reorganizing material, pointing out ways to pin the material together or to put more warmth and human interest in the story. She enjoyed suggesting titles. Carson usually knew, before Marie went to work on a piece, how it could be revised, and their solutions were always commonly arrived at.[22]

Rodell's role as morale booster was equally important and increased rather than diminished over time. Carson frequently came home from a hectic week at her Fish and Wildlife office too exhausted to write. By Saturday evening, however, she would have revived enough to begin another draft, often calling Rodell on the telephone during the weekend for moral support. Rodell's energy and her emotional involvement were contagious. So was her sense of humor and her realism. "I have sacrificed a black cock, put a hill of beans under the bed, poured a sacrificial libation for the waiting demons, and sent your piece off to the *Saturday Evening Post* tentatively entitled 'Another Beachhead'," Marie wrote. "I think it reads very well. Whether Mr. Brandt will consider it too academic I do not know—there is a chance he may. I applaud your decision about no more articles until a hunk of the book gets done. We do get distracted, don't we." Regardless of whether the results of their publishing efforts were favorable or not, Rodell's infectious energy and obvious faith in Carson's abilities provided the ingredient that Carson needed to move ahead.[23]

Over the course of the first six months, Rodell got a glimpse at how tough and how committed to her writing Carson was. When the *Post* rejected the Pacific Islands article, Carson wanted to know if they gave any definite reason. "Not that I was really surprised, you understand," she wrote Rodell, "but I just think some specific criticism, no matter how unflattering, would help in case we ever tried it again."[24]

In the middle of December Rodell left for a two-week vacation in St. Petersburg with her parents. She left a depressed Carson, who had just returned from her sad visit to Chicago and was anticipating news of Mary Scott Skinker's death, a fear that she confided to the compassionate Rodell. "I hope you are going to have a holiday in Florida," Rachel told Marie sincerely, "and that you can succeed in forgetting all your authors and their troubles for a couple weeks!" But even on vacation, Marie monitored Rachel's progress and kept her spirits buoyed. The solidity of their friendship and their professional relationship would be well tested over the next six months.[25]

"Another Beachhead" and the islands chapter, separately and jointly, continued to garner rejection slips from the magazine market. "What a lovely post-mortem we can hold on Another Beachhead when you come down," Rachel wrote Marie, naturally discouraged. Although Marie admonished her not to be faint-hearted, Rachel decided that trying to publish the articles was simply delaying the book. "I'm more than ever convinced these magazine things are a mistake, at least until the book has a solid start," she told Rodell. "So the next time I suggest one, please drop my letter in the nearest wastebasket." But Carson's search for publishing opportunities was insatiable and her resolve lasted barely a week.[26]

After she finished the islands chapter, Rachel began drafting chapters on the seasonal changes of surface sea life and undersea topography, but she made agonizingly slow progress. When Marie, who was a devout New Dealer, went down to Washington for the presidential inauguration of Harry S Truman, the two spent a day together in which Rachel poured out her frustrations and admitted her deep pessimism over her lack of meaningful progress, questioning whether she could ever write such a book. But shortly after Rodell's visit, which had obviously improved her spirits, Carson had an insight into her difficulties.

> I have just made a monumental discovery. I find that the reason—well anyway, one important reason—I've been having such a fiendish time with Chapters 2, 3 etc. is that I haven't done Chapter 1. So I've been absorbed for two days, (thinking, not writing) and have decided it's going to be pretty good. Best of all, it seems to me I can see the others falling into line in a way they just refused to do up to now. Absurdly obvious, isn't it?[27]

Marie professed herself "no end amused" at Rachel's discovery but delighted at anything that enabled her to move forward with her writing.

Although Carson's progress was uneven, she was able to promise Rodell the first four chapters, a revised islands chapter, and a slightly condensed outline by the first of April, when she planned to go to New York for a long weekend that included a day bird-watching with Edwin and Nellie Teale on Long Island. Rodell invited Carson to sleep on her living room couch while she was in the city and also made an appointment for her with William Beebe at the New York Zoological Society.[28]

Carson had made extensive use of Beebe's famous studies of deep-sea life made from his dives in the bathysphere and in a diving suit. Ever since he had included Carson's chapter on the odyssey of the eel from *Under the Sea-Wind* in his *Book of Naturalists*, Carson had sought his advice and enjoyed his support. "I am much impressed by man's dependence upon the ocean, directly, and in thousands of ways unsuspected by most people," she told the distinguished oceanographer. "These relationships, and my belief that we will become even more dependent upon the ocean as we destroy the land, are really the theme of the book and have suggested its tentative title, 'Return to the Sea.' " Now she had specific questions for him as well as a favor to ask.[29]

Rachel's early struggle with the material for *The Sea Around Us* was typical of her method of writing and repeated itself in more or less the same form whenever she embarked on any new project. Certainly her efforts to organize and interpret such a vast literature as that on the ocean were frustrating. But what Carson had to do was to wrestle with the subject until she found a personal approach to the material that satisfied her. Until she had discovered what that was, she endured real frustration and a certain necessary agony.

The April weekend with Marie in New York was a sort of turning point for Rachel. With about a third of the book in draft, both women agreed there was enough to allow Rodell to try to place it. Of nearly equal importance, Rodell had found a fellowship that would give Carson both the time and money she needed to finish the book. Through Mark Saxton of Harper & Brothers, she learned of the Eugene F. Saxton Memorial Trust, established by the publishing company, to provide assistance to writers of promise before they were recognized. Rodell accurately saw that Carson's credentials made her more competitive for the Saxton Fellowship in 1949 than she was for a Guggenheim whose grantees were typically more well-published scholars. With such a fellowship, Carson could take time off from her job at the Fish and Wildlife Service and still support her family.[30]

Rachel's meeting with William Beebe that same weekend was also fruitful. When she returned to Silver Spring, Rachel wrote Marie, "as a result of my talk with Beebe, I don't dare finish this book without getting under water, and he has me practically on the way to Bermuda, where he will make all sorts of advance arrangements so that I'll be sure of meeting the proper sharks, octopuses etc." More practically, Beebe consented readily to write a recommendation to the Saxton Foundation for Carson.[31]

Carson's application to the foundation reveals not only her initial conceptualization of the book but much about her needs as a writer. It confirms that she had started "specific research" during the previous summer and commenced writing very soon thereafter. Providing that she could arrange four months of uninterrupted work to concentrate exclusively on the book—two months in 1949, two in 1950—she estimated completion by the summer of 1950. She gave the names of William Beebe, Edwin Way Teale, Maria Leiper, and Elmer Higgins as references.

Carson's application emphasized that her project required extraordinary travel expenses that could not be financed by a publisher's advance. "In addition," Carson wrote, "I seriously need some early income from the book." She explained that her financial obligations included "the total support of my mother, with considerable medical care involved and assistance to another member of the family and money for rent."[32]

Carson's summary describes *Return to the Sea* as a blending of two things: "an imaginative searching out of what is humanly interesting and significant in the life history of the earth's ocean; and the answering of questions thus raised in the light of the best available scientific knowledge." Oceanography, she pointed out, was being studied on an unprecedented scale all over the world. Recent advances in oceanographic knowledge had completely altered scientists' conceptions of the sea.[33]

Less formally, she thought of it as a "book about the ocean that I myself would have enjoyed reading had some one else written it. Long before I became a student of biology, the ocean fascinated me. My mind was full of curiosity about it—of questions that remained largely unanswered through the years of formal education in zoology and later professional association with the field of marine biology." Never in doubt about her intended audience, Carson wanted it "to be read and enjoyed by everyone who has ever seen [the ocean] or who has felt its fascination even before standing on its shores." She also dared hope it would be a book "with which scientists will have no quarrel, and in which they may even find a fresh approach and a fresh interpretation of matters in a broad way familiar."

Convinced that human dependence on the resources of the ocean would increase in the years ahead, Carson reiterated what she had told William Beebe when she first embarked on the idea of an ocean profile. "The book will, I hope, carry something of my conviction of the dominating role played by the ocean in the course of earth history—how the very form and nature of our world has been shaped and modified by the sea—how all life everywhere carries with it the impress of its marine origin."[34]

Carson's objective was at one with her vision of her life's mission. She would educate and awaken as well as fascinate. She would tell the story of the intricate relationship between the life of the sea and the life of the land. Her focus would be on the long history of the ocean, revealing its beauty and its mystery. But her tale would not neglect the destruction that the human species had brought to the planet in its brief tenure here. "For the life that invaded the lands," Carson wrote, "has already so despoiled them it is being driven back more and more to its dependence on the sea." These themes would reappear in her work again and again.[35]

Soon after Rachel's visit to New York, Marie Rodell got an unexpected inquiry about her manuscript from Philip Vaudrin, the editor of Oxford University Press. The North American branch of the English press was in its early years of operation. Vaudrin was actively seeking books that would further Oxford's reputation in the United States for trade books, books for the general public rather than the academic books the press was known for.[36]

Vaudrin was a perfect choice to direct Oxford's American operations. He appraised individuals and situations quickly and usually accurately. He disliked extended negotiations. On April 10 he called Marie Rodell expressing an interest in seeing some of Carson's material. After a meeting with Vaudrin, Rodell sent Carson's four chapters and outline out on April 12, along with a letter telling Vaudrin that "Carson wants to go under the sea and Dr. Beebe is making arrangements for her to do so in Bermuda so an advance is even more imperative if she is to finish [the book] within a reasonable time."[37]

How *The Sea Around Us* was published is still the subject of apocryphal stories. At Oxford, the story persists that Carson's manuscript had been turned down by more than twenty trade houses before it came to them, when in fact the evidence is clear that Rodell had submitted it only to one other publisher.[38]

The part of the story that is credible is how Carson's book came to Vaudrin's attention in the first place. It seems that Oxford's East Coast sales representative heard about it from the owners of the Francis Scott Key Bookstore, a popular literary gathering place in Washington's Georgetown. He carried the news back to Vaudrin, who thought the subject sounded interesting and called Rodell. Oxford's in-house reading was positive, with one reader reporting that the manuscript "was particularly well written." Vaudrin sent it to only one outside reader, Daniel Merriman, the director of the Bingham Oceanographic Laboratory at Yale University. His evaluation was positive as well.[39]

Obviously anxious about the outcome of Oxford's interest, Rachel told Marie, "Be sure to let me know what the Oxford people say, whatever it is. This thing of sparing my feelings is all very well on some things but not on the book. If they are not interested there are some changes I want to make before you show it to anyone else." In early May Vaudrin wrote to Carson directly to arrange to meet her when he was in Washington for a bookseller's convention, telling her he hoped to conclude a "mutually satisfactory agreement" through Rodell for publication in the fall of 1950 and thoughtfully including a copy of Merriman's report. Rachel pronounced herself "profoundly satisfied with the whole business" thus far, but leaving nothing to chance and very little to Marie, she insisted on knowing exactly how close they were to a final contract before she met Vaudrin for lunch.[40]

Carson found Vaudrin charming, reporting to Rodell "I liked him immensely." Although they did not discuss contract details, Vaudrin told her Oxford was counting on an advance of $1,000 and wanted delivery of the manuscript by March 1, 1950—several months earlier than Carson planned. Jumping ahead in typical fashion, Carson was concerned about how Oxford would promote the book and how Marie intended to negotiate the all-important issue of foreign rights. Carson casually admitted that she had mentioned the subject of her next book to Vaudrin. "Mr. Vaudrin," Carson wrote Rodell with some amusement, "appears to have the impression that he extracted my book from you practically by force, when you came to see him about quite another matter; of course I did not disillusion him." To which Marie replied, "I am no end amused that Vaudrin never saw through that little strategy about your script—apparently in publishing as in sex, a man is always more eager for what one seems reluctant to offer him!"[41]

Rodell's skills in negotiating the Oxford contract established another dimension of the working relationship between writer and agent. Carson was always uncomfortable letting someone else handle her literary affairs, no mater how capable, and she fretted about every aspect of the proposed contract. Rodell exercised enormous patience and restraint, and terms were finally agreed on with some concessions on both sides.[42]

Carson adamantly rejected Vaudrin's demand that he see each chapter in draft as it was completed, complaining to Marie that it "would upset the scheme you and I worked out for just tearing ahead and getting the whole thing down, then revising." In reality, she was insulted that Vaudrin would treat her like a novice writer whose work he had to check. "He is not going to see any rough drafts!" Rachel told Marie. "That, my dear, is a privilege only you can have."[43]

Carson signed the Oxford contract on June 28. Less than a week later, much to her relief, Rodell sent the promised advance, less 10 percent commission. The Carson-Rodell team had their first winner. Manuscript delivery was set for March 1, 1950.

While Marie had been negotiating, Rachel worked on two more chapters, one dealing with the ocean surface, the other on shorelines. "Last week," she told Marie with light good humor, "was fairly productive, the only trouble being the fine weather that lured me to work in the back yard, where there are baby birds to be saved from cats, squirrels who want to be fed peanuts, and all manner of calls and movements overhead, requiring investigations. Please send me a pair of the things you put on horses (blinders?); also ear plugs." Rachel finished the drafts, working over the Fourth of July weekend and evenings, but she would not let Marie see them until she was satisfied with her revisions and her mother had retyped them. At the same time she was preparing her itinerary for two important research trips in July.[44]

Uncertainty about her finances and the difficulty of taking leave from her job forced Carson to revise her plans for diving in Bermuda. An invitation from Dr. F. G. Walton-Smith, one of the biologists at the Miami Marine Laboratory, to join his summer class in Miami convinced Carson that it would be better to take her "Great Undersea Adventure," as she called it, with his group in the more accessible waters of southern Florida. Diving there offered the advantage of combining research on the book with official Fish and Wildlife Service business. For the service publications' series, Carson wanted to visit the refuge in the Everglades as well as several FWS sites in the Florida Keys. In between, she could go out diving with Dr. Walton-Smith and his class.

Always ready for a naturalist outing, Shirley Briggs decided to take her vacation and keep Rachel company in Florida. Shirley was eager to photograph water birds, and since she enjoyed the ocean, she hoped she might have the opportunity to dive as well.[45]

Arranging for the other research trip was more difficult. Carson had been talking for some time with officials at the FWS Fisheries Station at Woods Hole about joining one of their research trips to the Georges Bank, a deeply submerged sandbank in the Atlantic Ocean 200 miles east of Boston and south of Nova Scotia, known for both its productive fishing and its dangerous cross-currents and fog. Service officials, however, were reluctant to allow a single woman to join the all-male crew, even as an observer. In late June Carson had the inspired idea of asking Marie Rodell if she would like to go along as a "chaperon." Marie was always ready to travel and delighted to play the part, vowing to write an article about the trip entitled "I Was a Chaperon on a Fishing Boat." This arrangement satisfied the Fisheries bureaucracy. Rachel planned both the Florida and Woods Hole trips back to back in July, barely giving herself enough time in between to see her mother and repack her bags.[46]

Rachel and Shirley left for Miami on the Atlantic Coast Line sleeper train on July 11 and arrived in Miami the next afternoon. There they found comfortable accommodations at the Atlantic Towers on Miami Beach and made contact with Jack Watson, a FWS patrolman, who took them out in his shallow-drafted speed boat for a memorable sixty-mile tour of the opalescent waters of Florida Bay.

The following day Fred Finneran, another FWS patrolman who lived in the interior of the Everglades with only his puppy and a seven-foot-long blue indigo snake, joined them for a trip into the outer areas of the refuge along the Tamiami Trail. Rachel was struck by the stark beauty of the Everglades. Once again she found qualities there in the inland terrain that reminded her of the sea. In her field notes she observed,

> The feeling here is of immense space, from the utter flatness of the land and the great expanse of sky. The cloud effects were beautiful and always changing, dark and ominous in the west and north—white and fleecy with rainbow lights in them. Rain came in over

> the grass, making a beautiful soft play of changing color—all grey and soft green. There is the feeling that the land has formed only the thinnest veneer over this underlying platform of the ancient sea. The feeling of space is almost the same as at sea, from the flatness of the landscape and the dominance of the sky.[47]

Both Rachel and Shirley wanted to see more of the refuge interior than the Tamiami Trail allowed. At Finneran's suggestion, they were able to arrange a trip deep into the Everglades interior with Don Poppenhager, a local guide, who had developed a conveyance known as a glades buggy. Poppenhager had never taken two women into the swamp before and was skeptical that they could endure the discomfort, the mosquitoes, and the long hours, but Carson and Briggs convinced him they could meet the challenge.

The next morning the two were up at dawn. Dressed in heavy work pants and shirts and armed with mosquito repellent, they were picked up at their fashionable hotel by a large Service truck at 5:00 A.M. and driven to the end of the Tamiami Trail to a little store where Poppenhager and his glades buggy were waiting. Rachel later recalled,

> It was built something like a tractor, with six pairs of very large wheels. Its engine was completely naked and exposed, and during the trip blasted its heat on the three of us perched on the buggy's single seat. There were various tools—pliers, screwdrivers, etc—in a little rack against the motor block, and from time to time Mr. Poppenhager leaned out as we jogged along and turned something or jabbed at the motor. It seemed to be in a perpetual state of boiling over; and now and then Mr. P. would stop and get out with a tin can and dip up some water—there was water everywhere—and pour it into the radiator.[48]

But the glades buggy worked fine, and Poppenhager miraculously knew where he was going in the roadless expanse of grass and sky.

"It clambers over old coral reefs with no more than severe lurching, creaking and clouds of steam from the radiator," Briggs wrote her mother in Iowa. "The man [Don Poppenhager] who took us gave us to understand, at the end of the 9 hour jaunt, that our deportment had been a pleasant surprise. Few men, he claims, would go out into those places, and we had done so without complaint, even when it rained in torrents.

We, in turn, were so enthralled by the whole experience, and our luck at finding him and his vehicle, that it was a mutual admiration society."[49]

Carson had better luck exploring the Florida Everglades than she did the ocean floor. On at least three separate occasions Rachel, Shirley, and Dr. Walton-Smith's class embarked in the little dive boat the *Nauplius* and attempted to find a suitably protected reef from which to dive. But the weather refused to cooperate. Overcast and stormy, sudden high winds whipped the water, making diving impossible, especially for a novice. Finally on the fourth trip, Walton-Smith told Carson he would give her a lifeline and let her go down the ladder at least. By the time they anchored on the shoal of the reef, the horizon was dark and thunder rumbled in the distance. Dressed in her Sears Roebuck work pants and a long-sleeved shirt over her bathing suit, Carson took the lifeline and went down the ladder to shoulder depth, where she donned the eighty-four-pound diving helmet.[50]

As she lowered herself into the water rung by rung, her first view was of waving sea fans. Feeling desperately for the next rung, she found that her foot was caught in a tangled patch of these gorgonians. Her field notes on this, her first and only dive, show that despite adverse conditions the experience of being underwater was like no other.

> Pressure on the ears at first annoying—relieved by repeated swallowing. Sound of air coming in an agonized gasping and gulping. Perhaps by suggestion I found myself breathing heavily. Bottom proved far from smooth or level—all mounds and crevices and slopes and hollows—big niggerhead corals as high as my head, gorgonians, sea fans. Visibility very poor due to London fog effect. Some small highly colored fishes nothing else moving. Considerable current running—because of this and slippery uneven, bottom, did not stray from ladder.[51]

Although Walton-Smith took them out again two days later, high winds sabotaged this attempt as well. Rachel was keenly disappointed that her experience underwater was so brief and that it could not have been more relaxed, or the visibility better. But she had at last experienced with her eyes and her body, rather than her imagination and intellect, what it was like to be under the sea and to look up at the water's surface. It was the perspective she had longed to see.

Writing to Beebe afterward, Carson realistically appraised what the dive had meant to her.

> I had the bad luck to strike stormy weather at Miami but after several abortive attempts I finally got down, under conditions that were far from ideal—water murky, the current so strong I could not walk around but hung onto the ladder. But the difference between having dived—even under those conditions—and never having dived is so tremendous that it formed one of those milestones of life, after which everything seems a little different.[52]

Several years later she forgot the adverse conditions. What remained was the memory of what "the surface of the water look[ed] like from underneath and how exquisitely delicate and varied the colors displayed by the animals of the reef, and I got the feeling of the misty green vistas of a strange, nonhuman world."[53]

The success of the Florida trip was complete when Maria Carson telephoned midweek to tell Rachel that she had received the Saxton Fellowship. Freed from financial anxiety about taking leave, Carson resolved to complete her research as quickly as she could. After a quick stop at home in Silver Spring to change clothes and gear, she was off to Woods Hole to meet Marie Rodell and the high seas.[54]

The Fish and Wildlife Services' *Albatross III*, a converted otter trawler commissioned in March 1948, was a worthy successor to the legendary *Albatross* that had explored the oceans of the world in the late nineteenth century. Built for the Fish Commission in 1882, it was the first vessel specifically designed for deep-sea research. Its dredge hauls were so plentiful that it took decades to classify its treasures. The *Albatross III* had been a gift of General Seafood in 1939 but had not been completely converted to research purposes when the war started. The U.S. Navy requisitioned it and rebuilt it as a patrol vessel. Converted yet again into a research ship in 1948, its various incarnations made it a long, narrow, strange-looking vessel with a distinctive superstructure.[55]

Carson's official mission was to collect material for future publications about the *Albatross III* and its mission in conserving the fishery resources of the New England banks. Unofficially, she could experience firsthand the currents, the winds, the fog, and the ever-changing surface of the sea as well as observe the contents of each catch from the ocean floor.[56]

Even as early as the 1940s commercial fish were becoming increasingly scarce on the Georges Bank. To find out how to maintain and increase the fish populations, the *Albatross III* was assigned to make a census of the ground fish population of the fisheries of the northwest Atlantic by systematically fishing over a selected series of stations on the New England banks, simultaneously collecting scientific data on the fish, the water temperatures, and depth.[57]

July 27 was an unusually hot, humid day on Cape Cod when Rachel and Marie arrived at the harbor in Woods Hole, clutching their bottles of Dramamine and trying to ignore the skeptical glances of the crew. Marie's first impression of the ship the night before had not been favorable. "No one could call her pretty," she wrote in her diary. But they had been assigned the comparatively elegant quarters of the vessel's chief scientist, Raymond Buller, which had the luxury of a washstand and desk. As they steamed out through the channel that led past Pollack's Rip Lighthouse into the embrace of the fog, the two women were given a tour of the scientific areas with wet and dry laboratories, the pilot house and chart room, and the galley and crew's quarters, which were reached down a spindly ladder from an open hatch in the center of the forward deck. They were treated to an explanation of the workings of the two huge dragging nets and the techniques of trawling.

The ship's officers also took pains to explain how the long, narrow ship rolled like a canoe at sea, how everyone got violently seasick, how bad the food was, and how gruesome the accidents that frequently happened handling the heavy fishing gear. Too tired to stay up until they reached the first trawling station at midnight, Rachel and Marie went off to bed, hoping they had enough food stashed in their room that they could avoid going down the galley ladder in a storm.[58]

As Rachel later retold the story of their first tow that night, their sleep was interrupted by a tremendous crash. "Surely," they thought, "we had been rammed by another vessel. Then a series of the most appalling bangs, chunks, and rumbles began directly over our heads, a rhythmic thundering of machinery that would put any boiler factory to shame. Finally it dawned upon us that this was fishing! It also dawned on us that this was what we had to endure for the next ten nights." The next morning the crew was eager to learn how well they had slept. When they feigned ignorance of any particular disturbance, they were accepted; soon they were able to sleep through the uproar of the late-night tows.[59]

For the next nine days, Carson and Rodell were on hand for all the daytime tows and waited expectantly for the bit net to disgorge its contents on the deck. Fish were counted, measured, and in some cases tagged and thrown back. One of the big nets was torn badly on the second day, when it was towed over a large bed of mussels, but that misfortune was offset by the later discovery of a large bed of sea scallops.

One of Carson's objectives on the cruise was to observe the oceanographic instruments on the ship: the bathythermagraph, which recorded ocean temperature, and the echo-sounder, which traced the contours of the ocean floor. She wrote later that "the high point of the cruise was seeing, with the aid of the echo-sounder, the great undersea canyons that cut into the outer rim of the Georges Bank. It was an extremely dramatic thing to watch the level ocean floor pass beneath us, then suddenly drop away in a deep, V-shaped chasm."[60]

For Rachel the most unforgettable impression of the voyage was the sight of the net coming into view from the deepest parts of the ocean with its cargo of fish, crabs, sponges, starfish, lobster, and other more exotic creatures that she had never seen before. "The deep-water starfish" she found "especially lovely, and sometimes there were heart urchins and such odd beings as sea mice. Scores of different species of fishes were brought up to give their own mute testimony as to who lived down in the undersea world of Georges Bank."[61]

Carson found the ocean at night a wondrous sight. "The sun was perfectly visible," she wrote, "a pale silver disk casting a soft radiance over its path through the fog. The most striking effect of the fog is that of being enclosed in a steadily shrinking room as the fog creeps in, shutting out all sight of what it has already engulfed." Fascinated by fog, the light, and the sea, she felt she was in a scene described by Samuel Coleridge. Nights on the *Albatross III* gave her once more the long perspective of geologic time and the ability to stand back from the immediacy of human perspective, conscious of the immensity of the water world.[62]

Carson drew directly upon her *Albatross* notes for the chapter "Wind, Sun and the Spinning of the Earth," writing there,

> Day after day the "Albatross" moved in a small circular room, whose walls were soft gray curtains and whose floor had a glassy smoothness. Sometimes a petrel flew, with swallow-like flutterings, across this room, entering and leaving it by passing through its walls as if by sorcery. Evenings, the sun, before it set, was a pale silver disc hung in the ship's rigging, the drifting streamers of fog

> picking up a diffused radiance and creating a scene that set us searching our memories for quotations from Coleridge.[63]

When Cruise 26 was over, Chief Buller pronounced it the most successful census of the Georges Bank yet. The scientific staff and the ship's crew cooperated well and together had documented an important nursery ground for immature haddock off the bank's northern ridge. From the diaries Marie Rodell kept of the voyage, she drew material for a three-part series later published in the bulletin of the National Academy of Sciences.[64]

When Carson got back to Silver Spring, she stayed up most of the night sharing her voyage with her mother. Enjoying the delights of civilization again, she wrote Marie in good humor, "I'm thinking of taking another Albatross cruise—I lost four pounds on this one. Also, have acquired a nasty cold." Marie found several crucial inches around her waist and hips missing and was invigorated by their expedition. Ten days on the *Albatross III* voyage had deepened their friendship, and they now closed their letters to each other with love.[65]

Their voyage had given Rachel time to talk to Marie about other book projects she had in mind. The most immediate and the most exciting was a color catalog of the dramatic Mexican bird plates drawn by the master bird painter Louis Agassiz Fuertes, plates that recently had been unearthed in the Fish and Wildlife Service Library. Carson wanted to write an extended introduction to the collection, including a biographical sketch of Fuertes. Rodell thought the idea worthy and Vaudrin's interest was piqued, so when Carson returned she began making inquiries about the status of the plates and even contacted Fuertes's estate.[66]

In addition to writing and revising chapters for the yet-unnamed book, she and Bob Hines began making an itemized inventory of the Fuertes birds of Mexico and looking for the artist's Mexican notebooks. Convinced it would be an easy book to get out and enthusiastic about its prospects, she invited Vaudrin to join Marie in Washington to see the paintings and discuss her idea with FWS assistant director Clarence Cottam.[67]

But in October Vaudrin decided the costs of color reproduction were too expensive and declined the book for Oxford. Undaunted, Rachel asked Marie to approach several other publishing houses, including Houghton Mifflin Company, the old-line Boston house that maintained a small New York office. Rodell made an appointment for them to meet with Paul Brooks, editor-in-chief of Houghton Mifflin's general book department, in mid-December when Carson would be in town.

After speaking to Rodell about Carson, Brooks read *Under the Sea-Wind*. "I liked it so much," he wrote Rodell, "that I read every word with pleasure and admiration. It is a superb job in a field where really good books are rare. If she has any further book projects that are not tied up, I'd like very much to hear about them. In fact, I have a somewhat uncrystallized idea myself that I'd like to discuss with her."[68]

Paul Brooks was only two years older than Rachel Carson, but his gracious, almost courtly manner, his Bostonian reserve, and his literary sophistication must have made him seem more her senior than he was. He was a man who exuded good taste, education, and cultural refinement. But his Brahmin image was softened by a contagious smile, a compassionate nature, and a delightful sense of humor. An antique illustration of a Wild West character wrestling a bear hung on his office wall in Boston. Below it, Brooks had captioned "The Author/Publisher Relationship."[69]

He already knew Marie Rodell, but he had never met the reserved Fish and Wildlife Service editor Rachel Carson, who sat primly with her agent in his Manhattan office dressed in a dark suit, gloves, and a proper pillbox hat with a short veil decorously covering the upper part of her face. Brooks and Carson had much in common. He was an accomplished naturalist and an enthusiastic amateur ornithologist. He was also a friend of the American ornithologist and illustrator Roger Tory Peterson with whom Carson served on the board of directors of the Audubon Society of the District of Columbia. Brooks was the editor of Peterson's field guides to the birds of North America and was well acquainted with Louis Fuertes's work. Without much enthusiasm, he agreed to consider Carson's idea for a folio edition of the newly discovered plates. In the meantime, Brooks had a project of his own he thought might interest her.[70]

Several months earlier one of Brooks's editors had come to him with the idea of finding an author to write a handbook or guide that would be biologically sophisticated enough to teach the general public about the life cycle of common shore creatures. Brooks liked the idea but had no one in mind to do it. As he spoke with Carson about her current book on the ocean, he wondered if she would have any interest in the idea.

She did, of course, telling Brooks of her earlier discussion with Edwin Way Teale on writing just such a book. Brooks and Carson concluded their amicable discussion with a verbal commitment for a seashore guide that Carson would begin after she delivered her manuscript to Oxford. Brooks would draw up a contract for Rodell to review, and he promised to get back to them about the Fuertes project.[71]

By the end of the year, Carson had been officially on leave for the month of October and several weeks in December, although various editorial crises kept bringing her back into the office. Nevertheless, the revised chapters on islands, waves, and currents were in the hands of Mrs. Frey, the typist Rodell had hired for Rachel in New York. Meanwhile Rachel struggled with the difficult chapter on bottom topography and the reorganization of separate chapters on sediments, tides, and shorelines. At the same time she sent completed chapters to various experts to evaluate and made plans to visit other East Coast scientists to check her information.

Throughout February and March, Rachel and Marie debated possible titles. Both were unsatisfied with *Return to the Sea*, which did not capture the whole epic. *The Story of the Ocean* satisfied Carson's desire that the title not sound textbookish nor be mistaken for poetry or fiction, but Rodell thought it boring. *Story of the Sea*, *Empire of the Sea*, and even *Sea Without End* were considered and rejected. Even Bert Walford and his imaginative gang at FWS were unable to think of something suitable. "Current suggestions from irreverent friends and relatives," Carson told Rodell "include 'Out of My Depth' and 'Carson at Sea.' If they would only employ their brains constructively."[72]

While Rachel searched for the perfect title, Marie continued to try to interest magazine publishers in first serial rights. But even the *Atlantic* turned Carson's chapters down. In what seems astonishingly bad judgment, many editors considered her writing too poetic for a work of nonfiction. As the rejections piled up, a frustrated Carson responded with a stream of frantic and often contradictory instructions to Rodell.[73]

But even with these occasional outbursts, Rachel doggedly turned out material, endlessly rewriting and reorganizing. With leftover travel money, she hired Ida Johnson, the FWS librarian, whom she described as a "perfect ferret at finding things," to help give her more time to write. Her final East Coast trip turned out to be logistically difficult. In the end she opted to consult with Maurice Ewing by mail instead of going to Woods Hole. She spent two days at the Harvard Observatory talking over new material on climate and meteorology with Charles Brooks, and a day at Yale with oceanographers Daniel Merriman and Carl Dunbar. As an unexpected bonus Thor Heyerdahl, the author and sailor who had just finished writing *Kon-Tiki*, agreed to read her chapter on the open sea and was enthusiastic in his praise of it.[74]

The closer Carson got to finishing, the more her tension and frustration mounted as she found it necessary to take work home with her from the office, making her leave time nearly worthless. In addition, her younger niece, Marjorie, who was struggling to put herself through college, came down with a serious sinus and ear infection complicated by her diabetes and required Carson's care and attention. "None of the present or future is very favorable for the last desperate push," she complained to Marie, "but I am grimly determined to finish somehow. I feel now that I'd die if this went on much longer!"[75]

Rachel had asked Kay Howe to do a few select drawings for the book: an illustrated chart of geologic time, an ancient sea serpent for the frontispiece, and one or two others that were never used because Carson could not afford to buy them. Kay gave Rachel suggestions for the book's general design and page layout and advised her on the best way to reproduce ancient maps of the ocean Carson had to line the front and back inside covers.[76]

But by mid-February it was obvious that she could not meet Oxford's deadline of March 1. Rodell negotiated a new date with Vaudrin that gave Carson the breathing room she needed. "I would have died if I'd had to get the book in about now," Carson told Rodell gratefully, "all the energy I had remaining deserted me last week, and so my accomplishments are nil."[77]

By the end of March, though, Carson's spirits were improving. The experts to whom she had been sending her chapters were exuberant in their praise. Wave expert Walter Munk at the Scripps Institute wrote, "It was really a pleasure to read your well written chapter on wind and water. Of all non-mathematical accounts I have read on this subject, yours is easily the best." And Henry Bigelow's review elated her. "Your book will stand for a long time . . . I have read every word of the manuscript with great pleasure."[78]

The first week of June brought word from *The New Yorker* that it was interested in several chapters for condensation in its "Profiles" column. Its editors asked for other chapters to consider. *Science Digest* and *The Yale Review* also made offers for some of the same chapters.[79]

While *The New Yorker* dithered over which chapters it wanted, sending some back and asking to see others a second time, Rachel finished up the manuscript. Back in April, she had written Philip Vaudrin at Oxford, "We have made so many title suggestions that I'm afraid I have lost track—did we ever mention 'The Sea Around Us'?" They had, but now author and editor agreed it seemed the most likely candidate. So the title was finally settled. Carson was already concerned about such issues as typeface, the size and thickness of the book, and the dust jacket's design. As an editor, she had definite opinions about how she wanted the book to look, and she intended to fight for them.[80]

Finally, at the end of June, Carson handed in the completed manuscript to Oxford. But she continued to revise and make additions to chapters so that she never had the sense of total completion. "Oddly enough," she told Marie, "I am less relieved at being delivered of my book than I expected to be." Thinking ahead of prizes and awards, Carson wondered which chapter she could submit for the American Association for the Advancement of Science's (AAAS) George Westinghouse Science Writing prize. To be eligible, it had to be published by the end of September. She suggested that Marie send the islands chapter to the *Yale Review* in place of the one she had withdrawn when *The New Yorker* initially was interested in it. "Authors' judgments are notoriously poor, I know," she told Rodell, "but I've always liked that chapter and it seems to me significant what with all our interest in far Pacific islands."[81]

Then there was the matter of the John Burroughs Memorial medal, a prize honoring the best book on natural history published in a given year. Through her service on the D.C. Audubon Society board, she had learned from Roger Tory Peterson that he had been named to the Burroughs prize committee. Peterson told her to be sure that Oxford submitted her book to the Burroughs trustees.

As soon as the manuscript had been accepted by Oxford, Carson wrote Rodell somewhat disingenuously, "I have heard several bits of gossip to the effect that the Burroughs people would like to consider my book for next year's award—all quite unofficial and off-the-record, of course, but from good sources. Perhaps you can see to it that advance copies are in the proper hands early enough to assure consideration. I can get the names of the Directors if you do not have them. . . ."[82]

Until the end of June, Rodell did not know for certain which of the *New Yorker* editors was interested in *The Sea Around Us*. Finally she learned that staff editor Edith Oliver had commended Carson's manuscript to editor-in-chief, William Shawn, who more than shared her enthusiasm for it. Several weeks later Oliver suggested to Rodell that, because the magazine was already committed to material for a year in advance, any serialization of *The Sea Around Us* would require Oxford to postpone publication by at least that long. Both Carson and Rodell vigorously opposed such a course.[83]

Negotiations came to a temporary halt in August when Edith Oliver told Rodell that Shawn still wanted to hold on to several chapters, promising a final decision by the middle of the month. "Darn the *New Yorker*," Rachel wrote her agent when she learned of the latest postponement, "I wish they'd get busy with waves and get it in print by September some time. It just might mean a thousand bucks, plus some nice advertising."[84]

Apologizing to Marie for a peevish letter in which she gave yet more directions on serial sales, Rachel told her "do what you think best. [My ideas] were the product of an afternoon when I was feeling too cussed with a cold to do anything but think up work for other people."[85]

True to his word, William Shawn called Marie Rodell on August 15 with an offer to buy not one but nine of the fourteen chapters of *The Sea Around Us*. He would condense the chapters himself and they would appear as a "Profile of the Sea" in three parts. His offer for first serial rights was $7,200, payable in three installments; two of $1,000, and a final payment of $5,200.

Carson's acceptance of Shawn's terms was made on the condition that Oxford's publication not be delayed. Rodell held firm and the next day *The New Yorker* editors agreed to Carson's terms. Serialization was set for late winter. The author, the agent, and the publisher expressed themselves well satisfied with the arrangements. In a single sale and even after Rodell's 10 percent commission, Carson made more money than her $6,400 annual government salary.[86]

Two days later the *Yale Review* offered $75 for "The Birth of an Island." After more hard negotiating by Rodell, the editors agreed to include it in the September issue so that it could be considered for the AAAS prize. *Science Digest* ended up with the chapter "Wealth from the Salt Seas," paying more for it than its editors originally offered. And this was just the beginning.

An exuberant Marie Rodell reported to Rachel that Edith Oliver had invited her out for a congratulatory drink. With her usual style, Rodell brought Oliver two tiny dark-red orchids for the occasion. Marie told Rachel she gave them to Oliver "with love and kisses from both of us." Carson cabled her plucky agent in response, "I am still in a daze about your news—all I know is how lucky I am to have you."[87]

8

"A Subject Very Close to My Heart"

After she delivered *The Sea Around Us* to Oxford and signed the contract for *The New Yorker* serialization, the first thing Rachel wanted to do was to get out of the muggy heat and humidity that oppresses Washington every August. She had planned two short trips that month. The first was a weekend jaunt to Island Beach, New Jersey, on the southern end of the Barnegat Peninsula, an area threatened by development that was much in the news. The other outing would take her to Amherst, Massachusetts, to visit her friend Alice Mullen, then on to the coastal town of Rockport, where Marie Rodell would join her for a long, cool Labor Day weekend. "I find it hard to separate avocations from vocation," she once wrote in answer to an author questionnaire, "for the things I most enjoy doing contribute to my writing, ornithology, walking the beach, exploring a tide pool."[1]

Island Beach, a private preserve owned by the Henry Phipps family, was one of the last remaining examples of pristine barrier ecology on the mid-Atlantic coast. The Phipps heirs needed to sell the property, and in order to forestall commercial development, the Island Beach National Monument Committee had organized under the leadership of Rachel's friend, conservationist Richard Pough. Carson wrote Pough in August, "The saving of some such place before it is forever too late is, of course, a subject very close to my heart."[2]

Rachel wanted to publish an article about Island Beach in a periodical where it would do some good. Pough arranged a private visit to the property so she could get the feel of it. Shirley Briggs and Rachel's niece,

Marjie Williams, would come with her. Pough was happy to have Carson visit, explaining to Captain Joseph Tilton, who controlled permits to the preserve, that Carson was "unquestionably the country's outstanding writer on seashore areas, and I know that her article . . . can do our cause a tremendous amount of good."[3]

Anticipating a quiet, relaxing holiday, Rachel planned to get to their hotel in nearby Tom's River, New Jersey, early so they could spend the afternoon at the beach. But her plans were spoiled when the brake cylinder in her car collapsed shortly after starting out, causing them to miss most of a sunny day of exploration and picture taking. Tilton opened the gates of the preserve for them the following morning.

Shirley Briggs described the area as the most varied beach she had seen. Although most of the bird breeding season was over, there were young herons, osprey still in their nests atop telephone poles, and an island ecology nearly undisturbed by humans, fire, or grazing. The group had plenty of time to picnic, swim, take photographs, and explore.[4]

The following morning, however, they found the sanctuary enveloped in an oppressive haze. A hurricane offshore at Cape Hatteras was expected to reach Island Beach in the early afternoon. After watching the surf breaking farther and farther out all morning, they reluctantly set out for home. Carson told Pough later "I think what I may do is to treat it along with other, as yet relatively unspoiled seashore areas (Hatteras, Ocracoke, etc.) in a piece about what we are going to lose if we're not careful."[5]

This support for Island Beach is the earliest expression of Carson's interest in saving wild areas, although her ideas about the preservation of natural areas, whether they were seashore, oceanic atoll, or inland wilderness, were clearly formulated and emotionally significant by the autumn of 1950. After World War II, she recognized that even the most enlightened conservation policies would not always and everywhere protect wild nature from the engines of industrial progress or from human greed and ignorance.

Carson enthusiastically supported the federal conservation policies that had created refuge and national park systems. But as her personal experiences deepened her intellectual and spiritual connections with nature, she became more troubled by the political implications of multiple-use conservation, especially the economic and technological pressures to reduce and transform the natural world. Her professional experience in the FWS, the experts whom she consulted in the course of her research in marine biology and oceanography, and her associations in the Audubon Society of the District of Columbia combined with her emotional response to nature to inform her ideas about the proper relationship between humans and the living world.

By 1950 Carson had been in the Fish and Wildlife Service bureaucracy for nearly fourteen years. Her experience in the field and on the policy-making staff of the Division of Information as well as the influence of her scientific associates in fishery and wildlife biology and those of the visiting scientists who came in and out of service headquarters cannot be underestimated as a source of her deepening connection with nature or of her commitment to the preservation of unspoiled natural areas.[6]

Throughout the 1940s Carson wrote speeches for Interior Department staff and others advocating a variety of conservation measures. She watched while conservation legislation introduced by her agency was altered by special interests such as timber, mining, grazing, and even recreation. As an editor she experienced firsthand how difficult it was to reconcile the values that dominated conservation policies within different agencies of the same department. Even within her own agency, scientists in the Divisions of Fishery Biology, Wildlife Research, Commercial Fisheries, and Predator Control often held conflicting views on wildlife protection measures, sometimes reflecting the varied interests of commercial fishermen, ranchers, loggers, and sport hunters.

Carson's friend Charles Alldredge was an avid supporter of The Wilderness Society and introduced Carson to Howard Zahniser, its low-key but passionate director, sometime in 1946. There is no record of exactly when Carson joined The Wilderness Society, but she was a member by 1950. She adamantly opposed the Bureau of Reclamation's proposal to build a dam in Echo Park that would flood the unique canyon formations and fossil beds of Dinosaur National Monument on the Utah-Colorado border.[7]

By this time Rachel Carson had put together an impressive network of scientific colleagues, experts who supported her oceanographic research and who were impressed by her ability to write not only beautiful but scientifically accurate explanations of the natural world. Some, such as Henry Bigelow, William Beebe, Robert Cushman Murphy, Richard Pough, Clarence Cottam, and Ray Fosberg, became personal friends. Others, such as Swedish oceanographer Hans Pettersson, and marine scientists Harry Ladd, Henry Stetson, Maurice Ewing, H. A. Marmer, and

Daniel Merriman, were cordial colleagues with whom she enjoyed an easy intellectual exchange. Such dialogues also helped forge Carson's views.

To these men of science, Carson added another network of naturalists and nature writers whose work she admired and drew from: writers such as Hendrik van Loon, Ada Govan, Edwin Way Teale, Thor Heyerdahl, Louis Halle, and Henry Beston. They did not necessarily have the same view of humankind's relationship to nature, but all of them confronted similar problems of writing about the natural world. With many of these associates Carson also shared not only the common bond of nature writing and natural history but also a passionate interest in birds.

Carson's early and lifelong interest in ornithology was another important source of her love of the natural world. Initiated into birding and bird lore by her mother, the Audubon Society of D.C., which in 1950 changed its name to the Audubon Naturalist Society of the Central Atlantic States (ANS), enlarged her interest. In the immediate postwar years, before Carson began writing *The Sea Around Us*, she was particularly active in their activities. Its magazine, *The Wood Thrush*, later *The Atlantic Naturalist*, was edited by Carson's friend Shirley Briggs. Carson often chaired the publications committee and frequently wrote book reviews.[8] What little social life she had centered around ANS activities. Birding trips to the Jersey shore, to Hawk Mountain in Pennsylvania, to Cheat Mountain in West Virginia, to the eastern shores of Maryland and Virginia, countless morning bird walks around Washington, and many enjoyable evening lecture programs were all events sponsored by the local Audubon Society.[9]

Irston Barnes, an indefatigable champion of environmental causes and the author of a nationally syndicated column for *The Washington Post* on naturalist topics, was president of the Society from 1946 to 1962. Barnes, Louis Halle, and Roger Tory Peterson had revived the languishing local Audubon group after the war and made it a voice on regional conservation issues.[10]

Carson was first elected to the Audubon Society Board in 1948. Her other colleagues on the board in the late 1940s included George Washington University zoology professor Paul Bartsch, who among other things had been Mary Scott Skinker's doctoral adviser; geographer, author, and philanthropist Millicent Todd Bingham; retired admiral and preservation activist Neill Phillips; conservation ornithologist William Vogt, who was then the conservation director of the Pan American

Union; the noted ornithologist Alexander Wetmore, then secretary of the Smithsonian Institution, who was an honorary vice president. Gilbert Grovesnor, the founder and president of the National Geographic Society, and his wife, were also active members. Carson went off the ANS board in the fall of 1950 but was reelected again in 1955, serving with Howard Zahniser and Clarence Cottam.[11]

Interest in and enthusiasm for birds brought not only this remarkable group together but also linked Carson to William Beebe, Robert Cushman Murphy, Richard Pough, Edwin Way Teale, and naturalist John Kieran, all enthusiastic birders who were active in their respective state Audubon societies. Carson's colleagues in FWS and ANS formed circles within circles. They were her earliest professional networks and ones she consciously cultivated. By the time Carson had finished *The Sea Around Us*, she was established in a broad community of scientists, naturalists, and writers in and outside the federal government, who knew and respected her work. Her social relationships, her professional work, and her writing all revolved around nature and the living world.[12]

While she waited impatiently for Oxford to decide on a publishing schedule, she found herself thinking about all the things she had left out of *The Sea Around Us*. Her files grew thick with additions and corrections to include in a second edition. But other projects demanded her attention. Driven by her emotional and financial need to produce as much as fast as she could, she worked on three or four pieces simultaneously, a necessary but precarious juggling act that often invited unexpected anxiety.[13]

Paul Brooks had inconveniently gone off on a western vacation before he and Carson could conclude their negotiations on the scope and content of the seashore guide or agree on when she would produce it. Because Marie cautioned Rachel not to spend too much time thinking about it until these issues were resolved, Carson worked on an outline for a book of essays on her reflections as a naturalist.[14]

Carson thought the essays would be the sort of thing *The New Yorker* would like. "If *The New Yorker* loves me," she wrote Rodell, "they should be ready for one or two of the essays next summer and fall. That seems to me the most important thing ahead—to keep contributing to *The New Yorker* as long as they want me to."[15]

Also high on Carson's agenda was finding a publisher to reissue *Under the Sea-Wind* as soon as *The Sea Around Us* was published. But at the moment she could not afford even the $150 that Simon & Schuster wanted for the publishing rights and the gravure negatives of Howard

Frech's illustrations, which were moldering in a warehouse where Marie Leiper, her former editor, protected them from being melted down until Carson could find the money. Rodell suggested that she might consider using some of *The New Yorker* payment when she got it or, alternatively, push Paul Brooks to buy the rights to *Under the Sea-Wind* at the same time as they negotiated the contract for the shore book. Eventually Rachel bought them herself.[16]

In spare moments at her Fish and Wildlife office, she captioned the Fuertes bird plates and sorted through correspondence about his drawings. Her new FWS boss, Alastair MacBain, supported her plan to reproduce the paintings and was prepared to help her obtain the necessary permissions from the service when she found a publisher.

MacBain had been named director of the Division of Information in the late spring of 1950, replacing Frank Dufresne. The change had given Carson a new lease on life at the service. MacBain, a fine professional writer, was not only enthusiastic about the Fuertes project but was also receptive to Carson's need for an extended period of leave without pay in order to research the seashore book. With MacBain's blessing, she decided once again to see if the guide might be the basis of a Guggenheim award.[17]

Prizes, fellowships, and publicity were very much on Carson's mind, especially with the September 1950 publication of "The Birth of an Island" in *The Yale Review*. Ray Fosberg, the tropical botanist, who had reviewed Carson's chapter, called it "the finest account of the creation and colonization of a oceanic island" that he had ever read. His assessment was later shared by many readers.[18]

"The Birth of an Island" vividly sets forth Carson's conception of the long rhythms of an orderly evolution. She contrasts the slow emergence of an island and its unique collection of flora and fauna and precarious existence with humankind's rapacious destruction of island habitats. In one of her strongest statements of outrage at humankind's shortsighted ignorance, Carson concluded,

> The tragedy of the oceanic islands lies in the uniqueness, the irreplaceability of the species they have developed, by the slow process of the ages. In a reasonable world men would have treated these islands as precious possessions, as natural museums filled with beautiful and curious works of creation, valuable beyond price because nowhere in the world are they duplicated.[19]

Quoting one of her favorite naturalists, W. H. Hudson, Carson ended the article with the chilling statement "the beautiful has vanished and returns not."[20]

Exhausted but unable to relax or rest, Carson had a physical checkup in late August. On the day before she was to leave for her vacation in Massachusetts, she wrote Rodell that she had decided to postpone the trip for a couple of weeks. "The reasons are several and slightly complex," she told her obliquely, "but about ten o'clock last night it seemed to me a good idea to forget it, and it still does. I had been wavering pretty badly about it for days anyway."[21]

Ten days later Rachel casually explained at the end of a long business letter to Marie that a medical examination had revealed a tumor in her left breast. "I'll probably be going into the hospital for a few days within the next week or ten days. There is a small cyst or tumor in one breast which the doctor thinks I should get rid of, and I suppose it's a good idea. Otherwise, my complaints seem to stem chiefly from nervous exhaustion—for which I am ordered to take that vacation as soon as the hospital episode is out of the way."[22]

A few days later Rachel responded to Marie's obvious concern. "Of course I'll let you know about the operation, but don't worry. It should be simple. My chief worry is finding a surgeon. The operation will probably turn out to be so trivial that any dope could do it; but of course there is in such cases, always the possibility that a much more drastic procedure will prove necessary. In any event, I'll be at Doctor's Hospital, where a very dear friend is a nurse, and I will be in excellent hands in that respect." Rachel hoped to get the whole thing over with as soon as she settled on a surgeon.[23]

Carson's casual reaction to the discovery of a breast tumor in September 1950 is surprising. Although this was the second such tumor in the same breast, an earlier small cyst having been removed sometime in 1946, she gave the impression of nonchalance when this larger one was discovered. Her search for a surgeon was extraordinarily casual for someone with her knowledge and research skills. She had been disillusioned by the ethical practices of the general practitioner whom both she and Kitty Birch had seen for some years, and she thought the head surgeon at Doctor's Hospital, a man in his early seventies, too old even though he had a fine reputation. The doctor who was, apparently, her first choice was himself in the hospital, so the surgeon she finally settled upon was someone relatively unknown to her.[24]

The operation was performed on September 21, 1950. The tumor was removed and the doctors suggested no further treatment. When Rachel specifically asked her surgeon whether the tissue biopsy showed any evidence of malignancy, she was told it did not. Carson remained in the hospital for four days. After a brief recuperation at home, she left for Nags Head, North Carolina, in early October for a week's rest combined with some seashore research. Just before leaving, she penned an afterthought to a long letter on the advantages and disadvantages of the seashore book to her anxious agent: "In case I haven't said so, the thing they took out of me was okay, though about walnut-size and very deep. I'm sore as heck, but otherwise very spry." A deeply relieved Rodell responded, "You were, frankly, scaring the daylights out of me by saying nothing—but I didn't feel I could ask!"[25]

Carson's conscious desire to minimize her health problems is further underscored by the several letters she wrote to Marie Rodell just before and just after the surgery that focused exclusively on literary and business affairs. A single letter to Edwin Teale hints at her emotional reaction to the surgery. After sharing the news of *The New Yorker* serialization and the other books she had in mind, she confided, "this time I'm not going to sit back for seven years before starting another! I seem now to have, as writers should, a sense of urgency and passing time—and so much to say! Of course Thoreau had the whole idea in a sentence—'If thou art a writer, write as if thy time were short, for it is indeed short, at the longest.' "[26]

Rachel's week on the North Carolina shore gave her more time to reflect on life's swift passage. After a morning on the beach at Nags Head, she wrote in her field notes:

> Walked south on the beach—a cloudy, grey morning with showers of rain. . . . Saw tracks of a shore bird probably a sanderling, and followed them a little, then they turned toward the water and were soon obliterated by the sea. How much it washes away, and makes as though it had never been. Time itself is like the sea, containing all that came before us, sooner or later sweeping us away on its flood and washng over and obliterating the traces of our presence, as the sea this morning erased the foot-prints of the bird.[27]

On her way up the beach that morning with the wind blowing stiffly, she saw a little one-legged sanderling hopping along hunting food. She thought of the miles of travel ahead of it and wondered how long he would last. Two days later Rachel encountered the bird again.

> This time I could see that his left leg is a short stump less than an inch long. I wondered if some animal maybe a fox, had caught it in the Arctic, or whether it had gotten into a trap. . . . He would hop, hop, hop, toward the surf; probing and jabbing busily with opened bill, turn and hop away from the advancing foam. Only twice did I see him have to take to his wings to escape a wetting. It made my heart ache to think how tired his little leg must be, but his whole manner suggested a cheerfulness of spirit and a gameness which must mean that the God of fallen sparrows has not forgotten him.[28]

Rachel's field notes also contained lighter moments, as when she picked up a dime-size baby ghost crab. Afraid it did not know its way home, she made it a new hole with her finger in the sand. "He darted into it," she wrote, "and we were both happy."[29]

Her solitary walks also gave her time to think about how she wanted to approach a seashore guide. When she and Brooks had first discussed such a project, he had in mind a kind of field guide to the coastal beaches. Carson's conceptualization of a shore guide took into account not only what she thought people wanted to know about the seashore and how they would use it but, as a practical publishing matter, the variety of ways she could sell it. A guide to American seashores would have no foreign sales and, she guessed, no subsidiary income from serial sales. It would not, she thought, be of interest to *The New Yorker*.[30]

But as she spent the week roaming the dunes of Virginia Beach and, more happily, Nags Head, she began to think of the book as less of a guide to specific sites than a narrative account of the biological principles that control life along the shore and of the ecology of shore animals. She was more interested in understanding why creatures live where they do and how they adapt to their natural environment than she was in a mere catalog. She reported to Rodell, "I'm satisfied that in these days of tramping the beach down here I have thought out an approach that will make this book completely different from any other, and I hope, the most practically useful."[31]

Impulsively, Carson decided to apply for a Guggenheim Fellowship to support the shore guide while she was in North Carolina. Her application's narrative reflects how she thought of herself as a forty-three-year-old writer, confident in her ability to write popular science and natural history. Carson proposed doing original research in several Atlantic coast biological laboratories and libraries from Maine to Florida and fieldwork in areas she knew of special interest ecologically. But she regarded the project "as chiefly a creative work" in which "an ecological concept" would dominate.[32]

Carson confidently told the fellowship committee that she knew of "no existing book on the Atlantic coast that stresses the ecological approach." Reviewing her past accomplishments, she noted that when she had turned again to writing after graduate school, she found her "purpose as a writer in the interpretation of scientific findings in terms that give them reality and meaning for the non-scientific reader." She was confident that this guide would not only be unique but that it also would be a "contribution to a better understanding of an interesting and important region of our world." The fieldwork she proposed would complement the writing of reflective essays on her experiences as a naturalist, which, she noted, would be a book she intended to "devote some leisure time to during the next several years."[33]

Rachel barely completed the application by the October 15 deadline. Impressive in its conceptualization and self-confident style, the application was supported by eight references: Henry Bigelow, William Beebe, Robert Cushman Murphy, Clarence Cottam, Richard Pough, and Edwin Way Teale, as well as editors Paul Brooks and Maria Leiper. Carson requested funding equivalent to six months' compensation from the FWS and estimated that the guide could be completed by the spring of 1952.

Instead of being rested and relaxed when she returned to the office from North Carolina in mid-October, Rachel was frantic at the lack of progress she had made on any of her projects. Nothing had been resolved on the guide with Brooks, and Oxford had been "fiddingly around," as she called it, for almost three and a half months and still she had no firm publication date for *The Sea Around Us*.

Carson's frustration with Oxford's progress, however, masked a deeper anxiety than just the financial market for her book. The uncertain impact of the U.S. involvement in military action in Korea was gnawing at her and kept her future in limbo. She worried that once again a foreign conflict would affect not only book sales but even its publication. *The Sea Around Us* could end up a victim of the Cold War.[34]

Carson always blamed the outbreak of World War II for the commercial failure of *Under the Sea-Wind,* although she acknowledged that Simon & Schuster's meager publicity had been a factor. Now, a decade later, Carson was about to bring out a far more important book with a relatively unknown trade publisher when another military conflict a world away was capturing national attention. On June 5, 1950, North Korean troops invaded the South, beginning what U.S. diplomat Averill Harriman called "that sour little war." By July United Nations forces in Korea were bogged down in heavy fighting. Carson's peevish letter about Oxford's delays was written just as U.S.-led forces massed at the Chinese border and the war seemed about to escalate.

At home, the so-called police action in Korea brought massive increases in military spending and research. President Harry Truman seized the nation's railroads to avert a general strike. Various other economic dislocations, including fuel shortages and price increases, followed throughout the summer and fall of 1950, including a serious paper shortage that affected publishing houses both here and abroad.[35]

Carson's position at the U.S. Fish and Wildlife Service was even more immediately affected by the widening Korean War. Many of her colleagues anticipated being called back into military service. Personnel changes and duty reassignments were announced daily throughout the Department of Interior. Once again there was talk of transferring the entire FWS out of Washington to make room for war personnel. A new rumor about the ultimate destiny of the service circulated every week.

As in 1941, there was nothing Rachel could do but wait. But the stress and anxiety of not knowing how to plan for the future was enormous, for Carson desperately needed to remain on the East Coast. The longer publication of *The Sea Around Us* was delayed, the more anxious she became.[36]

Other things kept her on edge as well. To everyone's surprise, Oxford University Press, England, declined to publish *The Sea Around Us.* While this meant that Marie was free to sell the English rights to another house, it also provoked a new uncertainty. Meanwhile, Carson found the Fuertes project, which at first had appeared so easy, was encumbered by a variety of newly discovered restrictions.[37]

In going through the FWS files, Rachel learned that the painter, who had originally charged the service almost nothing for paintings published in a government pamphlet, had stipulated that he should be compensated if they were ever published elsewhere. The book Carson had in mind required not only the permission of the Fuertes estate but also payment for reproduction. By the winter of 1950, Mary Fuertes Boynton, the painter's daughter and heir, had made it clear that she intended to play a larger part in the project than Carson had anticipated. Carson's efforts to clarify ownership of the paintings and her use of Fuertes's correspondence to describe the context of each one had apparently alarmed Boynton, who now planned a biography of her father.

Before Christmas, Rachel's beloved silver Persian cat, Tippy, died. Tippy was the last of the Carson family's original brood of Persians, and both Maria and Rachel grieved over his loss. Charles Alldredge kindly brought comfort, arriving on Christmas Day with a different species of companion for Rachel and her mother. "We got a bird," Rachel reported to Marie, "Charles' variety which I don't know how to spell. He is still nameless, and shy, but very sweet." But year's end also brought some good news.[38]

On December 8 Carson received an unexpected telephone call from a member of the AAAS Westinghouse Prize Committee telling her that her essay, "The Birth of an Island," had been honored by the thousand-dollar science writing award. The committee asked her to come to the Cleveland meetings on December 29 to accept the honor. Rachel was elated but not altogether surprised. However, the prestigious award did improve her mood and morale. Relieved when she learned she did not have to give a speech in Cleveland, she enjoyed the publicity in the local press, many phone calls of congratulation, and the excitement in her office.[39]

When Marie happened to discover that Rachel had neglected to inform the Saxton Foundation about either the AAAS award or *The New Yorker* serialization, she told Rachel bluntly, "I think, my dear, that it is time you got over your peeve against the Saxton people. After all, it was they who first made possible in large part all the pleasant things that have been happening." Although Rachel denied carrying a grudge, she admitted that she deserved to be scolded and dutifully wrote Saxton Foundation secretary, Amy Flashner, a note.[40]

Rachel offered to give Marie her customary commission on the AAAS prize money. Very touched, Marie of course refused, but Carson was not easily dissuaded. "I don't know anything about your old Agent's Association rules, but my reasoning tells me that you are entitled to your share of anything that comes in on a book you've handled. If I can't give you a check without getting you disbarred, you must at least tell me something handsome you want, that I can get you as a little share of the loot."[41]

Two days after she learned about the AAAS award, the first galleys finally arrived from Oxford. Although Carson returned from Cleveland exhausted and suffering from a bad cold and sinus infection, the AAAS prize was a turning point. Rachel recognized it for what it was—the first public affirmation of the quality of her work—and seemed to draw strength from it even though much of her future was uncertain.[42]

The announcement of agencies scheduled to move out of Washington permanently was expected any time. Rachel explained to Marie that she worried most about the emotional upheaval that relocating herself and her mother would bring.

"I also know what a terrible upset it was for months and months the other time, and there would simply be no writing done this winter. If I felt I were doing vital defense work I suppose there would be moral reason for just submitting, but I don't. Instead, I feel that unless I should transfer to direct war work, I'd be doing more for the things I believe in by writing than by staying in this job."[43]

"Maybe," she told Marie with uncharacteristic sarcasm, "they will decide to leave us here as targets."[44]

By the end of the month Rachel was feeling more sanguine. Her office was still in place and she had received the rest of the galleys from Oxford. She celebrated Marie's thirty-ninth birthday by sending a gift subscription to *Natural History Magazine*, a lovely copy of the *Apocrypha*, and a note that read, "May they remind you of my love and the very real gratitude for all the things you have done for me in many ways."[45]

Marie's birthday prompted Rachel to confide her latest pipe dream. "You may think me utterly mad, but after some comment was made the other day about movie rights I've been thinking, well, why not a documentary on the sea? I don't see why it couldn't be every bit as good as *The River* [a documentary directed by Pare Lorentz]. After all, lots of movies have rather a casual resemblance to the books on which they are based." Considering the world situation and the increased public awareness of the ocean's role, Carson thought the movie could "stress the impact of marine matters on human affairs. Maybe a sort of Pare Lorentz-ish narration which I wouldn't mind trying to do myself. Well with that I shall go back to the salt mines."[46]

Rachel's idea for a documentary version of *The Sea Around Us* drastically underestimated the challenge and frustrations of a film adaptation. But Marie also had considered the merits of a movie version and, with Rachel's expressed interest, began making inquiries in Hollywood through her friend and film agent, Shirley Collier.

February brought other positive developments. *The New Yorker* had a tentative publication date: June 2, 9, and 16 if publication took place in three parts. Editor William Shawn wanted to wait until March to see how the Korean War news might affect his schedule. Rodell relayed the dates to Vaudrin at Oxford, who set book publication for July 12. But there was more.

"I have been debating since late yesterday afternoon," Marie wrote, "whether or not to tell you another bit of news. With most of my clients my inclination would be not to but I think you can be trusted not to build your hopes too high. That news is that the Book-of-the-Month Club has sent for more galleys and labeled *The Sea Around Us* an 'A' book—that means it is definitely one of the contenders. The board will not meet until March sixth so there will be no further word until then." Rachel tried to remain outwardly calm at Marie's news, but her mind danced with the benefits Book-of-the-Month Club selection could bring.[47]

Two days later Bob Hines was at work in his office next to Rachel's when she went in and asked him to meet her in the hall. When Hines came out she motioned him toward the telephone booths in the corner of the cavernous hallway, squeezed into one with him, and closed the door. Sitting on his lap, Rachel told Bob her news with tears of happiness streaming down her face: *The Sea Around Us* had been nominated for the Book-of-the-Month Club. If selected, she told him, it could mean as much as $40,000, money that would enable her to leave the service and devote full time to her writing. After swearing him to secrecy, they extracted themselves from the phone booth and nonchalantly went back to work.[48]

In early March Carson signed a contract with Staples Press in London to bring out the British edition of *The Sea Around Us*. Rodell's British agent chose Staples because it had its own printing presses and an adequate supply of paper, something few other European houses were able to offer due to postwar shortages. Several days later Carson approved the final terms Rodell had negotiated with Paul Brooks at Houghton Mifflin for the seashore guide, which was tentatively titled *Guide to Seashore Life on the Atlantic Coast*. Harper & Brothers had agreed to publish the Fuertes book and wanted to close a contract as soon as Carson set a delivery date. Only the Guggenheim Fellowship and the Book-of-the-Month Club remained in the balance.[49]

Although Carson had planned to travel to the southern beaches with her mother shortly after the New Year, the uncertainty of the Korean War and the need to work on the galleys kept her at home. Once publication was set for July, Rachel's attention turned to production matters and to Oxford's marketing plans or lack thereof.

Rachel's involvement in the physical production of *The Sea Around Us* was more than mere professional interest. Her efforts to influence the marketing in particular were symptomatic of the perfectionism that she demanded of herself as well as of the control she wanted over all aspects of her writing.

Carson's previous experience with Simon & Schuster's lackluster promotion of *Under the Sea-Wind* had left a certain bitterness. Never again would she trust her work to others less capable or less concerned about the outcome. Even though she now had Marie Rodell to help her with such matters, Carson could depend on no one but herself. Her concern was rightfully heightened when Philip Vaudrin left Oxford in February 1951. Deprived of his intelligent intercession, Carson and Rodell were left to deal with Oxford's president, Henry Walck, whose background was in accounting, and with Walter Oakley, the head of marketing.[50]

Catherine Scott had come to Oxford in 1948 to direct their first real office of public relations and promotion. Scott was a likable, unpretentious woman who had been doing publicity for Columbia University Press for a number of years. But the requirements of organizing and promoting a trade book were quite different from what had been required at a university press.

Oxford's marketing campaign, however, was made easier by the fact that *The Sea Around Us* would first appear in *The New Yorker*; presumably a demand would exist for the book even before publication. But both Oxford's reputation as a conservative university press and Scott's background rendered each less able to take advantage of this prepublication publicity. In fairness to Oxford and Catherine Scott, probably no publisher would have been able to satisfy Carson's expectations or promote the book as well as she thought it should. Relations between Carson and Scott remained cordial, even friendly. But Carson was the source of most promotion ideas, sending them along to Scott for her consideration and, she hoped, implementation.[51]

At the end of March 1951, Carson received notice in the mail that she had been awarded a coveted Guggenheim Fellowship. With Alastair MacBain's blessing she applied for a year's leave of absence from the service beginning in June and tried to stop worrying so much about whether her office would be moved out of Washington.[52]

Marie Rodell called Rachel four days later with the news that the Book-of-the-Month Club had selected *The Sea Around Us* as its alternate selection for July or August. Although an alternate selection meant far less money, Rachel was elated. She even managed to ignore Walck's tactless response. "We are delighted the Book-of-the-Month Club is going to use the book as an alternate," he wrote Rodell, "although naturally we should have preferred a full selection." Shirley Briggs's reaction was much closer to Rachel's own. "Nothing left but the Burroughs medal," she wrote in her diary.[53]

Carson's telephone rang with requests from local reporters wanting to talk about her Guggenheim award and the imminent publication of *The Sea Around Us*. *Vogue* magazine surprised everyone by purchasing the chapter entitled "The Global Thermostat" in which Carson discussed how the ocean currents regulated climate. In late April the magazine sent photographer Irving Penn to Silver Spring to photograph Carson for a feature essay on Washington's famous residents. A relieved subject reported afterward, "Mr. Penn turned out to be a young man of great charm who turned the usual ordeal of photography into something almost pleasant. He exposes innumerable negatives, so presumably there might be something tolerable in the lot."[54]

With the aid of Charles Alldredge and journalist Else Strom, Oxford had scheduled a book party in Washington for June 20 at the National Press Club. Alldredge, who was friendly with local Washington bookseller Franz Bader, the managing partner of Whyte's Bookstore on Connecticut Avenue, had arranged an evening autographing party for Carson at Whyte's on publication day. Dissatisfied with Oxford's publicity efforts, Alldredge had taken it into his own hands to place news stories about Carson and her book with *Variety* as well as with *Washington Star* social columnist Betty Beale, a woman whom he occasionally escorted to Washington social and political functions.[55]

Alldredge provided copy to Beale without consulting Rachel, Marie, or Scott. When Beale devoted nearly half of her May 7 syndicated column "Exclusively Yours" to Carson and her book, Rachel knew immediately that Charles was behind it. "Few people realize it," wrote Beale, "but we have here in Washington—right in our midst—a woman whom some critics are saying is one of the great writers of our age. In fact it looks as though Miss Carson . . . is about to become the toast of Washington's highbrow circles." Describing Carson as a woman "in her late thirties with chestnut hair, blue eyes and a sweet face, the new-famed author is an extremely modest and shy person. She is, however, an unusual combination—a science scholar and a writer with style."[56]

Annoyed that Alldredge had done this without her knowledge, and embarrassed by some of Beale's extraneous social commentary, initially Rachel was angry with Charles, but she recognized its enormous publicity value and graciously called to thank him. "He was pleased as punch," Rachel reported to Marie. "For heavens sake tell him he's wonderful, whatever you think about it." Marie was livid with Charles for interfering, but agreed with Catherine Scott that it would be too bad not to take advantage of whatever Charles could do and so held her tongue and her pen.[57]

Carson was more upset by production problems at Oxford. After Walck finally agreed to change the binding, which was of such poor quality that Carson felt the book would fall apart as soon as it was opened, she focused on getting the right advance comments for the dust jacket. Although she asked Scott to get one from William Beebe at the outset, for one reason or another Scott had not done so, and now Beebe was in Trinidad. Scott had gotten statements from nature writer John Kieran and from Dr. Waldo Schmitt, curator of zoology at the National Museum of Natural History, but Carson had her heart set on one from Beebe.[58]

Marie went to Catherine Scott to see what could be done, but Scott told her she had written to Beebe and had received no answer. Scott had heard through the publishing grapevine, however, that Beebe was reviewing *The Sea Around Us* for the *New York Times*. Marie passed on the news to Rachel: "This is a wonderful break but I think it means he cannot be quoted before that, which is what may be holding up his reply to her." But Scott's information was inaccurate. Beebe was not the reviewer and Oxford failed to get any advance comment from the famous oceanographer.[59]

Rachel was furious with the publisher and complained to Marie, who responded calmly, "I am not trying to say with all of this that I think Catherine Scott is the genius of the age nor that I do not feel that Oxford could have done more trade promotion than it has. I am only trying to help you evaluate the situation in realistic terms."[60]

Rodell enclosed a check for $4,680 from *The New Yorker* representing the balance owed to Carson for the profile, hoping that the money and William Shawn's gracious note might improve her disposition. Shawn wrote, "Our check for the balance of the payment of Miss Carson's superb article. We are delighted about publishing this. Thank you for sending us off on the whole happy adventure."[61]

Rachel acknowledged being tired and irritable. In addition to being upset with Oxford's lack of initiative, she was on edge waiting for Shawn to go over *The New Yorker* page proofs and unable to plan any field research until that was finished. She was also busy training George Cain, her Fish and Wildlife assistant, who would take over most of her duties while she was on leave. Most distressing of all, the Fuertes project was unraveling amid acrimony and innuendo.

At the end of March, Rachel had written Mary Boynton that Harper had agreed to publish the Fuertes bird paintings in the fall of 1952. Boynton unexpectedly replied that she had decided to edit the book herself since she no longer considered Carson the best choice of author or editor because she had not known Fuertes.[62]

Boynton not only fired Carson from a project she had initiated but had the audacity to write Carson's boss, Fish and Wildlife Director Dr. Albert Day, informing him of her decision to remove Carson. Boynton gave no other reason for her change of heart except to quote the opinion of one of her father's ornithologist friends, George Sutton, who had asked, "What does Carson know either about Fuertes or about birds?"[63]

Rachel was furious. On April 3 she responded to Boynton.

> It is too bad you have waited until now to make your true position known. The choice of an author for any such book is seldom determined by the desires or willingness of prospective writers to undertake it, and in this instance the decision is in the hands of the Fish and Wildlife Service and the publishers. I do not feel that further discussion of this subject between you and me will serve any useful purpose.[64]

Maria Carson painstakingly typed out all the correspondence between Rachel and Mary Boynton since October 1949 and sent copies to Marie and Mr. Day.

At the office, Carson and MacBain spent hours going over it, trying to understand Boynton's behavior. MacBain, who grew more furious with "that woman" by the minute, called in a service lawyer to review it. At issue was whether the service had the right to make the paintings available for the proposed volume and whether Harper had the right to publish them.

Rachel was stunned by Boynton's inexplicable change of mind. She despised personal confrontations, but she was angry too, and stood her ground, refusing to abandon the book. Rachel told Marie, "I am sure now that she feels I am trying to make money out of it; but I wonder whether any writer worthy of the name could be found who would devote a half year of his time without expecting money for it. Perhaps the real truth is that she wants to have her own manuscript used—now that we have most conveniently found a publisher."[65]

Carson's tenacity throughout the dispute exhibits a characteristic stubbornness and a healthy competitive spirit. Boynton's letters to her and to her superiors were insulting and unprofessional. Her threat of legal action against the Fish and Wildlife Service, although upsetting, infuriated Carson more. Boynton's husband even wrote to Day, as did one of the ornithologists Boynton suggested as an alternative author.

Considering all the pressures on Carson with the imminent publication of *The Sea Around Us*, her pending leave of absence, and the need to begin work on the shore guide, it would have been simpler if she had walked away from the Fuertes project. But Boynton had violated Carson's code of ethical behavior by treating her as a personal friend then inexplicably turning on her. Boynton's insinuations insulted Carson's reputation as a naturalist and a professional writer.

One reason for Rachel's tenaciousness was her loyalty to Marie, who had invested many hours in the project that now appeared to be worthless. Marie used the occasion to set the record straight about her role as agent. Her response confirmed her devotion to Rachel and her conduct as a literary agent. "My dear," Rodell wrote Carson at the end of May, "you owe me nothing. A normal part of an agent's business is gambling time on projects which may never come to fruition. I, as an agent, do not handle this thing by Rachel Carson, and that thing by Rachel Carson; I handle Rachel Carson. What comes in as my share covers the whole obligation."[66]

The controversy with Boynton and the Fuertes estate dragged on until February 1953, at which point Carson bowed out. The Fish and Wildlife Service continued adjudicating its interest in the paintings, but by then

Carson was committed to other more important literary efforts. In the end, the primary reason Rachel dropped the Fuertes book was her personal distaste for any further dealings with Mary Boynton. Although Cass Canfield, the head of Harper & Brothers, believed the outstanding differences could be settled quickly, Rachel had had enough.[67]

9

"Kin This Be Me?"

"I would love to tear off to Beaufort [North Carolina] and rest for a week," Rachel told Marie early in May 1951. "I am really needing it very badly, and if I have to sit here for the next two weeks just because . . . [*The New Yorker*] can't or won't say when they will be ready for me, it isn't going to do my nervous system any good!" Rodell, who knew better than anyone that Rachel was on edge, urged her to get away. But as luck would have it, William Shawn was ready for Carson to go over his condensation of the nine chapters he had chosen.[1]

Shawn had read Carson's manuscript with enormous enthusiasm. Sensing immediately that she was a writer of first rank, he caused a literary stir first by publishing it serially as a *New Yorker* "Profile," the first ever about a nonhuman subject. Shawn anticipated that *The Sea Around Us* would be an important book, and he intended to introduce the public to a major American writer.[2]

In mid-May Shawn and Carson spent ten days editing page proofs together, requiring phone calls back and forth each day and a quick trip to New York for Carson. For her part, Rachel was delighted with the care Shawn had taken in condensing the chapters into three long profiles. Working together, Shawn was further impressed with Carson's literary craftsmanship and her scientific knowledge.[3]

"Shawn and I talked Monday," she reported to Marie; "he said the proofs were in such good shape that he might not have to call again, and he hasn't. I'm feeling almost neglected after one to three calls daily all the week before. Please tell Edith Oliver that I really think Shawn is wonderful. It has been a great experience to work with him and I can see why his staff seems to worship him as they do." Theirs was an effective and admiring collaboration that served the interests of author and editor well.[4]

Part 1 of "Profile of the Sea" appeared in *The New Yorker* on June 2. While the installments were running, Rachel had just enough time to slip away to Beaufort by herself, before Oxford's book party on June 20. Publication was now set for July 2, after which Carson naively looked forward to celebrating her personal freedom from *The Sea Around Us.*

Rachel had told her mother not to expect a letter every day and to tell the others she was too busy to write postcards. She did have time, however, for almost daily letters to Marie about marketing and publicity, concerns that were never far from her thoughts. Curiously, neither Carson nor Rodell speculated about the potential impact of *The New Yorker* serialization. While Carson had hounded Vaudrin to submit the book in time for the Burroughs medal and waited breathlessly for the results of the Book-of-the Month Club selection, she appears almost naive about being introduced in the pages of the nation's foremost literary magazine.

Perhaps what followed was inconceivable even to Rachel's wildest imaginings. Unsophisticated in the world of public relations, Carson underestimated the public attention to the author that follows sudden literary success. Since Rodell had never handled an author whose work appeared in *The New Yorker* before publication, even she failed to anticipate the popular response. But they both had a portent of what was to come when Marie learned that *The Saturday Review of Literature* would put Rachel's picture on the cover of the July 7 issue. Rachel's response was wary.

> Are they doing me against a background of squids, spouting whales, etc? Really, I grow more astounded by events every day. Maybe it is because a book, once it's between covers, seems to have very little to do with me. I felt that about *Under the Sea-Wind,* and perhaps more about this one. It's just itself—well, sort of as a child is different from its parents. I'm pleased to have people say nice things about the book, but all this stuff about me seems odd, to say the least.[5]

On June 12, after the second installment had appeared in *The New Yorker,* Marie wrote Rachel, "I had lunch yesterday with one of the editors of Random House and he told me that the entire town is talking about the profile of the sea."[6]

Even before publication, Washington literati were also reading and talking about *The Sea Around Us*. A surprise telephone call from Washington social maven Alice Roosevelt Longworth, President Theodore Roosevelt's daughter, a keen critic in her own right and a person of influence in Washington, was an indication of the kind of response Carson could anticipate. Bookseller Franz Bader had sent Mrs. Longworth an advance copy. He knew that if she took a fancy to a book, she told all her friends and ordered quantities as presents.

Alice Longworth telephoned Rachel Carson's home very early one June morning in a state of great excitement to tell the author that *The Sea Around Us* "was the most marvelous thing she had ever read." Finding Maria Carson instead, Mrs. Longworth described in detail how she had stayed up all night reading it through twice before dawn.[7]

Maria immediately conveyed Mrs. Longworth's enthusiasm to Rachel in Beaufort. "Your very exciting letter came this morning just as I was starting out on a collecting trip," Rachel replied. "When I got back I wired Catherine Scott, suggesting she wire Mrs. Longworth a special invitation to the Press Club party."[8]

Before she left Beaufort, *The New Yorker* was already getting fan mail from readers, but Carson's attention was fixed on the ugly, new plastic bindings in which Oxford was swathing the book. One of the copies Scott sent her was printed upside down and the others had obviously scuffed covers. She complained to Rodell, "This whole binding business is a mess!"[9]

Once again Betty Beale scooped Oxford's book party in her *Evening Star* column, announcing "Rachel Carson, brilliant author of the prize-winning *The Sea Around Us*, will be the honored guest at the National Press Club at a 5 to 7 affair on the 20th."[10]

The honored guest, her mother, brother Robert and his wife, Vera, Virginia and her husband, Lee King, and Marjie arrived early at the National Press Club for Oxford's official book party. Oxford President Henry Walck, Walter Oakley, and Catherine Scott represented the publisher. Marie Rodell, Charles Alldredge, and Else Strom joined a guest list that included officials from FWS, representatives from the press, the Congress, the navy, the Smithsonian Institution, the Washington scientific community, ANS members, a variety of literary critics and booksellers, and Alice Roosevelt Longworth. Carson's ANS friends Irston

Barnes, Shirley Briggs, and Howard Zahniser were there, as was the book's illustrator, Rachel's longtime friend Kay Howe, along with FWS colleagues Bob Hines and Bert Walford and his wife.[11]

Rachel wore a soft white silk dress printed with scattered wildflowers; it had cap sleeves and a mandarin collar. An elegant white feathered toque hat that had a short veil that she could wear up or down as the occasion required completed the outfit. Photographs of Carson taken during the evening show a very relaxed, attractive woman, conservatively but elegantly attired. She made a point of having a picture taken with Alice Longworth, who wore her signature black picture-book hat. Rachel enjoyed the accolades of the guests and endured the receiving line and the small talk without any hint of discomfort.[12]

In the ten days between Oxford's book party and publication, Rodell was besieged with speaking and writing requests for Carson. A representative of the Ford Foundation called to inquire if the television rights to the book were free. They were. RCA Victor Records asked if Carson would be interested in writing the jacket notes for a new recording of Claude Debussy's *La Mer* with Leopold Stokowski conducting the NBC Symphony Orchestra. She would. A contract was signed two weeks later. Catherine Scott called with a list of radio and TV requests but promised to make no commitments for Carson, who in typical fashion was preparing to leave for several weeks at the Marine Biological Lab and the U.S. Fisheries Station in Woods Hole as soon after Whyte's autographing party as she could get away. "Heavens," Rachel exclaimed to Marie, "is this all about me—it's really ridiculous!"[13]

Alastair MacBain and Bert Walford gave a going-away party for Carson and her Fish and Wildlife staff and friends after work on Friday, June 29, her last official day before starting her year's leave. Rachel and her friends gathered at their old favorite, the Watergate Restaurant, for a small celebration, which Rachel enjoyed far more than the crush of the Press Club party.[14]

Then suddenly it was Sunday, July 1. *The Sea Around Us* was the front-page feature review in *The New Times Book Review*. The reviewer was Jonathan Norton Leonard, the science editor of *Time* magazine, whose intriguing lead "—And His Wonders in the Deep: A Scientist Draws an Intimate Portrait of the Winding Sea and Its Churning Life" captured the biblical sweep of Carson's subject as well as her absorbing revelations of the sea's secrets. Leonard's appreciative review certainly pleased her, but it was not the review Beebe would have written.[15]

The Sea Around Us was published the next day, July 2, 1951. David Dempsey, the regular book critic for the *New York Times*, gave it a rather unimaginative but positive assessment in the daily edition. His review included an attractive formal photograph of Carson taken by the Brooks Studio in Washington originally for Oxford's use. Noting Carson's rare ability to make complex science comprehensible, Dempsey commended her for "removing the mystery of the sea, . . . while leaving us its poetry." Rachel did not share his appraisal and took pains later to correct his view of what she had added or subtracted from the sea.[16]

That evening Rachel and Marie, escorted by a proud Charles Alldredge, Mrs. Carson, and Rachel's nieces attended the autographing party at Whyte's Bookshop. Rachel, charmingly attired in a short-sleeved beige suit with a small white straw hat and short veil, sat amid piles of her book jacketed in sea green patiently autographing copies that Marie and Franz Bader piled in front of her. In between autographing requests, Carson talked to Tom Donnelly of the *Washington Daily News* and Dorothea Cruger of the *Washington Post*, among other Washington journalists who dropped by. Elderly gentlemen, well-dressed ladies, and teenagers alike were buying the book. "I read every word in *The New Yorker* and I wanted to read all the rest of it," one white-haired lady reported to Cruger.[17]

After Rachel inscribed a book to four members of one family for a customer, Marie Rodell was heard to comment humorously "We ought to charge them for four copies." When Donnelly asked Marie how she had come to think of sending the book to *The New Yorker*, she replied, "I don't know, I just took a chance. I never dreamed it would be such a big success. They told me they've had more letters on it than anything they've published. It's amazing for a book like this, a scientific book, to stir up such a response."[18]

When a journalist asked Rachel what she had hoped to accomplish in writing *The Sea Around Us*, she replied that she wanted people to appreciate the sea. "An ocean voyage, or a trip to the shore means so much more," she explained, "if you know a few things about the sea." She was also concerned about the need for seashore preservation. "What has taken centuries to develop is being destroyed in a few years," she told Dorothea Cruger, and went on to describe the seashore guide she was at work on.[19]

After nearly two hours of signing, Rachel told Donnelly she had "run out of sentiments" and asked if he minded if she simply inscribed her name in his copy. He didn't. Two days later both Donnelly and Cruger published enthusiastic articles about Whyte's book party, the charming author of *The Sea Around Us*, Carson's obvious love for the sea, and the enormous appeal of her book.[20]

Literary critics, scientists, and ordinary readers alike were surprised by Carson's ability to master such comprehensive information and to present a balanced picture with such lean yet poetic language. Drawn into the subject by Carson's own subjectively conveyed curiosity and delight, the first pages of the book introduce a writer of singular talent.

Carson's love of the ocean was contagious. Her prose was disarmingly natural, unassumingly competent. Specialists from all the physical and biological sciences could find something in these pages, a mere detail perhaps, that they did not know, or might be provoked to think about in a different way. Oceanographer Henry Bigelow, now director of Harvard's Museum of Comparative Zoology, told her, "the amount of material you have assembled amazes me. Although I have been concerned with the sea for fifty years, you have found a good many facts I hadn't." Generalists found this convention of sciences not only comprehensible but riveting.[21]

The Sea Around Us had something in it for everyone who ever drew the ocean's horizon across a large sheet of brown paper in a grade school far from the shore or who stood on a beach and looked out at the farthest point with wonder. Yet intriguing as this mix of science and poetry was, neither scientific explanation nor aesthetic language entirely explains why the American public bought the book in such record numbers in 1951, or what need Rachel Carson's epic of the sea fulfilled in them.

Carson anticipated one pragmatic reason for the book's popularity when she began her oceanographic research in 1948 and tried to publish some of it as "Another Beachhead" the following year. The American public in the immediate postwar years needed no reminder that their physical security and their economic future were dependent on a greater understanding of the seas that surrounded them and, until 1941, had kept them safe from invasion and attack. World War II reinforced human dependence not only on oceanographic science and continued research and exploration but on the resources of the ocean—"the wealth of the salt seas," as Carson called them.

Austin H. Clark, a marine zoologist and curator on the staff of the U.S. National Museum who reviewed *The Sea Around Us* for the *Saturday Review*, called attention to Carson's emphasis on the utility of the seas in human affairs—their effect on climate, mineral and biological resources, to "the commerce of all lands that must cross it." The *Newsweek* science critic who found Carson's prose "hypnotic" also highlighted the book's "practical significance," noting that the effect that submarine waves have on weather systems was only then beginning to be understood and that undersea oil fields, mineral deposits, and the mass migration of fish had obvious importance for contemporary society. In 1951 oceanography like other fields of multidisciplinary scientific research had to have practical application to ensure public funding.[22]

Another appeal of Carson's story of the sea was that it contained so much new information that was not available to the public prior to the end of World War II. The best-seller lists for both fiction and nonfiction in 1951 reflected the public's curiosity about the sea and their desire for the latest information in a form they could understand. Sea adventures and accounts of military activity on and under the sea enjoyed popularity as well.

For months James Jones's *From Here to Eternity*, a novel set in the Pacific about the peacetime army in Hawaii, occupied first place for fiction. In the early summer it was followed by Herman Wouk's *Caine Mutiny* and Nicholas Monsarrat's *Cruel Sea*. Both novels described an aspect of the human struggle with the sea as a mysterious and sometimes deadly adversary.

On top of the nonfiction list, Thor Heyerdahl's *Kon-Tiki* had held sway for over a year. His was a classic story of adventure at sea, crossing the Pacific on a raft in search of evidence that Western people might, at one time, have ruled the coral islands. Further interest in the Pacific islands was represented on the lists by James Michener's second Pacific voyage, *Return to Paradise*, and Agnes Newton Keith's *White Man Returns*, about the island of Borneo. But in spite of these titles, the popularity of Carson's book surprised most critics. "But who would have thought," *The Saturday Review* editorialized on October 27, "either that *The New Yorker* would print a great part of a book that is so alien to its normal purposes or that the public would promptly rush out and buy it by the thousands?"[23]

The popular response to *The Sea Around Us* cannot be explained simply because it contained fascinating fact, absorbing detail, economic utility, new scientific information, or even because of its literary appeal. Nor was its success attributable solely to the impact of *The New Yorker*'s unusual profile, although the total effect of that event can never be calculated completely.

Carson's fan mail revealed that *The Sea Around Us* had touched a deeper yearning for knowledge about the natural world as well as for a philosophic perspective on contemporary life. From these letters Carson sensed "an immense and unsatisfied thirst for understanding of the world about us, and every drop of information, every bit of fact that serves to free the reader's mind to roam the great spaces of the universe, is seized upon with almost pathetic eagerness." A nation fearful of the escalating nuclear arms race, made nervous by Joseph McCarthy's hunt for domestic Communists, and reluctant to send their sons to fight a war in a far-off Pacific nation like Korea found in *The Sea Around Us* a longer perspective on their problems and a larger dimension by which to measure human achievement.[24]

Her readers told her, "We have been troubled about the world, and had almost lost faith in man; it helps to think about the long history of the earth, and of how life came to be. When we think in terms of millions of years, we are not so impatient that our own problems be solved tomorrow." Another reader said: "This sort of thing helps one relate so many of our man-made problems to their proper proportions."[25]

Carson insisted natural history never provided an escape from reality or the problems of twentieth-century life. Rather she believed "the mysteries of living things, and the birth and death of continents and seas, are among the great realities." But her readers found those realities if not exactly an escape from contemporary anxiety, then a perspective that inspired as it reassured. It was this long view of "the stream of time" that Americans wanted in the summer of 1951. It became the leitmotif of all of Carson's writing.[26]

Most critics either missed this comforting quality or denigrated it. *Newsweek*'s reviewer, for example, regretted that the book fell into a weakness common to modern nature writing: "A kind of scientific piety pervades such prose, mournful references to endless cycles and astronomical distances which begin by being impressive and end by becoming almost magical incantations." Yet precisely these qualities put *The Sea Around Us* in a different category from other popular nonfiction and kept it on the top of the best-seller list for a record eighty-six weeks, thirty-two of them in first place.[27]

The volume received national press attention and was widely reviewed. Harvey Breit, book critic for *The Atlantic Monthly*, wondered that a "marine biologist would write what is a first-rate scientific tract with the charm of an elegant novelist and the lyric persuasiveness of a poet." E. H. Martin, book critic for Baltimore's *Evening Sun*, where Carson once wrote features, called it a "brilliant study of the sea" that was "not only a superb example of scientific reporting but also a work of art." Herpetologist M. Graham Netting, soon to be the director of the Carnegie Museum in Pittsburgh, wondered that the author of the charming and informative *Under the Sea-Wind* could "produce within a decade a book worthy of comparison with the works of [the great English naturalist] Thomas Henry Huxley."[28] But these glowing assessments were exceptions to the book's initial reception among scientists and science writers, who praised it but without enthusiasm. Some reviewers, most of whom were male science writers, were hesitant to give Carson or her book the critical accolades that such a display of learning and eloquence deserved. Their reviews of *The Sea Around Us* were prejudiced by qualities they held against the author: Carson's status as a scientist, the audience she addressed, and her gender.

Rachel Carson had, in effect, come in from outside the academic and professional establishment and scooped both the scientific and literary community with her book on the natural history of the earth's oceans. With only a master's degree in zoology and without a literary pedigree, this female editor of government wildlife publications produced a scientific book for the popular audience and became an overnight literary sensation.

The New Yorker's imprimatur meant that the literary crowd would read *The Sea Around Us* to discover a new and talented writer. The Book-of-the Month Club selection ensured that a diverse middle class would uncover a fascinating story embracing science and literature. Its eventual condensation by *Reader's Digest* broadcast Carson's epic to the general reader. Carson had caught the insiders flatfooted.

The sexism that greeted Carson and her sudden fame is not as surprising as its blatant crudeness is striking. Many male readers, and certainly the scientific community, were reluctant to admit that a woman could deal with a scientific subject of such scope and complexity. Perhaps thinking Rachel Carson was a pen name, one reader wrote, "I assume from the author's knowledge that he must be a man." But such attitudes were not limited to her readers.[29]

Almost every male who reviewed the book speculated about what a woman who could write such a book might look like. Even Jonathan Norton Leonard ended his praiseworthy review in the *New York Times* regretting that the book's publishers had not printed a photograph of Miss

Carson on the jacket. "It would be pleasant," Leonard thought, "to know what a woman looks like who can write about an exacting science with such beauty and precision." Even one of the Oxford editors, upon meeting Carson after the book was published, remarked, "You are such a surprise to me. I thought you would be a very large and forbidding woman."[30]

A *New York Herald Tribune* reporter obligingly supplied a physical description of the author. "Readers . . . are advised that she was born 44 years ago in Springdale, Pa., that she is attractive, as her picture suggests, and of medium height, quite slim, and blue eyed, and is credited by her friends with a very nice sense of humor but, on the other hand, not much small talk, and that she almost did not become a scientist at all." An interviewer from *Pathfinder Magazine* who found Carson at home in Silver Spring in late June reported she was "a quietly taut, fragile-looking woman."[31]

Carson found comic relief from this unwanted and demeaning gender speculation in a cartoon Shirley Briggs drew for her that fall. It depicted her as a female of Amazonian proportions striding the seas, long hair tossing in the wind, an octopus in one hand, sea spear in the other. Shirley titled it "Rachel as her readers seem to imagine her."

Shirley's illustration had unanticipated usefulness as well. During an interview Mrs. Carson had with an unqualified applicant for household work, she noticed that the woman was eyeing Shirley's drawing on the bookcase behind her with apprehension. "Oh," Mrs. Carson explained, "that's a painting of my daughter Rachel with whom you will have to work closely if you take this position." The obviously horrified woman decided it best to seek employment in another household.[32]

Once *The Sea Around Us* was published, Oxford's main problem was keeping enough books in print to meet popular demand. In spite of Rachel's and Marie Rodell's pleas for a larger first printing, Henry Walck was stubborn. He and Walter Oakley ordered only two printings in advance of publication, but by the day after publication, those were sold out, and Oxford began to ration reorders. A third, fourth, fifth, and sixth printing was ordered, but books were held up because the bindery was closed for vacation, because paper was in short supply, and because Oxford had made only one set of plates. The publisher was reduced to running ads explaining the stock situation in the *New York Times*, *Herald Tribune*, *Chicago Tribune*, and the *Washington Post*, but many buyers were turned away disappointed.[33]

A week after publication day, Rachel Carson's image, reproduced as a line drawing from the Brooks Studio photograph, appeared on the cover of *The Saturday Review* along with a lengthy review and biographical profile. By this time, however, the modest author had left her eighty-two-year-old mother at their home in Silver Spring with mounting piles of fan mail and assorted requests and had taken off for Woods Hole. In the wake of her departure she left a runaway best-seller.

Catherine Scott's list of requests for radio and television interviews kept growing, but Rachel, who found them "serious interruptions to writing," agreed to do only one television interview as a favor to Oxford. "I simply can't understand the way the public has gotten so mad about the sea!" Rachel told Marie. "Did you know the *Washington Star*'s list of best sellers for Washington last week, listed me second? How all this happens with no books is a mystery in itself."[34]

But despite her protestations, Carson was well aware of the financial implications of writing a best-seller. It was a condition she had hoped for all her adult life. Glad that the Guggenheim made any drastic decisions about her position at Fish and Wildlife unnecessary for a year, Rachel was eager to talk to Marie about future plans in general and future publishers in particular.

On July 22, 1951, three weeks after it was published, *The Sea Around Us* entered the *New York Times* "Best Seller List" in fifth place. Watching her book climb the list from her happy solitude at Woods Hole, Rachel told her agent that "it does look to me as though, with any sort of fore-sighted planning, the present book can carry me for several years, and if I'm not solidly established as a full time writer by that time I ought to be shot, anyway."[35]

Marie commented dryly that Rachel was "starting at the top with a vengeance," an especially remarkable feat since so many places were out of stock. Rachel wrote her mother the news from Woods Hole, "Imagine being second on the Washington list! But also, of course, imagine being fifth on the *Times*, which of course means the whole country. *Publishers Weekly* reports that it is a 'runaway best seller,' Kin this be me???"[36]

Letters from admirers, requests for interviews, and offers of writing assignments were of such volume that Carson had to hire a young woman in Woods Hole to take dictation just to acknowledge them. Her new fame also tested her relationship with her mother, whose need to be part of Rachel's life increased with her daughter's public recognition.

When Rachel left for Woods Hole, she instructed her mother to send all professional letters and inquiries from publishers up for her to answer. But she asked her mother to acknowledge fan mail. Maria Carson was indispensable to her daughter both emotionally and practically. She was secretary, office manager, and the filter through which most requests had to go. In between she sent Rachel clothes and other things she needed, did her laundry for her, and kept her updated on family matters. Maria's pride in Rachel's literary success, natural as it was, increased her anxiety about Rachel's health. It also heightened Maria's tendencies to screen Rachel's activities and manage her career.[37]

Maria wrote every day, sometimes three times in a single day, constantly fretting about whether Rachel was getting enough rest, and talked to her on the telephone several times a week. Rachel's patience with her mother was sorely tried but never seems to have wavered. She willingly shared all the excitement of her success and was generally content with her mother's help. Marie Rodell's management and opinion was a fact that Maria Carson acknowledged and had to make the best of. But she did not make taking second place to Marie a happy experience. While her jealousy was natural, it created difficult moments among the three women and imposed limitations on Rachel.[38]

When Rachel finished her research at Woods Hole, she planned to meet her mother in Boston and drive on to Boothbay Harbor, Maine. But even their time in Maine would not be exclusive as it had been in 1946. It was a working vacation for Rachel, who had invited Marie to join them for two weeks. Bob Hines, whom Paul Brooks had hired on Rachel's recommendation to do the illustrations for the shore guide, would also be there part of the time sketching marine life.

Bob Hines and Maria Carson always got along easily. He posed no threat to her daughter's attention to her, and she knew how important his work was to Rachel. But Hines was a keen observer of the mother-daughter relationship since he operated within it so often. He was genuinely fond of Maria Carson, but at the same time he chafed at the limits Maria placed on Rachel's friendships. Bob Hines was always charming and polite, but he also encouraged Rachel to make time for herself.[39]

Even at Woods Hole Rachel was not safe from inquiring journalists and photographers. Cyrus Durgin of the *Boston Globe* came down in mid-July to interview her and to take photographs. Rachel reported to her mother, "we went to lunch, then he took some pictures with the harbor as background. He really was a very nice person." But although

Rachel talked about her early interest in the sea and her scientific education, most of Durgin's published interview centered on Carson's gender.[40] He wrote:

> Would you imagine a woman who has written about the seven seas and their wonders to be a hearty physical type? Not Miss Carson. She is small and slender, with chestnut hair and eyes whose color has something of both the green and blue of sea water. She is trim and feminine, wears a soft pink nail polish and uses lipstick and powder expertly, but sparingly.[41]

Durgin garbled parts of his story, which was nationally syndicated, writing that Carson had taught part time in a "Maryland girls' college" and that her first "writing within covers" was a book entitled *Under the Seaweed.* He ended his feature on Carson without any serious evaluation of her writing but with another remark about the requisite polarity between biologist and woman. Durgin told his readers, "You figure out the line of demarcation between Rachel Carson, biologist, and Rachel Carson, the pleasant lady who is so definitely feminine."[42]

Shortly after the Durgin interview, Carson complained to her mother, "Mercy but I'm getting to hate all those interviews and picture-taking. Why can't they let poor authors alone." "Poor honey," Mamma responded, "shall I send you those disguises Shirley made for you, so that you can really travel around incognito?"[43]

In mid-August, after another Oxford luncheon for booksellers in Boston, Rachel picked up her mother at the train station and drove on to Maine. At the last minute Ethelyn Giles, the real estate agent in Boothbay Harbor from whom they had rented their cottage on the Sheepscot River in 1946, found a small log cabin on Wall Point on the east side of Boothbay, facing Linekin Bay. Set deep into tall pine trees, their porch looked directly out onto the water. Housekeeping conditions were fairly rustic but their surroundings made up for such inconveniences.

Hines arrived in Boothbay several days later. He and Rachel, sometimes with Maria, went out on collecting trips to Ocean Point, where they found abundant material for him to sketch. "Bob is out on the porch sketching and painting now," Rachel wrote Marie, who would be joining them soon. "Mamma is of course having a fine time. I am anxious to get you down among these rock pools and show you sea-green sponges and brittle stars and limpets." When Marie arrived, Rachel ushered her into the cottage with some relief. Marie later recalled Rachel saying "Now I can take the poker out from under the bed," and noted "And she wasn't joking!"[44]

With the success of *The Sea Around Us*, the time seemed right to reissue *Under the Sea-Wind.* Seeing the potential for two best-sellers at the same time, Henry Walck wanted to bring out Carson's earlier book in time for Christmas. But as much as Rachel wanted the book republished, she was unhappy about giving it to Oxford yet not ready to trust Houghton Mifflin, whose track record was still unknown.

Rodell took on the delicate issue with Walck in her usual bold but tactful manner. "Miss Carson," Rodell wrote, "has been sufficiently distressed by a number of things in connection with the publication of *The Sea Around Us* not to be entirely sure that she wants the earlier book to be reissued by Oxford." Itemizing Carson's complaints about the book's physical format, the sales lost by the small printings, and Oxford's lack of foresight for the book's demand, she complained "the current advertising schedule continues to reflect Oxford's caution rather than its enthusiasm." Rodell offered to discuss the matter with Walck again in the fall, after Carson had returned to Washington.[45]

In the end, Rodell's strategy worked to everyone's advantage. By the time Carson and Oxford agreed on terms for the sale of the rights to *Under the Sea-Wind*, just before Christmas 1951, *The Sea Around Us* had been number one on the best-seller lists for several months. Oxford offered to pay up to $20,000 by December 1952 on terms entirely favorable to Carson. The sale satisfied her desire for reissue and Oxford's wish for a second Carson title, and preserved amicable relations between the two.[46]

While Marie was in Maine with Rachel, they had reviewed the speaking invitations Carson had received. Uncomfortable with the idea of appearing before large audiences, Rachel turned down most, preferring autograph sessions in bookstores.

Her first test of will came when Irita Van Doren, the editor of the *New York Herald Tribune Book Review*, invited Rachel to speak to the newspaper's annual Book and Author Luncheon in October. Rodell recalled that Carson called Van Doren from a public telephone booth in Boothbay Harbor determined to decline. But Mrs. Van Doren somehow persuaded her to accept.[47]

Carson was happier accepting an invitation from the National

Symphony Orchestra to speak at a small benefit luncheon in late September on Debussy's *La Mer*, although at the time she accepted she did not know that President Harry Truman's wife Bess would be the guest of honor.[48]

Carson left Maine in early September and, on the twenty-fifth, appropriately dressed in hat and gloves, Rachel and her mother joined Mrs. Truman and a select group of contributors to the orchestra at the head table for luncheon at the Mayflower Hotel in Washington. In her brief remarks, Carson explained that RCA Victor Records had asked her to write the commentary for the Toscanini-NBC Symphony recording of Debussy's *La Mer* not because she had any special musical knowledge but because she had a certain feeling for the sea. While Carson commented briefly on how the sea influenced the music of Debussy, Rimsky-Korsakov, and Sibelius, the theme of her talk was the strength of spirit people derived from music and the arts in difficult times.

Drawing on her own experience, she told the gathering about the letters she had received about *The Sea Around Us*: "It has come to me very clearly through these wonderful letters that people everywhere are desperately eager for whatever will lift them out of themselves and allow them to believe in the future. I am sure that such release from tension can come through the contemplation of the beauties and mysterious rhythms of the natural world."[49]

Carson's brief speech at this luncheon marked the beginning of her effort to develop an environmental philosophy that would provoke her audience to consider the consequences of environmental destruction. In what would be the first of many references in her writing and public speaking to the anxieties produced by the Cold War, Carson told her audience "the symphony orchestras that present and interpret the music of the ages are not luxuries in this mechanized, this atomic age. They are, more than ever, necessities."[50]

About the same time, she also wrote a brief article for *This Week Magazine*'s widely syndicated feature "Words to Live By." Touching again on the theme of strength of spirit that the mystery and beauty of nature provided, Carson revealed that "in the darker hours of life" she had drawn on her rich store of memories of the earth's beauties for comfort and release from tension, and had found in them the calmness to face a world in turmoil.[51]

Her column for *This Week* was a first draft of one of the most memorable evocations of nature's beauty that later appeared in *The Edge of the Sea*. In this first version Carson wrote:

> There is symbolic as well as actual beauty in the migration of the birds; in the ebb and flow of the tides, responding to sun and moon as they have done for untold millions of years; in the repose of the folded bud in winter, ready within its sheath for the spring. There is something infinitely healing in these repeated refrains of nature, the assurance that after night, dawn comes, and spring after the winter.[52]

Such reflections on the eternal cycles of nature were not just idle public statements. Rachel was especially in need of the spiritual and emotional comfort she found in nature in the fall of 1951.

She and her mother had returned from Maine to Silver Spring to learn that Marjorie Williams had been having a relationship with a married man and was several months' pregnant. Even though Marjie was diabetic and too far along for a safe abortion, there never seems to have been any discussion of putting the baby up for adoption.

In addition to their concern for Marjie's health and well-being, her pregnancy presented a family crisis. Maria Carson and Rachel had to concoct a fictional account of Marjie's emotional involvement to mollify Robert and his wife, who were strict Baptists, and who would be judgmental and unforgiving if they knew the truth.

Robert Carson was self-righteous, arrogant, and cruelly critical of others. Like most bullies and cowards, he lived his own lie. He had never told his wife, Vera, a Canadian woman he had met on one of his fishing expeditions, that he had been married before and divorced, nor that he had a grown daughter whom he neither acknowledged nor supported.

His mother and sister gave him a plausible version of the truth, and for the time it kept him quiet. Marjie had already confided her difficulties to Rachel's friend Elizabeth Dickson. With her help they found a physician to care for Marjie and made arrangements to protect her privacy until the baby was born.

For a hundred reasons Rachel was anxious to keep the matter secret. Once again Maria Carson took charge of a difficult situation, leaving a distracted Rachel to worry about the future and deal with the demands of her new public persona.[53]

There was tragedy for everyone in this difficult situation, but in many ways Rachel's life was impacted the most brutally. Just at the moment of her greatest achievement, enjoyment and celebration were denied her by the sadness she felt for Marjie's life and the potential for public embarrassment to herself and her niece. Instead of basking in the limelight of literary success, her energies and attention were focused on the needs of her family. There was a sad irony to the fact that fame came at the very moment when Carson was particularly vulnerable and needed privacy the most.

Carson told no one except Marie Rodell what was happening within her family. Later she confided in her friend Dorothy Freeman and even later to her administrative assistant and friend, Jeanne Davis. The only remaining evidence of Rachel's emotional distress comes from a letter to Freeman in February 1955, in which Rachel recalled her feelings about the critical acclaim for *The Sea Around Us* in 1951.

> There is a bitter little corollary to the thought I expressed last week. . . . It is the awareness that all that followed the publication of *The Sea*—the acclaim, the excitement on the part of critics and the public at discovering a "promising" new writer—was simply blotted out for me by the private tragedy that engulfed me at precisely that time. I know it will never happen again, and if ever I am bitter, it is about that.[54]

On October 16, 1951, a very nervous Rachel Carson appeared as the featured speaker at the *New York Herald Tribune* Book and Author Luncheon at the Astor Hotel in New York. Apprehensive about how to hold the interest of such a large and critical audience, Carson planned a short speech on the sea as a place of mystery and armed herself with the latest Woods Hole Oceanographic Institute hydrophone recordings to illustrate the sounds made by shrimp, fish, and whales in the sea's middle regions.

The text of Carson's speech is interesting because of the way she called attention to her gender, although her hand notes indicated that she may have decided to omit some of these remarks at the last minute. "People," she wrote, "often seem to be surprised that a woman has written a book about the sea. This is especially true, I find, of men. Perhaps they have been accustomed to thinking of the more exciting fields of scientific knowledge as exclusively masculine domains. Then even if they accept my sex, some people are further surprised to find that I am not a tall, oversize, Amazon-type female. I can offer no defense for not being what people expect, but perhaps I might say a few words about why a woman, and only an average-size one at that, should have become a biographer of the sea."[55]

Carson's speech at this luncheon established the pattern of her response to journalistic interest in her. Clearly, the inference that she was a large woman rankled her. Carson was rightfully proud of her slim, petite figure and her femininity. She dressed plainly but neatly, had her hair styled and permed regularly, and kept her nails manicured and polished. Although she rarely wore any jewelry other than a lapel pin or broach, she wore makeup and applied it well. She had shapely legs, enjoyed wearing high heels occasionally, and liked hats. Carson was conscious of her physical appearance and determined to rebut the perverted image of the female scientist. Her public comments, however, had the effect of heightening interest in her private life rather than the opposite.

Some who heard Carson speak that day remember that she seemed shy and spoke so softly that they had to strain to hear her. Her remarks may not have seemed especially memorable, but her underwater recordings of shrimp clicking and snapping their claws made an impression.[56]

Nervous or not, the speech marked her first successful public appearance before a large group. Carson even found the photograph session afterward endurable. The ice had been broken. Rachel telephoned Mrs. Van Doren from the train station on her way back to Washington to tell her how nicely she thought everything had been handled. In spite of her reticence, she was ready for fame.[57]

Although Carson never enjoyed the prospect of public speaking, she became more confident in her delivery and more rhetorically skillful with each address. Like her other writing, each speech was the product of several longhand drafts. She typed the text onto three-by-five cards, with the first sentence of every paragraph printed in capital letters. She always made a backup copy typed in normal fashion.

Before delivering a speech, she often added marginal notes or eliminated phrases or sections. Once she began to speak, Carson rarely strayed from her notes or added extemporaneous details. Her delivery was steady, well modulated, and authoritative. As she became more relaxed, she included self-deprecating humor citing personal ancedotes and telling stories about her past.[58]

While Carson was perfecting the art of public speaking, Rodell was handling requests for foreign rights that were coming in every day. *The Sea Around Us* eventually was translated into thirty-two different languages. With film agent Shirley Collier in Hollywood, Rodell also was busy working out the terms of the option RKO studios had offered Carson for a documentary version of *The Sea Around Us* to be produced by Irwin Allen. At the end of December 1951 Carson signed the film option for $2,500. A complicated deal, it involved other institutions such as the Ford Foundation, which would supply film sequences of the sea for RKO. In addition to selling her book as the basis for the film script, Carson would be paid as a consultant to recommend film footage.[59]

The option was extended again in April 1952 and the deal finally signed August 21, 1952. Carson was paid $17,500 for the film rights in January 1953. The film *The Sea Around Us* was not released to the public until the summer of 1953. In the fall of 1951, when the deal was initiated, both Carson and Rodell naively believed they could exercise some control over its artistic content. Carson's contract called for script review and obligated her to publicize the film after it was released.[60]

Carson had agreed to promote *The Sea Around Us* with a three-day book tour to Cleveland and Pittsburgh after Thanksgiving. Arriving at Halle's Department Store in Cleveland on November 29, Carson found that Oxford and the booksellers had scheduled a full day of autographing, interviews, and photo sessions. The only saving grace was a reception that afternoon in the store where she meet Jane Halle Crile, the daughter of the department store founder and wife of Dr. George (Barney) Crile, Jr., a cancer specialist and son of the founder of the Cleveland Clinic. Jane and Rachel especially liked each other. After this meeting the Criles always called Carson whenever they were in Washington. Jane and Barney traveled widely and were accomplished underwater divers and amateur archaeologists. Some years later when they decided to write a book about their adventures, Rachel introduced them to Marie Rodell. Eventually the Criles became her clients as well.[61]

The next day Rachel arrived in Pittsburgh, where an even more elaborate promotion schedule awaited her. The *Pittsburgh Press*, claiming Carson as the city's own daughter, had published articles all fall about the successful Springdale girl who had learned natural history from her mother in the rocky hills along the Allegheny River. Rachel had not been back to Pittsburgh since her graduation from PCW in 1929. Mary Scott Skinker's recent death and her own still-bitter feelings toward the college made the visit awkward.

The booksellers at Gimbel's Department Store had arranged a morning press conference and an afternoon interview on radio station KDKA, in addition to autograph sessions at the store. Several family friends from Springdale made the trip in to see her, including Jane Collins, Carson's ninth-grade English teacher, and Angeline Sober, a Springdale High School teacher who had recently purchased the old Carson homestead.

Later in the day Oxford and Gimbel's hosted a reception at the store for PCW faculty and students, where Carson signed more autographs. She was polite to the college officials who came, but several of her former classmates who dropped by thought her manner stiff and aloof.[62]

Rachel returned to Maryland late the next day tired and annoyed. Complaining to Marie, she wrote, "In Cleveland and in Pittsburgh, I was left at the mercy of a bunch of eager beavers who thought only of how many minutes the day contained and how many events they could cram into it, and as a result I came home in a state of utter exhaustion. I will not submit to anything like that again."[63]

She had agreed to one other major promotional activity that fall, but it was hardly strenuous. She attended a small book party given by the Cunard Steamship Company Ltd., which wanted to use *The Sea Around Us* to advertise its transatlantic cruises. On December 7 Rachel and Marie were the guests of honor at a select literary gathering on board the luxury British cruise ship the SS *Mauritania.* Since Rachel already knew several of the guests and did not have to make any formal remarks, she enjoyed the conversation and was particularly at ease. Her sole responsibility was to present the captain with an autographed copy of the book.[64]

Honors and awards of all kinds were flooding in along with endless invitations to speak. The Philadelphia Geographical Society had selected her for its Henry G. Bryant Medal. Several colleges and universities, including her alma mater, wanted to bestow honorary degrees. Even more exciting, *The Sea Around Us* was one of the finalists both for the National Book Award in nonfiction and the Burroughs Medal in nature writing.

Late in January 1952 Carson learned that she had won the prestigious National Book Award for nonfiction. She was invited to attend the award ceremony and reception at the Century Room at the Hotel Commodore in New York on January 27, 1952, and was expected to make a speech. Joining Carson on the dais that evening were James Jones, the fiction winner for *From Here to Eternity*, and poetry recipient Marianne Moore, who won for her *Collected Poems.*[65]

They were a curious trio: the poet Moore dressed in black, but looking cherubic with recalcitrant wisps of white hair tumbling freely from under a large tricornered black hat; the flamboyant Jones in bow tie, sporting his signature pencil mustache, whose wisecracks and cigar smoking were unappreciated by both women; and Carson, looking stylishly polished but conservative in a dark silk dress and the same feathered toque that she favored for all her important public occasions. Both women stoically endured overly large orchid corsages.

Drama critic James Mason Brown was master of ceremonies. He read the citation for the nonfiction winner:

> Rachel L. Carson's *The Sea Around Us* brings to the attention of the public a hitherto unconsidered field of scientific inquiry of great importance to the spiritual and material economy of mankind. It is a work of scientific accuracy presented with poetic imagination and such clarity of style and originality of approach as to win and hold every reader's attention.[66]

Carson had been thinking about her acceptance speech ever since she had learned her book was a finalist. In part it was an extension of her two earlier speeches in which she shared the spiritual refreshment that readers had found in her book. But for the first time Carson talked about the culture of science in America and attacked the prevailing notion of science and literature as separate and exclusive methods of investigating the world and of discovering truth.

Her address reflected not only the new confidence she felt in herself as a writer, which the National Book Award symbolized, but her decision to take a public role as cultural commentator. Drawing upon her experience as a scientist and her philosophy as a naturalist, her speech exhibited her new boldness as a critic.

Although Carson would address the growing elitism of science many times more, her remarks that night announced the themes of her future work. She did not shy away from revealing her personal feelings about those who would isolate science from the public and unmistakably challenged the profession.

> Many people have commented with surprise on the fact that a work of science should have a large popular sale. But this notion that "science" is something that belongs in a separate compartment of its own, apart from everyday life, is one that I should like to challenge. We live in a scientific age; yet we assume that knowledge of science is the prerogative of only a small number of human beings, isolated and priestlike in their laboratories. This is not true.

> It cannot be true. The materials of science are the materials of life itself. Science is part of the reality of living; it is the what, the how, and the why of everything in our experience. It is impossible to understand man without understanding his environment and the forces that have molded him physically and mentally.[67]

Leaving no doubt exactly where she stood, Carson told her listeners, "the aim of science is to discover and illuminate truth. And that, I take it, is the aim of literature, whether biography or history or fiction. It seems to me, then, that there can be no separate literature of science." It was a truth Rachel had lived ever since she reconciled the dichotomy of the two disciplines in her own life in 1936, when she began to write again about what she knew and loved best.[68]

In his introduction of Carson, James Mason Brown, like so many reviewers, had commented on the fusion of poetry and prose in her writing. Carson addressed this quality of her work as well, claiming that she had no special gift. In lines that would be widely quoted and that she would use again, she demurred: "The winds," she said, "the sea, and the moving tides are what they are. If there is wonder and beauty and majesty in them, science will discover these qualities. If they are not there, science cannot create them. If there is poetry in my book about the sea, it is not because I deliberately put it there, but because no one could write truthfully about the sea and leave out the poetry."[69]

Although Rachel believed that she had written only as the subject demanded, her remark is self-deprecating and unusually disingenuous. Carson was intensely conscious of sound, alliteration, and rhythm in her writing. She reworked whole sections of *The Sea Around Us* over and over again until she was satisfied with the cadences, the sonority as well as the clarity of each sentence. Her editing of the manuscript shows tireless attention to poetic nuance and skillful use of poetic techniques. Her insistence that her mother read her writing out loud testifies to her concern for such matters. Carson was rightfully proud of her poetic and imaginative writing and understood that her creative encounters with the natural world was what made her work singular.

Rachel's conscious use of poetic technique does not take away from the accuracy of her claim that her guiding purpose was to portray her subject with fidelity and understanding, without consideration of whether she was doing it scientifically or poetically. Accuracy and beauty were never antithetical qualities in her writing. But the importance she placed on poetic technique does suggest that her now-famous public remark was carefully crafted to modestly deflect a deliberate literary quality.[70]

Rachel's speech underscored another point she had been thinking about as well—one she had touched upon briefly in her speech at the National Symphony Orchestra benefit—the proclivity of human beings to see themselves and their problems as too important and, in their consummate egotism, to be ignorant of their place in the vast stream of time. Once again she used the occasion to enlarge her public philosophy and to underscore humanity's dependence on its relationship with all of nature. In the shadow of a stalemated Korean War with its unsettling debate about expanding atomic warfare, Carson ended her remarks with the hope that "perhaps if we reversed the telescope and looked at man down these long vistas, we should find less time and inclination to plan for our own destruction."[71]

The very existence of the atomic bomb forced Carson to the ugly realization that human beings truly had the power to destroy all the beauty, mystery, and wonder that she knew for herself and communicated to others in her writing. After 1951, the specter of atomic destruction was ever-present, a prospect that increasingly shaped her vision of the future and moved her to action. By focusing on the immutable forces of nature, *The Sea Around Us* calmed atomic fears in others. But for Carson, the Bikini Island tests in the Pacific, the spread of nuclear arms among nations, and the war in Korea had fundamentally altered her private belief in the ultimate sanctity of nature. The science establishment was not the only group Carson urged to greater openness.[72]

The John Burroughs Memorial Association was established in 1921, the year the great naturalist died, to commemorate excellence in nature writing. Long affiliated with the American Museum of Natural History in New York, its first medal was awarded to William Beebe in 1926 for his published work to that time.

Of all literary and scientific awards, Rachel Carson coveted the Burroughs Medal the most. She had plotted and strategized to have Oxford nominate *The Sea Around Us* in time. With Roger Tory Peterson and Edwin Way Teale on the prize committee for 1952, Rachel had a reasonable expectation of success. But as she considered matters in the fall of 1951, she felt that the seashore guide, rather than the ocean profile, fell most completely within the Burroughs Medal guidelines. If she failed this time, there might be another chance.[73]

But her luck held. On April 7, 1952, Rachel claimed the Burroughs

Medal for *The Sea Around Us* in another gala ceremony in New York City. When it was hers, she felt an odd sense of unreality "in being linked . . . with the immortals in the field of nature writing." Citing those she so admired in the tradition of Burroughs, Richard Jeffries, W. H. Hudson, and Henry David Thoreau, Rachel proclaimed herself a pioneer, a new interpreter. But her remarks that evening broadened the cultural warnings she had already initiated.

> Mankind has gone very far into an artificial world of his own creation. He has sought to insulate himself, in his cities of steel and concrete, from the realities of earth and water and the growing seed. Intoxicated with a sense of his own power, he seems to be going farther and farther into more experiments for the destruction of himself and his world.[74]

After reminding her audience of the remedial effects of wonder and humility, Carson struck new ground. As she had previously criticized the dichotomy between science and literature, now she turned her criticism on the traditional practitioners of nature writing, urging them to write for a broader audience. "I am convinced," she said, "that we have been far too ready to assume that these people are indifferent to the world we know to be full of wonder. If they are indifferent it is only because they have not been properly introduced to it—and perhaps that is in some measure our fault. I feel," she continued, "that we have too often written only for each other. We have assumed that what we had to say would interest only other naturalists. We have too often seemed to consider ourselves the last representatives of a dying tradition, writing for steadily dwindling audiences."[75]

Certain that the popularity of *The Sea Around Us* was not singular, Carson urged the members of the Burroughs Association to "develop a more confident attitude toward the role and value of nature literature." Fearlessly defending the public's ability to absorb the "facts of science," Carson urged Burroughs members to shed their old attitudes.[76]

For Carson, nature writing and popular science writing were vehicles of human redemption. Every effort to confront the mystery and wonder of the natural world, no matter how inadequate, gave deeper meaning to human existence. Her scientific knowledge and her skills as a writer were now publicly bound with the mission of "working toward a better civilization for tomorrow." She invited others to join her "by focusing attention on the wonders of a world known to so few, although it lies about us every day."[77]

Energized by the critical acclaim of the National Book Award and the Burroughs Medal, Carson was eager to get on with her writing. *The Sea Around Us* brought her freedom on several levels. But most fundamentally the honors that accumulated provided her with the opportunity to describe her mission and stretch the dimension of her witness.

10

"An Alice in Wonderland Character"

Carson's contract with Houghton Mifflin called for her to deliver the shore guide in March 1953. She planned an intensive schedule of travel and field research along the southern beaches for late winter and spring of 1952. Summer would be spent in Woods Hole at the MBL library, visiting other New England beaches, and writing. But distracted by the demands of fame and family, and unhappy with her first conception of the guide, she made little progress on the book during most of that year.

The success of *The Sea Around Us* surprised even Rachel. Becoming a literary celebrity had been relatively easy compared to the public life that now seemed expected of her. In addition to the National Book Award for nonfiction and the Burroughs Medal, the *New York Times* had voted *The Sea Around Us* the outstanding book of 1951. The women's-page editors of the nation's newspapers voted Carson "Woman of the Year in Literature." By the end of 1951 over 250,000 copies of the book had been sold.

Two prestigious awards bracketed the new year. On January 9, 1952, Carson became the first woman to receive the Henry Grier Bryant Gold Medal for distinguished services to geography from the Geographical Society of Philadelphia. Almost exactly a year later, the New York Zoological Society, where Carson had once unsuccessfully applied for employment as a writer, presented her with its Gold Medal for her contributions as an interpreter of the sea, rounding out a full year of continuous public acclaim.[1]

Carson was expected to speak at the Geographical Society's award dinner held at the Barclay Hotel in Philadelphia. After debating whether to limit her remarks to a geographic topic, she decided to talk about the relatively new science of oceanography and the importance of creative imagination as a critical adjunct of technology and scientific discovery. One of the other speakers at the Philadelphia dinner was Dr. James Creese, president of Drexel Institute of Technology. Impressed by Carson's ideas and her presence as a speaker, he wrote her several weeks later, with the news that Drexel's faculty had voted to award her an honorary doctorate of letters at their June commencement. Rachel was particularly pleased to have the noted science institute honor her work; it further validated her view that science and literature were complementary avenues of discovery.[2]

Carson's brief remarks at the luncheon after the hooding ceremony addressed the increasingly separate cultures of science and the humanities. Carson told the Drexel gathering:

> Scientists are often accused of writing only for other scientists. They are even charged with opposing any attempt to interpret their findings in language the layman can understand. Literature is merely the expression of truth. And scientific truth has power to improve our world only if it is expressed. You have given your blessing to one of the most important functions of the writer today. This is to describe and to interpret, for the average man, the world that lies about us. I thank you for the encouragement you have given to me and to other writers who are attempting such a task.[3]

Drexel's doctorate followed an honorary doctorate in literature from her alma mater, Pennsylvania College for Women, awarded on "moving-up day" in May, and one in science from Oberlin College in Ohio in June. Although Carson was besieged with requests from other institutions, she agreed only to these three and to an honorary degree in literature from Smith College the following June.

PCW president Paul Anderson cited their distinguished alumna's eminence in the art of interpreting nature to human beings, her brilliant and clear writing, "and the promise of equally great contributions yet to come." In the receiving line later that afternoon at the college reception in her honor, Rachel whispered to her former classmate, Ruth Hunter Swisshelm, now the director of the college alumnae office who was standing next to her, that although she was very flattered by all the attention, she was much happier going barefoot in the sand than she was standing on a hardwood floor in high heels.[4]

The impetus for Oberlin College to give Carson an honorary doctorate of science came from zoology professor Hope Hibbard, who presented Carson for the degree. Hibbard was one of three female biologists on the Oberlin faculty, a college known for its early admission of female students, and one of the few women there who had achieved the rank of full professor. Rachel made no formal remarks at Oberlin or at the later ceremony at Smith College, but honors that acknowledged her contributions to science were especially gratifying.[5]

Edith Oliver, who, as theater critic for *The New Yorker*, had been in the audience when Carson spoke at the National Book Awards and who followed her progress in the press, commented to Marie Rodell "how gracefully and well Rachel had slipped into being a celebrity." Oliver could not have guessed at the physical and emotional effort the role required of her.[6]

"All these requests for personal appearances here and there are getting me down," Rachel complained to Oxford's publicity director, Fon Boardman. "To do even half the things people want, I'd have to be a sort of Alice in Wonderland character, rushing madly in all different directions at once. And needless to say, there would be no more Carson books, but of course the dear public does not stop to think of that." But other more serious aspects to her sudden fame oppressed her by the sheer time they demanded and the complicated arrangements they required her to make.[7]

For example, at the time of the Burroughs Award ceremony in April 1952, Rachel and her mother were in Myrtle Beach, South Carolina, where she was doing field research. Afraid to leave her mother alone for more than two nights at a time, Rachel set up alternative plans just in case she could not attend the ceremony, asking Edwin Way Teale to accept the award and to read her speech.[8]

She had hoped to spend the weekend after the award with the Teales at their home on Long Island, investigating the beach there. But even though the couple who owned the motel in Myrtle Beach stayed with her mother while she was gone, Rachel barely had time to "grab the medal and run." The beach walk would have to wait. "The longer *The Sea Around Us* stays at the top of the list," she complained to Teale sometime later, "the greater, it seems, become the pressures of correspondence, telephone calls and interruptions of all sorts. Even just the labor of saying 'No' in a way that doesn't make people mad takes a good deal of nervous energy and one cannot say no to everything."[9]

Oxford's publication of *Under the Sea-Wind* on April 13, 1952, when Carson's acclaim was at a peak, brought even more publicity and increased demands on her time. It was, of course, a wonderful event and a cause for personal celebration. Although the new edition was smaller in format and lacked Howard Frech's lovely pen-and-ink illustrations, Oxford ordered a large first printing and produced it on time. The Book-of-the-Month Club chose the work as an alternate selection for June, and *Life* magazine published all of Part 1 accompanied by striking pen-and-ink illustrations by staff artist Rudolph Freund. Nearly 40,000 copies of *Under the Sea-Wind* were sold even before publication.[10]

On April 27, 1952, the *New York Times* noted a "publishing phenomenon as rare as a total solar eclipse." *Under the Sea-Wind* appeared on the best-seller list in tenth place, while *The Sea Around Us* stayed solidly in second, having yielded first place to a sensational political exposé only the week before. Not only did Rachel feel vindicated by the popular reception of her once-neglected first book, but she took a certain delight in seeing how the book critics effused over what they had once ignored.[11]

Where *Times* critics had been somewhat reserved in their estimate of her achievements in 1951, they now compared Carson to literary giants. "Great poets from Homer, with his sonorous hexameters on the 'loud-sounding sea,' down to Masefield, with his poignant verses about sailing, have tried to evoke the deep mystery and endless fascinations of the ocean; but the slender, gentle lady who is editor of the United States Fish and Wildlife Service seems to have the best of it. Once or twice in a generation does the world get a physical scientist with literary genius. Miss Carson has written a classic in *The Sea Around Us*. *Under the Sea-Wind* may be another."[12]

Other critics, such as Harvey Breit, who had been modestly enthusiastic about *The Sea Around Us* in his column in *The Atlantic Monthly*, now warmly praised Carson's widely acknowledged literary talent. Meanwhile the honors continued to mount. Carson was elected a fellow of the Royal Society of Literature in England and to honorary membership in the national fraternity of women in journalism, Theta Sigma Phi. The Department of Interior honored her with its Distinguished Service Award, citing not only her exemplary government publications but her skill in interpreting science and advancing the cause of conservation through public appreciation and understanding. "I always think there is a special pleasure in turning out to be a prophet in one's own country," Marie Rodell told Rachel affectionately, and expressed her regret that Rachel, who was up in Woods Hole, would miss the ceremony.[13]

Carson turned down other attractive invitations to speak all over the country. "All of these invitations, no matter how pleasant, would absolutely wreck the writing program I am now laying out," she told Oxford editor Fon Boardman, who had taken Vaudrin's place. "What has gone on in the last six months is all very fine, but enough is enough." Ever the realist, Marie worried lest Rachel give the wrong impression and appear too aloof or arrogant. "I am frankly getting a little bit worried about the effect on people in general to your constant refusal to do things of this sort," she told Rachel when the latter balked at appearances to publicize the RKO film. "People never look at the motives but are simply apt to leap to the conclusion that you are being high and mighty." Rachel relented, but remembering how abused she had felt on her book tour appearances in Pittsburgh and Cleveland, insisted she must be consulted before any itinerary was finalized.[14]

Some of Carson's mail following *The Sea Around Us* was critical. A letter from James Bennet, an attorney and student of physical geography in New York City, is representative of a group of educated readers who took exception to Carson's account of the evolution of life from the sea. Bennet chastized Carson for ignoring God as Creator and for being dogmatic in her interpretation of how life began.

Carson's reply is a study in diplomacy, a well-crafted public response to the question of her religious beliefs, phrased perfectly for later quotation. As such it hides her deeper spirituality and simplifies her conception of both the Creator and the process of evolution. She told Bennet:

> It is true that I accept the theory of evolution as the most logical one that has ever been put forward to explain the development of living creatures on this earth. As far as I am concerned, however, there is absolutely no conflict between a belief in evolution and a belief in God as the creator. Believing as I do in evolution, I merely believe that is the method by which God created and is still creating life on earth. And it is a method so marvelously conceived that to study it in detail is to increase—and certainly never to diminish—one's reverence and awe both for the Creator and the process.[15]

What really got Carson's attention was not Bennet's accusation that she was an atheist but rather that he felt she had been arbitrary in her presentation of the various theories of creation. "As I look over it," she went on, "my text seems to me to be so full of expressions like 'perhaps'—'some scientists believe'—'it may be'—or 'we do not know' that I really did not expect to be charged with dogmatism, which all my training and instincts lead me to regard as a cardinal sin."[16]

Rachel deleted a paragraph from the draft of her reply to Bennet in which she denied she was an atheist, and she chose not to restate her understanding of material immortality as she had written of it in the last paragraphs of *Under the Sea-Wind*. She was content to let her commitment to the wonder and beauty of creation or, as she later described it, "the spectacle of life," stand as her spiritual credo.[17]

The acclaim for *The Sea Around Us* did not bring Carson only honors and awards. Its enormous sale, not to mention the republication of *Under the Sea-Wind*, produced a royalty income that brought her financial independence and a measure of security for the first time in her life. It also produced tax consequences requiring the services of an accountant as well as a literary properties lawyer, Maurice Greenbaum, who came highly recommended by Marie Rodell.

Although Carson was on a year's leave of absence from the Fish and Wildlife Service as a Guggenheim Fellow, she was still an employee of the U.S. Department of Interior. As such she accrued pension benefits and was paid a salary for the three months of the year that she had agreed to work. In March the Guggenheim Foundation informed its fellows that grants had been declared taxable and offered further compensation to help defray this unexpected expense. Rather than add to her already considerable taxable income for 1952, Carson returned the March stipend check and asked that no further payments be made to her; she could now count on royalties from *The Sea Around Us* to provide sufficient income and would prefer that the additional money be given to those who needed it. This gesture contrasted starkly with her earlier rather small-minded financial bickering over the Saxton Fellowship stipend. She completed her Guggenheim Fellowship at the end of May as scheduled.[18]

Carson's original conception of the *Guide to Seashore Life on the Atlantic Coast* was to interpret shore life in terms of its relation to the environment. The outline from which she began her field research in the fall of 1951 in Nags Head and later in Maine called for chapters dealing with the conditions of life on the shore, the equipment and collecting methods useful to a beachcomber, and a description of common specimens that placed them in their proper biological groups. These chapters framed five others on creatures found along rocky shores, sandy shores, mud and salt flats, wharf pilings, jetties and breakwaters, coral reefs, and offshore waters. Carson planned to suggest the special features of each environment to which creatures would have to adapt, their geological origins, and a selection of the animals commonly found in each area. She would provide a "biographical sketch" that illuminated the basic conditions of the more important life-forms.

Library research for the guide presented a formidable problem, involving the examination of literally thousands of references in a widely scattered literature. Field research was equally daunting, although much more fun. Once she selected the creatures to include, she had to study their life cycles and physical habitats, and identify the ways in which they had adapted to various and often continuously changing conditions.

When Carson arrived in Myrtle Beach, South Carolina, in the spring of 1952, she had changed her working title to *Rock, Sand, and Coral, a Beachcomber's Guide to the Atlantic Coast*. Her divisions were now primarily ecologic rather than geographic, but the groupings within remained substantially the same. Large gaps in her library research had to wait for summer months at the MBL library in Woods Hole. But she had yet to come up with the right way to present each creature without making the book repeat what other guides to shore life had done.[19]

Rachel and her mother made their base headquarters on the edge of Myrtle Beach State Park in the T & C Motor Court owned by the Thomases, a friendly couple who made the two women quite comfortable. Rachel brought along her newest research assistant, a handsome eight-month-old feline named Muffin, who turned out to be an unusually adaptable traveler. Rachel confided to Shirley Briggs that Muffin approved highly of the fish odor of the specimens she brought home at night, but that she had difficulty disposing of the larger and more redolent sponges and ascidians when she was finished looking at them. She resolved her problem by "slipping them into municipal trash cans after dark, to the surprise, no doubt, of the collectors of refuse." Shirley Briggs found the image of Rachel sneaking out to the city dump at night with a precious package of smelly beach specimens enormously amusing and made it the subject of another of her unique cartoons.[20]

By mid-April Rachel was roaming the wide sandy beaches of St.

Simons Island off the coast of Georgia just north of Brunswick. Her field notes from this trip are particularly rich with the detail of what she saw and what interested her: "the low tide beach deeply grooved with ripple marks—a pattern of wavelets sculptured and preserved for the tidal interval," clumps of *Alcyonidium* constructed on a foundation of small gorgonians, or attached to a clamshell.[21]

The sand flats yielded some of the most interesting treasures—sea pansies and many entrances of the elusive ghost shrimp that Rachel kept trying to coax out by dropping grains of sand down their holes. At dusk the birds came, their dark forms silhouetted by the bleak light reflected from the occasional pools of water in the sand. Rachel got very close to the sanderlings "scooting across the sand like little ghosts" and to the large, darker willets before they took alarm.[22]

The next day, out early on the same flats, she finally found a guide to help her see the ghost shrimp that she now realized were darting about in the pools left in the depressions of sand. She wrote in her notes:

> I first saw him away out on the flats, apparently by himself, and I thought he was chasing birds. But he was interested in the shallow pools of water and would wade in and go trotting around, his stumpy tail wagging constantly. I first wondered if he was noticing the little glittering reflections that were dancing all over the bottom for the breeze kept little ripples stirring and the sun was very bright. When I came back down the beach later, he was still out, trotting around in the same pool. Everyone had gone in; the tide had turned and I was worried for fear he might be cut off—he was very far out—get bewildered about where the shore was, and drown. So I decided to go out after him. He just wouldn't be diverted, but went on trotting in circles. Then I saw the darting of the little almost transparent forms of shrimp and knew what was attracting him. In the end I had to pick him up and carry him a little distance; then he scampered ahead to another pool and resumed his shrimp hunting, but since that was near the upper beach I didn't worry.[23]

The image of Rachel Carson, barefoot on the long flat beach of St. Simons Island, carrying a happy little dog back through the oncoming tide to the safety of the high ground is a defining one. Carson's field research was never so narrow and/or self-absorbing that she missed the wider angle of vision. Her delight in nature, in the wonder of creation that she saw everywhere, all around her, included the curiosity to follow a dog's adventures and be concerned for its well-being, grateful for what she had learned from observing it. Carson's concern for the dog, like her empathy for the one-legged sanderling, reflects her respect for all creatures. The joy with which she had viewed the natural world as a child and the poetic sense with which she endowed it as an adult were filtered through a scientist's knowledge and curiosity without any loss of initial wonder. Her field notes range from technically accurate taxonomic description to pure poetry, often in the same entry. At no time was Carson's focus bifurcated; in the field she always saw things in a single vision.[24]

All along the southeastern coastal beaches she visited, Rachel was fascinated by the sand dunes and the "peculiar magic inherent in that combination of sand and sky and water." The dunes were "bleak and stark" but not forbidding. To her, their bleakness was part of their quiet, calm strength. Sometime later she wrote a sketch of the dunes that included a special sort of epiphany of that moment when she suddenly understood the process of creation and the evolution of life in contemporary time. Perhaps she intended to include it in the shore guide, or perhaps it was just a private reflection, but her notes reveal her humility before the act of creation she witnessed on the beach.

> I stood where a new land was being built out of the sea, and I came away deeply moved. Although our intelligence forbids the idea, I believe our deeply rooted attitude toward the creation of the earth and the evolution of living things is a feeling that it all took place in a time infinitely remote. Now I understood. Here, as if for the benefit of my puny human understanding, the processes of creation—of earth building—had been speeded up so that I could trace the change within the life of my own contemporaries. The changes that were going on before my eyes were part and parcel of the same processes that brought the first dry land emerging out of the ancient and primitive ocean; or that led the first living creatures step by step out of the seas into the perilous new world of earth.
>
> Water and wind and sand were the builders, and only the gulls and I were there to witness this act of creation.[25]

From St. Simons Island, Rachel, Maria, and Muffin proceeded south to the Florida Keys. With their headquarters at Marathon Key, they spent days at various other nearby keys. On Big Pine Key, they joined Bob Hines and a FWS photographer on assignment to photograph and draw the rare Key deer. When that was done, Bob stayed on to draw sea creatures for Rachel.

Hines was a ruggedly handsome outdoorsman with an easy manner, a wry sometimes cynical sense of humor, and infinite patience. Years of working together had given Bob and Rachel an informal camaraderie as well as a thorough knowledge of each other's work habits. Although Bob found Rachel's mother a "frivolous, rather silly woman," he paid her kind attention but could not resist teasing her.

Hines and Carson spent the better part of the next three weeks in the Keys, ending their research in Key West. Most of that time the two spent long hours with camera, buckets, and other collecting gear, wading in mangrove swamps or in shallow coral shoals looking for specimens Rachel wanted Bob to illustrate. Clad in bathing suits, Bob shirtless, Rachel covered from the sun by a work shirt and visored cap, they worked easily and efficiently together. Hines remembered that Rachel talked to herself about what she was doing and what she was looking for as she waded around the shoals, but she did not impose her views on others. If you listened to her as she went along, Bob recalled later, she gave a small lecture on the creatures she was collecting and their habitat. She knew what she wanted and how to find it.[26]

Bob appreciated Rachel's sense of humor. He remembered that once she named the three crabs in her bucket after FWS people they both knew. Together they sent Shirley Briggs a postcard from Key West after an afternoon in the water, reporting that they had shaken hands with an octopus. "He was a baby about 10 inches long, and he did seem reluctant to part," Rachel wrote. "The Keys are really wonderful & I'll be sorry to head north."[27]

Before Carson left Florida there was one matter that she needed to resolve. All year long she had debated whether she dared leave the security of her government job and support herself by her writing. It was impossible to think of making any headway on the shore book if she went back to her editorial responsibilities. She was also aware that the political climate in the Department of Interior had changed while she had been on leave. Programs had been cut, and she realized it would be more difficult for her to support the prevailing policies. Her work would not only be less interesting but less vital. She could do more for the things she believed in out of government than in. Convinced that with some wise investing she could support herself and her family, she determined to make the break, a course that Marie Rodell, whose financial advice Carson trusted, encouraged.

On May 7, 1952, Rachel wrote to her FWS boss Alastair MacBain from Key West asking him for the forms she would need to sign in order to resign officially from government service. "It seems to me more than time that we got my long-discussed resignation on paper," she wrote, "for you must certainly be wanting to complete alternative arrangements." MacBain, who had been expecting such a request from Carson, replied, "I hate to do it but you asked for it, so here it is. After all, that's the price of fame, I guess."[28]

On May 15 Rachel signed the forms requesting that her resignation from the Service be effective as of June 3, 1952, the day her year's leave of absence expired. She stated her reason for resigning simply: "To devote my time to writing." After mailing the forms off, she called Hines and invited him to have dinner with her and her mother that night in Key West to celebrate. Rachel told him that she had just sent in her resignation from FWS and was no longer employed. "How do you feel?" Bob asked. "Ecstatic!" she replied.[29]

In July Rachel and her mother sublet their house on Williamsburg Drive, put their furniture in storage for the rest of the summer, and took off for Massachusetts. Rachel had made elaborate arrangements for her research at the Marine Biological Laboratory. She rented the house of her old friend Paul Galtsoff in Woods Hole, just across the street from the MBL, where she had invested in private laboratory space, a saltwater aquarium, and a high-powered binocular microscope. Maria kept house while Rachel worked at the MBL library during the day and returned to her laboratory at night. She hired a young woman to do some routine research and enticed Alice Mullen to come down from Amherst to do more. While Alice was there, Carson was elected to the MBL Corporation, an honor that underscored her contributions to marine science.[30]

In between studying oyster drills under her microscope and looking at baby starfish, Rachel entertained friends. Marie came for a week during which they discussed the virtues of various publishers and editors. Paul and Susie Brooks came one weekend, followed shortly thereafter by

Edwin and Nellie Teale, with whom Rachel went off to Nantucket and Monomoy.[31] While they were on Nantucket, the Teales introduced Rachel to their friends naturalist writer and bird enthusiast John Kieran and his wife, Margaret, a newspaper feature writer, who had a lovely home on the island. Later that month Rachel went back to Nantucket to explore the beach on her own. She had agreed to autograph her books at a special tea for the benefit of the Natural Science Department of the Maria Mitchell Association. The Kierans invited Rachel to spend the night and planned a small dinner party that evening. But when Rachel came in, Margaret sensed that she was already exhausted and kindly excused her from the party, serving her grateful guest her dinner on a tray in her room instead.[32]

Although Rachel enjoyed such outings, they invariably took time away from her work on the shore book. So when Bob Hines arrived in early September to do more drawings, she was ready for concentrated effort. Before he arrived, she had sent Hines a long list of marine creatures she wanted him to sketch. "Don't let it scare you to death," she told him. "I really think with the wonderful set-up I have here you won't have too much trouble, though I suppose it means working like a dog while you are here. But it is a pleasant place to do that." For a variety of reasons, most having to do with Bob's personal finances, he was far behind schedule on his illustrations.[33] They worked for two weeks in Rachel's lab, and although they made steady progress, Rachel confided to Marie, "Bob does not take one step unless I am behind him with a sharp needle. I am delighted with the way he is doing the drawings and cannot imagine anyone else who could do them half so well; but believe me, it gets done by the sweat of my brow as well as his." But she was also deeply indebted to Hines, who made her life easier in many small ways.[34]

They traveled up to Boothbay several weekends, staying at the Harbor Motor Court, so that Bob could do more drawings of tide-pool creatures at Ocean Point. Several times Rachel stayed out in the tide pools through an entire tidal interval. She got so cold and stiff in the icy water that she had difficulty getting back in over the rocks. Bob recalled that on those occasions he would wade in and carry Rachel out. Maria would wrap her in a blanket they kept for such purposes in the car until she warmed up and could go back to work.[35]

Rachel and her mother made several more weekend trips to the Maine coast in September, always with Boothbay as their base. On one visit

Rachel stopped by Ethelyn Giles's real estate office to inquire about homes for sale. She looked at a few cottages on the market but found nothing she could afford or that gave her enough space and privacy. Many were twenty or thirty years old and in need of expensive repairs.

After a visit one weekend tide pooling at Ocean Point, they were invited to dinner at the home of Canadian marine zoologist N. J. Berrill and his wife, Jacquelyn, with whom Rachel had become friends. The Berrills encouraged Rachel to look at property on which to build her own cottage instead of buying an existing one. When she did so, she quickly fell in love with a spot on Southport Island, just west of Boothbay Harbor, in a thickly wooded section along the shore of the estuary of the Sheepscot River known as Dogfish Head. With the Berrills' help, she hired a well-recommended builder and signed a contract for land and cottage.[36]

Back at Woods Hole, Rachel wrote Marie at length.

> I am about to become the owner (strange and inappropriate word) of a perfectly magnificent piece of Maine shoreline, and by next June I am to have a sweet little place of my own built and ready to occupy! The place overlooks the estuary of the Sheepscot River, which is very deep, so that sometimes—you'll never guess—*whales* come up past the place, blowing and rolling in all their majesty! And lots of seals, and there is a long pool left in the rocks at low tide, where sculpins and other fish sometimes get stranded. My frontage is 140 feet, and the lot runs back about 350 feet. Lots of evergreens and other trees. Are you excited?[37]

Rachel went back to Southport at least once more before she left for Maryland to go over the lot inch by inch with the builder to decide where to site the house and what trees would have to be cut. She would, of course, "have big picture windows for that magnificent view. I may have a little study tucked in for books, typewriter, microscope and me," she told Marie. She also added a screened porch on the side and a sun deck across the front.[38]

In Woods Hole as well as out in the field, Carson could lose herself in her work and forget the letters and requests that filled her mailbox. But the reality of her new public recognition intruded as soon as she left the laboratory or the tide line. It involved more than just the loss of privacy.

For a writer of Rachel's temperament, who already had more than enough built-in demands, being a celebrity was distracting, often annoying, and always stressful.

One day, while Rachel and her mother were traveling through the South, she went into a beauty parlor to have her hair done. Even sitting under the hair dryer in pin curls, she could not avoid being discovered by a stranger who wanted to meet her then and there. Another time, at the Thomases' motor court in Myrtle Beach, she was rudely awakened early one morning by an autograph seeker who pushed past her mother and presented Rachel, who was still in bed and had been asleep until then, with two books to autograph.[39]

Although Carson had been honest in March when she told Fon Boardman that her doctor had ordered her to get away and to reduce as much stress as she could, Rachel had told him only part of the story. She did not confide to anyone except Marie Rodell that family problems had become almost a greater source of anxiety and stress than any public demand. Nor did she indicate to any of her local friends that the several research trips that kept her and her mother out of town from March until late September 1952 were carefully calculated to deflect public attention away from her immediate family.[40]

Rachel had taken elaborate steps to see that the privacy of her niece Marjorie Williams would be protected during her medically risky pregnancy. Marjie lived in a small apartment in downtown Washington, not far from her sister, Virginia, on New Hampshire Avenue, and close to Doctor's Hospital and Rachel's doctor, Joseph A. Bailey, who was looking after her. Marjie continued to work during the day and attend her classes at night as long as she could, but the pregnancy proved difficult and she was in and out of the hospital several times.[41]

Marjorie's son, Roger Allen Christie, was born on February 18, 1952. Mother and baby continued to live downtown where Virginia and Rachel's friend and nurse Elizabeth Dickson could keep an eye on them. But Virginia herself had surgery for an ovarian cyst in early March, further delaying Rachel's departure to the southern beaches.

Rachel told Marie Rodell of Roger's birth and confided in Dorothy Algire and Alice Mullen, but no one else even knew Marjie had been pregnant. When Rachel and her mother got back to Maryland in mid-September, Roger was over six months old. Then slowly and deliberately Rachel mentioned to friends like Shirley Briggs that Marjie had been married briefly and now had a child. She gave no details and simply left the impression that, for whatever reason, Roger's father was no longer around.[42]

Roger's birth, Marjie's health, her mother's care, and the always unpredictable behavior of her brother Robert make it easy to understand why Rachel later told Dorothy Freeman she sometimes felt cheated out of the opportunity to enjoy the fame that *The Sea Around Us* had brought her. Little wonder too that Carson was frustrated with her lack of progress on the shore book and deeply relieved that she no longer had the additional responsibilities of the Fish and Wildlife Service job. No area of her life was without complication; no situation was simple. Only when she was out in the field could she forget her problems for a few hours and lose herself in nature.[43]

In August Carson had received an unusual invitation from Roger Revelle, director of the Scripps Institute of Oceanography in La Jolla, California, that offered real escape. She had first met Revelle during World War II, when he was with the Office of Naval Research. After the war Revelle became chairman of the committee studying the biological effects of radiation from the 1946 atomic tests in the Bikini Islands. Like many other government biologists and botanists, Carson opposed those tests. She edited the FWS's biological survey that was conducted on the islands before the tests and in the course of her editorial work had the opportunity to read Revelle's reports.

Now Revelle invited Carson to see the Pacific islands for herself, as the historian on an important four-month research expedition to the Central and South Pacific Ocean. The expedition, known as Operation Capricorn, involved two research vessels and their scientific crews from Scripps that would explore the little-known area of the Western Marshalls over the Tonga Deep. Revelle particularly wanted Carson for the leg of the trip that began at Kwajalein Island, but he hoped she could join them for the entire voyage, which began in November and returned to San Diego in February 1953.[44]

Rachel could hardly imagine a more exciting prospect than a research expedition to the far Pacific. Referring to it as her "great adventure," she got out books, maps, and schedules to see if there was some way she could manage it. She would be able to publish her ship's journal in book form and sell the articles she wrote as she went along. The trip offered her everything she had wanted, the opportunity to observe the ocean firsthand and to write about what she saw without restriction. But the timing was bad, and being away for four months presented difficult family decisions.

The seashore guide was already behind schedule. By the fall she realized she could not possibly make her promised spring deadline and that publication would have to be moved to a later date. If she went on the expedition, her work with Bob Hines would have to be rearranged as well. Then there was the even greater problem of finding someone to stay with her mother.

Carson tried to find a way to join the expedition if only for part of the voyage. But the realities of infrequent Pacific transportation and the complications of being away from home defeated her. Although she told Revelle her final decision was based on her book's publication schedule and on the fact that Hines had already arranged his government leave, the care of her elderly mother was the deciding factor. At the end of September, Rachel wired Revelle a final no. Only Marie Rodell knew how disappointed she was that she could not go. "I seem to be going around consoling everybody else about the Pacific trip," she told Marie, "now I wish someone would console me."[45]

When a copy of Henry Beston's review of *Under the Sea-Wind* arrived in the mail unexpectedly, she temporarily forgot her disappointment. Beston, whose writing deeply influenced Carson's, chose a small but influential monthly magazine, *The Freeman*, in which to publish his review, "Miss Carson's First." Beston's eloquent analysis of her writing must have almost made up for the neglect her book had suffered when it first appeared in 1941.

Reaffirming Rachel's own confidence in the knowledge obtained by the inner eye of the poet, Beston wrote lines that moved her deeply. "The poetic sense," he said, "is the justification of man's humanity; it is also the justification of his inexplicable world. No matter what astronomers make of the sun, it is always more than a gigantic mass of ions, it is a splendor and a mystery, a force and a divinity, it is life and the symbol of life. It is Miss Carson's particular gift to be able to blend scientific knowledge with the spirit of poetic awareness, thus restoring to us a true sense of the world." Rachel shared Beston's appraisal with a few friends, but it was so flattering that she was embarrassed by it. Although she had often thought about writing him to say how much she admired his work, she hesitated to do so even now. Beston's review was the best thing that happened to Carson that fall. The rest of it was taken up by a nasty dispute with film producer Irwin Allen and RKO studios.[46]

Allen, the writer, director, and producer of the RKO documentary *The Sea Around Us*, sent Carson a final draft of his script in early November.

"Frankly, I could not believe my first reading," she told Shirley Collier, her film agent in Hollywood, "and had to put it away and then sneak back to it the next day to see if it could possibly be as bad as I thought. But every reading sends my blood pressure higher." Carson sent Collier six pages of comment with the promise of a further response once she and Rodell had discussed it.[47]

Carson was shocked that instead of sticking to the atmosphere and basic concepts of her book and presenting the authoritative scientific knowledge of the ocean as she had, Allen's script was full of outmoded, unscientific concepts, presented in a distressingly amateurish manner. She particularly objected to the anthropomorphism of the language Allen used to describe ocean creatures and their relationships with each other. In her cover letter Carson told Collier, "the practice of attributing human vices and virtues to the lower animals went out of fashion many years ago. It persists only at the level of certain Sunday Supplements."[48]

In Rachel's estimation, the writing was "shockingly bad, riddled with clichés, and would be ridiculed." The whole script, in her opinion, amounted to nothing more than inaccurate sensationalism about the ocean, "a cross between a believe-it-or-not and a breezy travelogue."[49]

Marie Rodell shared Rachel's indignation at the scientific inaccuracies and sensationalism of the film, but as an editor and literary agent, she had her own list of grievances for Irwin Allen, who was unaccustomed to such stinging criticism of his creative work. "I am really staggered at Mr. Allen's impertinence, let alone his incredible egocentricity in rewriting Carson," she told Collier. "I have pointed out in the accompanying memo specific passages where in place of the prose which has conquered the imagination of half a million people, he has chosen his own largely ungrammatical paraphrases."[50]

Rodell reviewed the contract Carson had signed with RKO and realized that her right to review the script did not include the right to insist on any changes. Carson had sold RKO the right to use the book's title for the documentary, and her name, but Rodell thought perhaps the contract could be canceled without further payment. She warned Collier that if Allen failed to make the corrections Carson asked for, "Rachel would issue a statement to the trade journals and general press disclaiming any responsibility for the picture and deploring it strongly."[51]

In spite of Collier's efforts to mediate and Allen's willingness to make some corrections, relations between the parties deteriorated. When Carson and Rodell saw a screening of the finished film in New York in

January, it still contained misstatements of scientific fact. It was too late by then to make any more changes to the sound track. When Carson threatened to go public with her criticism, Allen made a few more cosmetic corrections but also threatened to sue her for libel and for breach of contract. It all ended in an unpleasant standoff. RKO released the film in May 1953, and Rachel signed an agreement promising to say nothing detrimental about the film or its producer in public.[52]

Carson got some private satisfaction from movie critics such as Richard Coe, whose column in the *Washington Post* deplored the film's narrative and pointed out that it bore nothing more than titular resemblance to Carson's book. "It has just opened at home," she wrote a friend that fall, "(how glad I am that I'm not in Washington) and the *Washington Post*, while liking some of the photography, roasted the script, for which I was duly grateful." But Allen and RKO were also vindicated when the film won an Academy Award for the "Best Documentary" of 1953.[53]

The whole filmmaking episode soured Carson from ever selling film rights to any other literary property and seemed to throw her off balance. It exposed a healthy stubbornness, a little arrogance, and obvious naïveté about the difficulties of working in other creative media. The prolonged option negotiations with RKO had given Carson and Rodell ample time to reconsider the sale and its terms. Carson ended the venture as she began it, stuck on the image of a certain kind of 1930s government documentary. Neither she nor Rodell had ever talked to Allen directly to see if their conceptions of a documentary on the sea held any common creative ground with his. Like her earlier dispute with the Fuertes estate, Carson ended up feeling morally wronged, this time by Allen's cinematic license with her text and his liberties with scientific fact.

Part of Carson's behavior can be attributed simply to having too much on her mind in the fall of 1952. Since her Houghton Mifflin contract had to be renegotiated, Rachel used the occasion to press Marie to get a better royalty rate from Paul Brooks. At the same time she fretted about making too much money in any one year and having to pay additional taxes since Marie had sold serial rights to *The Sea Around Us* to *The Philadelphia Inquirer* for a handsome fee.[54]

In mid-December Carson agreed to a contract with Harper & Brothers to do a volume on evolution she tentatively titled *Origin of Life* for their World Perspective Series edited by Ruth Nanda Anshen. She was also thinking seriously about writing a television script on clouds, or "air," as

Marie called it, for the *Omnibus* educational series. Distracted by too many decisions, pressured by the demands of others, and frustrated with her work on the seashore guide, Carson reacted to events and made commitments too hastily.[55]

Desperately needing to get away, Rachel flew down to the west coast of Florida shortly before Christmas to join Marie Rodell, who was visiting her family. They spent five days exploring the beaches of Sanibel and Marco Island. Even though the two women had several enjoyable visits together that year and took pleasure in each other's company, Rachel's literary success fundamentally altered their relationship.

Most of their letters, telephone conversations, and visits now concerned contracts, serial sales, and other literary matters. With fame and a measure of fortune, Rachel's emotional dependence on Marie lessened. While she still valued Marie's business savvy and her efficient management, Rachel was fully in charge not only of her career but of determining the degree of intimacy of their private friendship.

Success highlighted the temperamental differences between them that had always been there: Marie's tough, no-nonsense confrontation with life, her high-voltage energy, her head-on approach to problem solving, and her exuberant gregariousness now contrasted more glaringly with Rachel's reserved reactions to people and events. Rachel's reticence to confide her feelings or to take charge of the relationships in her life that sapped her energy must have frustrated Marie as well.

There was no one Rachel trusted more than Marie or whose literary opinion mattered more: That had not changed. But while they remained intensely loyal and deeply caring of each other, their interactions were more often those of closely allied author and agent rather than of emotionally connected friends. Rachel no longer looked to Marie for that uncritical devotion and emotional understanding that she had once hoped to find. Rachel still had a book to finish, and both Marie and Paul Brooks knew that she was stalled on it. Marie's job was to support her talented and exceedingly frustrated client.[56]

"You are being a model of virtue and patience not breathing down my neck at all," Rachel wrote Marie in March 1953. "Just keep it up—anything else would be unbearable. I know you are suffering, but just remember my sufferings are much worse. I'm getting into a horrid state of nerves and just possibly may conclude it will save time in the end to take off for Myrtle Beach for a week. . . . I'll let you know of course, before disappearing." To Nanda Anshen at Harper Rachel explained, "I have been working on the shore book with great intensity and now a terrible feeling of pressure (my own fault!) and as a result have developed a state of nervous tension that is not good. I've decided rather suddenly to take my doctor's advice to the extent of hurrying off to South Carolina for a week or ten days, where at least I can work in restoring surroundings."[57]

Carson had sent Brooks a new outline telling him she had found a unity of theme in the Florida Keys material that was lacking in the other sections. "As I write of it, it sounds so very easy; why is it such agony to put on paper?" After a visit with Rachel at the end of April, Rodell reported to Brooks that Rachel's new insights on the coral reef section seemed to improve the presentation. Author and agent felt encouraged.[58]

But no sooner had Rachel embarked on her new approach than she was laid low by a severe virus and felt even worse following a course of strong antibiotics. She improved enough to fly to New York for her first annual dinner as a member of the American Academy of Arts and Letters, but she returned the next day to rest before her trip to Smith College in Northampton, Massachusetts, ten days later, where she would receive an honorary doctorate of letters on June 8.[59]

Finally, in late June, her struggle with the material for the shore guide produced a new conception that freed her to restructure the book completely. Happy that she now knew how she wanted to present the material, Carson sent Brooks the chapter on the Florida Keys with a letter explaining

> Somewhere along in the Florida Keys chapter I decided that I have been trying for a very long time to write the wrong kind of book, and in dealing with the corals and mangroves and all the rest I seemed at last to fall into the sort of treatment that is "right" for me in dealing with this sort of subject. I seem to be doing the same sort of thing for the sand and feel I can for the marshes, not yet begun. It means that I shall have to rewrite quite a lot of the rocks chapter—but that is part of writing, I guess.[60]

Abandoning her attempt to write structureless chapters around thumbnail sketches of individual sea creatures, Carson now saw the shore guide as an interpretation of four types of shores, which she later reduced to three: rock, sand, and coral. The miscellaneous facts that had cluttered her style were now saved for picture captions or an appendix. "This solution frees my style to be itself," Carson wrote. The guide had now become a "sequel or companion volume" to *The Sea Around Us*, one dealing with the biological rather than the physical aspects of the sea. This new scheme allowed her to write about each geological area as a living ecological community rather than about individual organisms. On the rocky shores life was dominated by the tides; the waves ruled the sandy beaches; and the ocean currents determined life along the southern coasts. The Atlantic coast demonstrated these environments, common to shores all over the earth, "with the clarity of a well-conceived scientific experiment."[61]

By the time Rachel, her mother, and Muffin left Silver Spring for Maine in early July, Rachel was certain that she was on the right track and grateful for her editor's patience and understanding. The rocky shore section would have to be completely rewritten, but both Paul and Marie were convinced that with the material at her elbow, she could produce better results, although the pace continued to be agonizingly slow.

Rachel was eager to move into her dream cottage, which she had named "Silverledges." She was also looking forward to meeting Mrs. Stanley Freeman, her neighbor on the nearby Dogfish Head section of Southport Island, who had read in the local paper that Rachel Carson had bought property there and, just before Christmas, had written to welcome her. "I have loved the Boothbay Harbor area for years and do look forward to having a summer place to write in such beautiful surroundings," Rachel replied to Dorothy Freeman. "Do come see us. We look forward to knowing you, and I do appreciate your gracious welcome."[62]

11

"Nothing Lives to Itself"

Rachel Carson met Dorothy and Stanley Freeman on Southport Island in July 1953 shortly after she and her mother moved into their new cottage. The Freemans' only child, Stanley, Jr., and his wife, Madeleine, had given their father a copy of *The Sea Around Us* for his birthday in 1951, and the family had taken turns reading aloud from it as they sailed the Maine coast that summer. Dorothy and Stan Freeman were pleased to welcome that book's renowned author as their new neighbor on the island and to include Carson and her mother in their circle of summer friends.[1]

Rachel and Dorothy discovered they shared a love of nature, the ocean, and cats as well as the care of an elderly mother. They looked forward to their next visit, when Rachel promised she would take them tidepooling. The Freemans, who had been at their cottage since early June, left soon after their initial meeting for a long holiday in Canada.[2]

Rachel went about getting herself and her mother settled into their new home nestled in the spruce overlooking the wide stretch of the fast-moving Sheepscot River. She got very little writing done, but spent whatever time she could exploring her very own tide pools and relishing her surroundings. She had a steep stairway built down over the rocks to the shore so that she could carry material from her laboratory up to the cottage to look at under the microscope and then go back down and replace it. Maria would go down at low tide to feed the gulls while Rachel clamored over the rocks looking for creatures hidden in and under the seaweed. At dusk they sat on the deck above the water listening to the tide and the birds settling in for the night and watching the sunsets.

Marjie and baby Roger arrived several weeks later. Rachel always enjoyed Marjie's company, and together they explored the shoreline and woods. One morning they found a ten-inch starfish and brought it back to photograph Roger holding it. Since the tide was too high to return the starfish, Rachel waited until evening. "I took the flashlight and went slithering down to the low tide line and it was quite spooky," she wrote Marie. "The big crabs that usually stay down in crevices and under ledges in the day time were out scampering around and a drained anemone cave, by flashlight, with all the anemones hanging down, was quite Charles Addamsish." Before Marie came up for her first visit, Rachel warned her, "You have to get down to my low tide rocks if you have to crawl on your hands and knees, or wiggle on your stomach! I found a new part of it last night (on the lowest tide I've seen since we came) that is absolutely the most exciting, as to creatures, I've known anywhere."[3]

On the other side of her cottage was a dense woods of spruce and fir that included bunchberrys, reindeer moss, and lichens of all sorts. The trees began to turn to autumn flame in September, and almost every morning the woods was alive with migrant birds, warblers, kinglets, and grosbeaks. Out the living room's picture window Rachel and her mother could watch loons and seals, and sometimes a whale rolled within view at the nearby mouth of the Sheepscot. Carson's cottage in Maine was a dream come true, and Rachel was happier there than she had ever been.[4]

The Freemans returned to Dogfish Head just after Labor Day to close up their cottage. As promised, Carson invited them to go down to the low-tide world with her the following Sunday. Marie Rodell would be visiting for the weekend as well, and it was Rachel's favorite way of entertaining friends. Although it was only a neap tide, they could gather some interesting creatures to look at under Rachel's microscope and have a cup of tea together.

Their tide-pooling adventure allowed Rachel and Dorothy time to explore their common interests. Rachel's beloved cat Muffin had died of pneumonia shortly after they arrived in Maine, and both Rachel and her mother were still devastated. Dorothy understood how she felt and shared her sadness. The two women saw each other briefly several times more before Rachel penned a farewell letter to Dorothy. But in her own mail that same day, Rachel found a sweet thank-you letter from Dorothy that prompted her to add a postscript telling her new friend "how happy we are that you took the trouble to write me last winter and start this very pleasant friendship. I, too, feel a strong bond of common interests—and that we have the same feeling about many things." But Rachel wanted further assurance that Dorothy felt this bond as strongly as she, and so made an excuse that evening to walk down through the woods to the Head to say a last good-bye to the Freemans, this time impulsively leaving Dorothy with a kiss.[5]

Dorothy Freeman, at fifty-five, was nine years older than Rachel, but except for a few more wrinkles around her eyes and mouth when she smiled, she looked much the same age. Both women wore their hair in a similar style—short, rather tightly permed, and parted on the side. Dorothy had light brown hair with bangs covering a high forehead; Rachel's more auburn hair was swept back from her face. Dorothy was attractive but not stylish, preferring sensible, neatly tailored clothes. She was outgoing, exuberant, easily affectionate, and immensely empathetic. She loved people and collected devoted friends everywhere she went. But Dorothy also had a contemplative side. She was not particularly philosophical, but she read widely and searched for the larger meaning of life in the natural world about her rather than in any formal creed.[6]

While Rachel had loved the sea vicariously as a child but had never seen it until she was out of college, Dorothy had hardly ever known life away from clipper ships, salt air, and moving tides. Born Dorothy Murdoch in 1898, she and her family moved to the Massachusetts shore town of Marblehead, where she lived until she went off to Framingham State Normal School (now Framingham State College) in 1916. Her mother's family, the Whitneys, went to Southport to camp and bought land on Dogfish Head in the 1880s, one of the earliest families to settle there. Dorothy, an only child, first went to Dogfish Head as an infant on a steamer from Boston and was lowered into a dory in her baby basket. She spent the next eighty summers in the rustic family cottage sited with an almost panoramic view of the Sheepscot just to the left of the rugged point of rocks that was Dogfish Head.

Dorothy had grown up at the height of the nature-study movement. After teaching home economics in high school for several years, she took a job with the Massachusetts Department of Agriculture's Cooperative Extension Service in Amherst. She taught home economics to women and children for the 4H Clubs, rising to be regional director of 4H by 1924, the first woman to hold such a position. By the time of her marriage, she was an accomplished naturalist, completely comfortable in the outdoors, and particularly interested in birds, native plants, and marine life. Dorothy met Stanley Freeman, who was two years younger than she, at a basketball game at Massachusetts Agricultural College (now the University of Massachusetts), where he was studying animal nutrition. They were married on October 9, 1924, after Stan graduated and found a job as a county agricultural agent. Since married women were prohibited from teaching, Dorothy resigned from 4H and devoted herself to her family.

The Freemans' only child, Stanley, Jr., was born in 1926, shortly after the couple moved to West Bridgewater, a small town about two hours southeast of Boston. During these years Dorothy was a busy mother and homemaker. After 1938 she made a home for her widowed mother, Vira Murdoch, who came to live with them.

Stan Freeman joined the Wirthmore Feed Company, a large agricultural concern, where he rose to manager of the service department. His work involved visiting local dairy and cattle farmers who needed help with the chemical and nutritional composition of animal feed. Stan was knowledgeable about agricultural chemicals, animal pest control, and food processing.

After Stanley, Jr., went off to college and the navy, Dorothy spent much of her time writing letters to her many friends, including a group of her college classmates who had established a regular cycle of letter writing. It is hard to estimate the number of letters Dorothy wrote each day. For her, letter writing was a form of literary expression perfectly suited to her outgoing and affectionate personality. It was also an emotional outlet, a Christian duty, and a private passion. In addition, Dorothy faithfully kept a daily diary where she recorded her activities and thoughts as well as listed the poems, books, and articles she had read, the operas she had heard, and the natural life she had observed.[7]

When the Freemans met Rachel Carson and her mother in the summer of 1953, they had been married almost twenty-nine years. Their relationship was loving, affable, and devoted. Stan was a tall, large-boned man who had been fighting a receding hairline for a number of years. He had kind eyes, a ready smile, and an intellectual bent to his natural curiosity. A better than average amateur photographer, Stan particularly enjoyed nature photography. He had come to terms with the necessity of sharing his life and his home with his elderly mother-in-law, enjoyed his son's company, and delighted in his new baby granddaughter, Martha, who had been born in the spring of 1953.

Stan Freeman had his own interests in the sea, and during the summers on Southport he was an enthusiastic sailor and boatman. He was quieter and more reserved than his wife but had a steady depth and obvious compassion that drew people to him. Stan's business was hectic and he was under considerable pressure at work, especially after the company moved its offices to Boston. His exterior calm belied the stress he carried but rarely showed. From the time Stan and Rachel met in 1953, he was never again in robust health.[8]

That summer Carson sorely needed a devoted friend and kindred spirit, someone who would listen to her without advising and accept her wholly, the writer as well as the woman. She felt alone much of the time, without anyone with whom she could share her private world. The companionship she had known with her mother for so long was no longer available to her nor especially comforting. Maria Carson's emotional demands upon her daughter increased as her physical powers diminished. Rachel was now her mother's caretaker, still the center of her existence in a way that was more cloying than expanding, if indeed it ever had been the latter. Carson's daily schedule, particularly in the summer, revolved around her mother's needs. Maria remained the conduit between Rachel and the world, determining by her neediness when her daughter would be able to go out. By her presence as well as opinions, she still dominated Rachel's relationships with others, an arrangement Rachel had acceded to long before.

Carson appeared self-sufficient, and indeed in many ways she was, but fame, if anything, made it more difficult for her to open herself to others. Now further burdened by the secrets of other family members, she was more socially isolated and emotionally impoverished than when she had worked at Fish and Wildlife. Dorothy Freeman's easy warmth, her love of Maine, and knowledge of the natural world as well as her intelligence and quick empathy attracted Rachel and made her want to know the older woman better.

Months later they calculated they had been together only six and a half hours that summer at Southport, but their ensuing correspondence, begun after Dorothy returned to West Bridgewater, rushed them headlong into a deep and loving relationship based on shared sympathies, mutual understanding, and unwavering devotion. Each letter brought further confirmation that, as Rachel put it, "they shared the same feeling about the beautiful places and things of this earth!" They recognized a similar sympathy and spirituality in each other and sought through their letters to discover all that bound them as kindred spirits.[9]

Their letters were filled with descriptions of nature, the things Rachel collected in the tide pools, the birds and animals in Dorothy's backyard, and what she saw along her walks. They exchanged books and poems, Rachel introducing Dorothy to new favorites as well as to her oldest loves, Richard Jeffries and Henry Williamson.[10]

But however satisfying, Rachel had no intention of allowing this relationship to be based on letters alone. Even before she returned to Silver Spring, she began planning when and where she might see Dorothy again. In early October she casually mentioned that she would be in Boston for the American Association for the Advancement of Science (AAAS) meetings at the end of the year when she was taking part in a symposium on the ocean; perhaps Dorothy could come up for lunch.[11]

As their friendship progressed, Dorothy's quite understandable awe and self-consciousness at being the chosen intimate of the famous author of *The Sea Around Us* stood in the way of her complete acceptance of Rachel's proffered love. "A writer," Rachel reminded Dorothy as she was leaving Southport at the end of October, "is just an ordinary person, and could soon be a very lonely one if his friends started putting him on a pedestal, where he certainly doesn't belong, anyway!" Rachel took pains to reassure Dorothy not only that she had a special gift for putting herself into her letters but also of how much she needed all that Dorothy offered her. But Rachel seemed not to know how to trivialize her own talent and literary achievements, which made it more difficult for Dorothy to regard her as an equal and certainly never as "ordinary."[12]

When Rachel, her mother, Virginia, Marjie, and baby Roger went to Myrtle Beach for a week in November, she was still trying to reassure an uncertain Dorothy "that getting to know you and to count you among my friends is one of the nicest things that has happened to me in a very long time, and it happened, too, when I needed all that you have come to mean to me very much." By December Rachel was signing her letters "my dearest love always" and "all my love." For Dorothy, endearments such as "My dearest" and "Darling" came naturally; for Rachel to adopt such effusions was extraordinary.[13]

They made plans to meet after the AAAS meetings and for Rachel to spend the night with Dorothy and Stan in West Bridgewater. In joyful anticipation of seeing Dorothy in the next weeks, Rachel reflected on the breathtaking rush of their friendship and admitted a conscious desire to make up for all the years of sharing and knowledge that they had missed in each other's lives.

Rachel gave Dorothy verbal reassurance of her love that she hoped would end her doubts and speculations once and for all. Hereafter she could read Rachel's declaration over and over again for herself. Rachel told Dorothy,

> And, as you must know in your heart, there is such a simple answer for all the "whys" that are sprinkled through your letters: As why do I keep your letters? Why did I come to the Head that last night? Why? Because I love you! Now I could go on and tell you some of the reasons why I do, but that would take quite a while, and I think the simple fact covers everything.[14]

On Christmas Eve, Dorothy sent a special note for Rachel to put under her pillow to read before she went to sleep. Full of longing, they planned for the few short hours they would have together in Boston. "How can those hours Wednesday possibly be enough for all there is to say?" Rachel wrote the day after Christmas. "But I am so happy that we are to have them now."[15]

The AAAS symposium on the sea frontier, sponsored by Woods Hole Oceanographic Institution, was held at Mechanics Hall in Boston. Rachel was to speak in the afternoon about her research on the seashore and the challenges of studying the marine environment, but she wanted to get there in time to attend the morning session as well. Harvard's Henry Bigelow, the former director of Woods Hole Oceanographic, whom Rachel explained to Dorothy "I respect more than any other scientist in the world—and also love as a person," was chairing the session, and her former colleague and friend Bert Walford was one of the speakers.

Carson's paper, entitled "The Edge of the Sea," is the only purely scientific paper she ever gave to a professional academic organization. It reveals Carson as a meticulous, imaginative biologist who applied the latest theoretical research to her fieldwork and incorporated it in her writing. Her tone was scholarly and professional, equal to her audience, carefully setting out her observations for their consideration. Pursuing such ecological questions as "Why does an animal live where it does?" and "What is the nature of the ties that bind it to its world?" Carson reviewed the general subject of climate change and specifically examined the effects of temperature changes in sea water on the evolution of life at the shoreline. Most of her illustrations were drawn from her own observations of the changing distribution of marine species. She emphasized how dependent the adult marine animal was on the ecological conditions of the larvae and speculated on the effect the products of plant and animal metabolism had on the distribution of marine life. She called for creative research to match the wonderfully mysterious and complex pattern of life at the edge of the sea, reminding her audience "So, even in the waters of the sea, we are brought back to the fundamental truth that nothing lives to itself."[16]

Rachel had been anxious about her paper because of the notable scientists present in the audience, and she was relieved when it was over. To her surprise, she found Dorothy had arrived early and, instead of going on to the hotel as they had planned, was waiting in the crowd at the rear of Mechanics Hall. Rachel greeted her with a kiss, whispering, "We didn't plan it this way did we?"[17]

They returned to Rachel's room at the Sheraton, strangely shy now that they were at last together, then took the train to West Bridgewater. Thirteen hours later Rachel was back on another train to Washington sleeping fitfully, but with the remembered tenderness of Dorothy's presence. Both women must have worried that this meeting might be a letdown. "Reality can so easily fall short of hopes and expectations especially where they have been high," Rachel wrote Dorothy as soon as she got back to Silver Spring. "I do hope that for you, as they truly are for me, the memories of Wednesday are completely unclouded by any sense of disappointment, or of hopes unrealized. And as for you, my dear one, there is not a single thing about you that I would change if I could!" The visit had given Rachel "a little oasis of peace and sweet dreams where the other is." It was the first letter that Rachel addressed "My Darling." She closed it by reassuring a still sometimes skeptical Dorothy, "I can imagine no substitute for you in my life."[18]

The two of them were struck by the outrageous pace and intensity of their relationship. They made mutual fun of how many letters flew between Silver Spring and West Bridgewater, rejoicing that they were at least "both 'crazy' in the same way, and at the same time." But their absorption in each other created a certain awkwardness in both households. Rachel knew her mother's possessiveness and jealousy could be easily aroused by the frequency and volume of letters coming from

Dorothy. Feeling as if she could not share just one part of a fat letter from Dorothy, she chose to suppress their correspondence altogether.

Dorothy's domestic situation was less difficult and more open but probably no less stressful. The number of telephone calls between them and the number and length of her letters absorbed a great deal of Dorothy's time. Stan was aware that she was preoccupied and deeply involved in her friendship with Rachel.

To ease the tension, Rachel suggested to Dorothy that they occasionally write letters in two parts, a general letter that could be shared with her mother or with Stan without incurring any feelings of jealousy or exclusion and another just for their private reading. "After all," Rachel wrote, "our brand of 'craziness' would be a little hard for anyone but us to understand." They began the practice of putting a private letter inside another letter that was meant to be read out loud, referring to these letters within letters as "apples." When they both wrote of the same thing, or thought the same way about something, which happened with increasing frequency, they called it "stardust" or referred to it as being "stardusty."[19]

By February Rachel worried that they should relax a little. "After all, neither of us has any longer a shadow of doubt about the devotion of the other." Acknowledging that she felt guilty about disturbing the pattern and pace of Dorothy's life, Rachel told her: "I guess I'm just trying to say that the suddenness and intensity of this feeling between us has obviously brought great changes into both of our lives; that as far as I'm concerned, it is so exactly what I needed that it is all, not only beautiful and wonderful, but truly constructive; but for you I have sometimes feared I have too greatly disturbed the normal flow of your life, causing too much preoccupation with 'Us,' and too much emotional upset." Suggesting that they try to be calmer about their delight in the discovery of each other, Rachel told her "it's only because I do love you so deeply that I say this. If only we were where we could see each other very often, I'm sure there would be less tension about it—and how wonderful it would be. Maybe some day things will be so that we can."[20]

Part of the "craziness," at least for Rachel and probably for Dorothy as well, was a longing to be with each other. For Rachel, alone with her writing and hemmed in by her obligations, it was a driving force. At the end of January with the book still a millstone around her neck, Rachel found that talking to Dorothy on the telephone only made her long to be with her all the more. She began to fret about the summer, how long they would be in Southport together, and to plan for somehow seeing her again before then. "I know I need you terribly. (And I believe you need me, too. Shameless!)" Rachel wrote. "If we could only be near enough to talk often and be together even once each month. I really don't think I'd ever sink into the state of despair that so often comes over me. And it is so much better to talk than to write—for I think in a way writing magnifies things—makes what was perhaps a passing annoyance seem bigger or more lasting than it was."[21]

Many of Carson's letters in the first six months of their relationship concerned other family members or her frustration with her progress on the book because so much of her time was taken elsewhere. It did not seem fair to burden Dorothy with all her troubles when she was so far away and had never met most of Rachel's family. "I know you want me to write my thoughts," Rachel told her, "but I think I ought to write facts without being so harrowingly subjective about them." But Rachel, bottled up for so long, now had someone with whom she could truly share her feelings, no matter how passing they might be. The two solved the problem by agreeing that such letters would be destroyed, or put in "the strong box," which was their code word for the same thing.[22]

Rachel's despair was not only for the dreadfully slow pace of her book but the recognition that her complicated domestic situation could only become more encumbering with time. She spent hours taking care of her mother, helping Marjie, who was going through some difficult times, and seeing to baby Roger's care. Neither brother Robert nor her niece Virginia perceived any need to help out, or offered to relieve her. Rachel was increasingly isolated, with no office or colleagues to intervene or distract. She admitted to Dorothy that she should change her attitude; "as long as family health permits, I should shake myself out of my lethargy and make an effort to see other people more."[23]

Dorothy pleaded with Rachel to spare herself and not to spend what little private time she had writing letters to her. Frequently they vowed to write only on certain days or to limit the length of their letters, but each took pleasure in writing as well as receiving. As Rachel explained, "the lovely companionship of your letters has become a necessity to me, and that, just by being you, you are helping me more than you can imagine."[24]

Two of Carson's letters written a week apart in early February 1954 established the singular romantic nature of their friendship. In the first, a letter they referred to afterward as the "white hyacinth letter," Carson took pains to spell out to Freeman why she was so vital to her as a creative partner as well as a "dearly loved friend." Written in response to Dorothy's question, "Don't you ever marvel at yourself, finding yourself in such an overwhelming emotional experience?" Carson offered a rare glimpse into her emotional needs as a creative writer.[25]

She began by recalling for Dorothy the story of the man who said if he had two pennies, he would buy bread with one and with the other a "white hyacinth for the soul." Dorothy, she said, had become her "white hyacinth."

> I don't suppose anyone really knows how a creative writer works (he or she least of all, perhaps!) or what sort of nourishment his spirit must have. All I am certain of is this; that it is quite necessary for me to know that there is someone who is deeply devoted to me as a person, and who also has the capacity and the depth of understanding to share, vicariously, the sometimes crushing burden of creative effort, recognizing the heartache, the great weariness of mind and body, the occasional black despair it may involve—someone who cherishes me and what I am trying to create, as well.[26]

Implying no criticism of her family or friends, Rachel admitted that "the few who understood the creative problem," such as Marie Rodell, Paul Brooks, or even Bob Hines, "were not people to whom I felt emotionally close." Conversely, such friends as Elizabeth Dickson, Alice Mullen, Dorothy Algire, and Shirley Briggs, "who loved the non-writer part of me did not, by some strange paradox, understand the writer at all!"[27]

Then by some miracle, Dorothy came into her life. "I knew when first I saw you," Rachel told her, "that I wanted to see much more of you—I loved you before you left Southport—and very early in our correspondence last fall I began to sense that capacity to enter so fully into the intellectual and creative parts of my life as well as to be a dearly loved friend. And day by day all that I sensed in you has been fulfilled but even more wonderfully than I could have dreamed."[28]

Dorothy was overjoyed with Rachel's letter. Rachel's confession had touched her deeply, and she was reconciled without totally understanding how it could be as Rachel described. No stranger to giving and loving, Freeman would always struggle a little with the feeling that she did not merit Rachel's love and devotion, and although Rachel may have tried to deceive herself, theirs was never an entirely equal relationship. Rachel's work and her physical and psychological needs came first, and Dorothy, accustomed to the role of nurturer, accepted that and willingly endured the keen emotional deprivation that it sometimes brought her.

For her part, Rachel gave Dorothy's life renewed purpose and an intensity that she had never known before. Longing for an outlet for her own creative expression, but reticent to try and fail, she dared what would have intimidated many others, to love Rachel Carson and to live creatively by nurturing her.

Rachel acknowledged that Dorothy had not been drawn to her because of any lack of love in her own life. "No one could be with you and Stan even a short time without realizing how devoted and congenial you are," Rachel wrote. But the partnership that the Freemans had built over twenty-nine years was of a different order than the magic of finding such an intimate friend. "I was thinking today, with what depth of gratitude . . . how wonderfully sustaining is the assurance of your constant, day-and-night devotion and concern. Without it, I truly don't know what I would be doing now, when there are a good many otherwise dark days. And I do know that we are, to an incredible degree, kindred spirits. Our analysis has been beautiful and comforting and satisfying, but probably it will never be quite complete—never encompass the whole splendor and mystery."[29]

Dorothy shared parts of Rachel's letter about being kindred spirits with Stan. Certainly she wanted him to understand as best he could the love and devotion that Rachel needed, and on some level, she wanted his blessing. From Rachel's letters we learn that Stan's response to his wife's new relationship relieved her. Rachel reassured Dorothy that she understood her need to confide in Stan. "It means so very much to me to know that you have such an understanding, loving and wonderful husband," Rachel wrote. "And darling, I hope I made it clear in my little note that I was so glad you read him the letter—or parts of it. I *want* him to know what you mean to me."[30]

Looking back on this time a year later, Dorothy was amazed at the depth of their love and remarked, "What magic letters can work!" Certainly "The Revelation," as Dorothy called their February exchange of letters, was a milestone in the same way as their thirteen hours in December had been. While they grew more certain of each other's devotion, the longing to be together for hours and hours of uninterrupted talk intensified. Dorothy admitted shyly that she was physically and emotionally "stirred" whenever she saw or heard a public reference to Rachel, an admission that pleased Carson enormously.[31]

They planned a weekend visit in March when Rachel would go to Boston to visit her publisher. Rachel had accepted the fact that finishing the book in March was impossible and instead began a mad push for May or early June before going to Southport for the summer. She had committed to three speeches in April in the Midwest, which would take a month out of her writing. While she did not seem to care exactly when the book would be published, she did care enormously about when she finished it. "But oh," she bemoaned, "I am so agonizingly slow!"[32]

The exchanges of early 1954 brought Rachel a wonderful sense of relief. She felt she had destroyed the barrier that being a "famous author" had created and that kept Dorothy from accepting the truth of her love. "I was fighting to have you accept me as a simple human being first, an author second. (You know it makes such a difference which end of the telescope you look through.)" After their time together in December, Rachel knew she had made progress; now, she told Dorothy, "at last, my darling, I think I've won."[33]

Rachel's letters left Dorothy in no doubt about the responsibilities involved in loving Rachel Carson or with what other invisible forces she would have to share her. "The heart of [the creative struggle] is something very complex," Rachel wrote, "that has to do with ideas of destiny, and with an almost inexpressible feeling that I am merely the instrument through which something has happened—that I've had little to do with it myself. As for the loneliness—you can never fully know how much your love and companionship have eased that. Some of it, however, is an inseparable part of writing which someone accurately described as 'a lonely adventure of the mind' but how lovely to come in from the adventure at intervals to the warmth of your understanding and love!"[34]

Early in their correspondence Carson also shared with Dorothy Freeman not only her emotional responses to the world of nature but also her desire to help preserve the beautiful places of the earth. As postwar society became more and more materialistic, Carson, like many of her colleagues in the Wilderness Society, worried that the next generation would lose touch with the natural environment, with their origins, and the hope of saving places untouched by the industrial age.[35]

Although the Freemans were nominally Republican and Carson a Democrat, their love of nature provided common ground. As a government employee, Carson had of necessity been circumspect about criticizing government policies and careful not to express her political views publicly. After her resignation, she was no longer under such prohibitions and soon had occasion to speak out.

Even before the Democratic Party lost the White House in the election of 1952, changes in the nation's conservation policies were more beneficial to business interests, particularly in the West. But when Oregon businessman Douglas McKay was appointed Secretary of Interior in January 1953, critical personnel changes were made in the top staff of the department's agencies that reflected the Republican administration's desire to place more of the nation's natural resources in private hands. In late April McKay dismissed Carson's former boss, Albert M. Day, as director of the Fish and Wildlife Service. Deeply disturbed by Day's removal as well as by the firing of other experienced and competent career professionals and their replacement by nonprofessional political appointees, Carson took up her pen in protest.

In a letter to the editor published in the *Washington Post* on April 22, Carson suggested that Mr. Day's dismissal signaled the beginning of a "raid upon our natural resources that is without parallel within the present century." Reviewing Day's career in wildlife conservation and recalling his courageous opposition against those who demanded the relaxation of wildlife conservation measures for private gain, Carson interpreted McKay's decision to replace Day and others of like competence as part of a plan to "return us to the dark ages of unrestrained exploitation and destruction." In sharply critical language, Carson appropriated the images of McCarthy supporters to her own purposes. "It is one of the ironies of our time," she wrote, "that, while concentrating on the defense of our country against enemies from without, we should be so heedless of those who would destroy it from within."[36]

Her straightforward and compelling letter was picked up by the Associated Press, which called Carson for further comment about the situation at Interior. Carson was quoted as saying "The action against Mr. Day is an ominous threat to the cause of conservation and strongly suggests that our national resources are to become political plums." Her letter generated editorial comment in several other papers, including the Falmouth, Massachusetts, *Enterprise,* whose editors commented that Director Day was fortunate to have the authoritative and articulate Rachel Carson as his most conspicuous defender. Several months later *Reader's Digest* reprinted her letter to an even wider audience, identifying Carson as the author of *The Sea Around Us* and the former editor-in-chief of the Fish and Wildlife Service.[37]

Carson saw broad implications not only for government policy but for the future of science in the political changes at Interior and was pleased to have the opportunity to speak out. She was certain the dismissal of experienced scientists, who were dedicated to the public good, would lead to political decisions that would alter the public domain and irrevocably affect the preservation of wilderness.

Several months later Carson's fears were renewed by the steady expansion of private interests in the supposedly inviolate national park system. When local Audubon Society president Irston Barnes wrote a biting editorial in the *Atlantic Naturalist* in which he argued that the chief danger to the integrity of the national parks and to the National Capital Parks came from high officials in the Park Service, Carson supported him. She sent Barnes a telegram offering to contribute to a fund to reprint and distribute his indictment nationwide.[38]

National attention soon focused on the government's plan to build a dam that would flood the national monument areas of Colorado and Utah, including Dinosaur National Monument. Carson was outraged by the proposal and, as a member of the Wilderness Society, railed against it. Explaining the geologic as well as scenic importance of the area, Carson urged the Freemans to write to the president and suggested that Dorothy carry the message to her garden club and interest members in the conservation issue. "This is something we shall talk of much in the years and months ahead," Rachel told Dorothy prophetically. "It is part of the general problem that is so close to my heart—the saving of unspoiled, natural areas from senseless destruction. But in this particular case the time is short and perhaps you will find time and inclination to say something about it at your meeting next week."[39]

Rachel devoted the early spring to work on the sand section of her book; when it was finished, she planned to meet Dorothy for a long weekend in Boston. In spite of appointments at Harvard and meetings at Houghton Mifflin, Dorothy and Rachel conspired to find a few hours of private time together. When Rachel returned to Maryland, she had only a few days to finish her lecture for the Cranbrook Institute of Science. The lecture was an evening affair that included a slide presentation; afterward Carson would spend the evening with Cranbrook director Robert Hatt and his wife, Suzannah.[40]

Her lecture would be the first public preview of her new book, which now bore the title *The Edge of the Sea*. She flew to Detroit on April 9, arriving on a chill spring morning at Willow Run Airport, where she was met by a reporter and photographer from the *Detroit News*. Carson alighted from the plane wearing a pert white straw hat with a rhinestone-dotted veil and a chiffon scarf knotted softly at the neck underneath her fur topper and carrying her hat box. The reporter, startled by Carson's fashionable and feminine appearance, quickly uncovered the scientist as Carson answered questions about her research for the new book and told the now-familiar stories of her education and how she had come to write science for the public.[41]

Her lecture at Cranbrook concerned the problems and mysteries of seashore life on the rocky coast of New England and covered some of the same scientific material she had discussed at the AAAS meeting. In contrast, her speech two weeks later at the Theta Sigma Phi Matrix Table Dinner in Columbus, Ohio, hardly touched on the subject of her new book; instead, it challenged her listeners to think about the wonder and mystery of the natural world as real and vital to contemporary life. The Matrix Table Committee that had invited her hoped that she would talk about her experiences as a female writer. Rachel had the feeling that her speech to the nearly one-thousand-member sorority of women in journalism might be the place to mention some of the more personal things that had been on her mind; thus she spoke more autobiographically than she had ever dared before.

The first part of her talk was light and anecdotal, sharing some of the more humorous parts of being the author of a best-seller. She told listeners about the public's misconceptions of what a female scientist would look like and the reluctance of some readers to acknowledge that a woman could deal with a scientific subject. She shared her childhood love of nature, her earliest struggles to get published, and her disappointment with the initial reception of *Under the Sea-Wind*. Finally she came to her ideas about the meaning of life.[42]

"I am not afraid of being thought a sentimentalist," she told the sisters of Theta Sigma Phi, "when I stand here tonight and tell you that I believe natural beauty has a necessary place in the spiritual development of any individual or any society. I believe that whenever we substitute something man-made and artificial for a natural feature of the earth, we have retarded some part of man's spiritual growth."

Appealing to what she called women's "greater intuitive understanding," she gave some examples of "this substitution of man-made ugliness—this trend toward a perilously artificial world": the tract houses of Levittown, where individuality was crushed in sameness and all the trees were cut; the proposal to build a six-lane highway through the middle of Rock Creek Park in Washington, where the veery sings in the green twilight; and the invasion of the national parks with commercial schemes. "Is it the right of this, our generation," she asked, "in its selfish materialism, to destroy these things because we are blinded by the dollar sign?" She ended her speech by saying it was her belief that "the more clearly we can focus our attention on the wonders and realities of the universe about us, the less taste we shall have for destruction."[43]

According to the enthusiastic letter Rachel wrote to Dorothy late that same night, the women's response to her address was worth all the agony it had caused her. Her "thousand dragons," as she called the audience, had been moved by the obvious passion with which she spoke and the depth of her concern. As she left the room one woman, seated on the aisle, made a slight movement toward her with her hand and Rachel, equally impulsively, "stopped and took her hand." The Matrix Committee told Carson it was the best speech in their thirty-year history. "If it was," Rachel told Dorothy, "it was because of the importance of what I had to say, and my feeling about its importance. That feeling helped, I'm sure, to put me at ease so that I really was quite happy and relaxed during the giving of it."[44]

Although she never gave another speech of quite the same warmth, her success in Columbus enabled her to be more personal and approachable in other formal settings. The Theta Sigma Phi speech also marked a change in her style of delivery. For the first time she typed the text out completely instead of simply making outline notes to speak from. She had read this speech over so many times before giving it that she was able to speak informally with only an occasional glance at the script. She was much more relaxed and it showed.[45]

Such public appreciation only added to Rachel's already buoyant spirits. Earlier that same morning she received a telegram from the Limited Editions Club informing her that its jury had nominated her as one of the ten living American authors who had written a book in the past twenty-five years that seemed destined to be a classic, the only woman so honored. She was invited to New York to accept the Silver Jubilee Medal in early May. It would be an impressive formal ceremony, and it marked the beginning of the tradition that Rachel would wear a corsage from Dorothy whenever she spoke in public.[46]

Rachel used the occasion of the Limited Editions award to tell Marie Rodell, not entirely truthfully, that she would probably go on from New York to Boston to meet the Freemans and drive up to Southport with them to open her cottage. Actually, she met only Dorothy in Boston, and the two spent five days together at Rachel's cottage in Southport.[47]

Rachel had planned the getaway knowing that her private time with Dorothy during the summer would be short, particularly since the Freemans arrived and left earlier than Carson and her mother. Rachel also needed time with Dorothy to talk about her family situation, which she had not had the energy to do when they were last together. "There are stresses and worries in my general situation that I feel I must talk about with you—if I don't do it then, I don't know when I ever can or will," she wrote. "But that will be as brief as possible, then we'll shut the door on it and just be happy—so very happy, my dearest."[48]

During their spring visit to Southport, the two friends paid a special visit to the Nobleboro, Maine, home of Henry Beston and his wife, the poet and writer Elizabeth Coatsworth. Having vowed for over twenty years to write to the author of *The Outermost House* to express her joy in that book and to thank him for his review of *Under the Sea-Wind*, Carson finally had written Beston in hope that she and Dorothy could visit him while they were in Maine. But what had really roused Carson from that combination of procrastination and shyness was her desire to take Dorothy to hear the veeries while they were together in Maine, and Beston, an ardent birder, knew best where to find them at any time of year.[49]

Henry Beston was delighted to have Rachel Carson and her friend visit. It was the beginning of a close friendship among Beston, his wife, and Carson, and a yearly round of visits between them whenever Carson was in Maine. But it was too early in the year to hear veeries sing. Instead Rachel and Dorothy spent a day in Augusta that provided tender memories. They talked more than they slept, and Rachel was able to tell Dorothy how constrained she felt by her family obligations and how anxious she was about the future. "Darling," Rachel wrote when she had returned to Silver Spring, "I can't remember when I've had such a relaxed and happy time."[50]

The pace of their correspondence slowed after Rachel returned from Southport, where she faced the hard work of preparing sections of *The Edge of the Sea* for Marie to send out to magazines. In the middle of June Rachel received a new incentive to finish her book.

Marie had sent *New Yorker* editor William Shawn the section on sand,

and he telephoned her to say that he was considering buying first serial rights to the entire book, just as he had *The Sea Around Us*. Rachel was ecstatic, explaining to Dorothy how much she admired Shawn and how she would rather have her book published in *The New Yorker* than anywhere else. Her relief and excitement testified to how anxious she had been that this new book would measure up to what readers of *The Sea* expected. Ever since she had revised her conception of it the previous summer and rewritten the rocks section that fall, she had worried that she was still somehow off target. She told Edwin Teale, "I have been laboring under a bad psychological handicap, feeling this book was nowhere near the level of *The Sea*." But Shawn's interest now reaffirmed her earlier decisions.[51]

When Marie visited at the end of June, Rachel begged for every detail of Shawn's reaction. "She's done it again," Marie reported Shawn as saying when he telephoned to offer $2,500 for "Rim of Sand," with an option on the rights for the rest of the book. Even Paul Brooks was elated with the prospect of condensation in *The New Yorker*, since without Hines's illustrations, no reader would think they had read the whole book in the magazine. *Reader's Digest* wanted to consider it either for condensation in the magazine or for its quarterly book club volume, and a deluge of requests came in from foreign publishers. "So—all looks rosy," Rachel told Dorothy, "if the author just produces! All this is a tremendous stimulus, as you understand so well; also as you understand—there are still days and days of agonizing effort."[52]

Before Rachel and her mother and their new cat Jeffie left for Southport for the summer of 1954, Rachel bought a new car, a light-green Oldsmobile sedan with a white top, white-wall tires, and automatic everything. Her splurge bespoke her more relaxed financial situation and the promise of the financial success of her new book and another *New Yorker* sale. Little Roger was much impressed with his great-aunt's new car, reporting to his mother in garbled pronouns, "He's got me new car."

Also before leaving Maryland, Carson took precautions to protect the privacy and safety of her precious cache of Dorothy's letters. Although she had meant to discuss the matter with Dorothy when they were in Southport, there had been no time. Now she told her friend that she had bundled them up with a letter of instruction directing that if anything happened to her, the letters were to be destroyed unread. She urged Dorothy to write out similar instructions either to destroy Rachel's letters or send them back to her, but insisted she indicate her intent in writing.

"Ever since I became acutely aware of the public's prying curiosity about an author's life, I have shuddered every time I see announcement of the publication of some poor wretch's letters," Rachel wrote her.[53]

The summer in Maine was just as hectic as Rachel had foreseen, but she and Dorothy sandwiched in as much private time as they could, celebrating the anniversary of their first meeting on July 12, wandering the shore at both cottages, and finding more special places in the woods between.

Stan and Dorothy took Rachel out for a brief sail in their boat, but much to Stan's discomfiture, the boat scraped some rocks along the shore as they were showing Rachel how her cottage looked from the water, and they nearly capsized. Rachel claimed not to be as frightened as she appeared at the time, and Dorothy later remembered that the incident gave her an "excuse" to hold her hand. Rachel was never truly fond of boats, being an indifferent swimmer, but she was game to go out again—sometime.[54]

It was a strange summer in some ways, fragmented by the arrival and departure of visitors and by unexpected events. For one, Maria Carson suffered an acute attack of crippling bursitis in one knee and had to be hospitalized in Boothbay for a week—the same week that hurricane Carol hit the Maine coast. The Teales, the Bestons, and the Brookses all came for long weekends, followed by Rachel's brother, Robert, and his wife. They had planned a brief two-day visit, but Robert came down with a virus and stayed for a week, after which Rachel came down with the same bug.[55]

Southport was hit with two more hurricanes, Edna in September and Hazel a month later. Both threatened such damage that Rachel packed her manuscript in a box, ready to take it with her if they should have to evacuate the cottage. There were some benefits to the storms. Edna had blown one of Rachel's favorite spruces on the shoreline over onto the hillside. But before she could get it raised, Hazel hit from the opposite direction and righted the tree. "Now we have lost so many trees along the water that our skyline is sadly changed," Rachel told Marie Rodell. "However, we are thankful we still have a cottage and that no one was hurt."[56]

During their time together that summer, Dorothy and Rachel tried to think of ways to lighten Carson's domestic situation to give her more personal freedom and more time for her writing. Dorothy urged her to hire a full-time housekeeper who could see to her eighty-five-year-old mother's needs and fix meals, but Rachel was not convinced that such a plan would work, since her mother refused help from anyone but her daughter. Rachel promised she would try to spread her burden out, but she wrote to Dorothy at the end of the summer, "I want you to know that you have helped me to see more clearly what I have more or less known all along that the real difficulty is in me, and that I am the only one who can change things."[57]

Carson's self-imposed task of rewriting the rocky shore section of the book gave special stimulus to Stan Freeman's keen interest in nature photography. He had taken a variety of slides of shore life and was experimenting with techniques for underwater photography. Much of Rachel's time had been spent with both Stan and Dorothy finding specimens in various tide pools and along the shore, frequently with Stan taking pictures. Rachel wanted good slides to illustrate her lectures, and Stan had supplied her with several photographs she used in her presentation at Cranbrook. Anticipating more lectures on *The Edge of the Sea*, including a special one in December for the Audubon Society of the District of Columbia, they worked together to illustrate the points she wanted to make. His interest in photographing seashore life provided common ground for their own relationship, independent of Dorothy.

Stan and Rachel corresponded separately and fairly frequently. Rachel supplied him with books that were hard to find and helped him identify various biological and botanical specimens. Rachel was perfectly comfortable in Stan's company and valued him as her friend as well as Dorothy's loving husband. She had made it very clear that she wanted him to know how much Dorothy's friendship meant to her, and she knew that it was important for Stan to feel included in their relationship. For his part, Stan seems to have recognized the benefits of friendship with Rachel and contributed willingly to the feeling of family that the Freemans extended to Rachel and her mother. There is no evidence that he ever felt threatened by Rachel's love for his wife or hers for Rachel. It was, for him as for them, a friendship that was beyond definition or categorization, and Stan was wise enough to be happy about it, understanding that it was in a realm unto itself.[58]

Stan Freeman's personal friendship became of even larger significance to Rachel as her nephew, Roger Christie, grew. Baby Roger had visited Rachel briefly the previous summer, but in 1954 he was a toddler to be kept occupied. Dorothy and Stan were easy and comfortable with young children, and children were drawn to Stan's easy affability and always interesting activities. The Freemans' granddaughter Martha was about a year younger than Roger, so they often combined outings with the two, giving Rachel and Marjie time to work or rest. Stan was quick to realize that Roger needed male figures in his female-dominated life and made particular effort to include him in his summer routines whenever the boy visited Southport. Roger loved Uncle Stan and Aunt "Dorsey," as he called Dorothy. With each year, Stanley Freeman's surrogate role and influence became increasingly important to Rachel as well as to Roger.[59]

Rachel had promised Paul Brooks that she would have the finished manuscript to him by the end of January, with publication finally scheduled for the fall of 1955. When she returned to Maryland from Maine in late October, she imposed a tight schedule on her time and her letter writing. But before she buckled down to work, she put together a special package of books for Dorothy: first editions of both *Under the Sea-Wind* and *The Sea Around Us*. In each she enclosed a brief private letter and wrote an inscription on the flyleaf.[60]

In her letter accompanying *The Sea Around Us*, Rachel told Dorothy about the special line from Tennyson's *Locksley Hall* that had held such meaning for her on that long-ago rainy night at PCW. Rachel wrote:

> And so, as you know it has been. When finally I became its biographer, the sea brought me recognition and what the world calls success.
>
> It brought me to Southport.
>
> It gave me You.
>
> So now the sea means something to me that it never meant before. And even the title of the book has a new and personal significance—the sea around Us. Keep this for me, dear, and understand all it means.
>
> My deep love—Rachel[61]

Once back in Maryland, Rachel took Dorothy's summer advice about getting more household help. She already employed a kind, hardworking woman, Florence, once a week, to do some of the heavier housecleaning chores. Now she found another woman, Estelle, who had once worked for Alice Roosevelt Longworth and later in the White House. Estelle came the other four days to keep house and to do errands, the marketing, and some cooking. Temporarily relieved of the housekeeping chores, Rachel hoped she could work with fewer interruptions.[62]

The annual December Audubon Society lecture was one of the most prestigious events for the naturalist community in Washington. The lecture and dinner took place on December 13 in the Baird Auditorium of the Natural History Museum at the Smithsonian Institution. Carson had to speak twice, once in the afternoon and then again in the evening after dinner. Now an honorary vice president of the society, she looked forward to seeing many of her friends. Repeating the technique she had used for the Theta Sigma Phi lecture, Rachel typed out the text of her speech in case she needed to refer to it. She wore her navy taffeta dress with a wide white collar and a new white hat she bought to brighten up the outfit.[63]

Advertised as a preview of *The Edge of the Sea*, Carson's lecture drew a large and enthusiastic audience. Using Stan Freeman's latest summer slides, Carson described how life was shaped by the extremes of tides, temperature, geology of the shore, the force of the surf, and the currents. Her particular focus for this informed Audubon group was the variety of animals and plants that survived in community between the tide lines. Rachel's friend and Audubon editor Shirley Briggs, who was in the audience that evening, thought it a fine lecture and the slides remarkably good. This lecture marked Carson's last public responsibility before the Christmas holidays.[64]

Rachel and Dorothy exchanged presents, as they had the previous year, but what they treasured most was the now traditional private Christmas Eve letters each wrote in advance, to be read by the other before bed on Christmas Eve. In their 1954 letters both friends recounted the joys of the year past, the special moments that were, as Rachel wrote, "the steps by which our love and understanding have acquired that depth and firm foundation that will last for all time."[65]

In a similar vein, Dorothy's letters rehearsed specific moments of discovery and enumerated Rachel's gifts: "The glow you have brought into my life; the reawakening of an interest and a new insight into the natural world." But, Dorothy told her, the most precious of all was "to have found someone who understands me as you do, with whom I can be completely honest, is [a gift] beyond belief. And over and around and above all these the crowning joy is the gift of your Love for me."[66]

12

"Between the Tide Lines"

Carson welcomed the new year, 1955, with a mixture of happy anticipation, editorial weariness, and the familiar anxiety that comes with ending a project that had occupied her for over four years. Certain now that *The Edge of the Sea* would be published on schedule but tired of the endless details that remained, she allowed herself to think about the future. A variety of writing projects were awaiting her attention, but for the first time Carson was in no rush to start another book. Tired of deadlines, she looked forward to a freer time and to a summer in Maine without a book in progress.

As a prelude to what she hoped would be a more relaxing year, Rachel met Dorothy in New York City for a belated holiday weekend at the Barbizon Plaza. Anticipating an editorial meeting in Boston later in February, Rachel asked Dorothy and Stan to help her entertain Paul and Susie Brooks for dinner. She wanted the Brookses to see Stan's slides of the Maine shore and thought the occasion would provide the two couples an easy introduction.

Dorothy was understandably nervous about entertaining the sophisticated editor and his wife in her modest home, but Rachel assured her that the Brookses were very amiable. Dorothy's anxiety was heightened by the pressure she felt from Rachel to try her own hand at writing and publishing. Although Dorothy played with the idea that she might someday write something for children or about cats, she was genuinely uncertain of her abilities. She could not help being intimidated reading sections of Rachel's new manuscript, and she was also afraid that she might unconsciously imitate Rachel's style. The more Rachel urged Dorothy to write and suggested where and how to market her work, the more thorny the situation became. It was a subject that was never totally resolved; although Rachel understood Dorothy's lack of confidence on one level, she was quite insensitive to how her talent and success affected Dorothy's self-esteem about writing.

The evening with the Brookses turned out as Rachel had predicted. Both families found much in common, and there was no mention of Dorothy's would-be literary endeavors. Rachel's visit, however, was cut short unexpectedly by Maria Carson's anxiety at being left at home alone. Rachel's abrupt departure back to Maryland the next morning disappointed everyone.[1]

In the middle of March Carson sent Brooks most of her manuscript with an accompanying letter that left no doubt about her state of mind. She told him, "In thinking of how to celebrate this momentous event—the end of simply years of misery—I'm handicapped by the fact that the end seems never *quite* to come! There are always, as now, little bits left over to harass me." The prologue, epilogue, appendix, and picture captions remained unfinished, and she was bone tired. "It has been such a terribly long pull and I feel quite drained and exhausted," she lamented to fellow writer Edwin Teale, "but you know how it is!"[2]

"What a wonderful woman you are!" Brooks responded with evident pleasure upon receiving Carson's manuscript. "As I read this once again, I am convinced that it contains some of the best writing you have ever done and that there are passages here superior to anything in *The Sea Around Us*." Greatly relieved to have the book at last in his hands, he proposed only minor changes in organization, and suggested "The Marginal World" as the title for the still-unnamed first chapter, a suggestion Carson welcomed and adopted.

Rachel hired her old friend, zoologist Dorothy Algire, who had already done some library research for her earlier in the book's evolution, to help her finish. Algire knew the material well and enjoyed checking zoological facts and supplying the taxonomy for the appendix and captions. Dorothy and Rachel went to research libraries and the National Museum, enjoying the opportunity of working together again.[3]

To celebrate the end of her ordeal, Rachel had invited Dorothy Freeman to spend a week in Maryland at the end of March. Rachel warned Paul not to send her any editorial inquiries during that time because she intended "to forget I ever wrote a book, or ever thought of doing so." Rachel planned to introduce Dorothy to her brother and his wife, and worried about Robert's reaction, but even her hopelessly self-impressed brother was vulnerable to Dorothy Freeman's warmth and graciousness. Robert's approval allowed Rachel to be more open about her friendship with Mrs. Freeman and gained her a begrudging measure of cooperation from Robert in caring for Mamma when Rachel went out of town.[4]

To make certain that Dorothy understood how much a part of this new book she was, Rachel had decided to tell her during the visit that she had dedicated *The Edge of the Sea* to the Freemans. Her announcement caught Dorothy completely by surprise and overwhelmed her with happiness. Without any hesitation Dorothy and Stan agreed with Rachel's desire to include their surnames in the dedication.

Soon after Dorothy departed, *The New Yorker* galleys arrived and, with them, some unexpected good news. William Shawn had chosen some of Bob Hines's illustrations, enough to provide Hines with a substantial check and a preeminent publishing debut. Magazine publication had been moved to August, with the book to follow in October, a schedule Brooks disliked because it left too much time between the two events.[5]

By early May the publicists at Houghton Mifflin were putting together their final promotion plans. Rachel flew up to meet with Brooks and Anne Ford, Houghton Mifflin's publicity director, who turned out to be Mrs. John Kieran's sister and an energetic woman of experience and competence. As with *The Sea Around Us*, Carson had very definite ideas about the book's dust jacket, the layout of text and illustrations, what typeface to use, and what she wanted included in her biographical sketch. This time there would be a picture of the author, although she kept postponing her sitting.[6]

Rachel told Paul privately that she found Ford's initial sketch unbefitting an author of established reputation. "It seems to me that the account should establish my professional competence," and Ford's inclusion of the *St. Nicholas* League stories and Carson's graduate assistantships in zoology hardly accomplished that. "And from the standpoint of my place in the world of writers," Rachel continued with uncharacteristic arrogance, "I think it should be said that I am a member of the Institute of Arts and Letters and a Fellow of the Royal Society. The number of languages in which *The Sea* has appeared also seems worth specifying." Accustomed to working with temperamental writers, Ford suggested that Carson might like to write the copy herself, but after a halfhearted attempt, Rachel returned the job to Ford, this time providing a list of honors and awards she wanted included.[7]

Rachel was insistent that the jacket acknowledge Bob Hines's contributions. "I hope you are going to give some information on the jacket about the artist," she told Brooks, "apart from the fact that we share the hope that good things will come to Bob . . . it seems to me demanded by the fact that the art is such a substantial part of the book and is so beautifully and satisfyingly done." At Brooks's suggestion Carson also decided to drop her middle initial and never reclaimed it. Reassured that Ford understood how she wanted things done, Rachel left with Dorothy for a weekend in Southport. She had agreed to go back to Boston in three weeks to speak at Houghton Mifflin's spring sales conference and would use the opportunity to see how the promotion plans were progressing.

The sales meetings provided an important opportunity for Carson to promote her book and to introduce herself to the sales staff. Her remarks at the conference combined entertaining anecdotes about her fan mail with an informal introduction to the distinctive ecological theme of *The Edge of the Sea*. Carson told the sales representatives how the book had evolved from a field guide into an interpretation of the three basic types of shoreline—rock, sand, and coral—and the community of life found in each. She had tried, she said, to put into the book a sense of her own excitement about and endless fascination with the life that inhabited the low-tide world. As a testimony to her unabated enthusiasm, Carson confessed she could hardly wait to get back to Maine to explore the great spring tides.[8]

As much as she longed to be done with it, however, *The Edge of the Sea* seemed endlessly with her. Work on *The New Yorker* condensation collided with Houghton Mifflin's deadlines for finished page proofs and index. Rachel finished the galleys the first week of June, and although she had made an appalling number of changes, she was at last satisfied with the outcome. So was Brooks, whose sigh of relief was almost audible. The summer of 1955 would mark the literary preview of Carson's third sea book and establish her as the preeminent interpreter of marine science. But Rachel was less interested in her fame than in being able to spend the summer in Maine in Dorothy's company. "Somehow," she told Dorothy just before arriving with her mother and Jeffie at the end of June, "the sharing of beautiful and lovely things is so much more satisfying with *you* than it has ever been for me with anyone else."[9]

Much earlier that year, Carson had agreed to give a book talk in the neighboring town of Wiscasset using Stan Freeman's slides of Southport and at Ocean Point. Her lecture, entitled "Between Tide Lines on the Maine Coast," was a fund-raiser sponsored by the Lincoln County Cultural and Historical Association to restore and remodel the old county jail as a children's museum. The occasion provided Carson a happy prepublication forum to test public interest in her new book, and the enthusiasm with which the audience greeted her lecture lifted her spirits and gave a wonderful start to the summer.[10]

The Edge of the Sea appeared in *The New Yorker* in two installments on August 20 and 27, 1955. The letters Carson received from readers immediately afterward were duly complimentary, but their scantiness disappointed her. Carson was also puzzled by the fact that most of her initial fan mail came from male readers. After a month, Rachel agreed with Houghton Mifflin trade division director Lovell Thompson, who had predicted that the public's reaction to *The Edge of the Sea* would be quite different from what it had been when *The Sea Around Us* had appeared in *The New Yorker*. There was keen critical interest but not the same intense excitement at discovering a new author that there had been in June 1951.[11]

Readers of *The New Yorker* condensation could hardly appreciate how difficult it had been to bring a sense of anticipation and freshness to the subject of the seashore. Edwin Way Teale was one of the few who understood that as well as the personal price of her achievement. After reading the first installment, "The Rim of Sand," he wrote Carson: "If the rest of the book is as good as the first installment, the man [Shawn] is right: You have done it again! The wonderful part of it is that in spite of the strain and struggle and frustration that I know went into the shaping of the book in its final form there is no hint of 'tired writing.' It is serene and fresh and strong with no residue of fatigue or stress in it—and that in truth, is a very great accomplishment."[12] Teale's reaction reinforced Rachel's determination to spend the rest of the summer not thinking about any other writing projects so that when she did embark on something new, she would be truly refreshed.

There were plenty of visitors to Carson's Southport cottage that summer. Marjie and Roger came for several weeks. Rachel had purchased the lovely woodland lot to the south of the cottage, extending the boundaries of her property and adding more shoreline and privacy. Marjie helped Rachel plant wildflowers and perennials around the rear of the cottage and put in new shrubs. Rachel splurged on a 35mm Exakta camera that she and Stan could use for taking underwater shots, and she tried her hand at photographing marine subjects. By the end of September the Freemans were back in West Bridgewater. Feeling bereft in Southport, Rachel wrote Dorothy, "Life here will be so different without you, and nothing will seem quite right."[13]

Carson had plenty to do before her book was published on October 26. Houghton Mifflin planned a book party in New York at the 21 Club the evening before. Working with Anne Ford, Rachel made up a personal guest list that included the Freemans, William Beebe, Edwin and Nellie Teale, Robert Murphy, and Richard Pough. She invited various friends from Fish and Wildlife that Bob Hines knew, such as Alastair MacBain, and an assortment of writers and critics. With an eye to publicity, Rachel suggested inviting several feature writers from the New York newspapers who were interested in conservation topics as well as Carl Buchheister, president of the National Audubon Society, and anthropologist and author Margaret Mead.[14]

But Carson had no interest in a request from NBC television's *Today* show to send a crew to her cottage to film an interview with her for an eight-minute television segment. Marie agreed with Rachel's assessment and declined for her. Carson, who watched little or no television, had never heard of the show and was emphatically opposed to having a film crew invade her home. At that time television was young and its power as a publicity medium was still uncertain.[15]

When the Freemans went back to Southport on October 9 to celebrate their anniversary, Rachel surprised them with an advance copy of *The Edge of the Sea* with its special dedication. It read:

> *To Dorothy and Stanley Freeman*
> *who have gone down with me into the low-tide world*
> *and have felt its beauty and its mystery.*[16]

Deeply touched, Dorothy and Stan gave her a diamond pin in the shape of a seashell. She would wear it first on her dark-green taffeta dress at the book party in New York. The note that accompanied it explained what *The Edge of the Sea* meant to them. "We thought we knew the sea, but through you we discovered how slight was our knowledge. It was you who really unlocked its 'beauty and mystery' for us."[17]

Houghton Mifflin's gala book party was one of the happiest of celebrations for Rachel because the Freemans were there to share it with her. Other friends came too, many from Washington. Bob Hines's pleasure in his new acclaim was contagious, and everyone enjoyed the party. Rachel spent the night with Marie, but the next morning she joined the Freemans for breakfast and read the first favorable reviews of *The Edge of the Sea* over coffee.

Back in Silver Spring, Rachel reflected on just how much it meant to her to have Dorothy to share it all with. "This sharing, not only of events but of what is in my own thoughts and feelings, is exactly what I have longed for almost from the time you walked into my life," Rachel told her. This joyful publication of her third book contrasted sharply with memories of her earlier books. This time there was a different sort of anxiety. "The odd thing about *The Sea*," she wrote Dorothy, "was that, in writing it, I expected very little. I was just grateful I had a publisher for a book written as I wanted to write it. Now, . . . I have myself made it impossible that anything of the sort can happen to me again. I know that, even if this book achieves acceptance, acclaim, and sales that by any reasonable standards amount to 'success'—still, by comparison with *The Sea* it will fail. What I want for *The Edge of the Sea* is for it to be judged on its own merits, but that is most unlikely to happen. So of course I am tense, waiting for each review, each 'straw-in-the-wind.' " Her agony was not prolonged. Barely three weeks after publication, *The Edge of the Sea* entered the *New York Herald Tribune Best Seller List* as fifteenth of twenty. A week later it had jumped to number four and appeared on the *New York Times* list as number eight.[18]

About the same time, Rachel learned the board of directors of the Boston Science Museum, enthusiastic over her new book, had elected her an honorary fellow of the museum, citing her "contribution to the understanding of the world in which we live." At Paul's urging Rachel agreed to accept the award in person in early November on the condition that she did not have to make a speech; she would stay on for other promotional appearances in Boston. Her reaction to this newest honor was one of almost curious surprise. "I find people are fascinated by the thought that sand is not just sand," she told Paul, and suggested that the museum might like some different sand samples for part of its new exhibit on marine habitats.[19]

Although many of her friends, as well as her brother Robert, expected *The Edge of the Sea* to move to first place on the best-seller lists, Rachel was more realistic. The fall season was, as she explained to Dorothy, "murderously competitive." There was also an element of regionalism in the book, focusing as it did on the eastern Atlantic shore. To achieve a place among the top four or five on the national lists meant that it had to be a best-seller in bookstores outside the East Coast.[20]

By the first weekend in December, however, *The Edge of the Sea* had advanced to fourth place on the *Times* list, and Carson began to believe that she had, once again, written a best-seller. Just before Christmas it moved to number three, where it remained nearly five months. At the end of December, it had reached second place on the *Tribune* list just below Anne Morrow Lindbergh's immensely popular *Gift from the Sea.* "It looks odd," Rachel told Dorothy, "to see two sea titles in first and second place. As for my reaction, I continue to be genuinely amazed. Hereafter, I shall leave prophecy to the ground hogs."[21]

For a book that lacked the direct, philosophic appeal of Mrs. Lindbergh's little book, which had been published earlier that spring and remained in first place on all the lists for well over a year, the fact that *The Edge of the Sea* rose to numbers two and three was a remarkable achievement. For most of the time, second place rotated between Norman Vincent Peale's *The Power of Positive Thinking* and John Gunther's disturbing report *Inside Africa.* Rachel was pleased that Lindbergh's book topped the lists for she found much to admire in it herself. As she told Dorothy, "I'll be happy that it is Mrs. Lindbergh's book and not something sensational or trashy that holds that position." The public often confused the two books and their female authors. Carson's book suffered by being the second book to appear on what, at cursory glance, seemed to be a similar seashore topic. But her personal triumph as a writer meant more than the book's inevitable position on the best-seller list, although, of course, its financial success was always one of Rachel's major concerns.[22]

The Edge of the Sea had initially promised to be so pleasant to research and write, but it proved tortuous to organize and difficult to conceptualize. With its publication and acclaim, Carson had proven that the author of *The Sea Around Us* was no ephemeral star on the literary horizon but a writer to be reckoned with now and in the future. If there was not the same excitement of literary discovery that had greeted her in 1951, she had moved beyond an important psychological threshold as a creative writer.

Rachel's assessment of how this new book would be received was dispassionate. The nature of her subject was more limited and inevitably invited comparisons between the Odyssean account of the cosmic forces that shaped the sea and those seemingly less heroic ones that governed the struggle for life between the tide lines. Jacquetta Hawkes, the English anthropologist and author writing in the *New Republic*, thought Carson's choice of subject reflected a diminution of her literary power. *New York Times* critic Jonathan Leonard missed "the organ tones" of *The Sea Around Us*. To engage her reader, Carson had to capture the imagination for a different sort of maritime journey. In place of the epic story of the elemental forces that ruled the sea, Carson offered an intimate exploration of the "essential unity that binds life to the earth."[23]

The nature of her research and the circumstances of her writing insured that *The Edge* would have more of a naturalist's firsthand acquaintance with the living world and less of the biologist's theoretical explanation. Her conception of the book was a radical departure from what the public understood as a "field guide." Carson warned the reader in her preface "To understand the shore, it is not enough to catalogue its life" or "pick up an empty shell and say 'this is a murex,' or 'That is an angel wing.' " More was required than mere identification. "Understanding," she wrote, "comes only when, standing on a beach, we can sense the long rhythms of sea and earth that sculptured its land forms and produced the rock and sand of which it is composed; when we can sense with the eye and ear of the mind the surge of life beating always at its shores—blindly, inexorably pressing for a foothold."[24]

In spite of the smaller scale of Carson's drama, most critics found much to praise in *The Edge of the Sea*. William Hogan, reviewer for the *San Francisco Chronicle*, noted, as did many others, that Carson's reputation for writing with lucid yet poetic force and simplicity was well established. "If the new book does not seem as exciting a discovery as the first," he wrote, "it is perhaps because Miss Carson's direct, crystal-clear prose (a kind of factual poetry) is by now familiar." Harry Ellis of the *Christian Science Monitor* agreed that "Miss Carson's pen is as poetic as ever, and the knowledge she imparts is profound." Some critics found the level of her artistry less consistent than that of *The Sea Around Us*, but others were stirred by the beauty of her expression and the more spiritual quality of her journey. Nearly all reviewers commented on her use of poetic imagination as an adjunct to scientific understanding.[25]

Charles Poore, writing in the daily *New York Times*, gave *The Edge of the Sea* particularly high marks. "The main news about Miss Carson," he wrote, "is that she has done it again. Her new book is as wise and wonderful as the 'The Sea Around Us.' " Calling it a work of "sense and sensibility," Poore praised it as "profoundly learned yet unencumbered with the numbing jargon of the squid and seaweed set." Other critics thought it a "soothing book" and invariably compared it with the quality of "private peace" that characterized Anne Morrow Lindbergh's *Gift from the Sea*.[26]

Only Carson's friend Robert Cushman Murphy criticized her science, calling her discussion of the "wastefulness" of the superabundant fertility of marine life an "old-fashioned point of view" and taking exception to her statement that coastal coral reefs usually were found only on the eastern shores of the continents. On the other end of the scale, the book critic for *Time* magazine, in an extravagant metaphor, wrote that once again "Carson has shown her remarkable talent for catching the life breath of science on the still glass of poetry."[27]

Rachel was particularly touched by the evaluations of two steadfast friends. Henry Bigelow of Harvard wrote her that "plenty of people write about the sea . . . but no one else writes with the feeling for the sea that shows in your every sentence. And no one else equals the delightful way in which you express yourself." Bigelow was obviously touched by Rachel's preface where she acknowledged her debts to him of many years. In the November issue of the *Atlantic Naturalist*, Shirley Briggs wrote perceptively that Carson did not need to exhort her readers to take more care of the natural world as other writers must, because readers would share in "the infectious quality of her own joy in every manifestation of life" and have their own attitudes toward the natural world transformed.[28]

Rachel shared most of these reviews with Dorothy, secure now that she could do so without being misunderstood. Her public response to the critics was to wrap herself in a cloak of unreality, feeling as if they were talking about some person other than herself. When Dorothy told her of weeping over one review, Rachel replied, "As for myself, darling, I don't know that I have shed any tears, but that is only because I am protected by that feeling of unreality. If I believed what they say to be really true, I don't know just how I would react. But dear—truly—I am too conscious of the many flaws in my work to accept some of these high estimates without strong reservations. They are something to try to be worthy of in the future and perhaps that is the only way I can regard them." Rachel may have been overly modest as well as somewhat disingenuous in this reply since the critical response was, to some extent, what she had expected, and she was secure in her own literary estimate. Carson had a healthy ego, not only about her literary abilities but about her place as a literary figure. A frustrating correspondence with the bookkeeping department of the Musical Masterpiece Society reveals that when aggrieved, Carson could be both angry and arrogant.[29]

Rachel's enthusiasm for classical music, which had been rekindled by her friendship with Dorothy, led her to accept membership in the Musical Masterpiece Society, a mail-order subscription enterprise that offered an automatic monthly selection of classical records. Finding the quality of the recordings the society offered inferior, Rachel canceled her membership before she left for Maine. But records continued to be sent and her previous payment disregarded, so that soon the society was sending a barrage of insulting form letters threatening legal action and credit ruin over a bill Carson adamantly believed she did not owe.

By February 1956 Rachel was angry as well as frustrated with a situation that seemed beyond remedy or reconciliation. In a letter reviewing the history of the dispute, Rachel pulled rank. "In case my name is not familiar to you," she wrote the society's comptroller,

> I suggest you consult the membership records of the Author's Guild, the P.E.N. Club, and the National Institute of Arts and Letters. You might also look in Who's Who. After this research, you might conclude that I am a reasonable, responsible person, quite able to pay the small sum involved, and not at all likely to endanger my credit by neglecting it if I owed it. You have sent me one ultimatum after another. It is now my turn to send you one. If I have one more communication of this type from you, it will be my great pleasure to present the whole matter to a group which, I am sure, will be interested to look into just what sort of racket you are carrying on. You may conclude that this is an angry letter and you are quite right. The very least you owe me is an apology.

It was another month before the matter was finally resolved.[30]

Now, at the end of 1955, Carson had finished her biography of the sea and was ready to turn her energies to other projects. Full of optimism she told Dorothy, "it is hard now even to remember the dark roads of some of the preceding years, and the hours of despair in which I thought maybe they would never lead anywhere, and certainly never to such a peak. Really, darling, I think it was a very critical period in my writing career—

this first book after *The Sea*—and with it behind me, and happily so, I can't believe any of the future roads will ever be quite so dark and arduous."[31]

In early 1953 she had agreed to a book for Ruth Nanda Anshen's World Perspectives Series, and there were other smaller projects waiting for her consideration as well. Anshen was by all accounts a unique figure in the publishing world. Socially well connected and financially well-to-do, Anshen was trained as a philosopher but made her literary reputation as a super planner of several book series focused on universal themes. Contributions to Dr. Anshen's series were by invitation only, and she published those scholars and writers whom she believed understood that beyond their specialized knowledge lay a unity of human experience. The World Perspectives series was her most ambitious undertaking and eventually included over seventy titles.[32]

Shortly after signing the Harper contract and receiving a $5,000 advance, Rodell informed Anshen that Carson, in reaction to Julian Huxley's new book, *Evolution in Action*, wanted to shift the emphasis of her proposed book from evolution to the relation of life to its environment. Carson suggested *Remembrance of Earth* as the new title and put the Harper series out of her mind until after *Edge of the Sea* was published.[33]

Carson also had agreed to write an essay and select bibliography on the biological sciences for *Good Reading*, a reference book produced by the Committee on College Reading of the National Council of Teachers of English and published by the New American Library. Editors Atwood Townshend and J. Sherwood Weber at Pratt Institute in New York paid their contributors handsomely. But Carson found that putting together a bibliography of the best books in the biological sciences required a great deal more work than she had anticipated. She turned in her essay just after New Year's 1956, well over a month late.

Carson's brief introduction to the list of books she had selected provides insight into her attitudes toward science in general and biology in particular at a time when she was returning to research in those fields. Defining the scope of biology as "the history of the earth and all its life—the past, the present, and the future," she included a specific ecological dimension to her definition, explaining that "neither man nor any other living creature may be studied or comprehended apart from the world in which he lives." Carson was deeply concerned about the accelerated specialization of science that had become commonplace after World War II and lamented its increasing remoteness from the average citizen.

With some passion Carson reiterated her belief that "In the truest sense, there is no separate literature of biology or of any science. Knowledge of the facts of science is not the prerogative of a small number of men, isolated in their laboratories, but belongs to all men, for the realities of science are the realities of life itself." She was equally insistent on the value of emotion and direct experience in the apprehension of "the living creatures of the living earth" and recommended an exploration of the subject first in nature and in the writings of the great naturalists, such as Thoreau and W. H. Hudson, and only then in the laboratory.[34]

While Carson was reflecting on the bibliography for *Good Reading*, she began to think more about her book for the Harper series. At first she had been excited about the prospect of writing about evolution, describing it to Dorothy as "perhaps more important than anything else I've done." Now, almost a year later, she realized she was committed to writing this book for what she regarded as a minor series at Harper & Brothers and not, as she would rather, for Brooks at Houghton Mifflin.[35]

Unhappy with the prospect of losing one of his leading authors to another house, Brooks played with the idea of asking Cass Canfield, the distinguished editor of Harper & Brothers, to relinquish his contract with Carson, thereby freeing her to write the book for Houghton Mifflin. After meeting with Paul and Marie together, Rachel realized that Paul's plan amounted to nothing more than asking for her to be relieved of a contract that she had signed in good faith—a position neither she nor Marie could accept.[36]

Carson's solution was to do for Harper exactly the small series book Anshen had asked for on some aspect of evolution and to save the bigger and more important book on the ecology of man for Paul. Carson rationalized her decision in a forceful letter to Brooks, telling him that "writing this little dissertation on the origin and evolution of life will clarify my own mind on something that is basic to the other book. While I am writing it, the larger subject can be developing and growing in my mind, and to a certain extent, the work on the two can proceed together. Knowing me as you do," she continued more realistically, "you will understand that the larger subject will require several years to mature." Brooks could not argue with Carson's ethics on the Harper matter, but he was anxious to get on with the book and had a much more realistic appraisal of how very long it would take her to complete two books.[37]

Immersed in the latest research in evolutionary biology, Rachel confessed to Dorothy, "I am really laughing at myself for even supposing I could take any appreciable time off before beginning the new book. I am taking to this research like an old alcoholic to his bottle. Really, it is so stimulating, and I find my mind a ferment of ideas." She considered attending the AAAS meetings in Atlanta and planned a trip to the Massachusetts Institute of Technology and Harvard to see biologists at those institutions. But there were other offers to consider as well.[38]

With the publication of *The Edge of the Sea*, Carson was inundated with an array of projects. Although she had sworn off magazine writing more than once, she had been impressed with a proposal from the popular monthly magazine *Woman's Home Companion* for an article encouraging children's awareness of nature and one from *Life* magazine to write the text for a picture essay on the jet stream. An entirely different sort of invitation came from the TV-Radio Workshop, an arm of the Ford Foundation, to write a television script on clouds for *Omnibus*, the CBS Television Network's popular cultural information and entertainment show. These proposals appealed to Carson because of their novel subject matter and the opportunity they offered to reach new audiences.

After *The Sea Around Us* was published, magazine editors, particularly those from *Ladies Home Journal* and *Woman's Home Companion*, had tried to interview Carson for a feature story. Rachel refused to consider any such invasion of her privacy, and Marie Rodell, knowing the reasons, reluctantly agreed, all the while regretting the loss of publicity. Rodell seized on the *Companion* proposal, when it first came along, as a way to get Rachel to talk about herself, suggesting to the editors that they ask Rachel to include something about her experiences with her great-nephew Roger. Carson's price proved too high for the magazine, and the project collapsed on both sides. In February 1956, with *The Edge of the Sea* selling briskly, the magazine's editors called back, this time begging Carson to write the article at her price. She happily agreed, but she was already at work on the *Omnibus* script, which had to be finished first.[39]

The producers of the *Omnibus* show had approached Carson once before. Now they offered her any topic she might like, but suggested a "new look at clouds." The idea for such a show came initially from an eight-year-old viewer, who wrote *Omnibus* that she wanted to see a program "on something about the sky."[40]

Carson was intrigued by the idea of writing a television script on clouds and had been interested in the subject since her early research on tides. After discussing the proposal with Marie, Rachel confessed that regardless of her own "indifference to television," she realized it was the medium that reached the largest audience and that through television she could influence popular attitudes.[41]

The week before Christmas Carson met in New York with Boris Kaplan, the film supervisor for TV-Radio Workshop, and meteorologist Victor Schafer, the director of research for the Munitalp Foundation and the discoverer of cloud seeding whose film footage of clouds would form the basis of the show. Excited by the creative opportunity the script offered, she explained to Marie, "I can decide on the story to be told, rather than just writing something to go along with a film sequence already set."[42]

By mid-January Carson had a preliminary treatment ready for *Omnibus* producer Robert Saudek. She provided a sense of continuity to the subject by linking specific clouds and cloud patterns once again to the web of life. Carson wanted to change the popular conception that clouds were "just clouds with no particular meaning or significance" and to provide a framework that was "global or even cosmic, so that everything we later tell about clouds assumes meaning and significance against this broad perspective." She told Kaplan, "I hope we can establish an awareness of a dynamic process that is never completed, a sequence of events in time and space that is full of meaning for us as living creatures."[43]

Saudek, Kaplan, and the Ford Foundation staff were enthusiastic about Carson's treatment, but formal contract arrangements with *Omnibus* dragged on interminably. Working with television people proved almost as trying to Carson as her past dealings with film producers. But the delay gave her time to work on the *Companion* piece and to take several trips to New York on other business.

She attended the annual dinner of the New York Zoological Society where she found herself seated next to Lawrence Rockefeller, whom she had first met in 1953 when she received the society's medal. Rachel had found the taciturn Rockefeller "delightful," and reported to Dorothy that she took advantage of the occasion to talk to him about her "prime interest—the preservation of seashore areas in their natural state. So I was particularly glad for an opportunity to talk with him at greater length."[44]

Two weeks later Rachel was back in New York. *The Edge of the Sea* had been nominated for the National Book Award in nonfiction, but the award went to Herbert Kubly for *An American in Italy*, a book that generated little enthusiasm. Meeting with the *Omnibus* group the next day, Rachel and Victor Schafer finally got down to the task of fitting text to pictures. After several more delays and another trip to New York, "Something About the Sky" was scheduled for broadcast on March 11.[45]

In its final form, "Something About the Sky" was vintage Carson with its emphasis on the long journey of wind and water. "Now rain falls," she wrote, "the end of a long journey and yet not the end, for in a constantly renewing cycle there is no end." And in language reminiscent of the concluding chapter of *The Sea*, the script ended as it began with water from the clouds filling brooks and streams, returning to the sea. Happy with the finished production, Rachel watched it on television at her brother's house with Roger and the rest of her family gathered 'round. A few days later she capitulated and bought her own television set. "Already I can see what a hit it's going to make with Mamma," she wrote Dorothy enthusiastically. "I called a little while ago and she reported—sounding as happy as a cat with a saucer of cream—that Robert had it working beautifully and they were watching 'The Lone Ranger.' "[46]

The success of the *Omnibus* show intensified interest from *Life* magazine. Carson was genuinely receptive to writing about the jet stream, but when she met with the *Life* editors in mid-April, their coercive attitude toward her material renewed her "allergy" to the magazine. The essay they had in mind was part of a feature on weather, but they wanted a very specific slant on the jet stream and had a complete list of specifications she would have to include as well as what they wanted her to conclude. It was not at all the kind of essay Carson had any interest in producing. She told Dorothy, "Well I can't and I won't and they can go to you-know-where and ask the Proprietor there to write it for them."[47]

Back in Silver Spring, Rachel told Marie she was glad to find out early exactly what the *Life* editors had in mind. The whole episode served to remind her "that my proper field is books, where an author can call his soul his own." Rachel never did the article and never regretted it. When she met Dorothy in New York at the end of April to see the new musical *Carousel*, she needed to pour out her frustration with the constant distraction and burden she faced as caregiver.[48]

Maria Carson's nose had been badly out of joint ever since Rachel had started work on the *Omnibus* script. She resented the time and attention Rachel gave to Paul Brooks and especially to Marie Rodell, and felt that both had displaced her. Maria's care, and frequently Marjie's as well, robbed Rachel of energy and focus. "I did need very much to talk with you, and it did me a great deal of good," she wrote Dorothy after she returned home from their weekend. "I am thankful you realize that, as with most human situations, there is no cure-all that can suddenly take care of all aspects of the problem. I'm sure it will have to be worked at, a little at a time. But, dearest, you have helped me see some things much more clearly, and you have strengthened my determination to change some of the things I can change." But even with this renewed determination to take steps for herself, Rachel continued to feel both exploited and trapped by circumstances that seemed to grow only more complicated.[49]

Rachel also confessed to Dorothy that she could no longer discuss the domestic situation with Marie Rodell, because Marie "would come up with purely practical solutions that I—in my weakness or whatever it is—couldn't accept." Marie's energy and impatience with Rachel's endless complaining but passive acceptance of a situation that was destructive to her physical and emotional well-being led her to propose solutions that Rachel found out of character and too "hard boiled."[50]

By mid-March, with *Omnibus* behind her, Rachel was making progress on the *Companion* article and having fun involving Roger in selecting which adventures to include. He referred to it as "Rachel's article for the *Woman's Home Bepanion.*" She sent the article off in early April, only a week late, but worried that it was longer than they wanted.[51]

Rachel warned Dorothy that when Mamma and Marjie read it, both had wept. "Maybe *you* should have some Kleenex on hand, though I didn't intend it to be sad!" She also threatened to annotate the essay just for Dorothy, complete with all the interruptions and unanticipated crises that occurred during just one day's effort. But her humor reflected an inner happiness with a piece of writing she had clearly enjoyed.[52]

When Dorothy and Stan received their copy of "Help Your Child to Wonder" a few days later, Dorothy was as moved by it as Maria Carson and Marjie had been. She found Rachel's "signature" all through it. She also realized that with this article the public would discover the more private Carson that Marie Rodell had hoped would emerge when she suggested that Rachel write the piece. But Dorothy was understandably uncertain about sharing that Rachel with strangers. To Rachel she predicted, "the public is going to find a new you—the one that I've known from the start, the you of the Starry eyes, the elfin you, whimsical, fanciful you who appealed so much to me. Somehow, I wonder whether I'm going to like sharing that you with the world. But the deed is done and I guess I'm glad the world is going to have this glimpse of you."[53]

"Help Your Child to Wonder" appeared in the July issue of *Woman's Home Companion*, which went on sale the end of June. The essay was accompanied by Marc Roberts's photographs of several different little boys exploring the natural world. Rachel allowed the publication of only one picture of Roger—one she had taken the previous summer of him sitting on the deck of the cottage in Maine with a squirrel eating from a dish at his elbow.[54]

As in no previous piece of writing, this article reflected Carson's passion to help others to *feel* rather than to know nature. Wonder and awe were, for her, the highest emotions. In her outline she had written almost as a simple credo, "Once you are *aware* of the wonder and beauty of earth, you will want to learn about it." In the published version Carson elaborated on the significance of an emotional response to nature. "Once the emotions have been aroused—a sense of the beautiful, the excitement of the new and the unknown, a feeling of sympathy, pity, admiration or love—then we wish for knowledge about the object of our emotional response. Once found, it has lasting meaning."[55]

Making the most of a child's delight in discovery, she explored the natural world of sound, sight, scent, night, and the little things often significant to children and overlooked by adults who had outgrown the capacity for wonder. In one of the most memorable passages Carson wrote:

> A child's world is fresh and new and beautiful, full of wonder and excitement. It is our misfortune that for most of us that clear-eyed vision, that true instinct for what is beautiful and awe-inspiring, is dimmed and even lost before we reach adulthood. If I had influence with the good fairy who is supposed to preside over the christening of all children I should ask that her gift to each child in the world be a sense of wonder so indestructible that it would last through life, as an unfailing antidote against the boredom and disenchantments of later years, the sterile preoccupation with things that are artificial, the alienation from the sources of our strength.[56]

Marie Rodell urged Rachel to expand it into a book. Brooks had the same idea. "This particular article seems almost to cry out for expansion," he wrote. Rachel agreed but was far too pressed with other commitments to pursue it just then. The idea simmered in her mind, though, and in late 1958 she gave an expanded outline to Marie, who went to work to find new photographs to accompany the text.[57]

In a loving gesture to Roger, who had, after all, been the prime mover and chief actor in their exciting explorations, Rachel had her lawyer draw up a gift of deed giving Marjorie Christie the rights to "Help Your Child to Wonder." It was a token of her affection as well as a way of helping them out a little financially. Marjie promptly hired Marie Rodell as her agent, and Rodell sold the article to *Reader's Digest*, not only earning Marjie a tidy fee but providing enormous pleasure for a young mother whose life lacked for so much.[58]

The Edge of the Sea also brought Rachel unexpected friendship. W. Curtis Bok, sometime author, sailor, lover of literature, and distinguished jurist, soon to be associate justice of the Supreme Court of Pennsylvania, wrote to Carson at the end of October 1955 congratulating her on the book and complimenting her on her craft. "You have a special ability to get nature's crystal loveliness on paper," Judge Bok told her. "I never dip into that book [*Under the Sea-Wind*] without a catch in the breath for the sheer beauty of the writing."[59]

Carson acknowledged Bok's initial letter a month later. She was surprised when Bok continued to write her at an astonishing pace, which created some jealousy in Dorothy, who found their literary friendship disconcerting. Rachel received an invitation from Bok in early March to visit him and his wife at their home in Radnor, Pennsylvania, outside Philadelphia for an April weekend. "What do you think Emily Post would say to my handling of the situation?" Rachel wondered. "If I'm ever going to meet him I think it should be soon. Also, I have a feeling it's about time I knew Mrs. B. If she and I can be friends, well and good; if not perhaps it's best to let the correspondence die out, pleasant as it is." She also decided she would stay only for one night, "in case we all hate each other violently."[60]

Rachel embarked with her usual shyness but her reserve vanished with the pleasure she found in the Boks' company. In her thank-you note, she told them: "I'm not at all sure I can find words for what I really want to say. . . . All the time I was with you there was such a warm glow—such a sense of understanding and communication, of having found real friends—that this weekend getting acquainted became one of those unforgettable milestones of life."[61]

On her return, she recounted the details of the weekend to Dorothy, filling several letters. "Everything is all right, with everyone, and now I have no hesitation about continuing this friendship that has been so different from any I've ever known." Before long, Rachel was asking Bok for literary counsel and financial advice.[62]

Two particularly pleasant awards added to the gifts brought by *The Edge of the Sea* that brightened the spring of 1956. Carson's alma mater, Pennsylvania College for Women, had recently changed its name to

Chatham College; it wanted to present her with one of its Distinguished Service Alumnae Awards at the celebration of the twenty-fifth anniversary of the opening of the science building in early May. There was no speech to give, she simply had to attend. Her classmate Mary Lou Succop Bell invited Rachel to stay with them and also arranged a small tea. Carson's feelings of animosity toward the college had abated over the years since President Cora Coolidge's death, and she was flattered by this second award from the college.[63]

The award ceremony in the college chapel was a dignified academic affair. Chatham president Paul Anderson presented each of the four alumnae honorees with a copy of a lengthy citation, which he read aloud, and a sterling silver medal. Carson's citation recalled the time she had brought a bawling billy goat to the intermural hockey game as well as recounted the milestones of her professional career and her literary achievements. Carson wrote President Anderson afterward that she "thought the whole conception of the celebration was very fine and I am both proud and humbled to have a part in it."[64]

Similarly, the Achievement Award of the American Association of University Women (AAUW), which carried a cash prize of $2,500 for outstanding scholarship, required of Carson only the briefest address. But that address provided the occasion for the most revealing insights she had yet given into her creative processes.

The award dinner and reception were held in Washington, D.C., on June 22 at the Sheraton-Park Hotel. The affair was the highlight of the association's year, and identity of the recipient was kept secret. Rachel wore a full-length deep-blue evening gown with her sapphire and rhinestone earrings and bracelet, and the Freemans' shell pin. She reported to Dorothy the next day that nearly every woman present had come to greet her warmly afterward, many commenting that they were moved by her words.[65]

"Writing is a lonely occupation at best," Rachel told the AAUW women. "Of course there are stimulating and even happy associations with friends and colleagues, but during the actual work of creation the writer cuts himself off from all others and confronts his subject alone. He moves in to a realm where he has never gone before—perhaps where no one has ever been. It is a lonely place, and even a little frightening."[66]

Speaking of her own situation at that moment, she continued, "No writer can stand still. He continues to create or he perishes. Each task completed carries its own obligation to go on to something new. I am always more interested in what I am about to do than in what I have already done." Rachel shared something of her understanding of the relationship between writer and subject. "I believe, for example, that in some mysterious way the subject chooses the writer—not the other way around." To illustrate she used her own preoccupation with the sea, its physical realities, and then its life. "Then," she continued, "it seemed inevitable that the central riddle of life itself should begin to possess my mind."

She told her audience how she had been fascinated by the new understanding of the chemical and physical processes of life. "Until recently," she confessed, "I had been one of those who believed we should never be able to penetrate the mystery of how life arose. Now, studying the work of some modern pioneers in biochemistry, I have come to believe science can at least form a reasonable theory to account for that mystery of all mysteries." Commending those scientists who courageously abandoned preconceived ideas, she told the audience that she was privileged to have "the opportunity to interpret some of these discoveries for those who are not scientists."[67]

Although Carson's AAUW speech made it sound otherwise, her progress on the evolution book was frustrated by her lack of clarity on how to approach it. She told Bok, "The awful truth is, Curtis, that I myself don't quite know 'the scope of my thrust for the new book.' At present I am just feeling my way. Having contributed nothing to the subject myself, I had intended merely to present and interpret the current thinking, but I suppose that inevitably my own thinking must have a place in the book."[68]

Carson's confusion was largely the result of her encounters with series editor Ruth Nanda Anshen, who presumed too deep a relationship between author and editor. Anshen kept up a steady barrage of well-intentioned letters to Carson meant to encourage her. But these, combined with her insistence on luncheon meetings at her elegant Manhattan town house, only impressed Rachel with the futility of attempting any useful dialogue. After a particularly discouraging dinner meeting with Anshen, Rachel told the Freemans, "Dr. Anshen was so confusing that now I haven't the slightest idea what it [the book] is about! I told Marie if I ever had to see that woman again I didn't think I could write it. I've decided I shall never let her know when I'm to be in New York, and will always be setting out for the Antarctic if I hear she is coming here."

Curtis Bok put a lighter spin on her struggles with evolution, concluding "Yes, Rachel, face up to it like a big brave girl: what are you going to do about God?"[69]

Carson needed her sense of humor to keep from being utterly discouraged as her work routine collapsed around her mother's physical decline and Marjorie's continued poor health. Tests that spring had shown conclusively that her diabetes had worsened.

Frustrated and weary, Rachel succumbed to complaint. "Meanwhile, what is needed is a near-twin of me who can do everything I do except write, and let me do that! When I feel, as I do now, the pressure of all the things that seem worth doing in the years that are left, it seems so silly to be spending my time being a nurse and housemaid." Acknowledging to Dorothy that there was "a time when I longed so desperately just to run way from it all, and then in time I learned that you can't do that," Rachel spent much of the spring house hunting.[70]

She had given up the idea of remodeling their current house since Mamma would countenance no changes; now she considered building another house so that Marjie and Roger could move in with her and Mamma when Marjie could no longer live independently. The reality of her situation was made plain when Mamma had a bad fall just after Rachel returned from Pittsburgh and spent a week in the hospital at the end of May. Rachel hired a nurse practitioner for the weeks of convalescence but knew she would have to find a more permanent solution.[71]

As summer and the long hoped for trip to Maine approached, Rachel acknowledged just how comforted she was by her friend's steadfastness. On Dorothy's birthday Rachel wrote,

> You have come to occupy a place in my life that no one else could fill, and it is strange now to contemplate all the empty years when you weren't there. But perhaps we shouldn't regret those years—perhaps instead we should just give ourselves over to wonder and gratitude that a friendship so satisfying and so full of joy and beauty could come to each of us in the middle years—when, perhaps, we needed it most![72]

13

"One Must Dream Greatly"

Looking back, Carson realized that the summer of 1956 had been an omen of the difficult days to follow. Even then, on some level of her consciousness, Rachel knew she had crossed an invisible yet recognizable divide. Never after would she be free of nearly crushing family responsibilities or able to call her time her own even to the limited extent she had for the past five years. Increasingly her personal and creative life would be circumscribed and the despair that accompanies powerlessness would become a daily adversary.

Yet during that summer she also experienced unexpected renewal and great bursts of creativity. Not ready yet to commit herself to *Remembrance of Earth*, the World Perspectives book for Harper, Rachel's energies were captured by a dream she shared with Dorothy Freeman to preserve the tract of coastal forest that marched down the west side of Southport Island between Carson's road and Dogfish Head. It was a peaceful retreat that had become a central part of their summer lives. But it also symbolized much of what Carson believed that nature offered the human spirit. The hope of buying the "Lost Woods," as she and Dorothy called it, and preserving it from future development became an antidote to the helplessness she felt in every other aspect of her life. It gave her purpose, energy, and a sense of control over her life and work at a crucial time.[1]

Maria Carson's recuperation from her attack of arthritis continued into July, and Rachel was unwilling to risk the two-day automobile trip to Maine until the end of the month. They were barely settled in the cottage when Stan Freeman was rushed to the hospital with a mysterious and frightening bout of internal bleeding requiring blood transfusions and extensive tests. The Freemans returned to West Bridgewater, where Stan remained hospitalized. About the same time Marjie and Roger arrived in Maine for several weeks of vacation. Rachel left Mamma with Marjie in Southport and spent the first weekend in August with Dorothy and visited Stan in the hospital. The preliminary diagnosis was that he suffered from a bleeding ulcer. He was ordered to rest and begin a specialized diet. For most of August, the Freemans remained at their Massachusetts home while Rachel cared for her mother, Marjie, and Roger in Maine.[2]

The spring tides of the new moon had begun. One moonlit night not long after Rachel returned to Southport from West Bridgewater, she and Marjie went down to the beach near midnight to watch the surf and listen to the swell of the tide. Turning off their flashlights to get the full effect of the wildness, they found the surf full of phosphorescence, each wave throwing off the largest sparks of diamonds and emeralds Rachel had ever seen. As they watched the display, even trying to capture the elusive will-o'-wisps in the sand, Rachel noticed a firefly close to the surf signaling to those other twinkling lights as if to other fireflies. Soon it was caught in the rolling water, its light flashing urgently as it was tossed about in the wet sand. "You can guess the rest," Rachel wrote Stan and Dorothy early the next morning.

> I waded in and rescued him (the will-o-wisps already had me in icy water to my knees so a new wetting didn't matter) and put him in Roger's bucket to dry his wings. When we came up we brought him as far as the porch—out of reach of temptation, we hoped. I've already thought of a child's story based on it—but maybe that will never get written.[3]

Rachel filed the firefly story away with other notes she had collected for a time when she could expand "Help Your Child to Wonder" into a book. Meanwhile she salvaged some pleasurable moments, in between taking Mamma into town for treatments on her knees, to plant some black-eyed Susans, snapdragons, and portulaca around the cottage. She had decided to expand the Maine property either by building a separate little house to accommodate Margie and Roger or by enlarging the cottage. After working with a local contractor on various plans, she finally elected to add to the existing structure. At the same time, Rachel was seriously considering several suburban lots in Silver Spring on which to build a new home to solve the domestic problem there.[4]

Real estate matters were very much on Rachel's mind that summer as she explored the woods on Southport Island. She was not the only one who had bought more property on the island recently and was well aware that land was getting scarce and the island population increasing. Markers along the road indicated that the town had decided to widen Dog Fish Head Road. Rachel feared that the woods that she and Dorothy so loved would be affected. Most of the tract was owned by Gustav Tenggren, a well-regarded artist and illustrator of children's books, and Rachel feared he had plans for selling some of it off. "I explored all the woodland from Mahard's [Carson's neighbors] new lot back to the one where the woman is going to build," Rachel wrote Dorothy in late September, "and began to wish very much I *could* buy those lots."[5]

Two days after writing to Dorothy, Carson attended a meeting in Wiscasset to discuss the work of The Nature Conservancy in Maine. All of them were concerned about the disappearance of ecologically unique habitats as well as the increasing development pressures on the coastal areas and were frustrated by the lack of any coordination of conservation efforts in the state. The group had been called together by Dorothea Marston, an active local conservationist who represented The Nature Conservancy.[6]

Marston had asked Carson to say a few words to the group about her views on conservation. Rachel read a prepared statement in which she explicitly connected the need to preserve ecological habitats for the benefits they provided to wildlife with the well-being of humankind. "Our lives," she told the group, "are enriched by understanding the close inter-relationship between living things and their environment."[7]

After a lengthy discussion about establishing a general council on conservation in the state composed of existing organizations, Carson suggested that while such a group might be beneficial, there was an immediate need for a local Maine branch of The Nature Conservancy, as it was the "one group which encourages *practical action*." Carson thought there was an opportunity to save some of the natural areas in Maine, "but it would not last long."[8]

After further discussion, the group voted to organize a Maine chapter. Six members, led by Carson, signed the form requesting authority from the executive director to do so. Before the group adjourned, Charles

Bradford, superintendent of State Parks of Maine, asked Carson if she would serve as honorary chairman of the Maine chapter, which she consented to do with pleasure. Maine officially became the fourth field office of The Nature Conservancy on November 26, 1956.[9]

A week later she spent a windy October morning exploring the shore and adjacent woods some distance north of her property. "If only that could be kept always just as it is," she bemoaned afterward to Dorothy and Stan, "if ever I wish for money—lots of it—it is when I see something like that. Just for fun, tell me what you think, and let's pretend we could somehow create a sanctuary there, where people like us could go, as my friend said of the Bok Tower and grounds, 'and walk about, and get what they need.' Well if no one ever thinks of it, it certainly won't happen; if someone does think hard enough, it just might. Of course I am just thinking aloud, and quite confidentially, to two dear kindred spirits. But it's fun to dream of such things, isn't it?"[10]

The Lost Woods or Dream Woods, as she and Dorothy sometimes referred to the tract on Southport Island, encompassed not only acres of dense white pine forest but also a shoreline marked by deep rocky fissures. Carson's interest in buying this land was influenced not only by her emotional connections to it and its threatened development but also by her deepening friendship with Judge Curtis Bok, whose family had long been involved in philanthropic preservation.[11]

Bok's father, publisher and philanthropist Edward W. Bok, established The American Foundation before he died in 1930. Part of the foundation's income was used to build and maintain the Mountain Lake Sanctuary and Singing Tower in Lake Wales, Florida, where the Bok family had their winter home. The 205-foot gothic-style tower, made from Georgia marble and tan coquina rock from St. Augustine, housed a fifty-seven-bell carillon and looked out over nearly a hundred acres of beautifully landscaped public gardens. Designed by Frederick Law Olmsted, Jr., the gardens provided protection for rare and endangered birds and plants.[12]

Carson and Bok had talked about his plans for the further development of the gardens and sanctuary when she visited the Boks in Philadelphia in April. They continued their discussions when he, and his wife, Nellie Lee, and daughters Rachel and Enid visited Carson in Southport in August. In October Bok invited Carson to serve on the board of directors of The American Foundation, formally proposing her for membership at the November 9 meeting of the board, at which Carson was duly elected. Later that winter Bok invited Carson to join his family in their private Pullman car to go to Florida to spend a few days in Lake Wales and see the sanctuary for herself. Although Rachel longed to go, family illness prevented her from making the trip. But her interest in the development and work of the sanctuary remained keen.[13]

Through the activities of The Nature Conservancy and her involvement in the work of The American Foundation, Carson saw firsthand the impact such personal efforts could have in saving beautiful places, and she began to consider more seriously how she might act to preserve the small area of island forest and shoreline that was so irreplaceable to her. Ever since she had been able to devote full time to her writing, she had hoped one day to be able to contribute modestly to seashore preservation but had never thought of doing something on her own. But after the summer of 1956, Carson knew what she most wanted to save and had a model, at least in terms of spiritual intent, in the Bok sanctuary for how it might be done, if she could only put enough money together.[14]

Carson's newly quickened interest in seashore preservation in Southport increased her resolve to reorganize her domestic arrangements when she returned to Maryland; if she did not, she realized, she would never have time to do any of the things of which she dreamed. She had gotten very little rest in Maine, since she was up frequently during the night to dispense pain medication to her mother.

As if to underscore the urgency for her to act, Maria Carson "toppled over like a felled tree" on the cottage kitchen floor one morning in early October. With no neighbors around to help, Rachel had to see to her injuries alone. Luckily Dorothy arrived later that day to close up her own house and helped Rachel care for Maria. After that, it was clear that Maria could not go about without assistance and that Rachel could not leave her alone except for the briefest of time. Once again Rachel and Dorothy found themselves sharing similar burdens of caring for aging and increasingly frail mothers; Dorothy had the added strain of a husband who now had health problems serious enough to alter their future activities.[15]

Constrained from doing any sustained work by her mother's care but relieved somewhat by frequent and companionable summer visitors, Carson spent the rest of her time in Maine thinking about how to preserve the Lost Woods. Her first requirement was to raise enough money to make a serious offer to buy part of the Tenggren land. This practical necessity forced her to reconsider two writing projects she had previously dismissed and to discover in them genuinely creative opportunities.

Without revealing too much about her plans, Rachel explained to Marie that she was prepared to look favorably on some projects about which she had previously been almost stubbornly unreceptive. In fact, Rachel told Marie, "the prospect of additional cash for only a moderate investment of time and effort [was] definitely appealing."[16]

Through Carson's first editor Maria Leiper, Simon & Schuster had earlier proposed that Carson adapt *The Sea Around Us* for juvenile readers for their popular Golden Book series. Carson had rejected the idea initially because she did not have the time to rewrite the text herself and would not consider having anyone else do it. Now Rachel changed her mind. She told Marie she would agree to have S&S hire a writer to do the adaptation provided she had control over the final result. The Golden Book project, which became known as "Jr. Sea," involved complicated contract negotiations because Oxford University Press had an interest as well. Carson asked Marie to draw up the contract so that royalties from it were deeded to Marjie in the same way as those from "Help Your Child to Wonder." Although Rachel left Maine at the end of October knowing the trip back to Maryland would be difficult and her future uncertain, she was buoyed by the possibilities that lay ahead.[17]

Once home, Maria's health continued to deteriorate. Through the rest of the fall and into the winter she suffered increasingly serious respiratory infections and several times had to have oxygen. Rachel engaged a practical nurse to come in during the day and solicited advice from Shirley Briggs and several of her other friends about finding a full-time housekeeper, the need for whom became more critical with each passing day.[18]

One of the women who heard about Carson's search was a pleasant black woman in her late thirties who had a young son of her own and whose husband was an interstate truck driver. Ida Sprow was a tall, slim, stately woman with a pleasant smile. She was reserved, soft spoken, and self-effacing about her experience and fine references but clearly recognized her competence. In mid-November Maria and Rachel interviewed Mrs. Sprow in the living room together and were impressed that, among other good qualities, Mrs. Sprow did not object when Jeffie, Rachel's cat, jumped into her lap and demanded attention.

Ida Sprow began working for the Carsons in late November, traveling to Silver Spring from her house on Capitol Hill by bus. Maria Carson was still very much in charge of the household, and Ida did the cooking, cleaning, and the laundry at her direction. After the first month Rachel, who was still holding her breath because Ida seemed too good to be true, confessed to Dorothy, "Ida is still a joy to have, and it seems to me I'd have had an intimation of clay feet by now, if they existed. She keeps the house in excellent order, with no direction really necessary. Best of all—and if only *this* lasts!—she doesn't seem to be resented and there has been no friction." Soon Rachel was appealing to Ida to stay all night when she had to go out of town.[19]

During the next several months Carson's hope that she might be able to put together the necessary money to make the Tenggrens' an offer grew even brighter. Yale microbiologist Wolf Vishniac's efforts to find well-heeled backers for a film version of *The Edge of the Sea* seemed about to succeed. Carson had written Lawrence Rockefeller after her conversation with him at the New York Zoological Society dinner in the hope that he might be interested in underwriting the film. Rockefeller declined, but he did discuss it with Fairfield Osborn, president of the Conservation Foundation where Rockefeller was a board member. Osborn had known Carson professionally since the late 1940s and called her to express his interest in the film, agreeing to meet with Marie Rodell in December.[20]

About the same time Leiper asked Carson to reconsider another project: editing a multivolume anthology of natural history similar to S&S's best-selling anthology series, *The World of Mathematics*. S&S proposed the title, *The World of Nature*, and suggested a run of approximately 100,000 sets selling at $20 per set. Initially Carson had rejected Leiper's idea because she thought there were too many nature anthologies as it was, but now she had an idea of how to make one distinctive. Rodell and Leiper were to discuss it further. Finally, William Shawn of *The New Yorker* telephoned about an idea of his own. With all these projects in the air, Rachel hoped she might somehow end up "rich enough to buy all the Tenggrens' property" on Southport Island. Alive with possibilities, she went to New York City at the end of November to receive the award for outstanding book of the year given by the National Council of Women and to meet with Rodell and Leiper.[21]

The National Council's Book Award had been given for the first time to Anne Morrow Lindbergh at a fancy ceremony at the Waldorf Astoria Hotel in 1955. In 1956 the council's Letters Committee decided thereafter to give a cash prize of five hundred dollars and to hold the ceremony in less expensive quarters, since the intent of the annual award was to recognize outstanding female writers. In announcing its award to Carson for *The Edge of the Sea*, the committee noted Carson's success in working in a field that was dominated by men. "Miss Carson," the citation read, "has successfully invaded a man's field and with a poet's eye, a scientific mind, and a woman's intuition, has taught the world to wonder."[22]

The party at the Carnegie Foundation building following the award ceremony was smaller and less formal than Rachel had anticipated, and she was pleased that, of the hundred or more guests present, she knew so many of them. After the festivities, Marie Rodell invited a group of Carson's friends, including Teale, Paul Brooks, Maria Leiper, and Carson's literary lawyer Maurice Greenbaum, to a dinner party at her apartment.[23]

The next day Carson and Rodell had a successful meeting with Walter Oakley of Oxford and editor Albert Leventhal of Simon & Schuster on the contract for the juvenile adaptation of *The Sea Around Us*. A young woman had been hired to do the adaptation, but Carson retained veto power over the text and the illustrations. They hoped to publish the book for Christmas 1958.[24]

When Rachel got back from New York, she decided quite uncharacteristically to splurge, spending all her award check on a phonograph, something she considered an "enormous extravagance" but a pleasure she was tired of postponing.[25]

Carried away by the violin concertos of Mendelssohn and Beethoven one evening in early December as she listened to her new phonograph, Rachel had a vision that she would succeed in preserving the Lost Woods. She later told Dorothy she had been "almost overwhelmed by the thought that at last—*really*—I was seeing a way it *might* be accomplished."[26]

Carson's December letters to Rodell and to Freeman reflect a new level of energy and excitement that had been absent even when she began the fieldwork along the Atlantic coast for *The Edge of the Sea*. When Rachel and Dorothy made their scouting trip of the woods in July, Rachel had thought of getting others to help her in its preservation. The Nature Conservancy meeting in Wiscasset that fall reinforced that idea. But when she comprehended how much money she might realize from publication of "Jr. Sea" and from the nature anthology, she began to see a way both to provide for her disabled dependents and to achieve her dream of preserving the Lost Woods. Something creative had happened that December evening when she glimpsed what it might mean for her if these projects came through. "Quite suddenly and amazingly," she explained to Dorothy, "there are enormous potential changes on my horizon."[27]

> And now, like the scattered parts of a puzzle suddenly falling into place, everything seems possible! When I stop to pinch myself I can scarcely believe it. It's like an answer to prayer—and yet I confess I have not prayed for it, unless my life, not words, were the prayer. But for a good many years I have believed that in order to achieve one must dream greatly—one must not be afraid to think large thoughts. And now, suddenly, as though it was "meant to be," the way seems to be opening up.[28]

Carson's plan was to use the revenues from the junior edition of *The Sea* to take care of Marjie and Roger's living expenses, their medical care, and even the boy's education. Proceeds from the anthology would go toward the acquisition of the Lost Woods.[29]

Rachel's December 8 letter to Dorothy indicates that she was aware that such a project might appear to some as rank commercialization of her art, at least until she could explain what she needed the money for. But Carson believed in the dream and so long as Dorothy did, too, she did not care what the critics or the public thought. The anthology, she decided, should not be confined to nature as commonly understood but should instead "present the whole story of Life on our earth, the geologic setting, the beginnings of life, its amazing ramifications and adaptations, its relations to its physical and biological environment." Rachel conceived of it as a project as vast and noble as *The Sea Around Us*, and was certain it "would make a true contribution to popular thinking."[30]

Full of enthusiasm, Carson contacted James Newman, the editor of the S&S anthology *The World of Mathematics*. She also got advice on specific terms of land acquisition from The Nature Conservancy office in Washington. Next she wrote Curtis and Nellie Lee Bok explaining what she wanted to do and asking Curtis's advice about establishing a foundation to own and control the property. Yet she still had not mustered her courage to talk to the Tenggrens. "I go into a positive cold sweat at the thought of how, when and through whom to approach the Tenggrens," she moaned to Dorothy, "suppose they prove intractable!" But even such fears could not discourage her or dim her belief that the dream was "Meant To Be."[31]

Rachel drafted her letter to the Boks carefully, perhaps secretly hoping they would be interested in contributing to her sanctuary, but certainly wanting the benefit of Curtis's experience. Her letter explained that ever since she had become a financially successful writer, she had hoped to contribute some of her earnings to further the things she believed in so deeply. Her lyric description of the particular woodlands and coastline she wanted to preserve conveyed the intense beauty she found there and her determination to preserve it if she could.

> Its charm for me lies in its combination of rugged shore rising in rather steep cliffs for the most part, and cut in several places by deep chasms where the storm surf must create a magnificent scene. Even the peaceful high tides explore them and leave a watermark of rockweeds, barnacles and periwinkles. There is one unexpected, tiny beach where the shore makes a sharp curve and there is a protective jutting out of rocks. . . . I suppose there is about a mile of shoreline. Behind this is the wonderful, deep, dark woodland—a cathedral of stillness and peace. . . . It is a living museum of mosses and lichens, which in some places form a carpet many inches deep. Rocks jut out here and there, as a flat floor where only lichens may grow or rising in shadowed walls. For the most part the woods are dark and silent, but here and there one comes out into open areas of sunshine filled with woods smells. It is a treasure of a place to which I have lost my heart completely.[32]

The loveliness of her letter as well as her passion for the place caught Curtis Bok's enthusiastic attention because he cared deeply about the same things. He invited Carson to come to Philadelphia to talk it over before Christmas.[33]

In one respect, however, Curtis Bok was more realistic then Carson. He advised her to contact the Tenggrens soon to see if they would even entertain sale of the land before she proceeded to set up any legal entity. Bok feared that people who would bulldoze a road through such natural beauty as Carson described might not be amenable to arguments for its preservation. He told her frankly, "Tenggren may be more business man than artist and want top price by the inch." Bok's letter reinforced Rachel's resolve to write the Tenggrens about her interest and then to go up to Southport to talk to them.[34]

But first there was need for another trip to New York to conclude the negotiations on "Jr. Sea" and to talk to Maria Leiper about her new conception of the anthology. Rachel wrote Marie, "the theme should be not 'Nature' but 'Life.' And this means, not just a new slant, but a wholly different project. It is this project I want to unfold to Maria, insofar as I'm able to visualize it now. I am satisfied," she told her agent, "that it has enormous and exciting possibilities, and that it could attract many more readers than just another collection of nature writings."[35]

Carson was certainly aware that her dream was still just that, but she did not think her hopes were unfounded. "In one form or another," she wrote Dorothy in her private annual Christmas letter, "I believe something will result from this that will live on into the future, the symbol of what we both so dearly love. And because it is something we can share, it is doubly precious to me."[36]

Rachel admitted that since the idea of preserving the coastal woodlands had come to her, her whole outlook had been transformed, and she had been seized by a sense of purpose in ways she had never experienced before. "Despite those occasional moments of shock and alarm, I can't help feeling, darling, that it is all 'meant' to work out. And there is some of that feeling I've tried to describe in relation to the impact of *The Sea*—that it is something that will happen through me, rather than something I shall do." With such exciting prospects ahead of her, Carson looked forward to the happy possibilities of the new year ahead.[37]

But it began ominously when Carson's trip to New York had to be postponed because of a severe case of intestinal flu. To make matters worse, Mamma was still not well and Rachel had not been able to find anyone to come in at night.[38]

She wrote to her lawyer, Maurice Greenbaum, about setting up a tax-exempt foundation and was reassured to learn that it was a simple process. He advised going ahead with it, stating objectives in very broad terms so that other projects might be included in addition to or as an alternative to the Lost Woods. Rachel also had time to think about how she wanted to approach the Tenggrens, deciding boldly that there was nothing to be lost from speaking to them before the contract for the anthology was signed. She thought that her best approach was to tell them she had always hoped to preserve some tract of Maine coastal woodland and that their land was one of several that appealed to her. If she left the impression that she had alternative possibilities, she would not have to reveal "how fully my heart is lost to *that* one" and thereby have no bargaining power.

Curtis Bok cautioned Rachel not to make any arrangements that jeopardized her own financial security. But Carson's devotion to the Lost Woods went beyond her concern for anything more than the assurance of enough for a "reasonably rainy day." She had made good investments and, she reasoned rather simplistically, there would be other books. Besides, there was no such thing as absolute security. In spite of a demoralizing conversation with James Newman about the arduous process of editing and collecting an anthology of the scope she envisioned, Carson had been thinking about the rest of her life's work and was convinced that the anthology had a place in it.[39]

A week later events beyond her control brought quite a different reality. Marjie was hospitalized on January 15 for pneumonia and returned home a week later by ambulance, pale and weak, plagued by a severe anemia that was unresponsive to treatment. Rachel, unwell herself, spent time in the hospital with her niece but also had to care for Roger, now just weeks shy of his fifth birthday. He developed an influenza-type infection and fever of his own that required keeping him confined as much as a child as "lively as 17 crickets" could be.[40]

"Rachel has had someone sick on her hands all fall," Shirley Briggs wrote her mother in early January after she and Rachel had chatted by telephone. "Now the little boy has something and they can't find out what it is. She had sort of a vacation in Maine of course, but had all the housework and care of Roger. We recalled our Florida trip and she said it was hard to imagine being that carefree again ever."[41]

Rachel depended on Ida to help her care for her mother and Roger, and hired a nurse to stay with Marjie for the time being. But even so, she was exhausted, explaining to Dorothy "the possibility of working or even writing a letter, no matter how urgent—has been at least as remote as a personal trip to the moon. I have eaten a fair number of meals without sitting down—bolting a sandwich while doing something else. From the moment I get out of bed the Emergency has claimed me, until I fall into bed again. Last night I got into the tub for the first time in days and days. But I'm all right, dearest—really I am. Probably at such times one draws on reserve sources of strength unsuspected before. It must be so."[42]

Once back in her own home, Marjie's health did improve and she was able to go downstairs occasionally. Rachel began to think that all would be well. But all such thoughts were dashed when Marjie's condition suddenly deteriorated and she was rushed back to the hospital, where she died some hours later on January 30. She was thirty-one years old. Rachel had been alone with Marjie during the desperate hours before they could get her to the hospital, and the experience seared her heart. As Marjie's executor, once again Rachel was left to take care of funeral arrangements, to explain what had happened to an uncomprehending child who was suddenly orphaned, and to plan for his future.[43]

Dorothy Freeman left Stan, who himself was just home from the hospital, and joined Rachel the day after Marjie's death, staying for over a week to do what she could to assuage the sadness and the tragedy that once again engulfed her friend. Rachel and her mother conferred about what to do, but there never was really any choice—Roger was closest to his grandmother and his great-aunt Rachel, and he would remain with them. Maria, now eighty-eight, insisted she could manage, but Rachel knew the responsibility of caring for Roger would be hers.[44]

Marjie's sister, Virginia King, was in many respects a more natural choice to take Roger. She was half Rachel's age, but she worked full time and was married to a man whose job required frequent relocation and who had grown children by a previous marriage. Neither Virginia nor Lee King wanted to take on the task of raising a young child nor had they been particularly close to Roger. Robert and Vera Carson had no children of their own and wanted none. More important, Robert was openly hostile to Roger. There were no alternatives. Rachel had been totally unprepared for Marjie's death—at least not then, not when she had been improving—and she was devastated by its suddenness and by the loss of her sweet-spirited and companionable niece. Just months shy of her own fiftieth birthday, Rachel now faced the prospect of becoming a de facto parent.[45]

Paul Brooks had written Carson a sympathy note when Marjie died, but Rachel did not acknowledge it until early April. Her matter-of-fact explanation of her situation to Brooks hid any hint of her own despair. "Marjorie and I were very close all her life, and of course I miss her dreadfully. Among the many changes this has brought is the fact that I shall now adopt Roger as my own; he had lost his father before he could remember him, and in our small family I am the logical one to care for him and, I'm sure, the one who is really closest to him. He does not fully realize the finality of his loss, and seems quite happy with us. But it is not an easy undertaking—I should be 15 or 20 years younger!"[46]

After spending several more weeks searching without success for a larger house to rent, Rachel at last decided to build her own. She hired an architect, made the necessary mortgage application, and studied a variety of house plans. She chose a large, heavily wooded corner lot at 11707 Berwick Road in the Quaint Acres subdivision of suburban Silver Spring. Enthusiastic about her building venture, Rachel wanted a house with large picture windows and lots of light. The house would have a brick exterior but would be a contemporary, one-story rambler with carport and a full basement with an additional bedroom and bath. Construction began in March with completion promised for July 1. Up in Maine, the contractor was busy remodeling the Southport cottage, adding two bedrooms, a new, enlarged screened porch, and an expanded study; it would be ready for the summer.[47]

In between meetings with banker and architect, Rachel read Dr. Arnold Gesell's popular book *The Child from Five to Ten* in an effort to find out just what to expect from her anxious five-year-old charge. But, as she confided to Dorothy, Gesell's analysis proved more distressing than helpful, showing only "what little beasts children appear to be, with little relief in sight within the dreary wastes of time encompassed by his book—just progression from one phase to another even worse!" Although Roger had recovered from his virus, he was plagued by what appeared to be serious ophthalmologic problems, and Rachel was considering corrective eye surgery.[48]

Rachel's anxiety about her child-raising abilities was well founded. Not only was she constitutionally ill-suited for the firm, consistent love and discipline a five-year-old needs, but Roger Christie was not an easy little boy. Bright, alert, and curious, he was tall for his age, but uncoordinated and awkward, a condition certainly made worse because he had little opportunity for rough-and-tumble recreation or for competitive games and sports. Probably because he was most often around adults, his social interactions with other children were frequently unsuccessful. Roger may well have suffered from clinical hyperactivity. But certainly his short attention span and need for constant attention was aggravated by his emotional insecurity. Whatever the source, it produced a needy, demanding child with few self-entertainment skills or creative outlets.[49]

Rachel, deeply discouraged, wrote Dorothy, "I grow more conscious with each passing week that my life will never again be the same, and that when it might otherwise be possible to do the things I had thought to do, the sands will have run too low. But no more in that depressing vein—I was only recalling that while I may have thought myself 'encumbered' during our lovely 1956 Spring-time, I didn't know 'from nothin'!"[50]

Sometimes a desperate sort of anxiety washed over her and she felt powerless to cope with the situation. "Somehow I feel terribly alone with my problems, as I suppose I inevitably must be," she confided to Dorothy. "And sometimes I even have a panicky feeling that I *can't* go through with it, but then I see again that there is no gate in the wall; there is no alternative. And then I'm haunted by the thought 'What would become of Roger if something happened to me?'—and for that, as yet, I've found no answer and it frightens me."[51]

Rachel received more bad news in mid-April when word came that her dear friend Alice Mullen had passed away in Amherst just before Easter. Rachel was stunned. Alice Mullen was Rachel's oldest friend, a woman with whom she felt a deep bond and in whom she had confided. Sharing her grief with Dorothy, Rachel explained, "not often in one's whole lifetime does one find a real kindred spirit. In their different ways, both Alice and Marjie were that to me, and in an interval of less than three months they have both gone. My heart has been very heavy since the news came and the night had many sleepless hours, thinking of things we had shared and now can never share again."[52]

Two deaths in so brief a time were nearly too much for Rachel to bear, and even small problems began to appear insurmountable. "We must never again for a moment forget what a precious possession we have in our love and understanding," she wrote Dorothy, "and in that constant and sometimes almost puzzling longing to share with each other every thought and experience. There has never been anyone else, darling, with whom I have known that to a degree even approaching the way I feel it with you. And there never could be another, I know. If ever I have seemed to forget the wonder and fragile beauty of it, darling, know that I won't forget again."[53]

Rachel's dream of saving the Lost Woods as a sanctuary was still alive that spring, but her hopes had been somewhat diminished. She had written the Tenggrens of her interest in buying a portion of their land. They told her they had no real desire to sell any land at the moment, confident the land boom already under way in Maine would continue, but that they would consider her interest and her offer. As Curtis Bok had feared, they set their price far higher than Carson had imagined. While Rachel was not about to give up the idea, it seemed far wiser to think about joining forces with others and to give the Tenggrens more time to consider her proposal. Marjorie's death also forced her to put the anthology project on hold since she now had neither the time nor the energy to commit to it. She needed a writing project that was both quick and easy. Once again life events forced Carson to change her course.[54]

After the normal series of delays typical of housing construction, the builder finished his work. Rachel, her mother, and Roger moved into

11701 Berwick Road on July 14. They spent the next two weeks getting things stored and organized before leaving the sweltering heat of Washington for Maine on August 1. Rachel could not manage her mother, Roger, two cats, and the driving without help, so her sister-in-law, Vera Carson, drove up with them. Their stay would be briefer than usual since Roger was starting a prekindergarten program at the end of September.

Although Rachel enjoyed her more spacious cottage in Southport, the summer proved even more difficult than the previous one. She had hoped to be able to find a college student to come in several hours a day to keep Roger entertained and allow her some time to work, but instead she ended up taking care of both Mamma and Roger by herself. By her own admission, she was miserable much of the time.[55]

Rachel and Dorothy had to steal time for themselves most of August. Stan Freeman's health problems were still not under control or apparently correctly diagnosed, so Dorothy's freedom, like Rachel's, was constrained. Whenever they could, Dorothy and Stan took over entertaining Roger, allowing Rachel a few hours to work. The weight of her obligations exacted a toll. Rachel's despair was evident in a letter to Paul Brooks in early September explaining they could not stop in Boston to see him, nor did she foresee going to New York any time soon. "My freedom of movement is now greatly curtailed," Carson told Brooks, "and the sad truth is that I have done no new work for very many months."[56]

However, the adaptation of "Jr. Sea" was proceeding more or less on schedule. Carson had reviewed several chapters and had selected and captioned many new illustrations. But this sort of editorial work was all that she could squeeze in between her domestic duties. When the time came to leave Southport, Rachel feared that the door had indeed been slammed on her great dream and perhaps on most of the vision that she had held out for herself. Yet there was an unforeseen benefit to the rather desperate situation Carson found herself in as she returned to Maryland in the fall of 1957.

Without a book in progress to consume her or immediate necessity of decisions to preserve the Lost Woods to divert her, Carson was able to give closer attention than she had in some time to affairs around her. If she could not immediately save that particular coastal forest in Maine, perhaps she could use her influence to alert others to the disappearance of seacoasts everywhere.

She arrived back in Silver Spring just as the world learned that scientists in the Soviet Union had successfully launched *Sputnik I*, an artificial satellite that was orbiting Earth. The implications of this latest technological entry into the Cold War, with its capabilities for photographic reconnaissance, were ominous for future relations between East and West. The Soviet achievement also represented the intrusion of humankind into a dimension of nature that many, including Carson, had previously regarded as sacrosanct. Rachel reacted to this event and the launch of the second Soviet satellite, *Sputnik II*, a month later less as a scientist impressed at the technical achievement than as a philosopher disturbed by its potential for evil and destruction.[57]

Closer to home, Carson found other evidence of the hazards of scientific knowledge misapplied. Her friends in the D.C. Audubon Society, particularly Irston Barnes, were alarmed by the U.S. Department of Agriculture's (USDA) announcement of a new program to spray thousands of acres of crop- and forestland in the South and Southwest with powerful pesticides in an effort to eradicate the fire ant. The USDA's program was, in part, a response to complaints from southern farmers about crop and livestock losses due to the stings of a species of fire ant that had been introduced from Brazil during World War II. But it was motivated equally, if not more, by the desire of the department's bureaucracy to expand its influence and leadership in American agriculture through the application of science and technology.[58]

Research conducted by the Department's Agricultural Research Service (ARS) suggested the effectiveness of massive aerial spraying with powerful chlorinated hydrocarbon pesticides such as chlordane, dieldrin, and aldrin, chemicals that, like DDT, had been developed during World War II. Such weapons promised not only to control insects and other pests but to eradicate them altogether. These new chemicals were the agricultural equivalent of the atomic bomb—the ultimate weapon; these pesticides promised to redefine the ancient warfare between farmer and insect. But the American public knew just as little about the long-term effects of these chemical weapons as they did the effects of atomic radiation.[59]

Congressional appropriation hearings on the USDA's proposal for spraying took place in the spring of 1957, when Carson had been preoccupied with Marjie's death. By late fall, when ARS announced plans for fire ant eradication, Carson was immediately alert to the threat such a plan posed to wildlife. Barnes, along with the leaders of other concerned environmental organizations, such as the National Wildlife Federation, had written USDA bureau chiefs and scientists questioning their proposed course. Carson's old employer, the Department of Interior, through the Fish and Wildlife Service, objected to the USDA's plan and raised questions about the incompleteness of its scientific analysis of the effects of spraying.[60]

Overlapping this pesticide controversy between federal agencies were newspaper accounts of a pending lawsuit scheduled to be heard in the U.S. Federal Court in Brooklyn, New York, in early February. The plaintiffs were a group of Long Islanders, the most prominent being Carson's friend ornithologist Robert Cushman Murphy. The organizational energy and commitment behind the group came from two remarkable women, Marjorie Spock and Mary Richards, who lived and gardened on Long Island. Their suit intended to restrain the federal and state Departments of Agriculture permanently from the spraying of their property with DDT mixed in fuel oil. This spraying was part of a government effort to wipe out Dutch elm disease, but the mixture was also applied for fogging against mosquitoes. Testimony against the spraying would come from fish and wildlife advocates, sportsmen, nutritionists, vegetable and dairy farmers, and concerned property owners. Witness briefs already filed charged inestimable damage to birds, bees, fish, and beneficial insects, and also warned of hazards to children, pets, cattle, gardens, and pastures. Carson was well aware of the government's pesticide spraying programs and the increasing evidence that not only were the pesticides killing birds and beneficial insects but that a growing number of insect pests were becoming resistant to the chemicals. Along with her Audubon friends, Carson followed the progress of the Long Island case with increasing interest.[61]

Although Rachel had not been able to write much for many months, she was determined to change that situation. With Roger successfully enrolled at a private school run by educational innovator Cynthia Warner, and with Ida's household help, Carson accepted an assignment that came to her from *Holiday* magazine shortly before she arrived back in Maryland.

The editors of *Holiday* planned a special issue for the summer of 1958 devoted to "Nature's America." They wrote to Rodell to ask if Carson would contribute a short article on the nation's seashores. Marie was lukewarm about the proposal since the magazine's fee was below what she considered Carson ought to accept. But Rachel decided to go ahead since she thought she could do it with material already at hand and in her head. "Of course I'd like to wring every cent possible out of them, and hasten the day of Burning the Mortgage," she told Marie, "so—please stretch this just as far as it will go. On the other hand, don't slam the door completely, no matter what the response. I say that because it seems to me an opportunity to get in a few licks about how few seashores remain." It would be a pleasant piece to write, and she was ready to begin immediately.[62]

The *Holiday* editors, however, wanted more of a mood portrait of the seashore before the coming of humans. Carson objected, explaining to Rodell, "I definitely want to do the article for them and trust they will accept what seems to me a quite reasonable and logical condition. I don't propose to include an ill-natured diatribe against anyone or any group—just a presentation of the plight of the shore, even as I did for the islands in *The Sea*." If she could not have Lost Woods for herself, she could at least be an advocate for the preservation of America's seashores everywhere.[63]

The outline that Carson submitted to the *Holiday* editors through Rodell combined sketches of several specific shores, her favorites on the East Coast—Ocean Point, Peaked Hill Bars, Plum Island, Beaufort, and St. Simons—but also included one or two on the West Coast, evoking the different mood and atmosphere of each. She would emphasize the flow of time and change, describing shores taking millions of years to appear as well as those emerging after a single, violent storm. But as her outline makes clear, she intended to use the last section of the article to remind readers that few wild and pristine shores remained. She wrote:

> The dismal truth is that shores such as we are proposing to describe are fast disappearing, and may well do so completely within the life of some of us. This is not alarmist speculation, but a conclusion based on recent factual surveys and predictions by those qualified to know. Only vision, understanding, and bold action can better the situation. Feeling this so deeply as I do, I cannot write about the shores I love without pointing out their peril, even though briefly. For it is only as people are informed of dangers that threaten such priceless regions that they can be saved.[64]

The editors at *Holiday* seemed satisfied with her proposal, and Carson set to work.

Rachel collected vignettes about the seashore that she had written in her field notebooks and in letters to Dorothy, such as the firefly story and her early description of the sea cave at Ocean Point, that she thought she might include. The project seemed to renew her spirits and confirm for her that yes, she would write again.[65]

Although Carson had intended to finish the *Holiday* piece by the deadline of December 15, she was diverted by Roger's needs and another respiratory virus of her own. An evening listening to Beethoven's symphonies had prompted her to see the *Holiday* article, the Harper book, and the "Help Your Child to Wonder" article as opportunities to "say in different ways, some of the things I want to say before I lay down my pen." But in spite of her best intentions, sustained writing time was nearly impossible to find.[66]

Realizing how difficult Rachel's domestic situation was, Marie prodded her to find more household help. "You have not answered my question about the built-in baby sitter," Marie chided, "so I assume you've done nothing about it. I do think it is the most important thing you have to do just now and I intend to nag you til it's done. Fair warning!" But for Rachel the answer was not so simple, and she resented Marie's "brisk competence" and her "slide-rule solutions."[67]

As Christmas and the anniversary of Marjorie's death approached, Roger's insecurities increased to the point that after talking to Mrs. Warner at his school, Rachel felt she might need a psychiatrist's assistance. The boy was plagued by a variety of unexplainable aches and pains and legitimate bouts of tonsillitis, often staying home for a combination of real and imagined symptoms. Rachel reported to Dorothy on New Year's Eve that the physician who had examined Roger was "more inclined to think this is chiefly emotional, and believes the shock resulting from Marjie's death is only now coming to the surface."[68]

Roger's demands on her had, as she told Dorothy, "increased to the point where—even though understanding or trying to—I think I'll explode! He will scarcely let me out of his sight. And what this meant in terms of the *Holiday* article, I leave it to your good imagination to picture. For no matter how I explained the situation—yes, and no matter how hard-boiled I got about it—nothing helped very much—he was at my door every little while to see 'how much work' I had done. And I actually believe he convinced himself he was 'helping' by staying away even for a few minutes at a time."[69]

The "searing agony," as she called it, of finishing the seashore piece under such conditions was compounded by the feeling that no one could quite understand why she could not just sit down and write it. Some mornings, she confessed in another tearful letter to Dorothy, "I would open my eyes remembering everyone waiting and not understanding, and I'd only want to go to the bathroom and be sick!"[70]

But at last she did finish the seashore piece, entitled "Our Ever-Changing Shore," and sent it off to *Holiday* just after the first of the new year. Symptomatic of her emotional state, Carson had reduced the section on the vanishing seashores and need for their preservation to several paragraphs. The effort to get the article finished was enormous, and she told Marie, "I doubt very much I want to go on and write a save-the-seashore book now."[71]

Harry Sions, the magazine's editorial director, acknowledged its receipt and in a rather arch tone explained that "Miss Carson's article will require a little more work and some additional material." Carson had failed to include any descriptions of Pacific seashores as she had indicated in her original outline, and he thought she had devoted too much space to minute ocean and shore life instead of to grand and sweeping descriptions. Rachel did not finish her revisions until mid-February, overtaken as she was by other events. She took out "all the small creatures, substituted coastal scenery moods," and added what she had originally intended to say about vanishing seashores.[72]

"Our Ever-Changing Shore" was enthusiastically received when it was published in *Holiday*'s July 1958 issue. It combined the best of Carson's sweeping vision of the timelessness of the sea found in *The Sea Around Us* with the intimate attention to the details of shorelife refracted through her own experience that distinguishes *The Edge of the Sea*. There are familiar scenes in this piece, such as when Carson describes the intense awe she and Dorothy felt at dawn one morning in Maine as they stepped out of the mists of the spruce forest onto the dripping rocks and vast expanse of gray sea. Here, too, is an abbreviated account of the night of the autumn phosphorescence on her own Maine shore, but without the benighted firefly; the shades and colors of the changing seasons; the flat vistas of the salt marshes of Matamuskeet; and the vast expanse of beach at St. Simons.[73]

Her plea for preserving wilderness areas of seacoast "where the relations of sea and wind and shore—of living things and their physical world—remain as they have been over the long vistas of time in which man did not exist" is brief but powerful, juxtaposed as it is to her censure of "this space-age universe" where there is yet "the possibility that man's way is not always best."[74]

Carson's preoccupation in "Our Ever-Changing Shore" with the corrupting hand of man, which she found most conspicuous in the fabrications of modern science and technology, was a theme that she had decided to take up in the much promised book for Harper. She outlined that book and her views on modern science as she now conceived them in a letter to Dorothy in early February 1958 that revealed the atomic bomb's impact on her thinking.

> The theme remains what I have felt for several years it would be: Life and the relations of Life to the physical environment. But I have been mentally blocked for a long time, first because I didn't know just what it was I wanted to say about Life, and also for a reason more difficult to explain. Of course everyone knows by this time that the whole world of science has been revolutionized by events of the past decade or so. I suppose my thinking began to be affected soon after atomic science was firmly established. Some of the thoughts that came were so unattractive to me that I rejected them completely, for the old ideas die hard, especially when they are emotionally as well as intellectually dear to one. It was pleasant to believe, for example, that much of Nature was forever beyond the tampering reach of man—he might level the forests and dam the streams, but the clouds and the rain and the wind were God's. . . .
>
> It was comforting to suppose that the stream of life would flow on through time in whatever course that God had appointed for it—without interference by one of the drops of the stream—man. And to suppose that however the physical environment might mold Life, that Life could never assume the power to change drastically—or even destroy—the physical world.[75]

She had clung to these traditional beliefs because to have them vaguely threatened undermined everything she held dear. "I shut my mind," Rachel confessed, "refused to acknowledge what I couldn't help seeing. But that does no good, and I have now opened my eyes and my mind. I may not like what I see, but it does no good to ignore it, and it's worse than useless to go on repeating the old 'eternal verities' that are no more eternal than the hills of the poets." So, she explained, after another of those agonizing meetings with Nanda Anshen, she had decided she might as well be the one to write about "Life in the light of the truth as it now appears to us."[76]

Carson admitted that before the space age became a reality, she had dismissed many of the predictions of science as so much fantasy. Now she realized that was no longer possible. "And man seems actually likely to take into his hands—ill-prepared as he is psychologically—many of the functions of God." But in spite of all that science and technology promised, Rachel steadfastly maintained that "as man approaches the 'new heaven and the new earth'—or the space-age universe . . . he must do so with humility rather than arrogance." Unable to stop there, she added, "And along with humility I think there is still a place for wonder."[77]

All this she planned to put into the "Remembrance of Life," which, ironically, she had outlined for Dorothy while listening to the radio report of the disastrous attempt to launch the nation's first space satellite from Cape Canaveral, Florida. Carson had never been able to explain to anyone before, perhaps even to herself, what the theme of this book would be. The letter to Dorothy is remarkable in its preview of what Carson felt compelled to write and in her admission of what motivated her. In fact, she had outlined precisely the theme of her next book. Its context, but not its philosophic intent, was altered by a series of events that enveloped Carson in the winter of 1957–58 and swept her along in an intellectual and scientific adventure beyond even her considerable powers of imagination.[78]

14

"I Shall Rant a Little, Too"

Rachel Carson had been interested in the role of poisons in the environment since 1938, when she thought to write an article on naturally occurring arsenics. She had been skeptical of the ecological impact of synthetic chemical pesticides even before 1945 when, after studying the wildlife research done by Clarence Cottam and Elmer Higgins for the Fish and Wildlife Service, she tried to interest *Reader's Digest* in an article on DDT. At no time after that was she ever dispassionate about the use of synthetic chemical pesticides either in the wild or in agriculture.

Her negative assessment was reinforced by the shortsighted attitudes of predator and pest control scientists at FWS and USDA. Too often she thought they acted precipitously, without a comprehensive understanding of the long-term effects of these chemicals, their impact on pest life cycles, or the ecological value of the pest targeted for elimination. What she had read in the years since leaving government service in 1952 only confirmed her opinion that if these poisons were used indiscriminately, the delicate balance of nature would be threatened and with it the functioning ecology of the living world.[1]

Carson was first brought back to the subject of synthetic pesticides in the fall and winter of 1957 by the controversy surrounding the USDA's fire ant eradication program and by the Long Island suit seeking to halt the aerial spraying of private land with DDT. Carson made a few telephone calls to relevant government agencies in December and January 1958 that confirmed the tremendous expansion of the use of chlorinated hydrocarbon and organophosphate pesticides as well as the technology facilitating their wide application and potential misuse. Carson's inquiries, along with the information made public by the Long Island trial, led her to conclude initially that she wanted to write an article about the dangers associated with pesticide abuse.[2]

Less than a year later, however, Carson had committed herself to a three-part serial for *The New Yorker* and a book on the subject for Houghton Mifflin. In the process of her research she established a remarkable network of scholars in many fields all over the world and created an alliance of scientists, naturalists, journalists, and activists committed to helping her document a spectrum of environmental abuses. The evidence Carson gathered eventually convinced her that the ecological crisis brought about by the misuse of pesticides extended to and endangered human health as well as the nonhuman world. Along the way, she realized that this book might be her most important yet, but her investigation did not begin with that thought in mind.[3]

Irston Barnes, the indefatigable conservationist president of the D.C. Audubon Society, was opposed to the USDA's fire ant extermination program. In the fall of 1957, Barnes enlisted Carson in his efforts to get the department to make public the research upon which its pesticide policies were based. About the same time William Longgood, a dedicated young staff writer for the *New York World-Telegram-and-Sun*, began covering the Long Island spraying case, which was set for trial in the Federal District Court in Brooklyn in early February.[4]

The Long Island case was closely watched by many people, especially those in Pennsylvania, New York, and New England whose property had been sprayed in the spring and summer of 1957. The USDA and allied state agencies had covered the region with DDT mixed in fuel oil to combat infestations of gypsy moth, tent caterpillar, and mosquitoes. Beatrice Trum Hunter, an organic gardener and naturalist in Hillsboro, New Hampshire, was one of the more irate and articulate victims of that control effort. A friend of several of those involved in the Long Island case, Hunter lent her support to the activities of the Committee Against Mass Poisoning, a group of eminent naturalists that included John Kieran, Edwin Way Teale, and Robert Cushman Murphy, one of the plaintiffs, who opposed indiscriminate pesticide spraying and had created a legal fund to support the Long Island plaintiffs.[5]

Despite mounting citizen protest, state and federal agencies planned to expand their spraying campaigns again the following year. On January 12,

1958, the *Boston Herald* published an angry letter from Mrs. Hunter detailing the wildlife damage that had occurred as a result of the spraying, warning of the potential harm to humans, and urging citizen expression against what she called "this mass poisoning." Hunter's letter provoked another articulate New Englander, Olga Owens Huckins, to take action.[6]

Huckins, a writer, lecturer, and the former literary editor of the *Boston Post*, and her husband, Stuart, had a large bird sanctuary around their seashore home in Duxbury, Massachusetts. Huckins and Carson had been friends and correspondents since 1951, when Huckins gave *The Sea Around Us* a splendid review in the *Post* and Carson had written to thank her. Huckins's property in Duxbury, like Mrs. Hunter's in New Hampshire, had been sprayed for mosquitoes repeatedly in the summer of 1957; as a result, many songbirds had died and their nesting places, ponds, and birdbaths had been contaminated.[7]

Believing that aerial spraying was "inhuman, undemocratic, and probably unconstitutional," Huckins sent Carson a copy of Mrs. Hunter's *Herald* letter shortly after it appeared. Rachel shared Hunter's account of the harm to wildlife with her mother, who was so outraged that she called Agricultural Secretary Ezra Benson's office as well as the White House to protest.[8]

Hunter's letter elicited several responses that were also published in the *Herald*. The first came from one R. C. Codman of Waban, Massachusetts, who identified himself as active in the commonwealth's spraying program. He defended the state's action and categorically denied there had been any loss of wildlife. Denigrating Mrs. Hunter's claims, Codman dismissed the members of the Committee Against Mass Poisoning as "hysterical."[9]

This was too much for Olga Huckins, who penned her own biting letter to the *Herald* and sent a copy of it to Carson, along with a description of the damage to her birds as well as her efforts to find out what Benson and the state had in mind next. Huckins's letter only heightened Carson's interest in the issue.[10]

Huckins's letter was published in the *Boston Herald* on January 29. Blasting Codman's claim that there had been no wildlife loss, Huckins wrote, "The testers must have used black glasses, and the trout that did not feel the poison were super-fish." She then detailed how the "harmless shower bath" of poisons had killed her songbirds, which had died horribly, and how the mosquitoes that reappeared were more voracious than before, but that the bees, grasshoppers, and other insects had vanished.

According to Huckins, the answer to this intolerable situation was simple: "STOP THE SPRAYING OF POISONS FROM THE AIR everywhere, until all the evidence, biological and scientific, immediate and long run, of the effects upon wildlife and human beings [was] known." It was a position Carson could wholeheartedly endorse.[11]

Knowing of Rachel's interest in the controversy, Marie Rodell passed on news that *Reader's Digest* planned to publish an article favorable to aerial spraying. Annoyed that *Digest* editor DeWitt Wallace would make such a mistake in judgment, Carson collected information aimed at changing his mind. Rodell also confirmed that Carson's friend and former FWS colleague Durwood Allen was writing a piece on the dangers of insecticides for *Fisherman Magazine* and would be happy to share his material.[12]

Not long after receiving Beatrice Hunter's *Boston Herald* letter, Carson telephoned W. L. Popham, then the assistant administrator of the Plant Pest Control Division in the Agricultural Research Service (ARS) of USDA, who was in charge of the fire ant program. She asked him for data on the percentage of dieldrin and heptachlor, some of the newest and most toxic chlorinated hydrocarbon pesticides the USDA was using. She also requested certain ARS research bulletins, which Popham subsequently sent her.[13]

Following Durwood Allen's lead, Carson also telephoned the congressional offices of the House and Senate committees that were investigating wildlife damage as well as an official at the Department of Health, Education and Welfare who was concerned about pesticides in groundwater supplies. She found a friendly but cautious official at the Food and Drug Administration (FDA) willing to talk about a rumor that a leading baby food manufacturer had stopped production of one vegetable because of widespread pesticide contamination. He agreed to send her some information on the case.

Allen also told Carson that the Conservation Foundation had just issued a lengthy report on pesticides and that the National Audubon Society had recently released a bulletin critical of the fire ant control program. Rachel asked Marie to get copies of these reports and enclosed the letter she had written to DeWitt Wallace at *Reader's Digest.* To Wallace she said: "I cannot refrain from calling to your attention the enormous danger—both to wildlife and, more frighteningly, to public health—in these rapidly growing projects for insect control by poisons, especially as widely and randomly distributed by airplanes." Reviewing her own years in conservation work in the federal government, Carson told Wallace, "Many of my former colleagues, as well as representatives of other agencies directly concerned with public health as affected by food and water, tell me of their genuine alarm at what is happening. This alarm is shared by a large number of scientists, naturalists, physicians, and public health officials throughout the nation."[14]

Carson gave him some examples of the damage she had gathered, including reports of the contamination of cow milk from pastures sprayed by DDT and the reproductive failures of various birds after ingesting poisoned insects. The thrust of her argument was that human populations were being put at risk by the use of these chemicals. "I am sure," Carson told Wallace, "that a publication with the *Digest*'s enormous power to influence public thinking all over the country would not wish to put its seal of approval on something so potentially hazardous to public welfare."[15]

Carson had begun the new year with several projects awaiting her attention. Among them was an anthology of sea literature that Elizabeth Lawrence, a senior editor at Harper, had discussed with Rodell in January. But Carson's immediate attention had already been captured by the pesticide problem and the evidence that would be produced by the Murphy suit against the government.

Certain that the case would be of interest to *The New Yorker*, Rachel told Marie, "It has occurred to me that E. B. White might be interested for various reasons, and it is the sort of thing he could be devastating about if he chose. I thought I might write him." She also suggested that Marie might have a writer or two from among her clientele who could attend the trial in Brooklyn and write a magazine article. Carson knew that the expert testimony on both sides would be important. The case's precedent as a citizen-initiated effort to protect the environment and enjoin the government from abusing the property rights of private citizens would influence future policy.[16]

After a conversation with Rodell on February 1, Carson decided she would write the article. "Having spent a substantial part of two weeks," she told Marie, "in phone calls, correspondence and searching through references, and having finally struck what appears to be 'pay dirt'—I naturally feel that I should like to do an article myself. In the course of all this, I have made certain valuable contacts and discovered many leads still to be followed up; this in its full value would be difficult to transfer to another writer." Still chafing from the lack of interest in the subject at

Reader's Digest, Carson asked Marie to contact editors at *Ladies Home Journal*. Carson enclosed a three-page memorandum for Marie to use in trying to interest magazine editors. It summarized some of what Rachel had uncovered in her several weeks of investigation and reflects her initial attitude toward synthetic pesticides.[17]

Noting the increase in pesticide production and revenue since 1940, Carson argued that "the effect of these chemical poisons—some of great toxicity—is only beginning to be assessed in its relation to the lives and welfare, not only of the whole community of animals in the area subjected to ground and aerial sprays, but of the human population as well. There exists already, however, a large body of well documented evidence that these highly toxic poisons, as presently used, represent an alarming threat to human welfare, and also to the basic balance of nature on which human survival ultimately depends."[18]

Emphasizing the unknown effect of these chemicals on human reproduction, Carson quoted the comparison made by the National Audubon Society's president, John Baker, of the hazards of chemical poisons to those of radioactive fallout. Carson noted that scholars at the Institute of Agricultural Medicine at the University of Iowa and the Conservation Foundation had raised the possibility of human sterility and carcinogenic agency from pesticides. Armed with Carson's memo, Rodell began making editorial inquiries.[19]

Next Rachel sent off her promised letter to E. B. White. Repeating her conviction about the dangers of mass spraying, Carson told him of the upcoming Long Island trial in federal court. "A large amount of important testimony is certain to be presented," she told him. "Should the injunction be granted, the results would be far-reaching. It is my hope that you might cover these court hearings for *The New Yorker*."[20]

Rachel's attempt to enlist White was perfectly directed. E. B. White had been one of the first to question publicly what might happen if DDT were ever used promiscuously as an insecticide spray from airplanes. Carson reported that the USDA might include Maine in its summer gypsy moth control campaign, knowing that White, who now lived in North Brooklin, Maine, would be incensed by the news. "It would delight me beyond measure," Carson told him, "if you should be moved to take up your own pen against this nonsense—though that is far too mild a word! There is an enormous body of fact waiting to support anyone who will speak out to the public—and I shall be happy to supply the references."[21]

Carson's letter to White begs the question of why, having just told Rodell that she wanted to do an article herself, she attempted to entice him to do one for *The New Yorker*. Rachel had at least two outcomes in mind. Recognizing how important the testimony at the trial would be and how central it was to any article she might write later, she wanted someone who understood its ramifications to cover it, and given her responsibilities to Roger and Mamma, she had no hope of being there herself. She genuinely hoped White would join the cause. Her other reason for turning to White was more complex. If he was unable to cover the trial but understood its importance, he would certainly tell editor William Shawn about it. Then Carson would have two informed advocates at the magazine and a greater chance of placing some kind of an article there herself when she was ready. This is precisely what happened several weeks later.[22]

White's response on the question of DDT was just as impassioned as Carson hoped it would be, but he wrote that he could not take the assignment. He would, however, forward her letter to Shawn with a recommendation that he assign a reporter to cover the court proceedings.[23]

On the same day she wrote to White, Carson asked Marie Rodell to write to Marjorie Spock, one of the primary plaintiffs in the Long Island suit, requesting some background material. Delighted to learn of Carson's interest, Spock telephoned Rodell, mailed off a stack of documents, and wrote Carson what proved to be a prophetic note.[24]

"I think you know how grim this struggle with the U.S. government and the whole chemical industry is bound to be. We have marshalled some pretty solid scientific men and data, and are feeling confident." Unable to resist the temptation, Spock asked Carson if she would consider giving expert testimony and offered to pay her legal costs. Thanking Carson for her interest, Spock graciously wrote, "how deeply moved I have been by your marvelous way with a pen! No words suffice to express that!"[25]

Carson had made an inspired connection. Marjorie Spock was a woman of enormous courage, integrity, and indefatigable spirit who soon became one of Carson's inner circle of friends and the central point of her original research network. Marjorie was the eldest daughter of Benjamin Spock, the general solicitor of the New York, New Haven, and Hartford Railroad, and the younger sister of the renowned pediatrician Benjamin Spock. Raised in a large, boisterous, and erudite family in New Haven, Connecticut, she was a creative and intellectually independent spirit. Instead of entering Smith College as her family intended, she had fled to Switzerland, against her father's wishes, to study eurythmy, a holistic philosophy of the art of movement espoused by the Swiss thinker Rudolf Steiner. Spock returned home several years later, intending to teach the Steiner techniques in the United States, but first spent some years taking care of her widowed mother and raising her younger sister.[26]

In the early 1950s Spock and her friend, Mary (Polly) Richards, the wealthy daughter of a family friend, bought a house in Brookville, Long Island. They put in a two-acre garden where they could practice organic agriculture. Richards, a digestive invalid all her life, had to have the purest food available, and Spock, who had studied organic farming in Switzerland, was committed to it.

It was this garden that state and federal control planes sprayed repeatedly with DDT mixed in fuel oil—fourteen times in a single day—during the summer of 1957. Distraught that their food supply was ruined, their dairy animals contaminated, and their soil irrevocably compromised, Spock and Richards decided to sue. Spock asked Robert Cushman Murphy, one of their neighbors, to help her find an attorney to take the case. Although Murphy failed in that endeavor, he persuaded other landowners on Long Island, including Jane Nichols, the daughter of the financier J. P. Morgan, and Theodore Roosevelt's son, Archibald, to join them as plaintiffs.[27]

Spock and Richards were a formidable team, brilliant, erudite, and absolutely committed. For Richards, the issue was her life; for Spock, it was her friend's health, her desire to have what she considered healthful food, and her constitutional right as a property owner to keep her land as she wished it, free from trespass by the government.[28]

The day the trial began, February 10, the New York area was buried in five feet of snow. The trial lasted twenty-two days. Spock recalls that in spite of a fine legal team and mountains of evidence, "the government ran rough shod over any one who got in the way of the new technology. They brushed us off like so many flies." In the end the judge, a man recently appointed to the federal bench by President Dwight Eisenhower, threw out seventy-two uncontested admissions for the plaintiffs and denied their petition. It took three years to exhaust all legal appeals. When the case finally reached the U.S. Supreme Court in 1960, it was declined on a technicality. Associate Justice William O. Douglas, however, wrote a strong dissenting opinion supporting the case on its merits.[29]

Marjorie Spock had invested in one of the earliest models of thermofax machines, which she kept in her basement. It was a crude affair that continually overheated, belching smoke and vile-smelling fumes from odd sprockets and sending out scorched brown paper, sometimes completely burned and only barely legible at best. Nevertheless, when she got home from court each night, she wrote a summary of the day's events, called "Today in Court," copied it on the uncooperative machine, and sent it out to a large list of interested people, including the Committee Against Mass Poisoning, Beatrice Trum Hunter, Olga Huckins, and after February 14, to Rachel Carson.[30]

With still a week to go in the trial, Carson wired Spock asking how she could get a full transcript of the proceedings. Spock responded that between Polly Richards and Mrs. Thomas Waller, a plaintiff representing the interests of the State Garden Clubs, they would make one available to her, but it would take some time. In the meantime, Spock continued to send Carson other important documents, including a seminal article on insect resistance by C. J. Breijer, the director of the Dutch Plant Pest Control Service in the Netherlands.[31]

Through Spock, Carson discovered the work of two distinguished physicians and a young wildlife biologist whose research proved crucial. Both Morton Biskind of Westport, Connecticut, and Malcolm Hargraves of the Mayo Clinic worked at the edges of mainstream medical research. Biskind, a retired toxicologist and nutritionist with a world reputation, studied the effects of synthetic chemicals on human enzyme systems and their possible relationship to cancer. He was an expert on industrial contaminants and human cancer but was viewed suspiciously by the medical establishment for his unpopular conclusions and was hounded by the chemical industry after giving damaging testimony at the congressional hearings to amend the Pure Food and Drug Act. Hargraves, a hematologist, worked on the connection between chemical exposure and blood disorders, particularly leukemias. Although Hargraves was held in high regard, he was viewed with suspicion by some colleagues because of his willingness to give expert testimony and participate in public health debates rather than confine his energies to the laboratory. John George had documented DDT's immediate mortality to birds and fish after it was applied against spruce budworm in Clear Lake Junction, New York, in 1946 and was the primary investigator on the Conservation Foundation's controversial pesticide report. A wildlife biologist with ties to the government research community, George had just been appointed assistant chief of Wildlife Biology at the Patuxent Research Refuge.[32]

While Carson was collecting material, Rodell tried without success to interest a magazine in publishing an article on the dangers of pesticides. Negative editorial responses, many based on fear of lost advertising revenues, only heightened Carson's determination to push ahead. They represented just the sort of scientific ignorance she wanted to combat and convinced her of the public's need for information. But if placing an article was going to be difficult, she agreed with Marie that perhaps they should consider a brief book instead. Marie queried Paul Brooks, who was interested.[33]

On February 21 Rachel sent Brooks copies of some of the more important documents she had assembled along with a copy of her earlier memoranda. By this time she had collected "mountains of material" but was especially excited about finding a copy of the published hearings of the House Select Committee to Investigate the Use of Chemicals in Foods and Cosmetics. The so-called Delaney Committee hearings had resulted in the passage of the Miller Amendment to the Food, Drug, and Cosmetic Act in the early 1950s, and the expert testimony they contained was invaluable.[34]

Still somewhat ambivalent about how she wanted to handle her material, she responded to a wire from Brooks by saying:

> I don't know what I should do about this, Paul. As you know, I had various other plans, to be carried out as speedily as my rather difficult personal situation allows. I feel I should do something on this however. If I can do a magazine article that would also serve as a chapter of a book on this subject, then also perhaps an introduction and some general editorial work, this would probably be all I should undertake. But let's discuss it as soon as you hear more.[35]

While she waited for Brooks and Lovell Thompson, the head of the trade division at Houghton Mifflin, to confer, she took E. B. White's suggestion and sent a proposal to William Shawn at *The New Yorker* about an article on insect control and the effect of insecticides on the balance of nature.

Although that proposal follows the basic outlines of her earlier memorandum to Rodell, her more recent research is evident in the examples she selects, the sources she quotes, and the emphasis of her argument. She opened with a powerful quotation from Albert Schweitzer that she had discovered in a 1956 bulletin of the International Union for the Conservation of Nature and Natural Resources that summed up her thesis.

> Modern man no longer knows how to foresee or to forestall. He will end by destroying the earth from which he and other living creatures draw their food.[36]

This intriguing proposal captured Shawn's interest at once.[37]

By the time Rachel agreed to write an article for *The New Yorker*, she was also ready to move ahead on a book if she could find a collaborator. Brooks had suggested a collaboration originally, and Rodell and Carson concurred, apparently without giving too much thought to how such an arrangement would work out in practice. Uppermost in Rachel's mind was the need to have someone in New York who would have access to the trial transcript and could do other research that was precluded to her by distance and time. Brooks and Rodell thought what she needed was someone to do both research and basic writing to help speed the process. So while Rachel waited for Paul and Marie to come to some understanding about how work and profits would be divided, she began roughing out a chapter outline.[38]

Marie undertook the search for an editor or writer with whom Rachel could work. After she had been turned down by several leading science writers, Marie decided they might have more luck interesting a professional magazine writer who specialized in scientific topics. From the outset, Rodell and Carson were on two separate courses in their thinking about this project. Aware of Carson's other writing commitments, Rodell focused on how Carson could turn out a quick book; at the same time, Carson's interest in the subject and commitment to writing about pesticide abuse became deeper every day. The more she learned about the complexity of the impact of chemical poisons on the environment, the more convinced she was of the importance of the subject to her own mission as a writer.[39]

On March 4 Rodell wired Lovell Thompson that she had found a probable collaborator, and the process moved on despite his reservations about the project. The book, she told him, was tentatively entitled *How to Balance Nature*, and Edwin Diamond, science editor of *Newsweek*, had agreed to collaborate. Carson's outline would follow.[40]

The Diamond-Carson collaboration lasted barely four months. As a literary partnership it was doomed from the start, but the hard feelings that it left reappeared years later, in 1963, when Edwin Diamond authored one of the most devastating critiques of *Silent Spring* in the *Saturday Evening Post*. The episode marks one of the few times Marie Rodell's personal and literary judgment can be seriously faulted. But both Brooks and Rodell failed to understand the significance of Carson's project, and Carson herself was slow to articulate her altered perspective. As a consequence, she was put in a vulnerable situation that needlessly cast a shadow over her work.[41]

Edwin Diamond had joined *Newsweek* in the fall of 1957. A self-described "hard charging journalist" from Chicago, he was bright, ambitious, and determined to make a name for himself in scientific journalism. After several telephone calls and one meeting, Rodell offered Diamond joint authorship of a book with Carson and a fifty-fifty split of all monies. Carson would write the beginning and the end, Diamond would do the bulk of the research and write the middle. How much Rodell told him about Carson's approach to the topic of chemical pesticides and the environment is unknown, but she certainly gave Diamond Carson's outline and memorandum. Although Diamond's job at *Newsweek* was hectic and he traveled a lot, he told Rodell he would do it because he wanted the chance to work with Rachel Carson.[42]

In mid-March Diamond went down to Silver Spring to meet Carson. He remembers little about that meeting other than that Carson was very reserved. The project seemed straightforward, but Carson was vague about which chapters he would write. Rachel described Diamond simply as "a keen and intelligent young man."[43]

"Edward [*sic*] Diamond and Rachel Carson have met, talked, got on well, and agreed they would like to do the book together," Rodell reported to Lovell Thompson, "so I guess we have to do something about a contract." Diamond agreed to Rodell's rough division of labor and indicated he could start immediately. Rodell arranged to advance Diamond his share of the signing fee, $750, in advance of the contract. Marie was preparing for a lengthy business trip to Europe and was eager to get this deal concluded.[44]

The two writers could not have been more different in background, temperament, style, or outlook. Diamond apparently sensed at least some of these differences after their initial meeting, and perhaps Carson did as well. But Carson was focused on her need for research on the Long Island case and eager for Diamond to get in touch with Marjorie Spock so that he could read and take notes on the trial transcript and meet some of the other plaintiffs. She wrote a note to Spock in which she explained that she had decided to do a "small, quick book" in collaboration with Diamond, whose job it would be to "go through masses of material, assemble data, and write the more factual portions of the book."[45]

But on April 1 Carson's approach to the book and her attitude toward the collaboration with Diamond was fundamentally altered by William Shawn's decision that he wanted Carson to write a long two-part piece of about 20,000 to 30,000 words. Rachel, caught completely off guard by his expansive proposal with its handsome remuneration, was gratified about Shawn's enthusiasm for the topic and delighted by the prospect of a serial in *The New Yorker*. The article Shawn envisioned could stand for most of the book, and coauthorship of the *New Yorker* article was unthinkable. Carson had no intention of sharing the profits from it. Diamond's role would have to be redefined and, if necessary, limited.[46]

Brooks's original idea of hiring someone to string together sections of trial testimony and quotes from medical experts with Carson doing some reediting and writing of the introduction and conclusion was, as Rachel put it, "out." "If the collaboration is to be a help and not just a nuisance and an unjustified division of profits," Rachel wrote Marie, "I do think we must reexamine the situation and reach a firm agreement before we go farther." Privately, she told Dorothy that Diamond did not seem to be making the kind of progress she had expected.[47]

Unaware of Carson's altered attitude, Brooks presented the Carson-Diamond project to the executive committee of Houghton Mifflin on April 2, substituting for the title Carson proposed one of his own, *The Control of Nature*. Brooks recommended a contract for publication with an advance of $3,000, $1,500 on signing, to be divided equally between Carson and Diamond. But the contract was never signed by either party because Carson objected to the terms of the collaborative agreement. She did not, however, object to Brooks's substitute title, telling him it was all right as a working title, but what the final title would be "I have not the faintest idea at the moment."[48]

Carson and Rodell had another long talk about the agreement on April 6. Lovell Thompson insisted that Carson and Diamond meet again to discuss the division of labor. Accordingly Diamond went back down to Silver Spring, but little was accomplished. "Our conversation Sunday left me more perturbed than I had been, I confess," Carson told Rodell with unusual exasperation, "what I wanted was that a new way be found—and clearly defined—by which Mr. Diamond could earn his 50 percent." But on a deeper level Carson realized that what had once been a quick, short book had become a much larger and a much more significant undertaking. She told Rodell, "I know you have not had my opportunity to visualize the deep significance of the material—of tremendous importance in itself and also meaningful in relation to my broader concern with what life (and especially man) is doing to the environment."[49]

Rachel, frustrated because she could not get Marie to see that the collaboration was unworkable but fearful of legal action on Diamond's part should she try to end it, summarily told her agent, "out of regard for the integrity of my treatment, I shall spend a vast amount of time, exclusive of writing, on *The New Yorker* piece. It should be understood by you and Paul that my concern at the moment is to do a first class job for *The New Yorker*. The book use is secondary. This is implicit in the history and chronological development of the entire project."[50]

What Rachel really needed was a research assistant, not a coauthor, but Diamond would never have deigned to accept such a role. Given his geographical access to trial testimony and to special libraries such as the one at American Cyanamid Co., Carson was reluctant to give up the valuable legwork that he might do. Rodell redrafted the letter of agreement on April 18 incorporating Carson's concerns as best she could and sent it to Diamond. By now it was apparent to him that their collaboration was not working. But probably for the same legal and ethical reasons, Diamond was just as reluctant as Carson to be the one to end it.[51]

After several long conversations with Rachel, just before she left for six weeks in Europe, Marie Rodell took action. "Rachel feels that she simply can't work this way; that this is in fact no collaboration," she explained. "We feel, in other words, that we'd better not go on with this arrangement." Rodell asked Diamond to turn over to Rachel his completed digest of the trial and anything else he had collected. In return, she would consider the $750 payment for that research. For whatever reason, Diamond asked Rodell to reconsider the matter, but Rachel wanted no more of it and he was so informed.[52]

Over the course of the next month, in Rodell's absence, Joan Daves, her literary partner, and Paul Brooks both attempted, without success, to get Diamond to turn over his material. In early June Carson received a copy of the trial transcript from Spock and Richards, which obviated the need for Diamond's notes. Fearful that she would open herself to charges that she had used his material in the finished book, Carson insisted Brooks keep whatever material Diamond ever submitted. But Diamond refused to cooperate until Brooks hinted that he might take legal action. They finally agreed that Diamond could keep the advance and send only a portion of his notes.[53]

The whole affair ended sourly. Brooks regretted ever initiating the idea of a collaborator, Rodell was angry that she had so misjudged Diamond, and Carson, upset at losing more time, found the entire affair upsetting. She refused to sign the contract with Houghton Mifflin until August, when she felt more certain that the Diamond matter had been completely resolved. But Rachel was desperate for assistance. In early June she received a call from the daughter of a longtime Fish and Wildlife staff member who was looking for a summer research job. After a brief discussion of her qualifications, Carson asked the young woman to come out for an interview.[54]

Bette Haney was a senior biology major at Bryn Mawr College and had worked at Rachel's old Bureau of Fisheries laboratory in College Park after her high school graduation. There was much about the bright, attractive, serious young woman that must have reminded Carson of herself at the same age. Haney had won a science writing prize, was an excellent biology student, loved literature, and was a born researcher. Carson hired her at two dollars an hour.[55]

Carson quickly established a comfortable routine with Haney. At the beginning of each week, the two would meet and review the bibliography Carson had prepared on index cards. The evidence of what DDT and the other chemicals did to the land and to wildlife was available in the agricultural journals Carson assigned Haney to read. Bette would read the articles and write summaries of them. If an article was particularly important, Rachel starred it and asked for specific information. Carson would call the librarians and make sure the material she wanted was available before she sent Haney in to work. Sometimes Rachel wanted to read an important article or parts of it herself, in which case Bette went to the library, pulled the material, and had it laid out for Rachel.

Most of Haney's research was done at libraries in the Interior, the Department of Agriculture, the Food and Drug Administration, the Public Health Service, and sometimes the Library of Medicine at the National

Institutes of Health. She took notes in a small five-by-eight loose-leaf notebook, carefully noting the bibliographic citation at the top of each page. Carson then filed these sheets by author or subject, rearranging them later as her writing required.[56]

When Bette arrived at Rachel's house, she would find Carson already at work on her correspondence. They talked about Rachel's experiences at Johns Hopkins, a school Haney was considering for graduate work, about working at FWS, and about their mutual delight in Bob Hines. Haney recalls that most mornings, Maria Carson sat sleeping in the living room in her wheelchair next to Rachel's study. She was impressed by Rachel's caring and reverential attitude toward her mother.[57]

Roger was an extremely active six-and-a-half-year-old that summer. Rachel confided that she was concerned that she was not able to give him the attention he needed and invited Bette to go to Maine with them later that summer, where she could continue to help Rachel and also entertain Roger. However, Bette already had another job.[58]

Not long after Bette started working for Rachel, Carson went to New York on business. The most satisfying part of her trip was the nearly three hours she spent with William Shawn talking about her article. Rachel wrote Dorothy on the train back to Washington: "He is completely fascinated with the theme and obviously happy and excited at presenting it in *The New Yorker*. Best of all, I can (indeed he *wants* me to) present it strictly from my point of view, pulling no punches. He says, 'After all there are some things one doesn't have to be objective and unbiased about—one doesn't condone murder!' Besides the importance of the theme ('We don't usually think of *The New Yorker* as changing the world, but this is one time it might') he feels the material is just plain fascinating, and now thinks he'd like to have 50,000 words!!" This meant three installments, amounting to nearly all the book.

Energized by Shawn's own excitement and full of new ideas on how to approach the material, Rachel returned to Washington more committed to her new project than ever and much more certain of its ultimate importance.[59]

The only damper on her spirits was Dorothy Freeman's attitude. Dorothy felt that insect control was not a subject that merited her friend's talent for describing the beauty of the natural world. She also understood Rachel's work habits and knew the toll that the pressures of deadlines would take. She wanted to protect Rachel and was unhappy that Rachel had committed herself to such a large and depressing topic.

Freeman's attitude was also shaped by her own emotional needs. Already their correspondence had slowed dramatically, and even when she visited Rachel in April, it was clear that the topic took Rachel in directions that it would be hard to share with Dorothy. Whereas Dorothy had joined Rachel's tide-pool research and befriended the naturalist experts such as the Berrills, the Teales, and the Bestons, whom she met through Rachel, the Freemans were far less likely to have anything in common with the scientists with whom Rachel was corresponding now. Rachel was aware of Dorothy's fear of being excluded, telling her only enough about what she was doing to keep Dorothy involved but restraining her enthusiasm for the scientific mystery she had embarked upon.

In late June Rachel tried to explain to Dorothy just how important the book had become to her.

> You do know, I think, how deeply I believe in the importance of what I am doing. Knowing what I do, there would be no future peace for me if I kept silent. I wish I could feel that you *want* me to do it. I wish you could feel, as I do, that it is, in the deepest sense, a privilege as well as a duty to have the opportunity to speak out—to many thousands of people—on something so important.[60]

Rachel also tried to explain the joy she felt in immersing herself completely in such a fascinating subject, something she had not been able to do since *The Sea*. Rationalizing that it could not drag on forever, since she had a deadline to meet with *The New Yorker*, Rachel hoped Dorothy could begin to see the project differently.[61]

Carson planned to join her friend in Maine just after the Fourth of July, but her departure was postponed for various reasons. Arriving in Southport almost ten days later than planned, Rachel's time with Dorothy was curtailed by her mother's care, Roger's schedule, her need to work, and the Freemans' departure in early August.[62]

In spite of their best efforts, both Rachel and Dorothy felt isolated and misunderstood, unable to break through the tension between them until nearly the end of the summer. "I have been heavy-hearted for some time," Rachel wrote Dorothy just after the latter had left Southport for West Bridgewater, "and I think you have too. Most of the time you seemed so far away—and I was groping for you as through a fog. Today it seemed as though I found you again in that conversation, when you told me that you do understand and accept the things I felt had come between us. Somehow I feel now that you really do, and the weight has lifted. And although this summer has held fewer of those moments of beauty and loveliness that seem to belong especially to us, there have been some, and we shall cherish them through the months ahead."[63]

The summer unexpectedly brought Carson some new relationships. In July she received a fan letter from a young blind woman in New Jersey who also loved to write, telling Carson of her enjoyment in listening to a Talking Books version of *The Edge of the Sea.* Although Carson did not answer Beverly Knecht's charming letter until after she returned to Maryland, Rachel's pleasure in Knecht's prose and her compassion for her situation led to a lengthy correspondence and an intense friendship.[64]

Perhaps the most significant note Carson received during the summer came from Lois Crisler, one of Harper editor Elizabeth Lawrence's authors, who had recently published her first book, *Arctic Wild*, to critical acclaim. Crisler lived with her wildlife photographer husband, Herb (Cris) Crisler, in the wilds of Alaska, where they first saved and then raised a female wolf and her cubs. At Lawrence's urging, Lois wrote to tell how her own writing had been inspired by Carson's books.[65]

Rachel was deeply moved by Lois's book, and her attraction to Crisler followed naturally from their mutual passion for nature and their intense response to the wonders of the living world. For the first time since her early friendship with Ada Govan, Rachel had found another female writer of commensurate talent with whom she could share her own struggles and intuitively acknowledge a similar point of view.[66]

Through Fairfield Osborn, Carson had learned of the work of Robert Rudd, a brilliant young zoology professor at the University of California at Davis, who was writing a book, supported by the Conservation Foundation, on the effects of chemical control of animals on the biotic environment. Rudd's previous field studies of avian reproduction in California and the consequences of the ingestion of pesticides were highly regarded. Carson had written him in April requesting a copy of several bulletins and asking for reprints of his other papers.

Bob Rudd, an enormously forthright and politically sophisticated young scientist whose work was on the cutting edge of wildlife biology, was only too happy to share his publications with Carson. He described the ecological perspective of his new book and the changes he had witnessed in the philosophy of chemical use in agriculture over the last five years. Rudd was to be in Canada during the summer and suggested that he might visit Carson in Maine.[67]

Carson responded to Rudd's openness by telling him about her book as well as the one she planned for Harper on the relationship between life and the environment. She believed that the latter book, not the one on pesticides, might be similar in point of view to the one Rudd was writing. "I mention this merely to clarify the situation at the outset, and as a matter of interest," Rachel wrote. "It should cause no concern to either of us, for I learned long ago that it doesn't matter how many people write about the same thing; each will make his own contribution. And I have a feeling that the subject we both have in mind now is an extremely important one for our time, and I welcome the idea that others are dealing with it."[68]

Carson's keen interest in Rudd's work was reflected in her warm invitation to visit, and in mid-July Rudd, his wife, and their two daughters arrived for a brief visit at Carson's cottage. Rachel was eager to question Rudd since he had done far more work on the subject than she and was much further along on his book. For all of Rudd's self-confidence, he found himself much in awe of Carson, whom he considered one of the best science writers alive. He was, however, surprised by the shy, almost timid, and rather plain woman who met him.[69]

Since Rudd's children and Roger were the same age, Mrs. Rudd took them all off to the tide pools so the two biologists could talk. Unfortunately, their conversation was so dominated by Maria Carson that they never had any time to speak at length on their own. Mamma stayed in the living room with them, and any substantial intellectual discussion was precluded by her control of the conversation. Nonetheless, Rudd and Carson found much to like and admire in each other, and their discussion was lively and interesting. Their subsequent exchanges, consisting mostly of requests from Carson for more information and for clarification of something she had read, continued by mail. The research Rudd shared and his perceptive understanding of the sociology of pesticide use made him an especially valuable ally for her.[70]

Carson also had visits from Paul and Susie Brooks and from Elizabeth Coatsworth and Henry Beston. Then in August, just before she left Maine, Rachel had a delightful visit from Marjorie Spock, Spock's octogenarian mother, and Polly Richards. The three came by boat to visit on their way to Mrs. Spock's summer home on MacMahan Island, across the

Sheepscot, but not quite visible from Rachel's deck. At the last minute, Rachel declined to be picked up by boat and instead met her friends for lunch at the Newagen Inn, one of her favorite spots on Southport Island.[71]

By this time Spock and Carson had been corresponding for some months, during which time Spock had been an invaluable source of names, citations, references, and opinion, and Carson had come to depend on her. Even so, Spock was initially surprised by Carson's reserve. Spock later wrote of the occasion:

> Upon landing we went to meet her at the inn's parking lot. As we approached it, a slightly built woman came around the bend walking unhurriedly. Seeing us she smiled, but did not change her pace. When we knew Rachel better, we realized how typical it was of her to keep to her own way in everything. Neither at this nor further meetings did she strike us as an exuberant, outgoing nature. But there was no heaviness in her somewhat grave demeanor, no lack of warmth in her reserve, or unease in her incapacity for chit-chat. Rather did she seem so disciplined to concentration, so given to listening and looking and weighing impressions as to be unable to externalize.[72]

After lunch the Spocks suggested that Rachel join them for an afternoon cruise among the islands, but Rachel explained she could not be so long away from her invalid mother or her great-nephew, who was with a young neighbor for the afternoon. Instead she invited them back to the cottage, insisting that her mother would enjoy visiting with Mrs. Spock. Marjorie accepted with pleasure as they had hardly begun to talk, but as they were leaving the inn, Mrs. Spock, who had a wonderful sense of humor, wickedly remarked, "I don't think Miss Carson cares much for the sea around us."[73]

Leaving the two mothers happily chatting on the porch, Rachel showed Marjorie and Polly every inch of her cottage and in her study reviewed some of the clippings and articles Spock had sent recently. After the experience of Bob Rudd's visit, Rachel invited them down to the tide pools, a suggestion Spock recognized as an immediate lure to get some privacy and continue their conversation uninterrupted.[74]

Rachel was moved by Spock's affectionate and generous spirit as well as by her compassion and obvious commitment to halt pesticide spraying.

Spock remained Carson's "chief clipping service," sending material several times a week. It was through Spock's urging that Carson made contact with the Sport Fishing Institute. "I agree that hunters and fishermen are good allies," Carson responded, "and where I still have occasional contacts with writers and organizations of this sort left over from my days in Fish and Wildlife, I am trying to sow more seeds of discontent."[75]

By the first of September, Rachel was eager to get back to her research, although she always hated to leave Maine, especially when there was a full moon. Back in Maryland, she went into high gear. The focus of her research had expanded to include the work of more experts and a broader view of the problem. Marjorie Spock remained at the center of one group of scientists from whom Carson gathered most of her initial material about the relationship between synthetic pesticides and human health. Citations from the work of trial witnesses and experts such as M. S. Biskind and Malcolm Hargraves led Carson into a brisk correspondence with both men. Hargraves was particularly generous in sharing sources, including the names of hundreds of individuals who had experienced medical problems related to pesticide spraying and whose cases were documented as well as the results of his latest experiments in hematology. This line of research eventually led Carson to Wilhelm C. Hueper of the National Cancer Institute, one of the foremost authorities on environmental cancer.[76]

The expert testimony in the Long Island trial also centered around the research of wildlife scientists and augmented Carson's own considerable network of scientists at the U.S. Fish and Wildlife Service. In 1956, when FWS studies began on the gypsy moth spraying, John George played a central role in the field research. But it was Harvard entomologist Edward O. Wilson who brought George's research on the fire ant to Carson's attention in the fall of 1958.[77]

Wilson had heard of Carson's plan to write on the effects of pest control through a mutual friend and wrote Rachel encouragingly. "The subject is a vital one," he said, "and needs to be aired by a writer of your gifts and prestige." He sent Carson a reprint of one of his recent articles on the fire ant and told her about two other important sources. One was Charles Elton's *Ecology of Invasions*, which contained a wealth of material on the life cycle of insects, and the other was a mimeographed Conservation Foundation report containing a full account of the fire ant case by John George that had received only the most restricted distribution. Carson was grateful for both citations, telling Wilson "I am eager to build up, in every way I can, the positive alternatives to chemical sprays, for I feel that a book that is wholly against something cannot possibly be as effective as one that points the way to acceptable alternatives."[78]

When George joined the Physiological, Chemical and Pesticide Wildlife Studies Branch at the Patuxent Refuge that fall, he became central to Carson's network of government scientists and was an outspoken critic of the USDA's control entomologists who ran the fire ant elimination program. His involvement in the fire ant controversy indirectly led Carson back to her former FWS supervisor, Clarence Cottam.[79]

The trial also led Carson to George J. Wallace, an ornithologist at Michigan State University who, after noting the collapse of the robin population on campus, studied the effects of pesticides on avian reproduction. Wallace's work led her to Joseph Hickey, another ornithologist, who occupied the position once held by ecologist Aldo Leopold at the University of Wisconsin. Hickey studied the effects of pesticides on a spectrum of avian metabolic issues and confirmed that insecticides were responsible for the thin eggshell phenomenon and resultant population losses. Correspondence with scientists in the Netherlands led her to U.S. soil scientists working in groundwater studies and in arsenic toxicology as well as to entomologists studying insect resistance and biological controls, and finally to Edward F. Knipling, the leading U.S. authority in those fields.[80]

The Long Island trial had also produced scores of government witnesses and experts from the Food and Drug Administration, the Public Health Service, and especially the Agricultural Research Service of USDA. Bette Haney interviewed some of these officials; others Carson called herself. By the time she returned from Maine, Rachel had established correspondence with scientists in the most important federal agencies dealing with chemical pesticides and was following the hundreds of leads each new conversation gave her.[81]

An important but little recognized component of Carson's research network, however, came from her own connections with government scientists, librarians, Smithsonian Institution scientists, associates in conservation organizations at the national level, and the regional Audubon Society. Her nearly sixteen years in government were key to her ability to find the information she needed or the one person who knew where the information could be found.

When she began her research on pesticides, she had been out of government for only six years. Many of the people she had known then were still working; some had been promoted to even more influential positions. Others had moved into private research institutions and enjoyed broad access to government, corporate, and university research. Carson's network also included scientists who had helped with her previous books, especially *The Sea Around Us*, or government employees who just loved her writing. It was not unusual to have a congressional aide or a clerk in the Government Printing Office recognize her name and dig out the obscure document or citation that she needed.[82]

From this same wellspring of goodwill Carson found individuals in key places who, at great risk to their jobs and reputations, were willing to give her confidential information if she protected them. With their private help and that of anonymous friends, Carson's sleuthing, particularly inside government and other Washington-based institutions, was highly successful.[83]

Rachel made steady progress with her research during the early fall. By October she was compiling comparisons of data on the decline in bird population in different geographical areas that had been treated with chemicals. She also had begun to formulate some trenchant opinions on the politics of pesticide use. "One of my delights in the book," she wrote Edwin Way Teale, "will be to take apart Dr. Wayland Hayes' much cited feeding experiment on '51' volunteers. It was '51' for only the first day of the experiment; thereafter the experimentees rapidly lost their taste for DDT and drifted away until only a mere handful finished the course of poisoned meals." She criticized Hayes, the chief toxicologist of the U.S. Public Health Service, for failing to make any subsequent check on the welfare of his human subjects, knowing well that it took months or years for such damage to show up. But the government's selective use of evidence did not surprise her.[84]

When Paul Brooks visited Rachel in Maine that summer, he brought with him a copy of a new Houghton Mifflin publication, *The Affluent Society*, by Harvard economist John Kenneth Galbraith, which he left with Carson. She read it that fall with interest, telling Brooks that she had found much in Galbraith's analysis of contemporary society that carried over to her thinking about the problem of pesticides and human attitudes toward insect control. "I do feel that the rather sorry picture I have to paint can be illuminated with some broad conceptions that will reveal the futility and the basic wrongness of the present chemical program—

even better than by ranting against it, though doubtless I shall rant a little, too."[85]

From what she had read and from those she had interviewed, Carson tended to separate most scientists into two broad groups: positivists like Wayland Hayes, who denied any damage from pesticides because the evidence of damage had not been conclusively demonstrated, and those like George Wallace at Michigan State, who were willing to take the next logical step and assume damage might be possible and move on to consider alternatives to chemical spraying. She found entomologists, particularly those who worked in applied science rather than basic research, especially closed to any suggestion that alternatives to chemical spraying might exist.

The reaction among some local entomologists and ornithologists to C. J. Breijer's article on insect resistance surprised her. "The idea of biological control as something workable seemed new to them, and they were vastly intrigued with the idea of something positive that they could support, instead of just being 'agin' sprays," she told Brooks. "Incidentally," she wrote, thinking about the range of scientific reactions to the fire ant program, "I'm convinced there is a psychological angle in all this: that people, especially professional men, are uncomfortable about coming out against something, especially if they haven't absolute proof the 'something' is wrong, but only a good suspicion. So they will go along with a program about which they privately have acute misgivings. So I think it is most important [for me] to build up the positive alternatives."[86]

Unlike Marjorie Spock, who had firsthand experience with corporate and government advocates and had seen the kinds of cloak-and-dagger retaliation taken against those who disagreed, Rachel was still optimistic about changing official attitudes. She predicted that " 'The days of the squirt-gun control' of insects are numbered; there is a great deal of handwriting on the wall." Carson had recently learned that the Agriculture Department had quietly set up a new unit in the Agricultural Research Service for basic research to develop other methods of pest control and wondered how the chemical lobby would react to that news.[87]

Carson's outlook on the future of pest control and her understanding of the risks involved in going against the federal government's policies and the culture of pesticide use received a hard dose of political and economic reality when, in the late fall of 1958, she renewed her friendship with Clarence Cottam.[88]

Cottam, who along with Elmer Higgins had been one of the pioneers on the harmful effects of DDT, had left the Fish and Wildlife Service in 1954. After a year as dean of the College of Biological and Agricultural Sciences at Brigham Young University, he was appointed director of the Welder Wildlife Foundation in Sinton, Texas, a post that gave him national prominence in conservation and wildlife policy making. Like other areas of the Southeast, parts of eastern Texas had been infested by colonies of fire ants and subjected to a barrage of pesticides. The Welder Foundation biologists had been alarmed by the ensuing damage to wildlife; Cottam, who was highly regarded by Agricultural Secretary Ezra Taft Benson, had been outspoken in his criticism of the USDA eradication program from the outset.[89]

At the urging of Irston Barnes and John George, Carson wrote Cottam in November. She told him:

> The news seems to be out on the grapevine, so possibly you have heard, that my current writing project is a book dealing with the basic problem of the effect of chemical insecticides in present use on all living things and on their fundamental ecological relationships. This was something I had not expected to do, but facts that came to my attention last winter disturbed me so deeply that I made the decision to postpone all other commitments and devote myself to what I consider a tremendously important problem.[90]

Unsure about how deeply involved Cottam was in the fire ant issue, Carson asked him to send her any papers or speeches he had given on the subject and hoped that if he came to Washington anytime soon, they could talk it all over.

Cottam was delighted to hear from her, and responded immediately, saying, "I hope you include both insecticides, herbicides, rodenticides, and fungicides. The whole gamut of poisons should be considered, and I know of no one who is more able to summarize this situation than you." Making what he could not then have known would be such a prescient remark, Cottam predicted, "I am sure you will render a great public service, although I shall predict that your book will not be the best seller that *The Sea Around Us* has been. The total effect, however, might be infinitely more important to our national economy and well-being."[91]

A few days after receiving Cottam's encouraging reply, Rachel's attention was diverted from her research to her mother, who suffered a stroke on November 22 that was followed by pneumonia and a variety of other ailments. Rachel got a hospital bed for her and hired a nurse to help take shifts among herself, sister-in-law Vera Carson, and the ever-faithful Ida. By November 30 Rachel knew the end of her mother's life was near. She got an oxygen tent to keep her comfortable and kept her at home.

Several days later Rachel wrote Dorothy describing her mother's death.

> During that last agonizing night, I sat most of the time by the bed with my hand slipped under the border of the oxygen tent, holding Mamma's. Of course I didn't feel she knew, and occasionally I slipped away into the dark living room, to look out of the picture window at the trees and the sky. Orion stood in all his glory just above the horizon of our woods, and several other stars blazed more highly than I can remember ever seeing them. Then I went back into the room and at 6:05 she slipped away, her hand in mine. I told Roger about the stars just before Grandma left us, and he said, "Maybe they were the lights of the angels, coming to take her to heaven."[92]

Maria McLean Carson had named Rachel, not Robert, as her executor, so her daughter made the funeral arrangements. Presbyterian services were held at a funeral home in Silver Spring. Maria had requested that her body be cremated but that her ashes remain near Rachel and Roger in Maryland and not sent back to Pennsylvania. She was buried in Parklawn Cemetery nearby where she and Rachel had purchased adjoining plots. In Maria's brief obituary, Rachel testified to her mother's influence, writing, "Maria Carson had a life long interest in nature and land conservation, which was transmitted to her daughter Rachel, whose book, *The Sea Around Us*, was a best seller in 1952."[93]

When the official functions were over, Rachel wrote to Marjorie Spock of her grief and her concern for how Roger would take this latest loss. "Poor little fellow, this is a new blow for him, for he loved his Grandma, and her love for him was overflowing. Also it is obviously recalling to him all the memories of the loss of his mother, less than two years ago. It is good for me, I'm sure, that I am forced to think of him and of how to ease the readjustment which will be difficult, to say the least, for all of us."[94]

Maria Carson's spiritual legacy to her daughter had been given long since. In her loneliness and grief Rachel was able to summon it for her present courage. "Sometime I want to tell you more of her," she wrote Spock.

> Her love of life and of all living things was her outstanding quality, of which everyone speaks. More than anyone else I know, she embodied Albert Schweitzer's, 'reverence for life.' And while gentle and compassionate, she could fight fiercely against anything she believed wrong, as in our present Crusade! Knowing how she felt about that will help me to return to it soon, and to carry it through to completion.[95]

After the saddest Christmas she had ever known, Rachel poured out her gratitude to Dorothy, whose "constant, day by day, hour by hour caring" gave Rachel the knowledge that she was not alone. Her energy spent, her courage at an ebb, and her heart heavy with sorrow, Rachel ended the year in bed with the flu.

15

"The Red Queen"

If there was a great emptiness for Rachel in the loss of her mother, there was an equal legacy of determination to carry on their mutual crusade. Carson's sense of mission was deepened by her mother's belief in the importance of their shared vision. On a practical level, her mother's death released Rachel from the tremendous physical and emotional burdens that her care had imposed. She had a new measure of energy for her work, and for the first time in her life, she was free to make new friends and enter into new relationships. By the middle of January, Rachel was back in the research libraries of Washington.[1]

She spent most of her time at the Library of Medicine at the National Institutes of Health. Instead of working up entire chapters following her outline, she worked on a variety of topics simultaneously. First she examined the problem of resistance, then wildlife damage, the impact of pesticides on songbirds and other avian species, and most persistently on the various chronic threats pesticides posed to human health.

At the Library of Medicine and at the National Cancer Institute (NCI) she followed the tortuous trail opened by Otto Warburg, the German biologist whose research in cell physiology had led cancer scientists to look for connections between the wild proliferation of cancer cells and the physiological changes within the cell structure that researchers thought were controlled by various enzymes. Working in chemistry, physiology, and genetics, Carson spent the next six weeks overwhelmed with difficult new material but feeling instinctively that she was on the right course to finding a connection between pesticides and the physiological changes that signaled the onset of cancer. It was perhaps the toughest research problem she had ever endeavored to explicate, but she returned home every afternoon exhilarated by the challenge.[2]

By February she was ready to give her editors, William Shawn and Paul Brooks, a progress report. "I am sure it must seem a long time in the making" she wrote in identical letters, "but in the end I believe you will feel, as I do, that my long and thorough preparation is indispensable to doing an effective job. I can see clearly now that [what] I might have written last summer would have been half-baked at best. Now it is as though all the pieces of an extremely complex jig-saw puzzle are at last falling into place." Assuring them that she still intended to show how pesticides disturbed the basic ecology of all living things, she was certain that her most compelling evidence would emphasize how they menaced human health. "As I look over my reference material," she wrote,

> I am impressed by the fact that the evidence on this particular point outweighs by far, in sheer bulk and also significance, any other aspect of the problem. I have a comforting feeling that what I shall now be able to achieve is a synthesis of widely scattered facts, that have not heretofore been considered in relation to each other. It is now possible to build up, step by step, a really damning case against the use of these chemicals as they are now inflicted upon us.[3]

Her report included the fact that while the American Medical Association and the U.S. Public Health Service had been publicly vague about the dangers of pesticides to humans, their published statements constituted a broad indictment. With her unusual sense of political acumen, she told her editors she planned to take advantage of the weight of the professional standing of these organizations and let them scramble to make their public positions conform. In the same vein, Carson planned to use the debacle of the inadvertent effects of fire ant spraying in the South as her "Exhibit A," of "ill-advised, irresponsible Governmental actions."[4]

In addition to detailing her research on the slow, cumulative, hard-to-identify long-term effects of pesticide exposure, the special vulnerability of infants and children (human and animal), and genetic cell disturbance, Carson summarized the most recent research in alternative methods of pest control. Encouraged by the many different people working on controlling insects through hormones and through man-induced diseases, Carson wrote of her upcoming interviews with the scientists in the USDA's units on insect physiology where Edward F. Knipling was experimenting with insect sterilization using radioactive cobalt.[5]

Carson hoped her report would satisfy both editors, who really wanted to know what she could not tell them: when she thought she could finish. She suggested that Brooks come to Washington for an author's conference and hoped that she might see Shawn if she was able to get away to the National Wildlife Federation meetings in New York in March.

By coincidence, Carson's letter to Brooks overlapped one from him politely asking for just such an account. His letter told of a conversation he had with artist/ornithologist Roger Tory Peterson, at one time Carson's colleague on the District of Columbia Audubon Society board. Peterson had quite flatly predicted that pesticide use constituted the greatest threat to wildlife since the beginning of time and thought Carson's book could do more than anything else to apprise the public of that fact. Brooks also asked Carson for her opinion on spot spraying against mosquito infestations, an alternative that his town of Lincoln, Massachusetts, was considering.[6]

In her cover letter to Brooks, Carson noted that Peterson's prediction had been fully documented by George Wallace, who had recently presented his conclusions of the collapse of avian populations at the annual meeting of the National Audubon Society. As to advising Brooks about spot spraying, Carson admitted, "I know it is not realistic to take a flat position against any spraying at all. I am afraid there have to be compromises, much as I hate any part of it." But, she wondered, had the Lincoln town fathers considered that by spraying they would be creating "a race of fiercely resistant mosquitoes that will in the future be untouchable by any chemical means?" Carson was hopeful that sometime in the future new biological methods would yield better compromises.[7]

Brooks sent Carson's letter on to Lovell Thompson with the marginal comment that the book was "broadening and deepening" and that "Rachel seems to know where she is going far better than she did last summer." The irrepressible Thompson remarked that it was an "ill poison that doesn't give some publisher a good book," and wondered what to call it. He offered, *Who Are You Killing?*, *Let's Die in Bed*, or *Of Monsters and Mosquitoes*, hastening to add that the book did sound like a "landmark, if you'll pardon the expression."[8]

Thompson might not have been so glib had he known the difficulties Rachel was encountering. Several lengthy episodes of chronic sinus infections had kept her at home. Roger had been out of school for several weeks, first with a bad throat and then a severe penicillin reaction. If that were not enough, Rachel started her car one morning only to be greeted by a small explosion and an engine fire. Someone had stolen the carburetor during the night and wreaked general havoc on the car. She was forced to rent one in order to get to the library.[9]

Carson also mentioned to Brooks that she had turned down a tempting invitation from the National Wildlife Federation to speak on the health hazards of insecticides at a session moderated by Clarence Cottam at their annual meetings in New York. Although she was torn, Rachel had decided that "it would be premature and unwise for me to disclose the facts I have on this phase of the subject, for, I feel, they are pretty terrific and should not be revealed until they can form part of the total impact of the book."[10]

To Cottam, Carson explained that she had said very little to anyone about her project. "But as you know the whole thing is so explosive and the pressures on the other side so powerful and enormous, that I feel it far wiser to keep my own council insofar as I can until I am ready to launch my attack as a whole." Her decision turned out to be a good one, since in her place the federation invited Malcolm Hargraves of the Mayo Clinic to speak on the links between chemical spraying and leukemias.[11]

Rachel took the train up to New York on February 27 to attend the session as an anonymous observer and had a good visit with Hargraves, whose Mayo Clinic colleagues criticized his participation. He told Carson about data from a new control program in Memphis, Tennessee, where the USDA was dousing houses and yards with dieldrin in an effort to wipe out a white-fringed beetle.

The meetings also gave Carson an opportunity to talk further with Marjorie Spock and Polly Richards. Spock supplied her with more clippings and sent a small, handmade wren house for Roger with a secret note for him hidden inside. With her keen political antennae aimed just right, Spock reported that after the panel discussion, someone had announced that Carson was writing a book on pesticides. Most of the people had left the room when the announcement was made, but, Spock warned, "the government boys were all still there."[12]

Until this time, the USDA Agricultural Research Service entomologists had been naively untroubled by Carson's inquiries into the fire ant control program. Some, like W. L. Popham, failed even to identify the inquirer. But Carson's increasing association with Clarence Cottam and Malcolm Hargraves had been noticed and her access to material at ARS became increasingly restricted. Knowing how bitterly government and industry scientists had attacked Morton Biskind for his work on the public health hazards of pesticides, Carson tried to avoid any unnecessary publicity. But the expansion of the USDA's fire ant eradication in spite of mounting public criticism made it difficult for her to maintain her anonymity.[13]

In March Rachel, along with Irston Barnes, Shirley Briggs, and other officers of the D.C. Audubon Society, attended a preview of the USDA's new public service film, *Fire Ant on Trial*. It was the USDA's attempt to counter the adverse publicity of the eradication program, but instead it only created more of an uproar. As Rachel reported to Clarence Cottam afterward, "as might be expected, it denies all danger to wildlife and implies that the program has the full support of wildlife agencies and organizations. I assume this will be vigorously challenged by the many organizations that have been carrying on a fight against the program." Incensed by the USDA's bureaucratic arrogance as well as its obvious intent to deceive, Carson, Barnes, and Briggs drafted a letter on behalf of the D.C. Audubon Society to Agriculture Secretary Benson, asking that the film be withheld from distribution. Although Carson wrote most of it, she did not have to put her name on it.[14]

Labeling the film "flagrant propaganda in support of a program that has been widely challenged as ill-conceived, irresponsible, and dangerous," the letter mirrors many of the arguments against the broadcast use of chemical pesticides that Carson would use in her book. The authors confined their comments to the destruction of wildlife, the supposed cooperation of wildlife agencies, and the hazards to human health. Carson's hand is especially apparent in the latter section. Noting that the film failed to mention the high toxicity of the chemicals scattered over the southern states, they wrote:

> The poisons dieldrin and heptachlor are recognized, beyond possibility of denial, as extremely toxic even in minute traces. Both are absorbed through the skin as well as through other portals. Both are stored in the human body. Both are toxic to the human nervous system and to the liver, and almost certainly interfere with many of the basic processes of the body. The most dangerous effect

> is not . . . acute toxicity, but cumulative poisoning. This may not be revealed in its full and possibly disastrous impact for a number of years. The threat of the fire ant is insignificant compared with the serious and long-lasting damage inflicted by your efforts to control it.[15]

To Carson and her colleagues, eradication of the fire ant was as futile as the bureaucratic excesses of the ARS were astonishing. As expected, their letter drew no comment from the Agriculture Department, and the eradication program continued unabated. But their letter was widely reprinted in the publications of other conservation organizations that also sent letters of protest to the USDA. The only hint of annoyance came from Justus Ward, chief of the pesticides regulation branch, who became increasingly reluctant to answer Carson's requests for information.[16]

When Popham and Ward blocked her research at ARS, Carson turned to Reece Sailer. Sailer had been a systematic entomologist with the Bureau of Entomology and Plant Quarantine, in the Entomology Research Division of ARS. In 1957 he became the assistant chief of insect identification and parasite introduction. Sailer had a broad interest in ecology and was an outspoken advocate of biological control. A compassionate and generous man, he took great pride in helping Carson get whatever information she needed. It was understood between them that she would not reveal him as a source. Sailer proved an invaluable ally and remained keenly supportive of Carson's work as it progressed.[17]

About the same time that Carson discovered Reece Sailer in ARS research, she also found Harold Peters. Peters had been with the USDA's Bureau of Entomology and later was a flyway biologist for the Fish and Wildlife Service. A charming, gregarious, highly observant naturalist, Peters was a passionate ornithologist. He knew everyone in wildlife biology, from Ivy League scholars to garden club leaders. After years in government, Peters also knew most of the field scientists for both USDA and FWS.

In 1959 Peters left FWS to become a research biologist with the National Audubon Society. In this capacity, he roamed the southern states collecting data on the fire ant eradication and observing other wildlife damage from the government's pesticide programs. When Carson needed confirmation of wildlife losses, the percentage of ingredients of chemical sprays used in different geographical areas, or the facts about rumored USDA harassment of FWS field agents and suppression of data, Harold Peters supplied it. His information was accurate, his sources reliable, and his contacts absolutely invaluable. As a bonus, his chatty letters overflowed with observations and information that no one else could have supplied. One name that Peters mentioned to Carson again and again for his understanding of the damaging effects of pesticides was that of Frank Edwin Egler.[18]

Frank Egler, a brilliant ecologist and botanist whose education and wide expertise defies categorization, was perhaps the most broadly trained scientist Carson added to her inner circle of experts. Egler was a maverick who had worked for several years on the staff of the American Museum of Natural History in New York as director of the museum's committee for Brush Control Recommendations for Rights-of-Way. But Egler, whose intellectual independence often clashed with the policies of large organizations, left the museum after a bitter dispute. He settled in an isolated corner of northwestern Connecticut where he established his own private forest reserve on hundreds of acres of woodland.[19]

Egler was horrified by the ecological havoc wrought by the broadcast use of herbicides. His search for alternative methods of vegetation management was reinforced by the damage he saw on the atolls in the Pacific that had been subjected to heavy chemical assaults. Egler was an outspoken advocate of selective spraying and had successfully used this technique for the control of roadside brush. He was a longtime friend and colleague of Ray Fosberg, who correctly regarded him as a world expert in the field of vegetation management and on the uses of the most widely used synthetic herbicides, 2,4-D, and 2,4,5-T.[20]

Carson had known Egler by reputation long before she began her own work on pesticides. After she read his views in a Conservation Foundation bulletin, they began corresponding on the properties of herbicides in general and on the methods of vegetation management. Carson inadvertently discovered another side of Egler when she sought out Warren G. Kenfield, the author of an impressive little pamphlet, "The Art of Naturalistic Landscape." Mr. Kenfield turned out to be none other than Frank Edwin Egler with the letters of his name rearranged. Egler's work became the basis for Carson's chapter, "Earth's Green Mantle," as well as for her greater understanding of plant ecology.[21]

On April 3 the *Washington Post* published an editorial commenting on a National Audubon Society report on effects of the unusually harsh winter weather on migrating birds in the South. Knowing that climatic variations explained only a tiny part of the population decline, Carson wrote a response of her own exposing the role that the spraying of poisonous insecticides and herbicides played in the "silencing of birds." Titled "Vanishing Americans," it was published in the newspaper a week later. Her letter provided the first public clue that Rachel Carson was working on the subject of synthetic pesticides.[22]

Carson's letter is a small gem, outlining in miniature the argument of her book. Dismissing the notion that the reduction in bird populations stemmed from natural conditions, she provides a brief history of the use of synthetic chemicals from wartime to domestic application, and explains their persistent longevity in vegetation, soils, and the food chain. Using language that would appear in the book, she wrote, "To many of us, the sudden silencing of the song of birds, this obliteration of the color and beauty and interest of bird life, is sufficient cause for sharp regret." But, she asks, "if this 'rain of death' has produced so disastrous an effect on birds, what of other lives, including our own?"[23]

Her focus on birds offered a good opportunity to gauge the public's response to the problem of pesticides. The reaction bore out an intense interest in the subject. One writer, an Associated Press correspondent, urged her to expand the material she had used in the letter into a feature article, a suggestion that Rachel found most amusing. Her letter also brought responses from two highly connected Washington women, both of whom subsequently became personal friends.

One was from the owner of the *Washington Post*, Agnes (Mrs. Eugene) Meyer. "I am sure you started all the nature lovers on an important campaign," Meyer wrote. "At this moment the ginkgo trees in front of my house all have a sign to motorists to beware because the trees are going to be sprayed within a few days. I wish the birds could read." Like Meyer, all of her respondents had personal stories to tell.

Christine Stevens was president of the Animal Welfare Institute in New York, but she went to Washington frequently to lobby Congress and to support her husband, the arts advocate Roger Stevens. Mrs. Stevens expressed her gratitude to Carson for exposing the chemical "rain of death." "All humanitarians will be grateful to you for writing on this subject," she told Carson, "for your great gifts as a writer combined with those as a biologist would make your efforts of inestimable value in putting a stop to these poison campaigns."[24]

Carson graciously acknowledged both letters and correspondence between them continued, although Agnes Meyer was more likely to telephone just to check on Carson's progress. Greatly encouraged by the support of people and organizations such as those Stevens represented, Carson was happily reinforced in her conviction that there was an audience for her message. She told Marjorie Spock, "I think the book will be welcome when it finally comes."[25]

Rachel made one other public foray that spring that she viewed as safe as well as useful. Her Silver Spring, Maryland, neighbors in the Quaint Acres subdivision were considering a spraying program. Several of them were scientists and medical professionals and knew about her current work. The citizens association president asked Rachel if she would speak about her research at their June meeting.

When Carson addressed an outdoor meeting of the Quaint Acres Community Association, she was aware that there was no serious insect infestation in the community but that the listeners would vote on a spraying program after her remarks. Although she had made lengthy notes on both wildlife damage and the dangers to human health, the heat and humidity that night forced her to abandon her prepared text and to talk almost exclusively about the relation of insecticides to cancer. It was the first time that she had discussed this aspect of her research. Summarizing the work of scientists Hargraves, Biskind, and particularly W. C. Hueper, Carson gave examples from the letters she had received telling of individuals whose illnesses appeared to be directly related to pesticide exposure.[26]

After her remarks, the association voted decisively against the proposed spraying, which made her efforts especially gratifying. Telling Marjorie Spock about the event a few days later, Rachel wrote, "I felt this was a fair little test of the reception that may be given the book." Satisfied with her public ventures, Carson returned to her policy of secrecy.[27]

When Paul Brooks visited her at the end of April, Rachel had adopted the title *Man Against the Earth* as at least the temporary label for her book. Paul was inclined to like it, so it was under consideration as a permanent title. They had agreed that if she could get the manuscript to him in October, he could publish it in February. In early June Carson acceded to Brooks's pressure to announce the book by that title in the Houghton Mifflin spring catalog. "I am pressing ahead just as fast as I can," she told him, "driven by the knowledge that the book is desperately needed. Unquestionably, what it has to say will come as news to 99 out of 100 people."[28]

The notice that appeared in the catalog was immediately picked up by reviewer John Barkham of the *Saturday Review* syndicate and generated a rash of newspaper comment. Barkham's headline read "Miss Carson Probes into Health Menaces," and the text quoted Houghton Mifflin's description that *Man Against the Earth* was "an expression of the author's deep concern over the increasing menace to health from man's use of poisons in his efforts to control nature."[29]

Carson was distressed by the language of the catalog and its implications. As she explained to Anne Ford at Houghton Mifflin: "I think we had better make clear my broader ecological interests since the forthcoming book has not a drip of salt water in it. It is a very difficult book to describe, even I find it so—and because of the rather violent controversies that have raged around this subject we shall, of course, have to choose our words very carefully. It would be so easy to imply inadvertently a sensationalism that really has no place in my approach to the problem."[30] With a deadline looming, Rachel and Roger left for Maine at the end of June.

Carson had located a pleasant and, she hoped, able stenographer to help her with correspondence and had enrolled Roger at a nearby day camp and was infinitely relieved when he adjusted to it happily. With Roger occupied from early morning to late afternoon, Rachel had the whole day to work and, as she told Edwin Teale, hoped to have the book on paper before she returned in September.[31]

But once again her work had to be sacrificed to more pressing parental responsibilities. After little more than ten days at camp, Roger developed a severe respiratory infection accompanied by a spiking fever. With Dorothy's help, Rachel bundled him up and took him to the hospital, where he spent the week without a clear diagnosis. When a suspicious area was observed on one of his lungs, the doctors advised Rachel not to let Roger return to camp at all that summer. "This is sensible, I know, and quite in line with my thinking," Rachel told Marie, "but it is somewhat disastrous in terms of getting work done." She gave up all hope of substantive progress on the book, but postponed telling Brooks that his publishing schedule would have to be scrapped until after she got home.[32]

At least three other projects needed Rachel's attention that summer, and she made some progress on them. At the end of January Carson had agreed to publish an enlarged version of "Help Your Child to Wonder" with Harper. This was easy for her to work on in Maine since, she explained to Marie Rodell, the material "comes to my door without my half trying." She and Roger took a lot of walks and one evening watched "a whale cruise up and down the bay, blowing and rolling most beautifully as he apparently pursued a school of fish." She also interviewed several photographers and looked at a number of photograph collections trying to find just the right ones to accompany the text.[33]

Rachel also was able to do some work on a new edition of *The Sea Around Us* for Oxford. Realizing it would be impossible to revise the text to include all the new developments in oceanography and marine biology, she had decided to summarize the most important areas of new research in an introduction, add substantive footnotes, update parts of the appendix, and perhaps include some photographs.[34]

The other project was entirely new. Cass Canfield and Elizabeth Lawrence of Harper had both courted Carson for some time. Rachel returned their admiration, finding in that pair of notable editors a companionable literary fit. She had met with Canfield several times about the World Perspectives book, once describing him to Dorothy as her "ideal of the old-fashioned editor or publisher, a man of immense integrity, with good taste and good judgement, highly intelligent, courteous, urbane." Lawrence and Carson had liked each other immediately. When Lawrence renewed her proposal that Carson do a small sea anthology for Harper in addition to the other two books, and then came down to Washington to talk about it, Carson agreed.[35]

A contract for *Magic of the Sea* was drawn up in early April, with Harper paying Carson an advance of $3,000 in May. Neither Canfield nor Lawrence pressed Rachel to set a delivery date. Marie was left to break the news to Maria Leiper at Simon & Schuster that Rachel would not be able to do the *World of Nature* anthology, but Rachel could not bring herself to tell Brooks that she was now committed to three books, including "Help Your Child," with Harper.[36]

If the summer of 1959 did not offer Carson much progress on *Man Against the Earth*, it afforded her a new perspective on her life. It was the first time she had ever been in Maine without her mother. She was free to invite friends to visit, to entertain, and take what little solitude she could find from Roger's needs for herself.

Although Dorothy and Stan were there to help her deal with Roger's illness, the summer for Dorothy was exceptionally burdensome. Stan's health had continued to deteriorate, beginning with a serious heart attack in January just weeks after he had retired. Dorothy's mother was confined in a nursing home in the Boothbay area. With their positions now reversed, it was Dorothy who was the most restricted by family responsibilities and Rachel who was, at least emotionally, less encumbered. This reality, combined with Rachel's preoccupation with her book, continued to keep their relationship off balance.

Carson's new project and her mother's death also altered her relationship with Marie Rodell. Rodell had been as quick in her own way as Carson to see the importance of the topic of chemical poisons and had encouraged Rachel from the outset. She had been tough in negotiations with Houghton Mifflin, and while Rachel had been critical of her handling of the collaboration, Marie never once complained of having to make the hard calls. She had ably represented Carson's interest with *The New Yorker* and with Harper.

Maria Carson had tolerated but had never genuinely liked Rodell. Their worlds were too different, their personalities too dissimilar, and Marie too intrusive. Maria viewed Marie as a necessary and able influence in her daughter's life, but one she intended to moderate, and, for the most part, she had succeeded. With her death, Marie Rodell no longer had any competition in the management of Rachel's literary affairs, and Rachel no longer had to disguise Rodell's influence.

Rodell visited Carson in Silver Spring twice during the spring of 1959, and their partnership in Carson's controversial project provided them an opportunity to rediscover those qualities they had first enjoyed in each other and that bound them as literary partners as well as friends. Like any parent, Carson's friendships after 1957 were increasingly limited to those who took an interest in Roger, and Marie Rodell had always been one of Roger's favorite people. Rodell had nieces and grand-nieces and nephews upon whom she doted. Children gravitated to her because of her cleverness and energy, and because she genuinely enjoyed their company. Marie's kindness to Roger was an additional gift that Rachel acknowledged with gratitude.[37]

Carson's friendship with Marjorie Spock flourished for some of the same reasons. It was hard not to be thoroughly enraptured by Marjorie. Although Rachel saw her far less often than she would have liked, their occasional lunches in New York and their outings in Maine were memorable. Spock, too, genuinely responded to Roger. She remembered him at special holidays, sent him small surprises, and recognized his loneliness and his need for attention. In August Spock arranged to meet Rachel and Roger in Wiscasset for lunch and then took them to the old military fort in Edgecomb where the boy spent one of his happiest summer afternoons.[38]

Carson's more recent friendship with Lois Crisler and Beverly Knecht probably would not have occurred if Maria Carson had been alive. Both relationships deepened after Maria's death and reflected Rachel's need to love and care for someone. Crisler and Knecht shared in different ways and at different levels an emergent literary talent that Rachel wanted to encourage. Both were women whom Rachel could genuinely mentor, and they allowed her to repeat in some ways the role Mary Scott Skinker and Grace Croff had played in her own life years earlier. The physical and psychological isolation inherent in Lois's life in Alaska and later in Colorado, and Beverly's physical limitations due to severe diabetes and blindness allowed Rachel to minister to their emotional and spiritual needs at the same time as she encouraged them in their writing.

Lois touched Rachel by her kind words of sympathy when Maria died, even though she had not known her. When Carson heard that Crisler was coming to Baltimore in March to speak, she impulsively invited her to spend the weekend with them in Silver Spring.

By way of introduction Carson told her:

> "We" are myself, my adopted little boy, Roger, and two cats. Roger is really a grand-nephew who was orphaned by the early loss of his father and the death of his dear mother, my niece, two years ago. Roger was left quite alone so I adopted him. We live in a house that is too large for us, especially since my mother's death, and it would be a joy to entertain you. We can promise you the song of mockingbirds and cardinals, and by mid-March we might even manage the beginning of our frog chorus. I do hope you can say "Yes"![39]

Crisler went gladly, with tales of wolf pups and camping in the wilderness to enchant Roger and a compassion for life and all living things that mirrored Carson's. Rachel gave a rare party for Lois on Saturday evening, inviting her niece Virginia and her husband, Shirley Briggs, Dorothy Algire, Irston Barnes, and several others. Crisler showed her slides and photographs of the wolves, and told stories of their behavior. She fascinated them with her account of life in remote northern Alaska and of her husband's efforts to photograph caribou and wolves for a Disney film. The conversation was lively, and Mrs. Crisler was a delightful guest.[40]

After this meeting Carson and Crisler wrote each other with a regularity Rachel reserved for few others. Their letters touch on animals, both wild and domestic, on the problem of poisons, and particularly on their mutual writing. "Someday," Rachel told Lois, "I wish I could find time to turn my pen against the Fish and Wildlife Service's despicable poisoning activities! I do think I can work in references to this sort of thing in the present book—it is all part of the same black picture." Rachel confessed, "I guess I ought to be glad you have no phone—for I am notoriously weak-minded and unable to resist temptation when a kindred spirit is at the other end of a telephone line, no matter how long the line."[41]

Since from the start Crisler had been excited by Carson's new project, Rachel shared her progress easily and asked advice. "The title has been a dreadful problem," Carson had written her in May, "and finally in desperation I thought up what at least serves as an interim title—'Man Against the Earth.' If you have reactions pro or con I'd be interested—or new ideas. I still hope to get something better—although in truth man *is* against the earth! Did I tell you I plan to dedicate it to Albert Schweitzer, using his comment, 'Man has lost the capacity to foresee or to forestall. He will end by destroying the earth'?"[42]

Perhaps most illustrative of Carson's pleasure in her new friendships and the depth of her emotional involvement was the way she wove them together. "I am having a very interesting guest this week-end," Rachel had written Beverly Knecht. "Lois Crisler, who wrote a wonderful book called *Arctic Wild.* I know her only through correspondence—but, as you and I have discovered, that can mean real friendship."[43]

During Lois's visit, Rachel told her about Beverly and showed her some of the latter's letters. In a letter to Crisler afterward, Carson expressed her admiration for Knecht's talents, praising her unusual spirit in the face of so much adversity.[44]

Rachel's warmth and obvious affection for Beverly Knecht, and the intensity of her spontaneous friendship, was unusual, and probably slightly overwhelming. Carson was drawn to this young woman not only because of a literary talent that merited mentoring, but also because she perceived a spiritual bond between them. Knecht reminded Carson of her niece Marjie, who also had been diabetic, and with whom she had been so close and shared so much. Beverly was in love with words, in much the same way Carson had once been, and needed someone who challenged her. But although Knecht was imprisoned in her sickly body and deprived of her sight, she was free to express herself and her love of life in ways Carson, imprisoned by duty and emotional reticence, had never been. Rachel recognized that Knecht had lessons for her as well.

In 1959 when their friendship began, Beverly Knecht was about twenty-nine years old. Well read, well educated in art and music, Beverly had been an invalid since childhood. Stricken with polio and diabetes, she had been on the verge of success as an artist when acute glaucoma deprived her of her sight during her senior year in college. Challenged to outwit her oppressor, she turned to writing as an alternate means of self-expression. Before her diabetic condition worsened, she had been nearly self-supporting through a combination of handicrafts, lecturing for community groups, and the sale of a few stories and poems. After a long period of writer's block, Knecht had emerged at the time she first wrote to Carson serenely confident that she could write, but, ironically, too ill to sit at a typewriter.[45]

At Rachel's request, Beverly sent her a sample of her writing, including the beginnings of a manuscript, "The Texture of Mexico," and parts of an article on olfactory senses that she had offered to a magazine. For her part, Carson sent Knecht paperback copies of her other sea books, the "Help Your Child to Wonder" article, and her very first article, "Undersea."

Frightened by Knecht's physical decline and extended hospitalization in the spring of 1959, Carson telephoned Morton Biskind in May to get his opinion on a vitamin therapy that could speed the healing of an infection in her foot and increase her circulation. Carson wrote Knecht at least once a week and sometimes more frequently, but was hopelessly outpaced by Beverly's long letters, which in March came at the rate of one every other day. The two also had lengthy evening telephone conversations, similar to the ones Rachel enjoyed with Dorothy.[46]

Beverly's illness and her blindness allowed Rachel to be demonstrative in ways that she could not be with her other friends. Her manner of giving was not so much maternal as it was an expression of affectionate comforting. While Beverly was hospitalized, Carson sent a carton of assorted seashells that she had painstakingly labeled for someone to read to her while she turned them over in her hands. Rachel looked for recordings of Bach's cello music, a favorite of Beverly's, and bought her a bright pink nightgown because Beverly had loved the color and wearing it would cheer her. Later there were flowers, stamped envelopes, books of all sorts, a small, battery-operated tape recorder with tapes of the night sounds in Rachel's woods and garden, and a necklace made from the tiniest of clamshells.[47]

"It is amazing that one can feel so close to a person one has never seen, but I feel I know her so well," Rachel told Lois Crisler. "She [Beverly] is really a wonderful person—her mind and spirit seem to have soared above the prison of her poor tormented body! I have talked with her several times now, and our conversations are a delight—so full of laughter and happiness! In talking to her it is almost impossible to remember that she is blind. It may be because of a wonderful quality in her voice, which is soft and low, but also so *alive* and full of eagerness." All those qualities combined to draw Carson into a compelling friendship with this young woman. In April, after sixteen weeks in the hospital, Beverly Knecht returned home to Glen Rock, New Jersey, and Rachel flew up to meet and spend the day with her.[48]

Most of their letters, and presumably their conversations, were about writers and writing. They talked of writer's block and the things that stand in the way of writing. But they also shared some of the reasons why they wrote in the first place. "I think all of us might well ask ourselves that," Rachel confessed. "Each would have his own special reasons, I suppose, yet basically I think all of us would come down to the reason you express so well—a means of preserving our identity, even of projecting it into a future that our physical selves will never know."[49]

Rachel told Beverly about her friendship with Dorothy. "Our friendship began, much as yours and mine did," Rachel wrote, "because she wrote me about one of my books. Soon we discovered a kindred feeling about so many things that a really lovely association developed. Knowing how deeply she would appreciate them, I have sent her several of your letters."[50]

Dorothy was enchanted by Beverly's expression and wrote to her as well. But Dorothy's notes in the margin of one of the letters that Rachel had shared show that she did not miss the adoration in Beverly's letters to Rachel or feel some slight that she had not impressed Rachel with her literary ability as much as Beverly seemed to. When Beverly called Rachel her "dragon and leprechaun," Dorothy wrote in the margin, "Darling, through all this and her others I feel in her that need to pour everything out to you—just as I did—and do! I just know she's dying to say 'Darling' to you—her leprechaun and her dragon, indeed! Well after you've talked with her she will if she doesn't get up her courage first."[51]

The fall of 1959 brought the addition of one other person into Rachel Carson's life. In the case of Jeanne Davis, whom Rachel hired in September as part-time secretary, administrative assistant, and researcher, it was not just the discovery of a devoted associate but of a person with the perfect combination of talents to augment Rachel's and someone who would play a crucial role in helping Carson accomplish her witness.

When Carson returned from Maine, she was not only hopelessly behind schedule but overwhelmed with correspondence and research that still needed to be done. Bette Haney was off to medical school, so Carson placed an advertisement for a secretary and general assistant. One of the people who responded to it was Jeanne (Mrs. Burnet M.) Davis, a woman in her early forties whose teenage children were occupied during the day. After reviewing Davis's background on the telephone, Rachel invited her to the house for an interview. Only when they met was Davis certain that this was indeed the Rachel Carson whose books she had read and so admired.[52]

Jeanne Davis not only had, as Rachel said later, "an incredibly right background," she was also a woman of talent, intelligence, and compassion who had wide social and professional connections in Washington. Born to a distinguished Nebraska family, only much later did Jeanne and Rachel figure out that they were distantly related through Jeanne's father's family and the husband of Rachel's aunt Ida.[53]

Davis graduated from the University of California at Berkeley with a degree in economics and married Burnet Davis, a promising medical student. She was a research assistant and editor for two medical professors at Harvard University, where her husband did his surgical residency. While they lived in Boston, Davis completed a secretarial degree at Simmons College. Burnet Davis had enlisted as a public health physician during the Korean War and continued his distinguished career in the Public Health Service in Washington. Jeanne was thoroughly familiar with the intricacies of medical research and with a wide range of scientific and technical publications. In addition to her research and editorial experience, she had superb organizational and secretarial skills.

Jeanne's personality was perfectly suited to Rachel's. She was calm, soft-spoken, and quietly efficient. She had a wonderfully gentle manner about her and a keenly observant mind. Davis was much more broadly educated and more widely read than Rachel, but her demeanor was such that these qualities only enhanced her value to Carson.

As Rachel confided happily to Paul Brooks, "if I had set out to make someone up I could hardly have done better! The problem of the moment seems to be to find some hormone that will split both Mrs. Davis and me into twins!" Davis was privately horrified at the magnitude of work Carson had left to do with a book due in a matter of months. But she dug in to help with what she could.[54]

With Davis's assistance, Carson's medical research picked up momentum. Davis got a carrel in the library at the National Institutes of Health, where she sometimes spent whole days, working on bibliography and reading and abstracting articles. Carson introduced her to Dorothy Algire, and frequently the two worked together searching for documents Carson needed to see. As an NIH employee and a librarian, Algire was able to get documents unavailable to other researchers. Sometimes this material turned up in Davis's carrel for her to abstract. Other times Algire simply took the reports home with her at night, delivering them to Rachel to read and Jeanne to summarize and return the next day. Algire's access and Davis's technical abstracts were crucial to Carson's research.[55]

Carson continued her highly technical correspondence with Morton Biskind on the effects of pesticides on body cells and the possible relationship with cancer. The more Rachel read, the more she was convinced that this work on cellular metabolism was central to understanding the basic physiological and chemical response to pesticides and to carcinogenesis. It supported the research Wilhelm Hueper was doing at the National Cancer Institute. Hueper was one of the most controversial scientists working on the connections between cancer and chemical pesticides and one of the few who had rated DDT as a chemical carcinogen. Much of Davis's research at NIH and Algire's sleuthing revolved around Hueper's work.[56]

In early December Carson was ready to interview Hueper. But first she talked to another authority of cellular metabolism at NCI, to make certain of her own understanding. He was so interested in Carson's line of research that he gave her what amounted to a two-hour seminar on biological oxidations. Although Carson had already had a lengthy correspondence with Hueper, this was the first time they had met. From the outset, he had been supportive of her project and impressed by her grasp of the science involved. "Dr. H. says," Rachel explained to Dorothy, "he thinks the time now is right for the book for people are beginning to want the facts—sooner would have been premature, he thinks." Hueper, who himself was no stranger to scientific controversy, later remembered his interviews with Carson and his impression that she was "a sincere, unusually well informed scientist possessing not only an unusual degree of social responsibility but also having the courage and ability to express and fight for her convictions and principles."[57]

Although Carson understood from Biskind, Hargraves, Hueper, and other pioneers in the field that the relationship between pesticides and cancer was extremely controversial, the evidence to her, as to them, was incontrovertible. Her conclusions were based not only on the work of scientists on the cutting edge of their fields but on the case histories that filled her file cabinets. One of the most devastating examples was a case Malcolm Hargraves at the Mayo Clinic had shared with her. The victim explained his history:

> On a hunting trip in Northern British Columbia the latter part of August 1957, we sprayed a tent for twenty-one nights with DDT. We did not sufficiently aerate the tent. When I got back home in September, my marrow and white and red corpuscles were terribly impaired. I nearly lost my life. I have had forty-one infusions in my arm, each lasting from four to six to eight hours, in Philadelphia, and I am slowly coming back.[58]

Carson had followed up on the case with Hargraves later and learned that the man had died of leukemia in May 1959.[59]

The question in Rachel's mind was how to handle the information on cancer and how much emphasis to give it. "Just now I'm trying to put together a chapter on cancer hazards related to pesticides," she wrote Brooks.

> Until recently, I saw this as part of a general chapter on the physical effects on man. Now it looms so terrifically important that I want to devote a whole chapter to it—and that perhaps will be the most important chapter of the book. To tell the truth in the beginning I felt the link between pesticides and cancer was tenuous and at best circumstantial; now I feel it is very strong indeed. This is partly because I feel I shall be able to suggest the actual mechanism by which these things transform a normal cell into a cancer cell. This has taken very deep digging into the realms of physiology and biochemistry and genetics, to say nothing of chemistry. But now I feel that a lot of isolated pieces of the jig-saw puzzle have suddenly fallen into place. It has not, to my knowledge, been brought together by anyone else, and I think it will make my case very strong indeed.[60]

In October Shirley Briggs and Irston Barnes persuaded Rachel to present some of her research to a select group of officials from the regional

Audubon, ornithological, and natural history societies who were meeting at the Brookings Institution in Washington. Carson's remarks focused on the slow, chronic hazards chemical pesticides posed to humans rather than to wildlife. She did, however, include some comments on the toxicity of herbicides, particularly her conclusion on the dangers of 2,4-D and the problems of insect resistance.

Although the subject of her remarks was grim, Rachel managed to find some humor in the occasion. "I felt rather as though I were a professor lecturing to an extraordinarily attentive and diligent class," she told Dorothy. "I was surprised to discover they were all equipped with pencil and paper, and from the moment I began, throughout the 30 to 40 minutes I talked, they all scribbled away for dear life, taking notes. (Or, so I assumed—could they have been writing letters home???)"[61]

During the question-and-answer session that followed, Rachel clarified her position on the use of pesticides in domestic agriculture. A forester remarked how disastrous it would be to attempt to eliminate the spraying of crops entirely, and Carson quickly agreed. But she criticized the context in which chemical pesticides were used. Her analysis of the broader cultural problems of pesticides reflects the influence of John Kenneth Galbraith's critique of American society and its demands for immediate solutions.

> I am not one who feels you can eliminate all spraying, by any means. I think it would be fine if you could. I doubt that it is possible from the practical standpoint, but I do think that one great trouble—and I suppose it is the fault of the American public as a whole—is this desire for the quick and the easy way of doing something, without any consideration of the consequences. Even if the consequences are strongly implied or known, there is still a great temptation to go ahead and get the job done and let the future take care of itself. Maybe we will come up with a pill to take care of it, or something like that![62]

Just one month later Carson found herself much involved in the practical problems of pesticide contamination when she attended government hearings on the FDA's pre-Thanksgiving ban on the marketing of cranberries that had been sprayed with the herbicide aminotriazole. The "Great Cranberry Scandal" of 1959 exposed the inherent weaknesses in the USDA's pesticide registration process and in the testing procedures.

Aminotriazole had been registered with the USDA in 1956 for non-food use. Two years later it was approved for use on cranberry bogs after the berries had been harvested. But in 1957 many cranberry growers applied the herbicide prior to harvest. As a result, the plants took up the aminotriazole and some got into the berries. Since the FDA had not established a tolerance for the chemical, one-third of the 1957 crop from the Pacific northwestern fields was withheld from the market.

Meanwhile, the 1958 crop had been grown, processed, and marketed while toxicity studies were carried out by the manufacturers of aminotriazole, the American Cyanamid Company and the Amchem Co. Those studies established that the herbicide was a carcinogen, causing cancer of the thyroid in laboratory rats. With the danger of aminotriazole established, the FDA began checking the spraying practices of growers. The National Cranberry Association, dominated by Ocean Spray Cranberry Company, instituted a plan to withhold from shipment any lots in which it was suspected that the herbicide had been used. Nevertheless, as Thanksgiving approached, suspect cranberries were shipped to market.[63]

On November 9, 1959, Arthur S. Flemming, Secretary of Health, Education and Welfare (HEW), announced at a press conference that he was recommending no further sales of cranberries or cranberry products produced in 1957, 1958, or 1959 until the industry submitted a workable plan to test, separate, and destroy contaminated berries. Leading grocery chains took cranberries off their shelves and sales fell to zero.

Cranberry growers in New England, where little contamination had occurred, demanded that President Eisenhower fire Flemming for wrecking the industry, while an obviously irritated Agriculture Secretary Benson announced that he saw no reason to make any changes in pesticide registration procedures and expressed sympathy with the growers. Presidential hopefuls John F. Kennedy and Richard M. Nixon, then touring the country, publicly wolfed down large portions of Wisconsin cranberries to show their devotion to the growers, while other officials complained that even tainted berries posed no realistic health problem.

Most of the public was shocked and alarmed by Secretary Flemming's disclosure of toxic contamination. Congress and the chemical companies did not miss the significance of controversy or the ensuing media attention that offered an unexpected forum for consumer education. Aminotriazole was registered for use not only on cranberry bogs but also on cornfields, in apple and pear orchards for control of poison ivy, and on roadside weeds. The cranberry scare revealed that the laws protecting consumers from toxic chemicals were inadequate and exposed the need for legislation forcing manufacturers to demonstrate the safety of chemicals before, not after, marketing. The cranberry industry as well as the USDA worried that the question of tolerances in general would now be raised for other chemicals used in agriculture.[64]

On November 19 Carson, Irston Barnes, and others attended the much-anticipated public hearing on the FDA's ban called by HEW Secretary Flemming. Rachel was particularly impressed with the dignity and courtesy with which Flemming handled the hearing as well as with Oregon congressman Charles O. Porter who, contrary to her expectations, said the incident pointed up the enormous problem of pesticide and additive contamination of food and called for better laws and more rigid enforcement.[65]

Carson was not, however, the least impressed with the industry's chief spokesman, Edward B. Astwood, a professor of medicine at Tufts University and an agricultural proponent who used aminotriazole clinically in the treatment of thyroid disease. Carson reported to Dorothy, "his testimony can be shot so full of holes as to be absolutely worthless, and the disheartening thing is that he must know this full well. However it was good that Consumer's Union sent a man who gave the opinion of a leading specialist at the University of Chicago—exactly the opposite of the man from Tufts. And my files are full of things that refute the Tufts man!"[66]

Carson's letter to Clarence Cottam the day after the hearings reveals her understanding of the political significance of the cranberry crisis. "I am wondering," she asked him, "whether you could persuade Drew Pearson to investigate the all important subject of financial inducements behind certain pesticide programs. The cranberry crisis has, I believe, been a wonderful thing in opening up the problem for a public that has been blissfully unaware that food carries anything in the way of contamination." Cottam concurred with her analysis and carried out her request.[67]

The Great Cranberry Scare provided Carson with additional evidence of the misuses of toxic chemicals and helped create a climate of public opinion receptive to her message. If only she could get the book finished![68]

All in all, Carson made progress that fall and was encouraged by the response she was getting from those who learned of her work. "There are good developments on the book," she told Dorothy, "some wonderful letters and very influential people getting aroused through hearing of my project. I feel, darling, that this may well outweigh in importance everything else I have done."[69]

Christine Stevens certainly thought so. She and Carson had met for lunch shortly after Rachel returned from Maine. Carson had agreed to help Stevens with a booklet that her institute was preparing on more humane biology projects for high school students. Afterward Stevens told Carson, "I believe that your book on the poisons will be a kind of 'Uncle Tom's Cabin' for the wild birds and animals. I am very anxious to see it published."[70]

Carson's speeches and public appearances that fall energized her. Her happiness was apparent to Dorothy, who still remained skeptical.

> You thought you detected an exhilaration in my voice the other night, which you attributed—and rightly, I'm sure—to my happiness in the progress of The Book. The other day someone asked Leonard Bernstein about his inexhaustible energy and he said, "I have no more energy than anyone who loves what he is doing." Well, I'm afraid mine has to be recharged at times, but anyway I do seem just now to be riding the crest of a wave of enthusiasm and creativity, and although I'm going to bed late and often rising in very dim light to get in an hour of thinking and organizing before the household stirs, my weariness seems easily banished.[71]

Carson had other good reasons to feel confident. In early December she received the Lifetime Achievement Award for her contributions to the biological sciences from the northern Virginia chapter of the American Association of University Women, which included a stipend of $2,500. In a brief acceptance speech, Carson told the group that she would use the money for a new book probing "the basic problems of life, its origins, its evolution and its future."[72]

The only disappointing aspect of her work was how long it seemed to be taking. By December it was clear to everyone that she had no hope of keeping to the publishing schedule she had established with Brooks the previous spring. Finally she faced up to it in a frank letter. "You are the most patient of editors," Rachel told him,

> and often I am aware that I must try even your patience sorely. I guess all that sustains me is a serene inner conviction that when, at last the book is done, it is going to be built on an unshakable

> foundation. That is so terribly important. Too many people—with the best possible motives—have rushed out statements without adequate support, furnishing the best possible targets for the opposition. That we shall not have to worry about. I know you realize as fully as anyone not directly involved could that this is a very big job. But I don't think anyone but myself could know how big. I am very happy deep down inside with what I have been able to dig out and fit together, but I'm also horribly frustrated that it is taking so long.[73]

She told him she hoped she could finish by February but "I can only express the hope." She promised to send him the completed chapter on insect resistance and the cancer chapter within a week.

Brooks, of course, was not the only editor wondering when Carson would finish. William Shawn telephoned not long after, ostensibly to thank her for suggesting a piece in "Talk of the Town," on the cranberry scare, hoping to discover when she might finish. "He seemed patient as ever," Rachel told Marie afterward. "I did ask him if he'd like to see a small sample and he said he would. So would you send him your copy of the resistance chapter with outline so he can see where it fits."[74]

Rachel's Christmas letter to Marjorie Spock best summarized her feelings. "My own work goes on at a furious pace," she told Marjorie, who was trying to flee from the spray planes by moving her farm to a rural area deep in the Hudson River Valley, "but I feel a little like the Red Queen who had to run as fast as she could just to stay where she was." But unlike the grumpy Red Queen, Rachel's pleasure was evident. "Seriously," she continued, "I am very happy about the basis of all I have to say and continue to feel that the case against the insecticides can be made extremely convincing. I know it has been hard on everyone's nerves to take so long, but I feel in the end it will be very much better to have done so."[75]

Although she did not mention it to Spock, she had been elated by a surprise call on Christmas Eve from William Shawn, who had read her chapter and wanted to tell her how excited he was by what she was writing, how important it was, and how well he thought she was presenting it. "Did you realize how much that little Christmas Eve call from Mr. Shawn meant to me?" Rachel asked Dorothy. "I'm confident now about all of it."[76]

16

"If I Live to Be 90"

At the beginning of 1960, Rachel Carson was at the height of her analytical powers and fully in command of her material. She had drafted separate chapters on birds and wildlife, groundwater, soil, insect resistance, and two chapters dealing with cancer. She also had made a good start on the third and most difficult chapter on cell biology and genetic mutation and was encouraged by how it had turned out. She had Jeanne Davis's efficient assistance and, for the first half of the year, Bette Haney's help as well. Ida ran the household smoothly. Roger was happy with school, and Rachel was discovering more interests they could share. Dorothy Freeman was reconciled to Rachel's project and had even captured some of her excitement.[1]

Carson's friendships with Bok, Spock, Crisler, and Knecht brought new happiness to her, and she was energized by her far-flung correspondence with active and committed scientists Clarence Cottam, Robert Rudd, Frank Egler, George Wallace, Joseph Hickey, Harold Peters, Malcolm Hargraves, and Morton Biskind. She had followed up on hundreds of individual encounters with pesticides, and her files were full of evidence of ecological damage and illustrations of human harm. Carson knew what she had to say was important, and she was increasingly convinced that the public was ready to listen. Only the slow pace of her writing was discouraging, but even that had the benefit of reassuring her that her case would be as accurate as she could make it and could stand up against the criticism that would certainly come.

Her work now had a momentum and rhythm of its own. The prospect of finishing within the next four or five months was a realistic one. Thus the health crisis that beset her early in 1960 and escalated over the next year and a half was particularly tragic. It broke her hard-earned concentration, delayed the completion of her book, and forced her in upon herself. At times during these months only her indefatigable determination and inextinguishable spirit kept her from giving up. Long periods when she could do no work at all forced her to reconsider the whole concept of chemical pollution and entirely revamp the way she presented the case against pesticides. In the process, the moral dimension of Carson's social critique was expanded and sharpened. Challenged to dig deep into her inner resources and aware that this might be her only chance to speak out, she emerged from this initial illness confirmed in the importance of her message.

The discovery that she had a serious ulcer in early January was much more upsetting because of all she had achieved the previous fall, but Rachel seemed to take it in stride. "It's a duodenal ulcer," she wrote matter-of-factly to Marie, "so now I live on baby foods, Maalox, and Probanthine for a while. It's a horrid nuisance, but otherwise I'm not concerned." Certain that Dorothy would feel the stress of research and writing was to blame, Rachel was surprised by her friend's unexpected encouragement to get back to work as quickly as possible.[2]

In fact, Dorothy was relieved it was not cancer. She wisely attributed the ulcer not to the new book but to all the years of emotional strain Rachel had endured. "And," she told Carson, "you, I think, are the type—the person who, on the surface, keeps calm, shows no emotion, and goes along apparently unruffled with all the tensions bottled up inside. There have been times when, if I had been you, I would have screamed."[3]

That Rachel was frustrated, however, was apparent in the tone of her letters to Marie. Oxford insisted she submit the copy for the revision of *The Sea Around Us* in early March, and Marie suggested she take a break from the book while she got the new material ready. As far as Rachel was concerned, her ulcer had diverted her enough. "I am quite unable to think further about it now," Carson told her agent with annoyance, "and the way the situation has come up is doing me no good, either physically or in terms of undisturbed work on the present book—which I do consider by far the most important thing on the horizon."[4]

For a while Carson made good progress healing her ulcer with medications and diet, but at the end of January she was hit with a serious viral pneumonia followed by a sinus infection, which kept her very low for more than a week. Unable to work, Rachel sought solace from Marjorie Spock. Always compassionate, Marjorie wrote, "I am almost tongue-tied with shock upon reading your letter recounting the list of your present health afflictions. Our hearts are deeply stirred, and we wish our *hands* could do something to help, especially if that could mean removing these burdens."[5]

Carson's recovery was slow and days went by when she was barely able to crawl out of bed even briefly. Depressed and discouraged, she told Dorothy, "Sometimes I wonder whether the Author even exists anymore—it rather seems Fate has been otherwise minded these recent years. Very puzzling, to one who thought there were important things to be done." But she continued to work, and slowly her condition improved.[6]

In the middle of March she wrote Brooks: "I think I can feel now that by far the most difficult part is done and that the rest should roll along rather speedily. In a couple of days I am going to send you the two chapters that deal with the problem of cancer. To see how that has evolved, remember that originally cancer was going to be discussed as a small part of one chapter that would deal with all physical hazards to man. Then I realized cancer would require a chapter to itself, but as I worked that turned into two!"[7]

Annoyed that Rodell had not told Brooks just how ill she had been, Rachel told him she was not sure Marie knew "just how rough the going has been." With rare self-indulgence, she detailed her successive illnesses, commenting "I should think it [the ulcer] might have waited until the book is done!"[8]

Carson had sent the two cancer chapters to John J. Biesele, a research scientist for the Sloan Kettering Institute whose comments had been helpful. She wanted Brooks to read the chapters and give her a general reaction as to whether he found her explanations too difficult before he left for an extended trip to Europe. Brooks, who had some experience with an ulcer himself, offered to go down to Washington to talk about it but promised to read the chapters right away.[9]

When Rachel sent them off several days later, her letter contained more bad news. "I am entering the hospital soon—probably this week—for surgery that I hope will not be too complicated but that can't be known at the moment." Although she did not tell Brooks, Rachel had found what she thought were several cysts in her left breast and, based on her previous history of breast tumors, her doctor had recommended their removal. She was scheduled to go into Doctor's Hospital in Washington on March 24, but the surgery was postponed because both she and Roger shared another virus. An unexpected visit with Lois Crisler cheered her. They spent most of the night talking of life, nature, books, and writing.[10]

During the week before her surgery, Carson and Brooks carried out one of their most meaningful editorial exchanges. Carson told him about her plan to list her principle sources, including technical journals, in an appendix arranged by chapter as an alternative to footnotes in the text. Carson explained, "Doing this will, I think, serve a double purpose: it will make the book more useful to the serious student, and it will refute any claims that my views are personal and ill-founded. But most readers who won't care either way, can ignore them." Carson was considering having illustrations in addition to photographs. She thought a drawing or two of chromosomes during mitosis might help the reader visualize the process more easily.[11]

Rachel also wanted Paul's advice about the persistent title problem. Marie disliked *Man Against the Earth*, finding it misleading. Emphasizing again the parallels between pesticide poisoning and radioactive fallout, Rachel told Paul, "In my flounderings I keep asking myself what I would call it if my theme concerned radiation, having some illogical feeling that would be easier. As you have seen in the cancer chapter, I keep hammering away at the parallel. Whether radiation or chemicals are involved, the basic issue is the contamination of the environment."[12]

Brooks found the two cancer chapters impressive and convincing. He told Carson, "You have done a very good job of presenting and interpreting the evidence, and also of putting the whole thing in its historical setting." He thought her description of cell division particularly clear, questioning only the tongue-twisting names that would be stumbling blocks for nonscientific readers.

Grateful for Paul's encouragement, Rachel told him modestly that Dr. Biesele "did not find I had done any violence to the scientific facts" in her explanation of cell division and mutation, and she was now sending the chapters to a cell biologist at the University of Michigan. The chemical names were a problem but, she explained, "I believe the only solution seems to be not to drag them in unnecessarily. However, to be vague about which chemical does what, would destroy the usefulness of the book for the many who will turn to it with some serious purpose. Of course most gardeners are regrettably familiar with the names dieldrin, chlordane, malathion and the like." Stimulated by Brooks's reaction,

Rachel Carson, author of *The Sea Around Us*, 1951.

Rachel with Alice Roosevelt Longworth at a book party for *The Sea Around Us*, 1951.

Carson's cottage, West Southport, Maine, as seen from the Sheepscot River, 1955.

Carson on the steps of her Maine cottage, ca. 1952.

Dorothy Freeman, ca. 1950.

Rachel disposing of her day's marine specimens at midnight in Myrtle Beach, 1952.

Marie Rodell (left) with her client, Helen Gahagan Douglas, ca. 1954.

Bob Hines and Rachel Carson looking for marine specimens, Florida Keys, 1952.

Dorothy and Rachel, 1954.

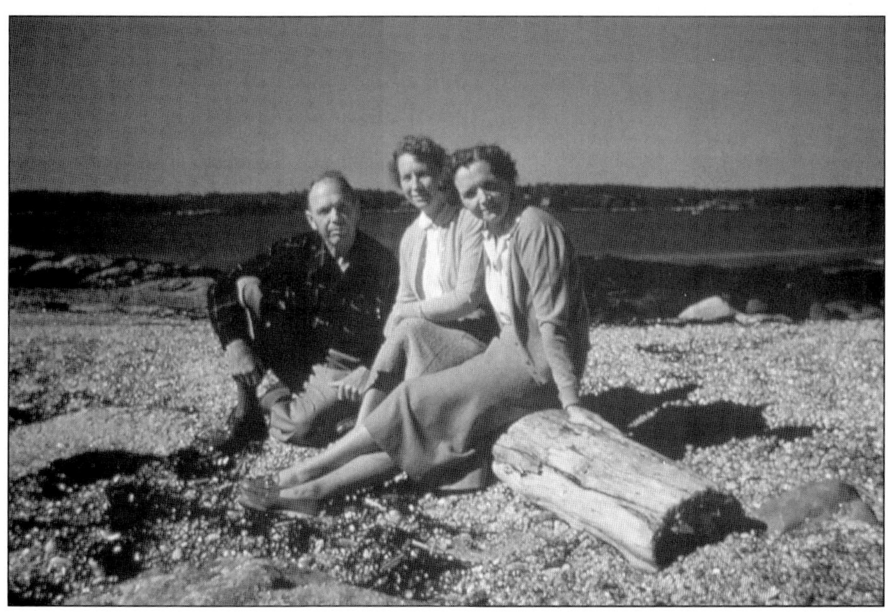

Stanley, Dorothy, and Rachel in West Southport, summer 1955.

Paul Brooks, ca. 1970.

Dorothy reading a Carson favorite, 1954.

Rachel exploring the tide pools, 1955.

Maria Carson in West Southport, ca. 1957.

Jeanne Vance Davis shortly before starting to work for Carson.

Roger Christie inspecting construction on the Berwick Road house, 1958.

Rachel on the steps of her new home, 1959.

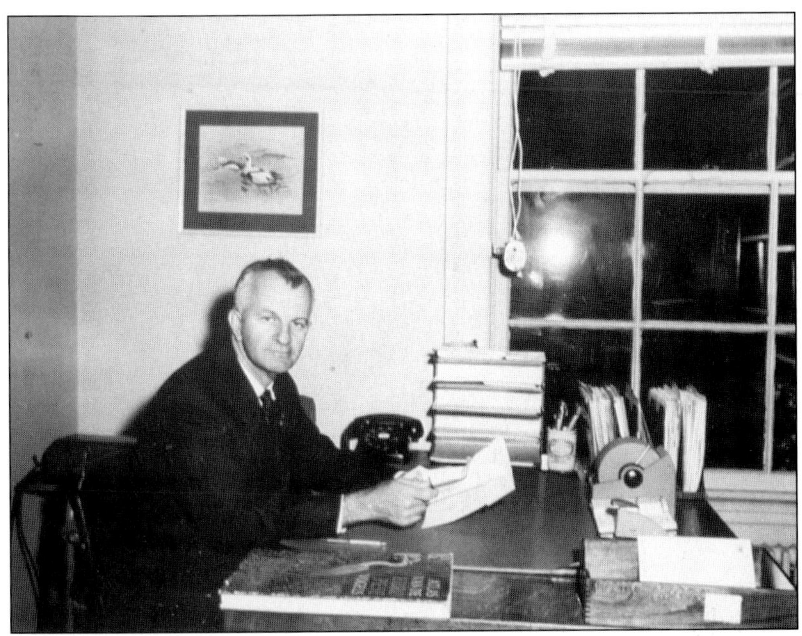

Roland C. Clement in his National Audubon Society office, late 1950s.

Frank E. Egler, ecologist and Carson supporter.

Robert Rudd, wildlife zoologist, ca. 1960.

Rachel tide-pooling, ca. 1956.

George Crile, Jr., M.D., ca. 1960.

Rachel on her deck in Maine, summer 1961.

Rachel, Roger, and Ruth Scott, West Southport, 1961.

Carson in the woods behind her cottage, summer 1961.

The author of *Silent Spring*, 1962.

Carson on the deck of her Maine cottage, summer 1962.

Rachel Carson as role model. (*Peanuts* © 1963, reprinted by permission of United Feature Syndicate, Inc.)

"I had just come to terms with fallout, and along comes Rachel Carson."

Drawing by Herbert Goldberg, *Saturday Review*, November 10, 1962.

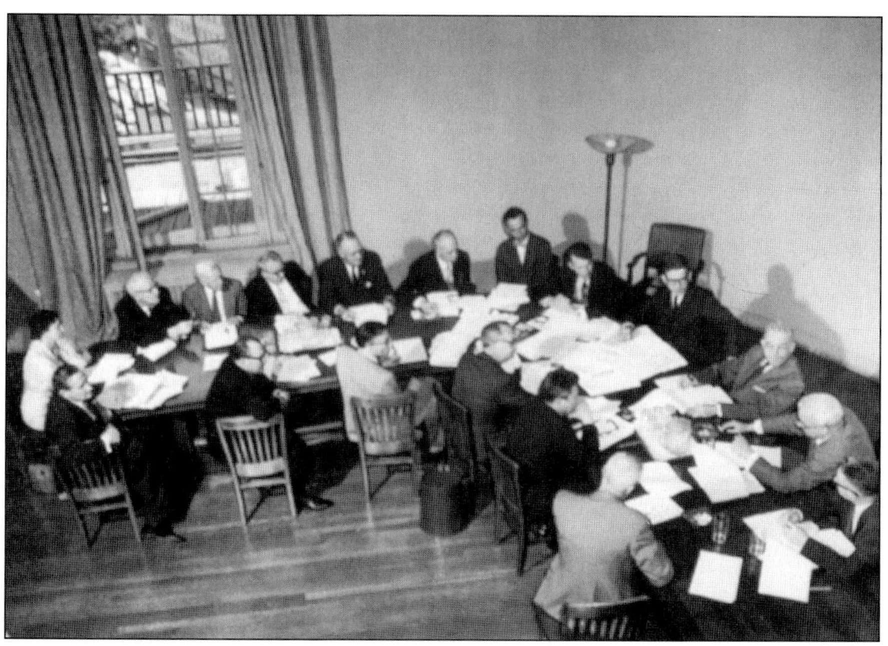

Carson (far left), meeting informally with the President's Science Advisory Committee, spring 1963.

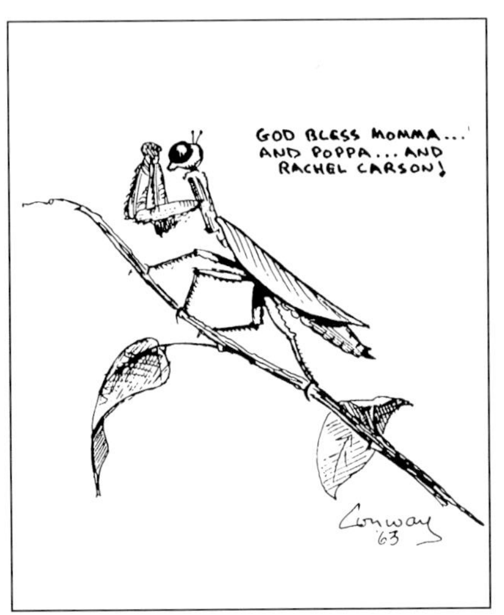

Praying mantis cartoon by Conway, 1963.

Carson during her *CBS Reports* interview with Eric Sevareid, December 1962, at her home in Silver Spring, MD.

The Sheepscot shore at Newagen, where Dorothy scattered Rachel's ashes.

Rachel planned to be back at work after a brief hospitalization. She entered Doctor's Hospital, where her friend Elizabeth Dickson was the floor nurse, on April 3 and underwent surgery the next day.[13]

According to Rachel's account to Marjorie Spock, the doctors found two tumors that she refers to as "cysts" in her left breast. One was apparently benign, the other, she explained, "suspicious enough to require a radical mastectomy." Carson asked her surgeon, a Dr. Sanderson, directly if the pathology report showed any malignancy. Sanderson told her she had "a condition bordering on malignancy," implying the mastectomy had been a precautionary measure. He recommended no further treatment.[14]

Her hospitalization was difficult, and she was in a great deal of pain. Even so, Carson insisted on going home barely six days later because she was anxious about Roger's emotional state. She told Marjorie Spock optimistically, "So far, I'm just concentrating on getting well, and the only possible attitude seems to be to feel thankful this discovery was made so early. I think there need be no apprehension for the future."[15]

It is clear from this letter that Carson was, however, concerned about the potential repercussions of any public disclosure that she might have cancer. "I am giving details to special friends like you," she told Spock, "not to others, but I suppose it's a futile effort to keep one's private affairs private. Somehow I have no wish to read of my ailments in literary gossip columns. Too much comfort to the chemical companies."[16]

Carson's friends were not as sanguine about her medical prognosis. Privately they were distressed about her postoperative situation and the vague nature of the pathology reports. Dorothy Algire, who worked at the National Cancer Institute, was especially concerned. At a party that week at Algire's parents' home, Dorothy, Shirley Briggs, Irston Barnes, and Dorothy's parents discussed the reports, feeling certain that both tumors must have been malignant and upset that Carson's doctors had not referred her for further treatment.[17]

Although Carson seemed reassured that her medical prognosis was good, she admitted that the surgery had been brutal. The lymph nodes on her left side had been removed as well as a good portion of the pectoral muscle. Recovery from such surgery took months, not weeks. Carson understood her recovery would be slow, acknowledging to Spock and Richards that her "hospital adventure" had wrecked her work schedule for the spring.[18]

But as Carson was to discover in December, Dr. Sanderson had lied to her about the results of the pathology reports. She explained to Paul Brooks just after Christmas, "I know now that I was not told the truth last spring at the time of my operation. The tumor was malignant, and there was even at that time evidence that it had metastasized, for some of the lymph nodes also were found to be involved. But I was told none of this, even though I asked directly."[19]

Medical protocols between a single, female patient and her physician in the 1950s and 1960s might help explain why Sanderson had not told Carson the truth. Typically, in the case of a married woman, the patient herself would not have been told she had a malignancy, but her husband, had he asked directly, would have been given the full account. But even these conventions do not explain why, knowing that the tumor had already metastasized, Sanderson failed to suggest further radiation treatment even as a precautionary measure. No explanation suffices except the possibility that he considered her cancer so far advanced that no treatment would make any difference in her life expectancy. However, given her physicians' continued dishonest response to her new symptoms later that year, the only available conclusion is that they consciously intended to hide the truth of her condition for as long as possible.[20]

Carson never uses the word "malignant" or "cancer" in her correspondence. While she might have done so to Dorothy on the telephone, it is doubtful. According to social protocol in the 1950s and early 1960s, cancer was most often referred to metaphorically or indirectly. Dorothy Freeman shared Rachel's reticence to talk about her mastectomy. After hearing from Rachel in the hospital, Dorothy wrote, "of the operation itself I have decided to shut it out of my mind as much as I can. When we can talk *together* maybe you will want to tell me what it means to you. In this era I'm sure that the future can be entirely hopeful." After two weeks at home, Rachel asked Dorothy to come down for the weekend. Dorothy was saddened to see Rachel so thin and so obviously worn by her physical suffering. She referred obliquely to Rachel's "hurt side," but Carson probably did not talk much about the details of her surgery or her prognosis. Rachel and Marie may have been slightly more forthright in their discussions, but they communicated mostly by telephone.[21]

By the time of Dorothy's visit, Rachel was driving a little and was back at her desk for a few hours every day. She had two assistants to direct and correspondence to answer even when she was too tired to edit or revise. As Carson gained strength, she moved back into the routine she and Jeanne Davis had established during the previous fall.[22]

Davis came three days a week. Rachel had arranged her study so that Jeanne used a desk placed at right angles to the large picture window that looked out on the woods. Rachel moved her chaise next to the desk. The birch-paneled office walls were lined with bookshelves and three large filing cabinets. She had placed several low file cabinets under the back window with a shelf on top where she kept her recording equipment.

Most of the time Rachel wrote in bed on a lap desk, propped up by cushions, and dictated all her editorial changes into her tape recorder. She worked into the night and slept late; when Jeanne arrived in the morning, Rachel was usually still in bed, but Davis would find a tape on her desk to transcribe. Jeanne retyped the manuscript and then took care of any routine correspondence, paid the bills, and made phone calls as directed. When Rachel got up, they would go over the manuscript changes and review bibliography, then Jeanne might do some filing or go on errands.[23]

The two usually ate a sandwich together at lunchtime, going outside on the patio in nice weather, but otherwise sitting by the window in the study watching the birds and the seasons change. Quite often they took a walk after lunch, sometimes just around the property, sometimes up Berwick Road to her friends the Rymers' house and back. Jeanne was an excellent gardener, and they often talked about plants and what was in bloom. After lunch, Rachel lay on her chaise with a stack of letters and dictated responses to Jeanne.[24]

Jeanne remembers Rachel spent a lot of time on the telephone that spring with the head of Roger's school. The boy, then eight years old, was going through a difficult time and was frequently in trouble. Some of Rachel's friends urged her to put him in a school where he would have more disciplined supervision. Since Jeanne had two children, Rachel valued her advice and often shared her anxiety over Roger's behavior. Although Carson knew her lack of consistent discipline contributed to the problem, she was constitutionally unable to provide a predictable structure.[25]

Bette Haney worked almost exclusively in the libraries, reading and taking notes on specific bibliographies. Rachel usually wanted direct quotes from the articles, so this took more time. One of Haney's most challenging assignments that spring was to interview Justus Ward, the chief of the Regulatory Division of the Agricultural Research Service, about the USDA's registration of two chemicals, aminotriazole and Chloral-1PC, a chemical being used as an antisprouting agent on potatoes.

Haney interviewed Ward at the ARS offices in Beltsville. They got through the registration of aminotriazole amicably, but Haney ran into trouble over Chloral-1PC. Ward got suspicious after explaining that the USDA had gained control of this plant regulator only in August 1959 and that it was first legally applied in March 1960. As Haney remembers it, he was just about to answer her question about registration dates and restrictions when he thought to ask her who she worked for. Apparently he had been under the impression that she was with a government bureau, for he was taken aback to discover that Haney was Rachel Carson's research assistant, and he ended the interview summarily.

Haney reported the incident to Carson, feeling as if she had been a failure. When she told Rachel just how nervous Ward appeared, Rachel remarked, "He should be," and went on to explain that she knew him and had expected that he might balk at giving out the information. She would, she said, find another way to get the data on Chloral-1PC. Carson later shared Haney's story with Wilhelm Hueper at NCI, telling him "Mr. Ward has displayed a very curious reluctance to divulge this information. He told a young assistant of mine that information was classified and has simply ignored several letters of mine in which I have asked for a summary of uses for which these chemicals have been registered." In the end Carson got the information she wanted from Reece Sailer.[26]

Bette Haney left Washington that fall for graduate work at Yale. Some years later, reflecting on her experience working with Rachel Carson, Bette wrote:

> Working with Rachel was like seeing the fable of the hare and the tortoise come alive. I honestly thought she would never finish that book. It was not because of all the obvious difficulties; her illness, her mother's death, care of Roger, but more with the pace of work . . . it seemed so slow. As a child of my culture, I had not yet learned to associate progress with that pace . . . and I did not know then the extent of her determination and what a powerful force that kind of determination can be. It was a valuable lesson.[27]

Rachel was very fond of Bette and appreciated her careful work. When Bette married Thomas Duff the following June, Rachel attended her wedding, one of her few social appearances that summer.

Carson had other writing obligations to finish. Before she left for

Maine, she wrote an introduction entitled "To Understand Biology" to the Animal Welfare Institute's educational booklet *Humane Biology Projects*, which she had promised Christine Stevens. In it Carson outlined the moral obligations scientists owed to the human and nonhuman world at a time of powerful technological influences. When the booklet was published, it received wide praise from science teachers. The first printing sold out before school opened that fall.[28]

Stevens was also responsible for introducing Carson to the work of British activist Ruth Harrison, whose book *Animal Machines* exposed the inhumane methods of rearing animals destined to become human food. In 1963 Carson wrote the foreword for that book in which she questioned humankind's moral right to the kind of domination over animals that Harrison described. These two contributions to animal welfare reflect Carson's mature philosophy of reverence for life. The humane treatment of animals was a concern and a cause she believed in passionately but one she kept relatively private. She supported Stevens and the Animal Welfare Institute by writing letters to congressmen and making select phone calls. But Carson was careful not to draw too much public attention to her advocacy, aware that critics would use it as a way to belittle her science.[29]

For similar reasons Rachel had taken a keen but detatched interest in the critical reaction to William Longgood's *The Poisons in Your Food*, a popular exposé of the inadequacy of the nation's food and drug laws to control chemical contamination, which appeared in February 1960. While she read several reviews, she assiduously avoided reading the book. When the chemical companies went on the offensive, Rachel told Marjorie Spock:

> It is too bad that Mr. Longgood is having such rough going with his book, although I suppose not surprising. His reporting of the trial would automatically make him a target of the New York State Department of Agriculture. I had felt I did not want to see the book now, so have no idea if there is any vestige of truth to the assertions that he is inaccurate. I do know from my own experience that one cannot accept any statement from whatever source as truth, until one takes the time to trace it to its original source. That, of course, is one reason I am being so slow, but with all my care I suppose there will be some slips.[30]

With her returning health, Carson was looking forward to going to Maine. She asked Jeanne Davis to come along and to help with the driving, since she was still too weak to manage the trip with Roger and the two cats by herself. They arrived in West Southport at the end of June, just in time for Roger to start camp. Rachel had found a housekeeper to come every day to cook and clean. Muriel Parlin, a local stenographer, had agreed to help her with correspondence and typing. Relieved to be back at her cottage, Carson began to feel restored.[31]

Rachel had reluctantly acceded to the pleas of the editor of the Johns Hopkins University alumni magazine to collaborate with Erich Hartmann, a rising photographer with Magnum Studios, on a photo essay for a special issue on the ocean. By happy coincidence, Hartmann and his family spent their summers in West Boothbay Harbor. Hartmann felt confident he and Carson could work together easily. But after several unsuccessful attempts to see her, he began photographing alone, taking shots of the ocean at Pemaquid and Ocean Point and other local spots. After borrowing a darkroom and making some enlargements, he called Carson again, telling her he had something to show her. Once at her cottage, Hartmann spread his photographs out on her dining room table. After admiring them silently a few moments, Carson told him quietly, "This is something quite different."[32]

Rachel found working with Erich Hartmann unexpectedly stimulating. She liked the way he worked and felt comfortable with him, even allowing him to take several shots of her. For his part, Hartmann was fascinated by her approach to the sea. The Hartmann/Carson essay was published as "The Sea" in the May/June 1961 issue of the *Johns Hopkins Magazine*. Carson's introduction and captions for Hartmann's photographs reflect her work on the revision of *The Sea Around Us* in its emphasis on the economic importance of the ocean's resources and the threats of pollution. Hartmann's photographs do not illustrate Carson's text so much as they enliven her philosophy of the sea and her distinctive sense of it.[33]

Rachel found that summer one of her most rewarding, even though she got very little work done. Certainly her illness had made her more aware of how much she loved that particular rocky shore. "As I sit here in the study for the last time this year," Rachel wrote Dorothy on the eve of her departure, "of course I find myself wondering what new changes will have entered our lives before another summer. It will be hard to say goodbye, darling."[34]

That September Carson took some of the ocean back to Silver Spring with her, since she was obligated to finish revising *The Sea Around Us*. Her eight-page preface seems, at first, a remarkably seamless addition in both style and voice to the earlier text. Reviewing the major achievements in oceanographic research in the decade since the book first appeared, she notes particularly those that contributed new knowledge of the ocean floor and the deep subsurface currents. Even in the deepest parts of the sea there were currents and movement, submarine landslides and internal tides and life-forms, suggesting a whole new dynamic of movement and formation.[35]

Proof of this dynamic nature provided Carson with the opportunity to comment on humankind's stewardship of the ocean's natural resources and on the hazards of the Atomic Age. In the last pages of the preface Carson's tone is more assertive and her language more didactic. No longer the lucid biologist explicating the wonders of postwar oceanography, she adopts a prophetic tone warning of the consequences of Cold War technology.

Having unlocked the secrets of the atom, Carson explains, humankind was confronted with the problem of disposing of the lethal by-products of atomic fission. Radioactive contamination of the world's oceans was another dimension of the pollution of the earth by toxic chemicals. Both were done without understanding the long-term effects and without public knowledge. Yet the real danger to humankind, Carson explains, is not just in the movement of radioactive elements but in the concentration of radioactive isotopes by marine life. Just as synthetic chemicals are magnified in the bodies of fish and wildlife, so radiochemicals move up the food chain of marine creatures. In both cases, Carson argues, we allow technology to outdistance knowledge, and the damage is irreversible. "To dispose first and investigate later is an invitation to disaster," she writes, "for once radioactive elements have been deposited at sea they are irretrievable. The mistakes that are made now are made for all time."[36]

The preface contains one of Carson's strongest statements on the perils of radioactive contamination. "It is a curious situation," she wrote, "that the sea, from which life first arose, should now be threatened by the activities of one form of that life. But the sea, though changed in a sinister way, will continue to exist; the threat is rather to life itself."[37]

Carson's views in October 1960 reflected contemporary concern about nuclear fallout. The Cold War had become more dangerous since 1957, when Soviet booster rockets and missile science had first threatened U.S. security. The nation's nuclear arsenal had tripled, and by 1960 both France and China had joined the United States and the Soviet Union as nuclear powers. Nuclear testing had been suspended in the United States temporarily in 1958 after a series of multimegaton thermonuclear blasts released dangerous amounts of radioactivity in the atmosphere that got into the rain and into the food chain. Public concern reached new heights when a study by the Committee for Nuclear Information at Washington University in St. Louis revealed the presence of Strontium 90 in baby teeth. The following year *Consumer Reports* revealed detectable levels of Strontium 90 in cow's milk. That September the *Saturday Evening Post* ran a feature called "Fallout: The Silent Killer," and scientists and physicians warned of leukemia, bone cancer, and long-term genetic alterations. By the end of 1959 a full-blown fallout scare gripped the nation.[38]

In May 1960 Soviet missiles shot down a high-flying American U-2 spy plane that had been photographing missile installations. The incident doomed the Geneva Summit Conference and with it hope of reducing the international arms buildup. While Carson was finishing her preface, diplomatic tensions escalated between East and West over control of West Germany. Closer to home, the bilateral agreements between the Soviet Union and the new Communist leader Fidel Castro in Cuba heightened the danger of nuclear confrontation. Evidence that the Soviets were shipping offensive weapons to Cuba made Americans feel vulnerable. Bomb-shelter building boomed in communities across the country. With wailing warning sirens and radio alerts a common occurrence, civil defense became a national preoccupation.[39]

While writing about the potentially deadly threat of one contaminant, Carson was acutely aware of its similarity to the type of deadly pollution that had gripped the public imagination. In August 1945 *Time* had published pictures of the first atomic bomb explosion in Alamagordo, New Mexico, alongside a report announcing DDT as the ultimate weapon in the war on insects. Now, fifteen years later, Carson drew similar parallels between the effects of atomic radiation and those of synthetic chemical pesticides. The two products of wartime science were forever linked in discovery, destruction, and debate.[40]

Paul Brooks was quick to see the publishing advantages inherent in Carson's comparison of pesticides and radiation. He told her, "the parallel between effects of chemicals and effects of radiation is so dramatic that people can't help getting the idea. In a sense, all this publicity about fallout gives you a head start in awakening people to the dangers of chemicals."[41]

During the fall Carson worked steadily, revising and incorporating the suggestions of the experts who had commented on her chapters. She had another long meeting with Wilhelm Hueper before he left for some months abroad. Hueper's reaction inspired her to tackle another revision of the cancer material, and by the end of September she felt it was much tighter and included constructive ideas for reform. She sent the revised chapter on birds to George Wallace and then to Paul Brooks.[42]

Carson was still trying out new titles in the hope that one would strike her. William O. Douglas's stinging dissent in the Long Island spraying case, which editor Norman Cousins published in the *Saturday Review of Literature*, suggested to Carson that *Dissent in Favor of Man* had some merit as a title and proposed it to Brooks, who did not think it had the right ring. He did, however, suggest that "Silent Spring" might be a good title for the bird chapter. Carson liked his idea but was more frustrated that she did not have a suitable title for the book.[43]

Carson found time that fall to work for the election of John F. Kennedy. At Agnes Meyer's urging, Carson had been invited to serve on the Natural Resources Committee of the Democratic Advisory Council. She accepted the invitation because she hoped a new Democratic administration would pay more attention to the problems of toxic pollution and force changes in the research priorities of government, industry, and agriculture. "But," she explained to the committee chairman, "my participation will have to be limited, because of temporary health problems and especially because of very heavy writing commitments. However, I do sincerely wish to do all I can."[44]

In early June she had outlined the issues she considered essential that the committee consider, mentioning pollution control, radioactive contamination of the sea, chemical poisoning of the environment, preservation of natural areas, and passage of the Wilderness Bill. Faulting the present administration for its eradication programs, Carson specifically recommended consultation with all those affected by spraying before undertaking any control program, suspension of any program if adequate research had not been conducted into the effects of the chemicals under the proposed conditions of use, and a new direction in research from development of new chemicals to alternatives to chemical control.[45]

Carson's ideas and language found their way into the committee's report on pollution control, which was largely written by film producer Pare Lorentz, whose conservation views Carson had long admired. The committee recommended the establishment of a Bureau of Environmental Health within the U.S. Public Health Service, which would be given regulatory jurisdiction over "our one imperative resource: the environment in which all of us live."[46]

Carson's enthusiasm for the creation of such an agency was evident in a letter she wrote to Lorentz. "I do not suppose any legislation relating to a Bureau of Environmental Health will be introduced by either side during August for I imagine effort will be concentrated on subjects that are more to the fore in the public mind. However, I do hope the next regular session may see some action." The Pollution Committee report, "Resources for the People," was submitted to John F. Kennedy in October.[47]

Agnes Meyer was also instrumental in naming Rachel to the Women's Committee for New Frontiers, which convened its only meeting at the Georgetown home of Senator and Mrs. Kennedy in October. One of forty-seven women leaders from a variety of fields including former Labor Secretary Frances Perkins and former First Lady Eleanor Roosevelt, Carson was deeply impressed by the caliber of the discussion and the poise and intelligence of Jacqueline Kennedy.

In acknowledgment of Carson's contributions to the committee, the Democratic National Committee sent her an invitation to the Distinguished Ladies Inaugural Reception at the National Gallery of Art in January, which she attended, and to the Inaugural Ball, which she did not. She also received a personal thank-you note from John F. Kennedy, which particularly impressed Roger.[48]

For Rachel, life was very focused during the fall of 1960. She had no time to read, or do anything that was not related to the book. The pressure as well as the press of time lent a sense of urgency to her work and to her thinking. Writing to Dorothy in October, Rachel was nostalgic about the past, which now, in retrospect, seemed more carefree. "I suppose as I grow older and become more aware that life is not only uncertain but short at best, the sense of urgency grows to press on with the things I need to say—things that may be less important than I think, but to me at least it is necessary that they be said. But I do think back with a bit of nostalgia, darling, to the times when this urgency seemed less. I like to *remember* at least, days when I spent a whole morning (or more!) writing a leisurely letter to you."[49]

With the big chapters complete, most of Carson's attention focused on alternative methods of pest control and specifically on Edward F. Knipling's research on biological controls. Knipling, who was now chief of the USDA's Entomology Research Branch, had worked at the Orlando Laboratory when the earliest experiments with DDT had been conducted. He was committed to the effectiveness of chemical pesticides, but in the early 1950s he also became interested in the biological challenges posed by insect resistance and embarked on a research program that aimed at total population management of insects through the sterilization and release of large numbers of males. By 1958 Knipling had carried out successful field tests using sterilized screwworm flies.[50]

Carson was intrigued by his research and visited his Beltsville laboratory several times, meeting with Knipling's assistant, Clarence Hoffman. She became convinced that if the basic research funds could be found, biological controls, particularly insect sterilization, offered one of the most promising alternatives to chemical pest management.[51]

By November Paul Brooks was wondering whether there was any chance that Carson could finish in time to publish the following summer. Carson scribbled a definitive no on Brooks's letter but sent him the revised cancer chapters as a consolation. She planned to attend the American Geographical Society dinner in late November, where Robert Cushman Murphy was delivering the Bowman Lecture on oceanography, and made arrangements to meet with Marie and Paul to go over the manuscript the day after. Before then Rachel hoped to finish revising the herbicide chapter, inserting material she had received from Justice Douglas, Frank Egler, and conservationist Olaus Murie. But at the last moment she was unable to make the trip.[52]

Paul and Marie met at Marie's office and went over the material that Rachel had sent them, each making notes on the copy to return. Paul made extensive editorial notes; Marie condensed hers in a letter. "In general," she wrote, "Paul and I agreed that when it was good, it was very, very good, and when it was not, it was difficult!" Both Rodell and Brooks thought that "the scientific word should be avoided whenever possible" and that the biggest problem was to simplify.[53]

Marie also thought the bird chapter read beautifully. "I wonder," she wrote Rachel, "if 'Silent Spring' mightn't make a title for the whole book?" Ever sensitive to the politics of Carson's writing, Rodell reminded her that "the references to and comments about the chemical companies need to be phrased very carefully not to set up a counter-reaction in the readers. We must at all costs avoid giving anyone the opportunity to yell 'crank'." All in all, Marie thought the book was shaping up impressively. "The problems you have had to cope with in making all this understandable and readable for the layman are of course ferocious, but it seems to me you are accomplishing it in most of the copy."[54]

Carson's absence from the editorial meeting in New York came as the result of her discovery in late November of a "curious, hard swelling, on the 3rd or 4th rib on the operated side, near the junction with the sternum." At first she was not sure it was anything, but after ten days, the swelling became obvious enough to send her back to Dr. Healy and then to the surgeon. X rays taken just before Thanksgiving showed a hard, immovable mass between the rib and the skin. Both doctors professed to be puzzled by it, but without further diagnostic work of any sort, they recommended she begin radiation therapy.[55]

Telling Dorothy what the X rays had revealed and that she would start treatment the next day, Rachel wrote, "The time this represents now when it is all so precious is of course horribly frustrating. But naturally there is no choice. Well, I shall believe the x-ray therapy will take care of this, and I shall try to cross no more bridges at this time. Of course it is true that I thought a door had been closed last spring, and now it has opened a little or so it seems."[56]

Carson had two radiation treatments on November 28 and 29 and "promptly became ill with what was at first thought to be either an unexpected reaction or the flu." She spent the next week in bed with fever, aching, and nausea, becoming so ill that she asked her sister-in-law, Vera Carson, to spend the nights with her.[57]

Confined to bed, Carson had time to think about the whole sequence of medical events and concluded that she had made decisions regarding her treatment too hastily the previous spring. She decided she did not want to resume any further radiation treatment until she had a thorough evaluation by someone else. As she later explained to Brooks: "My doctors still tried to keep me in the dark by pretending to be puzzled, but did recommend radiation. I had actually started treatment just before I got flu. But by that time I was beginning to realize the deception, and while laid up with flu did a lot of thinking, the result of which was a decision that I wanted a more skilled judgement brought to bear on the problem than any then concerned with it." In early December she wrote to George (Barney) Crile, the cancer specialist at the Cleveland Clinic, whom she had first met during her book tour for *The Sea Around Us*, describing her medical history and asking his opinion on how to proceed.[58]

Rachel told Crile that she was reluctant to begin treatment at the George Washington University clinic, which had been recommended, because she knew the clinic had a grant from the National Institutes of Health to study chemotherapy and that its doctors therefore were eager to try out chemicals. "I want to do what must be done," she told Crile, "but no more. After all, I still have several books to write, and can't spend the rest of my life in hospitals."[59]

After talking with Crile on the telephone, Rachel decided to fly to the Cleveland Clinic for an evaluation. Crile asked her to have her doctors send her medical records including operative notes and pathology reports. Only then did Dr. Healy admit in a notable understatement, "Dr. Sanderson did not tell Miss Carson that she had a malignancy, but said that she had a condition bordering on a malignancy. Because of her being informed that there was no malignancy, her present management is quite difficult."[60]

After settling Roger with their favorite neighbors, the Newtons, Rachel left for Cleveland in the midst of a fierce winter snowstorm that closed schools, froze the water pipes in her house, and left her stranded on a snowy street for over an hour waiting for a cab to the airport. After two days at the clinic, Crile confirmed to Carson that she had cancer and that it had metastasized to other lymph nodes. He recommended that she begin radiation therapy to the affected site only. But since she was still menstruating at age fifty-three, he directed that first she undergo sterilization by radiating the ovaries. Crile wrote Dr. Healy, "In the first place, I have discussed with her quite frankly what the situation is, pointing out that we view a tumor in lymph nodes as being local disease and do not think that it should be treated at this stage with chemotherapy or with wide field radiation therapy."[61]

The truth liberated Rachel to tap her strength, for now she could react as a scientist as well as a victim. She told Crile:

> Your kind of mind combines everything I wanted, and it would be hard to express fully the feeling of relief I have now that the direction of the treatment is in your hands. You smiled when I suggested that medicine could ever be scientific, but one of the things I appreciate in you, and one of the things I mean by "scientific," is

> your awareness of what is *not* known and your unwillingness to rush in with procedures that may disrupt that unknown but all-important ecology of the body cells. I appreciate, too, your having enough respect for my mentality and emotional stability to discuss all this frankly with me. I have a great deal more peace of mind when I feel I know the facts, even though I might wish they were different.[62]

Following Carson's wishes, Crile bypassed the radiologist at the Washington Clinic. Unable to get her into an experimental protocol at NIH, he settled on Dr. Ralph Caulk of the Washington Hospital Center as Carson's chief radiologist. Carson was sterilized and started the first series of ten radiation treatments in late January.[63]

By then the mass was receding, which indicated to the doctors that the tumor was endocrine-dependent. The radiation caused her ulcer to flare up, increasing her general discomfort. Carson looked forward to a visit from Dorothy just after the holidays when they could be together and talk about all that had happened since they left Maine in September. A note to Dorothy, probably slipped under her bed pillow on the first night of her visit to Silver Spring, quoted a stanza from poet William Blake that Rachel took particular comfort from:

> *To see the world in a grain of sand,*
> *And a heaven in a wild flower;*
> *Hold infinity in the palm of our hand,*
> *And eternity in an hour.*[64]

They needed to talk of death, and so they managed, at first hesitantly, but then honestly and lovingly. They spent hours reading by the fire, listening to music, and, as Rachel wrote in the note she left for Dorothy to read on the train, "a chance to share each other's thoughts and in their light to exorcise any lurking dark spirits."[65]

Rachel confided her medical situation quite candidly to Paul Brooks just after Christmas. "As far as the present trouble is concerned, there is a pretty good chance that it will be brought under control, at least temporarily, perhaps permanently. Of course the fact that the original tumor had metastasized means that other trouble *can* develop, but not necessarily that it will. As to what all this does to me and my work—for another week or more, and again when treatment is resumed, pretty serious diversion of time and capacity for work because there are some side effects. But in the intervals I hope to work hard and productively. Perhaps even more than ever, I am eager to get the book done." Rachel hoped Paul could come to Washington soon to work with her a little, telling him "I am so aware I need help seeing the wood in all this forest of trees. Maybe it always has to be written 'wrong' first and improved only through repeated revisions, but I keep hoping to find a more direct way for the chapters still to be written. In any event, your suggestions are always helpful to me—much more so than those of anyone else."[66]

Rachel confided to Paul that Marie, who had been in Europe on business, did not know this latest news yet and that she had been reluctant to tell her, but had finally decided she should. "After all, there is much that is hopeful in my case, and certainly now that I've had a chance to make some decisions for myself, I'm in excellent hands." But, she cautioned Brooks, "As far as other people are concerned, Paul, I don't want to have it discussed at all. Any such facts about a writer are immediately spread about in such a way that is most distasteful to me."[67]

Her spirits lifted by Dorothy's visit, Rachel felt well enough to attend the Inaugural Reception and made plans to take Roger with her to California in February, when she hoped to fulfill her long-overdue commitment to speak at Scripps College in Claremont, California. Afterward she wanted to visit Lois Crisler in Colorado. Dorothy felt it was a mistake for Rachel to think about taking Roger and offered to stay with him while Rachel traveled. But Rachel explained, "You know that I can see many reasons for a hopeful attitude, but you also know that I have faced all the possibilities. Out of that has come, I think, a deepened awareness of the preciousness of whatever time is left, be it long or short, and a desire to live more affirmatively, making the most of opportunities when they are offered, not putting them off for another day." She wanted to take Roger because it was a chance to give him the gift of a memory he could keep. "If it must be that his world has to be shattered again before he reaches manhood," Rachel told Dorothy, "at least I want while there is time to share as many 'wonders' as possible with him."[68]

The same awareness of time pervaded Dorothy's long letter to Rachel at the end of January. She wrote movingly about the ways in which Rachel had enriched her life and made her realize the depth of love she held for her own family and the wonder of finding a kindred spirit with whom she could share the things of the inner spirit.[69]

Rachel needed all of Dorothy's tender reassurance, for she had barely begun to cope with the regime of radiation when she was assaulted by a series of increasingly serious ailments. It began innocuously enough with a minor bladder irritation that became more severe; a culture showed a hemolytic staphylococcus. Two days after she began a course of antibiotics, she developed severe phlebitis in both legs; just as treatment was beginning to have an effect, her right knee and left ankle became inflamed and painful to the point that she was unable to walk or stand. Confined to bed or to a wheelchair, she began weekly hydrocortisone injections to the affected joints.[70]

Rachel attempted to keep up a good front for Roger, but the staph infection was a serious one and reminded her of Marjorie's death just four years earlier from the same ailment. Carson confided to Dorothy that on one afternoon she had slept heavily and awoke feeling "so indescribably weak and ill that I was frightened. I just had the feeling that at that moment life had burned down to a very tiny flame, that might so easily flicker out. I didn't want Ida to know how bad I felt (we were then marooned in a blizzard) but I kept her near me on some pretext. She rubbed me with alcohol, later got me some tea, and in a few hours strength was somehow coming back—and since then the trend has been up."[71]

The staphylococcus infection had settled in her joints. Dr. Healy and Dr. Darrell Crain, a specialist in arthritic disease, decided that given the inclement winter weather and the difficulty Rachel had traveling, it would be easier if she spent a couple days in the hospital where they could begin physical therapy on her joints and continue the radiation treatments.[72]

Carson went by ambulance to the Washington Hospital Center on February 12 and remained there for the next six days, returning home for Roger's ninth birthday on the eighteenth. Jeanne Davis visited several times garnering a pile of dictation, but Rachel was too ill to do any other work. During Carson's hospitalization, Roger and the cats went again to the Newtons after school, and then Ida, Mrs. Tenney, and Mary Hays, who had worked for Rachel and her mother, took turns spending the night with him. By the end of her stay, Rachel was halfway through the radiation treatments, but her joints reacted badly to heat treatments and to physical therapy, both of which were abandoned. Dr. Crain changed his diagnosis to acute infectious arthritis.[73]

After Rachel went home, she still faced a daily round trip to the hospital for radiation, a schedule that she maintained through the beginning of March. By then she was able to get around with a walker, but it had been five weeks since she was first stricken and, during most of that time, she had been too ill to do more than think about the book. She told Dorothy, "In the occasional intervals when my mind can rise above all this and *think*, I've tried to see how I could revamp the whole concept of the book to something much shorter and simpler. That may be the answer, when I can ever be creative enough in mind and strong enough in body to do it."[74]

Although outwardly resigned to a long convalescence, Rachel was inwardly in great distress and enormously frustrated. "Time flows on in such a monotonous way," she wrote Dorothy in a particularly vulnerable moment, "and as I've already told you, I daren't think ahead. When I do, a little, I feel I'll fly into a million pieces!" She was not even brightened much by the publication on February 23 of the revised edition of *The Sea Around Us*. But she was touched by a letter from oceanographer Henry Bigelow, who expressed his pleasure at the unexpected honor of having Carson dedicate the new edition to him. Her dedication read: "To Henry Bryant Bigelow who by precept and example has guided all others in the exploration of the sea."[75]

As signs of spring appeared through the snow in her yard, Rachel experienced mixed emotions. She explained to Dorothy:

> You know my high hopes for the goal I might reach by March—hopes I entertained last October! After that conversation with Paul Brooks when we laid out a schedule, I said to you one night on the phone, "I feel I *can* do it—if only nothing happens!" Now I look back at the complete and devastating wreckage of those plans—not only no writing for months but the nearly complete loss of any creative feeling or desire. I'm reminded of a quotation that has stuck in my mind since college days . . . "When the lamp is shattered, the light in the dust lies ahead."[76]

Occasionally she felt stirrings of a desire to sit down and get at the book again, but as she neared the end of her radiation treatments, often she was quite nauseated and slept a great deal of the time between treatments. She told Dorothy, "I sometimes have a feeling (maybe 100% wishful thinking) that perhaps this long period away from active work will give me the perspective that was so hard to attain, the ability to see the woods in the midst of the confusing multitude of trees. But the thought of continued long work on it, and at the expense of other things I want to write, is hard to bear."[77]

As the weather improved, Rachel often sat for a time in Jeanne's car after returning from her treatments enjoying the sunshine, the warm air, and the birdsong. Her garden was coming into spring bloom, but she could not walk about outside unassisted to see the bulbs open. She was reminded of a favorite passage in Richard Jeffries's "Hours of Spring," when he also wondered how spring could be happening without him. "Each spring is so precious," she told Dorothy. "I wanted this one, and feel cheated."[78]

When the longer than anticipated radiation treatments were finally over in early March, Rachel began to feel better. Only her painful knee and ankles remained unresponsive. Her mood was understandably bleak, and Dr. Crain gave her little hope that she would be walking anytime soon. She confided to Dorothy, "Of course I really don't know and I suppose no one does, how much it is going to interfere with my doing the things I love to do. I wonder, for example, whether I will walk on my beach this summer or even sit under the spruce!"[79]

It must have been during this time, after a fitful night, that she wrote a plaintive note in one of her small research notebooks that she kept beside her bed. Most of its pages were filled with notes on insecticides, but suddenly there is a page on which Carson had written, "I moan inside—and I wake in the night and cry out silently for Maine. I prayed very graciously to God that he would make it a nice day." The next page continues with her scientific notes. Some pages later is a handwritten ledger of her financial holdings, including her investments, real estate, retirement, insurance, and royalties made in an effort to calculate her current net worth. Both entries testify to Carson's emotional suffering during these months and to her despair.[80]

Dr. Crain was at a loss as to what to propose next. His diagnosis alternated between a staph infection and infectious rheumatoid arthritis. Rachel told Dorothy, "He is talking about the possibility of 'trying to speed things up' by using intra muscular injections of gold. I don't like this prospect much from what I know of it, and am not going to agree without some further investigation. . . . One of the possible toxic effects is depression of bone marrow, and I think my marrow has had enough abuse via radiation for the present."[81]

Carson was rightfully skeptical. Confiding her feelings to Dorothy

Algire, she asked her friend to see what she could find out about such a protocol. Crain's vacillating diagnosis disturbed Carson, for she realized he did not know why the membrane inflammation persisted. Her scientific training made her suspicious of being a guinea pig for any procedure. She wrote Dorothy Freeman: "I've already had a taste of having to submit to something I knew was dangerous and in theory undesirable (the radiation) but there the alternative left no choice. Here I feel I'd rather endure some arthritis than gamble with the bone marrow." Feeling solitary and alone, Rachel confessed she was "just spilling out to my dear one the occasional thoughts of the dark hours, but in general things are so much better than they might be. And I have you to love and be loved by."[82]

After talking to a scientist at NIH, Jeanne Davis reported that Crain's diagnosis of rheumatoid arthritis was very questionable. Rachel felt vindicated when Dorothy Algire read her the section on gold in the most recent pharmacology reference. It contained a specific statement that gold was contraindicated for anyone who had recently undergone a course of radiation. Crain had certainly been aware of this contraindication, yet he had recommended gold injections. Emboldened, Rachel stood her ground with him and would not consent to the treatment. She complained to Dorothy, "Yet this man, knowing perfectly well I'd just had radiation, was quite ready to give it to me. What this does to my already great cynicism about doctors you can perhaps imagine."[83]

At the end of March, Rachel learned that Marie had not informed Paul Brooks of Carson's newest medical complications. Telling Brooks that she was beginning to be able to get back to work in a limited way, Rachel reflected: "About the only good thing I can see in all this experience is that the long time away from close contact with the book may have given me a broader perspective which I've always struggled for but felt I was not achieving. Now I'm trying to find ways to write it all more simply and perhaps more briefly and with less exhaustive detail. Later, when I have enough in this new vein to make it worth while, I hope you can come down and talk it over."[84]

Rachel was finding that every day she was able to be somewhat less confined. "April will bring a new month and a new year," she told Dorothy, "for it was just a year ago I entered the hospital and started on a road I'd rather not have taken. But perhaps that detour is behind me." She was beginning to drive by herself again. The freedom to go out renewed her, and she was able to send more material off to Brooks, including a revised chapter on cellular biology.[85]

Shirley Briggs spent an evening with Rachel in late May looking at slides of Maine. She found Rachel much stronger than when she had last seen her and able to get about well except for going up and down stairs. Rachel planned to leave for Maine as soon as Roger was out of school. This time Bob Hines would drive them up and stay for a week in a nearby cottage. Roger adored Bob, whom he had known all his life. Hines had a grown-up son but had not forgotten how to entertain little boys. He and Roger planned to do some fishing and exploring so Rachel could work.[86]

All during her confinement, Carson had been anxious about Lois Crisler, worried about her isolation and the little time her rugged lifestyle allowed for her writing. Rachel tried to persuade Lois to apply for a Saxton Foundation grant and offered advice about publishers. The commercial success of Joy Adamson's *Born Free, A Lioness of Two Worlds* and of Gavin Maxwell's *Ring of Bright Water* convinced Carson that Crisler should focus her writing on her relationship with a female wolf named Alatna. She nominated Crisler for one of the grants offered by the National Institute of Arts and Letters, and some months later did persuade Lois to apply for a Guggenheim Foundation grant, writing in support of her friend's application.[87]

As promised, Paul Brooks arrived in Washington for a working visit in early June. The two went over revisions of the two chapters Carson had sent him, but they still struggled over titles. Carson had thought of a possible opening sentence: "This is a book about man's war against nature, and because man is part of nature it is also inevitably a book about man's war against himself." Consequently her new thinking about titles ranged from *The War Against Nature* to *At War with Nature*. Rodell, in mock exasperation, dubbed it, *Carson: Opus #4*. Brooks, apparently forgetting that Marie had already suggested *Silent Spring* as the title, proposed it again himself, arguing that metaphorically it fit the content of the whole book. But Rachel remained unconvinced.[88]

They also continued their earlier discussion of using illustrations rather than photographs to break up the text as well as to illustrate some of the more difficult concepts. Paul promised to gather some artwork for Rachel to consider.[89]

Rachel, Roger, the two cats, and Bob Hines reached Southport, Maine, on June 23. For Rachel, to be back another summer and to be able to walk around, even going gingerly down to her tide pool, was somewhat miraculous. This summer, she allowed few visitors to interrupt her privacy, but she did agree to meet two photographers. One was

Charles Pratt, a young man Marie had discovered, whose photographs of children, the surf, and of tide pools she thought would be perfect for an expanded "Help Your Child to Wonder." The other was Alfred Eisenstaedt, who had been assigned by *Life* magazine to photograph Carson for an essay on American naturalists. When Erich Hartmann reassured her about Eisenstaedt, she agreed to meet with him. So one foggy morning, Carson and Eisenstaedt spent two hours on the Southport shore. She was delighted with the portrait that appeared in *Life* just before Christmas.[90]

There was one visitor, however, Rachel was particularly looking forward to meeting that summer. Ruth Scott, a naturalist from Pittsburgh who was the state bird chairman of the Garden Club Federation of Pennsylvania, wrote Carson just before Rachel left for Maine. Scott and her husband, J. Lewis (Scotty), were going to be at Audubon Camp in Maine. Scott was launching a Roadside Vegetation Management Project in Pennsylvania aimed at educating people about ecological vegetation management and the dangers of using pesticides to kill roadside vegetation. Enormously interested in Scott's work and intrigued by her letter, Carson invited them to stop by on their way home at the end of July.[91]

Ruth Jury Scott had gone to Pittsburgh in the 1930s to study at what was then the Carnegie Institute of Technology. Forced by illness to drop out of college before she finished her degree, Scott made her way as landscape designer as she perfected her already considerable skills as a naturalist. Ruth applied her architectural talents to a small house on the edge of a dramatic ravine overlooking Powers Run, high above the Allegheny River, barely five miles from Springdale, an area she was determined to preserve in its natural state. She married Scotty, a prominent geological engineer for Gulf Oil Company, in the late 1940s, and together they became actively involved in a variety of environmental causes and conservation efforts.[92]

Scott had become a quiet but enormously effective leader in the Federation of State Garden Clubs, an organization she believed capable of educating women in the conservation ethic. By 1961 she had been named to the National Bird Committee. She and Scotty were also deeply involved in National and State Audubon Society activities and in the Nature Conservancy. Scott had conceived of her vegetation management project as a way of educating these organizations about the dangers of pesticides and as a natural project for the garden clubs.[93]

Scott's work in vegetation management and brush control had led her to Frank Egler, who was unusually impressed with her grasp of ecological relationships and her organizational abilities. Egler encouraged Scott to write Carson. "I really feel awed writing to you," Scott wrote, "a great author and naturalist, whose writing is a very real part of my life." Awed but not intimidated, she sent Carson a copy of "Conservation Report #1" that she had prepared to introduce her project to the residents of Pennsylvania.[94]

Carson sensed that Ruth Scott was a special person. It did not take much conversation to realize that they shared the same view of the natural world and were committed to the same causes. Carson admired Scott's energy and her organizational abilities. Ruth's manner particularly endeared her to Rachel. Soft-spoken, calm, and self-effacing, Scott had a quick mind, a lively wit, a ready laugh, and an ability to appraise people and their gifts with unerring accuracy. Carson sensed in Scott, both at their meeting in Maine and in their later correspondence, enormous strength of character and instinctive political awareness. "I have worked hard on the pesticide issue," Ruth had written Rachel in her first letter. "There are such powerful adversaries: the U.S. Department of Agriculture and the business empires and the ever-increasing practice of monoculture." Carson soon found that Scott's network of connections in the naturalist community were almost as broad as her own and included many of the same people. Scott quickly became part of Carson's small inner circle of friends.[95]

Among Scott's talents was an easy rapport with children. Childless, both she and her husband loved young people, and their interests in naturalist education were directed especially to children. Whenever the Scotts visited Rachel and Roger in Southport, it was a happy day for the boy. Ruth and Scotty recognized Roger's loneliness and drew him into their conversation and their explorations. Ruth later sent him postcards and pictures, and Scotty sent him rock samples, thereby becoming a particular favorite of Roger's.[96]

After that initial visit, Rachel and Ruth wrote each other and talked on the telephone frequently about vegetation management, the dangers of herbicides, and a wide range of conservation issues. Carson sent a copy of Scott's bulletin to Irston Barnes, telling him she thought it a model for other Audubon societies. She sent Scott citations that helped her get her project through various organizational hurdles and suggested ways to approach the Garden Club Federation about the misuse of pesticides at their annual meeting.[97]

For her part, Scott was crucial in convincing a reluctant Frank Egler to change his emphasis on the toxicity of 2,4-D, and 2,4,5-T and its potential danger to wildlife in a bulletin he had written for distribution by the National Audubon Society. Scott had been behind the Audubon decision to publish a statement on herbicides and after visiting Carson, she had a brief visit with Egler. Between Scott and Carson, Egler agreed to reconsider his statement. It was an important issue, one that showed just how advanced Carson's views were on the issue of toxicity.[98]

As their friendship progressed, Scott's organizational skills as well as her ties to conservation organizations and leaders became increasingly important to Carson. Scott's early collisions with hostile entomologists from the State Extension Service provided invaluable lessons to Carson. Her successful efforts to restrain the state from spraying DDT against Dutch elm disease in an area that was almost literally over the hill from Carson's childhood home in Springdale not only endeared her to Carson but demonstrated Scott's political acumen.[99]

Rachel worked steadily most of the summer. Being in Maine always had an energizing effect on her, and this summer was no exception. She told Lois Crisler, "I feel really over the hump now—there remain only two new chapters to do, plus of course a lot of final revision. There has been good solid progress this summer and at last it moves with its own momentum."[100]

She and Dorothy took walks in their Lost Woods, rejoicing in the song of the hermit thrush, the olive-backs, and of course the veeries. At the end of the year, Rachel recalled the summer's special moments, "the memory of the veery's song in the green dusk by the little church was one of our high points . . . that and the fog on the beach. And we shall add many more memories in '62 when my infirmities are even farther in the past." News of Beverly Knecht's death that summer lent her time at Southport a special poignancy.[101]

At the end of August, Marie Rodell joined Rachel and Roger in Southport. Marie had been thinking about the title problem too and still thought that *Silent Spring* suited the book very well. In an effort to persuade Rachel, Marie had done her literary homework. She found some lines from the English Romantic poet John Keats's poem "La Belle Dame Sans Merci" that amplified the title *Silent Spring* beautifully. The lines were: "The sedge is wither'd from the lake,/And no birds sing." Rachel acquiesced. And so finally the book became *Silent Spring*.[102]

Secure in her research and in her conclusions, Carson took the risk of going public on two occasions during that summer. The first came in response to Paul Brooks's request for something to "brandish" before his town meeting where DDT spraying against mosquitoes was again under consideration. Rachel's public letter summarized how self-defeating chemical spraying was, and how, after causing irrevocable ecological damage, all one got for the trouble was a new generation of chemically resistant mosquitoes. After listening to Carson's opinions, the Lincoln town meeting again rejected the proposal for DDT spraying.[103]

About a month later a column by Sidney Baldwin on the need to save trees from pests, published in the local paper, the *Boothbay Register*, provoked Carson to add a few thoughts. The fact that she took the time to write the letter in itself testifies to her improved stamina, but she exhibited a certain naïveté in thinking that her views on pesticides would be confined to readers of this small community newspaper.[104]

Carson first attacked the assumption that pesticide spraying was a cure for unhealthy, diseased trees, citing examples from Greenwich, Connecticut, and Toledo, Ohio, where spraying against Dutch elm disease had only made insect infestation worse. She suggested some alternatives to "drenching the landscape with highly lethal sprays, such as insect pathogens, insect predators and parasites and other biological methods that would cost much less than the money poured into chemical control."[105]

"Our choice is not, then, the stark and simple one: 'Shall we have birds or shall we have trees?' " Carson wrote. "If we continue our present methods we shall probably end with neither. If, on the other hand, an informed and aroused public demands it, we can turn our resources and talents to the development of methods that accomplish control without raining death and destruction on all living things." Her article produced a flood of letters from the Boothbay area, most of them strongly in support of her position and many wanting more information. The wire services picked up her letter, provoking publicity and correspondence Rachel had not intended or wanted. She admitted her error of judgment to Audubon executive Charles Callison, who wanted to publicize her book further: "To write as I did for a small and local paper seemed deceptively harmless and I should have known better."[106]

Back in Silver Spring in early September, having made the return trip without Bob Hines's help, Carson sensed that she was nearing the end and pushed herself hard. She wrote Dorothy:

> I am working late at night most of the time now. If I can fight off the desire to go to bed around 11:30 I seem to get my second wind and be able to go on. This chapter [on synthetic chemicals] has been very difficult but by now I understand myself and my way of working well enough to know I'm over the hump and it is now all fitting together about as it should. But with any chapter that presents difficult problems, as this one does, there is first a period when nothing moves and then it is hard not to be discouraged. What underlies the most important part of this chapter is a whole field of the most technical and difficult biology—discoveries only recently made. How to reveal enough to give understanding of the most serious effects of the chemicals without being technical, how to simplify without error—these have been problems of rather monumental proportions.[107]

Marie and Paul had lunch again in New York in early September. Paul was relieved that Rachel's health had improved and was pleased with her progress and choice of title. After considering several illustrators, he proposed hiring Louis and Lois Darling to do the illustrations for *Silent Spring*.

The Darlings were coauthors and coillustrators of a number of successful books in the biological sciences. Louis Darling had been a photographer, commercial artist, and landscape painter, and Lois, a biologist and illustrator of a number of natural science books, was on the staff at the Department of Paleontology at the American Museum of Natural History in New York. The couple lived in Westport, Connecticut, where they were neighbors and good friends with the ornithological illustrator Roger Tory Peterson. At Peterson's insistence the Darlings had placed their latest book with Houghton Mifflin. They had just finished *Bird*, an illustrated history of the evolution of birds with a foreword by Peterson, when Brooks approached them about Carson's book.[108]

Rachel had looked at some of the Darlings' drawings during the summer but was unexcited. She found their work "beautiful and meticulous," but she was uncertain those were the qualities she had in mind. Dismayed by Carson's lukewarm reaction, Brooks wrote her again in early October to ask her to look at the page proofs for *Bird*, just to make certain that they were not missing a good thing.[109]

By that time, without another illustrator whose work she liked any better, Carson agreed to have Brooks propose the project to the Darlings. Paul reported that Louis had been most enthusiastic. "The fact that he understands and cares about the issues involved is obviously all to the good," Paul wrote.[110]

The Darlings agreed to provide illustrations for chapter headings as well as a number of illustrations and decorations throughout the text. Most of these would have to wait until the text was in galley form so that drawings could be made to scale. But they sent a tentative list of twenty or so ideas for Carson to consider. Although she liked Lois and Louis when she met them, for some reason she was never much taken with their style or impressed with their creative imagination.[111]

After reading Carson's text, the Darlings, especially Louis, had equal reservations about their joint venture. Lois recalled later that Louis told Brooks, "We'll do it, of course, because Rachel Carson wrote the book, but it is bound to be a flop." He was afraid Carson had overextended her evidence and was simply inviting a damaging scientific backlash. He wondered aloud to Lois just "who would want to read it?" To which Lois, whose vision extended farther than her husband's, replied, "Anyone who ever held a spray can, and we all have."[112]

Paul Brooks held the collaborative effort together, reassuring the Darlings of the book's certain commercial success on the one hand and trying to impress upon an impatient Carson how difficult it was to conceptualize her material. In the end, Carson agreed to use the Darlings' illustrations only as chapter headings and on the title page.[113]

Rachel had revised most chapters and was working on the "fable for tomorrow," with which the book opens, by late fall. Her decision to begin a book on the ecology of pesticides with a brief story or fable had come to her as she gathered evidence of the havoc pesticides had played in particular places around the country. Its advantage as a literary device was apparent after she realized that the first chapter, which at one time was entitled "The Rain of Death," might be too serious and scientific to capture the nonscientific reader. She could choose from hundreds of case histories and anecdotes from individuals who had written to her, but the particular devastation that strikes "a town in the heart of America" was a composite of many stories and many towns.[114]

Rachel's experience growing up in Springdale, Pennsylvania, was embedded in the fable and in her decision to write it. It too had once been a little town nestled on the banks of a clean, beautiful river surrounded by prosperous farmlands and hillsides of blooming orchards, and later it was devastated by the pollution of an earlier technology but with the same human carelessness as beset the town in Carson's fable. She was also struck by two articles she had found. One by the naturalist writer and Audubon magazine editor John K. Terres, published in the *New Republic* and titled "Dynamite in DDT," described the death of songbirds in Moscow, Pennsylvania, after the town had been sprayed with DDT. The other was a guest editorial by the well-known writer Mark Van Doren in *Saturday Review* questioning the contemporary belief in the supremacy of science.[115]

Carson's first version of the fable gave the town a name, Green Meadows, and centered on a young man who returned after some years' absence only to find the town devastated by illness and ecological havoc. Brooks thought the name Green Meadows sounded like a real estate development rather than a real community. Carson rewrote the fable making it clear that the town was a composite of many real communities, eliminated the young man, and became its narrator.[116]

In retrospect, it was inevitable that Carson's improved physical condition could not continue indefinitely. But it was perhaps cruelest of all that she was assaulted again as she reached the last stages of revision of the book and had glimpsed its end. In November Carson developed severe iritis, an inflammation of the iris of the eye. Unable to read or to tolerate light and in terrible pain, she spent two weeks nearly sightless and completely unable to work.[117]

She took Roger and went to the Freemans for Thanksgiving, wanting to give him some holiday pleasure and find comfort herself. For the next month she could barely see to work at all. As Rachel reclined on the chaise in her office, Jeanne read the chapters to her, making corrections on the copy as they went along, but Rachel was frustrated beyond imagination.

By early January she could work several hours without pain, but that was all. In a letter to Dorothy, she recalled their bittersweet visit the year before and the premonitions that had haunted them then.

> Yes, there is quite a story behind *Silent Spring*, isn't there? Such a catalogue of illnesses! If one were superstitious it would be easy to believe in some malevolent influence at work, determined by some means to keep the book from being finished. Some of the earlier things have been more serious, but I don't think anything has been frustrating and maddening in quite the same way as this iritis. And of course having the end in sight when it struck makes it, in a way, all the worse. I just creep along, a few hours a day. And I know that before I can happily let it go to the printer, there is a tremendous lot of work that only my eyes can do. I have always known I am

> visual minded, and I've certainly been reminded of it now. Having Jeanne read is of such limited help. I have to see it, and on revision I have to keep going over and over a page—with my eyes![118]

Yet Rachel's frustration belies what she was able to create sightless. Forced to listen to her words with a different intensity than she had when her mother read *The Sea Around Us* out loud, Carson altered cadences and rewrote passages. She struggled in a different mode for clarity and simplicity. Who can say what the result would have been, had Carson not been forced to listen with different ears? Tragedy again compelled the process of creative distillation and lent a sharper edge to her prose.[119]

In spite of this latest physical and psychological burden, Rachel's letters to Dorothy were generally positive, her determination to finish against all odds more apparent each day. She derived a certain measure of confidence with every passing week. Referring to revelations of undreamed-of effects from exposure to untested drugs or chemicals that seemed to appear in the newspapers daily, she told Dorothy, "I'm glad all these other things are happening to emphasize that people are ready for the book, and need it now. I, too, think a couple of years ago would have been too soon. But now I know that there are many, many people who are eager to do something and long to be given the facts to fight with."[120]

Toward the end of January 1962, Rachel sent fifteen of the seventeen chapters of her manuscript to Marie, along with a copy for William Shawn at *The New Yorker*. Although she was still revising certain sections and several chapters were being reviewed by experts, the manuscript was complete enough for both editors to read. Sending it off gave Carson time to reflect on her present reality and the dreams she still cherished. She wrote Dorothy:

> Last year as I flew home from Cleveland I thought rather deeply, . . . and I knew then that if my time were to be limited, the thing I wanted above all else was to finish this book. Doing so, not swiftly and easily, but draggingly with the impediments of the arthritis and now the iritis, has been rather like those dreams where one tries to run and can't or to drive a car and it won't go. But now that it seems I shall somehow make this goal, of course I'm not satisfied—now I want time for the *Help Your Child to Wonder* book, and for the big "Man and Nature" book. Then I suppose I'll have others—if I live to be 90 still wanting to say something.[121]

During the summer she had written William Shawn, "The research job has been really tremendous, even bigger than for 'the Sea' but I think the material is quite impressive and should add up to a pretty overwhelming indictment of what man is doing to the earth." Now, six months later, Shawn read the nearly finished manuscript, picked up his telephone, and called Rachel Carson.[122]

" 'This is William Shawn', a mild voice said," according to Rachel's happy recollection of the phone call. She told Dorothy he had described it as "a brilliant achievement," telling her "you have made it literature, full of beauty and loveliness and depth of feeling." Shawn wanted to publish it in the spring, and Rachel experienced "a happy turbulence—aware of course of how very much [was] to be done with last minute checking, but so excited that the time is so close."[123]

But her immediate reaction upon putting down the receiver was more overwhelming than she had been able to express. In a later postscript to the same letter, Rachel revealed her deepest feelings about finishing the book and what Shawn's response had meant to her.

> It was odd—I really had not been waiting breathlessly for Mr. Shawn's reaction, yet once I had it I knew how very much it meant to me. You know I have the highest regard for his judgement, and suddenly I knew from his reaction that my message would get across. After Roger was asleep I took Jeffie into the study and suddenly the tensions of four years were broken and I got down and put my arms around Jeffie and let the tears come. With his little warm, rough tongue he told me that he understood. I think I let you see last summer what my deeper feelings are about this when I said I could never again listen happily to a thrush song if I had not done all I could. And last night the thoughts of all the birds and other creatures and all the loveliness that is in nature came to me with such a surge of deep happiness, that now I *had* done what I could—I had been able to complete it—now it had its own life![124]

For Carson, it was a brief cathartic moment; that was all she allowed herself. Then, her composure restored, she turned her attention to the last chapter and to preparing herself for whatever the publication of *Silent Spring* would bring.

17

"A Solemn Obligation"

"It is a busy time," Rachel wrote Lois Crisler in late January 1962, "with now the added spice of excitement . . . that I have almost reached the end of a long road." She admitted to Lois that she had felt "an enormous surge of relief" after Shawn's call, "as if now I knew the book would accomplish *what I long for it to do.*"

Paul Brooks was excited as well. After reading the whole manuscript in one sitting, he was more impressed than ever with Carson's achievement. He told Rachel, "I cannot imagine anyone else who possesses the combination of scientific understanding and literary skill to make such a fine book out of such difficult and complicated material."[1]

Nonetheless, Brooks was still not satisfied with chapter 3, "Elixirs of Death." "My feeling," he told Carson, "is that this Who's Who of poisons is the one big hurdle that the reader has to face. If he gets over this, the rest of it, despite any technicalities, will be relatively easy going. But if he bogs down here, all will be lost." He made a few minor changes in the first two chapters, primarily omitting some of Carson's introductory material and moving some of her recommendations to the end of the book. But he edited the third chapter heavily, cutting it by half, making it more of a reference chapter. He had it retyped and sent down to Rachel, who rewrote large sections with Brooks's editorial suggestions in mind.[2]

Brooks was understandably worried about the difficulty of enticing the general reader to read a subject that required a certain amount of scientific understanding. "We must get people to read it," he told her, "not just those who already understand the problem, but the thousands and thousands of intelligent persons who would care deeply if they only knew." With this problem in mind, Paul was already working on ways to promote the book and planning for the company sales conference in May. He had written to key individuals, such as Carl Buchheister, president of National Audubon, and Justice William O. Douglas for their suggestions. "This is not an easy book to tell people about," he warned Rachel. "We are going to have to work up something of a crusade—on a local level—if we are to reach a really wide audience."[3]

Deadlines were looming both at *The New Yorker* and at Houghton Mifflin. Still, Rachel hoped by the time she left for Southport in June, the copy editing and page proofs would be done and she could be free of her usual load of books and papers. A second letter to Crisler in early February reveals something of the passion and moral commitment with which Carson had endowed her crusade and her hopes for what the book might accomplish despite her publicly modest claims. It was one of the few times Rachel admitted to being motivated by anger as well as by beauty, a fact that was readily apparent in her choice of language throughout *Silent Spring*.

> No, I myself never thought the ugly facts would dominate, and I hope they don't. The beauty of the living world I was trying to save has always been uppermost in my mind—that, and anger at the senseless, brutish things that were being done. I have felt bound by a solemn obligation to do what I could—if I didn't at least try I could never again be happy in nature. But now I can believe I have at least helped a little. It would be unrealistic to believe one book could bring a complete change.[4]

Marie Rodell went down to Silver Spring for a working weekend, and the two went over the manuscript page by page in preparation for Carson's final revisions. They spent a long time making a preliminary list of people to whom they wanted to send advance copies. They consulted Charles Alldredge, their mutual friend and publicist, who had been so helpful promoting *The Sea Around Us* a decade earlier. Alldredge invited some friends for an informal gathering to meet Rachel and Marie and talk about the new book.[5]

From the beginning, Marie thought that there should be a luncheon in Washington to promote the book among key people and groups that had an obvious interest in reform, and Rachel, Marie, and Charles discussed who might host such an event and whom to invite. Marie wanted advance proofs out to people before *The New Yorker* installments were published and thought it was important for Rachel to meet with Houghton Mifflin publicity director Anne Ford the next time she went to New York.[6]

Rachel and Marie also reviewed copy for the dust jacket. Carson insisted that it establish her scientific credentials. Rachel wanted to include the fact that she had studied genetics with H. S. Jennings and Raymond Pearl at Johns Hopkins and studied radiation as a *cause* of mutation. She also wanted it to mention her early interest in the effects of synthetic pesticides after World War II. Carson drafted some sample copy for Ford: "Her basic interest in all her work has been the relation of life to its environment. In her earlier books, it was life of the seas and the shore; here she is concerned with the problem of how man is progressively making the environment unfit for life."[7]

Rachel remained unenthusiastic about the Darlings' illustrations. After reviewing their latest batch of sketches and rejecting most, she commented to Rodell, "It does seem to me they become less and less imaginative." As for Brooks's suggestion on chapter reorganization, Rodell explained to him after returning to New York that Rachel "is not in favor of the reshuffling of chapters, and has persuaded me that she is right. It is logical for all the chapters to be lumped that say: these are the effects; followed by the chapters that say—and it [the use of pesticides] was all in vain."[8]

From Rodell's letter to Brooks it is clear that she and Rachel had spent considerable time discussing the possibility of libel suits, a subject about which both women were deeply concerned. More than any other person, Rodell knew how financially vulnerable Carson was. It was not just Carson's ongoing concern about Roger's future that caused them disquiet but the unspoken acknowledgment that Rachel might face a long, incapacitating illness during which she would be unable to write. Litigation, even if filed as a form of harassment, would strain her finances, and a serious libel suit would be devastating to an independent writer who paid her own medical insurance and had no institutional affiliation. Rodell conveyed Carson's desire to have the manuscript read for libel by Houghton Mifflin's lawyers and also instructed Brooks to see if there was any such thing as libel insurance for an author.

When Brooks inquired of the firm's counsel, he was told that they had recently acquired libel insurance, but that it carried a $5,000 deductibility clause. There was, apparently, no protection available to the firm's authors.[9]

While Rachel worked on her list of principal sources, which she hoped would satisfy most readers and critics that her conclusions were thoroughly documented and in some sense protect her from frivolous litigation, Marie used the issue of advance copies to assert her direction of the promotion campaign. Once again Charles Alldredge's fine hand is discernible behind Rodell's efforts to bring the book to the early attention of people in a position to push it into the realm of policy debate as well as literary acclaim.

Carson and Rodell were well aware that publishing houses, especially conservative Boston ones, rarely liked to engage in anything that looked like lobbying and preferred to depend on their more predictable publicity channels of book reviewers, syndicated columnists, prestigious serials, and selective but well-placed advertisements to get the word out. Publishers tended to be especially reluctant to spend money sending out proof copies unless they were certain of getting a publishable statement in return. But Rodell and Alldredge had a more aggressive promotion campaign in mind. They wanted to put a copy of *Silent Spring* in the hands of policy makers, cabinet secretaries, White House staff, congressional committee chairmen and their staffs, conservation organization directors, and women's organization leaders.

As a Washington publicist, Alldredge knew the advantages that could come from ensuring support before the battle began. Carson, an old hand at the publicity game in Washington, had no desire to curb Alldredge's enthusiasm so long as promotion was done tastefully by someone unconnected to her. It naturally fell to Marie Rodell to let Houghton Mifflin know that as Rachel's agent, she expected them to market the book aggressively.[10]

Accordingly Marie wrote Anne Ford about what they hoped to accomplish with advance proofs and selective luncheons. Rodell explained that people such as William O. Douglas, Agnes Meyer, Howard Zahniser, and Senator Estes Kefauver had "a certain amount of advance knowledge of the book, and might feel slighted at being allowed to discover the book for themselves when it appears in the *New Yorker*." Douglas, she pointed out, had recently written Carson to inquire when her book would be out and had talked about pesticides in his new book. Rachel had drawn on sources Douglas had given her and had already promised him an advance copy.[11]

Marie was convinced that since Rachel would be attacked as a "crackpot and subversive," a backlog of highly respectable people who had read the book and discussed it would be an enormous help. Such organizations as the Garden Club and the League of Women Voters planned their fall activities well in advance. In order to sell the book to the members of such organizations when it came out, she argued, they had to sell it to the leaders now. Rodell proposed at least one women's luncheon to which important leaders who were familiar with the book would be invited to meet Carson.[12]

Ford was hesitant about hosting a luncheon, but Rodell dismissed her objections, pointing out "as for alerting the lobbyists . . . that will happen with the *New Yorker*—so we might just as well get our ammunition ready ahead." Ford and Brooks acquiesced with some grumbling about the expense of so many proof copies.[13]

By February Carson had sent most of her chapters to scientific experts for comment. Many found nothing they would change and simply said so. She held ongoing discussions with Biskind and Hueper on cancer research and genetic issues, but she was surprised by the kindness of two other scientists whose reviews went far beyond anything she had expected.

Frank Egler read the chapter "Earth's Green Mantle," that dealt with herbicides and roadside spraying, and responded with twelve single-spaced pages. He found no actual errors but pointed out several areas she had omitted and qualified or suggested different wording in other sections. "I am quite overwhelmed at the thought of the hours you must have spent in reading and commenting on my manuscript," Carson wrote the reclusive Connecticut ecologist. "I would never have dreamed of asking you for so much time and I am more grateful than I can say for the very substantial help you have given me."

Egler later recalled being so impressed by Carson's scientific thoroughness and by the precision of her language that he would have done anything to help. When she asked for references on the points he had made, Egler sent her complete copies of all the material she had inquired about. Egler was deeply pessimistic about the attack that he knew industry would launch against such a devastating critique. An old hand at scientific controversy, Egler had spent years battling industry and government over pesticide use on highway and roadside rights-of-way. A gallant gentleman as well as a ferocious intellectual opponent himself, he wanted to spare Carson needless hurt and prepare her for what was to come.[14]

For similar reasons Clarence Cottam, like Egler a veteran of government and industry infighting, also wrote an extensive critique of the four chapters dealing with wildlife that Carson had asked him to review. When he was in town for meetings of the Pesticide-Wildlife Committee working on part 3 of the National Academy of Sciences–National Research Council's (NAS-NRC) highly controversial report entitled "Pest Control and Wildlife Relationships," Rachel invited him to dinner at her house. She wanted Cottam's view of the two parts of the report that had just been published and to discuss his experience as a member of the subcommittee. Cottam found himself in the minority on this committee and was highly critical of the vested interests he found represented by several members, its chairman, and its executive director.[15]

Cottam was as certain as Egler that Carson's book would be subjected to the most critical examination and that she needed to be prepared for a personal attack as well. "Your writing is superb," he told her. "I am certain you are rendering a tremendous public service; yet, I want to warn you that I am convinced you are going to be subjected to ridicule and condemnation by a few. Facts will not stand in the way of some confirmed pest control workers and those who are receiving substantial subsidies from pesticides manufacturers." Certain that she would be especially condemned by operational people in the U.S. Department of Agriculture, Cottam was more critical of her manuscript that he would have been otherwise. In his ten-page comment on each of the four wildlife chapters, he discussed areas where he thought she needed to qualify her position or provide different evidence.[16]

Clarence Tarzwell, chief aquatic biologist for the Public Health Service, was another of Carson's expert readers who served on the Pesticide-Wildlife Committee and shared Cottam's frustration with its deliberations. He read Carson's chapter "Rivers of Death," and found nothing to change and much to commend. He told Carson about recent unpublished evidence that significant levels of DDT had been found in the livers of marine fish taken in the open sea, over one hundred miles from the Pacific coast. Although it was too late to include such evidence in *Silent Spring*, Carson made excellent use of it in her subsequent speeches.[17]

Carson benefited from the critical insights of all these scientists but was especially grateful to those who tried to prepare her for the battle to come. The bitter squabble between scientists on the Pesticide-Wildlife Committee and the publication of parts 1 and 2 of its reports just before *Silent Spring* appeared in *The New Yorker* increased the interest of a powerful group within the scientific and government communities in Carson's book. The controversy made it that much more certain that her book would be scrutinized by those who made recommendations on federal pesticide policy.

Cottam's experience made Carson particularly nervous about her claims that the USDA had tried to discharge several state and federal biologists after they reported wildlife damage as a result of government fire ant control programs. In the end, concerns about her legal vulnerability forced her to make only general comment on political repercussions.[18]

In the midst of last-minute critiques and revision, Rachel returned to Dr. Caulk for her two-month checkup. She had discovered several hard, painful lumps in the lymph glands on her right side. Before submitting to further surgery, she desperately wanted to go to Cleveland to consult with Barney Crile. But she hesitated, fearful of the effect another absence and hospitalization would have on Roger's emotional stability. Dorothy solved the problem by staying with the boy and running the household while Rachel went to the clinic.

Writing to Dorothy on the airplane to Cleveland, Rachel revealed a deeper spirituality than she had previously, sharing the old Scottish blessing she found so comforting. "I want you to know, darling, that I am not afraid. I was yesterday, but that is all behind me. I'm perfectly calm and steady now, and I have real faith that all will be well. So—the Lord bless you and keep you, while we are absent one from another."[19]

Crile's diagnosis was as certain as it was devastating. The biopsy he performed on Carson disclosed gross involvement of the whole mammary chain on her right side. Disdaining further surgery, Crile recommended to Dr. Caulk that he proceed with field radiation of the axilla and supraclavicular region.[20]

The "shadows in the background," as Dorothy referred to Rachel's spreading cancer, had enlarged, but when Rachel returned to Silver Spring, neither of them wanted to talk about them very much. Carson began another indeterminant round of radiation therapy with Caulk in mid-March. She spent most mornings working in bed and went to the hospital in the afternoon. Although she tried to keep her spirits up, she was nauseous by midday, not worth much in the late afternoon or evening, and rightfully worried about the long-term effects of such heavy radiation levels. Her biggest concern was what could be done to offset the radiation effects so she could get back to work.

Rachel shared her ambiguous feelings with Dorothy. "I don't question whether it is the right thing," she wrote forthrightly. "I know that 2-million-volt monster is my only ally in the major battle—but an awesome and terrible ally, for even while it is killing the cancer I know what it is doing to me. That is why it is so hard to subject myself to it each day. That's why I meant I would be happier if I knew less."[21]

Carson's mood was understandably low. "I was thinking today," she told Dorothy in one of the few times she allowed herself to look back, "if only I could set the calendar back two years. It was April 1 I entered the hospital. How differently I would handle it now—how carefully I should select the surgeon. It's hard to see how I could have given so little thought to the possibilities. But there's no use thinking of it now."[22]

Rachel admitted to Dorothy that her spirits were rather "mercurial." One moment she was optimistic and thought of taking impromptu trips to Texas and the Grand Canyon, and even more seriously of taking Roger and driving down to the South Carolina beaches she so loved during his school holidays. The next moment she was teary and completely without courage or hope. But her dogged determination usually resurfaced, allowing her to put her predicament in perspective.[23]

Paul Brooks went down to Silver Spring the first of April to go over final material. Carson had found a wonderful quotation from E. B. White that so accorded with her own views that it fairly begged to be included, along with lines from Keats. Brooks agreed that it was "too perfect to pass up." So it was included as an epigraph. White had written:

> I am pessimistic about the human race because it is too ingenious for its own good. Our approach to nature is to beat it into submission. We would stand a better chance of survival if we accommodated ourselves to this planet and viewed it appreciatively instead of skeptically and dictatorially.[24]

Brooks and Carson spent hours on the bibliography but barely made a dent in the number of titles Carson wanted to include. Helen Phillips, Carson's copy editor, called to tell her that the text would go to the printer the next day and that galleys would be ready in two to three weeks. Inconceivable as it was, the book was finished. "I'm going to celebrate by taking Roger and driving to Myrtle Beach for a few days!" Rachel told Brooks. "But it is quite impossible for me to realize that the book is done."[25]

Carson accepted the final chore and went to the Harris & Ewing Studio in Washington to have a new photograph taken for the book jacket and the sales conference in May. After that ordeal was over, she and her longtime hair stylist, Bea, went over to Elizabeth Arden's on Connecticut Avenue to "investigate wigs." Carson was anticipating the onset of public appearances at which she wanted to look her best, and the treatments had made her hair thin and lifeless. Finding the whole adventure more interesting than depressing, Rachel reported to Dorothy, "I'm in luck, because brown hair is cheapest! Gray is more. (I'll require a sprinkling of gray in mine, but not enough to put it above the $350 price!) It takes up to a month to get one made, so I want to order it next week."[26]

Agnes Meyer had offered to host a luncheon at her mansion in Washington for a few important women on May 14. Carson had been invited to the first White House Conference on Conservation the following week, and even if she did not attend the Houghton Mifflin sales conference in Boston, she had agreed to make a short speech to the Association of Librarians at the end of the month. Her long-awaited appearance as commencement speaker at Scripps College on the West Coast had been set for June 12.

The more Rachel anticipated the public attention that would focus on her, the more determined she was to hide her illness. After a dinner she attended with Clarence Cottam of the National Parks Association trustees where there had been comment about Senator Maurine Neuberger's cancer, Rachel made Dorothy swear to secrecy. She could not bear to think that there would be similar discussions of her condition and had no illusions about how gossip traveled. "You know something of how I feel about this," Rachel wrote her friend, who was on her way to Maine, "but probably not the depth of that feeling. There is no reason even to say I have not been well. If you want or think you need to give any negative report, say I had a bad time with iritis that delayed my work but it has cleared up nicely. And that you *never saw me look better*. Please say that."[27]

Rachel's medical report to Dorothy was upsetting no matter how positively she framed it. "The news is somewhere between my hopes and fears—better than my fears, or some of them, but worse than my hopes.

There is to be no more radiation just now, but soon I'll have to return for another course probably of two weeks duration." Another enlarged and painful node deep in her armpit signaled that the radiation had not been successful in stopping the cancer's spread. She also reported new soreness in her neck and spine. X rays showed nothing new, but that was little comfort. "The trouble with this business," Rachel explained, "is that every perfectly ordinary little ailment looks like a hobgoblin, and one lives in a little private hell until the thing is examined and found to be nothing much." Although she tried to deny it, Rachel was alarmed and wanted Crile's interpretation of this newest advance of the tumor.[28]

With publication in *The New Yorker* just a month away, Shawn was having trouble cutting out enough material to fit into three installments. He proposed extending the series, but Carson was reluctant for several reasons. Chief among them, she explained to Shawn, was her fear that readers would tire of pursuing a subject for longer than three weeks, and "so would miss some of the very important material in the concluding chapters."[29]

There was more editing to do than simply selecting and rearranging text. Bridges and transitions had to be made over cuts, and summaries had to be written for the beginning of each new installment. Robert Gerdy, one of Shawn's top editors, was detailed to help. After several sessions with Gerdy, Rachel came to admire him enormously, referring to him later as "that wonderfully brilliant man at *The New Yorker*." Unknown to Carson, Shawn had also asked wildlife biologist James DeWitt at the Patuxent Research Center to advise him on the scientific aspects of the condensation. Carson had high regard for DeWitt's work and would have been very relieved had she known of his involvement.[30]

Finally, Shawn decided to postpone the series until June 16, which pleased Carson since it would begin that much closer to book publication in September. She hoped, however, that the fact-checking could be completed before June 10, when she would be in California. She told Shawn she wanted to leave for Maine immediately upon her return. Although she did not say so explicitly, she wanted to be unavailable to the press when the first *New Yorker* installment appeared.[31]

Anne Ford at Houghton Mifflin did not learn about the plans for Agnes Meyer's May 14 luncheon until two weeks before the event, when Rachel called to give her a guest list. Carson's original list included Katharine Bain of the Children's Bureau, former Secretary of Labor Frances Perkins, Senator Maurine Neuberger, Congresswoman Leonor Sullivan, and the presidents of such organizations as the League of Women Voters, the National Federation of Women's Clubs, the National Council of Jewish Women, the Garden Clubs of America, the American Association of University Women, and the National Council of Women of the United States. In the end eight women accepted, but each of the sixteen invitees received a proof copy of *Silent Spring*. The group was small and congenial, the luncheon elegantly served, and the discussion heated.[32]

Rachel was pleased with the affair. She found Sylvia Ravitch of the National Council of Women particularly interested in the pesticide issue. Several weeks later Rachel received the first fruit of Meyer's luncheon: an invitation to be the featured speaker at the annual conference of the Council at the Waldorf Astoria Hotel in New York. The prestigious invitation was an indication that women's groups would be interested in efforts to curb the broadcast use of pesticides. Several days later the American Association of University Women asked Carson to attend a meeting of its Committee on Social and Economic Affairs, where the question of consumer protection would be considered.[33]

Although Carson decided not to attend the Houghton Mifflin sales conference in Boston because she was having radiation treatments, she did attend the White House Conference on Conservation convened at President Kennedy's request by Interior Secretary Stewart Udall. Rachel, invited as a distinguished guest, was accompanied by Ruth Scott, who was a delegate from Pennsylvania, and Scott's friend, Interior Department staff publicist Nicki Wilson.[34]

By the time of the White House conference, many delegates had received a proof copy of *Silent Spring* and many more had received personal notes from Houghton Mifflin notifying them of the June 16 issue of *The New Yorker*. Always adept at making connections between people, Ruth Scott saw to it that Rachel talked with Udall and other members of his personal staff as well as with Sierra Club director David Brower. William O. Douglas was there as was Howard Zahniser; both men went out of their way to tell Carson about their reactions to her book.[35]

Paul Knight, a senior member of Stewart Udall's personal staff, telephoned Carson after the conference to ask if he might come out to talk with her. Knight had long been interested in the public communication of scientific ideas, and Udall had assigned him to follow every phase of the book's publication and reception. Working in relative anonymity, Knight believed that by studying the response, he could offer Udall important political information as well as valuable suggestions for public policy. Knight and Carson met for the first time on May 27. Carson was delighted to have him involved in the cause.[36]

At the same time, Paul Brooks received a telephone call from Fred Friendly, the producer of CBS Television's popular news analysis program *CBS Reports*. After Friendly expressed interest in doing a segment on *Silent Spring*, Brooks promised to send him some proofs and told him to contact Marie Rodell.[37]

As the deadline for *The New Yorker* drew near, Carson was enlisted for a review of the final editing, which took her to New York just before she was to leave for California. At the same time she also was trying to finish her speeches for the Association of Librarians and for the Scripps College commencement. The first speech, "Man and Nature in a Chemical Age," was a brief prelude to the themes of the later address. Carson used the occasion to establish the basis of her larger critique against a culture that viewed man and nature as separate and unequal.[38]

Carson intended her Scripps Commencement address, "Of Man and the Stream of Time," as a major statement of her views on humankind's relationship with the natural world. In it Carson offers her understanding of ecology in whole cloth. Although the speech has much that is reminiscent of her discussion of the relationship between humankind and nature in her 1954 Theta Sigma Phi speech "The Real World Around Us," it is the maturity of Carson's moral philosophy that distinguishes the Claremont speech. In it Rachel displays the evolution of her development from nature writer to social critic and advocate of ecology.

"Man has long talked somewhat arrogantly about the conquest of nature," she wrote, echoing a passage from *Silent Spring*; "now he has the power to achieve his boast. It is our misfortune—it may well be our final tragedy—that this power has not been tempered with wisdom, but has been marked by irresponsibility; that there is all too little awareness that man is part of nature, and that the price of conquest may well be the destruction of man himself." She wanted to impress upon her young audience that "the flowing stream of time [is] unhurried, unmindful of man's restless and feverish pace." Harking back to similar themes from *The Edge of the Sea*, Carson admonished, "instead of always trying to impose our will on Nature we should sometimes be quiet and listen to what she has to tell us." Only then, she hoped, might we see the madness of our feverish pace and learn humility and wisdom.[39]

Rachel spent the first afternoon and evening of her transcontinental journey in Denver with Lois Crisler. Lois took her up to the bleak Crag

Cabin where she, Cris, Alatna, and the other wolves had their mountain home. While Rachel loved seeing it, it was an exhausting trip. The next day she flew on to Los Angeles and arrived in Claremont to find a telegram from Paul Brooks. "Hooray," Brooks wrote, "it's done!" The day after commencement, Marie Rodell sent an equally gratifying but much more surprising message: "BOM HAS CHOSEN SILENT SPRING FOR OCTOBER CHEERS CHEERS CHEERS HURRAY LOVE MARIE AND JOAN."[40]

Rachel wrote Dorothy that same evening:

> You know now that what I never counted on—really never even allowed myself to hope for—has happened and *Silent Spring* will be the October Book-of-the-Month. No one could say whether total sales and income will be greater this way but what gives me deep satisfaction is the feeling that this, added to other things we know of, will give it an irresistible initial momentum. And the BOM will carry it to farms and hamlets all over the country that don't know what a bookstore looks like—much less *The New Yorker*. So it is very, very good and tonight I am deeply and quietly happy.[41]

With a touch of uncharacteristic conceit she added, "It is perhaps not shameless to say that after three best-sellers one does not get wildly excited about such news, which is perhaps too bad, but the deep satisfaction is there."

Upon her return to Maryland, Marie Rodell greeted her with more good news. National Audubon Society president Carl Buchheister had been one of the first to receive a proof copy of *Silent Spring*. When *Audubon Magazine* editor John Vosburgh and staff biologist Roland Clement urged publication of a two-part excerpt in the magazine beginning in the September/October issue, *The New Yorker* surprisingly agreed. Brooks was particularly pleased since this added publicity would coincide with book publication.[42]

The first installment of *Silent Spring*, featured in the "Reporter at Large" department of *The New Yorker* for June 16, arrived at newsstands three days earlier and created an immediate sensation among readers. Mail to the magazine was heavier than anything they had ever experienced. Most of it was appreciative that Carson had exposed the problem. Many readers were angry at a government that made such excessive use of pesticides and seemed to support corporate greed. But not all readers appreciated Carson's point of view.

After the second installment appeared on June 23, a gentleman from California wrote a letter reflecting popular support for the dominant business culture and presaged a certain type of criticism that would be leveled against the female author of *Silent Spring*. He wrote:

> Miss Rachel Carson's reference to the selfishness of insecticide manufacturers probably reflects her Communist sympathies, like a lot of our writers these days.
>
> We can live without birds and animals, but, as the current market slump shows, we cannot live without business.
>
> As for insects, isn't it just like a woman to be scared to death of a few little bugs! As long as we have the H-bomb everything will be O.K. PS. She's probably a peace-nut too.[43]

By now Rachel, still stuck in Maryland with her galley proofs, was nearly desperate to get to Maine and escape the ringing phone, the requests for interviews, appearances, speeches, and questions. Feeling as if she had been living in another world, she wrote Dorothy for the first time in nearly a week, exclaiming there had been nothing quite like this in her life. "I never predicted the book would be a smashing success. I doubted it would, so this is all unexpected and wonderful to me, too. It was simply something I believed in so deeply that there was no other course; nothing that ever happened made me even consider turning back." Rachel recalled her earlier feelings: "I told you once that if I kept silent I could never again listen to a veery's song without overwhelming self-reproach."[44]

With Ida's help, Rachel, Roger, and the cats left for Maine on June 29. After several weeks of public clamor, Rachel wanted Dorothy to meet her at the cottage for a private reunion. "There is too much meaning, too much emotion involved—something about the end of the long, hard road, something of the undreamed of and dizzying promised success, something of Dr. Caulk's 'almost a miracle.' " Finally secluded in Maine when the last installment of *Silent Spring* appeared, Rachel's privacy was secure for a brief, luxurious time.[45]

Rachel and Marie were still anxious about the libel issue even though they had taken every possible precaution. In addition to asking Houghton Mifflin lawyers to review the manuscript, Carson had sent a memorandum directing the publisher's attention to chapter 9, "Rivers of Death," in which she talked about a number of commercial products.

Although she was careful not to mention any trade names, she had quoted statements from advertisements by which the products could be identified. The question of trade names was most troublesome. Carson knew that there could be a basis for legal action simply on the claim that she had hurt product sales even if she did not mention it by name.

She provided Brooks with a list of six trade names that could be identified from the context of her discussion, along with the manufacturers of each. But Carson explained, "apparently such names as dieldrin, chlordane, endrin, etc., don't rate as trade names, but apply to the basic chemicals from which a variety of trade named products can be made."[46]

Rachel also was concerned that she did not have specific permission to quote from letters that had been written to her describing an incident of pesticide abuse or a toxic reaction. "Although I feel confident that I have evidence for everything I say, I presume nuisance suits might be brought for the purpose of harassment. In such an event, I assume I would have to pay my own legal counsel even if the decision were in my favor."[47]

Marie Rodell, who was probably the most concerned about legal repercussions, renegotiated Carson's contract with Houghton Mifflin at the end of May to reflect her liability concerns. The new contract specifically limited Carson's liability to $2,500 or to half the cumulative total of any legal costs up to that amount.[48]

Although Carson tried to relax in Southport, she was preoccupied with promotion matters, particularly with what Houghton Mifflin did and did not plan to do. But others were spreading the word. Marie Rodell reported that Charles Alldredge wanted half a dozen advance copies and that he "would call on the key personnel in Congress before it recesses and see that advance copies get to them directly (not side-tracked on someone else's desk.)"[49]

John V. Lindsay, congressman from New York City, called attention to Carson's criticism of present methods of pest control on the floor of the House of Representatives and read into *The Congressional Record* the last several paragraphs of the final installment.

Lindsay had written to Carson earlier, suggesting that they meet to discuss existing pesticide legislation when she returned to Washington in the fall. His request was the earliest indication Carson had of congressional interest in drafting remedial legislation to regulate industry and impose restrictions on government departments charged with dispersing pesticides. The favorable remarks of Lindsay and other lawmakers, such as William Proxmire in the U.S. Senate, were alarm signals to industry trade groups.[50]

A *New York Times* editorial on July 2 also applauded what it called "Rachel Carson's Warning" and predicted that Carson would be "accused of alarmism" or at least a "lack of objectivity." But the editorial stated very clearly that Carson did not argue that pesticides should never be used, but only warned of "the dangers of misuse and overuse by a public that has become mesmerized by the notion that chemists are the possessors of divine wisdom and that nothing but benefit can emerge from their test tubes." The *Times* writer hoped that if the book aroused the public to force government bureaucracies to become advocates of public health and safety instead of doing the bidding of the chemical lobby, Carson "would be as deserving of the Nobel Prize as was the inventor of DDT."[51]

Publication of *Silent Spring* in *The New Yorker* set off a chain of events of which the flood of reader letters was only a part. *Reader's Digest* contacted Rodell about a condensation. Although Rodell was skeptical, she certainly would consider a proposal. She put off an inquiry from *Life* magazine to do a picture close-up of Rachel, in part because she knew Rachel disliked the format and because she thought the best time for such an essay was after the book had been published. The inquiry that came from Consumer's Union of U.S. Inc., a membership organization that encouraged consumer education, however, was more timely.[52]

Consumer's Union proposed to buy 40,000 copies of *Silent Spring* from Houghton Mifflin as a special softcover printing for resale to their subscribers. Lovell Thompson, who handled such matters, liked the idea, pointing out to Rodell that such a sale would ensure that *Silent Spring* reached an important audience. Carson was initially dubious about such an edition, fearful that it would cut into bookstore sales, but she finally agreed to go ahead when the Union assured her that any surplus copies would not be dumped on the market.[53]

Although Houghton Mifflin worried that the public would forget about *Silent Spring* between June and the end of September, two events in the middle of July focused attention on science and the public's growing distrust of government. The first was the public outrage over the disclosure that U.S. drug companies had attempted to market the drug thalidomide, which had been traced to appalling birth defects abroad. The other was the initial and uncoordinated response of U.S. Department of Agriculture officials and chemical manufacturing trade groups to Carson's articles in *The New Yorker*. These events reinforced the impact of *Our Synthetic Environment*, Murray Bookchin's sweeping indictment of environmental poisoning and urban and industrial pollution published in August, which reminded the public again of the threat from a spectrum of toxic chemicals and the consequences of humankind's estrangement from nature.[54]

Ever since the summer of 1961 families in Western Europe and Canada had reported an increased number of births of infants exhibiting a rare condition known as phocomelia, characterized by deformed limbs and other organs. Over the year, scientists had traced the condition to a new drug known generically as thalidomide, which had been widely prescribed for sedation and sleeplessness. When taken by women in the early months of pregnancy, this mild, supposedly safe drug was devastating to early fetal development.

Thalidomide drugs did not reach the U.S. market because of the stubborn questions raised by a cautious Food and Drug Administration scientist, Dr. Frances Oldham Kelsey. Kelsey, a staff physician and pharmacologist, was unhappy with the answers the American manufacturer of the drug, Richardson-Merrell, provided to her questions about the suspected neurological toxicity of thalidomide. The July 15 *Washington Post* carried banner headlines that read "Heroine of FDA keeps bad drug off market." A front-page article by *Post* columnist Morton Mintz recounted how Kelsey's delaying tactics and her persistent questions prevented what could otherwise have been an appalling American tragedy. Kelsey became an overnight heroine and for a while was the center of press and television attention. President John Kennedy acknowledged her role by awarding her a gold medal for distinguished service.[55]

The controversy over thalidomide, the thousands of tragically deformed children, and the agonized decisions by women and families to terminate pregnancies broke out just before *Silent Spring* was published and continued to occupy headlines through the fall. A reporter from the *New York Post* was the first to reach Rachel Carson, in New York for a press luncheon two weeks before book publication. Carson made the obvious connection. "It is all of a piece," she responded, "thalidomide and pesticides—they represent our willingness to rush ahead and use something new without knowing what the results are going to be."[56]

In late July a second article in the *New York Times*, this one in the Business and Financial Section, heralded the advent of the chemical industries' response to Carson. Headlines read " 'Silent Spring' Is Now Noisy Summer" and "Rachel Carson Stirs Conflict—Producers Are Crying 'Foul.' " The article reported that those who produced chemicals viewed *Silent Spring* as "crass commercialism or idealistic flag waving." "We are aghast," said one manufacturer. "Our members are raising hell," reported a trade association. Corporate attorneys meeting in Washington and New York were busy preparing briefs. Groups of agricultural chemists pored over Carson's work line by line. "Statements are being drafted and counter-attacks plotted," the *Times* reported.

Annoyed at Carson's claim that industry had not been alert or concerned about problems, some officials prefaced their remarks with a denigrating tribute to her writing skills but were forced to admit they had found few errors of fact in what had been published so far. Although some trade associations and government bureaus waited to examine Carson's sources before commenting extensively, industry spokesmen complained that Carson's case was one-sided at best.[57]

Others were reportedly upset "over the misrepresentation of an industry which has tried to do right. We don't intend to answer directly. We don't want to be on the defensive. But we are expanding our public information program and making available a number of new brochures." The Manufacturing Chemists' Association, another industry lobby, called Carson's work "a disappointment" and indicated it was considering several courses of action. The Department of Agriculture admitted receiving many letters expressing "horror and amazement at the department's use of potentially deadly pesticides" but wisely made no further comment. The public debate over pesticides was just beginning, but the *Times* reporter accurately predicted that the book reviews and publicity that would greet the book's publication would stir further controversy.[58]

Washington newspapers carried more details on the reaction to Carson's articles inside the USDA. The *Washington Daily News* reported that unnamed officials had accused Carson of a "one-sided approach" and "sweeping conclusions." Ernest G. Moore, spokesman for the Agricultural Research Service, pointed out that Carson had prepared her argument much like a legal brief, "putting down everything that favors her case and ignoring all else. The balance of nature," he added, "is a wonderful thing for people who sit back and write books or want to go out to Walden Pond and live as Thoreau did. But I don't know of a housewife today who will buy the type of wormy apples we had before pesticides." Moore did not fail to mention that the Department of Interior, especially

Carson's old employer Fish and Wildlife, had "done a good deal of nature-unbalancing itself, with poisons and bullets, to eliminate predators of certain favored animals."[59]

Moore reiterated the department's position that pesticides were safe and effective when used as instructed. Justus Ward, head of ARS Pesticide Regulation Division who had earlier deflected Bette Haney's questions, pointed out how few pests could be controlled by biological methods and how few people died from known pesticide poisoning compared to alcohol, sleeping pills, and aspirin. The calculated risk of adverse long-term effects were, he said, "well within the acceptable level."[60]

When the flood of letters protesting wide-scale dusting and spraying continued, Secretary of Agriculture Orville Freeman asked for a personal briefing on the subject of pesticide research and use. The *Wall Street Journal* reported that Freeman's staff was "trigger happy" and "anxious to take the offensive." But Freeman instructed ARS administrator Byron T. Shaw to muzzle any further criticism. He asked Shaw to draft a statement on the use of chemicals that could be sent in response to public letters and to review all materials used by the ARS to answer public inquiries to ensure they were in line with the latest research. Moore's remarks had been premature. He and the others were ordered to issue bland statements that amounted only to rhetorical diversions that praised Carson for raising the issue of pesticide safety.[61]

The official USDA statement put the department on the moral high ground. "Miss Carson presents a lucid description of the real and potential dangers of misusing chemical pesticides. . . . She expresses the concern of many people about the effect of chemical pesticides on birds, animals and people. We are fully aware of, and share, this concern."[62]

Over at Interior, Stewart Udall was also feeling political pressure. But unlike Freeman, he had been well advised about the problems in the FWS predator control program. Backing Carson from the beginning, Udall seized the opportunity *Silent Spring* presented to become the chief advocate for pesticide regulation and reform in the Kennedy cabinet.[63]

Paul Knight, who had been following reaction in the press and at other agencies, was reporting to Udall regularly. After the third installment, Knight wrote Rachel in Southport, "I believe you may have ignited a time fuse." Referring to the initial outburst from USDA spokesman Moore, Knight remarked, "If I were information officer for the Agricultural Research Service, or the National Agricultural Chemicals Association, I believe I would take extended leave." He reported conversations with several congressmen on committees having jurisdiction over food additives, suggesting that they might want to look into the matter.[64]

Neither Carson nor her publisher knew yet that Dr. Jerome B. Wiesner, Special Science Advisor to the President, had called a meeting of bureau chiefs from concerned agencies on the subject of pesticides and Carson's articles on July 30. The meeting was attended by representatives of HEW, Interior, Commerce, Defense, the Bureau of the Budget, and Agriculture. After considerable discussion, Wiesner appointed a task force under the chairmanship of Boisfeuillet Jones, special assistant to the secretary of HEW, to review the policies of all departments on pesticides and chemical pollution and to report to the president in two or three months.[65]

Marie Rodell was swamped with requests for interviews and articles. In late July she visited Rachel in Maine for a weekend to help organize correspondence, make decisions on public appearances, and prepare for her meeting at Houghton Mifflin. The *London Sunday Times* wanted an interview, and Richard Arlett of NBC called to ask if Carson would be interviewed on the *Today* show by Hugh Downs. National Educational TV wanted to film a segment on *Silent Spring*, and Caedmon Records wanted to discuss a record contract of Carson reading from sea books. Rodell gave a polite no to most of these on Carson's behalf.

Carson, however, agreed to several exclusive interviews, including one with Eric Sevareid for *CBS Reports*. Contract negotiations with CBS were concluded in early August. Rachel had also agreed to give *New York Times* critic-at-large Brooks Atkinson an exclusive interview in preparation for his review and feature column and had promised one for Agnes Meyer's *Washington Post*.[66]

Marie's agenda of items to be discussed with Houghton Mifflin included everything from handling fan mail, coordinating book publicity with Carson's speaking engagements, to interviews, press conferences, advance sales, and syndications. She was particularly anxious about Houghton Mifflin's handling of "free-loaders and the lunatic fringe—the ones with something to sell." She wanted to make sure no one placed ads in any Rodale organic gardening or Health Guild publications.[67]

Marie reported on the outcome of her meeting to Rachel in a long memo. Fan mail would be handled by form letters, which Ford and her staff would coordinate. Carson composed five different letters covering the standard questions or responses that had been raised by *The New Yorker* letters. There would be a press luncheon for book critics two weeks before publication, and Houghton Mifflin would host a cocktail party at the Carleton House on September 25. Finished books would be off the press on August 20, but none were to be shipped until just before the official publication date of September 27.[68]

Houghton Mifflin reported that requests for proofs from the press had risen enormously after the third *New Yorker* installment, including some from the chemical industry as well as industry trade group members. Representatives of E. I. DuPont & Company, one of the earliest producers of DDT and 2,4-D, also had contacted Brooks for proof copies.

Lovell Thompson thought that if DuPont was thinking about a lawsuit, the sooner they knew about it the better, but Carson was uncomfortable about letting the company have advance copies. "If the suit is good," Thompson argued, "we will be warned that much sooner. If it is not good, duPont's [*sic*] case will be weakened by their having had the book well in advance." Brooks was even more sanguine about the motives behind DuPont's request, telling Rachel naively that the company was moving increasingly into biological controls and had left the development of agricultural chemicals to others. Thompson was more concerned about "an organized campaign to discredit Rachel as a naive alarmist" than a lawsuit from DuPont.[69]

Brooks was more accurate when he told Carson that he thought *Silent Spring* would be "the most important book of the decade." He had ordered a second printing before publication, bringing the total to 60,000, a figure agent Rodell considered ridiculously meager, and said so.[70]

Brooks's estimate of the impact of Carson's book was shared by DuPont's public relations department. It was seriously alarmed that it would begin an era of increased government regulation and turn public opinion against the use of industrial chemicals. The department spent hours compiling a confidential press analysis of *Silent Spring*, which was ready in early November. The initial ten-page summary surveying periodicals, editorials, book reviews, news reports, and columnists concluded that early predictions of the impact of Carson's book on the public were conservative and that nationwide debate on pesticide safety was a certainty.[71]

On August 2, with nearly the whole publishing industry on vacation, Houghton Mifflin received a letter from Louis McLean, general counsel of the Velsicol Chemical Company of Chicago, sole makers of chlordane and heptachlor, to name two of their most valuable agricultural chemicals. Pointing out that the "disparagement of products manufactured solely by one company creates actionable rights to the company," McLean suggested there were a number of legal and moral questions arising from statements in Carson's articles. He assumed that the forthcoming book included substantially the same material. "The simple truth is that pesticides and other agricultural chemicals are essential if we are to continue to enjoy the most abundant and purest foods ever enjoyed by any country of this world," he wrote, and proceeded to enumerate the statements he found damaging to Velsicol's product reputation.

Taking exception to Carson's examples of accident, injury, and unsafe use, McLean invoked a traditional Cold War explanation for those who attacked the chemical industry, suggesting in McCarthyite tones that Carson might be part of a conspiracy. There were, McLean suggested, "sinister influences" at work. Their purpose was "to create the false impression that all business is grasping and immoral, and to reduce the use of agricultural chemicals in this country and the countries of western Europe, so that our supply of food will be reduced to east-curtain parity." McLean implied, rather than stated, that a lawsuit would follow if *Silent Spring* were published containing such inaccurate and disparaging statements.[72]

Paul Brooks was shaken by the possibility that legal action might delay publication and jeopardize the Book-of-the-Month Club edition. He asked Rachel if she could remember her sources for the statements McLean quoted so they could judge how best to respond. Meanwhile he sent the Velsicol letter and a copy of Carson's book to Dr. Arthur McBay, director of the State Police Chemical Laboratory, whom Brooks knew from Harvard Medical School, asking him to review Carson's comments for accuracy.[73]

Carson reacted calmly when Brooks told her about the Velsicol letter and read her its main points over the telephone. She urged Paul to make only the most routine acknowledgment of the letter until her lawyer, Maurice Greenbaum, was back from vacation and had a chance to see it. She supplied Brooks with the sources for all the statements McLean had challenged, which Brooks sent on to McBay. Rachel also told Brooks that she remembered hearing that someone from Chicago had tried to threaten *The New Yorker* out of publishing the third installment. They both wondered if it could have been the same company. It was.[74]

Milton Greenstein, legal counsel and vice president of *The New Yorker*, had received a phone call from Velsicol, and perhaps several other companies, informing him that a lawsuit would result unless the last installment was canceled. Greenstein's answer was the same to all: "Everything in those articles has been checked and is true. Go ahead and sue."[75]

Maurice Greenbaum took the same approach. Expressing "a notable lack of alarm about the whole thing," Greenbaum thought that Velsicol's letter was the sort of thing they should expect from other companies and that it contained very little charge of any specific nature. McBay found only one phrase about the risks of exposure to chlordane that seemed even potentially problematic and validated everything Carson had written.[76]

In the end, Houghton Mifflin's response to Velsicol, signed by Brooks, went to lengths to assure the company that the book was both fair and accurate. Miss Carson, they said, had provided very complete source references for all her material. But they invited Velsicol to provide other documentation in support of its position. The legal staff at Houghton Mifflin was still nervous. Some argued for a disclaimer printed on the cover. Brooks vehemently objected, telling President William Spaulding that Carson would take the book to another publisher if a disclaimer was insisted upon. Spaulding gave the order to publish the book as it was. Velsicol was left with the option of taking action to stop the shipment of *Silent Spring* to the nation's bookstores.[77]

Finding Houghton Mifflin immune to threat, lawyers from Velsicol next paid a personal call on the National Audubon Society. This time their approach was more heavy-handed. At lunch with *Audubon Magazine* editor John Vosburgh and Charles Callison, assistant to the president of the society, the Velsicol group suggested that the conservation organization might want to reconsider its decision to run the two-part excerpt of *Silent Spring*. Everyone had wives and children to feed, and it would be a shame, they thought, to jeopardize their financial security for a muckraking article containing unwarranted assertions about Velsicol pesticides.[78]

Audubon staff biologist Roland Clement, who was already taking the lead among conservation organizations defending Carson's work, was singularly unimpressed by Velsicol's veiled threats. Charles Callison agreed. Not only did *Audubon* publish the excerpts of *Silent Spring*, but Vosburgh wrote an editorial criticizing the chemical industry's response. He included several paragraphs from Velsicol's initial letter to Houghton Mifflin, to call attention to Velsicol's questionable ethics as exhibited in various pesticide control programs. None of Rachel Carson's publishers ever heard specifically from Velsicol again, but no one was naive enough to believe that this was anything but the industry's way of testing the waters.[79]

Book-of-the-Month Club members received their club *News* in early September offering *Silent Spring* as the October selection. Board president Harry Scherman took the rare step of urging members not to reject the opportunity to read this book, telling them, "The portentous problem it presents—of worldwide indiscriminate poisoning of all forms of life, including human—is in the same dread category as worldwide nuclear warfare."

The club's editorial board had asked Supreme Court Justice William O. Douglas to write the report on *Silent Spring* for club members. Douglas, who had already written a review comment for Houghton Mifflin in which he called *Silent Spring* "the most revolutionary book since *Uncle Tom's Cabin*," produced a daring review. "This book," he wrote, "is the most important chronicle of this century for the human race. The book is a call for immediate action and for effective control of all merchants of poison." Club promotion generated even more publicity and widespread newspaper comment. The club's first printing was 150,000 copies.[80]

About the same time that the Book-of-the-Month began mailing out its *News*, President Kennedy held one of his regular press conferences. The interest Carson's book had aroused even before its publication was dramatically illustrated in a question one of the reporters put to the president.

> Mr. President, there appears to be a growing concern among scientists as to the possibility of dangerous long-range side effects from the widespread use of DDT and other pesticides. Have you considered asking the Department of Agriculture or the Public Health Service to take a closer look at this?
>
> The President: Yes, and I know that they already are. I think particularly, of course, since Miss Carson's book, but they are examining the matter.[81]

Although Kennedy made no specific reference to the special interagency panel set up by the Federal Council for Science & Technology, his response made public for the first time the administration's interest in the larger issues addressed by Carson's book. Nor did Kennedy reveal that

Wiesner, already frustrated with the progress of the interagency task force, had instructed the Life Sciences Panel of the president's Science Advisory Committee to begin its own study of pesticide use.[82]

What Kennedy did say was sufficient to galvanize the chemical industry to take action. It was no accident that the day after this news conference, the National Agricultural Chemicals Association (NACA) issued its own pro-pesticide propaganda booklet, "Fact and Fancy."

Like the USDA, NACA initially viewed *Silent Spring* as a public relations problem. In anticipation of the lobbying effort to come, NACA dramatically expanded its public relations department, mailed out a number of new brochures reaffirming the benefits of pesticides when properly used, and suggested to magazine and newspaper editors that reviewing Carson's book favorably would adversely affect future advertising. In "Fact and Fancy" NACA writers took a number of unacknowledged quotations from *Silent Spring*, printed them in one column, and quoted references thought to refute them in another. Rachel checked the number of unauthorized quotations and Marie added up the number of words, wondering to Brooks if they had enough for a plagiarism case. "I think it would be delicious fun to threaten them with a suit if we have a case," Rodell wrote. "What do you think?"[83]

The summer of 1962 was different from previous summers in Southport in that Rachel's privacy came at the expense of keeping to her remote setting more than she was accustomed, and the mail monopolized her time. Remembering a long-ago summer on Plum Island in the Parker River Refuge when she and Kay Howe had wished for disguises, Rachel wrote Shirley Briggs, "So far I have not had to resort to disguises but I am about to have the telephone changed to an unlisted category, and even with that precaution I think I am about to be invaded by the press." But the news reaching her from friends more than made up for any inconvenience of notoriety.[84]

Perhaps the most meaningful letter Rachel received that summer was one from E. B. White thanking her for the autographed copy of *Silent Spring* she had sent him and acknowledging his pleasure at being "in the same bed with Keats" on Carson's epigraph page. White wrote that he thought her articles in *The New Yorker* "the most valuable articles the magazine had ever published." But after he carefully "and angrily" read the book, he came away with "the greatest respect and admiration for the courage you showed in putting on the gloves and going in with this formidable opponent, and for your skill and thoroughness. This will be," White predicted, echoing William O. Douglas, "an *Uncle Tom's Cabin* of a book,—the sort that will help turn the tide." Acknowledging that the writing of it must have been a difficult literary experience, he predicted it would be the work she would be proudest of. "I'm unable adequately to express my gratitude to you for attempting to decontaminate this lovely world, and when the thrush sings in my woods again (and I'm sure he will!) I will think of you every time, and give thanks." Deeply moved by White's tribute, Rachel told him, "I can think of no lovelier memorial than the song of a thrush."[85]

It had taken Marie Rodell some time to persuade Rachel to do the *Life* close-up essay. Finally when Rodell reminded her that if Henry Luce opened up his pages to the chemical industry, it would certainly seize the opportunity, Carson reluctantly agreed, as long as the emphasis was on writing the book and not on personal details. Her decision appeared particularly sound when she learned that *Reader's Digest* had dropped its plan to do a condensation. Rachel decided, however, not to allow anyone to take pictures of Roger and hoped no one would mention him in any interviews. As she explained to the editor of the *Washington Sunday Star Magazine*, "I feel quite strongly that it is better for a child to develop in his own way and at his own pace, shielded from the glare of publicity that from time to time may be directed to his elders."[86]

CBS Reports producer Jay McMullen along with his cameraman arrived at Carson's cottage in early September to film footage of Carson at her cottage and walking through the woods and along the shore. After talking with her, McMullen realized that she was seriously ill and was anxious to have the interview filmed as soon as possible. Because of a variety of scheduling conflicts, the interview did not take place until late November.[87]

Rachel's speaking engagements were set for the foreseeable future and her agreement with CBS precluded other television interviews for three months after the broadcast. When she and Roger left Southport, Carson was under no illusions that she had already become a public figure. She subscribed to an answering service for her old telephone number in Silver Spring and requested a new, unlisted one.

On September 17 Carson was in New York City for a private press luncheon at the Algonquin Hotel. Afterward she met briefly with writer Jane Howard from *Life* and with Roger Machell, editor of the

British publishing house of Hamish Hamilton, about the conservationist Lord Shackleton's offer to write the introduction for the British edition of *Silent Spring*.

A week later she was back again in New York wearing a dark-green silk dress decked with an orchid corsage for Houghton Mifflin's official publication cocktail party at the Carleton House. Book editors and journalists from all the major papers and magazines had been invited as had William Shawn and Edith Oliver from *The New Yorker*, illustrators Lois and Louis Darling, conservationists William Vogt and Robert Cushman Murphy, as well as good friends including Edwin Way Teale, Irston Barnes, and Shirley Briggs. With reviews already breaking in major newspapers and news magazines, *Silent Spring* was finally and officially published and available in bookstores on September 27.[88]

Carson was particularly interested in a *Times* report of an interview with Olga Huckins who was quoted as saying that she had asked Carson "to do something" to stop the spraying and that Carson's response to her plea had been to write *Silent Spring*. In her foreword Carson acknowledged that it had been Huckins's 1958 letter that "brought my attention sharply back to a problem with which I had been long concerned." The *Times* picked up the story from an article in the *Boston Herald* by Wayne Hanley, an old friend of Huckins's, whom Carson knew through Massachuetts Audubon.[89]

Although Olga later insisted that she had not made any such statement to Hanley, Rachel graciously embellished her account and Hanley's story, writing Huckins: "I think even you have forgotten, however, that it was not just the copy of your letter to the newspaper but your personal letter to me that started it all. In it you told what had happened and your feelings about the prospect of a new and bigger spraying and begged me to find someone in Washington who could help. It was in the course of finding that 'someone' that I realized that I must write the book."[90]

Carson spent publication day quietly at home in Silver Spring working on her upcoming speeches, particularly the one for the National Council of Women, and preparing for her book tour at the end of October. Her first postpublication speeches were both to Washington audiences and were somewhat informal because she was part of a group of speakers. The National Parks Association held its annual meeting at the Smithsonian Institution's Baird Auditorium. Besides Carson, featured speakers were Clarence Cottam and Carl Buchheister. Rachel wore her simple two-piece wool suit in sage green, which, as the *Washington Star* fashion editor noted, was a becoming choice for her auburn hair. CBS was on hand to film Carson for the upcoming *CBS Reports*, and the audience was large and responsive. Although Carson expected some tough questions from the government scientists present, the exchange was entirely friendly.[91]

In Carson's speech, "On the Origins of *Silent Spring*," she quoted many of the letters she had received from people all over the country. Over half were written by men, "which," as she observed, "pretty well disposes of the legend that it is only 'the ladies' who are concerned about pesticides." A great majority of the rest were from doctors. Carson humorously included the story of the gentleman who had written *The New Yorker* calling her a "communist" and a "peace nut."

She told her audience that she had been impressed by the sense of personal responsibility that came through in the letters, remarking that she thought this reflected a change in public attitude. People, she said, were beginning to challenge and ask questions. They no longer "assumed that someone was looking after things—that the spraying must be all right or it wouldn't be done."

Responding to the question that her readers asked again and again—"What can be done?"—Carson repeated that she did not advocate an end to the use of chemical pesticides but a change in emphasis. Part of that, she said, must come from making research into alternative methods of pest control a national priority. But she did not flinch from advocating grass-roots activities and community leadership in an effort to stop the use of toxic chemical sprays and chemical pollution. This was the first speech in which Carson outlined specific reforms and urged citizen activism. Her call for local responsibility was not lost on the chemical industry.[92]

Her brief remarks at the annual dinner meeting of the Audubon Naturalist Society several days later, where she shared the podium with Clarence Cottam, covered much the same ground. Among friends, she felt free to acknowledge the growth of a grass-roots movement in communities across the country.[93]

Dr. Frances Kelsey attended the dinner and responded briefly during the question-and-answer session. Rachel's admiration for Kelsey was reflected a week later in her speech at the convention of the National Council of Women in New York, where she underscored the need for the genetic testing of chemicals before they were released in the environment.[94]

In between the two events in Washington and New York was *Life* magazine's close-up essay by Jane Howard with photographs by Alfred Eisenstaedt, entitled "The Gentle Storm Center: A Calm Appraisal of *Silent Spring*." In late September the *Life* crew took the final photographs in Washington's Glover-Archibald Park, a site chosen by Shirley Briggs. Shirley had rounded up a group of "extras," including three children from the ranks of the Audubon Naturalist Society. Eisenstaedt approved both cast and background. Shirley noted in her diary that Rachel wore her "new Elizabeth Arden hairdo and looked younger and very pretty."[95]

Howard's essay depicted Carson as a miscast crusader who, while no stereotypic fanatic, was a "formidable adversary." "I have no wish to start a Carrie Nation crusade," Carson had told her. "I wrote the book because I think there is a great danger that the next generation will have no chance to know nature as we do—if we don't preserve it the damage will be irreversible." Howard noted that while Carson was unmarried, she was not a feminist. "I'm not interested in things done by women or by men," Carson told her, "but in things done by people." Although Howard joined the other journalists who framed the argument between Carson and the advocates of pesticides as one involving seemingly irreconcilable objectives, the essay commended Carson's views.

On balance, Rachel was pleased with the *Life* story and photographs. After seeing the proofs, she wrote Dorothy, "Hope you know me and are not unhappy with the new Me. I suspect you'll still like the Hartmann picture best—as I do." Rachel and Shirley were amused to discover that Eisenstaedt included a photograph of the group collectively looking skyward, some with binoculars, some without, that Rachel had dubbed "the second coming."[76]

Given the high level of public interest that surrounded the publication of *Silent Spring*, it was almost inevitable that Carson could find herself the subject of a *Peanuts* cartoon in the morning and receive an invitation from the Kennedy White House in the afternoon. The White House informed her that Secretary Udall wished her to attend a meeting of the "Kennedy Seminar" at his home.[97]

Not knowing exactly what to expect or who else might be there, Rachel had made detailed notes. Anticipating a challenge from Orville Freeman or someone on his staff, she dwelled at length on the inefficiency of chemical pesticides to eliminate crop destruction, the resurgence of insects after chemical spraying, and the increase of insect resistance. Criticizing the recent reports of the National Academy of

Science, she discussed several imaginative approaches in biological control, arguing for their support through increased government funding and public education.[98]

Udall remembers that he felt Carson was at a disadvantage that evening because of her gender and because of her very solemn style of speaking. Ethel Kennedy, the president's sister-in-law, who was present, seemed overwhelmed by the factual details. But regardless of how Carson had presented her case, the attention of the group would have been elsewhere. Attorney General Robert Kennedy never did attend the discussion. Instead he spent the evening closeted in Udall's study on the telephone, dealing with events that in a matter of days became the Cuban Missile Crisis.[99]

Writing Dorothy from Cleveland, where she had gone on October 23 for a reception at the Museum of Natural History and book signing, Carson referred to those frightening days in October when "it seemed as though time was standing still and there might even be no tomorrow." But her appearance at the Kennedy Seminar did reinforce the administration's interest in environmental contamination.[100]

It wasn't until after Thanksgiving that Carson's long-awaited interview with Eric Sevareid for *CBS Reports* took place. Cameramen and crew invaded her Berwick Road home and set up for several days of filming Carson in her study. Roger loved the excitement and Carson took it all calmly, being quite comfortable with Jay McMullen and Sevareid, but it was exhausting nevertheless. McMullen recalls being deeply impressed with the quality of Carson's responses, her logic and articulateness, and her quiet presence. Both reporters were pleased with how the interview had gone, but saddened by Carson's obvious ill health. McMullen remembers that as they were driving away, Sevareid agreed that they should get it on air as soon as possible. "Jay," he remarked, "you've got a dead leading lady."[101]

Carson's public remarks grew increasingly sharper as the fall progressed, particularly when it was obvious that many critics had failed to read her book. Commenting on how easily poisonous insecticides could be purchased by the average homeowner, she remarked, "they forget they are handling a dangerous substance and shop as if for Helena Rubenstein rather than Lucrezia Borgia." Spurred on by the publication of Frank Egler's devastating critique of the National Academy of Sciences–National Research Council's pesticide report in the *Atlantic Naturalist*, and by critics who misinterpreted science to plead their cause, Carson prepared a particularly scathing attack on a smugly self-satisfied industry when she spoke at the Women's National Press Club on December 5.[102]

"My text this afternoon," Carson began with a touch of wicked humor, "is taken from the *Globe Times* of Bethelem, Pa. After describing in detail the adverse reactions to *Silent Spring* by the farm bureaus in two Pennsylvania counties, the reporter continued: 'No one in either county farm office who was talked to today had read the book, but all disapproved of it heartily.' " With television cameras from ABC and CBS covering the event and Clarence Cottam on the stage beside her, Carson charged that basic scientific truths were being compromised "to serve the gods of profit and production." Deliberately squaring off against her critics, Carson described the liaison between science and industry. She used four examples from the *Journal of Economic Entomology* wherein researchers listed chemical industry support of their research, and she also disclosed that a newsletter from the American Medical Association had recently referred physicians to a pesticide trade association for help in answering patient questions on pesticide effects. "When the scientific organization speaks," Carson asked, "whose voice do we hear, that of science or of the sustaining industry?"[103]

"Rachel was wonderful at Women's Press Club luncheon today. I think her best and most newsworthy speech of all," Anne Ford cabled Marie Rodell, who was traveling. The audiotape of the speech certainly confirmed Ford's view. But no one could possibly have guessed what physical and mental resources Carson had called on to give such a taxing physical and intellectual performance. The following afternoon she was in Dr. Caulk's office waiting for the results of X rays on her spine.[104]

Hoping desperately that the pain she was experiencing was more arthritis, she was relieved when the X rays showed no physical change in the vertebrae. But when the pain worsened the week before Christmas, Carson went back to have Caulk take another look. Fearing further metastases, he advised five or six radiation sessions to her back. Barney Crile concurred, telling Rachel it might take two or three weeks to get the pain under control.

Christmas 1962 should have been a time of celebration for Carson with so many achievements behind her. *Silent Spring* had been number one on the *New York Times* best-seller list for most of the fall, dropped briefly, and returned before Christmas. Paul Brooks reported sales of 106,000 a week before Christmas. Instead Carson braved a blizzard and several ice storms to get to and from the Washington clinic, and two weeks of intense nausea. "The treatments themselves caused much less psychological distress than earlier ones," Rachel confided to Dorothy well after the fact, "largely, I think, because this time the machine was not the 2-million-volt monster but a much smaller one with a less awesome sound in a friendlier room."[105]

She tried to keep life normal for Roger, who was excited about being the king in the Christmas pageant at school. About a week before Christmas, Rachel was shopping at Woodward & Lothrop's department store in Chevy Chase, Maryland, where she had gone to buy a record player for him. With little warning, she suddenly collapsed over a table of records. It was the first time she had fainted in her life.[106]

Although Dr. Healy thought her fast heart rate was the result of stress and fatigue, Crile and Caulk knew better. Carson's recurrent chest pain and other symptoms signaled the onset of angina, a heart condition not unusual in patients undergoing frequent and heavy radiation and rapidly metastasizing cancer.

"It has been such a mixed year for both of us," Rachel acknowledged in her traditional Christmas letter to Dorothy, "joy and fulfillment, . . . and on the other hand, the shadows of ill health. For me, either would have been a solitary experience without you. Now, to you both, so much love and the hope that the new year will bring us all more joys than sorrows and renewed joys in being together—in belonging to each other."[107]

18

"Rumblings of an Avalanche"

In *Silent Spring,* Carson deliberately employed the rhetoric of the Cold War and the tone of moral crisis to persuade her readers of the urgency of her message. The crisis over the misuse of pesticides was, for her, perfectly analogous to the threat from radioactive fallout and justified her social and political criticism of the government and the scientific establishment as well as her implicit calm and reasonable call for citizen action.

One reviewer acknowledged the volatile culture that received Carson's message, but he nonetheless accused her of "emotionalism." "It isn't enough to have the threat of atomic warfare, a population explosion, communist aggression, irreligion [*sic*], youth dereliction and other menaces," he wrote, "we must also face the prediction that chemical warfare against insects is contaminating our air and sea and ground." A cartoon in *Saturday Review* captured the public mood. It showed a well-dressed gentleman at a restaurant with a friend bemoaning his state of crisis overload. "I just got adjusted to radioactive fallout, and now along comes Rachel Carson."[1]

Lorus and Margery Milne, who reviewed *Silent Spring* on the front page of the *New York Times Book Review,* accurately predicted that those Carson had accused of arrogance, stupidity, irresponsibility, and greed would respond in equally ideological terms. But even so most critics were surprised by the size of the campaign mounted against her. The pesticide industry trade group National Agricultural Chemicals Association (NACA) spent well over $250,000 in its efforts to persuade the public of

Carson's errors and to protect their threatened interests. It correctly understood that the public relations damage from *Silent Spring* could result not only in a drop in commercial demand for pesticides but also in a serious, perhaps even irreversible, loss of public confidence. Industry and its trade affiliates were even more worried about the possibility of new government regulations, expensive testing procedures, and stricter federal and state oversight. As a result, they sought to discredit Carson as a scientist by ridiculing her evidence as well as her conclusions. By denigrating Rachel as nothing more than an emotional female alarmist, they hoped to win the public relations battle in the marketplace and avoid a legislative battle in Congress.[2]

But many in science, government, and industry understood that the essential issue that Carson had raised was not one that could be won or lost by appeals to the consumer. They recognized *Silent Spring* for what it was: a fundamental social critique of a gospel of technological progress. Carson had attacked the integrity of the scientific establishment, its moral leadership, and its direction of society. Holding up before them their irresolute carelessness of the natural world, she dared to make their sins public. The fury with which they attacked her reflected the accuracy of her moral charges. Since her facts were essentially irrefutable, they disparaged Carson as the agent of a message that had to be suppressed.[3]

Over the course of the controversy, it became clear to her enemies as well as her allies that Carson had forced a public debate over the heretofore academic idea that living things and their environment were interrelated. It was the central theme of everything she had written before, and so it was at the core of *Silent Spring* as well.

The industry-led attack on Carson began early. Former Secretary of Agriculture Ezra Taft Benson is credited by some for framing it in its crudest terms in a letter to Dwight Eisenhower, but the remark was repeated so many times that its origin became inconsequential. Referring to Carson's articles in *The New Yorker*, Benson supposedly wondered "Why a spinster with no children was so concerned about genetics?" His explanation was that she was "probably a Communist." The question reflected increasing attention on Carson's gender by those who commented on *Silent Spring* and its reserved author. The press was inordinately interested in Carson's marital status. She was, after all, physically attractive, quiet, and feminine. A reporter from the *Baltimore Sun* asked her why she never married. "No time," Rachel responded, and went on to say that she sometimes envied male writers who married because they had wives to take care of them, provide meals, and spare them from unnecessary interruptions.[4]

News magazines, reflecting the dominant business culture, generally took a much dimmer view of *Silent Spring* than biologists, conservationists, book critics, and literary reviewers. A lengthy review in *Time* magazine's science section the day after the book's publication established the tenor of popular reports: "Miss Carson has taken up her pen in alarm and anger, putting literary skill second to the task of frightening and arousing her readers." Alluding to errors, oversimplifications, and scary generalizations, the *Time* correspondent concluded, "Many scientists sympathize with Miss Carson's love of wildlife, and even with her mystical attachment to the balance of nature. But they fear that her emotional and inaccurate outburst in *Silent Spring* may do harm by alarming the nontechnical public, while doing no good for the things that she loves."[5]

Once *Silent Spring* was published, the outlines of the industry's attack emerged quickly. It had three primary forms. First, Carson wrote for the public, a calling that somehow compromised her scientific credibility by implying that she was less than professional. She was an artist of acknowledged craft and merit, whose literary stock-in-trade was her ability to appeal to the public through their emotions. Point in fact: The opening fable was a scary hoax, pure science fiction. The fable was almost uniformly derided by reviewers unable to understand its basis in allegory and used it to further demean her credibility as a scientist. Second, Carson was not a professional scientist. She had only a master's degree in zoology, had little field experience, held no academic appointment, and had not published in any peer-reviewed journals. Although there was grudging acknowledgment that Carson had mastered the scientific literature, she had also relied on anecdote in equal measure, the sort of evidence no true scientist would select.

Finally, mixed in with all the other arguments was Carson's gender. She kept cats and loved birds. She was a nature writer, a mystic, a devotee of the balance of nature. Her arguments were exaggerations born of hysteria at worst and an overly sensitive nature at best. Reason had been sacrificed to sentiment. Behind these charges was understandable resentment of Carson's aggressive attack on the scientific establishment and on a male-dominated technology. Among her other errors, Miss Carson had overstepped her place.[6]

While the NACA and the Manufacturering Chemists' Association, two of the largest industry trade lobbies, were busy sending out a steady stream of brochures and bulletins denouncing things that Carson had never said and circulating "fact kits" to members, the Monsanto Corporation, an industry leader in the development and manufacture of agricultural pesticides, put its own public relations department to work. In early October 1962 it produced a parody on Carson's "Fable for Tomorrow" called "The Desolate Year." Mimicking Carson's style and tone, it described the horrors of a world without pesticides.

> Quietly, then, the desolate year began. Not many people seemed aware of danger. After all, in the winter, hardly a housefly was about. What could a few bugs do, here and there? How could the good life depend upon something so seemingly trivial as bug spray? Where were the bugs anyway? The bugs were everywhere. Unseen. Unheard. Unbelievably universal. Beneath the ground, beneath the waters, on and in limbs and twigs and stalks, under rocks, inside trees and animals and other insects—and, yes, inside man.[7]

Monsanto distributed copies of the parody to newspapers all over the country.

R. Milton Carleton, garden editor for a number of large midwestern papers and director of Vaughan's Garden Research Center outside Chicago, Illinois, was a ubiquitous critic for industry associations. As a fellow of the American Association for the Advancement of Science and a member of the National Association of Science Writers, Carleton strenuously objected to Carson's claim to scientific credentials. "*Silent Spring,*" he wrote in his garden column, "is NOT a scientific work. It is full of errors, perhaps not evident to the lay reader, but clear indices of a writer who has ventured into an unknown field and has absorbed all sorts of evidence, some of it sound, some of it worthless, and given everything equal billing."[8]

One of the scientific authorities Carleton deferred to was Dr. George C. Decker, principal scientist and head of economic entomology at the Illinois Natural History Survey and Illinois Agricultural Experiment Station. Decker was a frequent collaborator on insect control at USDA and a consultant to several chemical companies. Most recently he had chaired the NAS-NRC Pesticide-Wildlife Subcommittee. Decker was well connected in the agrichemical community. He spared no energy writing against Carson's claims, perhaps more ardently since his own role in the NAS-NRC report had been questioned as less than objective. "In her reckless misinterpretation of scientific facts, Miss Carson has done irreparable harm to the orderly processes of protecting human life from hazards far worse than the ogres she conjures up," he wrote.[9]

NACA supported a variety of efforts to counteract antipesticide propaganda, including the distribution of a brochure entitled "How to Answer Rachel Carson," which was offered by *County Agent and Vo-Ag Teacher*. It contained the admonition that readers could use the information in talks on television and radio and in newspaper articles, and was aimed at restoring confidence in the food industry. Among other corrections to Carson's evidence, this brochure offered the following dubious statement: "While residues of DDT *do* build up in stored fat in humans, they aren't permanent, and with no additional intake, they will disappear in 90 days." The brochure called Carson's book "more poisonous than the pesticides she condemned."[10]

The Nutrition Foundation, a research-sponsoring organization of the food industry whose leadership included executives from General Foods and Gerber Baby Foods and whose membership included fifty-four food, chemical, and nutrition companies, took the lead in attacking *Silent Spring* as a biased and unscientific account by an amateur. One of its earliest efforts was a mass mailing of reviews unfavorable to the book, which went first to all newspapers that had bought syndication rights to it.

Nutrition Foundation president C. G. King took particular umbrage at Carson for "maligning the integrity, objectivity and competence of executives and scientists in industry, agriculture, education and government." In King's view, the problem was made that much more dangerous because "publicists and the author's adherents among the food faddists, health quacks, and special interest groups were promoting her book as if it were scientifically irreproachable and written by a scientist." Getting to the heart of the matter, King continued, "Their alarmist advertising is aimed right at our pocketbooks. They poison minds for profit, and Miss Carson's book has become a tool in their hands." The Nutrition Foundation, like the members of NACA, thought that while Carson's book could be discounted successfully, it had set up a potentially dangerous chain of events.[11]

The Nutrition Foundation's packet of purportedly objective scientific appraisals of *Silent Spring* included one by I. L. Baldwin, chairman of the

NAS-NRC Pesticide Review Committee, William J. Darby, and Frederick J. Stare. Darby and Stare, representing the foundation's views but writing as third-party experts, were responsible for some of the fiercest attacks on Carson.

Darby, head of the Department of Biochemistry and director of the Division of Nutrition at Vanderbilt University School of Medicine, exhibited his lack of objectivity when he titled his review in *Chemical & Engineering News*, "Silence! Miss Carson." Referring to Carson's list of scientific sources, Darby sarcastically castigated her supporters as "organic gardeners, the antifluoride leaguers, the worshippers of 'natural foods' and those who cling to the philosophy of a vital principle, and other pseudo-scientists and faddists." Striking out at Carson's reliance on the research of controversial scientists such Morton S. Biskind and W. C. Hueper rather than the sound appraisals of the committees of NAS-NRC, the President's Science Advisory Committee, or scientists at the Nutrition Foundation, Darby advised readers that "in view of her scientific qualifications in contrast to those of our distinguished scientific leaders and statesmen, this book should be ignored."[12]

Frederick J. Stare, Ph.D. and M.D. with an appointment at Harvard Medical School, writing as a member of the Nutrition Foundation, was even more devastating in his criticism. Although Stare granted that Carson had rendered a public service by "arousing an apathetic, unscientific public" to the serious problem of providing "food for an exploding population and protecting man from the scourge of epidemic disease," he castigated her for "abandoning scientific proof and truth for exaggeration." Like Darby, Stare attacked Carson's scientific qualifications. "I have seen no evidence in *Silent Spring* which justifies calling Miss Carson a scientist." She was, he said, "a literary luminary—and one of splendid accomplishment whose book unfortunately only widens the gap between science and the public." But Stare's professionalism slipped at least once in print when he termed Carson's conclusions "baloney."[13]

The chemical companies banded together through NACA and employed a public relations firm, Glick and Lorwin, to attack the book. Robert White-Stevens, a biochemist who was assistant director of the Agricultural Research Division of American Cyanamid, and Thomas Jukes, a former employee who had recently joined the faculty of the University of California, Berkeley, were particularly upset about the evidence Carson had compiled against DDT. Both men were recognized research scientists, and both advanced the benefits of chemical pesticides in general and DDT in particular. They were afraid that *Silent Spring* would provoke legislative regulations that would hamstring agricultural technology, undermine Americans' confidence in their food, lower exports, and put the free world at risk to hunger and disease. Jukes wrote prolifically on the necessity for synthetic pesticides while White-Stevens, who made over twenty-eight speeches against *Silent Spring* in 1962 alone, became the chemical industry's chief spokesman.[14]

White-Stevens was a tall, distinguished-looking man who spoke with a clipped British accent. He was a formidable opponent in debate, exceptionally articulate, humorous, quick, and authoritative who routinely charged that Carson was "a fanatic defender of the cult of the balance of nature," as if she were a clandestine member of a Druid sect.[15]

Tom Jukes was a serious ideologue who pressed his friends at USDA to "gird their loins for the struggle ahead" and to go after Carson. In numerous well-placed scientific articles, he defended the safety of DDT and attempted to destroy Carson's credibility. Criticizing ARS director Byron Shaw for his mild statements about *Silent Spring* in an interview in *U.S. News & World Report*, Jukes told him, "Of course Miss Carson does not advocate halting the use of chemical pesticides. She merely states that they produce cancer and deformed babies. In the light of such statements it is not necessary to advocate halting their use."[16]

Carson read all the articles by Jukes and heard about White-Stevens's debating triumphs from friends. For the time being, she left her defense to Frank Egler, who took Jukes's measure in the pages of the various scientific journals, and to Roland Clement, who enjoined White-Stevens on at least three public occasions.[17]

Members of another industry affiliate, the National Pest Control Association, concerned that Carson's one-sided account would damage sales, followed NACA's example with a packet of negative reviews that included a lighthearted poetic effort by an honorary member intended to provide beleaguered members with some comic relief. Entitled "Rachel, Rachel," it mimicked the lyrics of the old song "Rubin, Rubin" and included the following stanzas:

Rachel, Rachel, we've been hearing,
All the dread words that you've said,
Were they true and Spring was silent,
Then I'm sure we'll soon be dead.

In those lands where stark starvation,
Stalk a child from birth to grave,
Gratitude for food production,
Calms the clamor, knights the brave.

Hunger, hunger, are you listening,
To the words from Rachel's pen?
Words which taken at face value,
Place lives of birds 'bove those of men.[18]

Silent Spring inspired a variety of creative literary efforts. One trade lobby produced a black-humored parody of the "Twelve Days of Christmas" that appeared in December 1962. Entitled the "Carsonoma Chorale" and sung by the "Chlorinated Choir," it described Carson giving twelve disgustingly sick and dying animals as Christmas presents to her friends.

Cartoons appeared routinely in major magazines and newspapers, including several in *The New Yorker*, and a total of three "Peanuts" episodes from the pen of Charles Shultz. Rachel found the humor and the social commentary in them genuinely amusing. In most cartoons, Carson's viewpoints were advocated by women or children who attempted to change the habits of skeptical males. The chemical lobby had cause to worry about homemakers, fearing that "no housewife can reach for a bug bomb without fear" and all because Carson had abandoned scientific reasoning.[19]

Letters to the editor reflected more female correspondents than male, although those who represented organizations were uniformly male. Women were concerned with a spectrum of pollution and contamination issues: fluoride in water, food additives, thalidomide, radioactive fallout, government secrecy, and corporate deception. They linked their concern with their primary roles as housewives and mothers and with the protection of future generations. Their outlook was not so much economic as humane.

Garden clubs across the nation reviewed and discussed *Silent Spring* at their meetings, but their response to Carson's message was by no means uniform or predictable. One of Carson's most influential critics was Dr. Cynthia Westcott, an entomologist with considerable literary skill, whom the chemical companies seized upon as their secret weapon.

Westcott was known to garden club women because of her popular column "The Plant Doctor," published in *American Woman* and syndicated in many influential women's magazines. A graduate of Wellesley College with a Ph.D. in plant pathology from Cornell University's School of Agricultural Science, Westcott had been chairman of the National Council of State Garden Clubs and had edited two major handbooks on plant pathology for the prestigious Brooklyn Botanical Garden. She was active in the Entomological Society of America and the American Horticultural Society and enjoyed the backing of both organizations.[20]

When Carrie Nettleton, president of the National Council of Federated Garden Clubs, had been unable to attend Agnes Meyer's luncheon in Washington, she sent the *Silent Spring* galleys to Westcott to review. Westcott, then chairman of the Council's Garden Enemies Committee, was not an objective reviewer. She had been the only female member of the NAS-NRC subcommittee on pest control and wildlife and had vigorously defended that committee's report. Mrs. Nettleton sent a copy of Westcott's review of *Silent Spring* in the *National Gardener* to Paul Brooks, who passed it on to Carson.[21]

In the review, which reached thousands of garden club members, Westcott took particular exception to Carson's evidence of a chemical threat to human health, arguing that it "can only be conjecture; no proof has yet been offered of any link with human cancer or other ailments." In addition to her monthly columns, in 1963 Westcott produced three bulletins critical of Carson's ideas for garden writers and club leaders. Along with her review, they were published and distributed by the Manufacturing Chemists Association. Westcott appeared regularly on public television, gardening shows, and produced a "Guide" for readers of *House and Garden* magazine, all belittling Carson's concerns. Westcott was bright, convivial, and well connected, exhibiting a sort of Julia Child affability. She always acknowledged Rachel Carson's service in jolting the public out of its complacency but adopted the NACA line that what was required was a balanced point of view and that Carson was an alarmist. "Throughout 'Silent Spring,' " Westcott wrote, "we are given pills of half truth, definitely not tranquilizing, and the facts are carefully selected to tell only one side of the story."[22]

Westcott made a careful distinction between herself as "Dr." Westcott, a scientist with a degree, and "Miss" Carson. She deliberately misstated Carson's position, telling her readers that without pesticides the American housewife would find it difficult to feed her family and warned that "unchecked" pests would bring "starvation and death." The Federation of State Garden Clubs of Pennsylvania, among other affiliates, endorsed Westcott's "unemotional and informative answers" to Carson's claims and praised her column in *The National Gardener*. There Westcott urged members not to be alarmed by Carson's unproven examples of chemical harm and admonished them to give "equal time to considering the good results of present programs of pest control." Through Ruth Scott's auspices Carson wrote her own rebuttal to Westcott, which was published in the Garden Club Federation of Pennsylvania *News*. In it she commented on the many new discoveries of damage to wildlife and the environment since her book appeared.[23]

Westcott and Carson had only one personal exchange. In July 1962 Westcott wrote Carson to tell her that she had read the galley Mrs. Nettleton had sent her. "For years I have been urging a middle-of-the-road policy for gardeners, an integrated program with the minimum of pesticides for practical results. I do think, however, that some of the results have not been quite as disastrous as you picture them." She told Carson flatly she "deplored" her suggestion that entomologists and other scientists were out for private gain but thought it would be a good thing if Carson's book made people more cautious.

The only area of agreement between the women was in the need for more research; Carson seized on this issue in her formal reply to "Doctor Westcott." "I am aware that we do not view the problems of pesticides in precisely the same way," she told Westcott graciously, adding that if her book helped to achieve increased support for research then she would consider the years devoted to it well spent. Knowing how closely Westcott was connected to industry, Carson wasted no effort in disputing her argument.[24]

Carson was not without her own powerful defenders, but many of the best—H. J. Muller, the Nobel Prize–winning geneticist, University of Pennsylvania anthropologist and historian of science Loren Eiseley, Clarence Cottam, and Frank Egler—were scholars and academics; as such, they had a more limited access to the broad vehicles of public opinion. Roland Clement, the best of Carson's public defenders, was busy speaking out to various groups and debating Robert White-Stevens on the radio and in person. But as Clement was the first to admit, "the birds and bunny boys" had only limited clout. Buchheister refused to commit the Audubon Society to an anti-DDT position, so Clement most often was left representing himself.[25]

But the National Audubon Society, with only 30,000 members, was no match for the power of a multimillion-dollar industry, and it was soon embroiled in a defense of its traditional Christmas bird count, which White-Stevens and Jukes seized on as showing that Carson's evidence for the population collapse of the American robin was bogus. Few other conservation organizations were willing to risk being unqualified advocates of Carson's position. The most serious scientific review of her ecological science came from Cornell zoologist LaMont C. Cole in the December 1962 issue of *Scientific American.* But even his fine review was not a wholehearted endorsement, as he differed with her on the evolutionary significance of insect resistance. Carson was pleased with Cole's comments nonetheless and with the supportive letters of private individuals whose opinions sustained her.[26]

Two such letters arrived in the winter of 1963, at a time when she needed particular courage. One was from Thomas Merton, the spiritual writer then in residence at the Abbey of Gethsemani, who had been moved by her book. Merton remarked on the culture of affluence that encouraged a mindless technology and on the parallels Carson had drawn between pesticides and radioactive fallout. The other was a handwritten note from Dr. Albert Schweitzer along with an inscribed photograph thanking her for her dedication and for writing *Silent Spring.* Rachel bought a special picture frame with glass on both sides to display Schweitzer's letter and kept it in her study. Ida Sprow, Carson's housekeeper, recalled that it was her most cherished possession.[27]

Carson wanted Houghton Mifflin to mount a positive advertising campaign to counter the negative criticism in the press. But the controversy was selling more books than the company's meager advertising budget ever could have generated. Marie Rodell and Carson were unimpressed with such a passive attitude. "Rachel wonders," Rodell wrote Brooks, "whether the public has not been by now so buffeted by statements from 'scientists' saying 'Silent Spring' is (to quote one of the most elegant) 'baloney' that the general effect may seem to be that all the scientists are on the other side. She wonders whether we ought not to collect a few scientists of our own, and make sure the public hears from them. In, presumably, a large ad full of quotes."[28]

Rodell suggested that they could quote the opposition scientists with each carefully identified as to his affiliations or special interests. For example: " 'Baloney,' says Dr. Frederick Stare of the National Nutrition Council, whose funds come from annual dues paid by Monsanto,

American Cyanamid and Union Carbide, the three largest manufacturers of pesticides in the U.S. In other words," Rodell continued, "let's kick 'em in the teeth. (*I* can be elegant too.)"[29]

Houghton Mifflin complied with an ad announcing "Unsolicited, unpaid-for comments by scientists about *Silent Spring*" and quoting nine scientists who praised the book at length, including several medical doctors, Hermann Muller, W. C. Hueper, and Loren Eiseley. Across the bottom was an adaptation of a "buyer beware" statement that read "Comment on *Silent Spring* which makes light of the dangers of chemical poisons may emanate from sources dependent on the expanding use of chemicals. Such comment may attribute to Miss Carson statements that she has never made. Weigh very carefully everything you read and hear."[30]

Carson's prodding encouraged Houghton Mifflin to take the unprecedented step of producing a pamphlet of its own. "The Story of *Silent Spring*" was to be mailed out to newspaper editors and bookstores across the country. Originally it was a condensation of quotes, first from critics, followed by Carson's true statements. But Carson thought that such an approach made the booklet little more than a weak echo of the industry's *Fact and Fancy* and suggested a narrative account instead.

She was too sick to contribute much to the pamphlet until March, when Brooks planned a visit to Maryland. In anticipation of his visit, she rewrote the section "Is the Author Qualified?" and inserted a new section highlighting some of the things that communities had done to improve the situation and take responsibility for pesticide use. Carson also cited requests for congressional investigations and the president's charge to the Life Sciences Committee of his Science Advisory Committee to study the uses of pesticides. She concluded that the principal purpose of the book, "to direct attention to a situation of which the general public was largely unaware, has been realized, perhaps because of, more than in spite of, the attacks."[31]

As she learned of more incidents of pesticide pollution and injury from other scientists and the public, she regretted that she had not had the time to state her case even more strongly. But she made use of this new information every time she spoke in public. Her speeches reflected her moral conviction that no "civilization can wage relentless war on life without destroying itself, and without losing the right to be called civilized."[32]

Early in January Carson went to New York to receive the Schweitzer

Medal from the Animal Welfare Institute and to give a major address at the Garden Club of America. In brief remarks after receiving the Schweitzer medal from Robert Cushman Murphy, Rachel shared some of her own understanding of "reverence for life." "What is important is the relation of man to all life," she said. "This has never been so tragically overlooked as in our present age, when through our technology we are waging war against the natural world. By acquiescing in needless destruction and suffering, our stature as human beings is diminished."[33]

To the women of the Garden Club, Carson spoke about a new phase of the struggle. Reiterating that she was not opposed to insect control but only the means used to do so, for the first time her speech focused on the political and economic forces that prevented changes in pesticide policy and the encouraging signs of grass-roots activities demanding reform. "People are beginning to ask questions and to insist upon proper answers instead of meekly acquiescing in whatever spraying programs are proposed," she said. "There is an increasing demand for better legislative control of pesticides."[34]

Addressing the stream of propaganda issuing from pesticide trade groups that hid their affiliations behind research organizations or educational institutions, Carson again urged citizen vigilance. "As you listen to the present controversy about pesticides," Carson told the audience, "I recommend you ask yourself—Who speaks?—And Why?"[35]

When Carson finished what Marie Rodell described as a "blockbuster" of a speech, they learned that the Garden Club did not believe in press coverage of their functions and had not notified the press of Carson's appearance. "I've asked her to incorporate the newsworthy stuff from it into her speech to the New England Wildflower people next week," Rodell grumbled to Ford, "but in case they too are shy violets, do you think you'd best alert the press?"[36]

Rodell need not have worried. The press appeared in Boston in full force to hear luncheon remarks by Carson and Esther Peterson, Assistant Secretary of Labor, who preceded her on the podium. Carson assumed the members of the New England Wildflower Preservation Society shared the same concern for the health and life of the natural world. "Are we being impractical when we protest the substitution of the 'brownout' for the color and beauty of flowers along our roads?" she asked. "Are we being sentimental when we care whether the robin returns to our dooryard and the veery sings in the twilight woods? A world that is no longer fit for wild plants, that is no longer graced by the flight of birds, a world whose streams and forests are empty and lifeless is not likely to be a fit habitat for man himself, for these things are symptoms of an ailing world."[37]

Carson gave particular attention to the work of Frank Egler and his new organization, Right-of-way Resources of America. Egler's program of roadside vegetation management and selective spraying, Carson explained, was an alternative to blanket spraying, which destroyed natural communities of shrubs, wildflowers, birds, and small animals.

Egler, in the audience that afternoon, heard Rachel Carson for the first time. He was the Connecticut chairman of the Wildflower Society and had come especially to meet her. Egler was not disappointed either in the content of her address or in the style of her speaking, recalling later that she was just as "intellectually tough" as he had expected from their correspondence and conversations. But he was unexpectedly charmed by her feminine demeanor and her calm, reflective manner of dealing with questions and admirers. She gave no indication at all that she had been in poor health.[38]

Rachel had looked forward to going to Boston, not only because she looked forward to meeting Egler and thanking him but because it gave her an excuse to spend the rest of the weekend with Dorothy and Stan in West Bridgewater. When Rachel returned home weary and anxious about the increasingly frequent pains in her chest, she found an invitation from the President's Science Advisory Committee to join it for an informal session on Saturday morning to discuss their ongoing study of pesticides. "I guess I should [go]," Rachel told Dorothy, understating the importance of the invitation; "perhaps it's a chance to straighten out some thinking."[39]

She also made an appointment with Dr. Bernard Walsh, a well-known cardiologist. "Dr. Healy clings to his theory [the pains are] radiation-caused, but since the result is the same (insufficient blood to the heart muscle) it really doesn't seem to matter much," she explained to Dorothy.[40]

Walsh confirmed Carson's angina and put her on a strict regimen. She was to do minimal walking, no stairs, no housework. She got a hospital bed to elevate her head and was given several different doses of nitroglycerin. Since her type of angina was unprovoked by exercise and the attacks were most frequent at night, Walsh felt it was wise if Carson did not plan to travel or to do any more public speaking until the attacks were under control.

Carson's scheduled speeches to accept the Constance Lindsay Skinner Woman of Conscience award from the Women's National Book Association in New York, and even the Conservationist of the Year Award from the National Wildlife Federation in Detroit in early March, had to be canceled. "So many ironic things," Rachel wrote Dorothy resignedly. "Now all the 'honors' have to be received for me by someone else. And all the opportunities to travel to foreign lands—all expenses paid—have to be passed up. Sweden is the latest." Carson had been invited by her Swedish publisher to lecture at the University of Stockholm. It was a great disappointment not to be able to go.[41]

Rachel kept up a good front in public, but privately she was often in pain and terribly frightened. As a measure of her despair and as insurance against regret, Rachel wrote a letter to Dorothy that she placed in "the strong box" in an envelope marked "For Dorothy Freeman" for her friend to read after her death.

Rachel wrote what became the first of three letters on January 24.

> I have been coming to the realization that suddenly there might be no chance to speak to you again and it seems I must leave a word of goodbye. But last night the pains were bad and came so often that I was frightened. No, that isn't quite the word, but I realized there might come a time when I wouldn't rouse from sleep in time to reach for the pills. And it seemed it might be a little easier for you if there were some message.
>
> I think that you must have no regrets in my behalf. I have had a rich life, full of rewards and satisfactions that come to few, and if it must end now, I can feel that I have achieved most of what I wished to do. That wouldn't have been true two years ago, when I first realized my time was short, and I am so grateful to have had this extra time.
>
> My regrets, darling, are for your sadness, leaving Roger, when I so wanted to see him through to manhood, for dear Jeffie whose life is linked to mine. What I want to write of is the joy and fun and gladness we have shared—for these are the things I want you to remember—I want to live on in your memories of happiness.[42]

In some ways Rachel saw her angina as a "secret weapon" against what she called "the grimmer foe," for it might take her quickly and spare her suffering.

Her mood of retrospection was apparent in a letter she wrote to Dorothy on the anniversary of their "white hyacinth" letter. "It seems strange," Rachel wrote, "looking back over my life, that all that went before this past decade seems to have been merely preparation for it. Into that decade (with a little stretching back to 1951) have been crowded everything I shall be remembered for. And most of the sorrows, tragedies, problems, and serious illnesses too, have been crowded into that period. I truly cannot imagine those years without you, darling. Because of you there has been far more joy in the happy things, and the hard spots have been more bearable. And so it will be in the time to come, I know."[43]

But moments of optimism were a luxury. A visit to Caulk revealed that there were new lymph tumors above the collarbone, midway to the shoulder, and another higher in her neck. Housebound and almost completely an invalid, Carson felt isolated. "I'm almost as confined as in a hospital," she told Dorothy, "but it's lonely in a different way. I've told almost no one, so everyone just thinks I'm still rushing around being busy—so there are no get well cards, inquiring calls, or any of the things that perhaps make sickness a little less solitary affair."[44]

Barney Crile was reassuring, but it was now certain that the cancer had entered her bones. After a conversation with him about how bone metastases yielded to radiation as easily as lymph tumors, Rachel felt less frightened. Caulk told Carson to pay attention to joint and bone pain and not to dismiss it as arthritis. Rachel was determined she was not going to lead an invalid's life and promised Dorothy they would still do most of the things they loved to do in Maine that summer.

"The main thing I want to say, dear," Rachel wrote Dorothy after her appointment with Caulk, "is that we are not going to get bogged down in unhappiness about all this. We are going to be happy, and go on enjoying all the lovely things that give life meaning—sunrise and sunset, moonlight on the bay, music and good books, the song of thrushes and the wild cries of geese passing over. So—let's think and live happily enjoying whatever time there is."[45]

"I still believe," she told Barney Crile, "in the old Churchillian determination to fight each battle as it comes . . . and I think a determination to win may well postpone the final battle." As she began another round of heavy radiation treatment in late February, Carson found she needed all her reserves to fight the tremendous weariness, the pain, nausea, and the depression that seemed the inevitable side effects.[46]

Rachel told Dorothy about the letter she had put in the strongbox, and she was relieved when she and Dorothy began to talk more openly about the certainty of death. "We both know that my time is limited," she wrote in early March, "and why shouldn't we face it together, freely and openly? I know you have dark thoughts and 'hard nights'—how could it be otherwise?" Quite naturally their letters turned to thoughts of immortality.[47]

Moved by Dorothy's thoughts on the immortality of consciousness, Rachel explained that as a biologist, she believed in the kind of "material immortality" that she had written about at the end of "Undersea." Thinking of the letter she had received from E. B. White, she said, "It is good to know that I shall live on even in the minds of many who do not know me, and largely through association with things that are beautiful and lovely." Immortality through memory, however, was insufficient, and she confessed she found "the concept of nothingness hard to accept."

Rachel thought that just because one did not know and could not imagine what kind of spiritual existence there might be did not mean that one rejected personal immortality. "Because I cannot understand something doesn't mean it doesn't exist. The marvels of atomic or nuclear physics, and the mathematical concepts of astronomy are wholly beyond my ability to grasp. Yet I know these concepts deal with proven realities, so it is no more difficult to believe there is some sort of life beyond that 'horizon,' and to accept the fact we cannot now know what it is." Barney Crile had once compared the life-death relationship to "rivers flowing into the sea," a concept Rachel told Dorothy she found "not only beautiful but somehow a source of great comfort and strength."[48]

These thoughts were also prompted by the unexpected death of her friend and sometime escort, Charles Alldredge. Too ill herself to go to his memorial service, Carson grieved at his passing. During the radiation treatments, Carson spent as much time as she could in bed, or at least reclining on the couch in her office while she and Jeanne Davis worked on correspondence. "Sometimes I wish I had nothing to do," she wrote Dorothy, "but probably it is better to keep my mind occupied. But the never dwindling piles of letters sometimes oppress me—like a treadmill—and I wonder how to get free to think about the book I still hope to write." She had been thinking about her approach to the man and nature book, but first, she wanted to finish the expansion of "Help Your Child to Wonder."[49]

Her spirits were lifted temporarily by an unexpected visit from Lois Crisler, who was anxious about Carson's declining health. Although she did not tell Crisler everything about the bone metastasis, Carson did talk openly about her cancer and about her hopes for the limited time she had left. "But I keep thinking," Rachel wrote Lois after their visit, "if only I could have reached this point ten years ago! Now, when there is the opportunity to do so much, my body falters and I know there is little time left. But this makes it all the more necessary to be rid of the tyranny of 'pieces of paper'—to use the months or years that remain to do what I can that is worth doing, not remain trapped in trivia."[50]

Paul Brooks had been worried about Carson's next book as well. He knew that both books had been promised to Harper, although he did not know that Carson had signed a contract and received an advance on a sea anthology. At each new honor for *Silent Spring*, Brooks became more and more unhappy with the idea that any Carson book would be published by a different house and editor. In October he finally spoke frankly about his frustration to Marie Rodell. "For better or worse, I have become so closely associated with the editing and publication of *Silent Spring* that the appearance of her next book on another list would be in the nature of a professional disaster." Acknowledging that Rodell had been dissatisfied with certain aspects of Houghton Mifflin's handling of *The Edge of the Sea*, Brooks argued that with the writing and publication of *Silent Spring* there was no justification for taking Carson's next book elsewhere. However Rodell responded to Brooks's letter at the time, by April 1963 circumstances had made the issue more problematic than Brooks knew. Rodell still held hope for the book on children but realistically knew Carson would not live long enough to complete another major work.[51]

By mid-March Carson could report that her angina was under control, but her gravest concern was the potential collapse of vertebrae. It was not so much the pain of walking but fear that kept her as inactive as possible. For the first time, Carson decided to try injections of the controversial anticancer substance Krebiozen, a course she knew most of her current doctors would attempt to discourage. Krebiozen had been the subject of bitter medical controversy for more than a decade. It was produced by injecting a mold preparation into horses, then extracting the substance from the blood serum. Adherents claimed it helped the whole body resist cancer, and in many patients it appeared to bring about considerable periods of pain relief and improvement. Dr. Biskind sent Rachel literature on Krebiozen, including a recent article in one of the medical association journals, and recommended that she consider it, but she had to find a doctor in Washington willing to give her the injections.[52]

After the massive doses of radiation therapy were completed in March, Ralph Caulk and Barney Crile discussed the possibility of initiating short-term androgen therapy when any new areas of bone pain occurred to see if the tumor was still endocrine-sensitive. But Carson rejected this protocol since the use of male hormones had unpleasant side effects and was primarily diagnostic. She was certain her cancer was endocrine-sensitive and understood that the final treatment available to her would be either some form of adrenalectomy or a hypophysectomy, the destruction of the pituitary gland, but that was a procedure she was reluctant to submit to. Rachel saw no reason not to give Krebiozen a trial. If she fell within the percentage of patients who lived longer and more comfortably, then well and good. At least, as she explained to Crile, it would do her no harm. "I am well aware of the controversy over Krebiozen and of the AMA's long-standing war against it—but then I have seldom if ever found myself in agreement with the AMA! Their attacks on Krebiozen resemble so closely some of the methods used against those critical of pesticides that the parallel is quite suggestive."[53]

Dr. Healy, who had treated Carson longer than anyone, agreed to give her the injections, but Caulk, as she had predicted, objected. His objections, as Rachel suspected, were more political than scientific. Although he told her he did not think Krebiozen would do any good, his real objection was evident in a letter he wrote to Crile. "I hope we can avoid having her receive the Krebiozen, because if any coincidental improvement should accrue, such benefit by a well known person, as she, would give the sponsors of this product unwarranted support." But Caulk did not pose further objections since Carson was willing to continue with radiation when her situation required it.[54]

Crile sympathized with Carson's desire to try something that had the possibility of systemic control and really was not against an experiment with Krebiozen. As Carson told him with a touch of sardonic humor, "If the Krebiozen gets me nowhere we can then think about other things later. If the past few months are typical there will be no dearth of symptoms to work on." Carson was eager to get started, hoping that new pains in the bones of her pelvis would be relieved. As she told Dorothy, "if these pains would yield to it, I would begin to recover some of the optimism I've lost." Carson began Krebiozen injections in April and stopped in July. The drug had no effect on her symptoms or pain whatsoever.[55]

At the end of March Carson had received the press release announcing "The Silent Spring of Rachel Carson," the *CBS Reports* television program scheduled to air on April 3. She was rather annoyed when she saw the program's outline. After reviewing the names of the others interviewed, noting whether they were reasonably on her side, neutral, or strongly negative, she told Dorothy, "the show is weighted against me." That conclusion was a realistic one, for the industry's efforts to discredit her ideas and to crush the positive forces for change were gaining in strength.

A rumor had reached her that the President's Science Advisory Committee had completed its preliminary report on pesticides and that several members of the Senate's Republican Policy Committee and the industry had exerted enormous pressure on the PSAC to water it down. She passed the information on to Paul Knight and to Paul Brooks, both of whom knew committee members personally. But it was an example of the political vulnerability of her views.[56]

Carson was doubly grateful when, just before the CBS show aired, Brooks Atkinson wrote a second column in the *New York Times* on the controversy. He commented on the soothing but meaningless statements coming from government officials and ridiculed the industry charge that Carson was a "fanatic defender of the balance of nature, as if the balance of nature were equivalent to nudism or skin diving." "Evidence," he wrote "continues to accumulate that she is right and that *Silent Spring* is the 'rights of man' of this generation."[57]

As the CBS broadcast date drew near, Rachel was also worried about how she would appear to television viewers. Remembering how weary she had been in November when Eric Sevareid and Jay McMullen interviewed her, she was not looking forward to seeing herself on screen. "Well, I just hope I don't look and sound like an utter idiot," she wrote Dorothy. "When I remember my state of extreme exhaustion those two days, plus the huskiness of voice, I can't be too optimistic."[58]

Producer Jay McMullen had worked over eight months, traveling from Maine to California, for interviews with individuals voicing a wide range of opinion about pesticides and their potential danger. In addition to Carson, on-camera interviews with government officials included Agriculture Secretary Orville Freeman, U. S. Surgeon General Luther Terry, Commissioner of the Food and Drug Administration George Larrick, chief toxicologist of the U.S. Public Health Service Wayland Hayes, director of the USFWS Wildlife Refuge Service John Buckley, and James Hartgering of the PSAC staff. Robert White-Stevens represented the chemical industry.

Press releases had gone out to journals about two weeks ahead announcing the subject of the show, but industry press agents complained they had difficulty finding out exactly who would appear. It was rumored that the program dipped into a philosophical argument about man's attitude toward nature and that McMullen's questions were probing. Anticipation ran high, causing a columnist for the Chicago *Sun Times* to remark, "DDT may be right up there with fallout as a subject of TV controversy once *CBS Reports* has put on its investigation of Rachel Carson's book."[59]

About the same time CBS was deluged by more than a thousand letters, more mail than had ever been received before a broadcast. All the letters were mimeographed, some signed, some not, asking that the program be fair about the issue. It was an obvious letter-writing campaign, and McMullen assumed it was directed by the chemical industry lobby.[60]

Then, two days before the broadcast, the three largest of the five commercial sponsors of the show withdrew from the program. A spokesman for Lehn & Fink Products, makers of Lysol Disinfectant Spray, cosmetics, and sanitary maintenance supplies, said, "It wasn't exactly the type of product to be advertising on a show about insecticides." The other two skittish sponsors were Standard Brands Inc. and Ralston Purina Co., both manufacturers of food products. They cited the show's controversial content, which they thought unsuited to their products' advertisement. The remaining two sponsors, Kiwi Polish Company and Brillo Manufacturing Co., stuck it out. Although the commercial loss hurt CBS, *Broadcasting* magazine reported that the time period opened up by the departing sponsors was devoted to an expansion of the program material.[61]

While there was great public interest in the show, *CBS Reports* had to compete with a more exciting scientific event taking place on the same evening. The earth-orbiting flight of the second Mercury space capsule, *Faith 7*, manned by the popular astronaut Gordon Cooper, contended for viewer attention. CBS was interrupted seven times by the Washington, D.C., affiliate and local stations in other cities to give the public updates of *Faith 7*'s progress.

With Eric Sevareid narrating, McMullen's show began with the acknowledgment that a pesticide problem existed. The question he probed was: How serious a problem was it? From the outset Carson's position was made clear. "In spite of her view that present pesticide safeguards are inadequate, Miss Carson does not advocate discontinuing the use of pesticides immediately. Instead she proposes a gradual shift to other methods of pest control."

Carson was seen in her wood-paneled study on Berwick Road wearing her sage-green suit and gold necklace. Sitting calmly in her office chair, she spoke unhurriedly and distinctly about what she had set out to do and why. She seemed entirely natural, even smiling slightly as she spoke. "We've heard the benefits of pesticides. We have heard a great deal about their safety, but very little about the hazards, very little about the failures, the inefficiencies and yet the public was being asked to accept these chemicals, was being asked to acquiesce in their use, and did not have the whole picture, so I set about to remedy the balance there."[62]

Carson then was shown reading passages from six different chapters of *Silent Spring* in her calm, deliberate, and unhurried way. During her reading, viewers saw examples of the pesticide use and abuse. Carson never changed her pattern of speech, never became excited or dogmatic, logically stating the facts as she believed them. She came across as a dignified, polite, concerned scientist, with no motive other than to alert the public to a significant problem. But it was obvious that her adversary in this controversy that was so well financed and so powerful that at any moment it could overwhelm even the most well-intentioned individual.

It would have been a masterful performance even if there had been no one else to compare her to, but in juxtaposition to the wild-eyed, loud-voiced Dr. Robert White-Stevens in white lab coat, Carson appeared anything but the hysterical alarmist that her critics contended. White-Stevens's opening statement, in stark contrast to Carson's quiet contention that pesticides presented a problem that the public needed to consider, called up a caldron of plagues that threatened human survival without chemicals. "If man were to faithfully follow the teachings of Miss Carson, we would return to the Dark Ages, and the insects and diseases and vermin would once again inherit the earth."[63]

In between Carson and White-Stevens was a parade of government witnesses. The overall impression these experts gave was that no one in authority knew very much about the chemicals that were being used so profligately nor seemed inordinately concerned about their long-term effects, which was precisely Carson's point. Taken together, the spectacle of the government's combined ignorance as well as its evasive answers to McMullen's questions was deeply disquieting. What viewers saw was a graphically compelling portrayal of Carson's thesis that "we know not what harm we face."

In the final portion of the report, McMullen transcended the specific issues of contention to examine the fundamental conflict in attitude over the proper role of humankind in the environment. It gave Carson a chance to explain her ecological view of the balance of nature as a series of interrelationships between living things and between living things and the environment. The program ended with a powerful statement from Carson: "We still talk in terms of conquest. We still haven't become mature enough to think of ourselves as only a very tiny part of a vast and incredible universe. Now I truly believe that we in this generation must come to terms with nature, and I think we're challenged, as mankind has never been challenged before, to prove our maturity and our mastery, not of nature but of ourselves."[64]

CBS Reports amounted to nothing less than a special printing of *Silent Spring*. The network estimated a viewing audience of 10 to 15 million people, a huge number of whom had not read the book but were concerned and confused by what they had been reading. Television allowed Carson and not her critics to define the issue. The show was devastating to public confidence in government officials, and it won few friends for the chemical industry. In a single evening, Jay McMullen's broadcast added the environment to the public agenda.[65]

When the show ended, Rachel's telephone rang with calls from friends congratulating her. CBS Television received hundreds of letters praising the show. The USDA, the Public Health Service, and the Food and Drug Administration were inundated with angry letters protesting their acquiescence in programs and policies threatening to human health and animal life and decrying their lack of scientific evidence about the long-term effects of what they were doing.

Carson also received hundreds of letters. Frank Egler was so pleased by her television triumph that he could scarcely contain himself. "Wonderful," he wrote Rachel. "You scored a notable triumph! You yourself came over *beautifully!*" Christine Stevens wrote, "You were superb on the television broadcast, and how delightful that Dr. White-Stevens looked so fiendish!" Carson was pleased with the show and called McMullen to tell him so.[66]

Most gratifying of all, the day after CBS Reports aired, Senator Hubert Humphrey (D-Minnesota) announced that he had asked Senator Abraham Ribicoff (D-Connecticut) to conduct a broad-ranging congressional review of environmental hazards, including pesticides. Ribicoff would chair a subcommittee of the Senate Government Operations Committee to hold hearings for that purpose. Two weeks later Carson accepted an invitation to testify before the Ribicoff committee.[67]

The CBS television broadcast shattered months of comparative quiet in Washington on the pesticide issue. But in a matter of days, it became clear that the White House considered the stage well set for the release of the long-overdue report by the President's Science Advisory Committee.[68]

The public had no advance warning of the final release of the report on May 15, but Carson, who had her own network, knew when it had been delivered to the president and had gone to the printer. Certain now that it would support her views, Carson told Brooks, "I think we should be ready to capitalize fully on whatever areas of agreement there are between *Silent Spring* and the report."[69]

The PSAC report, "The Uses of Pesticides," was not as harsh in its recommendations as many in government and industry feared. Nevertheless, in language that clearly vindicated Rachel Carson's evidence, the report concluded that "the accretion of residues in the environment can be controlled only by orderly reductions of persistent pesticides."

The PSAC criticized federal government agencies as well as the chemical industry and specifically challenged the government's current pest control program and its entire concept of pest eradication. It concluded that Carson's case against synthetic hydrocarbon pesticides was stronger than her critics had been willing to admit. The report recommended increased public education on the benefits and hazards of pesticide use, noting that "until the publication of *Silent Spring*, people were generally unaware of the toxicity of pesticides."[70]

Industry's reaction, according to the *Wall Street Journal*, was mixed. There was no threat that the government would move to withdraw highly toxic materials from interstate commerce or recommend stringent legislative controls. On the other hand, President Kennedy's statement, contained in the report, said that he would consider a variety of ways to implement the recommendations of the report, including new legislation. There was no way for industry to ignore the fact that the report was critical and that it cast a long shadow over governmental policies and industrial and agricultural practices.[71]

That same day the U.S. Senate Subcommittee on Reorganization and International Organization opened hearings on environmental hazards and called its first witness, Jerome Wiesner, Special Assistant to the President for Science and Technology. In his remarks Wiesner stated that pesticides may be "potentially a much greater hazard" than radioactive fallout. While pesticides should not be abolished, he recommended the need to study their long-range effect on humans.[72]

That evening CBS aired a special program produced by Sevareid and McMullen on the pesticide report entitled "The Verdict on the Silent Spring of Rachel Carson." Using some of the footage from the earlier broadcast of Carson reading and White-Stevens responding, CBS reported that the PSAC report called for major reforms in government regulation and in the standards and methods by which the government attempts to protect the public from the hazards of pesticides.

The CBS crew caught up with Carson in Philadelphia, where she had gone for a dinner and brief address to the Garden Club of America. CBS quoted her as saying "I think it's a splendid report. It's strong. It's objective and I think a very fair evaluation of the problem. I feel that the report has vindicated me and my principal contentions. I am particularly pleased by the reiteration of the fact that the public is entitled to the facts, which after all, was my reason for writing *Silent Spring*."

At the end of "The Verdict," Sevareid told viewers: "Miss Rachel Carson had two immediate aims. One was to alert the public; the second, to build a fire under the Government. She accomplished the first aim months ago. Tonight's report by the Presidential panel is prima facie evidence that she has accomplished the second."[73]

Paul Brooks wrote Carson the next day, "I have been reading the New York papers and am still in a happy glow." He had reason to be pleased, for no publishing company could ever have generated the publicity that Carson had by two appearances on CBS. Privately Rachel felt like gloating just a little. "I am sure you are as delighted as I am with the report of the President's Committee and the impact it is having in the press," she wrote Charles Callison at National Audubon. "I am told that the industry is wild." Callison had written proposing that she do a book on water pollution, but Carson demurred, telling him, "One crusading book in a lifetime is enough."[74]

Less than a week after the PSAC report was released, Rachel Carson made a rare appearance on *The Today Show*. She pushed herself to make these public appearances partly to assuage her fear that there were rumors about her ill health and also because she wanted to talk about how to bring about change.[75]

Rachel had been feeling well during most of May, but her angina was back and she was not sure how long radiation would continue to stave off the enemy. At the end of April her chest pains had been so intense that she had written another letter for Dorothy and put it in the strongbox. She had expected the Freemans to visit her, but they had to abandon their plans due to Stan's poor health.[76]

Thinking that Dorothy was on her way to her, Rachel wrote:

> You are starting on your way to me in the morning, but I have such a strange feeling that I may not be here when you come—so this is just an extra little note of farewell should that happen. There have been many pains (heart) in the past few days, and I'm weary in every bone. And tonight there is something strange about my vision, which may mean nothing. But of course I thought, what if I can't write—can't *see* to write—tomorrow?[77]

Rachel had thought more seriously about submitting to Crile's surgery to ablate the pituitary. But with her cancer in a period of remission and determined to get to Maine for the summer, she gathered all her energies in early June to draft her testimony for the upcoming hearings of the Ribicoff subcommittee and the Senate Commerce Committee two days later.[78]

Carson had been thinking about her recommendations for legislation and for policy change since beginning her research five years before. In the course of writing *Silent Spring*, she had contacted a variety of experts about their ideas for reform. Rachel wanted her testimony to provide specific recommendations that would bring improvement but at the same time be politically feasible. Rather than advocate wholesale reforms, Carson's years of experience in government kept her pragmatic and made it that much more impossible for legislators to dismiss her.[79]

Marie Rodell went down the night before Carson's appearance and Jeanne Davis and Rachel drove Carson's new Oldsmobile to Capitol Hill. Carson was not nervous. Jerome Sonosky, Ribicoff's legislative assistant who met with Carson before the hearings, recalled that it seemed she had been ready for this for a long time. Ribicoff remembers that the hearing room was jammed, and no one moved.[80]

Carson's testimony took over forty minutes. She established the context of the contamination of the physical environment of water, soil, air, vegetation, animals, and humans, and its many sources. Her focus was the evidence of pesticide pollution that had developed during the past year, emphasizing its wide dispersal from point of application: a new kind of fallout.[81]

Carson drew two major conclusions: that aerial spraying of pesticides should be brought under strict control and should be reduced to a minimum strength needed to accomplish the essential objectives and that a "strong and unremitting effort should be made to reduce the use of pesticides that leave long-lasting residues, and ultimately to eliminate them." Beyond that, she had several recommendations, the most important of which was "the right of the citizen to be secure in his own home against the intrusion of poisons applied by other persons. I speak not as a lawyer but as a biologist and as a human being, but I strongly feel that this is or should be one of the basic human rights. I am afraid, however, that it has little or no existence in practice."[82]

"There can be no doubt that you are the person most responsible for the current public concern over pesticide hazards," Senator Ribicoff told her when she had completed her testimony. When the chairman had finished his remarks, the questioning of the witness proceeded through the other four senators present—Ernest Gruening, James Pearson, Jacob Javits, and Claiborne Pell. Senator Gruening (D-Alaska) compared the impact of *Silent Spring* with that of *Uncle Tom's Cabin*, predicting that Carson's book also would change the course of history. The committee dwelt at some length on Carson's call for a bureau or some agency to carry out genetic testing of chemical pesticides. Carson was able to call the senators' attention to the type of advertising that lulled consumers into thinking pesticides were harmless. An hour and a half after she began, the subcommittee hearing moved to recess, and Carson's moment was over.[83]

Those who heard Rachel Carson that morning did not see a reserved or reticent woman in the witness chair but an accomplished scientist, an expert on chemical pesticides, a brilliant writer, and a woman of conscience who made the most of an opportunity few citizens of any rank can have to make their opinions known. Her witness had been equal to her vision.

Senator Ribicoff recalled that one of the reasons Carson's testimony that day and her responses during the whole controversy were so impressive was that she was a "true believer." Her testimony rang true, and no one who heard her that day could have questioned her integrity.[84]

Two days later Carson appeared in a different hearing room in the New Senate Office Building. She was to testify before members of the Senate Committee on Commerce, which was considering two bills introduced by Senator Maurine Neuberger to prevent federal spraying without state knowledge and require stronger warnings about pesticide hazards to wildlife. Committee chairman Warren Magnuson had called Carson and Roland Clement, staff biologist for the National Audubon Society, to testify.

Speaking as a government biologist for sixteen years who had seen the inevitable conflicts when several agencies attempted to carry out ambiguous mandates, Carson called for the formation of an independent board or commission set up within the Executive Department. This "Pesticide Commission," as Carson called it, would be made up of professionally competent experts in such fields as biology, medicine, genetics, and conservation and not drawn from professionals in government or industry. Its work would be supported by a small permanent staff and have authority to resolve problems arising from control programs and make decisions in the public interest. In the meantime, Carson had already spoken to a number of people, including Paul Knight, Frank Egler, and Ruth Scott, about the need to create some sort of private citizen's advisory committee to disseminate research on pesticides, answer consumer questions, and educate the public on the hazards of using toxic chemicals.[85]

Her public obligations fulfilled, at least for the moment, Rachel simply wanted to get to Maine. Stubbornly determined though she was, she recognized that it was risky putting six hundred miles between herself and Dr. Caulk's monster machine. Marie and Rachel's niece Virginia were concerned about her being alone with Roger in the cottage for seven weeks. Her heart condition was precarious, and her spine was now showing signs of compression fractures, making her walking risky.

With some misgivings about sacrificing her privacy as well as her time with Dorothy, Rachel asked Lois Crisler if she could go to Southport and stay for perhaps three weeks to start with. At first Crisler declined, probably reluctant to be a house guest for so long a time, but under strong pressure from Rodell, she did agree to go for one week at the end of August.[86]

Carson had one last formal appearance at a reception and dinner of the National Council of Women where she received their first "Woman of Conscience" award. After several false starts for Maine, caused by illnesses in Jeanne Davis's family and a death that took Ida out of town, Jeanne drove Rachel, Roger, and the two cats, Moppet and Jeffie, to Southport. Arriving on June 25, Roger promptly went off to camp for almost a month, leaving Rachel alone to enjoy her favorite spot in nature.[87]

Before her arrival Rachel had written Dorothy she was determined "that *nothing* must in any way mar our happiness together. There must be long days when we can go off together alone. There must be many opportunities for us to do together the things we love to do." A small note left for Dorothy one evening in August reflected Rachel's frustration with her debilitated physical condition and bespoke her desire to make memories to cherish when summer was over. "Would you help me search for a fairy cave on an August moon and a low, low tide? I would love to try once more, for the memories are precious."[88]

19

"I Shall Remember the Monarchs"

As the summer drifted by, each day seemed more bittersweet than the last. Rachel's mobility was compromised a little more each week, until by the beginning of September the pain in the bones of her pelvic girdle made each step a torturous effort. The inevitable prospect of leaving Maine, the serenity of Southport Island, the wild beauty of the Sheepscot, the birdsong in the shadowed forest, and her tide pools, which she could see from her deck but could not get to, was soon upon her. Sad as she was to leave Dorothy, Rachel knew she would see her again, but of her return to Maine and her cottage she was less certain.

Rachel had made arrangements with the ever-faithful Bob Hines to drive them all home. Her departure, however, was delayed not by sentiment or health, but by her cat Moppet. The cat had become so ill just before they were to leave that Rachel took her to a veterinary hospital in Brunswick, hoping that in a few days the cat would be well enough to travel. But Moppet died of pancreatitis on September 9. "Our sweet little Moppet died yesterday, so all we tried to do was of no avail," Rachel wrote Anne Ford the next day. "Now she is buried in a beautiful spot near our back door, to become part of the Maine she loved." Moppet's death made leaving Southport that much more wrenching and seemed particularly ominous.[1]

Dorothy drove Rachel down to the Newagen Inn, one of their favorite places on the little cape at the end of Southport Island, the day after Moppet died. With great difficulty Rachel managed to walk from the car to the wooden benches set in the field just above the rocky shore. It was a beautiful blue-skyed morning. The two talked of the joy and sadness of the summer while they listened to the sound of the wind and the water and watched the gulls wheel and turn overhead. As they looked out on Todd Point and Griffiths Head on the opposite shore, they remembered a day long ago when they were enveloped in a swirling fog on that remote beach and walked through it as in a dream.[2]

But on this warm, clear day Dorothy and Rachel spent the hours watching drifts of monarch butterflies feeding on the milkweed as they made their migration south. Later that afternoon Rachel wrote Dorothy, "a postscript" to their morning at Newagen, to leave her with some words of comfort she could not trust herself to speak. Rachel wrote:

> But most of all I shall remember the Monarchs, that unhurried westward drift of one small winged form after another, each drawn by some invisible force. We talked a little about their migration, their life history. Did they return? We thought not; for most, at least, this was the closing journey of their lives.
>
> But it occurred to me this afternoon, remembering, that it had been a happy spectacle, that we had felt no sadness when we spoke of the fact that there would be no return. And rightly—for when any living thing has come to the end of its life cycle we accept that end as natural.
>
> For the Monarch, that cycle is measured in a known span of months. For ourselves, the measure is something else, the span of which we cannot know. But the thought is the same: when that intangible cycle has run its course it is a natural and no unhappy thing that a life comes to its end.
>
> That is what those brightly fluttering bits of life taught me this morning. I found a deep happiness in it—so, I hope, may you.[3]

Finally, on the morning of the thirteenth Rachel, Roger, and Jeffie were ready to take leave of Maine. Rachel wanted some quiet moments on her deck to say farewell to the bay and to visit Moppet's mossy grave. Instead she found herself barely able to walk from the cottage to the car because of another fracture in her pelvic bones. Bob Hines almost had to carry her out. The long car trip was agony for Rachel. Bob decided it was best not to stop, so they drove all the way through, arriving in Silver Spring the next morning.[4]

Coming back to Maryland was always something of a systemic shock to Carson, a natural world and a cultural one so entirely different from Maine. It always seemed to Rachel as if "a curtain had fallen, separating one Act from the next." She was greeted by stacks of unopened mail, enough work to keep Jeanne busy for weeks. Four days later Rachel, under Ida's attentive supervision, was back at the Washington Hospital Center for tests.[5]

In less than three weeks Carson was scheduled to fly to San Francisco to deliver a major lecture to the Kaiser Foundation Hospitals and Permanente Medical Group's annual symposium at the Fairmont Hotel. Sitting that afternoon in Caulk's waiting room, aware that the X rays would certainly show new bone involvement, Carson could hardly contemplate being able to make such a trip.

"I've been x-rayed practically from chin to ankles," she wrote Dorothy. "All of the pelvic bones on the left side are involved, and there is ample explanation for the pain and lameness I've experienced most of the summer." Caulk conferred with Crile later that week and, with Rachel's consent, decided to begin a course of testosterone phosphorus to ease the pain and get her walking again. But first there would be further radiation treatments to the worst areas. The phosphorus program did not preclude surgery to ablate the pituitary, a procedure that now seemed inevitable. "I suspect before many months pass I shall try both treatments," Rachel told Dorothy matter-of-factly. "This [phosphorus], of course is for the bones only, while the pituitary implantation, if successful, might get the whole situation under better control."[6]

The one bright note was a call from Robert Cushman Murphy, notifying her unofficially that the American Geographical Society wished to award her the Cullem Medal at their annual dinner in New York on December 5. Rachel hoped Dorothy and Stan would be able to join her there for the festivities. Several days later Rachel received a letter from Murphy making it official. "You are the most thoroughly vindicated of prophets," he told her.[7]

Carson started the testosterone phosphorus treatment at the end of September. Dorothy tried to sustain her optimism with long letters describing her walks through the woods, an encounter with a marauding raccoon, another walk at Newagen, and a trip to Acadia. But her concern mounted when Rachel told her that walking was even more difficult than it had been. Caulk persisted in believing that she would be improved enough to make the California trip, but Rachel was doubtful.

At the end of one letter to Dorothy, she admitted, "Darling, you do know that my return [to Maine] is only a dream—a lovely dream." A few days later Rachel wrote to Dorothy, who was still at the Head, "I think of that little paradise you are inhabiting—the autumn loveliness, the birds, the seals, the sunsets and I don't want details of my very different days to break in upon the peace and contentment of this time. But give me your 'good thoughts' that somehow this ally I now have in my bones will be able to win this battle for me—your thoughts and your prayers, too."[8]

When she felt better, Carson worked on the piles of mail, dictating endlessly to Jeanne Davis and corresponding with supporters and friends about her desire to establish a citizen's advisory committee. Before leaving Maine, Rachel had written to Frank Egler that she wanted to talk to him about his ideas on how pesticide information could be disseminated and coordinated. She wrote similarly to her friend Ruth Scott who, like Egler, had wide experience with groups of the sort Carson had in mind. Rachel confided to Egler that her health had not been good that summer, but made him promise not to repeat it even to mutual friends such as Scott or Ray Fosberg.[9]

Earlier that spring Carson had a long conversation on the same subject with the Reverend Duncan Howlett, Alldredge's friend and the minister of All Souls Unitarian Church. After Alldredge's death, Carson had telephoned him, inviting him to come for tea. A man nearly the same age as she, Howlett was a fine writer and shared Carson's love of language. Although he had not seen Carson in many months, he realized by her puffy face and trembling hands that she was ill. She made tea, which they took out to her screened-in porch, where they sat and talked until it was too dark to see each other.[10]

They talked about the writer's craft. She told him about her mother's role as sympathetic critic and how she had read her books out loud to her. Howlett was concerned about the effect of the attacks industry had made on her. He was struck then, as he had been at an earlier meeting, by her quality of tenderness. Howlett unabashedly told Carson that he saw her as a prophet in her time, like Jeremiah, motivated by her love of the natural world, trying to persuade reasonable people how to behave. He remembers she did not demur from his description of her but quietly accepted it.

Carson shared with Howlett her concern over the number of letters she received from people wanting not only to have more information but to do something. After she explained her idea of setting up some kind of organization to continue her work, Howlett offered to pursue her idea with some of his associates.[11]

Carson also tried to finish a few small projects that she had promised but that, in the crush of activity over *Silent Spring*, she had been forced to put aside. In August she had somehow managed to make a start on a lengthy essay for the *World Book Encyclopedia Yearbook* on ocean resources that she had agreed to do in February. It was early September when she finally sent off a twenty-eight-page entry that incorporated the latest oceanographic research from Woods Hole.

Still gathering material for her larger book on man and nature, she wrote to Samuel Ordway, president of the Conservation Foundation, inquiring about research materials coming out of that organization's recent conference on carbon dioxide in the biosphere. Carson tried to do what she could on the manuscript that she referred to now as "the Wonder book." Marie sent her some new photographs Charles Pratt had taken of tide-pool creatures that seemed perfectly suited, but Carson made little progress.[12]

Public attacks on *Silent Spring* diminished after the PSAC report, while industry regrouped and waited for Ribicoff's Senate Subcommittee to finish hearing testimony. Industry spokesmen were fuming at the public vindication Carson had received from the PSAC, so it did not surprise her when, at the end of September, the *Saturday Evening Post* chose to publish a highly critical essay on *Silent Spring*. What did surprise her was that its author was none other than Edwin Diamond, Carson's one-time research collaborator.

In "The Myth of the 'Pesticide Menace,' " Diamond, who was then a senior editor at *Newsweek*, denigrated Carson's conclusions by mocking them and indirectly challenged her motives. "Thanks to a woman named Rachel Carson," he wrote, "a big fuss has been stirred up to scare the American public out of its wits. No matter that Miss Carson's conclusions were preconceived; no matter that her arguments were more emotional than accurate." Diamond's real quarrel with Carson was political. Angry that she had dared question the motives of industry and the integrity of science, thereby adding to what he called the "lamentably widespread distrust of scientists and their works," he accused Carson of employing the same kind of oversimplification and exaggeration that Joseph McCarthy had used against his mythical villains. The editors of the *Saturday Evening Post* prominently identified Diamond as "Miss Carson's collaborator at the start of the project that became *Silent*

Spring," stating that "a disagreement over how to proceed ended the collaboration."[13]

It was obvious to Carson, Rodell, and Brooks that Diamond was using this essay to get his revenge for being dismissed. Inundated with calls asking about her association with Diamond, Carson and Rodell wanted Brooks to write a letter to the editor stating the truth about their association and revealing the source of Diamond's vindictiveness; however, Brooks did nothing until Houghton Mifflin lawyers were certain that such a letter would not open them up for a libel action from Diamond.[14]

Rachel was deeply annoyed by Diamond's claims. "I don't think Mr. Diamond should be allowed to get away with his inference of high-level collaboration," she told Brooks. In Brooks's letter to the editor of the *Saturday Evening Post*, he stated the facts quite simply. "Mr. Diamond never did work with Miss Carson. To be more specific, Mr. Diamond was employed in March, 1958, to collaborate with her in the research for the book. By June, it had become apparent that he was not in a position to make a contribution to the book and his agreement with Houghton Mifflin was terminated." Brooks then quoted from his last letter to Diamond which stated that he was returning all the reporter's material without ever sending it to Carson.[15]

Another demeaning review, this one in the *Archives of Internal Medicine* by William B. Bean, M.D., was easier for Carson to ignore. Calling *Silent Spring* an impassioned tract and not a scientific document, Bean criticized Carson for her disregard for the conventions of scientific evidence. But, like Edwin Diamond, Bean's underlying pique was with Carson's temerity in criticizing the medical establishment for its lack of concern rather than with any legitimate scientific issue. In his conclusion, he said, "*Silent Spring*, which I read word for word with some trauma, kept reminding me of trying to win an argument with a woman. It can not be done."[16]

About the same time as these two reviews appeared, *Audubon Magazine* reprinted Carson's speech to the New England Wildflower Society as "Rachel Carson Answers Her Critics." It was perfectly timed to expose the motives and affiliations of her critics to the public. But as Roland Clement knew all too well, the National Audubon Society had limited public or political impact when matched against those who sought to undermine her message. The unfortunate publicity generated by Carson's decision not to speak at the American Forestry Association Congress in Washington at the end of October was another example of the power of those interests she had challenged to distort the truth. It also reflected the way her secretly declining health complicated the controversy.[17]

Carson had been invited to attend the congress in July and to participate in a panel entitled "Protection from Diseases and Insects." At the time she had been invited, the other participants on the panel had not been named. Rachel declined the invitation because of her uncertain health and her commitment to speak in San Francisco the previous week, and also because the forestry association leadership had close ties to the chemical lobby.[18]

Just before the congress opened, Carson learned that the association was distributing a press release to major newspapers and the wire services claiming that "Miss Rachel Carson, author of *Silent Spring*, had declined an invitation to share the platform with Dr. Westcott." The statement asserted that Westcott would "present the official scientific position on the treatment of insect and disease epidemics and defend the use of chemicals." The other panelist was a member of the ineffective Federal Pest Control Review Board.[19]

Upset and very angry at being misrepresented, Carson called Forestry Association officials, who admitted the statement was inaccurate. Assured that the matter would be corrected, Carson was shocked to learn that the association had continued distributing the offending statement. Carson demanded that it distribute a letter from her stating that her failure to appear had no relation to the appearance of anyone else on the program. Although she received apologies from the executives of the association, the damage was done.[20]

The atmosphere of innuendo and hostility made Carson all the more determined to present the opening lecture at the prestigious Kaiser Foundation symposium, "Man Against Himself," on October 18. Her appearance there would be widely reported in the press and provide an opportunity to reach an influential audience. For the same reasons, she accepted an invitation to speak at the Centennial of the Mayo Clinic in September 1964 along with her friend Loren Eiseley and distinguished scientists, Edward Teller and Peter Medawar.[21]

Rachel wondered if she would be able to endure the physical strain of a cross-country trip, but her speech, "The Pollution of the Environment," was a statement she very much wanted to make. Marie Rodell offered to accompany her to San Francisco since she had friends and clients there she needed to see. Jeanne Davis took care of Roger for the weekend.

Carson arrived at the Fairmont Hotel for the symposium in her wheelchair. Her official explanation for it, and the cane she used to get on and off the stage, was the old one of arthritis, which her hosts accepted without question. Carson sat to read her hour-long lecture and later wondered that she had endured even that. But given the enthusiastic reception by an audience of nearly 1,500 and the importance of what she had to say, she hardly noticed her infirmities.[22]

Her address, notable for its literary style as well as its calm but compelling message, was the first in which Carson publicly identified herself as an ecologist. Pointing out that since the beginning of biological time, there had been the closest possible interdependence between the physical environment and the life it sustains, Carson argued that humankind is "affected by the same influences that control the thousands of species to which he has evolutionary ties." The pollution of the environment, she argued, was a problem affecting the whole organism, in which the physical and biological environment acted on each other as a dynamic ecosystem. Carson emphasized that environmental contamination presented a problem of moral responsibility for present generations and for those yet unborn. It was time, Carson said, "that human beings admit their kinship with other forms of life."[23]

In her speech, there were reverberations of *Silent Spring*. She lamented that contemporary society seldom evaluated the risks of a new technology before it was "embedded in a vast economic and political commitment," becoming virtually impossible to alter. Carson argued that the most serious problem posed by modern synthetic pesticides was their long-term, widespread contamination of the environment. She gave dramatic new evidence of air pollution, with examples drawn from California, of the wide dispersal of pesticides beyond the point of application.[24]

It was one of her finest speeches, beautifully crafted and expertly delivered before a hushed and appreciative audience. A reporter for a San Francisco newspaper quoted large sections of her address, but insensitively described Carson as a "middle-aged, arthritis-crippled spinster," noting she "smiled faintly as the crowd applauded her, then picked up her cane and hobbled off the platform."[25]

Carson had made arrangements with David Brower, executive director of the Sierra Club, to do some sightseeing and the next morning, she and Marie joined Brower and his wife Anne for a tour of Muir Woods. A National Park Service ranger guided Carson's wheelchair through the great trees and down sun-dappled paths lined with enormous California laurel.

It was a trip Carson had always hoped to take, and while she delighted in it, she was also frustrated by her circumstances. "I longed to wander off, *alone*, into the heart of the woods, where I could really get the feeling of the place," she complained to Dorothy, "instead of being surrounded by people! And confined to a wheelchair! I was so grateful to the Browers for taking me, and to the Ranger for his hospitality and his fund of information, but the thing that would have made my enjoyment complete I couldn't have."[26]

Their next stop was Fort Cronkhite. David Brower remembers how moved he was as he watched Carson react to that Pacific Ocean beach. He gathered some pebbles for her from the shore's ancient stone formations. But then, taking charge of Carson's chair, Brower took her around to Rodeo Lagoon. "It was the first time I had seen them [the pelicans] there," Brower wrote later. "Not surprising, given what DDT had previously done to their eggs. But there they were, thanks to Miss Carson and her book—a whole gaggle of Brown pelicans, some two hundred of them, jubilant. So was she."[27]

Carson was intellectually stimulated by her exposure to the Pacific coast and deeply moved by its natural beauties, but she had been surprised by how physically dependent she was on Marie during the trip. At some point she realized that she could not possibly have made the long trip without her.

Upon her return, she admitted she was as sick as she had ever been and in constant pain. There was new involvement in her upper back affecting her arms. She could not walk or use the walker. Worst of all, she had difficulty writing because of numbness in her right hand. She read a little but slept a great deal, comforted by memories of the beautiful dreamlike flight she had taken across the continent. "A privilege," she called it, "to see it that way. I'm full of thoughts about water cycles and the role of water in sculpturing those strange canyon lands of the west," she told Dorothy, wishing they were together to share her thoughts.[28]

Dr. Caulk and Dr. Healy were both discouraged by Carson's failure to respond to the phosphorus and by the spread of the cancer through her bones. They began a regimen of steroids, which Crile recommended, to suppress Carson's adrenal function and retard the metastases.

Rachel's days were long, lonely, and often filled with despair. Dorothy's almost daily letters provided brief pleasure. When Rachel woke in the night she wondered if Dorothy, too, were lying awake in her bed thinking of her. "I believe, darling," Rachel wrote in early November, "that for the most part I do manage to be 'matter of fact' in my own thinking about the situation. Oh, I don't deny there are periods of depression and of dark thoughts." The worst of these moments involved her enormous desire to continue writing and her despair over what would happen to Roger when she was gone. The first problem Carson could discuss with Dorothy—the second, she was rarely able to face, let alone articulate.[29]

Carson's western sojourn led her to consider including a section on the water cycle in "the Wonder book." But with writing almost a physical impossibility, she was discouraged about attempting even that. "There is still so much I want to *do*, and it is hard to accept that in all probability, I must leave most of it undone," Rachel told Dorothy in anguish. "And just when I have attained the power to achieve so much I feel is important! Strange, isn't it? And there are times when I get so tired of the pain and especially the crippling that if it were not for those I love most, I'd want it to end soon." But the next moment Carson's ferocious spirit reasserted itself. "I want very much to do the Wonder book," she wrote. "That would be Heaven to achieve."[30]

The problem of Roger's future was so emotionally painful that Rachel could rarely bring herself to think about it realistically. Certainly she discussed the matter with Marie, but always obliquely. Their discussions had more to do with Carson's plans for a trust fund and for Roger's financial support than with her emotional pain at making specific arrangements for his future guardianship. Somewhere in the back of her mind, Rachel still hoped that Roger's aunt Virginia and Lee, her husband, would offer to care for the boy. She clung to that possibility since it offered the easiest solution, but they never did.[31]

Loving Roger as she did, Carson also had difficulty confronting the fact that Roger, at age eleven, was a difficult and undisciplined child and that the prospect of his care and education would be somewhat daunting to most of her friends and family. Rachel sensed, on some level, that Dorothy, and perhaps Marie as well, were privately critical of her parenting.[32]

The only alternative, and the one that she had thought about at least since the previous spring, was Paul Brooks. On a certain level it was an impossibly absurd notion, and yet Rachel began to believe it was the only good option. She had mentioned it once, confiding her idea to the only other childless writer she knew, Lois Crisler, after Lois's last visit with her.

> About Paul as guardian for Roger—this is not an easy thing to ask of anyone. Yet of all the people I know, I believe they could take on the responsibility more easily than any, and with no resentment at any disturbance of the flow of their lives. They are so adaptable. Susie is easy, warm, and outgoing. Paul is dear—more serious and reserved, but warm and kind. He was here for a few hours last Friday. He and Roger talked much about horses and we discussed choice of summer camp, next year's school, etc. Perhaps I shall write to him of the possibility, so that they may have it in their minds—no need to make a commitment.[33]

But Rachel never was able to write such a letter to Paul, and the time to talk to him about it never presented itself. Jeanne Davis believes that among the many reasons why Rachel could not face this subject was her real fear that whoever she asked might turn her down.[34]

Carson was quite up to facing another inevitable matter—that of establishing her literary estate and determining the disposition of her papers. When *The Sea Around Us* was finished, she had decided that Marie Rodell would act as her literary executor as well as literary agent. Over the course of several wills made in the 1950s, Rodell's authority over Carson's literary work and private correspondence was refined. The ultimate disposition of her literary papers, however, had never been settled.

After the American Academy of Arts and Letters exhibited Carson's manuscript for *Under the Sea-Wind* in 1953, Rachel indicated that she would leave at least part of her literary work to the academy. After some correspondence, however, it became clear that the academy library did not then have the facilities to hold large manuscript collections. Still, in a will made in 1953 Carson planned to give some of her material to the academy.

At the end of 1954 Carson received a letter from the chief of the Manuscript Division of the Library of Congress asking about a possible gift of her manuscripts there. Although Carson was favorably impressed with the library's facilities and decided to donate at least part of her material, she took no legal steps to do so.[35]

Over the years other librarians and archivists from Smith College, Syracuse University, and several western repositories inquired about her manuscripts and letters. The material Carson had amassed writing *Silent Spring* made it imperative that she find an archive that could process and house a considerably larger collection than she had originally offered the academy. By the fall of 1963 Marie Rodell and Carson's lawyer, Maurice Greenbaum, both urged her to make a decision and to leave everything to one repository.

With Ida's help, Rachel began to sort through material on the sea books in preparation for Marie's mid-November visit, when they would make a preliminary inventory. Rodell wanted Carson to go through as much material as possible herself so that what she gave would be her own decision. In going through the notebooks and drafts of *Under the Sea-Wind*, Rachel happily relived her first act of literary creation. "There was about it a sort of dewy freshness and innocence and wonder," Rachel wrote Dorothy later, "quite similar to our feelings when we remember the precious beginnings, of love and friendship in 1953–54. It is an odd feeling to be preparing it for the world, but also a privilege to be able to do it personally. I hope I can see the whole job through—on all four, [books] I mean."[36]

Rodell had been reading about Yale University's Beinecke Rare Book and Manuscript Library, a state-of-the-art facility for the preservation of rare materials, which had just opened that November in New Haven, Connecticut. The Beinecke would house Yale's extensive collection of western Americana, the Yale Collection of American Literature, and other important manuscript collections. Marie thought it an ideal repository for Carson's papers.

Her idea immediately appealed to Rachel, who had her own connections to the Yale faculty. She remembered the kind assistance Yale oceanographer Daniel Merriman had given her when she was doing research for *The Sea Around Us* and that the *Yale Review* had been the first periodical to accept and publish "The Birth of an Island," for which she won the Westinghouse Prize. Carson was also mindful of her debts to Paul B. Sears, former professor of conservation at Yale's School of Forestry, who read and commented on parts of *Silent Spring* and had defended it in several widely reprinted reviews. So it was settled. Marie would help Rachel get the manuscripts ready for the appraiser, and Maurice Greenbaum would prepare a deed of gift.[37]

Rachel and Marie spent a profitable but tiring weekend sorting manuscripts. Carson was scheduled to receive a trio of honors in less than two weeks from the National Audubon Society, American Geographical Society, and election into the American Academy of Arts and Letters, all in four heady days. Dorothy and Stan would attend the second event and stay with Carson at her New York hotel.

Anticipating these elegant occasions, Rachel decided that she would treat herself to a fur coat, something she had always wanted but never felt she could afford. So Rachel and Marie went shopping. Rachel bought a mink jacket with a large collar and full back that flattered her hair and coloring. Jeanne Davis remembers that Rachel was terribly pleased with it and looked "like a little girl in a party dress."[38]

Tired after shopping, Rachel was resting on the chaise in her office while Marie, full of energy, went out in Carson's yard to do something about the number of rotting apples that were attracting wasps in the fall sunshine. After spending some time bagging the apples, Marie went back inside, flopped into a chair, and remarked facetiously to Rachel, "It's a good thing NACA hasn't seen *your* apples!" Rachel was enormously amused by such a horrifying image.[39]

But laughter was in short supply that November as Carson made the rounds of neurologists and tried to find relief for her numb hand. The vertebrae in her neck were painful too, but she did not want to start treatment on that area until after she had returned from New York. Her spirits plunged further on November 22 when she and the nation learned that John F. Kennedy had been assassinated in Dallas. Thanksgiving was impossibly sad. Robert and Vera were in Canada, so rather than spending a cheerless holiday alone with Roger, Rachel invited Virginia and Lee and Lee's son for dinner, which Ida cooked ahead of time. Still, Carson found much to be thankful for. "For myself," she wrote Dorothy, "just to be here with the hope of accomplishing some of those 'dreams unrealized.' "[40]

By the fall of 1963 Carson had abundant evidence of the influence of her ideas and the enduring value of her work, though it by no means compensated for the writing she still wanted to do. She had known before she left for Maine that Secretary Udall was speaking at the dedication of a new research laboratory at the Patuxent Research Center in Maryland. The laboratory would enable FWS biologists to expand their research on the problems of pesticides. In his remarks at the dedication, Udall had commended Carson as "a great woman who awakened the nation by her forceful account of the dangers around us."[41]

Carson was deeply touched by Udall's speech, telling him:

> I am well aware that it took courage and forthrightness to make some of the statements contained in that speech. During the years I worked on *Silent Spring*, there were times when I wondered whether the effort was worthwhile—whether the warnings would be heeded enough to change the situation in any way. Of course I have been amazed and delighted by the many developments, but I can truthfully say that nothing has pleased me more than the tribute you paid. I hope the work down there may be a major factor in bringing about the changes we so urgently need.[42]

If further evidence was necessary to highlight the urgency of the situation, a massive fish kill on the lower Mississippi River in November provided it. Although there had been fish kills at the same time of year for the past three years, nothing compared to the magnitude of that kill, when over 5 million fish were floating, belly up, clogging the intakes to regional power plants and threatening public drinking water. This time Louisiana's Division of Water Pollution called in the U.S. Public Health Service to investigate.

Preliminary evidence indicated that a kill of this size could not be attributed to natural causes or even to pesticide runoff from the canefields in nearby Mississippi tributaries. Just before Carson left for New York, Donald Mount, a Public Health Service biologist, was able to confirm that the fish had died from minute amounts of the pesticide endrin in their bodies. What they did not yet know was where the endrin had come from.[43]

It was not until early April the following year that Carson learned from Paul Brooks that the source of the endrin in the Mississippi was a Memphis waste-treatment plant owned by none other than the Velsicol Corporation, the pesticide's developers and the company that had tried to stop the publication of *Silent Spring* in 1962. Senator Ribicoff and Secretary Udall finally had the kind of clear-cut evidence they needed to act. Ribicoff announced a new round of subcommittee hearings and dropped a draft for a Clean Water Bill into the Senate hopper. Udall issued a departmental ruling mandating that no pesticide be used where there existed a reasonable doubt as to its environmental effects.[44]

"How does Rachel Carson look now?" a reporter asked a group of Public

Health Service officials in Mississippi. "She looks pretty good," one scientist replied, still stunned by the tiny amount of endrin responsible for the catastrophe. A top official of the Public Health Service admitted, "this all opens up a new dimension in water pollution research."[45]

The season of honors began for Carson when she was awarded the second Paul Bartsch Award from the Audubon Naturalist Society for distinguished contributions to natural history. Too ill to go to the annual dinner, she had to accept the award in absentia. Irston Barnes stopped by her house with the award and a copy of his warm remarks. The citation read in part: "For steadfastly taking her place in the vanguard of scientific inquiry undaunted by controversy, facing attack with unfailing dignity and a gracious spirit." Saddened that she had not been present, Rachel was more determined than ever to attend "the extraordinary constellation of events" in New York City.[46]

Loaded down with baggage, Carson and Jeanne Davis took the train to New York on December 2, the day before the National Audubon Society dinner. Carson had boxes of manuscripts for *Under the Sea-Wind* and *The Sea Around Us* to take to the appraiser, in addition to a large suitcase containing formal attire, her mink jacket, and a large hat box. She stayed with Marie the first three nights, then when the Freemans arrived, she moved with them to the St. Regis Hotel, where the American Geographical Society dinner would take place.

The Audubon Medal, awarded to her for distinguished service to conservation, was presented on December 3 at the society's annual dinner at the Hotel Roosevelt. It was only the eleventh time the medal had been given and the first time ever to a woman. Carson was well aware that, as she spoke, the controversy over pesticides continued unabated. In fact, Roland Clement had spent that very day writing a rebuttal to an apologia for pesticides that Thomas Jukes had written in the *American Scientist*. Carson used the occasion to remark on how the current crisis reflected the same greed and shortsightedness that had historically characterized the struggle to conserve the nation's natural heritage. The capability of new technology to diffuse toxins in soil, air, and water, she said, made the pesticide crisis more urgent and actions taken, or not taken, irrevocable.[47]

Margaret Wentworth Owings of Big Sur, California, was also honored by National Audubon that evening. Owings received a special citation for successfully leading a campaign for the repeal of the California bounty on mountain lions. Owings and Rachel Carson had never met before, but Owings had written a year or so earlier to ask if Carson would consent to be on her committee to save the mountain lion.

Margaret Owings had come to her seat beside Carson at the Audubon dinner from a background as nearly opposite to Carson's as one could imagine. A daughter of one of California's most honored conservationists, she had grown up among wealth and privilege, carrying on a tradition of leadership in a variety of conservation causes in California. Her impassioned efforts to rescue the mountain lion from extinction made her spiritual kin to Carson.

After dinner, the two women found themselves in a lounge together. In her speech Owings had quoted some lines from the South African author Laurens van der Post that Carson did not recognize. Rachel asked Margaret about them. Seeing what others chose to ignore—that Carson was in pain and terribly ill—Owings told Carson about a time in her own life when she had found great comfort in having *The Sea Around Us* read to her. Moved by her confession, Rachel confided that she despaired over who would take up her work when she was gone. Margaret Owings promised Rachel that night that she would continue the fight.[48]

Two days later Rachel had a joyful reunion with Dorothy and Stan Freeman and moved into a spacious suite at the St. Regis. Before the Geographic dinner, Stan took pictures of the two friends in their formal gowns, and Rodell, who joined them for cocktails, took pictures of everyone. Rachel wore a floor-length, pale-blue sleeveless silk gown with a square neckline and her favorite blue sapphire and rhinestone necklace.

Carson's speech to the American Geographical Society was again a cry for recognition that all life, including the human species, depended on the environment. She pleaded for the need for humankind to recognize its unity with the natural world. It was a strong speech, delivered with authority in Carson's now-familiar cadences.[49]

Carson viewed her induction as a member of the American Academy of Arts and Letters at a luncheon meeting on December 6 as "the most deeply satisfying thing that has ever happened in the honors department." Membership in the academy was limited to fifty, and only when a seat became open was another elected to fill it from the ranks of the National Institute of Arts and Letters, to which Carson had belonged since 1953. When Rachel was elected, there were only three other female members. She became the sixth occupant of chair nineteen and considered her selection as a nonfiction writer a signal honor. Academy president Lew Mumford read a citation acknowledging Carson's moral leadership as well as her scientific achievements.

> A scientist in the grand literary style of Galileo and Buffon, she has used her scientific insight and moral feeling to quicken our consciousness of living nature and alert us to the calamitous possibility that our shortsighted technological conquests might destroy the very source of our being.[50]

Carson's six days in New York were triumphant and happy ones surrounded by her dearest friends and many admirers who delighted in the recognition given to her. Although she managed all these public occasions beautifully, when she returned to Silver Spring, she was ready to begin more treatments. Caulk found trouble at the base of her skull and radiated a large area down her back. One of her dorsal vertebrae had compressed, thereby explaining her chronic arm pain and numb hand. In hindsight, Carson wished he had started treatment weeks ago, so that she might have been able to write without so much distress. But Caulk kept hoping that Rachel would get more relief than she had from the phosphorus. Now her voice and her ability to swallow would be affected at least temporarily by the radiation. Carson hoped that if she could just get through these treatments, then she and Roger might go to the Freemans during his Christmas holidays.[51]

Rachel's only hesitation about making the trip was the illness of her dear cat, Jeffie, who had always been so dependent on her. The weather was foul. Carson could barely get to the hospital for her own treatments, let alone take Jeffie back and forth to the vet for shots that probably would not make much difference. Rachel was heartbroken over the cat's impending death.

"My heart is so burdened about Jeffie that I need to talk to you," she wrote Dorothy. "He is slipping so fast that I feel he will surely have left us by Christmas. You know that deep in my heart I feel I ought to be willing and even thankful to let him go while I am still here to care for him. But it is so very hard to think of doing without him. His little life has been so intertwined with mine all these ten years."[52]

That night Rachel sat up late with Jeffie and kept him in her room. She was awakened by his moans and difficult breathing. Sitting on the floor, stroking him, Rachel talked to her small companion comfortingly until finally he crawled under her bed. In the morning, as she was getting

Roger off to school, Jeffie died. Rachel curled him up in his basket and asked her handyman Elliott to bury him out under the pine trees by her study—a place she hoped would never be disturbed.

The dissolution of her little family, which had begun in September with Moppet's death, now included another that she loved. Rachel shared her anguish with Dorothy. "For exactly three years, since I flew to Cleveland in December and first understood my own situation, I have worried about my little family. I knew no one could take care of Jeffie, and I felt it unlikely that whoever takes Roger would want to adopt a cat, too, so even Moppet was a problem. But oh, I should be glad for Jeffie, and soon I know I can be, for it would have been awful for him, and so frightening, if he had survived me. Now that problem exists no more."[53]

Rachel's tenth Christmas message to Dorothy was especially poignant.

> I can only hope you know, darling, that even in spite of the miles that separate us, you are and have been my main comfort and support in these sometimes difficult days. Just what they would be without the knowledge of your constant devotion and concern is something I can't imagine. So it has been, of course, through all of this eventful and often troubled decade, but never more than now. I've been thinking recently, how wonderful it is for me that, if I couldn't have known you all my life, it is *now* that I do have you.[54]

Writing on the winter solstice, Rachel looked forward to the imperceptible but certain lengthening days, which always meant the coming of summer and Southport. Turning her back on the reality of her situation, she spoke of the roses she intended to plant later in the year. She wrote, "I had not, until recently, allowed my thoughts to range so far into the future. Now I do. We shall yet build more happy memories."[55]

Rachel and Roger celebrated the New Year in West Bridgewater with the Freemans. Carson found solace in an oasis of Dorothy's care. For Christmas, Rachel gave them the manuscript pages from the original draft of *Under the Sea-Wind* on which she had sketched the head of her cat Buzzie. "On two of these pages I had made sketches, first of his little head drooping with sleepiness, then of him after he had settled down comfortably for a nap," Rachel wrote. The notation "October—November—December" she explained was a reminder of how much time remained until the manuscript was due, December 31, 1941. Dorothy and Stan acknowledged it as a perfect bequest.[56]

Rachel and Dorothy had a chance to talk about the "lurking shadows." When Rachel left she felt there was nothing more that needed to be said between them. In her parting note, left under Dorothy's pillow, Rachel wrote, "And as long as either of us lives, I know our love 'will never pass into nothingness' but will keep a quiet bower stored with peace and with precious memories of all that we have shared. I need not say it again but I shall—I love you, now and always."[57]

Several days after Carson returned to Maryland, she began to have severe pains in her head and lost her sense of smell and taste. Dr. Caulk reminded her that it had been three years since she had come to him with seriously metastasizing cancer. He had told her then that she was "something of a miracle" but now reminded her of what she already knew. Her disease was widely disseminated, and few patients in such cases survived more than five years. Rachel knew he was telling her—"Don't expect too much more time"—but of course she hoped for more. "I am able to feel that another reprieve can perhaps be won. Now it really seems possible there might be yet another summer. But we do know that now every month, every day, is precious."[58]

The next death Dorothy had to confront, however, was not the one she was most prepared for but her husband's. Stanley Freeman suffered a fatal heart attack on January 14, seated at their kitchen table watching the birds. Rachel flew to Boston and went on to West Bridgewater to be with Dorothy for the funeral. It was a time of great sadness. The note she left for Dorothy this time contained a traditional Christian benediction: " 'The Lord bless you and keep you. The Lord lift up the light of his countenance upon you and give you peace.' You are very precious."[59]

Dorothy's son, Stanley Jr., drove Rachel back to the airport after the service. The long drive gave her a chance to get to know Stanley better. Much like his father in appearance and manner, Stanley was an assistant professor at the University of Maine at Orono, interested in educational policy but struggling to make ends meet with a young family to support. They talked about Stanley's children, Martha and Richard, and about Roger. Stanley stayed to see Rachel and her wheelchair onto the airplane.[60]

Rachel had undoubtedly considered the younger Freemans as possible guardians for Roger, but it seems unlikely that she ever specifically mentioned it to Dorothy, nor did she give Stanley any indication of her thoughts that day in the car. But Stanley's kindness to Rachel and the opportunity to know him better probably led her to consider him as a potential guardian.[61]

Stan Freeman's death left Dorothy freer from family responsibilities than she had been since she and Rachel met. Rachel selfishly hoped that they could see more of each other now that Dorothy could travel at will. "I do look forward to being with you more in the future, darling, now that in strange and sad ways the ties that held us both more or less immobilized have been broken. Almost ever since I have known you there have been reasons why it was usually so difficult to plan to be together except at Southport. Now, except for taking care of Roger, and my occasional inability to travel, this is changed."[62]

But two days later, as both of them were dealing with the difficulties of wills and estates but from opposite points, Rachel wrote more realistically, "I used to think when I let myself consider the possibility that you might be left alone, how wonderful it would be if you could then be close to me, somehow, somewhere. Now, with the uncertainties as to my own future, I know you should not build any long-range or permanent plans around me." But Rachel could not deny the hope that she and Dorothy could take a trip to California together.[63]

Rachel had several long meetings with her estate attorney, Richard Huhn, in late January to spell out the provisions of the trust she established for Roger in a new will. Revenues from *Silent Spring* had made quite a difference in calculating her estate taxes. Carson appointed Huhn together with the American Security & Trust Company to be the executors of her estate, having no confidence in her brother, Robert, to carry out her wishes. At the time Huhn drew up the will, Carson still had made no decision on the matter of a guardian for Roger.

At the end of January, Carson caught a respiratory virus from Roger and became acutely ill. In spite of antibiotics, her condition deteriorated. In early February she was hospitalized with staphococcal meningitis and contracted a serious case of herpes zoster, or shingles, in the hospital.

Dorothy, who had been planning to visit as soon as she had some of the most immediate estate matters taken care of, went to Silver Spring when Rachel returned from the hospital. But it was a poorly timed and a difficult visit for both of them. Dorothy was sad and preoccupied with her own affairs, and Rachel struggled to be cheerful but was in agony most of the time. Although Carson acknowledged again that "the time was beginning to feel precious," they were not able to talk about the things that weighed heavily on her heart: her will and Roger's guardianship.

After Dorothy returned to Massachusetts, she began worrying about the letters Rachel wanted her to have after her death. Dorothy had been reading about the correspondence of writer Dorothy Thompson, which had just been opened. She told Rachel: "There was one statement that really frightened me—I don't want to put it in writing but I'll just say that the same implication could be implied [inferred] about our correspondence. So, dear, please use the Strong Box quickly. We know even such volume could have its meanings to people who were looking for ideas. Having someone return them to me leaves possibility of miscarriage of your intentions and I really don't want them." Dorothy regretted that they had not had Ida burn them in the fireplace while they were together. "I really am uneasy about them," she told Rachel.[64]

Just after Dorothy's departure, Carson signed a new will and attached a codicil. Dated February 13, 1964, it left her papers to Yale University and established a literary trust with Marie Rodell as executor and trustee and a separate trust for Roger's support and education based on income from securities until he reached the age of thirty-five. Two-thirds of her residual estate were to be divided equally between The Nature Conservancy and The Sierra Club.[65]

Carson left cash bequests to her brother Robert, to her niece Virginia, to Ida Sprow, and to Dorothy Freeman, along with her Capehart phonograph and record collection. She wanted her Southport cottage to be maintained in her estate and given to Roger when he was twenty-five. She also bequeathed her microscope, Exacta camera, slides, and all her scientific books to Roger. All other personal property she divided between Robert and Virginia. Other than providing for Roger financially, Carson's will made no provision for his guardianship.[66]

A codicil appended to the will and signed the same day named Mr. and Mrs. Paul Brooks and Professor and Mrs. Stanley L. Freeman, Jr., as her nominees for guardians. Carson wrote in the codicil, "My choices are dictated in part by the conviction that Roger's best interests will be served if his guardianship or custodianship can be undertaken by friends who are parents of children of somewhat comparable age and who would undertake to rear him with affectionate care in the companionship of their own children."[67]

Certain now that she would not be able to make this decision during her lifetime, Carson added, "I therefore make the following nominations, with the request that at the time of my death, my executors discuss the matter with these persons, finding among them if possible, with due regard to the circumstances then prevailing, a person willing and able to act." The codicil was a shocking abdication of responsibility on Carson's part but testament to the psychic pain she experienced about Roger's future and her inability to confront emotional issues or deal with the possibility of rejection.[68]

From the middle of February on Carson was afflicted with uncontrollable nausea. Her doctors were unable to offer much help although they brought in a doctor from the National Institutes of Health for consultation. They considered doing the hypophysectomy at NIH so Carson would not have to endure the trip to Cleveland, but probably because of Rachel's trust in Crile, this idea was abandoned.

In spite of her nausea and pain, Carson continued to work with Jeanne Davis on her correspondence whenever she could. At the end of February she wrote to Frank Egler, explaining she had been "laid up for several weeks with a combination of flu and shingles." Telling Egler about a new pesticide bill that her local congressman and another from Maine had consulted with her about, she was gratified by the pace of pesticide legislation that had been introduced into several state legislatures. Rachel still talked of going to California later that spring. But she also wrote letters canceling her speeches at Chatham College's commencement in May and at the Mayo Clinic Centennial in September.[69]

At the beginning of March, Robert Carson, to whom Rachel had given power of attorney, insisted that someone stay in the house so that she could have care at night or when Ida could not be there. Mrs. Patterson, a kind and capable practical nurse, moved in. Despite Rachel's dislike of having someone about in the evenings, Roger liked her immensely and Rachel was grateful for the relief and reassurance she provided.[70]

Blood tests in February had revealed that Carson had become severely anemic from all the cobalt radiation. When she failed to respond to other measures, she received four or five blood transfusions at home. The transfusions relieved her nausea and made her feel stronger. Crile and Caulk agreed that Carson's improvement signaled the best opportunity to try the hypophysectomy. Only Jeanne Davis and her cardiologist husband, Burnet, felt that Rachel should not put herself through such torturous and risky surgery when it was clear she had very little time left. No one asked their opinion.[71]

Rachel asked Robert's wife, Vera, to accompany her to Cleveland, not knowing for certain if she could have the surgery or how long she would be hospitalized. Ida and Mrs. Patterson stayed with Roger, keeping his normal routine. Rachel wrote Dorothy just before leaving for Cleveland, "I feel there are things—about your problems and mine—which we should have talked about, but no time when you were here seemed right, and I doubt this is either. Perhaps when next we meet, whenever that may be. Meanwhile, we have only to remember the joys we have shared, the love each has felt for the other; all this is enough for a lifetime." Rachel did not ask Dorothy to go to Cleveland, knowing it would be too hard on both of them.[72]

Carson entered the Cleveland Clinic on March 13. According to medical records, her preoperative physical revealed that the cancer had metastasized into her liver. One physician noted that her heart condition made any surgery risky. Although Carson continued to be plagued by nausea and had lost weight, the doctors decided to go ahead. Marie Rodell arrived the night before. They implanted radioactive Yttrium-90 on March 18. For nearly a week Carson was near death. She became severely jaundiced and suffered from serious heart irregularities. But gradually her clinical condition stabilized.[73]

Vera telephoned Dorothy one night at the end of March to say that Rachel was in much less pain and that Crile believed the hypophysectomy was successfully remitting the cancer spread in her bones. The day before Easter Rachel telephoned her friend herself.[74]

She told Dorothy that at some point, either during the surgery or just after, she'd had "a Resurrection," or out-of-body experience. Rachel described herself surrounded by a brilliant white light and being lifted up, calmly and comfortably suspended in it. Floating in this otherworld, Rachel remembered it like being in the swirling fog at Todd Point. "Don't ever be afraid to die," Rachel told Jeanne Davis later. "It's beautiful."[75]

One of the other calls Rachel made from the Cleveland Clinic after the surgery was to the Reverend Howlett. He recalls a simple conversation in which Carson asked him if he would hold a memorial service for her at All Souls Unitarian Church when the time came. She gave him no details, other than suggesting he might read from the final section of *The Edge of the Sea*, leaving the rest to him; she simply wanted to be assured that he would do it. Howlett asked no questions, knowing from her voice that she was gravely ill. He gave her his word.[76]

Carson dictated some letters to other friends, but she also carefully hid her situation from most, reporting that she was in Cleveland for surgery for her arthritis and would be home soon. Keeping her up to date on the situation in the Mississippi River, Paul Brooks wrote, "News stories like this confirm my feeling that no book published in our generation is likely to have a more lasting impact." Vera had returned to Maryland earlier, so Marie flew back to Silver Spring with Rachel on April 6.[77]

The following weekend Dorothy Freeman flew down to be with Rachel and was relieved to find her so much more comfortable. They rejoiced in the hours they had together, but Rachel was only partly aware of what was going on around her. Dorothy left on April 12, and they spoke on the telephone that evening.

In what was her last letter to Rachel, written on the morning of April 14, Dorothy told her, "Dearest, I want you to know that yesterday I realized I had come home with a great sense of peace about you." Remembering their "oasis" of precious time at the New Year, Dorothy wrote, "Although my visit with you just now could not have the same tranquility, nevertheless there were very special moments when I felt we were in a 'quiet bower.' " Rachel never read Dorothy's letter.[78]

Late in the afternoon, on Tuesday, April 14, Rachel Carson suffered a coronary heart attack. She died just before sunset. It was as she had written: "For all at last return to the sea—to Oceanus, the ocean river, like the ever-flowing stream of time, the beginning and the end."[79]

Barely an hour later, mayhem broke out at 11701 Berwick Road when Robert Carson arrived to take charge. Although Rachel had instructed Ida and Mrs. Patterson to have her body cremated, Robert, belligerent, rude, and insensitive to all, was no respecter of the wishes of his younger sister. He refused to allow cremation and sent the body to Joseph Gawlers' Sons for preparation.

Instead of a simple memorial service at All Souls with Duncan Howlett, Robert planned an elaborate state funeral at the Washington National Cathedral on Mount St. Alban with William F. Creighton, the fourth bishop of Washington, leading a group of distinguished mourners on Friday morning, April 17.

By the time Marie Rodell arrived at Rachel's house the next afternoon, Robert Carson's plans were unalterable, and Rodell's only contribution was to arrange for honorary pallbearers who would be in keeping with Rachel's wishes. Duncan Howlett waited but never received a call from the Carson family.

In the hours after Rachel died, Robert Carson had managed to rampage through her files, destroying or removing precious personal documents and letters that displeased him. Roger's memories of that time are nightmarish. Robert, who had never liked the boy, stormed into his bedroom to confiscate the television set, the one thing that brought the boy a certain comfort, claiming that since Rachel had left her personal effects to him, the television was now his.

Marie Rodell had supplied the newspaper with material for Carson's obituary and handled calls from the media before she left New York. Richard Huhn, Carson's executor, discomfited by the obligation that fell to him of finding a guardian for Roger, called to inform a completely stunned Paul Brooks of his nomination in Carson's codicil. Preempting Huhn's other call, Marie Rodell telephoned Dorothy Freeman and then an equally astonished Madeleine Freeman to ask what their intentions for Roger might be. After talking to her children, Dorothy Freeman responded negatively on their behalf. The Brookses agreed to become Roger's guardians. Susie Brooks left for Silver Spring the next day, with Paul following for the funeral on Friday. Roger would go to the Brookses when school was out in June; he would stay with his next-door neighbors and friends until then, a solution that pleased him.[80]

Rachel's other friends learned of her death from an announcement on the radio or from front-page headlines the next morning. Most were surprised, having no idea she had been seriously ill. Only Ida and Dorothy Freeman went to Gawlers to view the body. Afterward they joined the nearly 150 others in the half-finished nave of the Washington Cathedral at 11:00 A.M. on the seventeenth for a traditional burial service according to the *Book of Common Prayer*. Six honorary pallbearers—Robert Cushman Murphy, Edwin Way Teale, U.S. Senator Abraham Ribicoff, Secretary of Interior Stewart Udall, Charles Callison of the National Audubon Society, and Rachel's loyal friend Bob Hines—carried Carson's bronze casket down the aisle and took their places in the front row opposite the family. Bishop Creighton offered prayers for those who had died at sea, at the request of Robert Carson, who somehow thought them appropriate. There were no memorial remarks. A large wreath of red and white flowers was prominently placed at the foot of the steps leading to the high altar, a tribute from Prince Philip of England.[81]

Thwarting Rachel's wishes further, Robert insisted that Carson's body be buried alongside that of her mother at Parklawn Cemetery. But enough of Rachel's friends as well as Huhn knew of her wish to be cremated and to have her ashes scattered at Southport that Robert was forced to compromise. He insisted, however, on burying half the ashes in the cemetery.[82]

Shirley Briggs drove to the eastern shore after the service and walked up to Cape Henlopen remembering other shores Rachel had shown her so long ago. Jeanne Davis and Marie Rodell worked at Rachel's house boxing up manuscripts and papers to ship to New York once the will was probated until Robert Carson returned and preemptorily asked Rodell to leave the house. Ida packed Roger's things.[83]

Without Robert Carson's knowledge, Marie got in touch with Duncan Howlett, who willingly cast aside the Sunday sermon he had planned for the memorial he had promised. Dorothy Freeman, Marie Rodell, Jeanne Davis, Irston Barnes, Bob Hines, and a few other close friends gathered at All Souls on a sparkling Sunday morning, April 19, to honor their friend in the simple manner she had wished. Dorothy had given Howlett a copy of the letter Rachel had written to her after their morning at Newagen; Howlett read it at the service after brief remarks of his own.

> Last week one of the true prophets of our time, Rachel Carson, died here in Washington. She had asked me to read at her funeral service certain passages which expressed her philosophy. Her wish was denied. I therefore take this opportunity to do as I promised, and in her memory shall read a passage from her own hand which expresses in a remarkable way the strength, the simplicity and the serenity that marked her character.
>
> We are already familiar with the extraordinary depth of insight and high poetic quality that marked her published writings. The following passage was not written for publication. It is a letter to a close friend, written but a few months ago when Rachel Carson already knew her time on earth might be short.[84]

Marie Rodell spent almost two years working in a small room she rented at the Yale Club of New York, meticulously sorting through Rachel's letters and papers. She returned letters to each of Carson's correspondents, asking them to review and to return only those they were willing to give permanently to the collection of material going to Yale.

Rodell also carried out Carson's wishes by organizing a committee of her friends and fellow scientists; they met for the first time on June 25 at Rockefeller University under the aegis of the Scientist's Institute for Public Information to discuss ways to carry on Carson's work. Rodell asked Ruth Scott and Shirley Briggs to take the lead in organizing what became The Rachel Carson Trust for the Living Environment. John George was later elected the first president, and Briggs, secretary.[85]

Rodell also saw to it that Carson's article, "Help Your Child to Wonder," was published posthumously as a short book by Harper, titled *The Sense of Wonder*, in 1965. It was dedicated to Roger Christie and included photographs by Charles Pratt.

Sometime in the late spring of 1964, Dorothy Freeman found a shoebox–size package wrapped in brown paper dangling precariously by its strings on the flag of her mailbox in West Bridgewater. Without note or explanation, it contained the remainder of Rachel Carson's ashes, sent by an unapologetic Robert Carson.[86]

That summer at Newagen Dorothy did as Rachel had asked, scattering her ashes along the rocky coast of the Sheepscot. As a benediction, Dorothy read the following lines from T. S. Eliot:

The sea has many voices . . .

The distant rote in the granite teeth . . .

And under the oppression of the silent fog
The tolling bell
Measures time not our time, rung by the unhurried
Ground swell . . .

When time stops and time is never ending;
And the ground swell, that is and was from the beginning,
Clangs
The Bell.[87]

Afterword

Senator Abraham Ribicoff learned of Carson's death when Marie Rodell telephoned his office to ask him to be an honorary pallbearer at Carson's funeral service at the Washington National Cathedral. That afternoon the senator opened the hearings with a tribute to Carson. "Today we mourn a great lady," he said. "All mankind is in her debt."

Three days later the senator and his legislative assistant, Jerome Sonosky, drove to the cathedral together for the Friday morning service. Ribicoff recalled how appropriate it seemed that Carson's last Christmas card had been a pen-and-ink sketch of the cathedral's great south facade with the traditional Scottish blessing as her greeting.

It was still a sparkling sunny day when Ribicoff and Sonosky emerged from the cathedral. They waited while the casket was loaded into the hearse, then walked with other mourners to their cars, which were parked along North Road. As they were getting into their car, something made both men look up at the same moment. The trees around the cathedral all had signs on them that read: "No Parking 7AM to 4PM. Trees to be sprayed with pesticides."

Abbreviations Used in the Notes

MANUSCRIPT COLLECTIONS

ANS/OSIA	Audubon Naturalist Society, Office of Smithsonian Institution Archives.
AWI	Papers of the Animal Welfare Institute, Washington, D.C.
Crile Papers	George Crile, Jr. Family Papers. The Cleveland Clinic Foundation Archives, Cleveland, OH.
EWTP/UC	Edwin Way Teale Papers, Archives & Special Collections, Thomas J. Dodd Research Center, University of Connecticut Libraries.
FFC	Freeman Family Correspondence.
UP/FFC	Unpublished Freeman Family Correspondence. Privately held.
FHA/JHU	Ferdinand Hamburger, Jr. Archives, Johns Hopkins University, Baltimore, MD.
FPR/OPM	Federal Personnel Records. Office of Personnel Management. St. Louis, MO.
NARA	National Archives and Records Administration, Washington, D.C./College Park, MD.
R/CA	Marie Rodell–Frances Collin Literary Agents Archive, Wayne, PA.
RCHP/RCC	Rachel Carson History Project, Rachel Carson Council, Inc., Chevy Chase, MD.
RCP/BLYU	Rachel Carson Papers, Yale Collection of American Literature, Beinecke Rare Book and Manuscript Library, Yale University, New Haven, CT.
SAB/D; SAB/L	Shirley A. Briggs, Diary and Letters. Privately held.

PUBLISHED COLLECTIONS

Letters	*Always, Rachel: The Letters of Rachel Carson and Dorothy Freeman, 1952–1964*. Edited by Martha Freeman. Boston: Beacon Press, 1995.

PERSONAL CORRESPONDENTS

RNA	Ruth Nanda Anshen
CB	Curtis Bok
PB	Paul Brooks
RC	Rachel Carson
CC	Clarence Cottam
LC	Lois Crisler
FE	Frank Egler
AF	Anne Ford
DF	Dorothy Freeman
BK	Beverly Knecht
MR	Marie Rodell
RR	Robert Rudd
RS	Ruth Scott
MS	Marjorie Spock
CS	Christine Stevens
EWT	Edwin Way Teale

Notes

1: "WILD CREATURES ARE MY FRIENDS"

1. Although Carson published her childhood writing under the name Rachel Louise Carson, she dropped her middle name in college in the 1920s. She used the middle initial L for some time, but for most purposes gave it up after 1941.
2. Rachel Louise Carson, "A Battle in the Clouds," *St. Nicholas Magazine* 45 (September 1918), 1048. Rachel Carson Papers, Yale Collection of American Literature, Beinecke Rare Book and Manuscript Library, Yale University, New Haven, CT. [Hereafter cited as RCP/BLYU.]
3. Rachel Carson, "The Real World Around Us," Speech, Theta Sigma Phi, April 21, 1954; Rachel Carson, biographical fragment, ca. 1954, RCP/BLYU.
4. A survey of the contents of *St. Nicholas Magazine*, vols. 34, 35 (New York: Century Publishing Company, 1907–1909). Story told by Carolyn Leiby, recounted by Claudia (James) Gianinni, ca. 1987, Rachel Carson Homestead, Springdale, PA. Mary H. Austin, *The Land of Little Rain* (Boston: Houghton Mifflin Co., 1903), 103.
5. N.A. [Commemorative publication] *Springdale: From Indian Village to Power City: Seventy-Five Years* (Springdale, PA, 1981). [Hereafter cited as *Springdale, 1906–1981.*] *Pittsburgh Leader,* May 1901. Wendy Wareham, "Rachel Carson's Early Years," *Carnegie Magazine,* 58, 6 (November-December 1986), 20–23. Joseph C. White, "Rachel Carson," *Famous Men and Women of Pittsburgh,* edited by Lenore R. Elkus (Pittsburgh: Pittsburgh History and Landmark Foundation, 1981), 138–145.
6. Interviews with Sarah Smith Totten, Claudia (James) Gianinni, Evelyn Hirtle George.
7. Bureau of the Census, *1880 Census Index,* Department of Commerce, C625. Bureau of the Census, *1900 Census,* vol. 27, E.D. 503, Sheet 10, l. 8. Harriet Branton, *Focus on Washington County,* vol. 3 (Washington, PA: Observer Publishing Company, August 1982), 81–82.
8. Ibid.
9. Obituary of the Reverend D. M. B. McLean, *The Canonsburg Herald,* Canonsburg,

PA, March 26, 1880. Nothing is known about Rachel Frazier Andrews's family background or where she and Reverend McLean were married. Her demeanor as the pastor's wife, however, suggests a woman of some education and training. See Records of the Washington County Historical Society, Washington, PA. I am grateful to James T. Herron of Canonsburg, PA, for his genealogical assistance. Branton, *Focus on Washington County*, 81. Information on the McLeans comes from Branton's columns in the *Observer-Reporter*. See Earle Forrest, *History of Washington County* (Chicago: J. Clarke Co., 1926), and *House of Romance* (Washington, PA: Washington County Historical Society, 1964).

10. Washington Female Seminary Catalogue, 1886–1887, Washington Seminary Collection, Citizens Library, Washington, PA. The seminary was founded in 1840 and closed its doors in 1948. Harriet Branton, "Sarah Foster Hanna, Just Let Me Try!" *Observer-Reporter*, March 31, 1979, Section B. Harriet Branton, *Focus on Washington*, vol. 3. See Keith Melder, "Mask of Oppression: The Female Seminary Movement in the United States," *New York History*, 55 (1974), 261–279. Margaret W. Rossiter, *Women Scientists in America: Struggles and Strategies to 1940* (Baltimore: Johns Hopkins University Press, 1982), 4–7. See Anne Frior Scott, "The Ever-Widening Circle: The Diffusion of Feminist Values From the Troy Female Seminary, 1822–1872," *History of Education Quarterly*, 19 (1979), 6.
11. The Vances had three children, one of whom, John Frazier Vance, became prominent in the magazine business, rising to production manager of the Robert L. Johnson magazine empire in New York City. Six years older than Rachel Carson, he died in 1939 from complications of an appendectomy. "J. Frazier Vance," Obituary, 1939, RCP/BLYU. Ida died of a mastoid infection in 1922 at age fifty-five. "Ida McLean Vance," Obituary, 1922, RCP/BLYU.
12. Maria McLean Carson to Ida and the other graduates of the Washington Female Seminary Class of 1887, May 30, 1950, Washington Seminary Collection, Citizens Library, Washington, PA.
13. Just after Rachel Louise Carson was born in 1907, Rachel McLean moved to Rock Island, Illinois, to live with Ida and her husband. Rachel McLean died in 1913, when her granddaughter Rachel was six years old. Allegheny County, PA, *Deeds of Record*, vol. 1076, 81.
14. "Preliminary Historic Structures Report on the Rachel Carson Homestead" draft. Prepared for The Rachel Carson Homestead Association by Landmarks Design Associates, May 1991. Interview with Sarah Smith Totten.
15. *The Springdale Record*, February 5, 1910: "For Sale, Large Level Lots, 46 × 130 feet. Fronting on 60 foot streets, a few minutes walk from the electric cars. Price $300. Cash or payments. R.W. Carson, Colfax Avenue."
16. Interviews with Sarah Smith Totten, Frances Carson Hoerner, Ruth Scott. Department of Commerce, U.S. Bureau of the Census, *Census 1920*, vol. 44, E.D. 815, Sheet 7, l. 46.
17. Nancy Chodorow, *The Reproduction of Mothering* (Berkeley: University of California Press, 1978), 57–91, 117–209. Of particular interest here is Chodorow's exploration of the consequences of unequal parenting.
18. Paul Brooks, *Speaking for Nature* (San Francisco: Sierra Club Books, 1980), 165–180. Harriet Kofalk, *No Woman Tenderfoot: Florence Merriam Bailey, Pioneer Naturalist* (College Station, TX: Texas A&M Press, 1989), xvi–xvii, 33, 52–53. Elizabeth Barnaby Keeney, "The Botanizers: Amateur Scientists in Nineteenth-Century America," Ph.D. diss, University of Wisconsin, 1985, 1–66.
19. Bailey referred to his curriculum as nature-study. When I refer to nature study, I mean the general field of natural history. Anna Botsford Comstock, *Handbook of*

Nature Study (Ithaca, NY: Cornell University Press, 1911, 1970), xi–xv, 1–24. Pamela M. Henson, " 'Through Books to Nature': Anna Botsford Comstock and the Nature Study Movement," in Barbara T. Gates and Ann B. Shteir, eds., *Using Nature's Language: Women Engendering Science 1690–1800*, (Madison: University of Wisconsin Press, 1997), 116–143. See Liberty Hyde Bailey, *The Outlook to Nature* (New York: Macmillan, 1905); *The Nature-Study Idea* (New York: Doubleday, Page & Co., 1903); *The Holy Earth* (New York: Scribner, 1915). Andrew Denny Rogers, *Liberty Hyde Bailey: A Story of American Plant Sciences* (Princeton, NJ: Princeton University Press 1949), 405–415. See Marcia Myers Bonta, "Anna Botsford Comstock." *Women in the Field: America's Pioneering Women Naturalists* (College Station, TX: Texas A&M University Press, 1991).

20. Keeney, "The Botanizers," 193–196. Ralph H. Lutts, *The Nature Fakers* (Golden, CO: Fulcrum Publishing, 1990), 16–36. I am indebted to Lutts for discussions over the years on the nature-study movement in general and its influence on Carson's girlhood. Clifton F. Hodge, *Nature Study and Life* (Boston: Ginn & Co., 1902), was the first great nature-study textbook. G. Kass-Simon, "Biology Is Destiny" in G. Kass-Simon and Patricia Farnes, eds., *Women of Science: Righting the Record* (Bloomington: Indiana University Press, 1990), 256–259. Rogers, *Liberty Hyde Bailey*, 299, 405. Bailey, *The Nature-Study Idea*, 14.
21. Comstock, *Handbook of Nature Study*, x, 1–2, 22. Marcia Myers Bonta, *Women in the Field*, 262–272. See also Peter J. Schmitt, *Back to Nature: The Arcadian Myth in Urban America* (New York: Oxford University Press, 1969), 14–44, 83–94, 144–145, on the impact of the nature-study movement.
22. Ann B. Shteir, "Botany in the Breakfast Room: Women and Early Nineteenth-Century British Plant Study," in Pnina G. Abir-am and Dorinda Outram, eds., *Uneasy Careers and Intimate Lives* (New Brunswick, NJ: Rutgers University Press, 1987), 15, 32–41. Shteir argues the home became the geographic center of botanical education. Botany was viewed as part of good mothering.
23. Maria M. Carson, Handwritten account of Rachel's first months, RCP/BLYU.
24. Ibid.
25. Records of Membership, 1911, 1912, Springdale United Presbyterian Church, Springdale, PA. Records of the Cheswick Presbyterian Church, Chronological Role, #209, #116–119, Cheswick, PA. Interview with Effie Dobner.
26. Carson, "The Real World Around Us."
27. Rachel Louise Carson, "The Little Book for Mr. R. W. Carson," RCP/BLYU.
28. Philip Sterling, *Sea and Earth: The Life of Rachel Carson* (New York: Thomas Y. Crowell Co., 1970), 18. Sterling's juvenile biography of Carson includes material from interviews with Robert M. Carson. Most of his recollections are inaccurate and suspect in both detail and motive. The identification of "Mr. Lee" as the owner of the laundry in Springdale seems plausible. Rachel Carson [hereafter cited as RC] to Marjorie Spock [hereafter cited as MS], December 4, 1958, RCP/BLYU.
29. Rachel Louise Carson, "The Little Brown House," RCP/BLYU.
30. Rachel Louise Carson, "A Sleeping Rabbit," RCP/BLYU.
31. As told by Robert M. Carson to Sterling, *Sea and Earth*, 22–23. I accept Sterling's version here because several of these books were in Carson's personal library at her death. Rachel read *Wind in the Willows* to her grandnephew Roger Christie when he was little. She and her friend Dorothy Freeman read it to each other in Maine during the summertime. See Rachel Carson, "The Battle of Mingo Pond," May 8, 1928, RCP/BLYU.
32. Lutts, *Nature Fakers*, 16–36. Brooks, *Speaking for Nature*, 176–180. Schmitt, *Back to Nature*, 125–137.

33. Rachel Louise Carson, "Dear Little Folks," RCP/BLYU. Frank Luther Mott, *A History of American Magazines*, vol. 4 (Cambridge, MA: Belknap Press, Harvard University, 1957), 212. "Mary Mapes Dodge," *Folio*, 20 (March 1991), 106,108. Paul Rosta, "The Magazine that Taught Faulkner, Fitzgerald, and Millay How to Write," *American Heritage* 37 (December 1985), 40–47.
34. *St. Nicholas* League, "Leaflet of Information and Rules," RCP/BLYU. The price of a subscription in 1917 was $3.00. The Century Company, publishers of *St. Nicholas Magazine*, advertised it as containing the finest writing for children in literature and art, and "never surpassed by any grown folks periodical." *St. Nicholas Magazine*, vol. 32 (New York: Century Publishing, 1904–1907).
35. *St. Nicholas* League, "Leaflet of Information and Rules."
36. Rosta, "The Magazine," 42, 45. Millay wrote the League in 1910, when she turned eighteen: "Although I shall never write for the league again, I shall not allow myself to become a stranger to it. You have been a great help and a great encouragement to me, and I am sorry to grow up and leave you."
37. Rachel Louise Carson, "A Battle in the Clouds." Although Rachel's surname was spelled correctly underneath the title of her story, it was written as "Carlson" in the listing of badge winners, 1047. Notice of Silver Badge Award, RCP/BLYU.
38. Ibid.
39. Rachel L. Carson, "A Young Hero," *St. Nicholas Magazine* 46 (January 1919), 280. This is a previously unknown story of Carson's. While the story is interesting on its own terms, its existence testifies to Rachel's determination to keep writing. Rachel L. Carson, "A Message to the Front," *St. Nicholas Magazine* 46 (February 1919), 375. Notice of Gold Badge Award, RCP/BLYU.
40. Rachel L. Carson, "A Famous Sea Fight," *St. Nicholas Magazine* 46 (August 1919), 951.
41. *St. Nicholas Magazine* paid Maria Carson for her musical settings of one of Mary Mapes Dodge's rhymes and published the song. William Fayal Clarke to Maria M. Carson, 1903, RCP/BLYU.
42. Frances W. Marshall to RC, July 18, 1921, RCP/BLYU. Payment was received August 10, 1921.
43. Rachel Carson to *The Author's Press*, July 13, 1921; editors, *St. Nicholas Magazine*, to Rachel Carson, August 9, 1921; story ledger, RCP/BLYU. Rachel Carson, "Just Dogs," RCP/BLYU.
44. Rachel Louise Carson, "My Favorite Recreation," *St. Nicholas Magazine*, 49 (July 1922), 999. Rosta, "The Magazine," 45. Rachel was fourteen when she wrote the story, fifteen when it was published. *St. Nicholas Magazine* editors to Rachel Carson, August 9, 1921, RCP/BLYU. This story is interesting not only because it reveals how observant of birds and nature Rachel had become since her early prose about the wrens but how romantic her view of nature was. That view was just what *St. Nicholas* encouraged in its readers.
45. Carson, biographical fragment, RCP/BLYU.
46. Interview with Sarah Smith Totten. *Springdale, 1906–1981*.
47. Department of Commerce, U.S. Bureau of the Census, *Census 1920*, vol. 44, E.D. 815, Sheet 7, l. 46.
48. Interviews with Sarah Smith Totten, Claudia (James) Gianinni.
49. Application for Marriage License, #J-14650, October 25, 1915, Case No. 121, October Term 1918, Court of Common Pleas, Allegheny County, PA.
50. Marian C. Frampton v. Lee F. Frampton, Case No. 121, October Term 1918, Court of Common Pleas, Allegheny County, PA. "Transcript of Official Notes of Testimony," February 25, 1919, Case No. 121, October Term 1918, Court of Common

Pleas, Allegheny County, PA. Department of Commerce, U.S. Bureau of the Census, *Census 1920*, vol. 44, E.D. 815, Sheet 7, l. 46. The divorce was final May 18, 1919. This census lists both Robert McLean Carson and Marian Carson Frampton as living at Colfax Lane.

51. Application for Marriage License. No. 19627. Office of the Register of Wills, Marriage Records Department, Allegheny County, PA.
52. Interview with Frances Carson Hoerner. *Springdale, 1906–1981*.
53. U.S. Bureau of the Census, 1920. Story told by A. W. Kennedy, recounted by Claudia (James) Gianinni.
54. Interview with Elizabeth Daugherty Shombert. Shombert was a member of the Parnassus High School Class of 1925. *Springdale, 1906–1981*.
55. Although Rachel did not participate in many social events, she seems to have been happy at Parnassus High School. One clue comes from a set of small tablet-paper drawings that date from her years there. The drawings of her classmates, some named, some not, are good-humored caricatures with accompanying limericks about each person. Tablet drawings, RCP/BLYU. Interview with Elizabeth Daugherty Shombert.
56. *Parnassus High School Year Book*, 1925.
57. Rachel Carson, "Intellectual Dissipation," June 1925, Thesis, Parnassus High School, Parnassus, PA, RCP/BLYU. Graduation photographs courtesy of Elizabeth Daugherty Shombert.
58. Interview with Helen Myers Knox. Many of Rachel's friends supplemented scholarships with campus jobs, but Maria was too proud to have Rachel work and was obsessed with her daughter's health. Unidentified newspaper clippings of scholarship awards, fragment, RCP/BLYU.
59. The "Alderside Addition No. 1, of August 2, 1924" is described in "The Preliminary Structures Report of the Rachel Carson Homestead," 6. Robert McLean Carson is listed as deeding these lots, which suggests again that the senior Carson was in poor health. *Springdale, 1906–1981*.

2: "THE VISION SPLENDID"

1. Laberta Dysart, *Chatham College: The First Ninety Years* (Pittsburgh, PA: Chatham College, 1959), 14–18, 19, 87–90, 141–145. Unless otherwise noted, I have relied on Dysart's history of the college for the years Carson was a student.
2. See ibid. for Cora Coolidge's style and personality. Other material is drawn from interviews with members of the classes of 1929 and 1930: Dorothy Thompson Seif, Helen Myers Knox, Ruth Hunter Swisshelm, Dorothy Appleby Musser. See also Dorothy Thompson Seif, "Letters from Rachel Carson: A Young Scientist Sets Her Course," Unpub. mss. Rachel Carson History Project/Rachel Carson Council, Inc., Chevy Chase, MD. [Hereafter cited as RCHP/RCC.] Correspondence that supports this manuscript is also held by RCHP/RCC. I am indebted to Dorothy Thompson Seif for the understanding she has given me of student life at PCW, her friendship with Carson, and science in the 1920s in interviews over an extended period of time. I am also grateful to her for giving me unlimited access to her manuscript and other papers and letters. I am grateful to Shirley A. Briggs, curator of the Rachel Carson History Project/Rachel Carson Council, for giving me access to the Carson correspondence that supports Seif's manuscript. Permission to quote from these letters is from Frances Collin, Trustee, u/w/o Rachel Carson.
3. Dysart, *Chatham College*, 147–155. Interview with Dorothy Thompson Seif.

4. Philip Sterling, *Sea and Earth: The Life of Rachel Carson* (New York: Thomas Y. Crowell Co., 1970), 43. Sterling got the story from Carson's brother. No college records exist about this loan. I give the story credence because it is consistent with Coolidge's philosophy and past practice. How long this private financing went on is unknown. Allegheny County Deed Book, vol. 2388, February 19, 1929. See Margaret Fifer, "I Remember Rachel" (Pittsburgh Poetry Society, April 13, 1973), 1, RCP/BLYU.
5. Interview with Dorothy Appleby Musser.
6. Interviews with Helen Myers Knox, Ruth Hunter Swisshelm, Dorothy Appleby Musser.
7. Ibid.
8. See H. Patricia Hynes, *The Recurring Silent Spring* (New York: Pergamon Press, 1989), 55–57, on mother as mentor.
9. Transcript of Divorce Hearing, January 10, 1930, Marian C. Williams v. Burton Williams. Divorce Case No. 1067, October Term, 1929, Allegheny County Records Center, Pittsburgh, PA.
10. Interview with Frances Carson Hoerner. Transcript of Divorce Hearing, September 20, 1928, Robert M. Carson v. Meredith B. Carson, Divorce Case No. 1444, July Term, 1928, Allegheny County Records Center, Pittsburgh, PA.
11. Rachel Carson, "Who I Am and Why I Came to P.C.W.," 1925, RCP/BLYU.
12. Ibid.
13. Grace Croff's background is unknown. It is likely that she also came from New England. She stayed at PCW only three years, leaving in June 1928. Thus Croff and Mary Scott Skinker both left the college at the end of Carson's junior year. *The Pennsylvanian*, 1928. Dysart, *Chatham College*, 260.
14. Rachel Carson, "Field Hockey," 1925, RCP/BLYU.
15. Interviews with Helen Myers Knox, Dorothy Appleby Musser, Dorothy Thompson Seif. Wendy Wareham, "Rachel Carson's Early Years," *Carnegie Magazine*, 58, 6 (November–December 1986), 27.
16. Rachel Carson, "Calvary Church," 1925, RCP/BLYU.
17. Rachel Carson, "Breakfast 'Chez Nous,' " 1926, RCP/BLYU.
18. Rachel Carson, "Dallas Lore Sharp," May 28, 1926, RCP/BLYU. She chose Sharp because she shared his view that "religion begins where science ends" and his belief that "good nature writing must have a pre-literary existence as lived reality."
19. Rachel Carson, "The Master of the Ship's Light," May 26, 1926, RCP/BLYU. Carson's evocation of the seacoast with its changes of weather, light, and mood are of such quality that Croff was taken aback when she learned that Rachel had never experienced it firsthand. Interview with Helen Myers Knox. Carol B. Gartner, *Rachel Carson*, (New York: Frederick Ungar Publishing Co., 1983), 9.
20. Interview with Frances Carson Hoerner. Transcript of Divorce Hearings, Carson v. Carson, Case No. 1444, July Term, 1928.
21. Ibid.
22. Ibid. Williams v. Williams, Divorce Hearing, Case No. 1067, October Term, 1929.
23. Interview with Helen Myers Knox. Knox recalled somewhat sarcastically that Mrs. Carson picked her as Rachel's roommate, whether she wanted to be or not. However, another alumna recalls that Dorothy and Rachel were left out when roommates were chosen and self-selected by default.
24. Rachel L. Carson, "Record of Secondary Education, Undergraduate College Credits," RCP/BLYU. Pennsylvania College for Women, *The Pennsylvanian, 1928*. Interview with Helen Myers Knox.
25. Rachel Carson, "The Golden Apple," March 11, 1927, RCP/BLYU.

26. My knowledge of M. S. Skinker's life comes from her letters to Rachel Carson, Mary Frye Llewelyn, and Dorothy Thompson Seif, some of which are collected in Dorothy Thompson Seif, "Letters," and other Carson letters held by the Rachel Carson History Project. I have had extensive interviews with Dorothy Thompson Seif and Mary Frye Llewelyn and with Skinker's surviving family members: Martha Skinker and Thomas M. Skinker and Dr. Thomas M. Skinker. Of utmost importance are various interviews with Frances Staley Skinker (Mrs. G. Murray Skinker). I will always cherish the memory of Mrs. Skinker's kindness and her intense interest in my work. Interviews with Martha Skinker, Thomas M. Skinker. Other information is drawn from the institutions of higher education where Skinker was a student. Registrar, The George Washington University; Registrar, Northern Colorado University; Registrar, Columbia Teacher's College.

    Seif's manuscript, written in the late 1980s, contains some errors of fact and memory. Skinker's family was only distantly related to the wealthy and socially influential family who owned large portions of St. Louis real estate, and Skinker attended but did not graduate from Washington University in St. Louis.
27. Skinker changed her major to science during the year she took courses at Colorado Teacher's College. The fact that Skinker went through essentially the same turmoil endeared her to Carson all the more. Coolidge required that department chairpersons have earned doctorates, so Skinker had risen as high as she could go at PCW in the fall of 1924.
28. Photographs of Mary Scott Skinker in author's possession. Interviews with Martha Skinker, Mary Frye Llewelyn, Dorothy Thompson Seif.
29. Interview with Ruth Hunter Swisshelm.
30. Dorothy Thompson Seif to Laberta Dysart, November 22, 1954, Chatham College Archives, Pittsburgh, PA.
31. Seif, "Letters," 24–25. Interviews with Dorothy Thompson Seif, Ruth Hunter Swisshelm. The grade issue was widely whispered about on campus. Coolidge criticized Skinker for her grading policy and her refusal to reconsider the girl's performance. It was the first of many discussions between Coolidge and Skinker over standards.
32. Seif, "Letters," 14, 24–25. Interview with Dorothy Thompson Seif.
33. Seif, "Letters," 16. I have used Seif's memoir cautiously, especially in terms of the accuracy of her recollected dialogue between Carson and herself. The historical context of the narrative and the correspondence, however, are invaluable sources.
34. Interviews with Dorothy Thompson Seif.
35. Ibid. *The Pennsylvanian*, 1929, 1930. Chatham College Archives.
36. Interviews with Mary Frye Llewelyn, Dorothy Thompson Seif, Helen Myers Knox, Ruth Hunter Swisshelm.
37. Rachel Carson, "The Return," February 25, 1927, RCP/BLYU. Croff appraised it highly, commenting particularly on Carson's descriptions of the tormented woman, the flower garden, and the story's ominous midnight setting. Rachel Carson, "Broken Lamps," May 27, 1927, RCP/BLYU. The story concerns the inner conflict of a young, self-confident engineer whose passion for building aesthetically pleasing bridges is at odds with the necessity that they also function perfectly. Evocative in its psychological portrait, "Broken Lamps" was her most serious effort yet to write about marital conflict.
38. Rachel Carson, autobiographical fragment, RCP/BLYU. Also discussed in Fifer, "I Remember Rachel," 4. It is difficult to determine precisely when Carson had this experience. Croff assigned "Locksley Hall" in the winter of 1926, but Carson read the poem often and the coincidence of the storm and the lines of the poem may

have been later than this. In Carson's mind, the vision of her destiny being somehow linked with the sea came from a particular reading of the poem.

39. Carson v. Carson, Case No. 1444, July Term, 1928. Interview with Frances Carson Hoerner.
40. She also enrolled in "Preventive Medicine and Hygiene" at the Johns Hopkins Medical School, but she withdrew from it, probably because the embryology lab required more than forty-five hours a week. Transcript, Office of the Registrar, The Johns Hopkins University, Baltimore, MD. Transcript, Registrar's Office, Cornell University, Ithaca, NY.
41. Skinker remained "acting head of biology." Dysart, *Chatham College*, 179–180. Margaret W. Rossiter, *Women Scientists in America: Struggles and Strategies to 1940* (Baltimore: Johns Hopkins University Press, 1982), 160–180.
42. Rossiter calls this "prestige-linked" antifeminism, which occurred at a time of relative prosperity at women's colleges. It also coincided with a modest tolerance to hire married women.
43. Rachel L. Carson, College Transcript, RCP/BLYU. Carson kept her own college transcript with precise grade point averages. Interview with Sarah Smith Totten.
44. *The Pennsylvanian*, 1928, Chatham College Archives. With Rachel on *The Arrow* and *The Englicode* staff that year were Peg Wooldridge, who was business manager and art editor, Betty MacColl, managing editor, and Marjorie Stevenson, Dorothy Appleby, and Dorothy Thompson. See *The Arrow*, March 28, 1928. Fifer, "I Remember Rachel," 4. I am indebted to Margaret "Peg" Wooldridge's daughter, Margaret Fifer, for giving me her mother's collections of *The Arrow* and *The Englicode*.
45. Interview with Helen Myers Knox. Stevenson graduated cum laude, went to graduate school at the University of Pittsburgh, and corresponded with Carson at Woods Hole and at Johns Hopkins. She was appointed to the PCW faculty in 1931 to teach ancient history for at least one year when Laberta Dysart was on leave. Stevenson never married. She was a distinguished teacher in the Pittsburgh Public School system and died in service in 1975. Other classmates hold vague memories of Stevenson. As a commuter and a scholar, Stevenson, like Rachel, was not popular.
46. Rachel Carson, "The Thumb of Gold," December 8, 1926; Rachel Carson, "They Call It Education," 1928, RCP/BLYU.
47. See Rachel Carson, "Draft for *Twentieth Century Authors*," 1st supplement. In 1928 Rachel herself did not see that biology "would give her something to write about." She anticipated that a career in science would be one in research or teaching. Skinker was her model. Writing, she thought, would become an avocation.
48. Rachel Carson, "Six Easy Pieces," November 15, 1927, RCP/BLYU.
49. Rachel Carson, "Triolet," December 6, 1927, RCP/BLYU. Croff commented: "This would be beautiful in a song—three sharps, written for a high voice. Lively, Excellent, Beautiful!!!" The poem was published in *The Arrow*, January 13, 1928.
50. Story told by Sterling, *Sea and Earth*, 53–54. I accept its accuracy because Sterling interviewed Betty MacColl, who was in this class with Rachel. See *The Pennsylvanian*, 1928, Chatham College Archives.
51. Ibid. No one was very happy about Coolidge's economy measure. This yearbook photograph is not Rachel's senior picture; it was taken when she was twenty years old. The other pictures of her in the yearbook were also taken in the early fall of 1928. Rachel's activities are listed through spring of 1928. Thus there is no mention of the science honorary, Mu Sigma Sigma, that she founded and was president of during her senior year. The 1928/29 yearbook was dedicated to Grace Croff.
52. Rossiter, *Women Scientists*, 313–316. See also Evelyn Fox Keller, *A Feeling for the*

Organism (New York: W. H. Freeman and Co., 1983), 39–77. Evelyn Fox Keller, "Gender and Science," in Sandra Harding and Merrill B. Hintikka, eds., *Discovering Reality* (Boston: D. Reidel Publishing Co., 1983), 187–205.

53. RC to Mary Frye, February 22, 1928, RCHP/RCC.
54. Ibid.
55. RC to Mary Frye, March 6, 1928, RCHP/RCC.
56. Rachel's date was Bob Frye, a junior at Westminster College. She wore a party dress with a pair of fashionable silver slippers. The day after the prom the two couples drove back to Westminster to see a basketball game. Interview with Ruth Hunter Swisshelm. Swisshelm's memory of Rachel's story is confirmed by an interview with Carolyn Leiby. RC to Mary Frye, March 14, 1928, RCHP/RCC.
57. Interview with Helen Myers Knox. RC to Mary Frye, April 24, 1928, RCHP/RCC. Except for Rachel's closest friends, her classmates' memories of her generally denigrate her appearance, her personality, her sociability, and her family. They told me of discussions among class members after Rachel had become famous for *The Sea Around Us*, when the question would come up of how she could possibly have achieved so much when their opinion of her had been so low. They were particularly surprised to find her so attractive and poised when she returned to campus to accept an honorary doctorate in 1952. Theirs was a common image of Rachel as an unattractive girl who kept entirely to herself, studied all the time, and had few friends. How, they wondered, could they possibly have ignored someone so talented and attractive who would bring more pride to their alma mater than all the rest?
58. RC to Mary Frye, March 14, 1928, RCHP/RCC.
59. Rossiter, *Women Scientists*, 18–22, for a discussion of the early "protégée chains." Hynes, *Recurring Silent Spring*, 60–61. See also Janice G. Raymond, *A Passion for Friends: Toward a Philosophy of Female Affection* (Boston: Beacon Press, 1986), 35–39. Raymond calls the process "prodigy lineage." She notes that not only did they last for several generations, but that they influenced many undergraduates to study science in the first place. Hynes and Raymond add the dimension of "female primacy" to the process Rossiter describes.

    Because there are few surviving letters between Mary Scott Skinker and her most famous student, I can only suggest the nature and extent of their relationship. Even without written evidence, it is clear that their friendship was an intimate one, which Rachel took great pains to protect.
60. Seif, "Letters," 21–22, RCHP/RCC. Mary Scott Skinker to Mary Frye, March 27, 1928. Author's possession, courtesy of Martha Skinker. Skinker spent the spring recess in Washington with her sister Anne, "where I most love to be." RC to Mary Frye, March 14, 1928, RCHP/RCC.
61. Rachel L. Carson, Application for Admission to the Faculty of Philosophy, April 27, 1928. Transcript from Pennsylvania College for Women, Rachel Carson File, the Ferdinand Hamburger Jr. Archives, Johns Hopkins University, Baltimore, MD. [Hereafter cited as FHA/JHU.] It is clear that Skinker and Carson agreed on this course of action before Carson sent in her application.
62. See correspondence between R. N. Dempster and H. S. Jennings, May 9–10, 1928, FHA/JHU. Application for Scholarship in the Faculty of Philosophy, May 11, 1928. R. N. Dempster to H. S. Jennings, May 9, 1928. H. S. Jennings to R. N. Dempster, May 10, 1928, FHA/JHU. Mary Scott Skinker to Committee on Scholarships, Johns Hopkins University, May 11, 1928, FHA/JHU. This letter indicates that Maria Carson had befriended Miss Skinker herself and approved of Rachel's efforts to leave PCW a year early.

63. RC to Mary Frye, April 23, 1928, RCHP/RCC.
64. Mary Scott Skinker to Mary Frye, July 11, 1928; RC to Mary Frye, August 27, 1928, RCHP/RCC.
65. RC to Mary Frye, August 6, 1928, RCHP/RCC.
66. RC to Mary Frye, July 23, 1928, RCHP/RCC.
67. *The Arrow*, October 19, 1928, Chatham College Archives.
68. Even though Rachel had no room for any composition classes in her schedule senior year, Croff's friendship had been important to her.
69. Seif, "Letters," 25, 53. RC to Mary Frye, August 27, 1928, RCHP/RCC.
70. *The Pennsylvanian*, 1928, Chatham College Archives. Dorothy Thompson Seif to Laberta Dysart, November 22, 1954. Whiting was a popular and undemanding teacher at PCW, remaining on the faculty from 1928 to 1936. In 1935 she introduced a course in eugenics and euthenics, which the students dubbed "the marriage course." Students applauded her "wholesome attitude" toward careers and marriage. Dysart, *Chatham College*, 179.
71. Quoted in Seif to Laberta Dysart. Interview with Dorothy Thompson Seif.
72. Anna R. Whiting to Scholarship Committee, December 18, 1928, FHA/JHU. Doxee's letter is pro forma and unremarkable. Although Carson had taken at least one course from him, he did not write in praise of her literary ability. Apparently Doxee was still smarting from Rachel's decision to leave his department for biology. ". . . though primarily interested in Biology, [she] has for the greater part of her college course been also a student in the English Department. In her English work Miss Carson has always stood with the highest."
73. RC to the President of the Johns Hopkins University, February 25, 1929, FHA/JHU.
74. Mary Scott Skinker to Scholarship Committee, February 25, 1929, FHA/JHU.
75. As Skinker predicted, Whiting was immensely popular. See Seif to Dysart, November 22, 1954, RCHP/RCC.
76. Clippings File, RCP/BLYU. "Rachel Carson '29 Wins Scholarship at Johns Hopkins," *The Arrow*, April 22, 1929, Chatham College Archives.
77. Robert M. Carson to Philip Sterling, in Sterling, *Sea and Earth*, 65. According to Carson's recollection, the college could charge 6 percent interest after October 1, 1930, on whatever balance remained. She began making payments in January 1931. See Rachel Louise Carson to Pennsylvania College for Women, Allegheny County, Pennsylvania, Deed Book, volume 2388, 28.
78. RC to Maria Carson, February 1929, RCP/BLYU.
79. *32nd Annual Report of the Marine Biological Laboratory*, 1929 (Woods Hole, MA: Marine Biological Laboratory, 1929), 28, 32.
80. Commencement Program, Class of 1929, Pennsylvania College for Women, Chatham College Archives.
81. Pennsylvania College for Women, Commencement Exercises, June 10, 1929, Chatham College Archives. RC to Dorothy Thompson, June 19, 1930, RCHP/RCC.
82. *The Pennsylvanian*, 1928, Chatham College Archives.

3: "THE DECISION FOR SCIENCE"

1. Philip Sterling, *Sea and Earth: The Life of Rachel Carson* (New York: Thomas Y. Crowell Co., 1970), 67–68. Sterling's description comes from Robert Carson, who lived at the homestead until 1930.

2. *Springdale: From Indian Village to Power City: Seventy-Five Years* (Springdale, PA, 1981).
3. H. S. Jennings to Rachel Carson, July 10, 1929, Rachel Carson Student File, FHA/JHU.
4. In her application for readmission to the graduate school in 1930, Skinker explained she had spent the previous year dividing her time between the USDA and illness. "Application for Readmission," The George Washington University Graduate School, Mary Scott Skinker Student File, Registrar's Office. Interviews with Dr. Thomas M. Skinker, Frances Staley Skinker. Frances Staley and Anne Skinker were roommates from the late 1930s until Staley married G. Murray Skinker in 1950. The couple lived in the same apartment building with his sister Anne for another decade. Staley first met Mary Scott about 1941.
5. RC to Dorothy Thompson, August 4, 1929, RCHP/RCC.
6. Margaret W. Rossiter, *Women Scientists in America: Struggles and Strategies to 1940* (Baltimore: Johns Hopkins University Press, 1982), 163–199. Carson received her M.S. in zoology in June 1932; Skinker was awarded her Ph.D. from George Washington University one year later. Both women were forced to work part time while studying for graduate degrees, a situation that markedly affected their research results.

   Skinker's date of birth is somewhat mysterious. She lists 1889, 1891, and 1893 on various educational applications, where she also changes the dates of her graduation from high school. I believe that 1889 is the correct date and that she alters it because of both ageist and sexist attitudes in the programs or jobs that she was applying for. A beautiful, stylish woman, she never looked as if she were in poor health and never looked her chronological age.
7. RC to Dorothy Thompson, August 4, 1929, RCHP/RCC.
8. Jane Maienschein, *100 Years Exploring Life, 1888–1988* (Boston: Jones and Bartlett Publishers, 1989), 19. E. F. Rivinus and E. M. Youssef, *Spencer Baird of the Smithsonian* (Washington, D.C.: Smithsonian Institution Press, 1992), 141–151. Paul S. Galtsoff, *The Story of the Bureau of Commercial Fisheries Biological Laboratory, Woods Hole, Massachusetts*, U.S. Department of Interior Circular 145 (Washington, D.C.: U.S. Department of the Interior, 1962), 1–52.
9. Maienschein, *100 Years Exploring Life*, 9–24. Philip J. Pauly, "Summer Resort and Scientific Discipline: Woods Hole and the Structure of American Biology, 1882–1925," in Ronald Rainger, Keith R. Benson, and Jane Maienschein, eds., *The American Development of Biology* (Philadelphia: University of Pennsylvania Press, 1988), 127–130. Baird's idea was to maintain the Marine Biological Laboratory (MBL) as a "private annex" of the Fish Commission lab. He invited universities to help purchase land for the laboratory in return for the privilege of sending faculty there for research on a regular basis (128–129). Rossiter, *Women Scientists*, 86–88. Cornelia Clapp, "Some Recollections of the First Summer at Woods Hole 1888," *The Collecting Net* 3, 10, Rare Book Library, Woods Hole Marine Biology Laboratory, Woods Hole, MA. Ellen Swallow of MIT was among those whose goodwill helped found MBL and who watched the diminishing role of women there with concern. See Robert Clarke, *Ellen Swallow: The Woman Who Founded Ecology* (Chicago: Follett Publishing Company, 1973), 147, 163–164. See Joan N. Burstyn, "Early Women in Education: The Role of The Anderson School of Natural History," *Boston University Journal of Education* 159, 3 (August 1977), 50–64.
10. See Pauly's article for a discussion of the implications of the "resort" atmosphere of Woods Hole on the professionalization of biology and on the creation of scientific networks, "Summer Resort."

11. Mary Scott Skinker had gone to Woods Hole in 1928 specifically to take Calkins's course in protozoology. Maienschein, *100 Years Exploring Life*, 134–142. Frank R. Lillie, *The Woods Hole Marine Biological Laboratory* (Chicago: University of Chicago Press, 1944), 34–61.
12. *32nd Annual Report of the Marine Biological Laboratory*, 1929 (Woods Hole, MA: Marine Biological Laboratory, 1929), 28.
13. Maienschein, *100 Years Exploring Life*, 16, 40, 42–45. Pauly, "Summer Resort," 134–138. Interview with Robert and Jane Huettner, volunteer archivists at the Marine Biological Laboratory Library, Woods Hole, MA. I am grateful for their help in checking MBL statistics.
14. RC to Dorothy Thompson, August 4, 1929, RCHP/RCC.
15. Rachel Carson, "Origins of the Book, *The Sea Around Us*," RCP/BLYU.
16. "Beginning Investigators, 1929" in *32nd Annual Report of the Marine Biological Laboratory*, 1929, 28. Mary Frye was one of twenty-eight female undergraduates enrolled as a student in the MBL classes. She paid her own way as a student in Calkins's course in protozoology. The next year she won the college seat instead of Dorothy Thompson.

    The annual reports for 1927, 1928, 1930, and 1931 show a similar ratio of men to women as in the class of beginning investigators for 1929. Not surprisingly, as the Depression deepened after 1931, the total number of beginning investigators dropped and the number of women fell off dramatically. See the 30th, 31st, 33rd, and 34th *Annual Reports of the Marine Biological Laboratory*.
17. Rachel had planned to work with Cowles that summer, hoping to benefit by this opportunity to accelerate her research during graduate school. RC to Dorothy Thompson, August 25, 1929, RCHP/RCC.
18. Interview with Mary Frye Llewelyn. The Fish Commission matured as an administrative agency and became the Bureau of Fisheries in the Department of Commerce and Labor in 1903. See A. Hunter Dupree, *Science in the Federal Government* (Cambridge, MA: Belknap Press of Harvard University, 1957), 237–238. It is possible that Rachel met Dr. Elmer Higgins, then assistant director of the bureau's Division of Scientific Inquiry, during the summer at Woods Hole. However, I think it more likely that Mary Scott Skinker arranged their introduction. Interview with Lynn Forbes, Librarian, Bureau of Fisheries, NOAH, Woods Hole, MA.
19. Interview with Dorothy Thompson Seif. Maienschein, *100 Years Exploring Life*, vii. Rachel describes this ritual in *The Edge of the Sea* (Boston: Houghton Mifflin Co., 1955).
20. Higgins was born in Iowa and educated in California, where he received degrees in zoology. He began his federal career with the Bureau of Fisheries in 1924, became the director of the Key West Biological Station in 1925, and was promoted to division chief in 1929. His interests and Carson's were similar: life history, ecology, conservation problems of marine fisheries, radiobiology, and atomic energy impacts on fish and wildlife. *American Men of Science* (Lancaster, PA: Science Press, 1944), 2283.
21. Interviews and extensive correspondence with Katherine Howe Roberts.
22. C. P. Swanson, "A History of Biology at The Johns Hopkins University," *IOS*, 22 (December 1951), 234–244. Keith R. Benson, "American Morphology in the Late-Nineteenth Century: The Biology Department at Johns Hopkins University," *Journal of the History of Biology*, 18, 2 (June 1985), 169–192. John C. French, *A History of the University Founded by Johns Hopkins* (Baltimore: Johns Hopkins University Press, 1946), 433–434.
23. William Coleman, *Biology in the Nineteenth Century: Problems of Form, Function, and*

Transformation (New York: John Wiley & Sons, 1971), 1–19. Garland Allen, *Life Science in the Twentieth Century* (Cambridge: Cambridge University Press, 1978), xi–39. Swanson, "History of Biology," 244–247. Sharon E. Kingsland, "A Man Out of Place: Herbert Spencer Jennings at Johns Hopkins, 1906–1938," *American Zoologist*, 27 (1987), 807–810. T. M. Sonneborn, "Herbert Spencer Jennings, 1868–1947," *Biographical Memoirs* 47 (Washington, D.C.: National Academy of Sciences, 1975), 182–200.

24. Swanson, "History of Biology," 244–245, 260. Pearl had been Jennings's student, both as an undergraduate at Dartmouth and as a graduate student at the University of Michigan. Jennings's interests in the mathematics of heredity and the application of mathematics to biological problems influenced Pearl. Later Pearl's biostatistical modeling in genetic research influenced Jennings. Sharon E. Kingsland, "Raymond Pearl: On the Frontier in the 1920s," Raymond Pearl Memorial Lecture, 1983, in *Human Biology*, 56 (February 1984), 1–18. Kingsland, "H. S. Jennings at Johns Hopkins," 812.
25. Kingsland's two articles on Jennings and Pearl make clear the pressures operating on the zoology laboratory at the time Carson was a graduate student there. Thomas B. Turner, *Heritage of Excellence: The Johns Hopkins Medical Institutions, 1914–1947* (Baltimore: Johns Hopkins University Press, 1974), 56–61, 358–362.
26. Sharon E. Kingsland, *Modeling Nature* (Chicago: University of Chicago Press, 1985), 7, 56–61. Swanson, "History of Biology," 261.
27. Johns Hopkins University *Register*, 1928–1929, 1929–1930, 1930–1931, FHA/JHU.
28. RC to Dorothy Thompson, November 10, 1929; RC to Mary Frye, February 8, 1930, RCHP/RCC. She describes the gender situation as "fun" but "stiff."
29. RC to Mary Frye, February 8, 1930, RCHP/RCC. Interview with Dorothy Thompson Seif.
30. Interview with Dorothy Thompson Seif.
31. Ibid. Rachel's letters are silent as to her father's health and financial reversals. Friends, such as Dorothy Thompson, who visited the Carsons remarked on Mr. Carson's poor health and his quiet demeanor.
32. RC to Dorothy Thompson, November 19, 1929, RCHP/RCC.
33. Interview with Dorothy Thompson Seif.
34. RC to Mary Frye, February 8, 1930.
35. Ibid.
36. Mary Scott Skinker to Dorothy Thompson, June 5, 1930, RCHP/RCC.
37. Ibid.
38. RC to Dorothy Thompson, June 19, 1930, RCHP/RCC.
39. Grace E. Lippy, Application for Admission to the Graduate School of Arts and Sciences, The Johns Hopkins University, 1924, Grace E. Lippy Student File, FHA/JHU. Interview with Grace E. Lippy.
40. *Johns Hopkins Half-Century Directory*, compiled by W. Norman Brown (Baltimore: Johns Hopkins University Press, 1926), 215. Lippy, Application for Admission. R. P. Cowles and S. O. Mast to the Board of University Studies, April 26, 1926, Grace E. Lippy Student File, FHA/JHU. Lippy was largely responsible for getting Rachel the teaching assistantship at the University of Maryland School of Dentistry. Interview with Grace E. Lippy.
41. Rachel lists her address as of March 25 as 3543 Newland Road, where the family stayed until the Stemmers Run house was ready to be occupied. Rachel Carson to Professor J. C. W. Frazer, March 25, 1930, FHA/JHU. On October 25, 1930, she wrote university president Joseph Ames: "In order to make possible the continuation of my University work, I have had to find some part-time employment and

have secured a position in the Institute of Biological Research. . . . Therefore I decline the scholarship of two hundred dollars which was granted me for the year 1930–1931." Rachel Carson Student File, FHA/JHU.

42. Rossiter, *Women Scientists*, 286, 206–207. According to Rossiter, the women on the faculty of the School of Medicine and the School of Hygiene and Public Health made Hopkins the largest center of female scientists in the 1920s and 1930s outside Columbia Teacher's College or the major women's colleges. French, *A History of the University*, 234.
43. RC to Dorothy Thompson, October 16, 1930, RCHP/RCC.
44. Rachel must have seen Mary Scott Skinker rather frequently during this period, as she mentions to Dorothy that she had just seen her the week before and knew about Skinker's plans for Thanksgiving in detail.
45. See Dorothy Thompson Seif, "Letters," for her recollection of the visit. Interview with Dorothy Thompson Seif, during which Seif elaborated on her memories of the 1930 Thanksgiving visit. She thought that Marian and the girls had moved down to Stemmers Run during the summer. She felt that Mrs. Carson was the key to Rachel's support during this difficult year in graduate school. Dorothy finished her M.A. in zoology in two years, then returned to Pittsburgh to teach.
46. RC to Mr. Shamel, February 6, 1931, Division of Mammals, RU 208, Office of Smithsonian Institution Archives, Washington, D.C. RC to Dorothy Thompson, August 23, 1931, RCHP/RCC.
47. Maria McLean Carson to the Graduates of the Washington Female Seminary, May 30, 1950. Washington Seminary Collection, Citizens Library, Washington, PA.
48. Rachel's letter to PCW is quoted in Sterling, *Sea and Earth*, 84. Chatham College Archives has no records. RC to Dorothy Thompson, August 23, 1931, RCHP/RCC.
49. R. P. Cowles to Professor C. J. Pierson, University of Maryland, Dental and Pharmacy Schools, n.d., 1931. Rachel Carson Student File, FHA/JHU. Interview with Grace E. Lippy.
50. *Annual Report of the President*, The Johns Hopkins University, 1932–1933, 782, FHA/JHU.
51. Allen, *Life Science*, 21–28.
52. RC to Dorothy Thompson, August 23, 1931, RCHP/RCC. Rachel Carson, "The Development of the Pronephros During the Embryonic and Early Larval Life of the Catfish *(Ictalurus punctatus)*," June 1932, 1–53, RCP/BLYU.
53. Rachel Carson to the Board of University Studies, October 16, 1931, Rachel Carson Student File, FHA/JHU. RC to Dorothy Thompson, August 23, 1931.
54. R. P. Cowles and E. A. Andrews to the Board of University Studies, May 14, 1932, Rachel Carson Student File, FHA/JHU.
55. Transcript, Rachel Louise Carson, Office of the Registrar, The Johns Hopkins University, FHA/JHU.
56. Legal documents are lost that would show when the college actually sold the lots and released Rachel of further obligation. But it was probably sometime after 1942, when the war stimulated the economy of rivertown communities like Springdale and employment began to bring in new families.
57. Interview with Dorothy Thompson Seif. Dorothy was teaching biology at the Winchester-Thurston School for Girls in Pittsburgh and married Charles Seif, an attorney, the following summer.
58. "Anguilla," the eel, made her debut in 1941 in Carson's first natural history of the sea, *Under the Sea-Wind*. Carson's careful observations of the eels in 1932 and 1933 were vividly employed in her story of the eel's life.

59. Registration Form, The Johns Hopkins University Bureau of Appointments, February 18, 1935, Rachel Carson Student File, FHA/JHU.
60. Mast said she had done "very satisfactory" work, and Pearl noted that Rachel was "extremely conscientious, hard-working and reliable as an assistant." Cowles last letter to Rachel's file in May 1935 elaborated on her teaching experience and her popularity with students and associates. He describes her as "clear-headed," "accurate," and "capable as an investigator." H. S. Jennings, Bureau of Appointments, "Rachel Louise Carson," March 29, 1935. Rachel Carson Student File, FHA/JHU. All of the recommendations are dated at the end of March, with the exception of Robinson's in April 1936.
61. Recommendation from Grace Lippy, Assistant Professor, Hood College, Frederick, MD, March 29, 1935, FHA/JHU. Interview with Grace Lippy. Lippy recalled that Rachel always had her head in a book, and although she was quiet, she knew all kinds of things, which she shared with her students. R. N. Dempster to R. C. Cranberry, April 26, 1935, FHA/JHU.
62. Account given by Sterling, *Sea and Earth*, 87. Interview with Dorothy Thompson Seif. Robert W. Carson, Death Notice, July 6, 1935, Circular of the United Presbyterian Church, Presbytery of Washington County, PA.
63. Announcement of the Final Examination of Mary Scott Skinker, The George Washington University, May 18, 1933. Registrar's Office, The George Washington University. Skinker studied under the renowned zoologist Paul Bartsch. Her dissertation was a study of all the varieties of meat-eating tapeworm. A list of Mary Scott Skinker's publications and presentations is in the *Index—Catalogue of Medical and Veterinary Zoology*, Part 15, April 1951 (U.S. Department of Agriculture, Washington, D.C.: Government Printing Office, 1951), National Agricultural Library, Beltsville, MD. Several other important articles by her appear in the Smithsonian Institution's U.S. National Museum Proceedings. Several deal with parasites in fish. Skinker was very active in the Helminthological Society of Washington, where she regularly presented her research summaries. Interviews with Dorothy Thompson Seif, Dr. Paul Underwood. Underwood was a colleague of Skinker's at the Bureau of Animal Industry.
64. Rachel L. Carson, Federal Personnel Records, Office of Personnel Management, St. Louis, MO. [Hereafter cited as FPR/OPM.] Application for Federal Employment, April 20, 1943. Interview with Frances Staley Skinker. Mary Scott Skinker's federal employment file has been lost.
65. Rachel Carson, "The Real World Around Us," RCP/BLYU.
66. Ibid. Rachel began her "intermittent" employment as a field aide on October 21, 1935, at the Baltimore Field Station. It ended on June 19, 1936. All information on Carson's federal employment comes from her official Federal Personnel Record.
67. Carson, "The Real World Around Us."
68. Carson's articles for the *Baltimore Sun* are collected in RCP/BLYU. "Mark Watson, Sun Writer, Dies at 78," Obituary, *Baltimore Sun*, March 25, 1966, Archives of the *Baltimore Sun*, Baltimore, MD.
69. R. L. Carson, "It'll Be Shad-Time Soon," *Baltimore Sunday Sun*, March 1, 1936, RCP/BLYU. The article was originally entitled "Shad Fishery in the Chesapeake Bay." Carson began using her initials in work for the Bureau of Fisheries, where she and her supervisors agreed her views would be taken more seriously if it were assumed that she was a man. She continued this practice almost without exception throughout her government career.
70. Rachel Carson Student File, FHA/JHU.

71. Carson, "The Real World Around Us." Ironically, after she became famous for writing *The Sea Around Us*, Rachel rather unfairly chided her early mentors in several public addresses for not seeing that she could combine her talent of writing with her interest in science and natural history. "What surprises me now is that apparently it didn't occur to any of my advisors, either."

4: "SOMETHING TO WRITE ABOUT"

1. Rachel Carson, "The Real World Around Us," RCP/BLYU. Philip Sterling, *Sea and Earth: The Life of Rachel Carson* (New York: Thomas Y. Crowell Co., 1970), 88–93. Sterling used this dialogue as the basis for an extended fictionalized conversation. Since Sterling interviewed Elmer Higgins, I have assumed the substantive accuracy of his account. Unfortunately, his fictionalized encounter has become near legend, instead of Carson's own recollection.
2. R. L. Carson to Contest Editor, *Reader's Digest*, April 30, 1936; R. L. Carson, "Numbering the Fish of the Sea," *Baltimore Sunday Sun*, May 24, 1936, RCP/BLYU.
3. Rachel L. Carson, FPR/OPM. Until 1972 the Civil Service Commission maintained its registers of applicants by sex. Rachel's rating on the junior aquatic biologist examination placed her first on the women's register. A probable myth has grown up around Carson's appointment that asserts she was the only woman taking the aquatic biology test and that she made the highest overall score. She may or may not have been the only woman taking the test in May 1935. The fact that the acting commissioner of the Bureau of Fisheries felt it necessary to write a special memorandum justifying the appointment of a female suggests that she was not the highest-scoring applicant.
4. Carson, FPR/OPM. Charles E. Jackson to Chief, Appointment Division, Department of Commerce, Memorandum, July 6, 1936, Carson, FPR/OPM. Jackson recalled that Dr. Vera Koehring had held a permanent appointment as associate aquatic biologist at the Beaufort, NC, laboratory, and that Miss Louella Cable currently held a permanent position as junior aquatic biologist in the Washington office.
5. Department of Commerce, Field Classification Sheet, June 27, 1936, Department of Commerce, Appointment Division to Miss Rachel L. Carson, July 13, 1936, Carson, FPR/OPM.
6. The *Baltimore Sun*'s syndicated papers included the *Richmond Times Dispatch*, the *Charlotte News Current*, and the *Raleigh News and Observer*. Mark S. Watson to RC, June 23, 1937, RCP/BLYU.
7. In the first half of 1937 Carson published "The Northern Trawlers Move South," "Shad Going the Way of the Buffalo," "Sentiment Plays No Part in the Save the Shad Movement," "Chesapeake Oystermen See Stars and They Don't Like It," "Farming Under the Chesapeake," and "Oyster Dinners at the Bottom of the Chesapeake," RCP/BLYU.
8. Burton Williams might have been serving in the U.S. Navy in 1937. His parents were aware of Marian's death and did, at some point, contribute to their grandchildren's welfare.
9. Little is known of Robert Carson's personal or professional activities during these years. His livelihood as an electrician was more stable, and he apparently had the means to support an active social life for himself but felt no obligation to his sister's children. His support of his ex-wife and daughter was also casual and increasingly sporadic.

10. Carson, FPR/OPM.
11. Rachel L. Carson, "The World of Waters," MSS, 1, 1936, RCP/BLYU.
12. Ibid., 9–11.
13. Edward Weeks to RC, July 8, 1937, RCP/BLYU. See Edward Weeks, *Writers and Friends* (Boston: Atlantic–Little, Brown, 1981).
14. Ibid.
15. R. L. Carson, "Undersea," *Atlantic Monthly*, 160 (September 1937), 322–325.
16. Weeks to RC, July 13, 1937, RCP/BLYU.
17. RC to Weeks, July 18, 1937, RCP/BLYU.
18. "Contributors' Column," *Atlantic Monthly*, 160 (September 1937), RCP/BLYU.
19. Carson, "The Real World Around Us."
20. Rachel Carson, "Memo for Mrs. Eales," n.d., RCP/BLYU. Mrs. Eales was probably on the staff of Simon & Schuster or of the Scientific Book Club. This memo provides background on how Carson wrote *Under the Sea-Wind* and gives an original synopsis of each chapter. The memo was written between 1941 and 1942.
21. Quincy Howe to Hendrik van Loon, September 9, 1937, RCP/BLYU. Hendrik Villem van Loon (1882–1944) was a Dutch journalist, world historian, illustrator, travel writer, explorer, and extraordinary man of letters. His first book with Simon & Schuster was *Ships and How They Sailed* (1935), which Rachel read with enthusiasm. At the time of his first letter to Carson, van Loon was completing his monumental *Story of Mankind* (1938). Carson, "The Real World Around Us."
22. Hendrik van Loon to RC, September 10, 1937, RCP/BLYU.
23. Ibid. RC to Gerard Willem van Loon, July 13, 1962, RCP/BLYU.
24. RC to Hendrik van Loon, n.d., handwritten draft, RCP/BLYU.
25. Van Loon gave Carson a copy of his 1937 book, *The Arts*, in which he sketched a frontispiece for her in full color. Naturally it featured a fish. RC to Sonia Bleeker, March 5, 1944, RCP/BLYU.
26. Van Loon to RC, September 10, 1937; RC to van Loon, October 6, 1937; van Loon to RC, October 8, 1937; RC to van Loon, October 13, 1937, RCP/BLYU. Carson was charmed by van Loon's letters, telling him "I am sure that not even the rarest species of those creatures gets as much enjoyment out of being discovered by an ichthyologist as I am getting out of being 'discovered by you.' "
27. Carson, "The Real World Around Us," RCP/BLYU.
28. RC to van Loon, February 5, 1938, RCP/BLYU.
29. Rachel Carson, draft for a review of Henry Williamson's *Tarka the Otter* and Henry Beston's *The Outermost House*, RCP/BLYU. RC to A. G. Ogden, April 26, 1938, RCP/BLYU.
30. Carson, "Memo for Mrs. Eales," 3. She told van Loon, "I think you expressed the essence of the matter very well at dinner when you said we must talk about the codfish—or any other fish—'chez elle.' "
31. RC to van Loon, February 5, 1938, RCP/BLYU.
32. Ibid.
33. Rachel Carson, Foreword, *Under the Sea-Wind: A Naturalist's Picture of Ocean Life* (New York: Simon & Schuster, 1941), xvii.
34. Ibid. Carol B. Gartner, *Rachel Carson* (New York: Frederick Ungar Publishing Co., 1983), 29.
35. RC to van Loon, February 5, 1938, RCP/BLYU. Carson told van Loon that it was Elmer Higgins's idea that she go undersea. Higgins may have encouraged her, but the idea had been in her mind for some time.
36. Ibid. Van Loon was working on *The Story of the Pacific* (1940) under contract to Harcourt, Brace and Company.

37. RC to Edward Weeks, February 5, 1938, RCP/BLYU.
38. A. G. Ogden to RC, February 9, 1938; RC to A. G. Ogden, April 26, 1938, and review June 20, 1938, RCP/BLYU. These reviews for the *Atlantic* are signed "Rachel L. Carson."
39. R. L. Carson, "Fight for Wildlife Pushes Ahead," *Richmond Times Dispatch Sunday Magazine*, March 20, 1938, 8–9, RCP/BLYU.
40. Rachel L. Carson, "How About Citizenship Papers for the Starling?" *Nature Magazine* (June/July 1939), 317–319.
41. RC to Mark Watson, November 4, 1938, RCP/BLYU. This is the earliest indication of Carson's interest in poisons and their impact on humans and wildlife. She kept all her research notes on selenium and used them in writing *Silent Spring*.
42. Undated notebooks from various North Carolina trips are in the RCP/BLYU. Carson's observations of the particular sandpipers known as sanderlings provided the setting for several chapters. During another visit to Beaufort in 1938 she observed the eel migration, which appears several times. See R. L. Carson, "Chesapeake Eels Seek the Sargasso Sea," *Baltimore Sunday Sun Magazine*, October 9, 1938.
43. Charles E. Jackson to the Secretary of Commerce, June 16, 1939. Carson, FPR/OPM.
44. Carson, FPR/OPM.
45. Oliver C. Short to Mr. Kerlin, June 20, 1939, Department of Commerce Memorandum. Carson, FPR/OPM.
46. Linda J. Lear, "Harold L. Ickes," in Otis Graham Jr. and Megan Robinson Wander, eds., *Franklin D. Roosevelt: His Life and Times* (Boston: G. K. Hall and Co., 1985), 199–202.
47. Department of Interior Memorandum, "change in official station," July 20, 1940. Carson, FPR/OPM.
48. Carson, FPR/OPM.
49. Interviews with Dr. Paul C. Underwood, Dr. Aurel O. Foster. Underwood, a research parasitologist, was the head of the Beltsville Laboratory during this period. Foster, a distinguished agricultural parasitologist, replaced Schwartz as division chief in 1939.
50. Margaret W. Rossiter, *Women Scientists in America: Struggles and Strategies to 1940* (Baltimore: Johns Hopkins University Press, 1982), 230, 234. Shortly thereafter Cram became the head of the helminthological section of NIH's Laboratory of Tropical Diseases. She was the only woman at the NIH in the 1930s to become a section chief, the lowest level of management, held back largely because her supervisor would not give raises to single women.
51. Interviews with Judith Shaw, Dr. Marion M. Farr. Shaw worked as a librarian at USDA and later helped produce a history of the Division of Zoology. Farr, a poultry parasitologist, worked with Skinker from 1934 to 1938, when Farr was reassigned to the Beltsville laboratory.
52. Interviews with Judith Shaw, Dr. Marion M. Farr, Martha Skinker. Mary Scott Skinker, Official Transcript, Columbia University Teacher's College. Skinker's career becomes more difficult to follow. One application indicates that she taught twelfth-grade English for several months in Oakland, CA. Interviews with Dr. Thomas M. Skinker, Frances Staley Skinker.
53. Rossiter, *Women Scientists*, 228, 233–234.
54. RC to Edward Weeks, June 34, 1939; RC to Edward Weeks, July 29, 1939, RCP/BLYU. Carson was to come up against Peattie at Simon & Schuster as well. Van Loon told her, "Max Schuster thinks that there werent [*sic*] no greater nature writer than donald concross peatty whom most of us detest . . . and we are using our detes-

taion [*sic*] as a way to boom your work." Van Loon to RC, June 21, 1939, RCP/BLYU.

55. RC to van Loon, June 2, 1939, RCP/BLYU.
56. Van Loon to RC, June 5, 1939, RCP/BLYU.
57. Van Loon to RC, June 25, 1939, RCP/BLYU. Carson was desperately in need of money to finance her research but also may have been emboldened by the fact that "Undersea" had been reprinted in an anthology of college readings by Harper.
58. Interviews with Stephen and Betty Algire, Anne Algire Moretti. I am indebted to Dorothy Hamilton Algire's children for providing photographs, family memorabilia, and their memories of their mother's friendship with Carson. Dorothy Hamilton Algire, Federal Personnel Record/ Office of Personnel Management, St. Louis, MO. Documents from Algire's file will be cited hereafter as Algire, FPR/OPM.
59. Quoted in Paul Brooks, *The House of Life: Rachel Carson at Work* (Boston: Houghton Mifflin Co., 1972), 33. Rachel gave Dorothy Freeman one of the pages, on which she had sketched "Buzzie's" head, as a Christmas present in 1963. The other sketch remains with the manuscripts of *Under the Sea-Wind*, RCP/BLYU.
60. See Brooks, *The House of Life*, 4–5, on Carson's writing habits.
61. Carson, "Memo for Mrs. Eales," 2; Howard Frech, preliminary sketches, RCP/BLYU.
62. Interview with Anne Algire Moretti. Dorothy Hamilton and Glenn Algire were married in early May 1940 in Great Barrington, MA, but were back at Woods Hole for the summer where both Dorothy and Glenn had ongoing research projects. Dorothy continued to work for Fish and Wildlife until late 1941, when she retired to raise a family of three children. Rachel was godmother to her first child, Anne.
63. Rachel Carson, "Memo for Mrs. Eales," 2.
64. Photographs of Carson, RCP/BLYU. Interview with Katherine Howe Roberts. She drafted a chapter, "The Harbor," with the Woods Hole harbor in mind. Rachel L. Carson, "The Harbor" from *Under the Sea-Wind* reprinted in *The Falmouth Enterprise*, May 16, 1952, RCP/BLYU.
65. Interview with Anne Algire Moretti. Dorothy Hamilton Algire's photograph album, courtesy Anne Algire Moretti.
66. Brooks, *The House of Life*, 32. RC to Henry Beston, May 14, 1954, RCP/BLYU. In this letter she told Beston of the first time she found the house and what it meant to her.
67. Carson, "Memo for Mrs. Eales," 3.
68. See Curtis Bok correspondence for her discussion of writing *Under the Sea-Wind*, RCP/BLYU.
69. Legend has it that Carson's manuscript was the only one that has ever been received by Simon & Schuster without a single typographical error.
70. Van Loon to RC, October 14, 1941, RCP/BLYU.
71. Sterling, *Sea and Earth*, 91. Van Loon to RC, November 2, 1941, RCP/BLYU.
72. See Kenneth Johnson, "The Lost Eden: The New World in American Nature Writing," Ph.D. diss. (Albuquerque, NM: University of New Mexico, 1973), 188–191.
73. Richard Jeffries, *The Pageant of Summer* (Portland, ME: Thomas B. Mosher, 1905), 10.
74. I am indebted to the criticism offered by Carol B. Gartner, *Rachel Carson*, 29–46, and to Cheryll Glotfelty for sharing a draft of her splendid essay on Rachel Carson in *American Nature Writers*, edited by John Elder (New York: Charles Scribner's Sons, 1996), 151–171. See also Thomas R. Dunlap, "Nature Literature and Modern Science," *Environmental History Review* (spring/summer 1990), 33–44.

75. Carson, *Under the Sea-Wind*, xiii.
76. Reviews are all quoted from publicity produced by Simon & Schuster, RCP/BLYU.
77. William Beebe, review of *Under the Sea-Wind* by Rachel Carson, *Saturday Review of Literature*, December 27, 1941, 5. William Beebe, ed., *The Book of Naturalists: An Anthology of the Best Natural History* (New York: Alfred A. Knopf, 1944). Beebe paid Carson $100 to reprint her chapters. RC to Sonia Bleeker, February 2, 1942, RCP/BLYU.
78. Carson, "The Real World Around Us."
79. Publisher's statement, RCP/BLYU. The first year's sales were 1,348 copies.
80. RC to Maria Leiper, January 25, April 9, 1942; RC to Sonia Bleeker, March 31, 1942, RCP/BLYU.
81. RC to Maria Leiper, January 24, March 15, 1942, RCP/BLYU.
82. Ibid. Interview with Thomas M. Skinker.
83. RC to Maria Leiper, April 9, 1942, RCP/BLYU.
84. Carson, FPR/OPM.
85. Ibid.
86. There is little information available on exactly what Virginia and Marjorie Williams were doing during this period. Possibly Marjorie went to Chicago with Rachel and Maria, but since the girl wanted to enter some kind of technical school in the fall, it is unlikely. Exactly where the nieces lived is unknown.
87. Brooks, *The House of Life*, 72–74. See "Food from the Sea" series: "Fish and Shellfish of New England," U.S. Department of the Interior, Office of the Coordinator of Fisheries, Fish and Wildlife Service, Conservation Bulletin #33 (Washington, D.C.: 1943). Carson coauthored "Fisheries of the Pacific Coast" with Elmer Higgins, which was completed in Chicago and went to press about the same time as the other conservation bulletins.
88. Carson's contributions to the "Food from the Sea" series are: "Fish and Shellfish of New England," Conservation Bulletin #33 (1943); "Fishes of the Middle West," Conservation Bulletin #34 (1943); "Fish and Shellfish of the South Atlantic and Gulf Coasts," Conservation Bulletin #37 (1944); and "Fish and Shellfish of the Middle Atlantic Coast," Conservation Bulletin #38 (1945). All published by U.S. Department of the Interior, Office of the Coordinator of Fisheries, Fish and Wildlife Service. See Glotfelty, "Rachel Carson." For example, see Carson's piece on "The Clam," reprinted in Brooks, *The House of Life*, 72–74.
89. Carson, FPR/OPM.
90. Carson, "Undersea," 325. Brooks, *The House of Life*, 74. Carson told Bleeker that she wanted a list of periodicals that paid well so she could concentrate her literary efforts on those that had wide readership and paid respectably. RC to Sonia Bleeker, April 5, 1943, RCP/BLYU.

5: "JUST TO LIVE BY WRITING"

1. David Brinkley, *Washington Goes to War* (New York: Alfred A. Knopf, 1988), 52–84. Constance McLaughlin Green, *Washington: A History of the Capital, 1800–1950* (Princeton, NJ: Princeton University Press, 1976), 387–440, illustration #44. David W. Look and Carole L. Perrault, *The Interior Building: Its Architecture and Art* (Washington, D.C.: Government Printing Office, 1986). See T. H. Watkins, *Righteous Pilgrim: The Life and Times of Harold L. Ickes, 1874–1952* (New York: Henry Holt and Company, Inc., 1990), 448–449.
2. Rachel Carson, FPR/OPM.

3. Ibid. RC to Maria Carson, n.d., 1944, RCP/BLYU.
4. RC to Maria Carson, n.d., 1944, RCP/BLYU. Interview with Katherine Howe Roberts.
5. RC to Sunnie Bleeker, March 5, 1944, RCP/BLYU. Carson tried to help Bleeker's husband, Dr. Howard Zim, a wildlife expert, find a position at the Patuxent Research Refuge. RC to Sunnie Bleeker, February 27, 1944, RCP/BLYU.
6. Rachel L. Carson, "Ocean Wonderland," *Transatlantic* (March 1944), 35–40; Rachel L. Carson, "Indoor Ocean," *This Month* (June 1946), 31–35, RCP/BLYU.
7. RC to Sunnie Bleeker, March 3, March 17, 1944, RCP/BLYU. *Reader's Digest* rejected the piece in February 1944. Carson mentions Allen Devoe's column, "Down to Earth" in the *American Mercury*, as a model for a monthly series on nature appreciation. Enormously fond of Thoreau's writing, Carson kept a copy of *Walden Pond* by her bedside. Her own sensitivity to the subtle changes of season, week by week, marked her personal correspondence and almost all of her creative fragments during this period. Bleeker to RC, March 11, 1944, RCP/BLYU. For an early evaluation of the transcendental influences in her writing, see Donald Fleming, "Roots of the New Conservation Movement," *Perspectives in American History* Vol. 6 (Cambridge, MA: Belknap Press of Harvard University, 1972), 12–14. List of subjects for nature column is in RCP/BLYU.
8. Rachel L. Carson, "Lifesaving Milkweed," *This Week*, September 4, 1944, RCP/BLYU.
9. Rachel L. Carson, "He Invented Radar—Sixty Million Years Ago!" RCP/BLYU.
10. Herbert Asbury to RC, September 8, 1944. RC to Herbert Asbury, September 11, 1944. Rachel L. Carson, "The Bat Knew It First," *Collier's*, November 18, 1944, RCP/BLYU.
11. Sunnie Bleeker to RC, November 28, 1944, RCP/BLYU. RC to Sunnie Bleeker, December 29, 1944, RCP/BLYU. Carson kept offering articles to *Reader's Digest* because of its high fees. Initially the *Digest* offered $200 for the article. Harold Lynch to RC, March 8, June 25, July 6, 12, 1945, RCP/BLYU. RC to Harold Lynch, June 28, July 10, 1945, RCP/BLYU.
12. Paul Brooks, *The House of Life: Rachel Carson at Work* (Boston: Houghton Mifflin Company, 1972), 75. Correspondence with the various reprint publishers is convoluted. Carson kept *This Month* hanging until she heard from *Reader's Digest*, and then she withdrew it. See correspondence with managing editor Ingrid Hallen of *This Month* and with Harold Lynch of *Reader's Digest* in RCP/BLYU. See also RC to Aldrain Berwick, Office of War Information, December 4, 1944, and from F. A. Hardy, U.S. Navy Recruiting Office, December 9, 1944, RCP/BLYU.
13. RC to DeWitt Wallace, November 20, 1944; Charles Alldredge and Rachel Carson, Advance Release, Information Service, Department of the Interior, November 12, 1944, RCP/BLYU. This is the first mention of her friendship with Alldredge.
14. Alldredge and Carson, Advance Release, November 12, 1944, RCP/BLYU.
15. Correspondence between Carson, *Reader's Digest*, and *Coronet* is in RCP/BLYU. RC to Sunnie Bleeker, March 5, 1945, RCP/BLYU.
16. Rachel Carson, unpublished fragment, RCP/BLYU.
17. RC to Quincy Howe, May 31, 1944, RCP/BLYU.
18. Ibid.
19. Ibid.
20. M. L. Schuster to DeWitt Wallace, June 12, 1944; RC to DeWitt Wallace, August 7, 1933, RCP/BLYU. Wallace's invitation resulted in the reprinting of "The Bat Knew It First" but no other articles.
21. RC to William Beebe, October 26, 1945, RCP/BLYU.

22. Fairfield Osborn to William Beebe, November 5, 1945, and William Beebe to Rachel Carson, November 10, 1945, RCP/BLYU. Brooks, *The House of Life*, 76.
23. RC to Richard Pough, n.d. [November 1945]; RC to John H. Baker, November 2, 1945, RCP/BLYU. Brooks, *The House of Life*, 76–77. In all these letters Carson explains that she "did not want my own thinking in regard to 'living natural history' to become set in the molds which hard necessity sometimes imposes upon Government conservationists! I cannot write about these things unless I can be sincere." RC to William Beebe, October 26, 1945, RCP/BLYU. Interview with Richard Pough. Pough was very impressed with Carson's FWS pamphlets on fish as well as *Under the Sea-Wind*. He remained one of Carson's lifelong advocates.
24. For a history of *Reader's Digest* during this period, see John Heidenry, *Theirs Was the Kingdom* (New York: W. W. Norton & Co., 1993). The war years at National Audubon are briefly touched on in Frank Graham, Jr., *The Audubon Ark* (New York: Alfred A. Knopf, 1990).
25. Various interviews with Roland C. Clement. I am grateful to Clement for sharing his manuscript history of National Audubon Society and other relevant documents in his possession.
26. Susan Schlee, *The Edge of an Unfamiliar World: A History of Oceanography* (New York: E. P. Dutton & Co., 1973), 272–285. Roger Revelle, "The Oceanographic and How It Grew," in M. Sears and D. Merriam, eds., *Oceanography: The Past* (New York: Springer-Verlag, 1980), 10–24. See especially H. U. Sverdrup, Martin W. Johnson, and Richard H. Fleming, *The Oceans: Their Physics, Chemistry, and General Biology* (Englewood Cliffs, NJ: Prentice-Hall, 1942), 1–8, 98–152, 605–761. This book was the basic text for all oceanographers after it appeared, even though the outbreak of World War II prevented the inclusion of classified research.
27. "Toxicity of DDT to Certain Species of Mammalian Wildlife," Patuxent Research Refuge, U.S. Fish and Wildlife Service, Department of the Interior. Economic Investigations Laboratory, Project 12, Quarterly Reports (October–December 1944). John H. Perkins, "Reshaping Technology in Wartime: The Effect of Military Goals on Entomological Research and Insect-Control Practices," *Technology and Culture* 19, 2 (April 1978), 169–186. Clarence Cottam and Elmer Higgins, "DDT and Its Effect on Fish and Wildlife," *Journal of Economic Entomology* 39 (February 1946), 44–52. Cottam was an outstanding economic ornithologist who had moved to FWS from the USDA's division of wildlife research in 1940.
28. RC to Harold Lynch, July 15, 1945, RCP/BLYU.
29. Ibid. This is the first evidence of Carson's interest in DDT but not the first indication of her interests in the effects of toxins on the environment or their impact on human health. The enclosed press release is missing, but the Patuxent tests had begun in the summer of 1944 and preliminary information was beginning to circulate among FWS biologists. The proximity of the Patuxent Research Refuge in Laurel, Maryland, was crucial for Carson's continued interest in the subject of DDT. The *Digest*'s response was similar to Mark Watson's earlier reaction when Carson proposed a feature on selenium and naturally occurring fluoride poisons. There is no indication that Carson tried to interest any other publication in the subject of DDT.
30. "DDT and Other Insecticides and Repellents Developed for the Armed Forces," USDA, Orlando, Florida, Laboratory of the Bureau of Entomology and Plant Quarantine (Washington, D.C.: Government Printing Office, August 1946). E. F. Knipling, "Insect Control Investigations of the Orlando, Florida, Laboratory During World War II," *Annual Report of the Board of Regents of the Smithsonian Institution* (Washington, D.C.: Smithsonian Institution, 1948), 331–348. Knipling was head of the Orlando laboratory from July 1942 to the end of the war. Interview with E. F. Knipling.

31. Early concerns about DDT's safety are discussed in Thomas R. Dunlap, *DDT: Scientists, Citizens, and Public Policy* (Princeton, NJ: Princeton University Press, 1981), 63–75; John H. Perkins, *Insects, Experts, and the Insecticide Crisis: The Quest for New Pest Management Strategies* (New York: Plenum Press, 1982). "DDT . . . A Deadly New Bug Killer," *Better Homes and Gardens* (May 1944), and "Coming Freedom from Insect Pests," *Reader's Digest* (May 1944), 44, quoted in Edmund P. Russell III, "Safe for Whom? Safe for What? Testing Insecticides and Repellents in World War II." Unpublished paper, March 7, 1993. I am grateful to Ed Russell for extended conversations over the years on DDT and its use and marketing. Russell's complete research will be published soon, but I have made use of his published and unpublished papers and dissertation throughout this study.
32. "DDT Dangers," *Time*, April 16, 1945, 91; "War on Insects," *Time*, August 27, 1945, 65. Edwin Way Teale, "DDT," *Nature Magazine* 38, 3 (March 1945), 121–124, 162–163. "Our Next World War—Against Insects," *Popular Mechanics* 81 (April 1944), 66–70. "Total Insect War Urged," *Science News Letter*, January 6, 1945, 5. C. H. Curran, "How DDT Really Works," *Popular Science* 148, 2 (February 1946), 71–74. Ed Russell first called my attention to the irony of the dual reports in *Time*. Tony Heyl sent me the issue containing Curran's important article.
33. Rachel L. Carson, "Origins of the Book, *The Sea Around Us*," RCP/BLYU.
34. Henry B. Bigelow, *Oceanography: Its Scope, Problems, and Economic Importance* (Boston: Houghton Mifflin Co., 1931). Susan Schlee, *The Edge of an Unfamiliar World*, 273–316. M. Sears and D. Merriman, eds., *Oceanography*, 16–24. Sverdrup, Johnson, and Fleming, *The Oceans*, 331–388. I am indebted to Gary Weir, Historian, Contemporary History Branch, Naval History Center, Washington, D.C., for extended discussions on the state of naval oceanography and prewar classification, and for sharing a chapter from his forthcoming history of naval oceanography.
35. See "Suggestions for Further Reading" in the revised edition of *The Sea Around Us* (New York: Oxford University Press, 1961).
36. Alice Mullen's background is unknown. Elizabeth Dickson was a nurse at Doctor's Hospital, but it is unclear exactly when she met Maria and Rachel. Information about Dr. Catherine Birch comes from interviews with Shirley Briggs and Katherine Howe Roberts.
37. Interview with Shirley Briggs.
38. Interview with Katherine Howe Roberts. Howe was educated at the Walnut Hill School and Syracuse University before getting her M.A. in art and art history at the University of Iowa, which had one of the finest art departments in the country. Kay's father died suddenly when she was quite young. Kay's mother lived with Kay and Shirley in Essex, Maryland, not far from the Martin plant.
39. Interviews with Shirley Briggs and Katherine Howe Roberts.
40. Shirley Briggs, Personal Diary, September 9, 1945. Briggs's diaries and letters to her parents are her private property. I am indebted to her for sharing this incomparable source and for giving me permission to quote from them. They will hereafter be cited as SAB/D and SAB/L respectively.
41. SAB/D, January 22, February 20, 1946.
42. SAB/D, February 20, 21, 1945.
43. Interviews with Shirley Briggs.
44. SAB/D, March 1, 13, 1946. Interview with Mary Frances Howell. Howell was Kay Howe's friend and housemate.
45. Various interviews with Bob Hines.
46. Interview with Katherine Howe Roberts. Ady worked in the Secretary's Office. He

was a political appointee and, according to Carson and her colleagues, knew next to nothing about the art or mechanics of printing and publishing. Interview with Shirley Briggs.

47. Interview with Shirley Briggs.
48. SAB/D, April 11–14, 1946. Interview with Shirley Briggs.
49. Rachel Carson, unpublished fragment "Road of the Hawks," RCP/BLYU. SAB/L, October 16, 1945.
50. SAB/L, October 16, 1945. Briggs's letter of October 16, 1945, to her parents is particularly rich in details about this first Hawk Mountain trip. On this trip as well as one a year later when Shirley accompanied Rachel and Dorothy Algire, she and Rachel took pictures of one another on the promontory. There is no evidence that Carson ever finished this fragment or ever sent it to any publisher although there are several drafts of it. Possibly she found it too personal.
51. SAB/L, October 16, 1945. SAB/D, November 29, 1945. It was at this initial meeting with Mrs. Carson that Briggs learned that Rachel supported her mother and two grown nieces.
52. SAB/L, October 21, 1946. SAB/D, October 19, 1946.
53. Rachel Carson, unpublished fragment, "Road of the Hawks," RCP/BLYU.
54. RC to Robert Murphy, June 27, 1945, RCP/BLYU. Robert Murphy to RC, July 6, 1945, and *National Geographic Magazine* to RC, December 21, 1945, RCP/BLYU.
55. The other two bird banders discussed in her article, Canadian Charles Broley, who banded bald eagles, and Edward McIlhenny of Avery Island, Louisiana, who specialized in ducks and geese, were well known to Audubon Society and Fish and Wildlife scientists. Richard Pough of the Audubon Society introduced Carson to Broley. RC to Maria Corporale, December 17, 1945. RC to Edward Strode, March 24, 1946. Ada Govan to RC, January 13, 23, 1946, RCP/BLYU.
56. RC to Ada Govan, January 7, 1946, RCP/BLYU.
57. Ada Clapham Govan, *Wings at My Window* (New York: Macmillan Company, 1940), preface, 1–54. Ada Govan to RC, January 13, 1946, RCP/BLYU. Interview with Roland Clement. Millicent Taylor, "Children Can Be Taught to Walk in Audubon's Own Wonderland," *Christian Science Monitor*, December 14, 1940, RCP/BLYU. I believe that Carson's "Help Your Child to Wonder" owes much to Govan's earlier writing, which Carson admired deeply. It was a subject they discussed when they visited in 1946.
58. Ada Govan to RC, March 9, 1946; RC to Ada Govan, March 22, 1946, RCP/BLYU.
59. Ada Govan to RC, March 25, 1946; RC to Ada Govan, April 1, 1946; Ada Govan to RC, December 2, 1946, RCP/BLYU.
60. Ada Govan to RC, February 12, 1947; RC to Ada Govan, February 15, 1947, RCP/BLYU.
61. RC to Ada Govan, February 15, 1947, RCP/BLYU.
62. Ibid.
63. Ibid.
64. Ibid.

6: "RETURN TO THE SEA"

1. Rachel Carson, FPR/OPM. RC to Mrs. W. S. Cole, November 3, 1951, RCP/BLYU.
2. SAB/L, April 1, 1947. Carson wrote four in the series herself and coauthored a fifth. She assigned other numbers to other FWS divisions and staff. Briggs contributed illus

trations to the first number, and Bob Hines, who took Kay Howe's place in 1948, illustrated the eighth.

3. Rachel L. Carson, *Guarding Our Wildlife Resources, Conservation in Action #5*, designed by Katherine L. Howe, U.S. Fish and Wildlife Service, Department of the Interior (Washington, D.C.: Government Printing Office, 1948), 1.
4. Rachel L. Carson, *Chincoteague: A National Wildlife Refuge, Conservation in Action #1*, illustrations by Shirley A. Briggs and Katherine L. Howe, U.S. Fish and Wildlife Service, Department of the Interior (Washington, D.C.: Government Printing Office, 1947).
5. SAB/L, April 22, 1946.
6. Recollections of the Chincoteague trip come from interviews with Shirley Briggs and from her letters and diary. SAB/D, April 17–20, 1946; SAB/L, April 22, 1946.
7. Ibid.
8. RC to Maria Leiper, November 18, 1946, RCP/BLYU.
9. Paul Brooks, *The House of Life: Rachel Carson at Work* (Boston: Houghton Mifflin Company, 1972), 86. Carson rented the cottage through Ethelyn Giles, the daughter of a prominent Southport Island family who had started a real estate agency in Boothbay in 1935. I am grateful to Giles and her sister, Phyllis Cook, for assisting my research, helping me locate the Scott cottage, Carson's other Maine cottages, and providing a wealth of information about the sea and the Carsons.
10. RC to Dorothy Algire, July 7, 1946; RC to Shirley Briggs, July 14, 1946; RC to Maria Leiper, November 18, 1946, RCP/BLYU.
11. RC to Dorothy Algire, July 7, 1946; RC to Shirley Briggs, July 14, 1946, RCP/BLYU. Interview with Dr. Clarice Yentsch. I am grateful to the Scott family heirs for providing me hospitality and access to the little cottage. As of January 1995, Indiantown Island, which had so enchanted Carson, was placed in protection of the Newagen Colony Partnership and the Boothbay Regional Land Trust. Letter from Yentsch to author, January 15, 1995.
12. RC to Dorothy Algire, July 7, 1946, RCP/BLYU.
13. RC to Shirley Briggs, July 14, 1946, RCP/BLYU.
14. Maria Carson to Mrs. Williams, June 1946, RCP/BLYU. In this long letter to Virginia and Marjorie's paternal grandmother, Maria describes their trip up to Maine, their cottage, and their daily activities in detail. RC, fragments, July 6, 1946, RCP/BLYU.
15. RC to Maria Leiper, November 18, 1946, RCP/BLYU.
16. Carson, fragments for "An Island I Remember," RCP/BLYU.
17. RC to Shirley Briggs, July 14, 1946, RCP/BLYU.
18. Rachel L. Carson, "Conservation Pledge" and "Why America's Natural Resources Must Be Conserved," July 29, 1946, RCP/BLYU.
19. RC to Raymond J. Brown, October 15, 1946, RCP/BLYU. SAB/D, December 13, 1946. SAB/L, December 14, 1946.
20. Interview with Katherine Howe Roberts. Rachel Carson, field notes, "winter conditions on the refuge," "Galtsoff's Survey," September 1946, RCP/BLYU. Rachel L. Carson, *Parker River, Conservation in Action #2*, with drawings and photographs by Katherine L. Howe, U.S. Fish and Wildlife Service, Department of the Interior (Washington, D.C.: Government Printing Office, 1947). The refuge area had previously been a bird sanctuary owned by the Massachusetts Audubon Society. It became a federal refuge in 1942, but because of labor and equipment shortages during the war, its data collecting had been neglected and outbuildings had fallen into disrepair.
21. RC to Shirley Briggs, September 28, 1946; Katherine Howe to Shirley Briggs, September 25, 1946, RCP/BLYU.
22. Interview with Katherine Howe Roberts.

23. RC to Shirley Briggs, September 28, 1946, RCP/BLYU. Rachel L. Carson, "Parker River—A New England Conservation Project," with photographs by Katherine L. Howe, *Massachusetts Audubon Society Bulletin* 31, 2 (1947), 51–61. An editor's note identifies Carson as the author of *Under the Sea-Wind* previously reviewed in the *Bulletin* and notes that "Edwin Way Teale said that if he were cast on a desert isle with a hundred books to read this would be one of them," RCP/BLYU. Carson also joined the Massachusetts Audubon Society during her visit to Parker River.
24. RC to Shirley Briggs, September 25, 1946, RCP/BLYU. Interview with Katherine Howe Roberts. Henry B. Bigelow, *Oceanography* (Boston: Houghton Mifflin Co., 1931), 126–184. Carson was especially interested in his chapter entitled "Life in the Sea." Carson's dedication of the 1961 edition of *The Sea Around Us* to Bigelow testifies to her gratitude for his encouragement and the scholars and scholarship he made available to her.
25. Interview with Katherine Howe Roberts.
26. RC to Ada Govan, February 15, 1947, RCP/BLYU. The final text of the booklet on Mattamuskeet mirrored Carson's letter to Govan. Rachel L. Carson, *Mattamuskeet, Conservation in Action #4*, illustrated by Katherine L. Howe, U.S. Fish and Wildlife Service, Department of the Interior (Washington, D.C.: Government Printing Office, 1947), 4–5.
27. Interviews with Shirley Briggs and Katherine Howe Roberts. SAB/D, June 20–22, 1947.
28. SAB/D, May 4, May 10, 1947, SAB/L, May 11, 1947. Louis J. Halle, *Spring in Washington* (Baltimore: Johns Hopkins University Press, 1988), 194–202. Originally published in 1947.
29. SAB/D, June 3, 1947. It is unclear just how Carson's correspondence with the Teales began, but it probably occurred naturally after Carson's "Undersea" and excerpts from Teale's *Grassroot Jungles* appeared in the *Atlantic Monthly* in 1937. Their interests in nature, birds, DDT, and Audubon Society activities kept them in frequent contact thereafter. RC to Edwin Way Teale [hereafter cited as EWT], February 2, 1947. Correspondence File, Edwin Way Teale Papers, Thomas J. Dodd Research Center, University of Connecticut Library. [Hereafter cited as EWTP/UC.]
30. Louis J. Halle, "Recollections of Rachel Carson," RCP/BLYU. Apparently Halle did not remember he had met Carson at the Seneca lock nor that she was the author of *Under the Sea-Wind*, and she did not remind him.
31. Interview with Katherine Howe Roberts. *Guarding Our Wildlife Resources* was the last *Conservation in Action* booklet Carson wrote entirely herself.
32. Unless otherwise cited, details of the western trip come from letters and interviews with Katherine Howe Roberts.
33. RC to Maria Carson, September 21, 1947, RCP/BLYU.
34. Interview with Katherine Howe Roberts. RC to Shirley Briggs, September 29, 1947, privately held.
35. Katherine Howe Roberts, letter to author, September 29, 1994.
36. Carson took extensive notes on salmon climbing the fish ladders into the hatchery pools and the horrors of the Bonneville turbines. RC, field notes, Willamette River Valley, RCP/BLYU.
37. Katherine Howe Roberts, letters to the author, June 22, September 29, 1994. Rachel L. Carson and Vanez T. Wilson, *Bear River, Conservation in Action #8*, illustrations by Bob Hines, U.S. Fish and Wildlife Service, Department of the Interior (Washington, D.C.: Government Printing Office, 1950), 1–6.
38. Various interviews with Bob Hines. Interview with Michael Lawler Smith, Assistant Director, Public Relations, FWS.

39. Rachel Carson, DOI, Information Service release, "Scientists' Finds on Florida Red Tide Reported," #PN29938, RCP/BLYU.
40. Rachel Carson, "Killer from the Sea," RCP/BLYU. Rachel L. Carson, "The Great Red Tide Mystey," *Field & Stream* (February 1948), 15–18. What Carson was paid for this article or whether she chose the photograph that accompanied it is not known.
41. SAB/D, 1946–1948. Interview with Katherine Howe Roberts. Sonia Bleeker to RC, February 20, 1945, RCP/BLYU. Rachel Carson, Medical History, Archives of the Cleveland Clinic, Cleveland, OH. I am grateful to Roger A. Christie for permission to use these records.
42. SAB/D, January 10, April 15, August 1, September 11, September 15, 1947. Interview with Katherine Howe Roberts. SAB/L, April 1, September 14, 1947. Briggs's position was in fact abolished and she was reassigned to the Bureau of Reclamation. Kay Howe's job was temporarily salvaged after a fight, but she remained in government service only about six months longer.
43. RC to Maria Leiper, February 23, 1947, RCP/BLYU. In this letter Carson tells Leiper she also spent a week in Chicago, followed by several days at Mattamuskeet and "a very slight operation which I had to have." It is not clear whether Rachel paid for Robert's surgery or not. Doubtless she contributed to his care.
44. SAB/D, January 3, 1948. Interview with Katherine Howe Roberts.
45. Interview with Bob Hines. Carson, FPR/OPM. Carson did not move into Walford's administrative position or grade, another gender-based decision, but she was given his editorial responsibilities and received a grade and pay increase.
46. Interviews with Bob Hines, Isabel Duncan Aldous. Aldous was on Carson's staff as Fish and Wildlife reference librarian.
47. Interviews with F. Raymond Fosberg. Fosberg was the foremost scholar on Pacific Island botany and coral reef atoll formations. He was also a founding director of The Nature Conservancy.
48. Brooks, *The House of Life*, 99, note. Howard Zahniser, one of the founders and the executive director of the Wilderness Society, told Brooks that Carson had ghost-written speeches for congressmen and lobbyists while she was with the Service. Brooks did not know that Charles Alldredge had been the one who solicited the work from her. RC to Marie Rodell, n.d., RCP/BLYU.

    Alldredge and Carson remained friends until he died in 1963. He was particularly instrumental in the success of *The Sea Around Us* and *The Edge of the Sea*. Alldredge also published a book of poetry, *Some Quick and Some Dead*. See Estes Kefauver Papers, University of Tennessee Archives, Knoxville, TN. Charles Haden Alldredge, Obituary, March 12, 1963, *Washington Evening Star* and *Washington Post*. Interview with the Reverend Duncan Howlett.
49. By the terms of her release from Simon & Schuster, the plates of the book were left at the warehouse until Carson could afford to buy them back. Leiper helped work out the deal that released Carson.
50. Both Rodell and Alldredge moved in a wide circle of writers and journalists. Rodell and Alldredge first met through mutual friends Nelson and Henrietta Pointer. Nelson Pointer was also a southern newspaperman, at one time the editor of the *St. Petersburg Times*, who later moved to Washington. Rodell knew them in Sarasota, where her family had a home. When Rodell went to Washington to see Carson, she always stayed with the Pointers. Interview with Joanne Ellman. Marie Rodell [hereafter cited as MR] to Paul Brooks, March 18, 1971, Marie Rodell–Frances Collin Literary Agents Archive, Wayne, PA. [Hereafter cited as R/CA.] Marie discovered later that Carson interviewed a total of three agents before selecting her.

51. Interview with Shirley Briggs. SAB/D, November 30, 1948. Information on Skinker's career at Hockaday was supplied by the school archivist, Mrs. Christopher, and alumnae director, Beth Mikeska, The Hockaday School, Dallas, TX, July 28, 1994. *The Hockaday*, Alumnae Issue (January 1947).
52. Interviews with Martha Skinker, Thomas M. Skinker, Dr. Thomas M. Skinker. I am grateful to Rose Novil, reference librarian of the National Louis University, for research and information on Skinker's tenure at the National College of Education. Interviews with Helen Challand, Mary Louise Neumann. Dr. Challand was a young instructor in biology and Neumann was the assistant librarian when Skinker was on the faculty. Challand's vivid and compassionate account of Skinker's style, manner, and collegiality was particularly insightful.
53. Interviews with Martha Skinker, Frances Staley Skinker. Frances Skinker recalls that it was Rachel who telephoned Anne Skinker and G. Murray with the news of Mary Scott's death. RC to Marie Rodell, December 12, 1948, RCP/BLYU.
54. Mary Scott Skinker, Obituary, December 21, 1948, *St. Louis Globe-Democrat*. A great deal of the information provided by Skinker's family in the obituary notices of her death is inaccurate.

7: "SUCH A COMFORT TO ME"

1. I am indebted to the following people who contributed to my understanding of Marie Rodell's life: Shirley Briggs, Paul Brooks, Knox Burger, Roger Christie, Eugenie Clark, Frances Collin, Jeanne Davis, Joanne Ellman, Ada and Frank Graham, Lucy Kavaler, Geraldine Rhoades, Corleis Smith, Ann Zwinger. Frances Collin provided special assistance by giving me access to certain business documents and memorabilia from the archive of the Rodell-Collin Literary Agents. Rodell's books are: Marion Randolph (Marie Rodell), *Breathe No More* (1940), *This'll Kill You* (1940), *Grim Grow the Lilacs* (1941), and Marie Rodell, *Mystery Fiction: Theory and Technique* (New York: Duell, Sloan and Pearce, 1943), for which she was awarded an Edgar by the Mystery Writers of America. For Paul Brooks's assessment of the relationship, see *The House of Life: Rachel Carson at Work* (Boston: Houghton Mifflin Company, 1972), 112–113. Various interviews with Paul Brooks.
2. Rodell wanted to have children but was persuaded to end a pregnancy by John Rodell, who later had children in another marriage. It was one of the great sadnesses in her life.
3. RC to Robert Cushman Murphy, n.d. [1948], RCP/BLYU.
4. The Rodell/Carson strategy is apparent in their earliest correspondence. Carson turned over her Simon & Schuster records, her copyright files, and her correspondence with *Holiday* magazine. In the summer of 1948 Rodell was sharing an office with Elsie McKeogh, another literary representative, on lower Fifth Avenue. See Rodell correspondence for August 1948, RCP/BLYU.
5. MR to RC, August 10, November 4, 1948, RCP/BLYU.
6. Carson's trip to Woods Hole was postponed because Sears and Ewing, among others she wanted to see, were not in residence. In the end Mary Sears proved unwilling to allow Carson access to unpublished material. RC to Mary Sears, August 12, 1948, and n.d. [1949], RCP/BLYU.
7. RC to MR, August 11, 1948, RC/BLYU. For a good while thereafter Carson signed her letters "Yours, Ray" and Rodell followed suit.
8. RC to MR, September 2, 1948, RCP/BLYU. Alldredge figured prominently in the production of the outline for the book. Carson showed him each draft and clearly

respected his reactions to it. She would later change her mind about the sufficiency of one chapter and an outline.

9. MR to Helen Taylor, September 7, 1948, RCP/BLYU.
10. RC to MR, September 28, 1948, RCP/BLYU. Submission card for R. L. Carson, R/CA, September 7, 1948.
11. RC to MR, October 6, 1948, RCP/BLYU.
12. RC to MR, November 11, 1948, RCP/BLYU. Raymond C. Cochrane, *The National Academy of Sciences: The First Hundred Years, 1863–1963* (Washington, D.C.: The National Academy of Sciences, 1978), 483–490. Pamela M. Henson, "The Smithsonian Goes to War: The Increase and Diffusion of Scientific Knowledge in the Pacific during World War II," paper presented to the History of Science Society, December 1992, 6, 11, 14–21. Philip F. Rehbock, "Organizing Pacific Science: Local and International Origins of the Pacific Science Association," in Roy MacLeod and Philip F. Rehbock, eds., *Nature in Its Greatest Extent: Western Science in the Pacific* (Honolulu: University of Hawaii Press, 1988), 197–200, 211–215. *Annual Report of the Smithsonian Institution*, 1946, 1947, Washington, D.C., 1946, 1947. See also Records of the Division of Marine Invertebrates, 1946–1947, Smithsonian Institution Archives. Carson's interest in the subject of coral atolls initiated her lifelong friendship with F. Raymond Fosberg to whom she sent the final draft of the islands chapter for review. Interviews with F. Raymond Fosberg.
13. RC to MR, September 30, 1948, RCP/BLYU.
14. Ibid.
15. MR to RC, October 4, 1948; RC to MR, October 5, 1948, RCP/BLYU.
16. RC to MR, November 11, 1948, RCP/BLYU. Carson explained her interest in the evolution of islands in a letter about the same time to Robert Cushman Murphy. RC to Robert Cushman Murphy, September 22, 1948, RCP/BLYU.
17. MR to RC, October 11, 1948, RCP/BLYU.
18. RC to MR, October 13, 1948, RCP/BLYU.
19. RC to MR, October 17, 1948, RCP/BLYU. The Sloan story comes by way of Sheldon Meyer at Oxford University Press who is familiar with the publishing history of *The Sea Around Us* at Oxford.
20. RC to MR, October 23, 1948, RCP/BLYU.
21. RC to MR, October 28, 1948, RCP/BLYU.
22. MR to RC, November 15, 1948, RCP/BLYU.
23. MR to RC, November 4, November 15, 1948, RCP/BLYU. Rodell also made important practical suggestions, telling Carson on one occasion to make her carbons on regular white paper because "editors hate onion skin."
24. RC to MR, December 12, 15, 1948, RCP/BLYU. This letter includes the only reference in Carson's papers to the work of nature writer Sally Carrighar. When *Beetle Rock* appeared, Carson had been impressed with the similariaties between it and *Under the Sea-Wind.* She pointed out to Rodell that when Howard Zahniser reviewed Carrighar's book, he "gave me credit for starting a new trend in nature literature which she was following." Carson's discussion of Carrighar's work underscores her disappointment that *Under the Sea-Wind* had sold so poorly and her determination to get it reprinted.
25. RC to MR, December 12, 1948; MR to RC, January 5, 1949, RCP/BLYU.
26. MR to RC, January 5, 1949; RC to MR, January 9, 1949, RCP/BLYU.
27. RC to MR, January 24, 1949, RCP/BLYU.
28. RC to EWT, April 3, April 18, 1949, EWTP/UC. EWT to RC, April 4, 1949; RC to EWT, April 5, 1949, RCP/BLYU.
29. RC to William Beebe, September 6, 1948; RC to MR, March 26, 1949, RCP/BLYU.

William Beebe, ed., *The Book of Naturalists: An Anthology of the Best Natural History* (New York: Alfred A. Knopf, 1944).

30. Flier from *Harper News*. Rodell had gotten an application for the Saxton Fellowship before Carson went to New York. See RCP/BLYU.
31. RC to MR, April 10, 1949; MR to RC, April 13, 1949, RCP/BLYU.
32. Rachel L. Carson, application to the Eugene F. Saxton Foundation, May 1, 1949, RCP/BLYU. Carson was supporting Marjorie while she was in college.
33. Ibid.
34. Ibid.
35. Ibid. Unlike her stance in *Under the Sea-Wind*, Carson intended to introduce humankind not just as a powerful participant in the life of the ocean but as a despoiler of potentially unprecedented proportions.
36. Submission card, RC/A. Interview with Leona Capeless.
37. Ibid.
38. Brooks, *The House of Life*, 112–113.
39. The Oxford account comes from Vice President Sheldon Meyer's notes. MR to Philip Vaudrin, April 12, 1949, RCP/BLYU. Interview with Vivian Brown, February 11, 1995, Washington, D.C., the current owner of the Francis Scott Key Bookstore. The hand of Charles Alldredge is evident, for he was very active in Washington literary circles and lived not far from the Georgetown bookstore. See Rodell's letter to Carson, May 21, 1949, RCP/BLYU, for discussion about including Alldredge in conversations about the book contract with Oxford.

    Marie Rodell, Notes on conversation with Philip Vaudrin. Vaudrin sent Carson a copy of Daniel Merriman's comments. Philip Vaudrin to RC, May 9, 1949, RCP/BLYU. Merriman had worked in the U.S. Bureau of Fisheries in the early 1930s and moved to Yale in 1938 as an aquatic biologist. He became director of the Bingham Laboratory in 1942. There is no indication that Carson knew Merriman at Fisheries, but he was one of the experts she consulted in 1950 about wartime advances in oceanography.
40. RC to MR, May 10, 1949, RCP/BLYU.
41. RC to MR, May 18, 1949; MR to RC, May 21, 1949, RCP/BLYU.
42. RC to MR, May 23, 1949, RCP/BLYU. MR, Memo of phone conversation May 4, 1949, with Philip Vaudrin of Oxford about Carson's "Return to the Sea." MR to RC, June 6, June 27, 1949. RC to MR, June 29, 1949, RCP/BLYU. Rodell successfully negotiated both a better delivery date and more money. Both women pushed for a bankruptcy clause because Oxford's American operations were young and still financially uncertain. Ironically it would be "Return to the Sea," as *The Sea Around Us* was first titled, which would ensure Oxford's stability and make its reputation as a trade house.
43. RC to MR, June 8, 1949, RCP/BLYU.
44. Ibid.
45. The FWS had responsibility for protecting wildlife in what became Everglades National Park, SAB/D, May 31–July 11, 1949.
46. RC to MR, June 8, June 23, June 27, June 29, 1949, RCP/BLYU. The Florida trip lasted from July 11 to 22 and the voyage on the *Albatross III* from July 26 to August 5. Both trips were carried out as "official business." In years past Maria Carson might have accompanied her daughter on such adventures; however, in 1949 her arthritis and recent surgery prevented her from going on these rigorous trips. RC, "The Real World Around Us," RCP/BLYU.
47. SAB/D, June 12, 13, 14, 1949. Rachel Carson, Field Notes, "Florida Bay;" Rachel Carson, Field Notes, "Tamiami Trail," RCP/BLYU. Much taken with Fred Fin-

neran's ability and knowledge, Carson put him in touch with Marie Rodell. SAB/D, July 15, 1949.

48. Carson, "The Real World Around Us," RCP/BLYU.
49. Shirley Briggs to Mrs. John Briggs, July 20, 1949, privately held. Rachel Carson, "The Real World Around Us," RCP/BLYU. The material for this speech came almost entirely from the field notes Carson took on her Everglades trip with Briggs, Finneran, and Poppenhager and on the *Albatross III* with Rodell.
50. Rachel Carson, Field Notes, July 16, 18, 19, RCP/BLYU.
51. Rachel Carson, Field Notes, July 19, 1949, RCP/BLYU.
52. RC to William Beebe, August 26, 1949, RCP/BLYU.
53. Rachel L. Carson, "Origins of *The Sea Around Us*," n.d. [1951], RCP/ BLYU. In this account of her dive written for publicity purposes, Carson inflates the experience and distorts the facts, leading the reader to understand her diving was more than a brief submersion while clinging to a dive boat ladder in stormy, turgid water. "To write with understanding about the ocean one needs to pay a first-hand visit to the undersea world, and with this in mind I did a little helmet diving, a couple of years ago, on the coral reefs off the southern coast of Florida."
54. Although Shirley was delighted with the flora and fauna she found on the reefs, she was disappointed that she had turned down the opportunity to go underwater herself. Confiding to her diary, "Great disappointment not to have been down at all—annoyed at myself for letting Ray discourage me from going Tuesday." SAB/D, July 21, 1949. Amy Flashner to RC, July 14, 1949, RCP/BLYU. Maria Carson to Marie Rodell, July 17, 1949, RCP/ BLYU. Maria Carson had not been well when Rodell visited in mid-June and so had not yet met her daughter's literary agent.
55. "Albatross III," U.S. Department of Interior, Fish and Wildlife Service, March 19, 1948. Northeast Fisheries Science Center Library, Woods Hole, MA, National Marine Fisheries Service. [Hereafter cited as NFSC/NMFS.] Paul S. Galtsoff, *The Story of the Bureau of Commercial Fisheries Biological Laboratory, Woods Hole, Massachusetts* (Washington: D.C., U.S. Department of Interior Circular #145, 1962); Marie F. Rodell, "The Albatross III," part 2, *Frontiers* (December 1950), 50.
56. Carson's Theta Sigma Phi speech cited above, "The Real World Around Us," does not mention her previous effort to join the *Albatross III*. Details of the voyage are taken from this speech, Carson's field notes, the three-part article published by Marie Rodell in *Frontiers*, the in-house bulletin of the National Academy of Sciences, and the official reports of Cruise 26 of the *Albatross III*. Brooks, *The House of Life*, 114–118. Paul Galtsoff was now one of the world's foremost experts on oysters and was permanently stationed at the Fisheries Laboratory. He and his wife entertained Carson and Rodell the night before they sailed on the *Albatross III*.
57. Summary reports of Cruise 26 of the *Albatross III*. William F. Royce, Chief North Atlantic Fishery Investigations, August 16, 1949, NFSC/NMFS.
58. Carson, "The Real World Around Us," RCP/BLYU. Marie Rodell's "Albatross Diary," quoted in Brooks, *The House of Life*, 115.
59. Rachel Carson, "The Real World Around Us," RCP/BLYU.
60. Rachel L. Carson, "Origins of *The Sea Around Us*," n.d. [1951], RCP/ BLYU. This piece was written for Oxford University Press to publicize the book after it was published.
61. Carson, "The Real World Around Us," RCP/BLYU. Rodell, "The Albatross III," part 2, *Frontiers* (December 1950), 51.
62. Rachel Carson, Notes from Albatross notebook, 1949, RCP/BLYU. Carson, "The Real World Around Us," RCP/BLYU.

63. Rachel Carson, *The Sea Around Us* (New York: Oxford University Press, 1951), 125.
64. U.S. Fish and Wildlife Service, Narrative Report of Cruise #26, "Albatross III," August 19, 1948. Raymond Buller's only suggestion to his chief at the end of the cruise was that a small radar be installed because of the necessity of running the boat in thick fog.

    Marie Rodell's articles in *Frontiers* provide an invaluable account of the trip and also indicate Rodell's engaging writing style. Her diary of the trip on which the articles were based is gone. Marie Rodell, "The Albatross III," *Frontiers*, part 3 (February 1951), 92–94. For a report on a recent closing of the Georges Bank, see "Fished Out. Georges Bank Closes, Ending an Era," *The Christian Science Monitor*, December 12, 1994, 1, 20.
65. RC to MR, August 13, 1949, RCP/BLYU. Carson's return from Woods Hole was marred by domestic stress. The previous February her eldest niece Virginia Williams had married Liston Lee King and settled nearby in the District of Columbia. With one less person at home, Carson tried unsuccessfully to buy another house, but ended up renting a small but charming place on Williamsburg Drive in Silver Spring. During the same time she had to care for Virginia who returned to convalesce after an appendectomy. SAB/D, February 5, August, 18, August 23, September 12, 13, 1949. RC to MR, August 18, August 22, 1949, RCP/BLYU.
66. This documents Carson's first interest in the Fuertes bird paintings, a project that not only sidetracked her book but dragged on for nearly four years. RC to MR, August 30, 1949, "Fuertes project," R/CA.
67. RC to Amy Flashner, October 13, 1949, RCP/BLYU. SAB/D, September 26, 28, October 3, 1949. RC to Mary Fuertes Boynton, October 6, 1949, "Fuertes project," R/CA. Carson had learned from Robert Cushman Murphy that Boynton had been at work on a memoir more than eight years ago. She hoped that Boynton's project had been abandoned, but couched her letter in terms that suggested hers was a complementary project. Boynton responded that she would look favorably on Carson's project. RC to MR, October 9, 1949; MR to Mary Boynton, October 11, 1949; RC to MR, October 13, "Fuertes project," R/CA.
68. Paul Brooks to MR, n.d. [December 1949], RCP/BLYU.
69. Brooks recounts the origins of the idea for a seashore guide in *The House of Life*, 151–153. Interviews with Paul Brooks, Shirley Briggs.
70. Interview with Paul Brooks.
71. Brooks, *The House of Life*, 152 and note. Interview with Paul Brooks. Edmund Wilson's daughter, Rosalind Wilson, was at that time one of Brooks's editors. She had been at her father's Provincetown house for a weekend literary soiree and recounted a tale of biological ignorance to Brooks when he returned the following Monday. As Brooks tells the story, a group of Wilson's guests had gone out to the beach the morning after a storm to find it littered with horseshoe crabs all upside down and piled on top of each other. Thinking the havoc a product of the storm, the visitors conscientiously gathered up the crabs and returned them to the sea. Recounting their adventure back at the house, another guest chastised them for their ignorance of the reproductive habits of horseshoe crabs: They had interrupted natural mating and egg laying and had jeopardized the next generation. Wilson suggested the right kind of popular seashore guide might help prevent such mishaps in the future. See Brooks's account in Paul Brooks, *Two Park Street: A Publishing Memoir* (Boston: Houghton Mifflin Company, 1986).
72. RC to MR, n.d., RCP/BLYU.
73. Rodell correspondence with Edward Weeks, R/CA. Brooks, *The House of Life*, 122.

RC to MR, January 14, 1950, RCP/BLYU. Rejection notices, R/CA. Rodell Correspondence, RCP/BLYU.

74. RC to MR, January 20, 24, 1950, RCP/BLYU. She also sent chapters on ocean tides and geology to experts at Scripps Institute. After her research in the summer of 1949, she abandoned her original plan of visiting experts in California. RC to MR, February 9, 1950, RCP/BLYU.
75. RC to MR, February 19, 25, 1950; MR to RC, February 24, 1950, RCP/BLYU.
76. Interview with Katherine Howe Roberts.
77. RC to MR, March 20, 29, 1950, RCP/BLYU. There was still no consensus on titles, leading Rachel to call it "the nameless" book.
78. RC to MR, March 16, 1950, RCP/BLYU.
79. Helen Grey to MR, April 20, 1950, RCP/BLYU. According to Marie Rodell's ledger, *The New Yorker* offer to buy chapters for a condensation was made June 6, 1950. *The Yale Review* offered to buy "The Birth of an Island" on August 17, 1950. RC/A. These records differ with Brooks's narrative, *The House of Life*, 122–123.
80. RC to Philip Vaudrin, April 15, 1950; Philip Vaudrin to MR, June 13, 1950; MR to RC, June 13, 1950, RCP/BLYU.
81. RC to MR, July 20, 31, 1950, RCP/BLYU.
82. RC to MR, April 30, June 2, 1950, RCP/BLYU. Brooks, *The House of Life*, 127. Interview with Paul Brooks.
83. RC to MR, July 20, 1950, RCP/BLYU.
84. Rodell had Oliver over to her house for a party in mid-July and learned from her that Shawn was considering more than one chapter. MR to RC, July 17, 1950; RC to MR, July 17, 1950, RCP/BLYU.
85. RC to MR, July 17, 1950, RCP/BLYU.
86. Ledger for first serial sale of *The Sea Around Us*, R/CA. Carson reported to Edwin Way Teale later that Shawn's offer was for ten chapters, but Rodell's records clearly show the purchase of nine. RC to EWT, September 19, 1950, RCP/BLYU. Carson, FPR/OPM, February 5, 1950.
87. RC to MR, August 17, 1950, RCP/BLYU.

8: "A SUBJECT VERY CLOSE TO MY HEART"

1. Author questionnaire [Chatham College], n.d. [1952], RCP/BLYU.
2. RC to Richard Pough, August 7, 1950, RCP/BLYU. Interviews with Shirley Briggs, Richard Pough.
3. Pough to Captain Joseph Tilton, August 15, 1950, RCP/BLYU. Pough had been one of Carson's advocates when she was searching for employment in 1945.
4. Shirley Briggs, "Island Beach," *Atlantic Naturalist* 6, 5 (May/August 1951): 214–219.
5. SAB/D, August 18, 19, 1950. Carson's surgery in September prevented her from getting back to Island Beach. RC to Richard Pough, November 3, 1950, RCP/BLYU.
6. Carson's criticism of some FWS refuge management practices, particularly those regarding hunting and predator control, was the source of her surprising lack of interest in Aldo Leopold's posthumously published *A Sand County Almanac*. I suspect that Carson never read Leopold's book and took his preservationist credentials on faith since Howard Zahniser praised the *Almanac* in a review he wrote for *The Wood Thrush*. He did not emphasize Leopold's philosophy of the land ethic but simply commended him for his "knowledge and understanding of the wild things in

our world . . . his sense of belonging to the whole community of life." See *The Wood Thrush* 5, 3 (January-February 1950), 132.

7. Her support for the integrity of the national park system was well known around the office, especially after historian and journalist Bernard DeVoto published his eloquent critique of the federal government's raid on the national parks in the *Saturday Evening Post.* Bernard DeVoto, "Shall We Let Them Ruin Our National Parks?", *Saturday Evening Post,* July 22, 1950, 17–18, 42–48. Interview with Bob Hines.
8. The Audubon Society of D.C. drew its membership from the Washington, D.C., metropolitan area where many members were employed as scientists for the federal government or were faculty at area universities. Although scientific research during World War II had increased the overall number of government scientists, they were still a comparatively small group within the federal bureaucracy and their membership in organizations such as Audubon was a natural extension of their professional activities.
9. Records of the Audubon Society of the District of Columbia and Records of the Audubon Naturalist Society of the Central Atlantic States, Inc., RU 7294, Archives of the Smithsonian Institution. Office of the Smithsonian Archives, Washington, D.C. [Hereafter cited as ANS/OSIA.] Interview with Shirley Briggs. *The Wood Thrush/Audubon Naturalist,* vols. 4–19, 1948–1964. Carson published an early version of her chapter on island formation in *The Wood Thrush*: Rachel L. Carson, "Lost Worlds: The Challenge of the Islands," *The Wood Thrush* 4, 5 (May-June 1949), 187.
10. Interview with Chaplin Barnes. "Irston R. Barnes," Obituary, January 19, 1988, *Washington Post.* Courtesy, Chaplin Barnes. Interview with Shirley Briggs.
11. "Community Mourns Wetmore, Past Secretary, Ornithologist," *Smithsonian Torch* (January 1979). Louis Halle, author of *Springtime in Washington,* introduced Carson to the nesting veeries in Rock Creek Park. Louis J. Halle, Jr., "Notes on the Veeries of Washington, D.C.," *The Wood Thrush* 4, 5 (May-June 1949), 188–189. Roger Tory Peterson had at that time published only one volume of his *Field Guide to the Birds.* Peterson was in the military service during World War II, stationed at Quantico, VA, where he worked on military camouflage. When the war was over, Peterson, like Barnes, stayed on, although in his case the draw was the proximity of so many good natural history museums. Barnes, Halle, Peterson, Carson, Zahniser, and Vogt were contemporaries. See Richard H. Stroud, ed., *National Leaders of American Conservation* (Washington, D.C.: Smithsonian Institution Press, 1985), ANS/OSIA. See records for 1947. Interviews with Shirley Briggs, Edward Zahniser, Roger Tory Peterson.
12. ANS/OSIA. SAB/D, 1947–1952. Louis Halle to Paul Brooks, n.d. quoted in Paul Brooks, *The House of Life: Rachel Carson at Work* (Boston: Houghton Mifflin Company, 1972), 98.
13. RC to Robert Cushman Murphy, October 19, 1950, RCP/BLYU.
14. Paul Brooks [hereafter cited as PB] to RC, September 1, 1950, RCP/BLYU. Brooks wrote Carson formally inviting her to write the shore guide and outlining his ideas for its design and then left for a month's vacation. RC to MR, September 13, 1950; RC to Marie Leiper, October 26, 1950, RCP/BLYU. The option question bothered Rachel and Marie. While Oxford had given up its legal option when it turned down the Fuertes book, no other publisher had taken it. Brooks took the position that his invitation to write the shore guide fell outside the option agreement. Interview with Paul Brooks.
15. RC to MR, September 29, 1950, RCP/BLYU.
16. RC to Maria Leiper, October 26, 1950, RCP/BLYU. Sometime during the war, Simon & Schuster had remaindered 1,500 copies of *Under the Sea-Wind* without notifying Carson until 1948. The firm found about twenty copies, which it sent to

her without charge, but Carson was furious that she had not had the chance to buy back as many copies as she could. Albert Rice Leventhal to RC, February 26, 1948, and Tom Torre Bevans to RC, March 24, 1948, R/CA. RC to MR, September 13, 1950, RCP/BLYU.

17. RC to MR, September 10, 1950, RCP/BLYU.
18. Interview with F. Raymond Fosberg. This was Fosberg's view both at the time he read the draft of the chapter and when he was interviewed forty-one years later. William Shawn's failure to select this chapter for his condensation of *The Sea Around Us* appears to have been an unfortunate oversight.
19. Rachel L. Carson, "The Birth of an Island," *Yale Review* 40, 1 (September 1950), 123, 126.
20. Ibid., 126.
21. RC to MR, August 30, 1950, RCP/BLYU.
22. RC to MR, September 10, 1950, RCP/BLYU.
23. RC to MR, September 13, 1950, RCP/BLYU. The head nurse at Doctor's Hospital was Carson's longtime friend Elizabeth Dickson. Although not a highly educated woman, Dickson was a very affectionate one. She had cared for Rachel during her previous surgeries and was privy to most of the family's private concerns. Their relationship may have gone back as far as Marian's death in 1937. The only surviving correspondence from Dickson is from 1952. See Dickson Correspondence, RCP/BLYU.
24. RC to MR, September 13, September 18, 1950, RCP/BLYU. SAB/D, September 20, 24, 1950. Briggs notes, "Rachel going in for *another* [italics mine] breast tumor." About the same time Carson told Mary Fuertes Boynton, "Now it seems I'm doomed to spend a few days in the hospital for some surgery—minor, I think,—but still hope to spend the end of the month somewhere I love." September 10, 1950, RCP/BLYU.
25. RC to MR, September 29, 1950; MR to RC, October 2, 1950, RCP/BLYU. Carson apologized to Rodell a week later from Virginia Beach: "That was wretchedly thoughtless of me not to tell you directly before that the results of the operation were satisfactory, I really meant that by my 'everything okay' in the wire from the hospital but I guess it wasn't very specific. I'm really sorry!" RC to MR, n.d. [September 1950], Virginia Beach, VA, RCP/BLYU. It is unclear whether Maria Carson went along with Rachel on this trip or not. Since Rachel was just out of the hospital and accompanied by quantities of surgical dressings, it is likely that she did.
26. RC to MR, September 29, 1950, RCP/BLYU. Carson's attitude toward this second and more serious breast tumor, and to her long-term health care, is remarkably casual, but consistent with previous medical history. She seems not to have questioned the laboratory results of the biopsy, nor her physician's opinion that no further treatment was necessary. It was an attitude she maintained a decade later when a third tumor was discovered.
27. Rachel Carson, Field Notes, Nags Head, October 9, 1950, RCP/BLYU.
28. Ibid.
29. Ibid.
30. RC to MR, September 5, 1950; RC to PB, September 9, 1950, RCP/BLYU.
31. RC to MR, n.d. [October 1950], RCP/BLYU. Carson also began to plan a seashore piece for *Holiday* magazine that would be ready by summer 1952.
32. Rachel L. Carson, Fellowship Application, John Simon Guggenheim Memorial Foundation, October 14, 1950, RCP/BLYU. RC to MR, n.d. [September 1950], Virginia Beach, VA, RCP/BLYU.
33. Ibid.

34. RC to MR, October 19, 1950, RCP/BLYU.
35. William H. Chafe, *Unfinished Journey: America Since World War II* (New York: Oxford University Press, 1986), 248–256. Stephen J. Whitfield, *The Culture of the Cold War* (Baltimore: Johns Hopkins University Press, 1991), 1–25, 32. See Richard Rhodes, *Dark Sun: The Making of the Hydrogen Bomb* (New York: Simon & Schuster, 1995), for details of Truman's crash H-bomb research program.
36. RC to MR, November 7, 1950, RCP/BLYU.
37. Rodell dealt with G. E. Shklovsky, a British literary agent in London.
38. RC to MR, December 11, 1950, RCP/BLYU.
39. RC to MR, December 9, 1950, RCP/BLYU. Judges for the Westinghouse Science Writing Award for 1950 were: Norman Cousins, editor of *Saturday Review*; Henry Aldrich of the Geological Society of America; Detlev Bronk, president of The Johns Hopkins University; and Howard Meyeroff of the AAAS.
40. When Carson signed the contract with Oxford, the Saxton Trustees reduced the amount of Carson's fellowship by the amount of her advance. Carson interpreted this as being penalized because she had found a publisher and was furious. The focus of her anger was Saxton board secretary Amy Flashner, who held to the decision despite Rodell's attempts at compromise, with the result that Carson received no stipend for the last quarter of the year. Amy Flashner to RC, August 4, 1949; RC to Amy Flashner, August 9, 1949; RC to MR, August 13, 1949, RCP/BLYU.
41. MR to RC, December 13, 1950; RC to MR, December 16, 1950, RCP/BLYU.
42. RC to Philip Vaudrin, January 24, 1951, RCP/BLYU.
43. RC to MR, January 2, January 7, 1951, RCP/BLYU.
44. RC to MR, January 7, 1951, RCP/BLYU.
45. RC to MR, January 30, 1951, RCP/BLYU.
46. Ibid. *The River* and *The Plow That Broke the Plains*, by filmmaker Pare Lorentz, were prize-winning documentaries produced in part by the Soil Conservation Service in the late 1930s. They were appropriate models for Carson to consider.
47. MR to RC, February 14, 1951, RCP/BLYU. As with the Westinghouse Award and the Burroughs Medal, Carson had done as much as she could to influence the BOMC selection committee. Shy at social occasions, Carson was assertive about marketing her writing and getting it noticed by those in a position to advance her work.
48. Interview with Bob Hines. Hines recalled this incident with tears in his eyes, commenting that he never could get over the fact that she had confided this secret to him.
49. G. E. Shklovsky to RC, March 1, 1951; RC to MR, March 3, 1951, RCP/BLYU. The Shklovsky-Staples sale was completed on February 23, 1951. The English edition of *The Sea Around Us* was published on October 15, 1951. Contracts, R/CA.
50. Vaudrin went to Alfred A. Knopf. Interviews with Leona Capeless, Walter Oakley. Oakley, who was in charge of domestic marketing and distribution, confirmed that in the early 1950s, Oxford's College Department had much more clout internally than did the Trade Book Department. Vaudrin had done well to bring Carson in. After Walck and Vaudrin disagreed over how much control Walck should have in editorial affairs, Vaudrin left. Walck left Oxford in 1958, taking the Children's Book Department with him. Catherine Scott left Oxford shortly after publication of *The Sea Around Us* to take a position with the U.S. Information Agency.
51. Ibid.
52. RC to MR, April 1, 1995, RCP/BLYU. Carson, FPR/OPM. Carson proposed that during the fellowship period, she would continue to carry on limited duties at FWS,

coming in one month out of every four for three months' salary, which would allow her to meet her budget. RC to James F. Mathias, April 2, 1951, RCP/BLYU.

53. Henry Walck to Marie Rodell, April 8, 1951, RCP/BLYU; SAB/D, April 3, 1951.
54. *Baltimore Sun*, April 16, 1951, RCP/BLYU. *The Department of Interior Magazine* featured Carson as the AAAS Science Writing Winner in January 1951 with a picture. "Famous in Washington," a photo essay by Irving Penn, *Vogue*, August 15, 1951. RC to MR, April 19, 1951, RCP/BLYU. R/CA. Carson was never very pleased to be photographed. Although she had studio portraits done by Brooks Photographers in Washington for the dust jacket, they were never used.
55. Interviews with Virginia Bader, Betty Beale, Else Strom.
56. Betty Beale, "Exclusively Yours," *The Evening Star*, May 7, 1951, RCP/BLYU.
57. Interview with Betty Beale. RC to MR, May 7, 1951, RCP/BLYU. "I have had a really awful letter from him. In my younger and less wise days, my reply would be the end of any relationship between us. It won't be. I am too fond of Charles and too indebted to him to blow him up. But it does mean that you are going to have to handle this delicate matter until he simmers down." MR to RC, May 8, 1951, RCP/BLYU.
58. RC to MR, April 24, 1951, RCP/BLYU.
59. MR to RC, May 4, 1951, RCP/BLYU.
60. MR to RC, May 11, 1951; William Shawn to MR, May 9, 1951, RCP/BLYU.
61. Shawn to MR, May 9, 1951, RCP/BLYU.
62. Mary Fuertes Boynton to RC, March 25, 1951, RCP/BLYU. After learning that Carson would produce a book with text as well as drawings, apparently Boynton wanted to write the text to accompany the drawings or to have an ornithologist of her own choosing, such as Robert Cushman Murphy or George Sutton, editor of *The Wilson Bulletin*, write it.
63. Mary Fuertes Boynton to Albert Day, April 9, 1951, RCP/BLYU.
64. RC to Mary Fuertes Boynton, April 3, 1951, RCP/BLYU.
65. RC to MR, March 24, 25, 1951; MR to Joan Daves, March 26, 1951; RC to Robert Cushman Murphy, March 24, 1951; Robert Cushman Murphy to RC, March 27, 1951; RC to Alastair MacBain, March 30, 1951, RCP/BLYU.
66. MR to RC, May 28, 1951, RCP/BLYU.
67. Cass Canfield to RC, February 5, 1953, RC/A. MR to Cass Canfield, February 10, 1953, RCP/BLYU.

9: "KIN THIS BE ME?"

1. RC to MR, May 7, 1951; MR to RC, May 11, 1951, RCP/BLYU.
2. William Shawn had been named editor of *The New Yorker* within the year and had already put his imprimatur on the magazine when he serialized John Hersey's controversial *Hiroshima*. Running *The Sea Around Us* as a "Profile" was another example of Shawn's new editorial leadership.
3. I have relied on material in the R/CA, and on conversations with Paul Brooks, who knew William Shawn.
4. RC to MR, May 31, 1951, RCP/BLYU.
5. RC to MR, n.d. [June 1951], RCP/BLYU.
6. MR to RC, June 12, 1951, RCP/BLYU.
7. RC to MR, June 14, 1951, RCP/BLYU.
8. Ibid.
9. Ibid.

10. Betty Beale, "Exclusively Yours," *The Evening Star*, June 18, 1951, R/CA.
11. Tentative Oxford University Press Club Party List, RCP/BLYU.
12. See photographs with Alice Roosevelt Longworth. Official guest lists to National Press Club Party, June 20, 1951, RCP/BLYU. SAB/D, June 1951.
13. RC to MR, June 14, 1951, RCP/BLYU.
14. Henry Walck to RC, June 30, 1951; MR to RC, n.d. [June 1951]; RC to MR, n.d. [July 1951], RCP/BLYU. SAB/D, June 29, 1951.
15. Jonathan Norton Leonard, "And His Wonders in the Deep" (Review of *The Sea Around Us*), *New York Times Book Review*, July 1, 1951, 1.
16. David Dempsey, "Books of the Times," *New York Times*, July 2, 1951, 21.
17. Interview with Virginia Bader. Vera Carson, a naturalized Canadian, married Robert Carson after World War II. They lived in Tacoma Park, MD, not far from Rachel and her mother. Robert Carson now had a good job at the U.S. Bureau of Standards but gave his wife very little for herself. They did not attend the book signing, but Rachel was fond of Vera and glad that her book parties provided the opportunity for her sister-in-law to get some nice dresses. RC to MR, n.d. [June 1951], "Tuesday night," RCP/BLYU. Tom Donnelley, "What Are the Wild Sea Creatures Saying?" *Washington Daily News*, July 4, 1951, 22. Dorothea Cruger, "Object of Her Affection Is the Ocean," *Washington Post*, July 4, 1951, R/CA.
18. Donnelley, "What Are the Wild Sea Creatures Saying?"
19. Cruger, "Object of Her Affection."
20. Donnelley, "What Are the Wild Sea Creatures Saying?" and Cruger, "Object of Her Affection." Paul Brooks, *The House of Life: Rachel Carson at Work* (Boston: Houghton Mifflin Company, 1972), 126.
21. The most complete literary analysis of Carson's writing remains that given by Carol B. Gartner in her chapter "Return to Oceanus: *The Sea Around Us*" in *Rachel Carson* (New York: Frederick Ungar Publishing Co., 1983). For a discussion of Carson's effective use of personal pronouns, see Cheryll Glotfelty, "Rachel Carson," in John Elder, ed., *American Nature Writers* (New York: Charles Scribner's Sons, 1996), vol. 1, 151–171. Mary A. McCay's analysis of *The Sea Around Us* in her *Rachel Carson* (New York: Twayne Publishers, 1993) compares Carson's nature philosophy in the 1951 edition with that of the revised edition of 1961. Henry Bigelow to RC, May 4, 1951, RCP/BLYU.
22. Austin H. Clark, "From the Beginning of the World" (Review of *The Sea Around Us*), *Saturday Review of Literature*, July 7, 1951, 13–14. Rachel Carson, *The Sea Around Us* (New York: Oxford University Press, 1951), 188. "Deep Waters," *Newsweek*, July 16, 1951, RCP/BLYU.
23. *New York Times Best Seller Lists*, 1950, 1951. "Best Sellers," *Saturday Review of Literature*, October 27, 1951, RCP/BLYU.
24. Rachel Carson, Speech (annotated copy), National Book Award, January 29, 1952, RCP/BLYU. See, for example, Paul Boyer, *By the Bombs Early Light* (New York: Pantheon Books, 1985), 334–355. The continuing debate over nuclear tests on the Bikini Islands after 1946 heightened interest in Pacific Island matters.
25. Rachel Carson, Speech, National Book Award, January 29, 1952, RCP/BLYU.
26. Thor Heyerdahl's *Kon-Tiki* was popular for some of the same reasons, but as an adventure story, it was more of an escape book than *The Sea Around Us*. Rachel Carson, "Design for Nature Writing," Speech, John Burroughs Medal, April 7, 1952. Reprinted in *Atlantic Naturalist* 7, 5 (May/August 1952), 234.
27. "Deep Waters," *Newsweek*. See Edwin Way Teale's explanation in his introduction to a chapter from *The Sea Around Us*, reprinted in Teale, *Green Treasury: A Journey*

Through the World's Great Nature Writing (New York: Dodd, Mead & Company, 1952), 28.

28. E. H. Martin, "Brilliant Study of the Sea," *The Evening Sun*, June 30, 1951, RCP/BLYU. Mark Watson, Carson's friend and former editor of the *Baltimore Sun*, wrote her, "What a long leap this is from your first piece in *The Sunday Sun*, which stirred my own confident belief that you would do large things one day. Never was hope more fully sustained." Mark Watson to RC, April 19, 1951, RCP/BLYU. See Margot Doss, "Long Time No Sea," *Baltimore Sun*, November 25, 1951, 11, 21, for a lengthy personal interview with Carson including photographs. M. Graham Netting, "The Naturalist's Bookshelf," *Carnegie Magazine*, 25 (November 1951), 320–321. Harvey Breit, "Reader's Choice," *The Atlantic Monthly*, 188 (August 1951), 82–84.
29. Rachel Carson, "The Real World Around Us," RCP/BLYU. Brooks, *The House of Life*, 132.
30. Leonard, "And His Wonders in the Deep," 1.
31. Clippings file, RCP/BLYU.
32. Shirley Briggs, Illustration, "Rachel as her readers seem to imagine her" (1951). Interview with Shirley Briggs. Briggs remembers Maria Carson phoning her gleefully to recount the interview.
33. RC to MR, July 6, 1951, RCP/BLYU. *Publishers Weekly*, July 14, 1951, R/CA.
34. RC to MR, July 19, 1951, RCP/BLYU.
35. RC to MR [Monday night], July 1951, RCP/BLYU.
36. RC to Maria Carson, July 18, 1951, RCP/BLYU. Carson and her mother, both somewhat obsessive about correct grammar, wrote humorous letters to each other using a kind of country dialect. It was an affectionate code between them.
37. See letters between Rachel and Maria Carson, July–August 1951, RCP/BLYU.
38. After Maria Carson's death, Rachel confided such difficulties to Dorothy Freeman and Jeanne Davis. Bob Hines had his own evidence of Maria Carson's domineering behavior. Interview with Bob Hines. When Rodell went through Carson's papers in 1964, she eliminated any letters that might have made Maria the subject of comment. But when Paul Brooks was writing *House of Life*, Rodell suggested that he might "delicately" get in the idea of "how totally tied down Rachel was by Mrs. C. Her literary output aside from trips abroad, etc.—suffered badly from having to match her pace to her mother's; to her mother's refusal for a long time to have adequate help in the house, to let anyone but Rachel help her across the room, do the marketing, etc., etc." MR to PB, March 18, 1971, R/CA.
39. Interview with Bob Hines. Carson collected letters between her and her mother and saved them with her papers. Rachel's letters hardly ever bear a date, only the day of the week. Maria Carson's sometimes are dated. Her first letter to Rachel was written within two hours of her daughter's departure from Silver Spring. Maria's letters are particularly valuable for their information on family matters. RCP/BLYU.
40. RC to Maria Carson, July 18, 1951, RCP/BLYU.
41. Cyrus Durgin, "Overnight Miss Carson Has Become Famous," *Boston Globe*, July 20, 1951, 1, 4.
42. Ibid.
43. RC to Maria Carson, July 22, 1951; Maria Carson to RC [n.d.], Tuesday evening, RCP/BLYU. The reference to Shirley's disguises is to those she made for Rachel and Kay Howe when they were working at Parker River and fearful of local antipathy toward U.S. Fish and Wildlife personnel. Maria Carson to RC, July 17, 1951, RCP/BLYU. Carson notes that she still had not met Dr. Mary Sears.
44. RC to MR, n.d. [August 1951], RCP/BLYU. Wall Point was then one of the more

remote points of land at the eastern end of Boothbay, and there were no other cottages nearby. The cottage, which still remains, although it has been much enlarged, had a lovely view of the Linekin Bay. MR to PB, March 18, 1971, R/CA.

45. MR to Henry Walck, August 14, 1951, RCP/BLYU.
46. RC to MR, November 4, 1951; MR to RC, December 7, 1951, RCP/BLYU. Terms between Oxford and Carson for *Under the Sea-Wind* were agreed upon on December 7, 1951, and Carson signed the contract on December 27. Carson was paid a royalty of $14,302.76 for 42,831 copies on April 30, 1952. Contracts and Ledgers in the R/CA. Oxford Press Publicity, RCP/BLYU.
47. Brooks, *The House of Life*, 126. *New York Herald Tribune Book Review*, October 7, 1951, 4.
48. The National Symphony Orchestra Luncheon, given to raise funds for the orchestra, was held September 25, 1951, in Washington, D.C.
49. Rachel Carson, Speech, National Symphony Orchestra Luncheon, September 25, 1951, RCP/BLYU.
50. Ibid. This is the first public reference Carson made to the atomic bomb and the cultural anxieties it produced. See Christine Oravec, "Rachel Louise Carson," in Karlyn Kohrs Campbell, ed., *Women Public Speakers in the United States, 1925–1993: A Biocritical Source Book* (Westport, CT: Greenwood Press, 1994), 8–84.
51. Rachel L. Carson, "The exceeding beauty of the earth—" "Words to Live By," *This Week Magazine*, Draft, RCP/BLYU. Although written in late September–early October 1951, the column did not appear until May 25, 1952. Carson quoted from one of her favorite works by English naturalist Richard Jeffries, *Pageant of Summer*.
52. Ibid.
53. Letters of Elizabeth Dickson; letters of Maria Carson to Rachel Carson, summer 1951, RCP/BLYU. Interviews with Else Strom, Shirley Briggs, Katherine Howe Roberts, Jeanne Davis, Frances Carson Hoerner, Roger Christie.
54. RC to Dorothy Freeman [hereafter cited as DF], February 1, 1956. Martha Freeman, ed., *Always, Rachel: The Letters of Rachel Carson and Dorothy Freeman, 1952–1964* (Boston: Beacon Press, 1995) [Hereafter cited as *Letters*.] Unless citation refers to the editor's preface or introduction, dates of published letters will be given rather than page numbers. Interview with Jeanne Davis.
55. Rachel Carson, Speech, Book and Author Luncheon, October 16, 1951, RCP/BLYU.
56. Interview with Roland Clement.
57. RC to MR, October 29, 1951, RCP/BLYU.
58. Ibid. See "Speech File," RCP/BLYU.
59. MR to RC, September 26, November 2, 1951, RCP/BLYU. Translation figures from R/CA.
60. Ledgers, R/CA. Brooks, *The House of Life*, 133. RC to DF, September 28, 1953, *Letters*. MR to Edward Colton, October 10, 1951, RCP/BLYU.
61. Interview with Helga Sandburg Crile. This meeting marked the beginning of Carson's friendship with Jane and George "Barney" Crile and, nearly a decade later, led to her choosing Crile as her surgeon. Jane Crile died after a valiant fight against breast cancer in January 1963. See George Crile, Jr., *The Way It Was* (Kent, OH: Kent State University Press, 1992), 46, 51–52, 293–294.
62. Interview with Ruth Hunter Swisshelm. Several details of Carson's Pittsburgh visit are drawn from Angeline J. Sober's unpublished manuscript, "With Every Good Wish, Rachel." Sober's work contains so many errors that it cannot be relied on for fact or interpretation. However, Sober did meet Carson at Gimbel's that day and

later interviewed Springdale residents, Carson's cousins in Pittsburgh, and some PCW classmates, including Swisshelm, and a few faculty.

63. "Pennsylvania Author Writes Book-of-the Month," *Pittsburgh Press*, September 1, 1951; Fon Boardman to Marie Rodell, October 9, 1951; *Publishers Weekly*, December 1, 1951; RC to MR, September 18, 1952, RCP/BLYU.
64. MR to RC, November 30, 1951, RCP/BLYU.
65. The jury that judged nonfiction nominees in 1952 for the American Booksellers Association, the American Book Publishers Council, and the Book Manufacturers Institute included Crane Brinton, Huntington Cairns, Marquis Childs, Luther H. Evans, and Horace M. Kallen.
66. Remarks by John Mason Brown, National Book Award, January 29, 1952, RCP/BLYU.
67. Rachel L. Carson, Speech, National Book Award, January 29, 1952, RCP/BLYU.
68. Ibid.
69. Ibid.
70. I am indebted to Carol B. Gartner for first calling my attention to this quality in Carson's remarks. This passage has been widely quoted but without the necessary context to see it as a rhetorical conceit. See Gartner, *Rachel Carson*, 55. See draft copies of *The Sea Around Us* and changes made in Carson's hand, RCP/BLYU. When expert copy editor Margaret Nicholson altered the word patterns in *The Sea Around Us*, Carson restored them, explaining "The departure from the normal order in these places is a matter of style, sometimes for emphasis or for the sound or rhythm of the words." RC to Margaret Nicholson, November 6, 1950, RCP/BLYU.
71. Carson, Speech, National Book Award, January 29, 1952, RCP/BLYU.
72. Ibid.
73. Carson told Philip Vaudrin as early as July 1950 "The internal politics and contrivings of the [Burroughs Association] group are said to be fearful to behold. . . . Just between us, I think my next book will come much closer to the Burroughs tradition, but we need not tell them about that." RC to Philip Vaudrin, July 24, 1950, RCP/BLYU.
74. Rachel L. Carson, "Design for Nature Writing," Remarks made on acceptance of the John Burroughs Medal, April 7, 1952. Published in *Atlantic Naturalist* 7, 5 (May/August 1952), 232–234.
75. Ibid.
76. Ibid.
77. Ibid.

10: "AN ALICE IN WONDERLAND CHARACTER"

1. Rachel Carson, Speech, "New York Zoological Society," January 14, 1953, RCP/BLYU.
2. Rachel Carson, Speech to the Members of the Geographical Society of Philadelphia, January 9, 1952, RCP/BLYU. "Author of Book on Sea Honored," *Philadelphia Evening Inquirer*, January 10, 1952. Archives of the *Philadelphia Inquirer*, Philadelphia, PA. See Christine Oravec, "Rachel Louise Carson," in Karlyn Kohrs Campbell, ed., *Women Public Speakers in the United States, 1925–1993, A Biocritical Source Book* (Westport, CT: Greenwood Press, 1994), 83.
3. Rachel L. Carson, Remarks at Commencement Luncheon, June 14, 1952, Drexel Institute of Technology, Philadelphia, PA, RCP/BLYU. Carson's speech is reminiscent of the views espoused by English physicist and writer C. P. Snow in 1959.

4. Citation, Honorary Degree Awarded to Rachel Carson, May 26, 1952, RCP/BLYU. Interview with Ruth Hunter Swisshelm. The dialogue that Philip Sterling gives to Rachel is not an accurate quote from Swisshelm or Carson. Philip Sterling, *Sea and Earth: The Life of Rachel Carson* (New York: Thomas Y. Crowell Co., 1970), 117.
5. Oberlin's citation noted her "genius as a biologist," but above all "her skill, so rare among scientists, in setting forth the findings of science in such a way as to make them a part of the cultural store of all men." Honorary Doctorate of Science, Awarded to Rachel Carson, June 1952. Presidential Papers of William E. Stevenson, Archives of Oberlin College, Oberlin, OH. *Oberlin College Alumni Magazine* (July 1952). Hope Hibbard was a noted aquatic biologist who had completed her doctorate at Bryn Mawr in the early 1920s. Carson stayed with Hibbard while at Oberlin and found much in common with her. William E. Stevenson to RC, November 15, 1951; Presidential Papers of William E. Stevenson, Archives of Oberlin College, Oberlin, OH.
6. MR to RC, February 1, 1952, RCP/BLYU.
7. RC to Fon Boardman, March 1, 1952, RCP/BLYU.
8. RC to EWT, March 5, March 22, 1952, EWTP/UC. Carson herself was ill with a stomach virus just before the award but had decided if she was at all up to the trip she would go. "I know it will be considered an affront to the award if I don't. Edwin Teale is ready to represent me as a 'last, last resort' but he begs me to come if I possibly can." RC to MR, March 31, 1952, RCP/BLYU.
9. Ibid. EWT to RC, February 10, 1952, EWTP/UC.
10. Rachel Carson, "Life at the Edge of the Sea," *Life*, April 14, 1952, 64–79. Paul Brooks, *The House of Life: Rachel Carson at Work* (Boston: Houghton Mifflin Co., 1972), 130. Publication figures from R/CA.
11. The book that displaced hers was the personal diaries and private letters of Harry S Truman by William Hillman (New York: Farrar, Straus and Young, 1952). "Two Best Sellers," *New York Times*, Sunday April 27, 1952, RCP/BLYU. The sequence and occasion of these critical reviews has been ignored.
12. Ibid.
13. Harvey Breit, review of *Under the Sea-Wind* in the *New York Times*, April 6, 1952, 33. A. C. Aces, review of *Under the Sea-Wind* in the *Chicago Sunday Tribune*, April 6, 1952, 3. J. H. Jackson, review of *Under the Sea-Wind* in the *San Francisco Chronicle*, April 4, 1952, 20. Citation for Distinguished Service from the Department of Interior, September 23, 1952. Carson was in Woods Hole when the award was made and did not attend the ceremonies in Washington, much to the disappointment of her former colleagues.
14. RC to Fon Boardman, February 15, 1952; MR to RC, September 12, 1952; RC to MR, September 18, 1952, RCP/BLYU.
15. James E. Bennet to RC, September 19, 1952; RC to James E. Bennett [*sic*], November 1, 1952, RCP/BLYU.
16. Ibid.
17. Rachel L. Carson, "The Land Around Us," *This Week Magazine*, May 25, 1952, RCP/BLYU.
18. Henry Allen Moe, Memorandum to Fellows, March 6, 1952; RC to Henry Allen Moe, March 19, 1952; Henry Allen Moe to RC, March 21, 1952, Archives of the J. S. Guggenheim Foundation. RC to James F. Mathias, April 2, 1951; RC to Henry Allen Moe, April 10, 1952, RCP/BLYU. Carson received a monthly stipend of $250 as a Guggenheim Fellow for a total fellowship of $3,000. At the time she requested no further payments, she had received $2,500. Carson did not resign her

fellowship. Fellowship data courtesy of the Archives of the J. S. Guggenheim Foundation, NY.

19. Field notebooks, RCP/BLYU. Outline for "Guide to Seashore Life on the Atlantic Coast," RCP/BLYU.
20. RC to MR, March 31, 1952, RCP/BLYU. RC to SAB, March 17, 1952, SAB. Shirley Briggs's father, John Briggs, a political science professor at the University of Iowa, died quite suddenly just before Rachel left for South Carolina. Rachel's letter to Shirley is a sympathy note written with the hope that her adventures would at least provide some amusement.
21. Rachel Carson, Field Notes, "St. Simons Island," n.d. [April 15, 1952], RCP/BLYU. Rachel Carson, *The Edge of the Sea* (Boston: Houghton Mifflin Co., 1955), 136. Hereafter cited as *EOS*.
22. Ibid.
23. Ibid.
24. Ibid.
25. Rachel Carson, Field Notes, fragment on dunes, RCP/BLYU. Unlike the little dog story, Carson typed out her reflections on the dunes. Her spacing indicates that she intended to add at least two paragraphs. The last paragraph, not cited, suggests that she thought about it as a short piece that could be published on its own.
26. Interview with Bob Hines.
27. Ibid. RC to SAB, May 13, 1952, SAB.
28. RC to Alastair MacBain, May 7, 1952; Alastair MacBain to RC, May 9, 1952, RCP/BLYU.
29. Rachel L. Carson, "Notification of Personnel Action," May 15, 1952, Carson, FPR/OPM. Interview with Bob Hines. RC to Fon Boardman, May 14, 1952, RCP/BLYU. Hines remembers that Carson took him out for lobster and that he ate more than one.
30. RC to EWT, July 31, 1952, EWTP/UC. RC to MR, August 12, 1952, RCP/BLYU. Carson's election to the Marine Biological Laboratory Corporation was August 12, 1952. She remained a member of the corporation until her death and regularly attended its meetings until 1961. Annual Reports of the Marine Biological Laboratory, 1952–1960, MBL Library, Woods Hole, MA.
31. RC to EWT, July 31, 1952, EWTP/UC. Rachel could go off and leave her mother in Woods Hole because she had friends there who would look in on her, including Bert Walford and his wife, who were also at the Fisheries Station that August.
32. EWT to RC, February 10, 1952; May 30, 1952; RC to EWT, July 31, 1952, EWTP/UC. RC to John and Margaret Kieran, August 22, 1952, RCP/ BLYU. Interview with Margaret (Mrs. John) Kieran. I am indebted to Margaret Kieran for providing me with photographs and memoirs of Carson from her personal papers, as well as from those of her husband and her late sister, Anne Ford. Anne Ford, biographical sketch of Rachel Carson, 1964, RCP/BLYU and original typescript, courtesy Margaret Ford Kieran.
33. RC to Bob Hines, n.d. [August 1952], RCP/BLYU.
34. RC to MR, October 1, 1952, RCP/BLYU.
35. Interview with Bob Hines. Sterling tells of similar incidents in Florida, but Hines only described and confirmed an occasion while tide-pooling in Maine in my interviews with him. Sterling, *Sea and Earth*, 134.
36. RC to MR, September 9, 1952, RCP/BLYU. N[orman] J[ohn] Berrill, Jack to his friends, was the author of *The Living Tide* (1951), a naturalist's account of near shore marine life that was published shortly before *The Sea Around Us*; at one time Rachel

regarded it as possible competition. Berrill and Carson were again doing similar marine research and often made common interest together at Ocean Point, Pemequid, or the salt pond over in New Harbor. They shared good sites and good tides and a love of the Maine coast. Jacquelyn Berrill wrote nature books for children, including *Wonder of the Seashore* (1951) and *Strange Nurseries: Another Wonder Book* (1954). RC to MR, September 9, 1952, RCP/BLYU.

37. RC to MR, September 9, 1952, RCP/BLYU.
38. Ibid. RC to MR, September 24, 1952, RCP/BLYU.
39. Rachel Carson, "The Real World Around Us," RCP/BLYU. Carson's irritation reflected the stress she felt from family as well as fans. RC to Fon Boardman, February 15, 1952, RCP/BLYU. She declined invitations from the Literary Club of Pelham, NY, The Richmond (VA) Book and Author Luncheon, and the Society of Chicago Geographers. RC to Mrs. Malcolm J. Edgerton, October 27, 1952, RCP/BLYU.
40. RC to Fon Boardman, March 1, 1952, RCP/BLYU.
41. RC to EWT, March 5, 1952, EWTP/UC.
42. RC to MR, March 24, 1952, RCP/BLYU. Interview with Shirley Briggs.
43. Elizabeth Dickson to RC, n.d. [March 1952] and May 1952, RCP/BLYU. These several letters from Dickson reveal how difficult the situation was for Carson.
44. Roger Revelle to RC, August 11, 1952, RCP/BLYU.
45. RC to Roger Revelle, August 21, 1952; telegram from RC to John Isaacs, n.d. [September 1952], RCP/BLYU. Rodell underscored the attraction of privacy when she told Carson, "If it does nothing else, it will give you a month of isolation from pressure by your public, your publishers, and me, and ought to be a wonderful rest." MR to RC, September 22, 1952; John Isaacs to RC, telegram, September 25, 1952; RC to Roger Revelle, October 1, 1952; RC to PB, October 3, 1952; RC to MR, October 1, 1952, RCP/BLYU.
46. Henry Beston, "Miss Carson's First," *The Freeman*, November 3, 1952, 100. She did tell Ruth Nanda Anshen about the review without any apologies or false modesty. RC to Ruth Nanda Anshen [hereafter cited as RNA], March 17, 1953, RCP/BLYU.
47. RC to Shirley Collier, November 9, 1952, RCP/BLYU.
48. Ibid.
49. Ibid.
50. MR to Shirley Collier, November 11, 1952, RCP/BLYU.
51. Ibid.
52. Shirley Collier to RC, November 12, 1952; RC to RKO Pictures, Inc., January 19, 1953, RCP/BLYU. Thomas Wood, " 'The Sea Around Us' Filmed," *New York Herald Tribune*, January 31, 1953, 4. SAB/L, March 8, 1953. Fon Boardman to MR, August 6, 1953, RCP/BLYU.
53. Richard L. Coe, "Little of Author in 'The Sea Around Us,' " *Washington Post*, n.d. [September 1953], RCP/BLYU. See RC to DF, September 3, September 28, 1953, *Letters*.
54. The contract with Houghton Mifflin concluded February 5, 1953, gave Carson $7,500 a year and some left over. Rodell negotiated an additional advance of $12,000 less the $1,000 already given in the previous contract. R/CA. The new delivery date was July 1, 1953. MR to RC, February 5, 1953, RCP/BLYU.
55. RC to MR, November 18, 1952; MR to RC, November 19, 1952; MR to RC, February 5, 1953; RC to RNA, February 27, March 17, 1953, RCP/BLYU.
56. Perhaps the most telling incident was Rachel's reticence to share with Marie her excitement at buying property in Maine. Earlier she would have confided the whole idea to Marie before ever going ahead with it. See RC to MR, September 9, 1952,

RCP/BLYU. The tone of their letters also changed during the spring of 1953 when Carson was traveling in the South. Carson became more aloof and less intimate. Their correspondence over the handling of literary property in Carson's new will was typical of their difficult exchanges. See correspondence in RCP/BLYU.

57. RC to RNA, March 17, 1953, RCP/BLYU.
58. RC to MR, April 29, 1953; RC to PB, March 11, 1953, RCP/BLYU.
59. RC to PB, May 28, 1953, RCP/BLYU.
60. RC to PB, June 24, 1953, RCP/BLYU.
61. Ibid. Brooks, *The House of Life*, 159. Rachel Carson, Speech, Audubon Naturalist Society, December 13, 1954. RCP/BLYU.
62. RC to DF, December 15, 1952, *Letters*.

11: "NOTHING LIVES TO ITSELF"

1. Linda J. Lear, "Dorothy Murdoch Freeman Rand, A Chronology of Her Life," mss., 1993. This chronology was prepared after several interviews with Stanley Freeman, Jr., and Madeleine Freeman, in July and September 1992, in Southport, ME, with reference to Freeman's diaries. Interviews with Martha Freeman. See Martha Freeman, ed., preface, *Letters*, xiv–xvi. Carson had stationery printed with that name on it.
2. RC to DF, September 3, 1953, *Letters*.
3. RC to MR, August 28, 1953, RCP/BLYU.
4. RC to MR, September 27, 1953; MR to RC, October 2, 1953, RCP/BLYU.
5. Rachel blamed herself for taking Muffin on long car trips in changing temperatures. "I must never have a cat again, I guess . . . besides I can't go through this grief again. I had loved the others dearly but Muffie was different." RC to MR, July 18, 1953, RCP/BLYU. RC to DF, September 10, 28, 1953, *Letters*.
6. Interviews with Jeanne Davis. See portrait photograph of Dorothy Freeman, Freeman Family Photographs. [Hereafter cited as FFP.] This formal portrait of Freeman was taken not long before she met Carson. A copy was in Carson's personal effects when she died. Interviews with Roger Christie, Shirley Briggs, Ruth Scott.
7. Stanley Freeman, Jr., estimates that she was in regular correspondence with about one hundred people from all over the world when she died in 1978. Interview with Stanley and Madeleine Freeman.
8. Photographs of Stanley and Dorothy Freeman, FFP. Interviews with Stanley and Madeleine Freeman.
9. RC to DF, October 18, 1953, Unpublished, Freeman Family Correspondence, privately held. [Hereafter cited as UP/FFC.] RC to DF, September 28, 1952, *Letters*.
10. They discovered that Margaret Cooper's wonderfully funny *How to Live with a Cat*, edited by Rachel's first editor and friend, Maria Leiper, was their favorite cat book.
11. RC to DF, October 5, 1953, *Letters*.
12. RC to DF, October 18, 1953, UP/FFC.
13. For example, she addressed letters to Jeanne Davis and to another friend Jean Reller with similar endearments. Personal collection of letters, courtesy of Jeanne Davis. Correspondence with Jean Reller, courtesy of Jeanne Davis. Interviews with Jeanne Davis, Stanley and Madeleine Freeman. Without Dorothy's letters to correct balance, we are left with Rachel as the initiator, the one who shaped the relationship, made the plans to meet, as well as the confident partner who reassured a tentative and self-effacing friend of her worthiness. But Rachel's letters show clearly that the

longing and anxiety to be certain of each other's love and commitment were mutual.

14. RC to DF, December 11, 1953, *Letters*.
15. RC to DF, December 26, 1953, *Letters*.
16. Rachel Carson, "The Edge of the Sea," Speech to the AAAS General Symposium, The Sea Frontier, December 29, 1953, RCP/BLYU.
17. DF to RC, "For Christmas Eve" [1954], UP/FFC.
18. RC to DF, January 1, 1954, *Letters*.
19. RC to DF, January 25, 1954, *Letters*. See Martha Freeman, ed., preface, *Letters*, xvii.
20. RC to DF, February 3, 1954, UP/FFC.
21. RC to DF, January 30, 1954, *Letters*.
22. Ibid. Martha Freeman, ed., preface, *Letters*, xvi.
23. Ibid. This letter makes clear that a large part of the letters Rachel asked Dorothy to destroy or destroyed herself when they were together were ones that contained references to Carson's family.
24. Ibid.
25. RC to DF, February 6, 1954, *Letters*.
26. Ibid.
27. Ibid.
28. Ibid.
29. RC to DF, February 13, 1954, *Letters*. Carson sent Freeman a copy of Henry Beston's review of *Under the Sea-Wind*, which she had received not long before.
30. RC to DF, February 20, 1954, *Letters*.
31. RC to DF, February 17, 1954; DF to RC, January 31, 1955; RC to DF, February 20, 1954, *Letters*. DF to RC, "For Christmas Eve" [1954], UP/FCC.
32. RC to DF, February 20, 1954, *Letters*.
33. Ibid.
34. Ibid.
35. Olaus J. Murie, "Wild Country as a National Asset," *The Living Wilderness* 45 (June 1953), 11–12. Carson underlined several paragraphs, including Murie's idea that he could only plead that somehow wild country "had to do with the spiritual well being of people, that it has had an effect on us similar to that of music or poetry."
36. Rachel Carson, "Mr. Day's Dismissal," *Washington Post*, April 22, 1953, RCP/BLYU.
37. "Miss Carson Also Speaks For Us," *Falmouth Enterprise*, RCP/BLYU. RC to Dr. Bently Glass, May 6, 1953, RCP/BLYU.
38. RC to Irston R. Barnes, telegram, October 12, 1953, RCP/BLYU. I suspect that there are other undocumented incidents that reflect Carson's political activism on behalf of preservation.
39. RC to DF, January 21, 1954, *Letters*.
40. RC to DF, March 12, 1954, *Letters*. Before their visit on March 29 Rachel wrote, "Oh, darling, lets be thoroughly 'selfish' this time—after all its our first real visit. And the time will be so short at best. So why not save friends for another time? I'm only daring to tell you how I really feel about it because I think you, too, want every moment we can have together."
41. Pauline Zimmermann, "Rachel Carson Previews New Book at Cranbrook," *Detroit News*, Cranbrook Institute Archives, Bloomfield Hills, MI. Given Carson's views about hunting, her ownership of a fur topper and later a mink stole seems an anomaly. I do not know when she acquired this coat. Rachel Carson, "The Edge of the Sea," Cranbrook Institute of Science, April 9, 1954, RCP/BLYU.
42. Rachel Carson, "The Real World Around Us," Matrix Table Dinner, Theta Sigma

Phi, Columbus, Ohio, April 21, 1954. This was the most personally revealing speech Carson ever gave. RC to DF, April 21, 1954, *Letters*.

43. Carson, "The Real World Around Us," April 21, 1954, RCP/BLYU.
44. Ibid. RC to DF, April 21, 1954, *Letters*.
45. RC to DF, May 3–4, 1954, *Letters*. Carson had given another speech in April at Western Indiana University, which was a shorter version of the Cranbrook slide lecture.
46. MR to RC, April 20, 1954, R/CA. RC to DF, April 21, 1954, and May 3–4, 1954, *Letters*. RC to MR, n.d. [May 1954], R/CA. Carson had been voted the single honoree for 1954, but since it was the club's twenty-fifth anniversary, it awarded medals to ten authors, including Carl Sandburg, Bernard DeVoto, and William Faulkner.
47. RC to MR, April 22, 1954, R/CA. Rodell had met the Freemans in July 1953, when they all went tide-pooling together, but Rachel had not mentioned the subsequent flowering of her friendship with Dorothy. RC to MR, May 27, 1954, R/CA.
48. Rachel took the train to Boston and met Dorothy on May 17, and they drove to Southport, returning to Boston May 21.
49. Carson had gone so far as to call Carl Buchheister, the president of the National Audubon Society, to ask him whether veeries would be singing that early in the year in Maine. Buchheister recommended she call Beston, who would know. Carson told Beston about discovering his book in the Pratt Library in Baltimore when she was just starting to work for the Bureau of Fisheries. "I hesitate to guess how many times I have read the book since then, but I don't hesitate to say that I can think of few others that have given me such deep and lasting pleasures, or to which I can return with such assurance of a renewal of my original enjoyment." RC to Henry Beston, May 14, 1954, RCP/BLYU.
50. Elizabeth Beston to RC, May 30, 1951, RCP/BLYU. RC to DF, May 23, 1954, *Letters*.
51. RC to MR, June 20, 1954, *Letters*. RC to EWT, August 14, 1955, EWTP/UC.
52. Sale and payment for first serial rights to "Rim of Sand," July 24, 1954, R/CA. Shawn bought the balance in May 1955. RC to DF, June 26, 1954, *Letters*.
53. RC to DF, June 26, 1954, *Letters*. Later that fall they would burn some letters when they were together. This accounts for the absence of Freeman letters between September 1953 and December 1954. Martha Freeman suggests that this was the case in her preface; see *Letters*, xvi. Interview with Martha Freeman.
54. RC to DF, July 28, 1954, UP/FFC.
55. RC to EWT, August 23, 1954, EWTP/UC. RC to DF, August 3, 1954, UP/FFC. RC to PB, November 2, 1954, RCP/BLYU.
56. RC to MR, September 7, 24, 1954, R/CA. RC to EWT, September 16, November 11, 1954, EWTP/UC. "The recent hurricane hit us directly . . . and we were lucky to save the house and inhabitants!" SAB/D, October 15, 1954. Henry Beston to RC, September 22, 1954, RCP/BLYU.
57. RC to DF, September 13, 1954, *Letters*.
58. RC to MR, September 24, R/CA. See Martha Freeman, ed., preface, *Letters*, xviii. RC to Stan Freeman, November 1, 1954, UP/FFC. Interviews with Stanley and Madeleine Freeman.
59. RC to DF, September 30, 1954, *Letters*.
60. MR to William Shawn, November 3, 1954, R/CA. Carson worried about the inscriptions, fearing them too private to be read outside the Freeman family circle. Later Dorothy put the accompanying letters into tiny envelopes and pasted them into each book. RC to DF, November 5, 1954, UP/FFC. Letters and inscriptions, courtesy of Stanley and Madeleine Freeman.

61. RC to DF, November 5, 1954, UP/FFC. As an inscription, Rachel wrote:

> There is another, inner way, a way that is not accessible to everyone. It leads from the unconscious within ourselves to the imponderable and invisible in the earthly environment.
>
> He who walks this trail, sees the beauty of the earth, and hears its music.
>
> Hans Cloos
>
> To Dorothy, to whom the "inner way" is accessible. Rachel.

62. Florence had been coming once a week for the past two years. Rachel also employed Mrs. Rivera, a typist, who handled her correspondence and typed her corrected manuscript chapters. RC to DF, October 28, 1954, *Letters*. RC to MR, November 1, 1954, R/CA. The whole arrangement depended on whether Maria Carson approved of the housekeepers and whether she was willing to let them do the work. Most domestic arrangements did not last long.
63. RC to DF, December 11, 1954, *Letters*.
64. Rachel Carson, speech, annual meeting of the Audubon Society of the District of Columbia, December 13, 1954, RCP/BLYU. SAB/D, December 13, 1954. "Events and Activities," *Audubon Naturalist*, 10, 2 (November–December 1954), 96.
65. RC to DF, Christmas Eve, 1954, *Letters*. Carson quoted a passage from Albert Einstein's 1931 book *Living Philosophies* that seemed to her to describe the wonder, mystery, and almost spiritual quality she found at the heart of their relationship. "The most beautiful and most profound emotion we can experience is the sensation of the mystical. . . ."
66. DF to RC, December 23, December 24, 1954, *Letters*. DF to RC, December 24, 1954, UP/FFC.

12: "BETWEEN THE TIDE LINES"

1. RC to DF, February 7, 19, 20, 1955, *Letters*.
2. RC to PB, March 14, 1955, RCP/BLYU. RC to EWT, February 24, 1955, EWTP/UC. See Paul Brooks, *The House of Life: Rachel Carson at Work* (Boston: Houghton Mifflin Co., 1972), 162–163. Brooks suggests that Carson was exaggerating and that her phrase "years of misery" should not be taken literally. However, in the early 1970s when Brooks wrote, he was not aware of the extent of Carson's family difficulties or how real her complaints had been.
3. Curriculum vitae for Dorothy H. Algire, 1960. Courtesy of the Algire Family. Algire's children were now in school and she had time for part-time research work.
4. RC to PB, March 14, 1955, RCP/BLYU. What seemed to matter most to Carson was that she would be spared Robert's insulting remarks about people whom he felt were inferior. RC to DF, March 30, April 12, 1955, *Letters*.
5. RC to PB, April 7, 1955; PB to RC, April 12, 1955, RCP/BLYU.
6. "My sister is Mrs. John Kieran and I've heard them speak affectionately of you." Anne Ford to RC, March 16, 1955, RCP/BLYU. Anne Ford had been a drama editor at the *Boston Herald* and then an advance agent for the Theatre Guild. She served as public relations director for Little, Brown and Company and Harcourt Brace before returning to Boston as director of publicity for Houghton Mifflin Company in 1953. Obituary, *Glouster Times*, November 18, 1993. Interview with Margaret Ford Kieran. Family Papers of Anne Ford, courtesy Margaret Ford Kieran. RC to DF, March 20, 1954, UP/FFC. RC to PB, April 27, 1955, RCP/BLYU.
7. RC to PB, May 8, 1955, RCP/BLYU.

8. Rachel Carson, speech at Houghton Mifflin Sales Conference, May 26, 1955, RCP/BLYU. RC to DF, January 14, 1955, UP/FFC.
9. RC to EWT, August 16, 1955, EWTP/UC. PB to RC, August 15, 1955, RCP/BLYU. RC to DF, June 12, 1955, *Letters*.
10. RC to DF, May 7, 1955, *Letters*. Carson's Wiscasset lecture was adapted from the one she had given at Cranbrook and at the D.C. Audubon Society with the addition of Freeman's latest slides. "Author Finds Maine Coast Ideal Lab to Give Talk"; "Author Rachel Carson to Lecture at Historical Assoc Benefit"; "Capacity crowd hears Rachel Carson tell of Marine Life"; lecture ticket, "Between Tide Lines on the Maine Coast"; advertisement from the "Smiling Cow," RCP/BLYU.
11. RC to MR, September 28, 1955, RCP/BLYU.
12. EWT to RC, August 22, 1955, EWTP/UC. Teale was referring to William Shawn's comments on reading Carson's original chapters.
13. RC to DF, September 18, 1955, UP/FFC.
14. RC to PB, September 30, 1955; MR to RC, October 6, 1955; Houghton Mifflin Publicity, RCP/BLYU.
15. MR to RC, October 6, 1955, RCP/BLYU.
16. Rachel Carson, *The Edge of the Sea* (Boston: Houghton Mifflin Co., 1955). To that published statement, Rachel wrote a special message on the inside title page:

    > As you turn these pages, may you remember always the world we shared—the fairy pool, the green sea caves, the smell of dripping rockweeds under early fog, anemones waiting for the tide's turning, the fragile beauty of the hydroid's flowers. Remember too, the gulls rosy-feathered at dawn, waterfowl in a sunset sky, the song of thrushes in spruce woods along our Island shores. And may these pages lead your thoughts to other shores we may explore together in the years of happy friendship ahead.

    Inscription, *The Edge of the Sea*, courtesy of Stanley Freeman, Jr.

17. Dorothy and Stanley Freeman to RC, October 26, 1955; DF to RC, October 26, 1955; RC to DF, October 26, 27, 1955, *Letters*.
18. RC to DF, October 29, 1955, *Letters*. N. J. Berrill, "The 'Drama-Filled Fringe,' " *Saturday Review of Literature*, December 3, 1955, 30. DF to RC, November 24, 1955, *Letters*. RC to N. J. Berrill, December 9, 1955, RCP/BLYU. RC to DF, December 27, 1955, UP/FFC.
19. RC to PB, September 30, 1955; MR to RC, September 30, 1955, RCP/BLYU. "Rachel Carson Given Honor by Science Museum," *Boston Daily Globe*, November 9, 1955, RCP/BLYU.
20. RC to DF, November 19, 1955, *Letters*. RC to DF, November 11, 1955, UP/FFC.
21. RC to DF, December 31, 1955, UP/FFC.
22. RC to DF, November 20, 24, 1955, *Letters*. *New York Times Best Seller List*, November 1955–November 1956, RCP/BLYU. Carson's book was on the list for a total of twenty-three weeks.
23. Robert Cushman Murphy, review of *The Edge of the Sea*, *New York Herald Tribune Book Review*, October 30, 1955, 3. John Norton Leonard, review of *The Edge of the Sea*, *New York Times Book Review*, October 30, 1955, 5. Jacquetta Hawkes, "The World Under Water," *The New Republic*, January 23, 1956, 17–18. Carson thought there were "elements of truth in her [Hawkes's] viewpoint, but also a strangely myopic complaint that I did not write the same book twice!" RC to DF, January 29,

1956, UP/FFC. Rachel Carson, *The Edge of the Sea* (Boston: Houghton Mifflin Co., 1955), viii. [Hereafter cited as EOS.]

24. *EOS*, vii–viii. Cheryll Glotfelty, "Rachel Carson," in John Elder, ed., *American Nature Writers*, vol. 1 (New York: Charles Scribner's Sons, 1996), 151–171. Vera Norwood, *Made From This Earth: American Women and Nature* (Chapel Hill: University of North Carolina Press, 1993), 143–171. Carol B. Gartner, *Rachel Carson* (New York: Frederick Ungar Publishing Co., 1983), 69–83. Mary A. McCay, *Rachel Carson* (New York: Twayne Publishers, 1993), 57.
25. William Hogan, "The Strange World at Water's Edge," *San Francisco Chronicle*, November 6, 1955, 16. Harry B. Ellis, "Between Pounding Surf and Dry Land," *Christian Science Monitor*, November 10, 1955, 8. Fanny Butcher, "Fabulous Cosmos at Sea's Edge," *Chicago Daily Tribune*, October 30, 1955, 3. Charles J. Rolo, "Reader's Choice," *Atlantic* (December 1955), 92.
26. Charles Poore, "Books of The Times," *New York Times*, October 26, 1955, 17.
27. Murphy, review of *EOS*, *New York Herald Tribune Book Review*, October 30, 1955, 3. "Marine Demimonde," *Time*, November 7, 1955, 128.
28. Henry B. Bigelow to RC, October 14, 1955, RCP/BLYU. Shirley Briggs, "The Edge of the Sea: A Review," *Atlantic Naturalist* 11, 2 (November/December 1955), 90.
29. RC to DF, November 27, 1955, *Letters*.
30. RC to Leon Powers, February 15, March 12, 1955, RCP/BLYU. Carson sent copies of her letters to Marie Rodell to handle if she was harassed further. When Carson reissued her check, the matter was resolved.
31. RC to DF, December 31, 1955, UP/FFC.
32. Interview with M. S. Wyeth, Jr., New York, NY. Harold Rosenberg, "The Woman Behind Great Thinkers," *Vogue* (August 1978), 5. Joann Giusto, "PW Interviews: Ruth Nanda Anshen," *Publishers Weekly*, January 9, 1978, 10–13. Interview with Ruth Nanda Anshen.
33. MR to RNA, February 27, 1953; RNA to RC, October 28, 1954; RC to RNA, November 11, 1954, RCP/BLYU. Carson had learned that British biologist Julian Huxley was about to publish two books on evolution. The origins of the contract with Anshen and Harper & Brothers remain unclear. Anshen's letter to Carson inviting her to contribute to the series states "only those spiritual and intellectual leaders who possess full consciousness of the pressing problems of our time with all their implications are invited to participate in the Series. Those who realize that the centrifugal force which has scattered and atomized humanity must be replaced by an integrating structure and process giving meaning and purpose to existence; those who accept the principle of individuality and universality, dynamics and form, freedom and destiny." RNA to RC, December 18, 1952, RCP/BLYU.
34. Rachel Carson, "Biological Sciences," in *Good Reading* (New York: New American Library, 1956). Draft in RCP/BLYU. The books Carson included in her bibliography reflect the richness and diversity she found in biology and include some titles that "stray over the line of 'pure' biology, and others that might be classed as natural history or 'literature.' " RC to J. Sherwood Weber, January 4, 1956, RCP/BLYU.
35. RC to DF, January 16, 1955; DF to RC, November 24, 1955, *Letters*.
36. RC to DF, November 26, 1955, UP/FFC. RC to PB, November 27, November 21, 1955, R/CA.
37. RC to PB, November 21, 1955, RCP/BLYU.
38. RC to DF, November 23, December 2, 1955, *Letters*. Carson particularly wanted to see Harvard biologist George Wald, who was working on the physiology of vision and its evolution.

39. RC to DF, April 13, 1956, February 2, 1956, *Letters*. RC to PB, March 3, 1953, RCP/BLYU.
40. " 'Omnibus' producer seeks one Robina Storm, an 8-year-old Miss with her head in the clouds." CBS Television Press Release, March 2, 1956. Department of CBS Audience Services, New York, NY. Storm had written, "Will you please put on your show something about the sky. I have herd [*sic*] so much about the sky. I am interested. I like your show very much. I am 8 years old." *Omnibus*, created by TV-Radio Workshop of The Ford Foundation, began broadcasting in November 1952.
41. RC to MR, November 29, 1955, RCP/BLYU. RC to DF, December 2, 15, 1955, *Letters*.
42. RC to MR, December 27, 1955, RCP/BLYU.
43. RC to Boris Kaplan, January 16, 1956, RCP/BLYU.
44. RC to DF, January 19, 1956, UP/FFC.
45. RC to DF, February 14, 1956, UP/FFC. RC to PB, February 25, 1956, RCP/BLYU. " 'Omnibus,' March 11," CBS Press Information, March 6, 1956. Carson's essay was the first of three segments on the show that evening, which marked the 100th broadcast of *Omnibus*.
46. "Something About the Sky," script notes in RCP/BLYU. RC to DF, April 8, 14, 1956, *Letters*.
47. RC to DF, April 17, 1956, UP/FFC.
48. RC to DF, April 18, 1956, *Letters*. Contract cards, R/CA. RC to DF, February 2, 1956, *Letters*.
49. RC to DF, February 25, 1956, *Letters*. See also Carson's earlier letters about the same subject: RC to DF, August 29, 1955, UP/FFC. DF to RC, October 26, 27, 1955, *Letters*.
50. DF to RC, October 26, 27, 1955, *Letters*. Carson was paying the rent on Marjie's house and helping her niece with medical bills. But Marjie needed physical help with household chores and child care and often was stricken without warning, leaving Rachel to cope with Roger. Mamma still refused personal care from anyone but Rachel, insisted that she could manage the household without outside help, and resisted all of Rachel's ideas for remodeling the house, including repainting the walls.
51. RC to Curtis Bok (hereafter cited as CB), March 12, 1956, RCP/BLYU.
52. RC to DF, March 15, 1956, April 8, 1956, *Letters*.
53. The passage appears on p. 47. DF to RC, April 11, 1956, *Letters*.
54. DF to RC, April 11, 1956, *Letters*.
55. Rachel Carson, holograph notes for "Help Your Child to Wonder," RCP/BLYU. Rachel Carson, "Help Your Child to Wonder," *Woman's Home Companion* 83 (July 1956), 25–27, 46–48.
56. Rachel Carson, "Help Your Child to Wonder," 46.
57. PB to RC, July 3, 1956, RCP/BLYU. Brooks deflects his own intense interest, making it seem as if the suggestion came from other publishers. Brooks, *The House of Life*, 201. RC to MR, January 22, 1959, RCP/BLYU. Carson seemed surprised by the reaction "Help Your Child to Wonder" evoked in her family, Dorothy, and Marie.
58. Deed of Gift, Rachel Carson to Marjorie W. Christie, May 3, 1956. Records of the R/CA.
59. CB to RC, October 28, 1955, RCP/BLYU. At the time Bok, who was president judge of the Pennsylvania Court of Common Pleas in Philadelphia, was recuperating from a mild heart attack. He was appointed associate judge of the Pennsylvania State Supreme Court in 1958. RC to DF, February 3, 1956, *Letters*. William Curtis

Bok, *Current Biography, 1954* (New York: H. W. Wilson Company, 1954), 99–100. "Curtis Bok," Obituary, *New York Times*, May 23, 1962.

60. RC to DF, March 12, 1956, *Letters*. RC to DF, n.d. [March 10, 1956] UP/FFC. Bok knew and enjoyed Herbert Kubly and suggested that he come for the same weekend, but Carson was unwilling to share her time. RC to DF, April 3, 1956, UP/FFC.
61. RC to Curtis and Nellie Lee Bok, May 1, 1956, RCP/BLYU.
62. RC to DF, May 1, 1956, UP/FFC. RC to DF/SF, May 1, 1956; RC to DF, May 2, 1956, *Letters*. Carson told Freeman that Bok reminded her a little of Hendrik van Loon, and in some ways the relationship proved a source of avuncular comfort for Carson.
63. RC to DF, April 21, 1956, UP/FFC. Mary Lou Succop Bell, who was still the motivating force behind the activities of the PCW class of 1929, kept in regular touch with Carson. Bell was a large contributor and no doubt encouraged Carson's selection for the award. Interview with Ruth Hunter Swisshelm.
64. Distinguished Alumnae Citation, May 10, 1956, Chatham College, Pittsburgh, PA. Carson's letter to Anderson, whom she liked and admired for what he had done for the college, reflects her now more amiable attitude toward her alma mater. RC to Paul R. Anderson, June 11, 1956, RCP/BLYU; RC to DF, May 12, 1956, UP/FFC.
65. RC to DF, June 23, 1956, *Letters*.
66. Rachel Carson, "Acceptance of AAUW Achievement Award," June 22, 1956, Washington, D.C., RCP/BLYU.
67. Ibid.
68. RC to CB, July 12, 1956, RCP/BLYU.
69. RC to DF and DF/SF, May 3, 6, 1956, UP/FFC. CB to RC, June 16, 1956, RCP/BLYU.
70. RC to DF, February 3, 28, 1956, *Letters*.
71. RC to DF, May 27, 1956, UP/FFC.
72. RC to DF, June 12, 1956, *Letters*.

13: "ONE MUST DREAM GREATLY"

1. Carson and Freeman adapted this name from one of H. M. Tomlinson's essays in *Out of Soundings* (1931), which Dorothy had first read aloud to Rachel in May 1954. See note 75 in *Letters*.
2. Freeman was stricken on July 27. An early diagnosis of diverticulitis was later revised to a bleeding ulcer. RC to DF, August 3, 7, UP/FFC. RC to Ethel Harvey, August 13, 1956, RCP/BLYU.
3. RC to the Freemans, August 8, 1956, *Letters*. RC to DF, August 8, 1956, UP/FFC. RC to DF, August 13, 1956, *Letters*.
4. RC to DF, September 1, 1956, UP/FFC. Dorothy met Marjie at the Boston station and helped her transfer from one train to the other on their return to Maryland. Rachel realized that eventually she would have to merge households in order to care for Marjie.
5. RC to DF, September 23, 1956, *Letters*.
6. Minutes of Meeting of Nine Persons Interested in Conservation, Wiscasset, ME, September 25, 1956, Maine Chapter, The Nature Conservancy, Brunswick, ME. I am indebted to Bruce Kidman, Executive Director, Maine Chapter, for finding these minutes and making them available to me. Carson's friend Richard Pough was then president of The Nature Conservancy.

7. It is clear from the minutes that Carson and Marston had discussed their strategy beforehand.
8. Minutes of Meeting, The Nature Conservancy, September 25, 1956.
9. In addition to Carson, the signers were Dorothea M. Marston, Charles P. Bradford, Mrs. John Parker, Christopher M. Packard, and Mrs. Paul Hannerman. The national organization dates from its incorporation in 1951. "The Nature Conservancy Historical Timeline," The Nature Conservancy Communications Office, Arlington, VA. Bruce Kidman to author, April 8, 1996. Carson kept the honorary office the rest of her life. RC to DF, September 23, 1956, *Letters*.
10. RC to Freemans, October 7, 1956, *Letters*. See RC to Richard Pough, August 7, 1950, RCP/BLYU. Carson read Olson's book in April 1956 and thereafter began a brief and complimentary exchange of letters with him about wilderness preservation. See RC to DF, April 17, 1956; RC to DF, December 13, 1956, UP/FFC. See RC to DF, April 21, 1954, *Letters*.
11. RC to DF, October 5, 1956, *Letters*. Carson's conversations about preservation with men like Lawrence Rockefeller were formal and professional and never on the intimate level that she enjoyed with Judge Bok.
12. *Bok Tower Gardens*, The American Foundation, 1981. Edward W. Bok, *America's Taj Mahal* (Lake Wales, FL: Bok Tower Gardens Foundation, 1989). Curtis Bok, "Memorandum," March 13, 1961, Archives of The American Foundation, Lake Wales, FL, courtesy The Bok Tower Gardens Library.
13. I am grateful to Derek Bok, Rachel Bok Goldman, and A. Margaret Bok for aiding my understanding of the Bok family philanthropy. Interviews with Derek Bok, Rachel Bok Goldman. RC to DF, November 15, 1956, *Letters*. See Johannes Leendert Kraabbendam, *The Model Man: The Life of Edward W. Bok* (Utrecht: privately published, 1995). Interview with Jonathan Shaw, Director, Bok Tower Gardens. Minutes of the Board of Directors, The American Foundation, November 9, 1956. Carson replaced Mary Louise Curtis Zimbalist, Bok's mother, on the board. CB to Board of Directors, September 21, 1956. Carson voted by proxy at the March 1957 meeting. Her letter of resignation was accepted by the board at a meeting on June 13, 1958, in Philadelphia. She gave as her reason "changes in her life due to adopting her grand-nephew and illness preventing her from taking an active interest." Minutes and Correspondence, Archives of The American Foundation, Lake Wales, FL, courtesy the Bok Tower Gardens Library.
14. See Paul Brooks, *The House of Life: Rachel Carson at Work* (Boston: Houghton Mifflin Co., 1972), 210–212. Brooks bases his view on Carson's letter to Bok about the Lost Woods in December 1956, but Carson's activities in preservation antedate this by at least a decade.
15. RC to MR, October 2, 1956, RCP/BLYU.
16. Ibid.
17. Ibid. RC to MR, October 4, 1956, RCP/BLYU.
18. SAB/L, October 31, 1956.
19. Interview with Ida Sprow. Sprow worked for Carson from November 1956 to July 1964. She remembers Maria Carson as a deeply religious woman who went about singing hymns as she worked. Ida had difficulty staying the night because of her own family but often accommodated Rachel by staying until after dinner. RC to DF, December 28, 1956, *Letters*.
20. RC to DF, December 1, 1956, *Letters*. Vishniac had proposed making a film of *The Edge of the Sea* and was trying to find financial backing for the project.
21. Ibid.
22. National Council of Women Citation, 1956 Book Award to Rachel L. Carson,

RCP/BLYU. Carson's brief remarks reflect the influence of Judge Bok's recent opinion of censorship.

23. Carson was disappointed not to have met Anne Morrow Lindbergh, who was not able to attend. Although they exchanged letters and both regretted the opportunity denied them, they never met. Their correspondence has not survived.
24. RC to DF, December 1, 1956, *Letters*. Anne Terry White did the adapting with Carson's approval and admiration.
25. RC to DF, n.d. [early December], 1956, UP/FFC.
26. RC to DF, December 5, 1956, *Letters*.
27. Ibid. RC to DF, December 8, 1956, *Letters*.
28. RC to DF, December 8, 1956, *Letters*.
29. Ibid.
30. Ibid. The more Carson thought about the anthology, the more she endowed it with some of the broad features she had previously proposed for the evolution book for Harper's World Perspectives.
31. RC to DF, December 8, 1956, *Letters*.
32. RC to Curtis and Nellie Lee Bok, December 12, 1956, RCP/BLYU.
33. RC to DF, December 18, 1956, UP/FFC.
34. Ibid. Interview with Stanley Freeman, Jr.
35. RC to MR, December 30, 1956, RCP/BLYU. See Brooks, *The House of Life*, 212. Brooks's view is understandable considering he was never involved in Carson's anthology project, nor did Carson seek his advice on its scope.
36. RC to DF, "For Christmas," 1956, *Letters*.
37. RC to DF, December 29, 1956, *Letters*.
38. RC to MR, January 9, 1957, R/CA.
39. RC to DF, January 7, 1957, *Letters*.
40. RC to MR, telegram, January 16, 1957, R/CA.
41. SAB/L, January 6, 1957.
42. RC to DF, January 24, 1957, *Letters*.
43. RC to DF, November 2, 1957, *Letters*. Marjorie's death was a result of a streptococcus infection. Filing of Letters Testamentary for the Estate of Marjorie W. Christie by Rachel L. Carson, February 26, 1957, Montgomery County, MD, Orphans Court, Rockville, MD. Carson had given Marjorie Christie publication rights to the junior edition of *The Sea Around Us* just before she died and now had to deal with it as part of Marjie's estate. Contract between Western Printing and Lithographing Co. to Marjorie W. Christie, January 17, 1957, R/CA.
44. Note 3, March 23, 1957, *Letters*.
45. Interviews with Roger Christie, Stanley L. Freeman, Jr., Jeanne Davis. Death notice, Marjorie W. Christie, January 31, 1957, Orphans Court, Montgomery County, MD. Interview with Ida Sprow. Sprow was surprised that Virginia King, Roger's aunt, did not offer to take him. Rachel did not tell her friends about Marjie's death. Shirley Briggs learned of it accidentally when she telephoned Rachel several weeks later on an unrelated matter. Interview with Shirley Briggs. SAB/L, February 10, 1957.
46. RC to PB, April 8, 1957, RCP/BLYU. This explanation was Carson's official account of Roger's family circumstances. Letters to Marie Rodell are missing, but it is clear that Rachel was in close contact with her about the situation. In all likelihood Rodell also came down to help.
47. The carport was later dropped in favor of a larger porch in the rear. The house was sited on the lot so that the front door opened to the woodland and was rarely used by anyone coming in the driveway. Rachel parked her car along the side of the house. Interviews with Jeanne Davis, Julia Ulrick.

48. RC to DF, March 28, 1957, *Letters*.
49. RC to DF, March 23, 28, 1957, *Letters*. Interviews with Stanley and Madeleine Freeman, Shirley Briggs, Roger Christie, Jeanne Davis, Martha Freeman.
50. RC to DF, March 28, 1957, *Letters*.
51. Ibid.
52. RC to DF, April 20, 1957, *Letters*.
53. RC to DF, April 22, 1957, *Letters*.
54. RC to MR, September 16, 1957, R/CA. Carson had purchased her Southport lot for just under $2,000 and based her bid on a conservatively figured estimate of land appreciation. The postwar land boom, however, had already driven the price of coastal land up substantially. It is not clear that she revealed her intent to create a sanctuary when she made her initial proposal. Interviews with Stanley L. Freeman, Jr., Ruth Gardner, Stanley Brower. Based on sales of other parts of the tract, Brower estimated the Tenggrens' asking price could well have been over $100,000.
55. RC to MR, June 14, 1958, R/CA.
56. RC to PB, September 4, 1957, RCP/BLYU. Carson's letter is intriguing because very probably she continued describing with some specificity just how burdensome her life had become now that she was responsible for Roger's care. But the remaining section of the paragraph has been excised with scissors, doubtless the protective censorship of Marie Rodell acting as literary executor before turning over the letter to the Beinecke Library. There is enough left of the letter to judge how low Carson's spirits were as she prepared to leave Maine, facing the reality of parenting a troubled and solitary child, and feeling completely frustrated that she had no time for herself or the writing she was longing to do. The excised portion of the letter probably revealed more about Roger's past than Rachel had previously told Brooks.
57. David Halberstam, *The Fifties* (New York: Villard Books, 1993), 623–628. The Soviet satellites were launched on October 4, and November 3, 1957. RC to DF, November 7, 1957, *Letters*.
58. Pete Daniel, "A Rogue Bureaucracy: The USDA Fire Ant Campaign of the Late 1950s," *Agricultural History* 64, 2 (spring 1990), 99–103. Daniel's germinal article elaborates a line of argument set forth initially by Thomas R. Dunlap, *DDT: Scientists, Citizens, and Public Policy* (Princeton, NJ: Princeton University Press, 1981), 36–37. Both Dunlap and Daniel stress the connection between the atomic bomb and chlorinated hydrocarbon pesticides and use the analogue of war as a means to access public policy pursued by a bureaucracy within the USDA. The most complete discussion of warfare against insects is Edmund P. Russell III, " 'Speaking of Annihilation': Mobilizing for War Against Human and Insect Enemies, 1914–1945," *Journal of American History* (March 1996), 1505–1529. Ernest Swift to Ezra Taft Benson, November 21, 1957, from the family of Irston Barnes, private papers.
59. Daniel, "Rogue Bureaucracy," 101. Ernest G. Moore, *The Agricultural Research Service* (New York: Frederick A. Praeger, 1967), 75–82.
60. The debate on the USDA's fire ant program can be followed in the records of the Agriculture Research Service, RG 310; of the Secretary of Agriculture, RG 16; and of the Fish and Wildlife Service, RG 22, National Archives and Records Administration. [Hereafter cited as NARA.] See Clarence Cottam's draft for Oscar Chapman to Charles F. Brannan, August 8, 1950, RG 22, (FWS) Entry 254, NARA. The scientific debate between entomologists is laid out by John H. Perkins, *Insects, Experts, and the Insecticide Crisis: The Quest for New Pest Management Strategies* (New York: Plenum, 1982), and the scientific debate among wildlife managers by Robert L. Rudd, *Pesticides and the Living Landscape* (Madison: University of Wisconsin Press, 1964). For a discussion of Carson's early involvement in pesticide issues, see Linda J. Lear, "Bombshell in Beltsville: The USDA and the Challenge of 'Silent Spring,' " *Agricultural History* 66, 2 (spring 1992), 151–159.

61. Carson had worked with Clarence Cottam and Elmer Higgins when they were writing scientific papers about the long-term consequences of DDT on wildlife after World War II. Marjorie Spock, June 26, 1957, on Long Island trial, quoted in newsletter of "The Committee of a Thousand," RCP/BLYU. Interview with Marjorie Spock.
62. Rodell thought *Life* magazine a better candidate for the seashore article, but Carson correctly assumed that the *Life* editors would not allow her to include an appeal for seashore preservation. Rodell had asked *Holiday* for a fee of $3,500, but Dick Field, production director, turned that down. Carson was paid $1,500 less commission to Rodell. RC to MR, Tuesday [n.d.]; Dick Field to MR, October 16, 1957, R/CA.
63. Dick Field to MR, October 21, 1957; RC to MR, October 26, 1957, R/CA.
64. RC to MR, October 26, 1957, RCP/BLYU. Brooks hoped Carson would expand the *Holiday* piece into a book on seashore preservation, an idea that appealed to Carson, who also considered doing a longer article for *The New Yorker*'s "Reporter at Large" column.
65. RC to DF, November 7, 1957, UP/FFC. She expanded on what she understood as her mission as a writer: "I consider my contributions to scientific fact far less important than my attempts to awaken an emotional response to the world of nature. I don't think straight scientific exposition is my 'contribution' to the world. It is, I agree, what you call lyricism." RC to DF, November 4, 5, 1957, *Letters*.
66. RC to DF, November 4, 5, December 2, 1957, *Letters*. MR to Richard Field, December 10, 1957, R/CA.
67. MR to RC, November 6, 1957, RCP/BLYU. Carson hired Mary Johnson to stay the night several weekends so Rachel could get some unbroken sleep. But she still could not get any sustained work done during the day. RC to DF, Wednesday, A.M. [January 1, 1958], *Letters*.
68. RC to DF, December 31, 1957, *Letters*.
69. Ibid.
70. RC to DF, Wednesday, A.M. [January 1, 1958], *Letters*.
71. Richard Field to MR, January 2, 1958; RC to MR, Saturday, n.d. [January 1958]; MR to RC, January 6, 1958, R/CA.
72. Harry Sions to MR, January 10, 1958; RC to MR, February 11, 1958, RCP/BLYU. MR to Harry Sions, January 13, 1958; RC to MR, January 29, 1958; R/CA. RC to MR, February 11, 1958, R/CA.
73. CB to RC, June 14, 1958, RCP/BLYU. Successor magazines regularly reprint parts of her article. See, for example, Rachel Carson, "The Shores of Autumn," *Travel Holiday* 173 (October 1990), 130.
74. Rachel Carson, "Our Ever-Changing Shore," *Holiday* 24 (July 1958), 71–120.
75. RC to DF, February 1, 1958, *Letters*.
76. Ibid.
77. Ibid.
78. Ibid. The context of this letter includes a rare discussion with Freeman of religion in which Carson admitted, "of course part of my trouble is finding anything definite I can really feel is true. But I am sure, there is a great and mysterious force that we don't, and perhaps can never understand." See RC to DF, Wednesday, A.M. [January 1, 1958], *Letters*.

14: "I SHALL RANT A LITTLE, TOO"

1. RC to Harold Lynch, July 15, 1945, RCP/BLYU. Carson used the same language in 1958 as she had in 1945: "The experiments at Patuxent have been planned to show . . . whether it may upset the whole delicate balance of nature if unwisely used." Clarence Cottam and Elmer Higgins, "DDT and Its Effect on Fish and Wildlife" (Washington, D.C.: Government Printing Office, 1946). Their article was based on the wildlife research going on at Patuxent, which was well established by 1945. See Joseph P. Linduska and Eugene W. Surber, "Effects of DDT and Other Insecticides on Fish and Wildlife, Summary of Investigations During 1947" (Washington, D.C.: Government Printing Office, 1947). The fieldwork summarized in this FWS bulletin included that done by William and Lucille Stickel, John L. George, Chandler Robbins, and Allan Duvall. Carson also had read certain military reports on the use of DDT, particularly in the Pacific Islands during the war and immediately after, as well as studies done by E. F. Knipling and his group at the Orlando Research Laboratory. See E. F. Knipling et al., "DDT and Other Insecticides and Repellents Developed for the Armed Forces," USDA Bulletin #606 (August 1946). John H. Perkins summarizes this research in "Reshaping Technology in Wartime: The Effect of Military Goals on Entomological Research and Insect-Control Practices," *Technology and Culture* 19, 2 (April 1978), 169–186. Carson's view of nature was a classical one in which the concept of a balance was central to its operation and maintenance.
2. I use the term "pesticides" to include all categories of synthetic chemical toxins. Beginning in 1957, Carson more often used the term "insecticides," but she changed her terminology gradually after 1960. By "insecticides" she meant that whole category of chemicals used against agents that society considered "pests."
3. The writing of what came to be *Silent Spring* can be usefully divided into two distinct stages. The first consists of Carson's research and writing from the spring of 1958 to the spring of 1960, when she gathered most of the evidence. The second, from the spring of 1960 to the spring of 1962, encompassed an enforced incubation of her ideas from which emerged a much enlarged critique of contemporary science and society.
4. These articles formed the basis for William F. Longgood, *The Poisons in Your Food* (New York: Simon & Schuster, 1960).
5. As he was the best known of the group, Murphy lent his name to the suit even though he did not initiate it. Interviews with Marjorie Spock, Roland Clement. The committee raised money as well as advised on expert testimony. Mrs. Hugo R. B. Newman to Roger Hinds, January 21, 1958, RCP/BLYU.
6. Beatrice Trum Hunter, "Aerial Spray Program Imperils Wildlife," *Boston Sunday Herald*, January 12, 1958, sec. 3, 2.
7. Carson and Huckins sometimes had lunch together when Carson was in Boston, and Huckins called Carson when she was in Washington. Olga was a cat lover as well as literary critic, book reviewer, and writer. She was also fond of Rachel's mother, whom she inaccurately but affectionately called "Lady Marie."
8. Olga Huckins to RC, January 27, 1958, RCP/BLYU.
9. R. C. Codman, "Prefers DDT Control to Moths, Mosquitoes," *Boston Herald*, January 16, 1958, sec. 3, 28.
10. Huckins to RC, January 27, 1958, RCP/BLYU. "Olga Owens," in *Who's Who of American Women*, vol. 2 (Chicago: A. N. Marquis Company, 1958, 1962). "Olga Owens Huckins," Obituary, *Boston Herald Traveler*, July 10, 1968, 12. Obituary, *Boston Globe*, July 10, 1968, 39. Huckins and her husband were politically well connected, but she wanted more facts before she wrote the governor. Huckins did not

ask Carson to help her, and Carson did not reply to her letter. This point is important in light of the near-legendary status of the later story that Huckins had begged Carson to find someone in Washington to help stop the spraying, in the course of which her interest in pesticides began. Here my intention is to correct Huckins's role in the origins of the book that became *Silent Spring* as reported by Paul Brooks, *The House of Life: Rachel Carson at Work* (Boston: Houghton Mifflin Co., 1972), 233, and by Frank Graham, Jr., *Since Silent Spring* (Boston: Houghton Mifflin Co., 1970), 1–18, and repeated endlessly by others. Carson acknowledged Huckins's role in bringing her attention "sharply back to a problem with which I had long been concerned" in her acknowledgments to *Silent Spring*. It is important to put Carson's own early inquiries in proper sequence and context.

11. Olga Owens Huckins, "Evidence of Havoc by DDT Air Spraying," *Boston Herald*, January 29, 1958, sec. 3, 14.
12. MR to RC, January 23, 1958; Dolores Gentile to RC, February 16, 1958, R/CA. Gentile was Marie Rodell's secretary and assistant. Durwood Allen, "What Pesticides Mean to Our Hunting and Fishing," draft, RCP/BLYU. Allen joined FWS in Maryland in 1946 and became assistant chief of the Branch of Wildlife Research in the Washington, D.C., FWS office in 1951. He had been president of the Wildlife Society and in 1957 became a distinguished professor of wildlife biology at Purdue University. William F. Longgood, "DDT Found in Air Month After Spraying," *New York World-Telegram and Sun*, August 7, 1957, RCP/BLYU.
13. W. L. Popham to RC, January 28, 1958, Regulatory Crops, Fire Ant, RG 310, ARS, NARA. Popham sent Carson a number of the latest ARS research bulletins and press releases on the fire ant and gypsy moth program and invited her to stop by the department to see photographs of crop devastation caused by fire ants. See my discussion of the Carson-Popham correspondence in Lear, "Bombshell in Beltsville: The USDA and the Challenge of 'Silent Spring,'" *Agricultural History* 66 (spring 1992), 159.
14. RC to MR, January 27, 1958; RC to DeWitt Wallace, January 27, 1958, R/CA. It is important to note that Carson's letter to Marie was written on the same day that Huckins wrote to Carson; hence it reflected the results of Carson's own inquiries, which predated Huckins's letter by at least two weeks.
15. Senior editor Walter B. Mahoney acknowledged Carson's letter in Wallace's absence, assuring her "we shall weigh all facts at hand in this situation before publishing a gypsy moth story." Walter Mahoney to RC, January 30, 1958, RCP/BLYU. Rodell had also learned that a regular staff writer at *Life* was preparing an article on pesticide spraying and that *McCall's* had dropped a piece on the subject because it could not get medical authorities to agree on whether the spraying was dangerous to humans. *McCall's* expressed some interest in reviving the article if Carson would write it. Rodell also learned that the Conservation Foundation was reluctant to circulate its pesticide report because they did not want it used as a basis for popular magazine articles. "Are they crazy?" Marie naively wondered aloud to Rachel, who was becoming more aware of the political and economic pressures such publicity would generate. MR to RC, January 28, 1958, RCP/BLYU.
16. Carson's choice of E. B. White, whom she had never met but whose *New Yorker* articles she admired, was based on his known love of nature and in particular their shared love of Maine. Graham is in error in suggesting that White's column influenced Carson. "These Precious Days" first appeared in *The New Yorker* on May 16, 1959. Graham, *Since Silent Spring*, 18. See Carson's comments about the Long Island case in *Silent Spring* (Boston: Houghton Mifflin Co., 1962), 158–159. To my knowledge, neither Carson nor Rodell made any attempt to contact William Long

good, who was already covering the trial and would have been a natural collaborator. The most likely explanation for this rather obvious omission is that they were aware that Longgood already intended to write a book on the subject. See Marjorie Spock's impassioned suggestion that Carson contact Longgood, MS to RC, June 6, 1958, RCP/BLYU.

17. RC to MR, February 2, 1958, R/CA. This letter and the accompanying memorandum summarizing her investigation was written the day before her letter to E. B. White. Carson's view from the outset was that more than one article on the subject could be written to good advantage. Marie Rodell corrected Brooks's original account, telling him in 1971 "It [the spray controversy] triggered her calling me to say I ought to get one of my clients, *not* Rachel, to write an article on the subject. Then a few days letter she decided she would do the article." MR to PB, January 11, 1971, R/CA.
18. MR to PB, January 11, 1971, R/CA.
19. Rachel Carson, "Memorandum on the effect of commonly used insecticides on man and animals," February 2, 1958, R/CA. In this memorandum Carson uses the terms "pesticides," "insecticides," and "chemical poisons" interchangeably.
20. RC to E. B. White, February 3, 1958, RCP/BLYU.
21. Ibid. "DDT" in "Talk of the Town," *The New Yorker*, May 26, 1946, 18. In this remarkable article, White warns "If DDT should ever be used widely and without care, we would have a country without fresh-water fish, serpents, frogs, and most of the birds we have now. Mind you, we don't object to its use to save lives now. What we're afraid of is what might happen when peace comes." White discussed the use of DDT in the South Pacific and quotes interviews with Edwin Way Teale and Richard Pough, who both expressed alarm over the peacetime application of DDT. There is no indication that Carson knew of White's 1946 editorial when she wrote her 1958 letter to him.
22. See Graham's speculation on this question in *Since Silent Spring*, 18–19. Graham did not know Carson had already committed herself to writing something on the subject. See Brooks, *The House of Life*, 236–237.
23. White responded, "The whole vast subject of pollution, of which this Gypsy Moth business is just a small part, is of the utmost interest and concern to everybody. It starts in the kitchen and extends to Jupiter and Mars. Always some special group or interest is represented, never the earth itself." E. B. White to RC, February 7, 1958, RCP/BLYU.
24. Carson had learned of Spock's involvement from Longgood's newspaper articles.
25. MS to RC, February 5, 1958, RCP/BLYU. Interview with Marjorie Spock.
26. Interviews with Marjorie Spock, Frank and Ada Graham, Jr. The Grahams are friends and near neighbors of Spock and the late Mary Richards.
27. Interview with Marjorie Spock.
28. Ibid. Marjorie Spock to the Committee of a Thousand, June 26, 1957, RCP/BLYU. Richards was willing to use her considerable wealth to pay the legal costs of the trial and related expenses, including expert witnesses and a transcript of the testimony. Mary Richards died in 1991.
29. Interview with Marjorie Spock. During the course of the trial, Spock became disillusioned with what she considered underhanded procedures and tactics used by the federal government. *Robert C. Murphy* v. *Ezra Taft Benson*, U.S. District Court, Eastern District of New York, May 24, 1957, 1511 F. Supp. 786. *Murphy et al.* v. *Benson et al.*, U. S. Court of Appeals. Second Circuit. Brief for Defendant-Appellee Butler. #25,448, March 1959. The court's summary can be found in U.S. District Court, Eastern District of New York, Robert Cushman Murphy et al., and Archi-

bald B. Roosevelt et al. Plaintiffs, against Ezra Taft Benson, etc., et al., Defendants, Civil No. 17610, June 23, 1958. Supreme Court of the United States, October Term. 662, *Robert Cushman Murphy et al.*, v. *Butler et al.* Dissenting opinion, March 28, 1960, of Mr. Justice Douglas upon the denial of petition for Writ of Certiorari to the United States Court of Appeals, Second Circuit.

30. Interviews with Marjorie Spock.
31. Spock and Richards had translated Breijer's article from the original Dutch. Breijer's research excited Carson, who thought it went to the heart of the insect control problem and wrote to him immediately. The ensuing correspondence was central to Carson's understanding of the problem. The trial transcript was a treasure trove of material, which Carson recognized from the outset. R. C. Murphy to PB, telegram, February 25, 1958, R/CA. Arrangements were made subsequently to have a copy available to Carson's editorial assistant in New York. R. C. Murphy to RC, March 28, 1958; RC to MS, March 14, 1958; RC to MS, March 19, 1958, RCP/BLYU.
32. MS to RC, February 15, 1958; RC to MS, March 14, 1958, RCP/BLYU. C. J. Breijer, "The Growing Insensitivity of Insects to Insecticides," Trans. M. Spock and M. T. Richards, *Mededelingen Directeur van de Tuinbouw*, New York: 1956. Breijer's article not only confirms the rapidly developing resistance of many insects to insecticides but argues that the failure to develop effective controls was caused by the faulty, overmechanical techniques of the specialists and their lack of understanding of the life cycles of living creatures. Breijer's article was later published in the *Atlantic Naturalist* 13, 3 (July/September 1958), 149–155, at Carson's suggestion. Biskind had studied diseases caused by chemicals used in dry cleaning, becoming ill himself from toxic exposure. Hargraves was an expert witness, Biskind attended but did not testify, and George's field studies were admitted as expert evidence. George had previously worked as a consultant at various federal agencies. Interviews with John L. George.
33. Rodell's queries were based on Carson's February 2 memorandum. MR to Biffie Page, February 5, 1958; MR to Maggie Cousins, February 21, 1958; RC to MR, February 11, 1958; A. A. Schaal & R. R. Bien, Good Housekeeping Bureau, to Herbert Mayes, February 26, 1958, RCP/BLYU.
34. The Delaney Committee hearings of 1950 and 1951 and the resulting Miller Amendment focused on pesticide residues in food and recommended stronger FDA regulation, including the establishment of tolerance levels. It legitimized the use of pesticides by establishing legal doses that were thought to be insignificant. The oversight of pesticides registration, however, remained with USDA, which was firmly in control of administering the Federal Insecticide, Fungicide, and Rodenticide Act of 1947, otherwise known as FIFRA. See Christopher J. Bosso, *Pesticides and Politics: The Life Cycle of a Public Issue* (Pittsburgh: University of Pittsburgh Press, 1987), 21–78.
35. RC to PB, February 21, 1958, RCP/BLYU. Later she sent the same proposal to Brooks that she had sent to Shawn. Rachel Carson, proposal for article on insecticides, n.d. [February 1958], R/CA.
36. Carson uses several versions of this quotation from a letter from Albert Schweitzer to a French apiarist. Its source has been the subject of heated discussion. This proposal represents her first use of it, although even here, she leaves out the last sentence, which reads "Poor bees, poor birds, poor men . . ." The incomplete passage from Schweitzer's letter was published in the December 1956 issue of the *Bulletin of the International Union for the Conservation of Nature and Natural Resources*, which

Marjorie Spock sent to Carson along with many other clippings. Undoubtedly the reason why Carson never documented the citation when she used it in even briefer form as part of her dedication of *Silent Spring* to Albert Schweitzer is because the *IUCN Bulletin* failed to quote it in full or to supply the name of Schweitzer's French correspondent. See *Bulletin* in RCP/BLYU.

I am indebted to the research of the late Adele "Nicki" Wilson, whose files of *IUCN Bulletins* were incomparable, and grateful to her for sharing her many "networks," and to Ann Cotrell Free whose journalistic sleuthing also uncovered the same source.

37. *IUCN Bulletin* (December 1956), RCP/BLYU. There is no record of Shawn's response, but Rodell's letter to Lovell Thompson of March 21, 1958, indicates that Carson had agreed to prepare an article for *The New Yorker*. It would have been typical of William Shawn to indicate he wanted an article from Carson without specifying terms until much later.
38. RC to MR, March 1, 1958, RCP/BLYU.
39. MR to RC, February 26, 1958, RCP/BLYU.
40. Lovell Thompson to PB, March 3, 1958; MR to PB, March 4, 1958, RCP/BLYU.
41. Edwin Diamond, "The Myth of the 'Pesticide Menace,'" *Saturday Evening Post* September 28, 1963, 16, 18.
42. Rodell probably saw Diamond's byline in *Newsweek*. MR to Edwin Diamond, May 5, 1958, RCP/BLYU. Interview with Edwin Diamond.
43. Interview with Edwin Diamond. RC to MS, March 26, 1958, RCP/BLYU.
44. RC to MS, March 26, 1958, RCP/BLYU. MR to Lovell Thompson, March 21, 1958, R/CA. Rodell's letters to Thompson are unusually vague about how the collaboration would work. The fact that Rodell consistently mistook Diamond's given name is indicative of her rare inattention to detail.
45. RC to MS, March 26, 1958, RCP/BLYU. Interview with Edwin Diamond. Carson was vague about the particulars of what she wanted a collaborator to do from the beginning.
46. RC to DF, April 2, 1958, *Letters*. Carson first mentioned the "poison-spray" material to Freeman on February 8, 1958. The dearth of letters between February and April testifies to Carson's absorption in her new project and also to the tension the project caused between them. Freeman found the subject matter genuinely distasteful, referring to the book as "Rachel's poison-book," a term Carson found objectionable. Carson intentionally diminished the importance of Shawn's call, casually telling Freeman, "This will greatly increase its impact, so I'm glad of that. Also, they will of course pay more, and since I'd be doing as much for the book anyway, that's good!"
47. RC to MR, April 3, 1958, R/CA. RC to DF, April 2, 3, 1958, *Letters*.
48. Paul Brooks, "Report to the Executive Committee, K5040. 'The Control of Nature' (working title)," Rachel Carson and Edward Diamond [*sic*], April 1, 1958; RC to PB, April 20, 1958, RCP/BLYU.
49. Diamond has no particular memory of this meeting. Interview with Edwin Diamond. Carson's letters to Rodell show that Carson was dissatisfied over the inequity of time and labor, and with the possible division of subsidiary rights. Here I do not mean to minimize her unhappiness at what she saw as an unfair and unfortunate division. She was always sensitive about financial remuneration, but the financial terms of the contract obscured the real source of Carson's discontent over the whole idea of collaboration. RC to MR, April 9, 1958, RCP/BLYU.
50. RC to MR, April 14, 1958, R/CA.
51. RC to MR, April 14, 1958, RCP/BLYU. Two weeks had passed since Carson had

heard from Diamond, who had said he would call to discuss his reading of the trial testimony. Gertrude Rodenhiser to MR, April 1, 1958; MR to Gertrude Rodenhiser, May 1, 2, 1958, RCP/BLYU. Interview with Edwin Diamond.

52. MR to Edwin Diamond, May 5, 1958, RCP/BLYU. Rodell's letter is the only indication of what kind of material Diamond might have collected. Contract between Rachel Carson and Houghton Mifflin for a book tentatively titled "The Control of Nature," May 22, 1958. Ledgerbook, R/CA. Diamond has no recollection of asking for reconsideration. He recalls that their approach to the subject matter was entirely different. He was scientifically detached about pesticides, Carson was not. Interview with Edwin Diamond. Joan Daves to Edwin Diamond, May 9, 1958, R/CA.
53. Joan Daves to RC, May 20, 1958; PB to Edwin Diamond, May 26, 1958; Joan Daves to Margaret Minahan, June 11, 1958; Margaret Minahan to Joan Daves, June 12, 1958; MS to RC, June 6, 1958, RCP/BLYU. Spock shipped down the three volumes by railway express, insuring it for $10,000. Her letter is an important summary of her personal experience as a witness and her disillusionment with the government's tactics and witnesses. PB, telegram to Edwin Diamond, June 9, 1958; PB to Joan Daves to Margaret Minahan, June 11, 1958; Edwin Diamond to PB, June 24, 1958, RCP/BLYU. Diamond's material arrived at Houghton Mifflin on June 30 and was never forwarded to Rodell or Carson. Margaret Minahan to Joan Daves, June 30, 1958, RCP/BLYU. Brooks's pencil jottings during his conversation with Diamond indicate that "legal recourse" was mentioned and that Brooks made clear that Diamond had been more than paid for the work he did. PB, pencil notes, R/CA. Brooks returned Diamond's material to him with a note saying he had not forwarded it on to Carson since he was sure she already had it in her files. PB to Edwin Diamond, July 21, 1958, RCP/BLYU. Diamond responded, "Someday, I would like to make clear the other side in this mess." Edwin Diamond to PB, June 24, 1958, RCP/BLYU. Interview with Edwin Diamond.
54. The contract was signed on August 19, 1958, and Carson was paid an advance of $3,000. The royalty terms remained the same as they had been when Diamond was a coauthor. Royalties were to accrue until publication, but Carson could draw down a portion after a year. Gertrude Rodenhiser to MR, July 28, 1958; Margaret Minahan to MR, August 21, 1958, R/CA. See Brooks, *The House of Life*, 239. RC to MR, September 11, 1958; MR to RC, October 1, 1958; Maria Leiper to MR, November 21, 1958, R/CA. Dorothy Algire had returned to government employment in 1956 as a biologist at the National Cancer Institute in cancer and chemotherapy and worked in the Literature Research Section, eventually becoming the head of that group, but she was unavailable to Carson for daily assistance. Dorothy H. Algire, FPR/OPM. Curriculum Vita, Dorothy H. Algire, Courtesy of the Family of Dorothy H. Algire. Carson also hired a young man from George Washington University for a brief time, but for whatever reason, he did not continue on the job for long. Interview with Bette Haney Duff. I am grateful to the Reverend Duff for sharing letters and other material about her employment with Carson.
55. Interview with Bette Haney Duff.
56. Ibid. While she was in Maine that summer, Rachel had time to read Bette's notes and research summaries. When she returned home in September, Rachel telephoned Bette before she went back to Bryn Mawr to say how much she appreciated her careful notes and fine summaries.
57. Interview with Bette Haney Duff.
58. Ibid.
59. RC to DF, June 12, 1958, *Letters*. Shawn may have given Carson a copy of White's column for "Talk of the Town" at this meeting. Pough, Teale, and Ray Fosberg were

all scientists who had written immediately after the war about the dangers DDT posed to the natural order if used domestically. Fosberg had first talked to Carson about the impact of DDT on the South Pacific atolls when she was writing *The Sea Around Us*. The importance of Carson's early and continuing association with these scientists cannot be underestimated. John K. Terres's 1946 article for *The New Republic*, "Dynamite in DDT," 114, March 25, 1946, 415–416, also belongs in this category of early essays, although it is doubtful if Carson read it when it was published.

60. RC to DF, June 28, 1958, *Letters*.
61. RC to DF, July 5, 7, 1958, *Letters*.
62. Rachel employed one of Dorothy's younger friends to take care of Roger several days a week, but that barely gave her enough time to keep up with her correspondence. RC to DF, July 9, 1958, *Letters*.
63. RC to DF, August 22, 1958, *Letters*.
64. Beverly Knecht [hereafter cited as BK] to RC, July 22, 1958; RC to BK, October 1, 1958, RCP/BLYU. Carson suggested Knecht get her earlier books in Braille or from Talking Books and talked about creating images in words. Knecht wrote on a Braille typewriter.
65. Crisler's first letter to Carson is missing.
66. RC to Lois Crisler [hereafter cited as LC], September 24, 1958, RCP/BLYU.
67. Robert L. Rudd and Richard Genelly, "Pesticides: Their Use and Toxicity in Relation to Wildlife," *California Department of Fish and Game Bulletin*, no. 7 (1956). Richard E. Genelly and Robert L. Rudd, "Chronic Toxicity of DDT, Toxaphene, and Dieldrin to Ring-Necked Pheasants," *California Fish and Game* 42, 1 (1956). Robert Rudd [hereafter cited as RR] to RC, April 17, 1958, RCP/BLYU. Interviews with Robert Rudd. Rudd has generously given his time and shared his professional papers, his knowledge of the field, and patiently answered my questions.
68. RC to RR, April 27, 1958, RCP/BLYU.
69. RR to RC, May 5, 1958, RCP/BLYU. Interview with Robert Rudd. At the time of this first exchange, Rudd was an instructor in zoology and junior zoologist in the USDA Agricultural Experimental Station at UC Davis. He had earned his Ph.D. in wildlife biology at the University of California at Berkeley and had been given a full-year fellowship from the Conservation Foundation to carry out research for what became *Pesticides and the Living Landscape* (Madison, WI: Wisconsin University Press, 1964). Rudd told Carson, "It was my pleasure to hear of your current thoughts on the chemicals-balance of nature theme. I quite agree that there is an opportunity for many authors to explore this area. And I think we will find a favorable public reception."
70. Interview with Robert Rudd. Rudd thought Maria Carson was a very domineering woman and a "tough lady." Rudd's book, *Pesticides and the Living Landscape*, was his ticket to tenure. He finished it in 1962, but its publication was delayed by University of Wisconsin Press, while the entire entomology department and then the president's office reviewed it. His tenure decision was postponed until the book appeared in 1964, but Rudd was relieved of his appointment at the UC Davis/USDA Agricultural Experimental Station because of his writings and not reinstated until some years later.
71. RC to DF, August 29, 1958, *Letters*. Interview with Marjorie Spock.
72. Interview with Marjorie Spock. Marjorie Spock with Polly Richards, "Portrait of Rachel," 1964, unpublished, RCP/BLYU. Spock and Richards's typescript in author's possession.
73. Spock with Richards, "Portrait of Rachel."
74. Interview with Marjorie Spock. Enormously observant of people, Spock noted that

Rachel's reserve was so great that she could not permit herself many changes of reaction. She also sized up Mrs. Carson as an "innocent powerhouse," who was both domineering and controlling. It was not until a month later that Rachel suggested they begin to use their given names.

75. RC to MS, September 15, 1958, RCP/BLYU. Spock and Carson had much in common, both sharing the care of elderly mothers and the love of the same part of Maine. Spock's broad intellect, her independence of life and spirit, and her high passion about the dangers of pesticides energized Carson. RC to MS, October 17, 1958, RCP/BLYU. The last letter Maria Carson wrote was to Marjorie Spock, on November 6, 1958; MS to RC, September 26, 1958, RCP/BLYU. Spock's frequent and very amusing letters to "Jolly Roger," as she called him, recounted canoeing down the Penobscot River and sharing her picnic lunch with a bear.
76. RC to DF, August 30, 1958, *Letters*. Spock's experience as an organic farmer gave Carson contacts and resources that would have been unavailable to her otherwise. RC to Malcolm Hargraves, April 14, 1958; Malcolm Hargraves to RC, April 30, 1958, RCP/BLYU.
77. Carson had already received many of George's papers from Marjorie Spock.
78. Edward O. Wilson to RC, October 7, 1958, RCP/BLYU. Although Fairfield Osborn had led Carson to Robert Rudd, he did not send Carson George's pamphlet until she specifically asked for it. Carson's correspondence with Wilson is important because it substantiates that from the beginning of her research she wanted to present positive, alternative methods of pest control. RC to E. O. Wilson, October 17, 1958, RCP/BLYU.
79. Interview with John L. George. Carson was careful not to contact George directly very often, only telephoning or dropping by the office occasionally, but she kept informed about his research.
80. Carson initiated correspondence with key scientists on the following dates: Morton Biskind, March 30, 1958; Malcolm Hargraves, April 14, 1958; C. J. Breijer, April 15, 1958; Robert Rudd, April 20, 1958; E. O. Wilson, October 7, 1958; Clarence Cottam, November 18, 1958; Harold Peters, June 29, 1959; George J. Wallace, December 7, 1959; Joseph Hickey, February 7, 1960, RCP/BLYU.
81. RC to MS, June 30, 1958, RCP/BLYU.
82. RC to PB, April 20, 1958, RCP/BLYU.
83. Interviews with Shirley Briggs, Harold Peters, F. Raymond Fosberg, Roland Clement, Edward Knipling.
84. RC to EWT, October 12, 1958, EWTP/UC.
85. RC to PB, September 11, 1958, RCP/BLYU.
86. RC to PB, September 24, 1958, RCP/BLYU. Carson had attended a D.C. Audubon committee meeting at the National Museum where John Aldrich, a FWS ornithologist who also worked at the Smithsonian, commented on the discussion Breijer's article had provoked among his colleagues.
87. RC to EWT, October 12, 1968, EWTP/UC. RC to MS, October 17, 1958, RCP/BLYU. An article in *Life* on insect control using hormones had exaggerated the benefits of such a course, but Carson was in correspondence with the scientists who had been cited and thought that "it is one straw that shows that the wind is beginning to veer away from chemicals as now used." Ibid.
88. RC to MS, November 6, 1958, RCP/BLYU.
89. Cottam and Benson were both high-ranking officials of the Church of Jesus Christ of the Latter Day Saints and had personal as well as professional ties.
90. RC to Clarence Cottam [hereafter cited as CC], November 18, 1958, RCP/BLYU. Cottam's tone with Carson was often somewhat paternal, which gives the

impression that he was considerably older than she; in fact, he was only eight years her elder.

91. CC to RC, November 21, 1958, RCP/BLYU.
92. RC to DF, December 4, 1958, *Letters*.
93. Interview with Ida Sprow. Death notice, "Maria M. Carson," *Washington Post*, December 2, 1958. Maria Carson had made a will just before leaving for Maine in July 1958. In it she left all her personal property to Rachel and named their attorney, Richard Huhn, as alternate executor. She left no estate to probate. Last Will and Testament of Maria M. Carson, Registrar of Wills, Orphans Court, Montgomery County, MD.
94. "I wish you could have known her better," she told Marjorie, "but I'm happy you had the little exchange of correspondence recently. And your warm and understanding letter to me, chiefly about Roger, came after my mind had been filled with apprehension, but I was still free enough to read it with deep gratitude for your affectionate comprehension of the problem. So few understand. I wish I had known you sooner." RC to MS, December 4, 1958, RCP/BLYU.
95. RC to MS, December 4, 1958, RCP/BLYU; RC to DF, "Christmas, 1958," *Letters*.

15: "THE RED QUEEN"

1. Clarence Cottam had responded to Carson's letter just after Maria Carson died. When Rachel replied she told him "We had been very close all my life and this leaves a great emptiness so that I am only now able to resume my work." RC to CC, January 8, 1959, RCP/BLYU. With a certain toughness that Carson needed, Cottam responded, "I knew that you and your mother were very close and my heart, therefore, goes out in sympathy despite the fact these are realities of life we all must face one time or another." CC to RC, January 12, 1959, RCP/BLYU.
2. RC to MS, February 12, 1959, RCP/BLYU.
3. RC to William Shawn [and PB], February 14, 1959, RCP/BLYU.
4. Ibid.
5. Ibid.
6. PB to RC, February 13, 1959, RCP/BLYU. Peterson had heard George Wallace's paper, "The Greatest Threat to Life on Earth," at the 1958 National Audubon convention and had taken up the cause. Roland Clement to author, January 4, 1996.
7. RC to PB, February 14, 1959, RCP/BLYU.
8. Marginal notes by Paul Brooks and Lovell Thompson on RC to PB, February 14, 1959.
9. Ibid. RC to MS, February 12, 1959, RCP/BLYU.
10. RC to PB, February 14, 1959; RC to CC, January 19, 1959, RCP/BLYU.
11. RC to CC, January 19, 1959; RC to MS, February 12, 1959; RC to CC, January 8, 1959, RCP/BLYU. Spock had filled Carson in on the pressures that Hargraves and especially Morton Biskind had suffered and applauded her decision not to participate. Carson told Cottam, "I may seem unduly cautious, but from all I know of the extremely powerful pressures that can be applied and from advice given me by those in position to know, I think it wise to keep my project under wraps just as long as possible." RC to CC, January 19, 1959, RCP/BLYU.
12. RC to CC, January 19, 1959; RC to PB, March 3, 1959, RCP/BLYU. Carson told Brooks her visit with Dr. Hargraves made the whole trip worthwhile. The Memphis Garden Club led the campaign against the USDA eradication. Hargraves spoke at their January 16 meeting, as did Robert Cushman Murphy and Harold Peters. Peters

sent Carson an account of the meeting, RCP/BLYU. SAB/D, March 1, 1959. MS to RC, February 22, 1959; MS to RC, March 3, 1959; MS to RC, March 7, 1959, RCP/BLYU. Carson hoped to take Roger with her to visit the Spock/Richards farm during the boy's Easter break from school in March, but once again illness kept her from doing so.

13. Biskind had become sensitized to DDT during his work in dry-cleaning establishments, where he had been doing chemical experiments on workers' blood. Widely accused of distorting and misrepresenting the facts in his scientific papers, he was abused by his fellow scientists. Carson viewed him as "a casualty in the fight against the unwise uses of chemicals." Like Spock, she had checked Biskind's citations and found his research absolutely reliable. Carson spoke with him often by telephone during this period. RC to CC, February 9, 1959, RCP/BLYU. Interview with Marjorie Spock.
14. RC to CC, March 18, 1959, RCP/BLYU. Pete Daniel, "A Rogue Bureaucracy: The USDA Fire Ant Campaign of the Late 1950s," *Agricultural History* 64 (spring 1990), 107–109. See my discussion of the controversy and Carson's role in "Bombshell in Beltsville: The USDA and the Challenge of 'Silent Spring,' " *Agricultural History* 66, 2 (spring 1992), 157–159. SAB/D, March 16, 1959.
15. Irston Barnes to Ezra Taft Benson, March 23, 1958, Records of the Audubon Society of the District of Columbia, Inc., Smithsonian Institution Archives, Washington, D.C. The letter was also published in the *Atlantic Naturalist* 14, 2 (April/June, 1959), 118. In *Silent Spring* Carson called the fire ant eradication effort "an outstanding example of an ill-conceived, badly executed and thoroughly detrimental experiment in the mass control of insects." Rachel Carson, *Silent Spring* (Boston: Houghton Mifflin Company, 1962), 162.
16. RC to MS, April 23, 1959, RCP/BLYU. The "Market Newsletter" in *Chemical Week*, March 21, 1959, excerpted in Carson's "Fire Ant" files, RCP/BLYU, indicates that industry already was nervous about the adverse publicity.
17. "Reece I. Sailer," Obituary, *Bulletin of the Entomological Society of America* 33, 2 (Summer 1987). Interview with Curt W. Sabrosky. With thanks to Dr. Christopher Thompson, Systematic Entomology, Museum of Natural History, Smithsonian Institution, Washington, D.C., who graciously provided me with information about Dr. Sailer's career. Carson went out of her way to protect Sailer's identity. Only Jeanne Davis knew his name, and she kept his material secure. When Rodell was sorting Carson's papers to give to the Beinecke Library, she remembered Rachel's undercover source and her desire to protect him and, with Davis's help, made certain that his correspondence did not get into the collection. MR to Jeanne Davis [hereafter cited as JD], August 12, 1964, R/CA.
18. Peters's work was cited in the Long Island trial and by Mrs. Waller, but Carson probably got his name from Cottam, who held Peters in esteem. Peters's extant correspondence with Carson dates from June 29, 1959, when she telephoned about livestock and poultry losses from the fire ant program, but they probably corresponded before this. Interview with Harold S. Peters.
19. Carson first knew of Egler through Ray Fosberg. Egler and Fosberg had worked together in Hawaii before the war. Egler joined Fosberg for several expeditions to the Pacific atolls. Interviews with F. Raymond Fosberg, Frank Egler. Egler has contributed significantly to my understanding of the impact of Carson's work on ecology as well as the storm of protest that greeted her book in 1962. He has generously provided important primary documents, patiently answered questions, and has actively contributed to this work. Curriculum Vita of Frank Edwin Egler, Papers of Frank E. Egler, Aton Forest, Norfolk, CT, privately held.

20. Interviews with F. Raymond Fosberg, Frank Egler.
21. RC to Frank Egler [hereafter cited as FE] November 7, 1960; FE to RC, November 9, 1960, RCP/BLYU. RC to Warren G. Kenfield, January 4, 1961, Papers of Frank E. Egler. Kenfield's pamphlet was published and distributed by the Litchfield Audubon Society, Litchfield, CT. A longer version, Warren G. Kenfield [Frank Edwin Egler], *The Wild Garden in the Wild Landscape: The Art of Naturalistic Landscape* (New York: Hafner Publishing Company, 1966) was published much later. See Carson's discussion of Egler's work in *Silent Spring*, 74–79. RC to FE, January 17, 1962; FE to RC, January 25, 1962, RCP/BLYU.
22. "Vanishing Americans," editorial, *Washington Post*, March 30, 1959. Rachel Carson, "Vanishing Americans," *Washington Post*, April 10, 1959. See draft in RCP/BLYU.
23. Carson, "Vanishing Americans." The phrase "rain of death" is from Charles Elton.
24. Christine Stevens [hereafter cited as CS] to RC, April 21, 1959, RCP/BLYU. Interview with Christine Stevens. The Animal Welfare Institute (AWI) was started by Stevens's father, a surgeon, and several of his medical colleagues in 1951. Later they established the Society for Animal Protective Legislation, a lobbying arm. When Carson met Stevens, the Animal Welfare Institute was working on the passage of the Laboratory Animal Welfare Act.
25. Agnes M. Meyer to RC, April 21, 1959; RC to CS, April 23, 1959; RC to MS, April 23, 1959, RCP/BLYU. CS to RC, May 14, 1959, courtesy of the Animal Welfare Institute. Meyer, some years Carson's senior, took an almost maternal interest in Carson's well-being.
26. Rachel Carson, Speech to the Quaint Acres Citizens Association, June 11, 1959, RCP/BLYU. Spock put Carson in touch with Mrs. Thomas Waller, the president of the Bedford, New York, Garden Club and one of the Long Island plaintiffs. Waller and her husband owned a large dairy farm, and their herd's milk had been contaminated during the 1957 spraying. Waller was well connected among women's civic groups and a frequent and effective speaker against pesticide spraying. Carson and Waller corresponded about the contamination of food and dairy products, and Carson quoted from several of Waller's speeches and used several of her sources. Waller, like Hunter, was a source of personal accounts of pesticide poisoning and an important conduit to women's organizations. Mrs. Thomas Waller, Speech to the President's Council Annual Meeting, Garden Club of America, May 6, 1959, Richmond, VA, RCP/BLYU.
27. RC to MS, June 19, 1959, RCP/BLYU.
28. RC to BK, April 29, 1959; RC to MR, May 4, 1959; PB to RC, May 25, 1959; RC to PB, June 3, 1959, RCP/BLYU. "My original doubts [about the title] seem to have evaporated. Now that I have lived with it a few weeks, it seems to wear pretty well."
29. John Barkham, "Of Books and Authors," *Youngstown, Ohio Vindicator*, June 20, 1959, R/CA. MR to PB, June 24, 1959, RCP/BLYU; PB to MR, June 29, 1959, R/CA.
30. RC to Anne Ford, July 6, 1959, RCP/BLYU.
31. RC to EWT, June 9, 16, 1959, EWTP/UC. RC to MS, July 1, 1959, RCP/BLYU.
32. RC to MR, July 22, 27 1959, R/CA. It was finally ascertained that Roger had acute pneumonitis. Dorothy helped get the boy to the hospital, and she and Stan took turns staying with him. RC to EWT, July 16, 1959, EWTP/UC. RC to MR, August 10, 1959, R/CA. Carson considered going back to Maryland, but Ida was recuperating from surgery and could be of no assistance there.
33. RC to MR, August 10, 1959; RC to MR, July 6, 1959; RC to MR, September 4, 1959, R/CA.
34. RC to MR, October 2, 1959, R/CA.

35. RC to DF, February 4, 1956, January 12, 1959, *Letters*.
36. MR to RC, January 26, 1959, R/CA. Carson's contract with Harper for *Magic of the Sea* called for a total advance of $5,000, larger than what Rodell had gotten from Houghton Mifflin for "The Control of Nature." Harper & Brothers, Remittance Advice, April 28, 1959; Marie Leiper to RC, February 2, 1959; Elizabeth Lawrence to MR, April 3, 1959; MR to RC, April 6, 1959, R/CA. Marie wanted to tell Brooks then and there about Rachel's decision on "Help Your Child to Wonder," but Rachel demurred.
37. Interviews with Roger Christie, Barbara Kobrak.
38. MS to RC, August 30, 1959, RCP/BLYU. Interview with Marjorie Spock.
39. RC to LC, March 4, 1959, RCP/BLYU. Carson had sent Stan Freeman a copy of *Arctic Wild*, which he read and enjoyed in the hospital while recuperating from his heart attack. See RC to DF, January 12, 1959, *Letters*.
40. RC to DF, January 12, 1959, *Letters*. SAB/D, March 14, 1959. The Freemans were fascinated by Crisler, and soon Dorothy and Lois had their own lively correspondence.
41. RC to LC, April 16, 1959; RC to LC, May 7, 1959, RCP/BLYU.
42. RC to LC, May 7, 1959, RCP/BLYU.
43. RC to BK, March 10, 1959, RCP/BLYU.
44. RC to LC, April 16, 1959; RC to LC, May 7, 1959, RCP/BLYU.
45. Knecht was the eldest of eight children. She attended the University of Syracuse on scholarship, finally graduating with the aid of the New York State Sight Commission and a group of young mothers who read to her. BK to RC, October 15, 1958, RCP/BLYU. Knecht's companion, Helen Coffman, supplied this background for Carson. See Knecht file, RCP/BLYU.
46. RC to MS, March 3, 1959; RC to Morton Biskind, May 4, 1959, RCP/BLYU.
47. RC to BK, May 5, 1959, RCP/BLYU. The necklace or rope of white, pink, and blue shells had been a present from Marie Rodell but Carson had never worn it.
48. RC to LC, May 7, 1959, RCP/BLYU.
49. RC to BK, March 8, 1959, RCP/BLYU.
50. RC to BK, March 8, 1959; DF to RC, marginal notes, March, 1959, RCP/BLYU. Carson shared the idea of "star dust" as she and Freeman used it, telling Knecht "I have been aware more than once that we were thinking the same thoughts independently, using the same words—and just generally being completely in tune." RC to BK, March 25, 1959, RCP/BLYU.
51. Ibid.
52. On the way home from Maine Carson's car had been struck by a truck outside of Baltimore. Lucky not to have been seriously injured, she shrugged off the incident but was plagued by the paperwork of insurance claims and the necessity of testifying against the driver who hit her. RC to MS, September 18, 1959, RCP/BLYU. Interview with Jeanne Davis.
53. The Vances of Nebraska originally came from Pennsylvania and settled on the plains at the end of the Civil War. Jeanne and her twin brother both live in the Washington, D.C., area. Ida McLean had married a Vance from Pennsylvania who was a minister, and they eventually settled in Illinois.
54. RC to PB, December 3, 1959, RCP/BLYU. Interview with Jeanne Davis. Carson told Davis when she hired her that she still hoped she could finish by the end of the year, an idea that Davis found impossible from the outset. Interview with Paul Brooks.
55. Interview with Jeanne Davis. Interview with Dorothy Algire, conducted by Carol B. Gartner, July 20, 1979, Silver Spring, MD. Used by permission. Interviews with Stephen Algire, Anne Algire Moretti.

56. RC to Morton Biskind, December 3, 1959; Morton Biskind to RC, December 12, 1959; RC to Morton Biskind, January 8, 1959, RCP/BLYU. Carson, *Silent Spring*, 225.
57. Carson, *Silent Spring*, 225. Carson met with Hueper at least three or four times between December 1959 and September 1961. W. C. Hueper to PB, June 18, 1969, copy in author's possession. Quoted in Paul Brooks, *The House of Life: Rachel Carson at Work* (Boston: Houghton Mifflin Co., 1972), 255.
58. Robert A. Uihlein to F. L. Larkin, August 20, 1958, RCP/BLYU.
59. Ibid. Carson wrote across the bottom of the letter: "Died of leukemia, May 1959."
60. RC to PB, December 3, 1959, RCP/BLYU.
61. Rachel Carson, Speech, "The Pesticide Problem," Transcript of the meeting of the State and Regional Audubon, Ornithological and Natural History Societies, Washington, D.C., October 18–19, 1959, 24–30, RCP/BLYU. RC to DF, October 18, 1959, *Letters*.
62. John Kenneth Galbraith, *The Affluent Society* (Boston: Houghton Mifflin Co., 1958). Rachel Carson, Speech, "The Pesticide Problem."
63. Irston R. Barnes, "Cranberry Scandal Discloses Problem," *Washington Post*, November 11, 1959, RCP/BLYU. William M. Blair, "Pesticides Both Boon and Threat," *New York Times*, November 22, 1959, sec. 2, 3.
64. "What Follows That Cranberry Crackdown?" *Farm Journal* 83 (December 1959), 33. "The Cranberry Scare—Here Are the Facts," *U.S. News & World Report*, November 23, 1959, 44–45. "A Lesson from Cranberries," *Consumer Reports*, January 25, 1960, 47–48.
65. RC to DF, November 19, 1959, *Letters*. Carson had written Mrs. Robert Cushman Murphy, who was the official head of the Citizens Against Mass Poisoning, asking her to wire Secretary Flemming in support of his attempt to curb the sprayers. RC to Grace Murphy, November 16, 1959; Statement by Congressman Charles O. Porter, November 18, 1959; Laura Olson to RC, November 18, 1959; RC to Laura Olson, November 20, 1959, RCP/BLYU. Carson called Porter's office the next day to get a copy of his statement and the address of the public health officer Porter had cited.
66. RC to DF, November 19, 1959, *Letters*. "What Follows That Cranberry Crackdown?" *Farm Journal* 83 (December 1959), 33.
67. RC to CC, November 20, 1959, RCP/BLYU. Cottam also praised Flemming for exposing the growers' nefarious practices. He agreed with Carson that the episode had served to alert the public that "our agricultural foods carry more than calories and vitamins." CC to RC, November 23, 1959, RCP/BLYU. Washington political commentator Drew Pearson did devote several columns of his "Washington Merry Go Around" to the controversy. RC to CS, November 30, 1959, RCP/BLYU.
68. Howard K. Smith, *CBS News*, "Weekly News Analysis," November 15, 1959, Washington, D.C., RCP/BLYU. I am grateful to Julie Hemler, an undergraduate student of mine at the University of Maryland, Baltimore County, for research on the cranberry scare of 1959. Carson, *Silent Spring*, 225–226. Carson used the incident in her chapter, "One in Every Four," commenting on the fact that although medical men challenged the fact that aminotriazole was a carcinogen, it was another example of premature use when the full effects of chlorinated hydrocarbon pesticides were simply not known.
69. RC to DF, October 2, 1959, *Letters*.
70. Stevens's knowledge of congressmen and congressional staff was especially valuable to Carson, who, in turn, put Stevens in touch with experts who could help in her legislative efforts. They met for lunch on September 23, 1959, at Carson's home. CS to RC, September 29, 1959; RC to CS, June 5, 1959; CS to RC, July 23, 1959; RC to CS, July 30, 1959; Estella Draper to RC, September 14, 1959, AWI. I am grateful

to Stevens for giving me access to her invaluable correspondence with Carson in the institute files.

71. RC to DF, Sunday [October 18, 1959], *Letters*.
72. Rachel Carson, Acceptance Speech, Virginia Chapter American Association of University Women, December 9, 1959, RCP/BLYU. Carson had received a number of other honors after publication of *The Edge of the Sea*. She had been named an associate of the Woods Hole Oceanographic Institute, elected as a member of the Corporation of the Woods Hole Marine Biological Laboratory, and made an associate member of the Bermuda Biological Station. See Corporate Minutes, Woods Hole Marine Biological Laboratory.
73. RC to PB, December 3, 1959, RCP/BLYU.
74. RC to MR, December 11, 1959, R/CA. In Carson's outline, dated December 14, 1959, the resistance chapter was chapter 8 of twelve chapters. Cancer was part of chapter 9 dealing with pesticide chemicals as a hazard to man. She stated as the book's major thesis: "that in at least one major area of man's efforts to gain mastery over nature—the reduction of unwanted or 'pest' species—the control operations are themselves dangerously out of control, with the result that normal and necessary relations of living things to each other and to the earth have been destroyed."
75. RC to MS, December 30, 1959, RCP/BLYU. Carson returned a copy of Beatrice Trum Hunter's latest address on pesticides, commenting to Spock, "She is certainly a well informed person isn't she? I'm always impressed with her documentation of what she has to say."
76. RC to DF, December 29, 1959, *Letters*.

16: "IF I LIVE TO BE 90"

1. DF to RC, January 9, 1960, *Letters*. Bette Haney had dropped out of medical school and worked for Carson from January to June 1960. Interview with Bette Haney Duff.
2. RC to MR, January 7, 1960, R/CA.
3. Ibid.
4. RC to MR, February 3, 1960; RC to Whitney Blake, February 17, 1969, R/CA.
5. MS to RC, January 22, 1960, RCP/BLYU.
6. RC to DF, February 10, 1960, *Letters*.
7. RC to PB, March 16, 1960, RCP/BLYU. These two chapters she called 9a and 9b and were titled "The Chemical Time Bomb" and "The Last and the Greatest Danger."
8. RC to PB, March 16, 1960, RCP/BLYU. Rodell kept all news of Carson's health private, feeling that Carson should be the one to provide details. This attitude would be especially true of professional relationships, such as the one with Brooks. As she was sorting Carson's papers in 1964, Rodell wrote across the bottom of this letter to Brooks, "Marie was being discreet."
9. PB to RC, March 18, 1960, RCP/BLYU.
10. RC to PB, March 21, 1960, RCP/BLYU. DF to RC, March 25, 1960, *Letters*. Although Carson told Rodell and Freeman about her pending surgery, she did so on the telephone. Crisler and she discussed it when Crisler visited. Dorothy Algire, Shirley Briggs, Jeanne Davis, and Bette Haney all knew about it as well. SAB/D, March 30, 1960. Carson's general internist was Michael Healy. She left the selection of a surgeon to Healy and was not much involved in discussions about the various outcomes. Perhaps Carson's casual attitude was the product of her absorption in her work, her past experience with benign cysts, or just an unwillingness to

think about unpleasant possibilities. It was in keeping with her earlier response, but an attitude she later regretted. RC to DF, March 28, 1962, *Letters*.

11. RC to PB, March 23, 1960, RCP/BLYU.
12. Ibid.
13. RC to PB, April 1, 1960, RCP/BLYU.
14. Dr. Sanderson's given name and medical background is unavailable. RC to Marjorie Spock and Polly Richards, April 12, 1960, RCP/BLYU. Michael Healy to George Crile, Jr., December 13, 1960, George Crile, Jr., Family Papers, The Cleveland Clinic Foundation Archives. [Hereafter cited as Crile Papers.] I am grateful to Helga Sandburg Crile for giving me access to the valuable correspondence between Crile and Carson, and to the archivists of the Cleveland Clinic Foundation for their assistance and for locating other relevant medical correspondence.
15. RC to Marjorie Spock and Polly Richards, April 12, 1960, RCP/BLYU.
16. Ibid.
17. SAB/D, April 9, 1960.
18. Rachel L. Carson, Medical History, Cleveland Clinic Foundation Archives, Cleveland, OH. RC to Marjorie Spock and Polly Richards, April 12, 1960; RC to PB, December 27, 1960, RCP/BLYU.
19. RC to PB, December 27, 1960, RCP/BLYU. This is the letter Brooks refers to obliquely in *The House of Life: Rachel Carson at Work* (Boston: Houghton Mifflin Co., 1972), 265.
20. Michael Healy to George Crile, Jr., December 13, 1960, Crile Papers. This letter sustains the conclusion that Carson had been lied to. Healy writes: "Dr. Sanderson did not tell Miss Carson that she had a malignancy but said that she had a condition bordering on a malignancy." Clearly Healy went along with this code of silence as well. I am indebted to Sandra Steingraber for ongoing discussions on the subject of Carson's cancer. The conclusions, however, are my own.
21. DF to RC, April 30, 1960, *Letters*. I am grateful to Stanley L. Freeman, Jr., for providing a record of Dorothy's and Rachel's telephone conversations from 1960 onward as Dorothy and then Stan Freeman, Sr., reported them in their diaries. I have not, however, had access to these diaries. Dorothy's entries may well deal more specifically with Rachel's understanding of her medical diagnosis. A note from Carson to Rodell written on April 2, 1960, directs her to call Virginia King in the evening if she has had no word on the outcome of the surgery. Rodell wrote "radical mastectomy" across the bottom of this note. While Rodell was by nature more forthright, her previous behavior in not asking Carson about her earlier tumor suggests she shared the same social convention.
22. Davis had worked for Carson for only three months before Carson's illnesses in January. But the routine described was their normal one. Interview with Jeanne Davis. I am grateful to Robert Ulrich and Julia Ulrich, who bought Carson's home in 1970 and graciously allowed me to conduct interviews there as well as have access to the house and grounds, which remained substantially unchanged since Carson's ownership.
23. Interview with Jeanne Davis.
24. Ibid.
25. Ibid. SAB/D, April 9, 1960.
26. Notes by Bette Haney on her interview with Justus Ward, Chief, Regulatory Division, ARS, n.d. [ca. spring 1960], RCP/BLYU. Interview with Bette Haney Duff. Bette Haney Duff to PB, February 24, 1969, copy in author's possession. RC to W. C. Hueper, August 12, 1960, RCP/BLYU.
27. Bette Haney Duff to PB, February 24, 1969. Interview with Bette Haney Duff. RC to DF, June 13, 1961, *Letters*.

28. Rachel Carson, "To Understand Biology." In *Humane Biology Projects* (Washington, D.C.: Animal Welfare Institute, 1960). Interview with Christine Stevens. CS to RC, February 16, 1960; RC to CS, February 24, 1960, AWI.
29. CS to RC, November 23, 1960; RC to CS, January 4, 1961, AWI. Ruth Harrison to RC, November 9, 1962; RC to Ruth Harrison, November 23, 1962, RCP/BLYU. Statement of Rachel Carson in support of HR 1937, Hearings on Humane Treatment of Animals Used in Research, 1962 in AWI. Rachel Carson, "Foreword," in Ruth Harrison, *Animal Machines: The New Factory Farming Industry* (London: Vincent Stuart, 1964).
30. RC to MS, May 18, 1960; RC to CC, April 1, 1960, RCP/BLYU.
31. RC to PB, June 1, 1960, RCP/BLYU. Davis's mother had died suddenly in Nebraska, and Bette Haney had returned to Yale for graduate study. RC to MR, telegram, June 23, 1960, R/CA.
32. Interview with Erich Hartmann and Ruth Baines Hartmann. Erich Hartmann to RC, May 15, 1960; RC to Ronald Wolk, July 11, 1960, RCP/BLYU.
33. RC to MR, August 10, 1960, R/CA. Interview with Erich Hartmann. As an added bonus of working with Hartmann, Carson discovered that he had a son exactly Roger's age. They subsequently arranged several visits for the boys to play together. Hartmann also took several photographs of Roger Christie, but none was ever published. RC to Ronald Wolk, August 23, 1960, RCP/BLYU. U.S. Senator Warren G. Magnuson, Chairman of the Senate Committee on Interstate and Foreign Commerce in 1961, claimed that the essay, along with several others in the same issue, aided materially in the passage of his omnibus oceanography bill. See undated letter to Ronald Wolk in R/CA. Carson finished writing the text in mid-April 1961.
34. RC to DF, September 8, 1960, *Letters*.
35. Rachel Carson, "Preface 1961," Revised Edition, *The Sea Around Us* (New York: Oxford University Press, 1961). Many of the new footnotes deal with specific research on the ocean floor, marine sounds, life-forms found on the abyssal floor, and new current tidal data.
36. Ibid., xii. Carson had relied on the research provided by her correspondence with Stanley A. Cain, chairman of the Department of Conservation in the School of Natural Resources at the University of Michigan, an expert on atomic pollution.
37. Carson, "Preface 1961."
38. For a discussion of the nuclear arms race and the heating up of the Cold War in the late 1950s, see Allan M. Winkler, *Life Under a Cloud: American Anxiety about the Atom* (New York: Oxford University Press, 1993), 84–104; Walter LaFeber, *America, Russia and the Cold War* (New York: Alfred A. Knopf, 1985), 195–223; Paul Boyer, *By the Bombs Early Light: American Thought and Culture at the Dawn of the Atomic Age* (New York: Pantheon Books, 1985), 352–367; Steven M. Spencer, "Fallout: The Silent Killer," *Saturday Evening Post*, August 29, 1959, 26, 89, and September 5, 1959, 86; Robert A. Divine, *Blowing on the Wind: The Nuclear Test Ban Debate, 1954–1960* (New York: Oxford University Press, 1978), 262–280; Spencer Weart, *Nuclear Fear* (Cambridge, MA: Harvard University Press, 1988), 69–82.
39. Paul Boyer, "Fallout Shelters," *Life*, September 15, 1961, 98–108. "Survival: Are Shelters the Answer?" *Newsweek*, November 6, 1961, 19. "Fall-Out Shelters Speeded by Hundreds in Suburbs," *New York Times*, October 3, 1961, 41.
40. "War on Insects" and "The First Atomic Blast," *Time*, August 27, 1945, 65. See Ralph H. Lutts, "Chemical Fallout: Rachel Carson's *Silent Spring*, Radioactive Fallout and the Environmental Movement," *Environmental Review* 9 (Fall 1985), 214–225. I am grateful to Lutts for many conversations about the connection

between fallout and pesticides and Carson's perceptions of both. "Danger—Strontium 90," *Newsweek,* November 12, 1956, 88–90.

41. PB to RC, March 29, 1960, RCP/BLYU.
42. RC to PB, September 5, 1960, RCP/BLYU. Wallace put Carson in touch with Mrs. F. L. Larkin of Milwaukee, WI, an amateur observer whose testimony Carson included in the book.
43. RC to PB, September 5, 1960; PB to RC, September 13, 1960; RC to PB, September 27, 1960, RCP/BLYU. After reading Douglas's opinion, Brooks predicted that the justice would be one of Carson's staunch supporters when the time came. Carson talked with Douglas about her book at the Audubon Naturalist Society's annual dinner at the end of September, where he was the featured speaker. RC to PB, October 3, 1960, RCP/BLYU.
44. RC to C. Girard Davidson, June 8, 1960, RCP/BLYU.
45. Ibid.
46. Pare Lorentz, "Air, Water and Places." Draft Statement on Pollution Control for the Natural Resources Committee of the Democratic Advisory Council [July 1960], RCP/BLYU.
47. RC to Pare Lorentz, July 26, 1960, RCP/BLYU.
48. Committee list, Women's Committee for New Frontiers Meeting at the Home of Senator and Mrs. John F. Kennedy, Washington, D.C., October 10, 1960, RCP/BLYU. RC to DF, January 4, 1961, *Letters.* Carson's participation at the Women's Committee meeting caused one of her more unpleasant misunderstandings with Dorothy Freeman. RC to DF, October 21, 22, 1960, *Letters.*
49. RC to DF, October 12, 1960, *Letters.* Carson's reminiscence was occasioned by the death of Dorothy's mother, Vira Murdock.
50. The best analysis of Knipling's background and research is that given by John H. Perkins, *Insects, Experts, and the Insecticide Crisis: The Quest for New Pest Management Strategies* (New York: Plenum Press, 1982), 97–127. Knipling grew up on a cotton and livestock farm in Texas, where he was familiar with screwworm fly infestations on livestock. In 1953 he became the chief of the Entomology Research section; hence he was not only the chief scientist but the chief administrator. Interview with Edward F. Knipling.
51. Interview with Edward F. Knipling. In the final chapter, "The Other Road," Carson describes and praises Knipling's research at length. See Carson, *Silent Spring,* 277–285. CC to RC, November 28, 1960; RC to CC, January 4, 1961, RCP/BLYU.
52. PB to RC, November 10, 1960, RCP/BLYU. RC to MR, November 17, 1960; MR to RC, November 18, 1960, R/CA. By mutual agreement Rodell told Brooks Rachel had the flu.
53. MR to RC, December 2, 1960, R/CA.
54. Ibid.
55. RC to George Crile, December 7, 1960, Crile Papers.
56. RC to DF, November 25, 1960, RCP/BLYU.
57. RC to George Crile, December 7, 1960, Crile Papers. DF to RC, December 4, 1960, *Letters.*
58. RC to PB, December 27, 1960, RCP/BLYU. Carson had known Jane and Barney Crile since 1951, when she met Jane Halle Crile during her book tour at Halle's Department Store in Cleveland. She admired Crile's book *Cancer and Common Sense* (New York: Viking Press, 1955). George Crile, Jr., *The Way It Was* (Kent, OH: Kent State University Press, 1992), 293–294.
59. Crile, *The Way It Was,* 293–294. RC to George Crile, December 7, 1960, Crile Papers. A letter three days later to Edwin and Nellie Teale tells them of her ulcer,

her current flu, and her mastectomy. Regarding the latter, she told them, "the permanent sections disclosed no more than 'suspicious' tissue." RC to Edwin and Nellie Teale, December 10, 1960, EWTP/UC.

60. Michael Healy to George Crile, December 13, 1960, Crile Papers.
61. George Crile to Michael Healy, December 16, 1960, Crile Papers. Roger stayed with friends during the day, and Ida came for the nights for the two days Rachel was away.
62. RC to George Crile, December 17, 1960, Crile Papers. DF to RC, December 31, 1960, *Letters*.
63. RC to George Crile, December 17, 1960, Crile Papers.
64. RC to DF, December 28, 1960, *Letters*. Dorothy visited from January 9 to January 13, 1961. RC to DF, January 9, 1961, *Letters*. Stanley L. Freeman, Diary 1961, FFC. Courtesy of Stanley L. Freeman, Jr.
65. RC to DF, January 13, 1961, *Letters*.
66. RC to PB, December 27, 1960, RCP/BLYU.
67. Ibid. It was difficult for Carson to tell Marie about her cancer since Marie had lost many close friends and relatives to the disease and would be very upset by Rachel's news.
68. RC to DF, January 17, 1961, *Letters*. Scripps College president William Hard had been trying to get Carson to speak at a college commencement since 1953.
69. DF to RC, January 31, 1961, *Letters*.
70. RC to George Crile, March 23, 1961, attachment, Crile Papers.
71. RC to DF, February 2, 1961, *Letters*.
72. The tumor had enlarged during the weeks of nontreatment; more treatments than expected were needed before there was any response. RC to DF, n.d. [February 1961], UP/FFC.
73. Neither Virginia King nor Robert and Vera Carson appears to have helped look after Roger while Rachel was in the hospital.
74. RC to George Crile, March 23, 1961, Crile Papers. RC to DF, February 16, 19, 20, 1961, *Letters*.
75. RC to DF, February 6, 1961, UP/FFC. Carson, *The Sea Around Us*, rev. ed., 1961. RC to DF, February 23, 1961, *Letters*.
76. RC to DF, February 24–25, 1961, *Letters*.
77. RC to DF, March 2, 3, 4, 1961, *Letters*. Carson was also depressed by Beverly Knecht's declining condition, although Knecht still managed to dictate regular letters to her.
78. Interview with Jeanne Davis. RC to DF, March 4, 13, 14, 1961, *Letters*.
79. RC to DF, March 20, 1961, *Letters*.
80. Notebooks for *Silent Spring*, RCP/BLYU.
81. RC to DF, March 17, 1961, *Letters*. RC to George Crile, March 18, 1961, RCP/BLYU. RC to George Crile, March 23, 1961, Crile Papers.
82. RC to DF, March 17, 1961, *Letters*.
83. RC to George Crile, Jr., March 23, 1961; George Crile to RC, March 24, 1961, Crile Papers. Crile investigated the gold treatments and told Carson that the injections would probably not cause any problems, but he gave this advice in regard to the tumor and not to her bone marrow. RC to DF, March 25, 1961, *Letters*.
84. RC to PB, March 25, 1961, RCP/BLYU.
85. RC to DF, April 13, 1961; DF to RC, June 8, 1961, *Letters*.
86. Interview with Bob Hines. Hines remembered being shocked at how thin and frail Rachel looked.
87. RC to DF, March 17, 1961, *Letters*. DF to RC, June 8, 1961, *Letters*. Marie Rodell

was supervising Crisler's Guggenheim application. Through Carson, Crisler was introduced to Supreme Court Justice William O. Douglas, who also wrote in support of Crisler's application. RC to DF, September 26, 1961, *Letters*. Rodell became Crisler's agent but handled only the foreign sales of her second book, *Captive Wild* (New York: Harper & Bros, 1968).

88. PB to MR, May 26, 1961, R/CA. Brooks's letter makes no mention that Rodell had already suggested just this strategy and for the same reasons. Brooks admitted that several Houghton Mifflin editors, including Lovell Thompson, found *Silent Spring* a "blank title."
89. RC to DF, June 13, 1961, *Letters*.
90. MR to RC, June 5, 1961: RC to MR, July 14, 1961, R/CA. Interview with Erich Hartmann. "A New Elite of American Naturalists: Heirs of a Great Tradition," Photographed for *Life* by Alfred Eisenstaedt in "Our Splendid Outdoors," *Life*, December 22, 1961, 107.
91. Ruth Scott [hereafter cited as RS] to RC, June 16, 1961, RCP/BLYU. Carson was working on the herbicide chapter using Egler's material. RC to Irston Barnes, June 22, 1961, RCP/BLYU.
92. Interviews with Ruth Scott, Joseph B. C. White. White is an environmental journalist and writer and longtime friend and neighbor of the Scotts.
93. Interview with Ruth Scott.
94. Ibid. RS to RC, June 16, 1961, RCP/BLYU. Scott had known Ray Fosberg for many years, primarily through her work in the Nature Conservancy and her colleagues at the Carnegie Institute.
95. Carson consulted Scott, who was active in the Nature Conservancy as well as the Audubon Society, about the terms of the legacies in her will. Interview with Joseph B. C. White. RS to RC, June 16, 1961, RCP/BLYU.
96. Interviews with Ruth Scott, Roger Christie.
97. RC to Irston Barnes, July 26, 1961; RS to RC, September 10, 1961, RCP/BLYU.
98. Frank E. Egler, *60 Questions and Answers Concerning Roadside Rightofway Vegetation Management* (Litchfield Hills, CT: Litchfield Hills Audubon Society, 1961). RS to RC, September 13, 1961; RC to RS, September 18, 1961; RC to Frank Egler, September 14, 1961; Frank Egler to RC, September 20, 1961; RC to Frank Egler, September 24, 1961, RCP/BLYU. The new research on the toxicity of herbicides to wildlife was the work of James DeWitt at Patuxent Research Center and had not yet been published. The fact that Carson was able to convince Egler to reword his bulletin was an impressive exercise of her scientific understanding. RC to RS, October 6, 1961, RCP/BLYU. Carson's postscript on her letter to Scott expresses her frustration that Egler was making this such an emotionally charged issue. Letter in author's possession. Interviews with Frank Egler, Ruth Scott, Roland Clement, Harold Peters.
99. RS to RC, December 6, 1961, RCP/BLYU. Interviews with Ruth Scott, Jeanne Davis, Adele "Nicki" Wilson.
100. RC to LC, August 19, 1961, RCP/BLYU.
101. RC to DF, "Christmas 1961," *Letters*. DF to MR, August 19, 1964, R/CA. Beverly Knecht died sometime during the summer of 1961, R/CA. Freeman gives only a general date for Knecht's death, but Rachel had been expecting it all spring. Extant correspondence between Knecht and Carson ends early in 1961, but Beverly wrote often and Rachel telephoned frequently after that time. Rodell disposed of many of Knecht's letters before turning over the collection to Yale University.
102. The title for the first chapter, "The Obligation to Endure," which sets forth Carson's argument on the dangers inherent in the broadcast use of chemical

pesticides and the public's right to know, came from a speech by the French scientist Jean Rostand. Carson took the line "The obligation to endure gives us the right to know" from Rostand's speech accepting the Kalinga Prize for outstanding contributions to the dissemination of scientific knowledge on April 21, 1960, and quoted in *Science*, May 20, 1960, 1.

103. RC to PB, June 26, 1961, RCP/BLYU. Brooks, *The House of Life*, 268–269.
104. RC to Roy M. Kelley, July 26, 1961, RCP/BLYU. Rachel Carson, "Letter to the Editor," *Boothbay Register*, July 27, 1961, 5.
105. Carson, "Letter to the Editor."
106. Ibid. RC to Charles M. Callison, August 9, 1961, RCP/BLYU.
107. RC to DF, September 26, 1961, *Letters*.
108. Kate Bernard at Houghton Mifflin suggested the Darlings to Brooks, but Brooks and Peterson had been friends since childhood. Interviews with Paul Brooks, Roger Tory Peterson. Lois and Louis Darling, *Bird* (Boston: Houghton Mifflin Co., 1962). Lois and Louis Darling Papers, Drawings and Correspondence about *Silent Spring*, Uncatalogued, BLYU. RC to MR [September 1961], R/CA. Interview with Roland Clement.
109. RC to PB, July 14, 1961, RCP/BLYU.
110. PB to RC, October 9, 1961; PB to RC, October 27, 1961, R/CA.
111. PB to RC, November 20, 1961; RC to MR, n.d. [February 1962], R/CA. Lutts, "Chemical Fallout," 222, comments on some of the Darlings' suggestions, including a mushroom cloud to illustrate Carson's comparison of the Swedish farmer's experience with the hapless sailors on the *Lucky Dragon* in the South Pacific. This was an example of what Carson viewed as unimaginative and trite.
112. Lois Darling, personal recollections, May 30, 1979, RCP/BLYU. Interviews with Roland Clement, Paul Brooks.
113. Louis Darling to PB, May 1962, RCP/BLYU. Houghton Mifflin paid for the illustrations. The fee was not backed out of Carson's advance. Interview with Roland Clement.
114. Marie Rodell supported Carson's idea of a fable to set the mood and capture the reader. R/CA. Brooks liked the idea as well but suggested major editorial changes in the fable's first draft. Interview with Paul Brooks. See Christine Oravec, "An Inventional Archaeology of Rachel Carson's 'A Fable for Tomorrow,' " in Kandia Salomone, ed., *Proceedings of The Conference on Communication and Our Environment* (Chattanooga, TN: University of Tennessee School of Journalism, 1997), for a discussion of the literary invention of this first chapter.
115. Both these articles were among Carson's files for the fable in RCP/BLYU.
116. PB to RC, November 20, 1961, RCP/BLYU.
117. Interview with Jeanne Davis. No one seems to have questioned the relationship between Carson's iritis and her heavy radiation treatments, although it seems impossible that the two were unrelated.
118. RC to DF, January 6, 1962, *Letters*.
119. Interview with Jeanne Davis, Ida Sprow.
120. Interview with Ida Sprow. Carson had traveled to Westport, CT, to talk with Morton Biskind in December after she had sent him her chapters to review. RC to Morton Biskind, December 11, 1961, RCP/BLYU.
121. RC to DF, January 6, 1962, *Letters*. RC to Morton Biskind, December 11, 1961, RCP/BLYU.
122. RC to William Shawn, July 20, 1961, RCP/BLYU.
123. RC to DF, January 23, 1962, *Letters*.
124. Ibid.

17: "A SOLEMN OBLIGATION"

1. RC to LC, January 23, 1962, RCP/BLYU. PB to RC, January 30, 1962, R/CA.
2. PB to RC, January 30, 1962, R/CA.
3. PB to RC, February 2, 1962, R/CA.
4. RC to LC, February 8, 1962, RCP/BLYU.
5. Rodell and Alldredge remained good friends. When Rodell was in town, the three of them frequently got together. Among those Alldredge invited to this gathering was Duncan Howlett, pastor of All Souls Unitarian Church, where Alldredge was active.
6. Anne Ford [hereafter cited as AF] to MR, April 13, 1962, RCP/BLYU. Ford was in favor of getting the book to prominent club women in the smaller cities and towns where pesticide spraying had been the greatest. Ford was afraid of looking like they had a propaganda book on their hands. Alldredge was the prime mover behind holding a political luncheon.
7. RC to MR, February 3, 1962, R/CA. After her experience with her two previous jacket covers in which she felt her credentials were inadequately described, Carson was careful to make sure the text was exactly as she prepared it.
8. MR to PB, February 16, 1962, RCP/BLYU. See RC to PB, April 20, 1962, RCP/BLYU.
9. MR to PB, April 16, 1962, RCP/BLYU. Notations in the margin indicate the lawyer's response to Brooks's inquiry.
10. Rodell in particular had been unhappy with Houghton Mifflin's marketing of *The Edge of the Sea* and was not about to let the company make a similar mistake with *Silent Spring*. This was the source of her strained relations with Lovell Thompson and to a lesser degree with Brooks.
11. "Anne Ford," Obituary, *Gloucester Times*, November 18, 1993. Interview with Margaret Ford Kieran. Douglas had written Carson on March 2, 1962, recalling a conversation about her book at the Audubon dinner the year before. His book, *My Wilderness: East to Katahdin* (Garden City, NY: Doubleday, 1960), had impressed Carson. William O. Douglas to RC, March 2, 1962; RC to William O. Douglas, March 5, 1962, RCP/BLYU. This was a crucial exchange that ultimately led Douglas to review *Silent Spring* in the *Book-of-the-Month Club News*.
12. MR to AF, April 20, 1962, R/CA.
13. AF to MR, April 13, 1962, RCP/BLYU; MR to AF, April 20, 1962, R/CA.
14. Frank Egler to RC, January 26, 1962, Papers of Frank E. Egler, copy in author's possession. RC to Frank Egler, January 29, 1962, RCP/BLYU. Carson later telephoned Egler several times to check on a few points before she sent the manuscript off. Egler and Carson did not meet until January 1963, but they spent considerable time on the telephone and in correspondence. Interview with Frank Egler.
15. For an analysis of the work of the NAS-NRC on this issue, see "Pesticides: The Academy Versus Rachel Carson" in Philip M. Boffey, *The Brain Bank of America: An Inquiry into the Politics of Science* (New York: McGraw-Hill Book Company, 1975), 199–226.
16. CC to RC, February 14, 22, 26, 1962, RCP/BLYU. Frank Graham, Jr., *Since Silent Spring* (Boston: Houghton Mifflin Co., 1970), 36–47, gives a summary of the NAS-NRC report and the subsequent controversy. NAS-NRC chairman I. L. Baldwin was professor of Agricultural Bacteriology at the University of Wisconsin. The committee's executive director was W. H. Larrimer, who had been division chief of the USDA's Insect Control Division and was an ardent believer in the benefits of synthetic hydrochlorinated pesticides. The committee included George C. Decker, an

economic entomologist at the Illinois Natural History Survey and a frequent consultant to the chemical industry, who was responsible for the subcommittee report on "Pesticide-Wildlife Problems," and Mitchell R. Zavon, a professor of industrial medicine at the University of Cincinnati and a consultant for the Shell Chemical Company, a maker of pesticides. The three reports were published as *Pest Control and Wildlife Relationships*. National Academy of Sciences-National Research Council Publications 920-A, 920-B, and 920-C (Washington, D.C.: 1962, 1963).

17. Clarence Tarzwell to RC, August 31, 1962, RCP/BLYU. All three scientists saw that the publication of Carson's book was of immense value in their struggle within NAS-NRC.
18. RC to CC, March 19, 1962; CC to RC, April 11, 1962, RCP/BLYU. See letter from Joseph Hickey to Carson about "l'affaire Rosene." Although these episodes of political retribution were well known in the field, even scientists such as Hickey wanted to distance themselves from any public disclosure.
19. RC to DF, February 27, March 5, 1962, *Letters*.
20. George Crile to Ralph Caulk, March 9, 1962, Cleveland Clinic Archives. Crile was becoming increasingly well known as a surgeon who did not believe in the generally accepted practice of radical mastectomy.
21. RC to DF, March 28, 1962, *Letters*.
22. Ibid.
23. RC to DF, April 1, 1962, RCP/BLYU.
24. E. B. White as quoted in *Silent Spring* (Boston: Houghton Mifflin Company, 1962). PB to RC, April 3, 1962, RCP/BLYU.
25. RC to PB, April 20, 1962, RCP/BLYU. They never went because of her radiation treatments.
26. RC to DF, April 5, 1962, *Letters*.
27. RC to DF, May 20, 1962, *Letters*. Rachel implored Dorothy to make sure of the confidentiality of anyone in Southport who did know her true situation.
28. Ibid. This letter, written over the course of several days, included more than one entry. In fact, the cancer had invaded her spinal vertebrae, although it took Caulk several more weeks to confirm it.
29. RC to William Shawn, May 8, 1962, RCP/BLYU.
30. Wallace White to James Dewitt [*sic*], July 19, 1962, letter in author's possession. PB to MR, April 9, 1971; MR to PB, April 12, 1971, R/CA. RC to William Shawn, May 8, 1962, RCP/BLYU.
31. RC to William Shawn, May 8, 1962, RCP/BLYU. RC to DF, June 13, 1962, *Letters*.
32. AF to Agnes Meyer, May 1, 1962; AF to RC, May 2, 3, 1962; AF to PB, May 3, 1962, RCP/BLYU. AF to MR, May 4, 1962, R/CA. Invitation List; List of Acceptances, Regrets; AF to PB, May 15, 1962, RCP/BLYU.
33. AF to PB, May 15, 1962; MR to AF, May 23, 1962; Agnes Meyer to RC, June 18, 1962; RC to Agnes Meyer, June 24, 1962, RCP/BLYU.
34. RS to RC, May 16, 1962, RCP/BLYU.
35. Interviews with Ruth Scott, Adele "Nicki" Wilson, David Brower. Nicki Wilson was the unofficial hostess for anyone coming to Washington to work for the cause of conservation. Longtime activists in the effort to create a Department of Natural Resources, Wilson and Scott were members of a national committee for its creation. It was a cause that had been around since the days of Harold Ickes, and Carson endorsed it. Interview with Stewart Udall.
36. Paul Knight produced several memoranda including "Some Thoughts on *Silent Spring*," (October 1962), RCP/BLYU, and a lengthy manuscript account of the con-

troversy. See Paul Knight, "A Case Study on Environmental Contamination," n.d.1964], unpublished manuscript, Rachel Carson Council, Chevy Chase, MD.

37. Diane Davin to AF, May 27, 1962, RCP/BLYU. This is the first record of interest from CBS.
38. Helen Phillips to RC, June 8, 1962, RCP/BLYU. Phillips and Carson had great admiration for each other's skills and enjoyed working together in spite of the pressures. Phillips offered her own assessment of Carson's work: "Your book has made a deep impression on me, and I am sure that a great many other people will feel the same way. I hope that a copy will find its way to President Kennedy's desk." Helen Phillips to RC, April 25, 1962; Rachel Carson, "Man and Nature in a Chemical Age," Speech, Association of Librarians, May 28, 1962, RCP/BLYU.
39. Rachel Carson, Speech, "Of Man and the Stream of Time," Lectern Copy, Scripps College Commencement, Claremont, CA, June 12, 1962, RCP/BLYU. The text that Scripps College published under its own imprint in July 1962 has been edited.
40. RC to Dorothy and Stan Freeman, June 11, 1962, *Letters*. MR to RC, telegram, June 13, 1962, R/CA.
41. RC to DF, June 13, 1962, *Letters*. This is one of the few times when it seems that Carson is writing to Dorothy with half a mind toward how posterity might view her reputation. MR to AF, June 11, 1962, RCP/BLYU.
42. MR to PB, May 23, 1962; MR to RC, May 31, 1962, RCP/BLYU. Interviews with Roland Clement, John Vosburgh. Buchheister, however, refused to have the society endorse the conclusions of *Silent Spring*.
43. H. Davidson, San Francisco, California. June 29, 1962, published for the first time in *The New Yorker*, 70th Anniversary Issue, February 20 & 27, 1995, 18. The P.S. was not included in the anniversary edition, but Carson quotes it in her speech to the National Parks Association. I am indebted to Cheryll Glotfelty for bringing the published letter to my attention.
44. RC to DF, June 27, 1962, *Letters*.
45. Ibid.
46. RC to PB, April 6, 1962, RCP/BLYU. The six trade names were Aramite, Chloro IPC, IPC, Diazanon, Penta, and Systox.
47. Carson's lawyer, Maurice Greenbaum, recommended some minor changes in the manuscript but cautioned her to avoid even the shadow of a suggestion that she had or would ever endorse any program, product, or commercial enterprise. MR to Lovell Thompson, July 17, 1962, RCP/BLYU.
48. Modification of contract between Rachel Carson and Houghton Mifflin Company of May 22, 1962, dated July 9, 1962. R/CA. MR to Craig Wylie, June 19, 1962, RCP/BLYU. They discussed printing a disclaimer statement on the copyright page of the book stating "Neither the Author nor the Publisher have authorized the use of their names nor the use of any of the material contained in this book in connection with the sale, promotion or advertising of any product. Any use is strictly illegal and in violation of the rights of Rachel Carson and Houghton Mifflin Company." But the disclaimer was never printed. Lovell Thompson to David Harris, August 14, 1962, RCP/BLYU.

    Rodell's concerns about potential liability proved justified when a Boston garden-supply house sponsored a radio commercial claiming they "carried pyrethrum and rotenone as recommended by Rachel Carson." There was little Rodell or Houghton Mifflin could do about such advertisements except to disclaim any association. MR to Lovell Thompson, May 23, 1962, RCP/BLYU.
49. MR to AF, June 26, 1962, RCP/BLYU. Alldredge did as he promised and might well have been responsible for getting the first copy of the book to President Kennedy,

who was known to have read the installments in *The New Yorker*. Interview with Stewart Udall.

50. Hon. John V. Lindsay, "Silent Springs" [*sic*]. Remarks in the *Congressional Record*, June 2, 1962, A5256; *Congressional Record*, July 11, 1962, copy in RCP/BLYU. John V. Lindsay to RC, June 30, 1962; RC to John Lindsay, July 2, 1962; RC to CS, July 20, 1962, RCP/BLYU. Proxmire wrote to both USDA and Interior secretaries asking for a full report on pesticide use.
51. Editorial, "Rachel Carson's Warning," *New York Times*, July 2, 1962, copy in R/CA.
52. RC to CS, July 5, 1962, AWI. Anne Ford, who was forwarding the mail to Carson from *The New Yorker*, calculated that the reaction was 98½ for and 1½ against. AF to MR, July 12, 1962; Lovell Thompson to MR, July 16, 1962, R/CA. MR to Laurence Pottinger, July 9, 1962, RCP/BLYU.
53. MR to Laurence Pottinger, July 9, 1962, RCP/BLYU; RC to Lovell Thompson, July 29, 1962, R/CA.
54. Lewis Herber [Murray Bookchin], *Our Synthetic Environment* (New York: Alfred A. Knopf, 1962). Bookchin's discussion of the poisoning of the human environment considers toxicants in food, pesticides, radioactivity, X rays, wildlife, and nuclear waste. His remedy lies in moving to the countryside and reestablishing a balanced relationship between man and nature. Bookchin's book was well received among a certain intelligentsia but had not much notice from the general public.
55. Helen B. Taussig, "The Thalidomide Syndrome," *Scientific American*, 207, 2 (August 1962), 29–35. The Insight Team of *The Sunday Times of London, Suffer the Children: The Story of Thalidomide* (New York: Viking Press, 1979), 64–85. Morton Mintz, "Heroine of FDA Keeps Bad Drug Off Market," *Washington Post*, July 15, 1962, A1. Some American women got the drug from overseas sources and gave birth to deformed infants, but thalidomide was never dispensed legally in the United States.
56. Rachel Carson, *New York Post*, September 14, 1962, RCP/BLYU.
57. John M. Lee, " 'Silent Spring' Is Now Noisy Summer," *New York Times*, July 22, 1962, RCP/BLYU. Lee reported that Carson's agent said Carson was on "extended vacation and not available for comment on the industry's rebuttal." Houghton Mifflin referred all questions to Rodell.
58. Ibid. MR to AF, July 19, 1962, RCP/BLYU.
59. Walter Wingo, "How Deadly Are Bug Sprays? Agriculture Dept. vs. Rachel Carson," *Washington Daily News*, July 13, 1962, 20. Robert Caro, then a reporter for *Newsday*, interviewed Moore and wrote a series of five articles in August. He was one of the first to emphasize the connection between pesticides and thalidomide, pointing out the dangers of genetic damage in both. Robert A. Caro, "Pesticides: The Hidden Poisons," *Newsday*, August 20, 1962, RG 310, ARS, NARA.
60. Caro, "Pesticides." "Insecticides: Hiss of Doom?" *Newsweek*, August 6, 1962, RCP/BLYU.
61. Shaw prepared a feature article for the October issue of *Agricultural Research* that emphasized the development of biological controls at ARS.
62. "Freeman Squelches Trigger-happy Underlings . . ." *Wall Street Journal*, August 3, 1962, RCP/BLYU. ARS staff felt victimized by Freeman's order and were chagrined when their overzealousness was reported in the press. "Comments on Rachel Carson's Articles in *The New Yorker*," RG 310, ARS. NARA. Ernest G. Moore, *The Agricultural Research Service* (New York: Frederick A. Praeger, 1967), 197. Interview with Orville Freeman. Orville Freeman to B. T. Shaw, Memorandum, July 16, 1962, RG 16, Office of the Secretary of Agriculture [hereafter cited as SOA], NARA. B. T. Shaw to Orville Freeman, Memoranda, July 31, 1962, RG 16,

SOA, NARA. Linda J. Lear, "Bombshell in Beltsville: The USDA and the Challenge of 'Silent Spring,' " *Agricultural History* 66, 2 (spring 1992), 161–165.

63. William Proxmire to Stewart Udall, July 20, 1962, RG 16, SOA, NARA. Interview with Stewart Udall.
64. Ibid. Paul Knight to RC, July 5, 1962; RC to Paul Knight, July 10, 1962, RCP/BLYU.
65. According to Stewart Udall, Wiesner brought up the subject of pesticides to President Kennedy and deserves credit for initiating action in the White House. Interview with Stewart Udall. B. T. Shaw to Orville Freeman, Memorandum, July 31, 1962, RG 16, SOA, NARA. Lear, "Bombshell in Beltsville," 165.
66. The first indication of Rodell's negotiation with CBS is on July 9, 1962. Approval from CBS executives took time and producer Jay McMullen had to complete another documentary first. Interview with Jay McMullen. Brooks Atkinson to RC, July 25, 1962; RC to Brooks Atkinson, August 8, 1962, RCP/BLYU. Although Atkinson asked Carson to respond to his questions in writing, she was unable to do so within the time he needed, and they ended up talking several times on the telephone. Brooks Atkinson, "Critic at Large," *New York Times*, September 11, 1962, RCP/BLYU.
67. MR to Brooks, Thompson, Ford, and Carson, August 7, 1962; AF to Brooks and Thompson, August 8, 1962, RCP/BLYU.
68. MR to RC, August 14, 1962, RCP/BLYU. Carson's form letters were coded by letter, A through I, & V. V said "thank you for your interests, Miss Carson is currently on vacation." Carson marked each letter with the appropriate symbol and sent them to Ford to coordinate the replies. The originals came back to Carson for her files. RC to AF, October 19, 1962, RCP/BLYU. Form letters are also in RCP/BLYU.
69. MR to Lovell Thompson, July 20, 1962; Lovell Thompson to MR, July 26, 1962; MR to RC, memo, July 30, 1962, R/CA. PB to RC, August 3, 1962, RCP/BLYU. Carson's attitude arose in part because Wilhelm Heuper had left DuPont intensely critical of the firm's failure to do systematic toxicological research. See Wilhelm C. Hueper, "Adventures of a Physician in Occupational Cancer" (Bethesda, MD: National Library of Medicine, 1976). See Robert N. Proctor, *Cancer Wars* (New York: Basic Books, 1995), 36–57, for an evaluation of Hueper's work. David Hounshell and John Kenly Smith, *Science and Corporate Strategy: DuPont R&D, 1902–1980* (New York: Cambridge University Press, 1988), 451–464. Interview with Gideon D. Hill. Hill, the DuPont scientist who headed the task force in urea herbicides in the 1950s, confirmed the view that DuPont scientists took little interest in Carson's book. Research and development of pesticides at DuPont experienced its greatest growth after 1962, when technology mushroomed.
70. Lovell Thompson to MR, August 1, 1962, R/CA. PB to RC, August 3, 1962, RCP/BLYU.
71. "Special Press Analysis of Rachel Carson's *Silent Spring*," November 1, December 6, 1962, Confidential reports, Public Relations Department, E. I. DuPont et Nemours. Hagley Museum & Library, Wilmington, DE. This remarkable document testifies to the importance the public relations department at DuPont gave to *Silent Spring*. The November 1, 1962, document concludes that the cries of danger were much louder than the reassurances that pesticides were safe to use. The December report concentrated on the growing heat of the controversy and the rebuttals to Carson. DuPont scientists were nearly oblivious to the public debate, and their research priorities remained unaffected by it. See "Buzz, Buzz, Buzz," *The New Republic*, August 13, 1962, 7.

72. Louis A. McLean to William E. Spaulding, President, Houghton Mifflin Company, August 2, 1962, RCP/BLYU. Interview with Paul Brooks.
73. Interview with Paul Brooks. PB to RC, August 6, 1962, RCP/BLYU.
74. RC to PB, August 8, 1962, RCP/BLYU.
75. "Milton Greenstein," *The New Yorker*, August 19, 1991, 79. Brooks sent a copy of Velsicol's letter to Harry Scherman at Book-of-the-Month Club alerting the latter that the club would be vulnerable as well. BOMC was ready to ship books; it was too late to make any textual changes even if it had wanted to.
76. MR to RC, August 14, 1962, R/CA.
77. PB to Louis McLean, August 10, 1962, RCP/BLYU. Greenbaum thought this letter went into too much detail. MR to RC, August 14, 1962, R/CA. PB to Lovell Thompson, August 22, 1962, RCP/BLYU. Even Thompson had been away when the Velsicol letter had come, leaving Brooks very much alone. Thompson pushed for the disclaimer. Interview with Paul Brooks. Subsequent printings contained slight changes of wording on pages 23, 24, and 25. PB to RC, August 23, 1962, R/CA. Velsicol's response, delivered August 14, offered "partial documentation" that amounted to little more than general assertions, including the charge that Carson had misunderstood insect resistance. McLean asked for a meeting prior to August 24 to discuss their contentions; Houghton Mifflin declined. Louis McLean to William Spaulding, August 14, 1962; Paul Brooks to Louis McLean, August 22, 1962, RCP/BLYU.
78. Interview with John Vosburgh.
79. John Vosburgh to Roland Clement, August 11, 1995, privately held. Interview with John Vosburgh. Roland Clement to John Vosburgh, August 16, 1995, Papers of Roland C. Clement, privately held. Interview with Roland Clement. Rachel Carson, "Poisoned Waters Kill Our Fish and Wildlife," *Audubon Magazine* 64 (September/October, 1962), 250–265. In the same issue Vosburgh reviews Lewis Herber [Murray Bookchin], *Our Synthetic Environment*, 286. Rachel Carson, "A Beetle Scare, Spray Planes—and Dead Wildlife," *Audubon Magazine* 64 (November/December 1962), 318–323. Clement reviewed *Silent Spring* in the November/December 1962 issue, "Three Reviews by Roland C. Clement," 356. "We must learn eventually not only what these chemicals do to our environment, but what they are doing to us, since we, too, are of nature," he wrote. "Miss Carson does not shirk this troubling question." "The Editorial Trail," *Audubon Magazine* 64 (November/December 1962), 306–307.
80. William O. Douglas, Report, *Book-of-the-Month Club News* (September 1962), 2–4. Brooks wrote the accompanying essay on Carson for the *News*. When Carson reviewed it, she asked Brooks not to use the word "organic." It was a "bad word," she explained, "because the enemy will immediately brand me an organic gardener." RC to PB, n.d. [June 1962], RCP/BLYU. "Are We Poisoning Ourselves?" *Business Week*, September 8, 1962, 36–38.
81. John F. Kennedy, Presidential News Conference, August 29, 1962. Copy of text in Knight, "Case Study," 41.
82. Kennedy's response underscored the sensitivity of Administration officials to the public anxiety over the unknown effects of toxic chemicals provoked by the thalidomide controversy and by Carson's book. See Knight, "A Case Study on Environmental Contamination." See also Graham, *Since Silent Spring*, 48–62, and Paul Brooks, The *House of Life: Rachel Carson at Work* (Boston: Houghton Mifflin Co., 1972), 294–305.
83. MR to PB, September 5, 1962, RCP/BLYU. Greenbaum, however, thought that if left alone, the industry would present them better legal opportunities.

84. RC to SAB, August 1, 1962, SAB, privately held.
85. E. B. White to RC, August 24, 1962; RC to E. B. White, September 5, 1962, RCP/BLYU. Carson told White how much his own occasional comments in *The New Yorker*'s "These Precious Days" had meant to her.
86. RC to AF, September 17, 1962, RCP/BLYU. Last-minute publicity arrangements severely strained the relationship between Anne Ford and Marie Rodell, but they managed to get along remarkably well considering the pressure. MR to AF, September 17, 1962; AF to MR, September 18, 1962, R/CA. RC to Harry Bacas, August 29, 1962, RCP/BLYU. There was never any explanation from *Reader's Digest*, but Rodell suspected outside pressure. RC to DF, October 4, 1962, *Letters*.
87. Interview with Jay McMullen.
88. MR to P. T. MacManus, September 11, 1962, RCP/BLYU. MacManus ran the publicity at Houghton Mifflin's New York office. MR to RC, September 11, 1962, RCP/BLYU. Major newspapers reviewed *Silent Spring* on Sunday, September 23, 1962, even though publication was not until the following Thursday. Pulitzer Prize–winning scientist Hermann J. Muller reviewed *Silent Spring* as the lead article for *New York Herald Tribune Books*, and Lorus and Margery Milne did the same in the *New York Times Book Review*. Walter Sullivan, *Times* science editor, reviewed *Silent Spring* again on publication day.
89. Interview with Wayne Hanley. Hanley, a longtime columnist and reviewer for the *Boston Herald*, had known Huckins for a long time. Hanley went out to interview Huckins and wrote the story that has since become legend.
90. Wayne Hanley, "The Way Through Insecticidal Fog," *Boston Herald*, September 24, 1962, 12. Anne Ford, a friend of Huckins's and Hanley's sent John Fenton of the *New York Times* out to interview Huckins. Olga Huckins to RC, September 25, 1962; RC to Olga Huckins, October 3, 1962, RCP/BLYU. Interview with Wayne Hanley. I am grateful to Hanley, who remembered interviewing Huckins and writing the story, and to the Microfilm Research Division of the Boston Public Library for helping me solve this longstanding mystery.
91. She also finished a statement to the chairman of the Congressional Subcommittee of Health and Safety in support of HR 1937. Christine Stevens and the AWI had lobbied for hearings on a bill that would regulate the conditions under which research animals were maintained and prevent their mistreatment. Stevens hoped that Carson could testify, and when that proved impossible, Carson sent in a statement. RC to Kenneth Roberts, September 27, 1962, "Statement in Support of HR 1937"; Kenneth Roberts to RC, October 3, 1962; CS to RC, October 3, 1962, RCP/BLYU. The bill Carson supported was the basis for the Laboratory Animal Welfare Act, which was not passed until 1966.

    This was the first time Washington audiences had seen Carson in her new wig. "The Eye," *Washington Star*, n.d. [October 4, 1962], RCP/BLYU. Cottam spoke about his experience with pesticides while supervising research at FWS. Roland Clement, who wrote Buchheister's speech, laid the pesticide problem at the door of the USDA and committed National Audubon to an active role in questioning the use of DDT. Buchheister, however, never allowed the society to publicly support a ban on DDT. See Roland C. Clement, "From Birds to People: The Politics of the Audubon Movement" [unpublished mss., 1993]. Interview with Roland Clement.
92. Rachel Carson, "On the Origins of *Silent Spring*," Speech to the National Parks Association, October 2, 1962, RCP/BLYU.
93. Rachel Carson, Speech, Audubon Naturalist Society Dinner, October 5, 1962, RCP/BLYU. D.C. Audubon had taken this new name in December 1959.

94. "Questions and Discussion," Audubon Dinner, October 1962, RCP/BLYU. Paul Knight, from Secretary Udall's office, was also present and answered questions. Rachel Carson, "Tomorrow's Spring," Conference speech, National Council of Women of the United States, October 11, 1962, RCP/BLYU. In this later speech Carson mentions Lewis Herber's [Murray Bookchin] recent book *Our Synthetic Environment* in the context of the staggering number of pollutants and their random and unknown combinations. To my knowledge Carson was not aware that Herber was a pseudonym, but she had specific knowledge of the contents of the book.
95. *Life*, October 12, 1962, 105–106, 109–110. SAB/D, September 20, 21, 1962.
96. SAB/D, September 20, 21, 1962. RC to DF, October 4, 1962, *Letters*.
97. Interview with Stewart Udall.
98. Udall did not recall whether Orville Freeman attended the seminar that night or not. Interview with Orville Freeman.
99. Interview with Orville Freeman.
100. RC to Stewart Udall, October 24, 1962, Private correspondence. Interview with Stewart Udall. RC to DF, October 25, 1962, *Letters*. Rachel Carson, Kennedy Group Speech, RCP/BLYU. The exact date of the Kennedy Seminar is unclear, but it was sometime around October 16 or the beginning of the week-long Cuban Missile Crisis. Carson left for Cleveland on October 23, the day after President Kennedy's ultimatum to the Soviet Union to remove the nuclear missiles from Cuba.
101. Interview with Jay McMullen.
102. Rachel Carson, Speech to the Associated Clubs of Virginia for Roadside Development, October 29, 1962, RCP/BLYU. Frank Egler's review of the NAS-NRC pesticide reports in which he criticizes the dominance of the profit motive in contemporary society was published in *Atlantic Naturalist* 17 (October/December 1962), 267–271. In the same issue, Paul B. Sears, former chairman of Yale's Department of Conservation, reviewed *Silent Spring*, 276–278. Carson told Egler after the speech that the timing of his review and another paper of his had influenced her thinking and encouraged her "to take a few pokes myself at the industry-science relationship." RC to Frank Egler, December 7, 1962, RCP/BLYU.
103. Rachel Carson, Speech to the Women's National Press Club, December 5, 1962. Carson had Greenbaum review the speech beforehand, knowing that NACA and the AMA would try to discredit her.
104. AF to MR, Telegram, December 5, 1962, R/CA. Audio recording of Women's National Press Club Speech, Rachel Carson Council, Chevy Chase, MD. RC to DF, January 1, 1963, *Letters*.
105. *New York Times Best Seller Lists* in RCP/BLYU. RC to DF, December 19, January 1, 1962, *Letters*.
106. RC to DF, January 1, 1963, *Letters*. *New York Times Best Seller Lists*, in RCP/BLYU.
107. RC to DF, "For Christmas" [December 1962], *Letters*.

18: "RUMBLINGS OF AN AVALANCHE"

1. J. F. Rothermel, "Rachel Carson's *Silent Spring* is too emotional," *Birmingham News*, October 21, 1962, RCP/BLYU. Carson subscribed to the Romeike Press Clippings Service. Drawing by Herbert Goldberg, *Saturday Review of Literature*, November 10, 1962. These clippings and cartoons are preserved in her papers at BLYU.
2. Lorus and Margery Milne, "There's Poison All Around Us Now," *New York Times*

Book Review, September 23, 1962, 1, 26. There is no evidence that any lobby group, industry, or individual ever actually filed a suit against Carson or her publishers.

3. Paul Brooks put this eloquently in *The House of Life: Rachel Carson at Work* (Boston: Houghton Mifflin Co., 1972), 293, writing: "she was questioning not only the indiscriminate use of poisons but the basic irresponsibility of an industrialized technological society toward the natural world." See last paragraph especially, Rachel Carson, *Silent Spring* (Boston: Houghton Mifflin Co., 1962), 297. Robert Rudd, "Review of *Silent Spring*," *Pacific Discovery* (November–December 1962), RCP/BLYU. Interview with Robert Rudd.
4. Ezra Taft Benson to Dwight D. Eisenhower, n.d. The Benson letter was first called to my attention by Blanche Wiesen Cook (see *AHA Perspectives* [November 1992], 14), but archivists at the Eisenhower Library have not been able to locate it. Frank Graham attributes the remark to a disgruntled member of the Federal Pest Control Review Board. Frank Graham, Jr., *Since Silent Spring* (Boston: Houghton Mifflin Co., 1970), 60. "Rachel Carson Shuns Lecture Hall," *Baltimore Sun*, October 3, 1962, RCP/BLYU. The reporter focused on the influence of Carson's mother.
5. "Pesticides: The Price for Progress," *Time*, September 28, 1962, 45–46, 48.
6. News articles are legion. See, for example: "*Silent Spring* Makes Protest Too Hysterical," *Tucson Arizona Star*, October 14, 1962; "Critics Call *Silent Spring*, One-Sided, Unbalanced Book," *Richmond Times Dispatch*, December 2, 1962; "Exaggeration Weakens Rachel Carson's Book," *Fort Wayne News-Sentinel*, October 6, 1962. See Linda J. Lear, "War in the Garden? Rachel Carson, Gender and Pesticides" [unpublished paper, American Society of Environmental History, 1993], for an extended discussion of the gender issue and Westcott's role as critic. See also H. Patricia Hynes, *The Recurring Silent Spring* (New York: Pergamon Press, 1989).
7. "The Desolate Year," *Monsanto Magazine* (October 1962), RCP/BLYU. Appended to the fictitious parody were two pages of facts about insect pests underscoring the dependence of domestic food supply on the use of chemical pesticides. Interview with Roland Clement. Clement recalls that most scientists were particularly turned off by the opening fiction. They just did not understand what Carson was trying to do or what the allegory was about. They were too literal and unimaginative to understand it.
8. R. Milton Carleton, "*Silent Spring* Merely Science Fiction Instead of Fact," *Chicago Sunday Sun-Times*, September 23, 1962; R. Milton Carleton to AF, March 8, 1963, RCP/BLYU.
9. George C. Decker, "Insecticides as a Part of the 20th Century Environment," Speech to the Ecological Society of America, August 1958; "Justification for the Use of Chemicals in Agriculture," Speech at the University of Illinois Farm and Home Festival, April 1960; "Pros and Cons of Pests, Pest Control and Pesticides," *World Review of Pest Control* (spring 1962), 6–18, reprinted in *Chemical World News*, RCP/BLYU.
10. "How to Answer Rachel Carson," *County Agent and Vo-Ag Teacher* (November 1962), RCP/BLYU.
11. Walter Sullivan, "Pesticides Book Called One-Sided," *New York Times*, September 13, 1962, RCP/BLYU. C. G. King to membership of The Nutrition Foundation, January 1963; Parke C. Brinkley to Rodney E. Leonard, August 29, 1962, RG 16, SOA, NARA. Brinkley, executive director of NACA, had a meeting the previous day with Leonard, a USDA official, to discuss the damage from Carson's book. Brinkley wrote, "I am concerned about the many other pieces that will be written as the result of it."

12. William J. Darby, "A Scientist Looks at *Silent Spring*," *Chemical & Engineering News*, October 1, 1962, RCP/BLYU. The title of Darby's review was changed from "Silence! Miss Carson," after readers complained that the review was bad-tempered and irresponsible and sent out in the Nutrition Foundation packet with the above heading. See "Letters," *Chemical & Engineering News*, November 5, 1962, 5–6.
13. Frederick J. Stare, "Some Comments on *Silent Spring*," *Nutrition Reviews* (January 1963), later published as "Two Buckets of Water," *Morning Globe*, February 4, 1963, RG 310, ARS, NARA. Carson and Rodell found Stare's distortions particularly offensive. When they learned that Stare recently had been sued for libel by the Boston Nutrition Society, Carson sent the legal citation to Greenbaum asking him to look into it. RC to Maurice Greenbaum, January 11, 1963, R/CA.
14. This was an argument taken seriously by health leaders, including Carson's friend conservationist William Vogt, who had become the director of the World Health Organization and who believed her position worked against the effective control of disease. MR to PB, October 24, 1962, R/CA.
15. See, for example, Thomas H. Jukes, "People and Pesticides," *American Scientist*, 51, 3 (September 1963), 355–361. Ironically, White-Stevens died in 1978 as a result of a reaction to massive wasp stings.
16. Byron T. Shaw, "Are Weed Killers, Bug Sprays Poisoning the Country?" *U.S. News & World Report*, November 26, 1962, 86–94. Thomas H. Jukes to Byron T. Shaw, May 10, 1963; Thomas H. Jukes to Orville Freeman, April 8, 1963, RG 310, ARS, NARA. The argument that pesticides were necessary to expand the food supply at a time of enormous crop surplus has been criticized as bogus by various scholars. See John H. Perkins, "Insects, Food, and Hunger: The Paradox of Plenty for U.S., Entomology, 1920–1970," *Environmental Review*, 7 (Spring 1983), 71–96.
17. Interviews with Frank Egler, Roland Clement. MR to PB, August 27, 1962, R/CA.
18. W. E. McCauley, "On *Silent Spring*," National Pest Control Association, September 13, 1962, RG 310, ARS, NARA.
19. "The Carsonoma Chorale" [Christmas 1962], RG 310, ARS, NARA. *Tucson Arizona Star*, October 14, 1962, RCP/BLYU.
20. Cynthia Westcott, *Plant Doctoring Is Fun* (Princeton, NJ: D. Van Nostrand Company, 1957). This is Westcott's successful account of her life and work as a "plant doctor."
21. Westcott was trained as an entomologist and received support from the Entomological Society of America, which promoted her in its pages as a calm, rational, trained scientist, the counterpart of Rachel Carson. I am grateful for material on Westcott given me by Frank Egler. Egler considered Westcott Carson's most damaging and dangerous opponent. Interview with Frank Egler.
22. Cynthia Westcott, "Half Truths or Whole Story? A Review of *Silent Spring*," distributed by Manufacturing Chemists Association, 1962. Courtesy Frank Egler.
23. She spoke particularly about the DDT residues in the bald eagle and in fish taken hundreds of miles at sea and asked for moderation and sanity in the use of chemical pesticides. Garden Club Federation of Pennsylvania *News*, February 14, 1963. Interview with Ruth Scott. Papers of Ruth Scott, privately held. Westcott, "Half-Truths or Whole Story? A Review of *Silent Spring*." Cynthia Westcott, "The Question Has Two Sides," *The National Gardener* (September/October 1962), 30–31. For evidence of Westcott's influence, see Helen S. Hull, "*Silent Spring* Becomes an Uproar," *Flower Grower Magazine* (December 1962), 18–19. *Flower Grower* depended on the agri-

cultural industry and the greenhouse lobby for most of its advertising. Carson and Westcott never met. See Lear, "War in the Garden."

24. Cynthia Westcott to RC, July 7, 1962; RC to Cynthia Westcott, August 6, 1962, RCP/BLYU.
25. Loren Eiseley, "Using a Plague to Fight a Plague," *Saturday Review of Literature*, September 29, 1962, 18, 19, 34. Clarence Cottam, "A Noisy Reaction to *Silent Spring*," *Sierra Club Bulletin* (January 1963); and Clarence Cottam and Thomas G. Scott, "A Commentary on *Silent Spring*," *Journal of Wildlife Management*, 27, 1 (January 1963), 151–155. In both articles, Cottam challenges George Decker's criticism of Carson. Clement, "From Birds to People." Clement's experience on the front lines against the chemical industry is a remarkable documentation of the power of big business and of the resilience of the committed individual. Interview with Roland Clement.
26. "Rachel Carson's Indictment of the Wide Use of Pesticides," review of *Silent Spring* by LaMont C. Cole, *Scientific American* (December 1962), 173–180. Frank Graham remarked on how resilent Carson was throughout a long period of devastating personal attacks and distortions of her work. Interview with Frank Graham.
27. Thomas Merton to RC, January 12, 1963, RCP/BLYU. Interview with Ida Sprow. Christine Stevens had a hand in getting the Schweitzer letter through a friend who visited the scientist in Africa. RC to CS, March 28, 1963, RCP/BLYU. Interview with Christine Stevens.
28. MR to PB, October 16, 1962, R/CA.
29. Ibid.
30. Houghton Mifflin advertisement for *Silent Spring*, RCP/BLYU. They also got free advertising from agricultural trade journals such as *Agrichemical West*, which ran a collage of sensational newspaper headlines featuring fish kills, pesticide warnings, and poisonings of agricultural workers that critics collected hoping to show the public how ridiculous Carson's book charges were, but which had just the opposite effect. "Editorial," *Agrichemical West* (November 1963), RCP/BLYU.
31. "The Story of *Silent Spring*," Houghton Mifflin Company, 1963, RCP/BLYU. RC to Joan Daves, November 29, 1962, R/CA.
32. "*Silent Spring* Author Calls Critics Unfair," *Chicago American*, January 29, 1963, RCP/BLYU. Carson, *Silent Spring*, 99. Yaakov Garb in his fine essay in *Dissent* (Fall 1995), 539–546, and expanded in "Change and Continuity in Environmental World-View: The Politics of Nature in Rachel Carson's *Silent Spring*," in David Macauley, ed., *Minding Nature* (New York: Guilford Press, 1996), 229–256, argues that Carson framed her case against pesticides primarily as an epistemic and moral problem rather than a political or economic one, and it was on this basis that her work was so broadly accepted by the public.
33. Rachel Carson, Speech, Animal Welfare Institute, January 7, 1963, RCP/BLYU. Interview with Christine Stevens. CS to RC, December 19, 1962, AWI.
34. Rachel Carson, Speech, Garden Club of America, January 8, 1963.
35. Ibid.
36. MR to AF, January 10, 1963, RCP/BLYU.
37. Margaret Clark, "Author Rachel Carson Is Small, Pretty and Dynamic," *Brocton Enterprise*, January 19, 1963. Carson's speech was entitled "A Sense of Values in Today's World." Rachel Carson, Speech, New England Wildflower Preservation Society, January 17, 1963, RCP/BLYU. Interview with Frank Egler. Egler was later instrumental in getting Carson's speech published in the April issue of *New Englander* magazine.
38. Interview with Frank Egler.

39. RC to DF, January 19, 1963, *Letters*. Carson met with the President's Science Advisory Committee on January 26, 1963, in what turned out to be a lengthy and very productive session. Interview with William L. Drury.
40. RC to DF, January 23, 1963, *Letters*.
41. Interview with William L. Drury. Carson's brief remarks were read by the president of the Women's National Book Association, February 13, 1963. Marie Rodell accepted an award made to Carson by the Rod and Gun Association a week later, where Rodell spoke about her trip with Carson on the *Albatross* and the origins of *Silent Spring* and read a brief statement by Carson. Rachel Carson, Speech, Rod and Gun Association, February 21, 1963, RCP/BLYU. Clarence Cottam accepted the Conservationist of the Year Award on Carson's behalf and read her remarks in Detroit, March 2, 1963. CC to RC, March 11, 1963; RC to CC, March 11, 1963, RCP/BLYU. RC to DF, March 2, 1963, *Letters*. Interview with Else Strom.
42. RC to DF, January 24, 1963, *Letters*.
43. RC to DF, n.d. [February 7, 1963], *Letters*.
44. RC to DF, February 14, 1963, *Letters*.
45. RC to DF, February 19, 1963 (in February 18 letter), *Letters*.
46. RC to George Crile, February 7, 1963, Crile Papers.
47. RC to DF, March 2, 1963, *Letters*.
48. RC to DF, March 27, 1963, *Letters*.
49. DF to RC, March 31, 1963, *Letters*. "Charles Alldredge," Obituary, *Washington Post*, RCP/BLYU. Interview with the Reverend Duncan Howlett. Carson always intended her next book to be the expansion of "Help Your Child to Wonder." RC to DF, March 2, 1963, *Letters*. See RC to Walter Minton, December 7, 1962, R/CA.
50. RC to LC, March 19, 1963, RCP/BLYU. The context of this unusually candid reflection was a letter Carson had received from "a woman in Big Sur" [Margaret Wentworth Owings], which had made a deep impression on her and increased her desire to live long enough to finish more of what she had planned.
51. PB to MR, October 23, 1962, R/CA.
52. RC to DF, March 19, 1963, *Letters*.
53. RC to George Crile, April 3, 1963, Crile Papers.
54. Ralph Caulk to George Crile, April 11, 1963, Crile Papers.
55. George Crile to RC, April 5, 1963, Crile Papers. Crile's letter goes into detail about a new method of ablating the hypophyses by implants of radioactive Yttrium, which he recommended as a potential treatment. Presumably Carson knew that this was a highly risky and experimental treatment that the Cleveland Clinic had been doing. In retrospect, as well as to Jeanne and Burnet Davis at the time, this drastic procedure was unwarranted. Interview with Jeanne Davis. RC to George Crile, April 3, 1963, Crile Papers. RC to DF, April 1, 1963, *Letters*.
56. Interviews with Paul Brooks, William Drury. RC to DF, March 28, 1963, *Letters*.
57. Brooks Atkinson, "Critic at Large," *New York Times*, April 2, 1963, RCP/BLYU. "Your column was really superb in getting directly to the heart of the controversy and stating the issues clearly. So many millions of words have been wasted talking about the wrong things. The timing could scarcely have been improved upon, coming just before the CBS program." RC to Brooks Atkinson, April 5, 1963, RCP/BLYU.
58. RC to DF, April 1, 1963, *Letters*.
59. *Houston* (Texas) *Post*, April 3, 1963; *Minneapolis Tribune*, March 19, 1963; Allan Gill, *Chicago Sun Times*, March 30, 1963, RCP/BLYU.
60. Interview with Jay McMullen.
61. Ibid. Curt Beck to Fred Friendly, May 10, 1963; Val Adams, "Sponsors Quit Pesticide Show," *New York Times*, April 3, 1963; *Broadcasting*, April 1, 1963; "Three

Sponsors Quit CBS TV Program," *Denver Post*, April 2, 1963; RCP/BLYU. Kiwi Shoe Polish gained immense benefits, and so presumably did Brillo. Kiwi president Lawrence Emley wrote Carson that "in the fifteen years of sponsorships and various advertising presentations in the U.S., we have never had such a fine reaction." Lawrence Emley to RC, May 24, 1963, RCP/BLYU.

62. AF to RC, August 7, 1963, RCP/BLYU. Before the CBS interview, Ford wrote a long letter on how to dress, not to wear makeup, and how to smile to relax her facial muscles. Frank Egler had asked Roland Clement to elaborate on his experience debating White-Stevens. Clement's letter gave her a very clear idea of White-Stevens's style and what to expect from him. Roland Clement to RC, November 27, 1962. Papers of Roland Clement. "The Silent Spring of Rachel Carson," *CBS Reports*, April 3, 1963, transcript. Interview with Jay McMullen.
63. "The Silent Spring of Rachel Carson," *CBS Reports*, April 3, 1963, transcript.
64. Ibid. Carson was paid $2,000 less commission for her appearance on *CBS Reports*. April 12, 1963, R/CA.
65. See Linda J. Lear, "Rachel Carson's *Silent Spring*," *Environmental History Review* 17, 2 (summer 1993), 23–48.
66. FE to RC, April 4, 1963; RC to FE, May 6, 1963; CS to RC, April 11, 1963, RCP/BLYU. Hundreds of angry letters to USDA are in RG 310, ARS, NARA. McMullen remembers poignantly that he told Carson when she called to tell him how much she had liked the documentary that he had enjoyed her company very much and hoped he would have the opportunity of seeing her again. There was a long pause on the telephone when he said this, and finally Carson said simply, "Good-bye, Mr. McMullen," and hung up. Interview with Jay McMullen.
67. On April 16, a week after the CBS broadcast, Rachel received a letter inviting her to testify before a House Subcommittee on Government Operations. She replied that she would be glad to do so, providing her physicians approved. Robert E. Jones to RC, House of Representatives, Natural Resources and Power Subcommittee. This invitation was immediately superseded by a call from Senator Ribicoff's legislative assistant, Jerome Sonosky, asking her to appear as a witness before the Senate Committee. Ribicoff himself called Carson the following day. Interview with Jerome Sonosky.
68. "And No Birds Sing," Editorial, *Washington Post*, April 13, 1963; "Pesticide Study Awaits White House Release," *Chemical & Engineering News*, April 8, 1963, RCP/BLYU. The industry journal recommended that pesticide producers brace themselves for a critical report.
69. RC to PB, May 11, 1963, RCP/BLYU. Carson had a pipeline through Paul Knight, and Brooks was in contact with members of William Drury's staff.
70. Drury, the director of the Hatheway School of Conservation Education, Massachusetts Audubon Society, was a close friend of Paul Brooks and of Roland Clement. *The Uses of Pesticides: A Report of the President's Science Advisory Committee*, The White House (Washington, D.C.: Government Printing Office, May 15, 1963), 23. Paul Knight, "Case Study on Environmental Contamination," 54–56. Interview with William L. Drury. Drury recalled that Carson did not have to make an impression on the PSAC when she came before them in informal session. She had already done her homework remarkably well. Drury's understanding of the issues presented and his dispassionate synthesis of them was apparent in my several interviews with him, the last he gave before his untimely death. Lear, "Rachel Carson's *Silent Spring*," 39–40.
71. Jonathan Spivak, *Wall Street Journal*, May 16, 1963. Headlines in the *Christian Science Monitor* were more dramatic. The day following release of the report, it

declared, "Rachel Carson Stands Vindicated!" I. L. Baldwin, "Chemicals and Pests," *Science*, September 28, 1962, 1042–1043. "Rachel Carson can be legitimately charged with having exceeded the bounds of scientific knowledge for the purpose of achieving shock: but her principal point—that pesticides are being used in massive quantities with little regard to undesirable side effects—permeates the PSAC report. . . ." Editorial, *Science*, May 24, 1964, 878–879.

72. "Rachel Carson Stands Vindicated!," *Christian Science Monitor*, May 16, 1963. "Pesticides: New Warning," *Washington Sunday Star*, May 19, 1963. Jerome B. Wiesner, *Where Science and Politics Meet* (New York: McGraw-Hill Book Company, 1961). "Jerome Wiesner," Obituary, October 23, 1994, *Washington Post*, B6.
73. CBS Reports, "The Verdict on the Silent Spring of Rachel Carson," May 15, 1963, Transcript in RCP/BLYU. The spokesman for the chemical industry on this report was Parke C. Brinkley, president of NACA.
74. PB to RC, May 16, 1963; RC to AF, May 21, 1963, RCP/BLYU. RC to Charles Callison, May 17, 1963, RCP/BLYU.
75. The increased publicity and her appearance on *The Today Show* were reflected in increased book sales. RC to AF, May 18, 1963, RCP/BLYU.
76. RC to DF, April 11, 1963, *Letters*.
77. RC to DF, April 30, 1963, *Letters*.
78. Carson wrote an article analyzing the PSAC report for the *New York Herald Tribune News Service*; it was syndicated in papers across the country. Copies in RCP/BLYU. Carson's testimony was originally scheduled for May 28 but was postponed by the committee to June 4.
79. RC to Olaus Murie, February 1, 1961; Olaus Murie to RC, February 6, 1961; RC to Clarence Cottam, April 10, 1963; RS to RC, May 12, 1963, RCP/BLYU. Ruth Scott visited Carson in Washington on May 21 when she was there to attend hearings and conservation meetings. Interview with Ruth Scott. RS to RC, May 22, 1963, RCP/BLYU. RC to Frank Egler, May 7, 1963, Papers of Frank E. Egler.
80. MR to AF, May 29, 1963, R/CA. Interviews with Jerome Sonosky, Abraham Ribicoff. Ribicoff noted that none of the other senators or staff left the room during Carson's testimony, a rare tribute.
81. Testimony of Rachel Carson, Hearings before the U.S. Senate Subcommittee on Reorganization and International Organizations of the Committee on Government Operations, "Interagency Coordination in Environmental Hazards (Pesticides)," June 4, 1963, 88th Congress (1 sess.) (Washington, D.C.: Government Printing Office, 1964).
82. Ibid. Carson also called for expanded programs of medical research and education in the field of pesticides, legislation restricting the sale and use of pesticides to persons incompetent to know how to handle them, the registration of chemicals by all agencies of government, the need to limit the number of pesticides in use, and government support of research on alternative methods of pest control.
83. Hearings. Interview with Abraham Ribicoff. Remarks of Ernest Gruening, Hearings, 220–221.
84. Remarks of Ernest Gruening, Hearings, 220–221. Ribicoff went on, "I have always known philosophically that one who believes is a majority because most people don't believe in anything, and here was a person who deeply believed in what she was saying."
85. Statement of Rachel Carson Before the Senate Committee on Commerce at Hearings on S. 1250 and S. 1251, June 6, 1963, 88th Congress (1 sess.), RCP/BLYU. See list of names Carson suggested to Scott for a "Citizens Advisory Committee." Papers of Ruth Scott, author's possession.

86. RC to DF, June 13, 1963, *Letters*. MR to LC, June 17, 1963, RCP/BLYU. Carson also wrote letters to congressmen speaking against the use of the steel jaw leg hold and the trapping and poisoning of wildlife in support of AWI initiatives.
87. Mrs. Yarnall Jacobs to RC, June 3, 1963, R/CA. Carson also spoke briefly at a meeting of the Federation of Homemakers, a group that had supported her since *The New Yorker* articles first appeared.
88. Rachel took Roger out of this camp after several weeks when she became distressed by its inadequate care. RC to DF, n.d. [August 1963], *Letters*.

19: "I SHALL REMEMBER THE MONARCHS"

1. DF to Jeanne Davis, July 14, 1963; RC to Jeanne Davis, August 8, 1963, Papers of Jeanne V. Davis, author's possession. These two letters reveal that the summer had not been tranquil or easy, particularly with regard to Roger. Interview with Bob Hines. Interview with Jeanne Davis. RC to AF, September 10, 1963, RCP/BLYU. Ford responded, "I'll bet Moppet is the cutest little black cat in heaven." RC to DF, September 16, 1963, *Letters*. After working closely with Anne Ford for nearly two years, Rachel had become very fond of her.
2. DF to Duncan Howlett, April 18, 1964, Papers of Duncan Howlett. Copy in author's possession.
3. RC to DF, September 10, 1963, *Letters*. Freeman recognized the rare quality of Carson's thoughts and cherished this letter. See DF to RC, September 12, 1963, *Letters*.
4. Interview with Bob Hines. RC to AF, September 23, 1963, RCP/BLYU. DF to RC, December 9, 1963, *Letters*.
5. Interview with Ida Sprow. RC to DF, September 16, 1963, *Letters*.
6. RC to DF, September 18, 1963, *Letters*.
7. Ibid. Robert Cushman Murphy to RC, September 21, 1963, RCP/BLYU.
8. RC to DF, October 3, 1963, *Letters*.
9. RC to FE, September 4, 1963, Papers of Frank E. Egler. FE to RC, September 12, 1963, RCP/BLYU.
10. Interview with Duncan Howlett. Howlett had preached a sermon on *Silent Spring* on October 7, 1962, which Senator Wayne Morse of Oregon placed in the *Congressional Record*. Alldredge sent Carson a copy. Duncan Howlett to RC, September 24, 1963, Papers of Duncan Howlett. Copy in author's possession. Howlett and Carson visited one other time when he came over to plant a shrub she had admired.
11. Ibid.
12. She also began drafting an introduction for a new British edition of her sea trilogy. Rights to *The Sea* had been sold to MacGibbon and Kee; it was not published until July 1964, with an introduction by Brian Vesy-Fitzgerald. A fragment of Carson's introduction is extant in R/CA. MR to RC, October 12, 1963, R/CA. RC to Roy M. Fisher, August 13, 1963, RCP/BLYU. Roy Fisher to RC, September 7, 1963, R/CA. Carson was paid $2,000 for the *World Book Encyclopedia Year Book* essay. RC to Samuel Ordway, June 10, 1963; MR to PB, June 22, 1963, RCP/BLYU.
13. Edwin Diamond, "The Myth of the 'Pesticide Menace,'" *Saturday Evening Post*, September 28, 1963, 16, 18.
14. RC to PB, October 3, 1963, RCP/BLYU. PB to MR, October 4, 1963, R/CA. PB to RC, October 4, October 10, 1963; Stuart Huckins to AF, November 4, 1963; RC to

Francis Silver, October 11, 1963, RCP/BLYU. Brooks did not think that a letter of correction hidden away in the letters column would do much to set the record straight.

15. RC to Helen Cruickshank, October 21, 1963; PB to Editor, *Saturday Evening Post*, October 4, 1963, RCP/BLYU. Diamond recalls no intention on his part to get even with Carson but rather a genuine disagreement with her science. Interview with Edwin Diamond.
16. William B. Bean, "The Noise of *Silent Spring*," *Archives of Internal Medicine* 112, 3 (September 1963), 62–65. MR to RC, December 17, 1963, R/CA. It is likely that Carson did not see Bean's review until December.
17. Rachel Carson, "Rachel Carson Answers Her Critics," *Audubon Magazine* 65 (September/October 1963), 262–265, 313–315. Interview with Roland Clement. Clement had continued to be the front man speaking in Carson's defense and taking on industry. Thanks to Charles Callison, Roland Clement, and John Vosburgh, *Audubon Magazine* had kept its readers' attention focused on the problems of pesticide contamination, the reluctance of the government to pass even the most moderate of control measures, and new evidence of harm that had appeared since Carson's book was published. See issues for the first six months of 1963.
18. RC to Kenneth Pomeroy, July 23, 1963; Kenneth Pomeroy to RC, July 12, 1963, RCP/BLYU.
19. RS to RC, September 8, 1963, RCP/BLYU. Scott and Ray Fosberg had already heard enough of Westcott's views to know what she would be saying. RC to Kenneth Pomeroy, October 12, 1963, RCP/BLYU. Interview with Ruth Scott.
20. Ruth Scott, who had gone to the Westcott panel to ask questions that would expose Westcott's industry affiliations, discovered the offending press release. At the same time she reported to Carson that rumors of Carson's ill health were circulating among industry delegates along with the story that she had declined to appear because she did not wish to confront Westcott in person. Interview with Ruth Scott. Fred E. Hornaday to Editor, *New York Times*, November 14, 1963; F. Hornaday to RC, November 14, 1963; Kenneth Pomeroy to RC, November 14, 1963, RCP/BLYU. Scott did what she could during the congress to dispel any notion that Carson had snubbed Westcott and to squash the persistent rumors that Carson's illness was caused by pesticide exposure.
21. The Kaiser Foundation symposium was intended to further the knowledge of "man and his environment" and was open to the scientific community by invitation. Carson was the only woman invited to participate in the Mayo Clinic's centennial. See invitation and program in RCP/BLYU.
22. The press account of Carson's speech is from George Dusheck, "An Echo of 'Silent Spring,' " *San Francisco News Call Bulletin*, October 19, 1963, 13.
23. Rachel Carson, Speech, Kaiser Foundation Symposium, "The Pollution of Our Environment," October 18, 1963, RCP/BLYU.
24. Carson's speech touched again on the problem of radioactive waste, its dispersal at sea, and the biological recycling of radioactive materials through the food chain. "We have not yet become sophisticated enough to view these matters as the ecological problems which they are, or to remember that we have introduced these things into dynamic systems."
25. Dusheck, "An Echo of 'Silent Spring,' " *San Francisco News Call*.
26. RC to DF, October 26, 1963, *Letters*.
27. David Brower, *For Earth's Sake* (Salt Lake City, UT: Gibbs and Smith Publisher, 1990), 214–215. Interview with David Brower. RC to DF, October 21, 1963, *Letters*. Carson did some shopping at Gumps Department Store, where she bought an

expensive Japanese screen that she hung as the centerpiece in her Berwick Road living room. RC to LC, n.d. [November 28, 1963], RCP/BLYU. Sadly, none of her family recognized its value; it was sold at public auction after her death for $25. Estate of Rachel L. Carson, Orphans Court, Montgomery County, MD.

28. RC to DF, October 21, 1963, *Letters*.
29. RC to DF, n.d. [early November 1963], *Letters*. To have done so would have meant first confronting her own death, which she was never completely able to do, even though she acknowledged her time was short. Comments made by Rodell after Carson's death indicate that Carson was in deep denial much of this time. See MR to PB, January 11, 1971, R/CA.
30. Ibid.
31. Interview with Jeanne Davis. Knowing that her brother Robert disliked Roger intensely, Rachel sought a male figure who had expressed some affection for the boy or at least essential goodwill. Virginia King's husband had at least one adult child from a previous marriage and his business required frequent travel. There is no evidence that Carson ever asked Virginia directly if they would take Roger. Interviews with Jeanne Davis, Shirley Briggs, Paul Brooks.
32. Interviews with Stanley and Madeleine Freeman, Martha Freeman, Paul Brooks, Jeanne Davis, Marjorie Spock, Shirley Briggs, Ruth Scott, Frank Egler, Ida Sprow.
33. RC to LC, March 19, 1963, RCP/BLYU. It is revealing that the only recorded discussion of Roger's guardianship is the one with Crisler, who raised wolves not children, and not with Marjorie Spock, who while single was knowledgeable about child development and fond of Roger. Carson also strangely never discussed the matter with Jeanne Davis, a successful mother of two. There exists the possibility that letters other than the one with Crisler existed but were destroyed by Rodell. Interviews with Marjorie Spock, Jeanne Davis.
34. Interviews with Paul Brooks, Stanley and Madeleine Freeman, Jeanne Davis, Ruth Scott, Roger Christie, Marjorie Spock.
35. RC to David G. Mearns, December 18, 1954; David G. Mearns to RC, December 29, 1964, RCP/BLYU. The next letter from Mearns appears to be April 4, 1964, well after Carson's deed of gift to Yale and ten days before her death.
36. RC to DF, November 14, 1963, *Letters*. Carson had not yet made the decision to give her papers to Yale.
37. The Beinecke opened in November 1963. Carson signed the first deed of gift December 21, 1963, which was redrafted to include her correspondence and signed January 24, 1964. University librarian, James T. Babb was not notified of Carson's gift of manuscripts and letters until April 1, 1964, when he received a letter from Maurice Greenbaum. After Carson's death, Babb was quoted in the *New Haven Register* as saying he had learned of Carson's wishes shortly before her death. RCP/BLYU. Donald T. Gallup, the curator of the Yale Collection of American Literature, made the decision to include Carson's gift in that collection. Records of the University Librarian, Series III, 1951–1964, Yale University Archives, Yale University, New Haven, CT.
38. Interview with Jeanne Davis.
39. Interview with Shirley Briggs. Marie Rodell told the story to Shirley after Carson's death when they were remembering her wonderful laugh.
40. RC to DF, November 27, 1963, *Letters*.
41. Stewart L. Udall, Speech, Dedication of the Department's Wildlife Research Laboratory, Patuxent Research Center, April 25, 1963, RCP/BLYU.
42. RC to Steward Udall, May 3, 1963, RCP/BLYU.
43. Frank Graham, Jr., *Since Silent Spring* (Boston: Houghton Mifflin Co., 1970),

96–109. See also Graham's study of water pollution including the Mississippi disaster, *Disaster by Default* (New York: M. Evans, 1966).

44. Interview with Jerome Sonosky.
45. Ibid. PB to RC, March 24, 1964, RCP/BLYU. Stuart H. Loory, "Science Tracks Down a Fish Killer," *New York Herald Tribune*, March 23, 1964, RCP/BLYU.
46. Irston Barnes, remarks at the annual dinner of the Audubon Naturalist Society, October 3, 1963, published in *Atlantic Naturalist* 18, 4 (October/December 1963), 207–208.
47. Rachel Carson, Speech, acceptance of Audubon Medal, December 3, 1963, RCP/BLYU. Roland Clement, Letter to *American Scientist*, December 3, 1963, RCP/BLYU. Interview with Roland Clement.
48. Interview with Margaret Wentworth Owings.
49. Rachel Carson, Speech, American Society of Geographers, December 5, 1963, RCP/BLYU.
50. RC to LC, n.d. [November 28, 1963], RCP/BLYU. Citation read at the election of Rachel Carson to membership in the American Academy of Arts and Letters, December 6, 1963, RCP/BLYU.
51. RC to DF, December 12, 1963, *Letters*.
52. RC to DF, December 18, 1963, *Letters*.
53. Ibid.
54. RC to DF, December 21, 1963, *Letters*.
55. Ibid. MR to PB, January 11, 1971, R/CA.
56. Carson also gave them a Sierra Club book of Eliot Porter's photographs. RC to DF, notes on three manuscript pages, December 25, 1963. Unpublished letters, UP/FFC.
57. RC to DF, January 2, 1964, *Letters*.
58. RC to DF, January 9, 1964, *Letters*.
59. RC to DF, January 18, 1964, *Letters*.
60. Interview with Stanley Freeman, Jr.
61. One of the great mysteries is whether Rachel ever hinted to Dorothy of her intention. Stanley and Madeleine Freeman do not believe she did, or that Dorothy knew about the codicil until Rodell called to inform her. Jeanne Davis shares this opinion.
62. RC to DF, January 18, 1964, *Letters*.
63. RC to DF, January 20, 1964, *Letters*.
64. DF to RC, February 29, 1964, *Letters*. Rachel insisted that Dorothy save them for the descriptions of the natural world they contained.
65. She had discussed bequests to these conservation organizations with Richard Pough and Ruth Scott, whose opinions she trusted. Interviews with Richard Pough, Ruth Scott.
66. "Last Will and Testament of Rachel L. Carson," February 13, 1964, Orphans Court, Montgomery County, MD.
67. "Codicil to the Last Will and Testament of Rachel L. Carson," February 13, 1964, Orphans Court, Montgomery County, MD. Having failed to discuss the issue with Dorothy when she had visited, Carson seemed to have given up all hope of confronting the issue before she died.
68. "Codicil."
69. RC to FE, February 23, 1964, RCP/BLYU. Interview with Jeanne Davis. Carson's name was never removed from the Mayo program.
70. Mrs. Patterson's given name is unknown.
71. Interview with Jeanne Davis. Dorothy felt the same way but knew that Rachel was determined to try everything.

72. RC to DF, March 10, 1964, *Letters*.
73. Rachel L. Carson, Medical Records, The Cleveland Clinic Foundation Archives.
74. DF to RC, March 30, 1964, *Letters*. Rachel dictated a letter taken down by a nurse for Dorothy on March 22, 1964, thanking her for her telephone calls and for her flowers, but it is mostly incoherent. RC to DF, March 22, 1964, UP/FFC.
75. Interview with Jeanne Davis. DF to RC, April 12, 1964, *Letters*.
76. Interview with Duncan Howlett.
77. SAB/D, April 1, 1964. PB to RC, March 24, 1964, RCP/BLYU. Vera had called Biskind from the clinic to report on Carson's improvement. Morton Biskind to RC, April 14, 1964, RCP/BLYU.
78. DF to RC, April 14, 1964, *Letters*.
79. Ida Sprow and Mrs. Patterson were with Carson in her bedroom when she died. Roger was in his room across the hall, watching television. Interview with Ida Sprow. According to George Crile's medical notes on Carson's record, "the hypophysectomy seemed to give remission of skeletal metastasis, but not liver." Physicians' notes, Rachel L. Carson Medical Records, The Cleveland Clinic Foundation Archives. Rachel Carson, *The Sea Around Us* (New York: Oxford University Press, 1951), 196.
80. Interview with Stanley and Madeleine Freeman. Stanley Freeman was out teaching when Rodell called Madeleine. Dorothy Freeman was extremely unhappy with Rodell's usurpation of Huhn's obligation. This tangle began a precipitous chill in relations between Freeman and Rodell, who had never been entirely comfortable with each other.
81. Parish Register, Washington National Cathedral, Washington, D.C.
82. SAB/D, April 18, 1964. Interviews with Ida Sprow, Jeanne Davis. Funeral Records, Joseph Gawlers' Sons, Washington, D.C.
83. SAB/D, April 17, 18, 1964. Interviews with Jeanne Davis, Bob Hines, Duncan Howlett.
84. Interview with Duncan Howlett. Remarks by the Reverend Duncan Howlett, April 19, 1964, All Soul's Unitarian Church, Washington, D.C. Courtesy, Duncan Howlett. DF to Duncan Howlett, April 18, 1964, Papers of Duncan Howlett. Dorothy offered the letter to Howlett, telling him, "I am so happy to do this for the beauty of its writing and the lovely thoughts that Rachel had expressed about dying."
85. The Rachel Carson Trust for the Living Environment was incorporated on December 25, 1965. Original committee members and those who met with Rodell in June 1964 included Irston Barnes, David Brower, Roland Clement, Clarence Cottam, Frank Egler, Ray Fosberg, Richard Goodwin, Robert Cushman Murphy, Richard Pough, Robert Rudd, Ruth Scott, Christine Stevens, Edwin Way Teale, and George Wallace. This organization was renamed the Rachel Carson Council, Inc., in 1978.
86. Interview with Stanley and Madeleine Freeman.
87. T. S. Eliot, from "The Dry Salvages," *Four Quartets* (New York: Harcourt Brace Jovanovich, 1943). A note in Dorothy's hand found in a copy of Brooks's book *The House of Life* that she had given to a local friend reads: "This is the quote I used in my notes on the scattering of Rachel's ashes." I am grateful to Jennifer Logan who now owns the copy of the book and shared it with me.

Bibliography

WRITINGS OF RACHEL CARSON (FIRST IMPRINTS ONLY)

Carson, Rachel Louise. "A Battle in the Clouds." *St. Nicholas Magazine* 45 (September 1918), 1048.

———. "A Young Hero." *St. Nicholas Magazine* 46 (January 1919), 280.

———. "A Message to the Front." *St. Nicholas Magazine* 46 (February 1919), 375.

———. "A Famous Sea Fight." *St. Nicholas Magazine* 46 (August 1919), 951.

———. "My Favorite Recreation." *St. Nicholas Magazine* 49 (July 1922), 999.

Carson, R. L. "It'll Be Shad-Time Soon." *Baltimore Sunday Sun*, 1 March 1936.

———. "Numbering the Fish of the Sea." *Baltimore Sunday Sun*, 24 May 1936.

———. "The Northern Trawlers Move South." *Baltimore Sunday Sun*, 3 January 1937.

———. "Shad Going the Way of the Buffalo." *Charleston, S.C. News-Current*, 14 February 1937.

———. "Sentiment Plays No Part in the Save the Shad Movement." *Baltimore Sunday Sun*, 28 February 1937.

———. "Chesapeake Oystermen See Stars and They Don't Like It." *Richmond Times Dispatch*, 28 March 1937.

———. "Oyster Dinners at the Bottom of the Chesapeake." *Richmond Times Dispatch Sunday Magazine*, 25 April 1937.

———. "Undersea." *Atlantic Monthly* 160 (September 1937), 322–325.

———. "Ducks Are Coming Back." *Baltimore Sunday Sun*, 16 January 1938.

———. "Baltimore Is Mecca of Conservationists This Week." *Baltimore Sunday Sun*, 13 February 1938.

———. "Fight for Wildlife Pushes Ahead." *Richmond Times Dispatch Sunday Magazine*, 20 March 1938, 8–9.

———. "Giants of the Riptide." *Baltimore Sunday Sun*, 3 August 1938.

———. "Open Season for Oysters." *Baltimore Sunday Sun*, 21 August 1938.

———. "Chesapeake Eels Seek the Sargasso Sea." *Baltimore Sunday Sun*, 9 October 1938.

———. "Whalers Ready for New Season." *Baltimore Sunday Sun*, 20 November 1938.

———. "Housing of Starlings Baltimore's Perennial Problem." *Baltimore Sunday Sun*, 5 March 1939.
———. "Shad Catches Declining as 1939 Season Opens." *Baltimore Sunday Sun*, 26 March 1939.
———. "Food from the Sea": "Fish and Shellfish of New England," U.S. Department of the Interior, Office of the Coordinator of Fisheries, Fish and Wildlife Service, Conservation Bulletin #33. Washington, D.C.: Government Printing Office, 1943.
———. "Food from the Sea": "Fishes of the Middle West," U.S. Department of the Interior, Office of the Coordinator of Fisheries, Fish and Wildlife Service, Conservation Bulletin #34. Washington, D.C.: Government Printing Office, 1943.
———. "Food from the Sea": "Fish and Shellfish of the South Atlantic and Gulf Coasts," U.S. Department of the Interior, Office of the Coordinator of Fisheries, Fish and Wildlife Service, Conservation Bulletin #37. Washington, D.C.: Government Printing Office, 1944.
———. "Food from the Sea": "Fish and Shellfish of the Middle Atlantic Coast," U.S. Department of the Interior, Office of the Coordinator of Fisheries, Fish and Wildlife Service, Conservation Bulletin #38. Washington, D.C.: Government Printing Office, 1945.
Carson, Rachel L. "How About Citizenship Papers for the Starling?" *Nature Magazine* (June/July 1939), 317–319.
———. *Under the Sea-Wind: A Naturalist's Picture of Ocean Life*. New York: Simon & Schuster, 1941.
———. "Ocean Wonderland." *Transatlantic* (March 1944), 35–40.
———. "Lifesaving Milkweed." *This Week Magazine*, 4 September 1944.
———. "The Bat Knew It First." *Collier's*, 18 November 1944.
———. "Sky Dwellers." *Coronet* (November 1945).
———. "Indoor Ocean." *This Month* (June 1946), 31–35.
———. *Chincoteague: A National Wildlife Refuge. Conservation in Action* #1. Washington, D.C.: U.S. Fish and Wildlife Service, Government Printing Office, 1947. Illustrated by Shirley A. Briggs and Katherine L. Howe.
———. *Mattamuskeet: A National Wildlife Refuge. Conservation in Action* #4. Washington, D.C.: U.S. Fish and Wildlife Service, Government Printing Office, 1947. Illustrated by Katherine L. Howe.
———. *Parker River: A National Wildlife Refuge. Conservation in Action* #2. Washington, D.C.: U.S. Fish and Wildlife Service, Government Printing Office, 1947. With drawings and photographs by Katherine L. Howe.
———. "Parker River—A New England Conservation Project." *Massachusetts Audubon Society Bulletin* 31, no. 2 (1947), 51–61. Photographs by Katherine L. Howe.
———. *Guarding Our Wildlife Resources. Conservation in Action* #5. Washington, D.C.: U.S. Fish and Wildlife Service, Government Printing Office, 1948. Designed by Katherine L. Howe.
———. "The Great Red Tide Mystery." *Field and Stream* (February 1948), 15–18.
———. "Lost Worlds: The Challenge of the Islands." *The Wood Thrush* 4, no. 5 (May–June 1949), 179–187.
Carson, Rachel L., and Vanez T. Wilson. *Bear River: A National Wildlife Refuge. Conservation in Action*, #8. Washington D.C.: U.S. Fish and Wildlife Service, Government Printing Office, 1950. Illustrations by Bob Hines.
Carson, Rachel L. "The Birth of an Island." *Yale Review* 40, no. 1 (September 1950), 112–126.
———. "The Sea" (excerpt) in "Profiles," *The New Yorker*, 2, 9, 16 June 1951.
———. *The Sea Around Us*. New York: Oxford University Press, 1951.
———. " 'The Exceeding Beauty of the Earth—' Words to Live By." *This Week Magazine*, 25 May 1952, 5.

———. "Mr. Day's Dismissal." *The Washington Post*, 22 April 1953, A26.
Carson, Rachel. "The Edge of the Sea" (excerpt) in "Profiles." *The New Yorker*, 20, 27, August 1955.
———. *The Edge of the Sea*. Boston: Houghton Mifflin Company, 1955.
———. "Biological Sciences." *Good Reading*. New York: New American Library, 1956.
———. "Help Your Child to Wonder." *Woman's Home Companion* (July 1956), 25–27, 46–48.
———. *The Sea Around Us*. Special Edition for Young Readers, adapted by Anne Terry White. New York: Simon & Schuster, 1958.
———. "Our Ever-Changing Shore." *Holiday* 24 (July 1958), 71–120.
———. "Vanishing Americans." *The Washington Post*, 10 April 1959, 26.
———. "To Understand Biology." *Humane Biology Projects*. Washington, D.C.: Animal Welfare Institute, 1960.
———. "The Sea." *The Johns Hopkins Magazine* 12, no. 8 (May–June 1961), 6–20. Photographs by Erich Hartmann.
———. "Letter to the Editor." *The Boothbay Register*, 27 July 1961, 5.
———. *The Sea Around Us*. rev. ed. New York: Oxford University Press, 1961.
———. "Silent Spring" (excerpt) in "Reporter at Large." *The New Yorker*, 16, 23, 30, June 1962.
———. *Silent Spring*. Boston: Houghton Mifflin Company, 1962.
———. "Of Man and the Stream of Time." Claremont, CA: Scripps College, 12 June 1962.
Carson, Rachel L. "The Living Ocean: A Year Book Special Report." *The World Book Encyclopedia Year Book*. Chicago: Chicago World Book, Childcraft International, 1963, 52–64.
Carson, Rachel. "Rachel Carson Answers Her Critics." *Audubon Magazine* 65 (September/October 1963), 262–265, 313–315.
———. "Foreword" to Ruth Harrison, *Animal Machines: The New Factory Farming Industry*. London: Vincent Stuart, LTC., 1964.
———. *The Sense of Wonder*. New York: Harper & Row, 1965. Photographs by Charles Pratt.

PERSONAL INTERVIEWS

Aldous, Isabel Duncan. Hillsboro, VA, November 9, 1994.
Algire, Stephen and Betty. Silver Spring, MD, August 27, 1994.
Andrews, Ella (Mrs. John). Silver Spring, MD, June 20, 1994.
Anshen, Ruth Nanda. New York, NY, June 3, 1996.
Bader, Virginia (Mrs. Franz). Washington, D.C., June 13, 1995.
Barnes, Chaplin. Stonington, CT, May 31, 1995.
Beale, Betty. Washington, D.C., June 13, 1995.
Bell, Mary Lou Succop. Pittsburgh, PA, December 12, 1993.
Bok, Derek. Cambridge, MA, April 11, 1996.
Branton, Harriet. Washington, PA, December 11, 1993.
Briggs, Shirley Ann. Bethesda, MD, August 10, 1990.
Brodeur, Paul. New York, NY, October 12, 1993.
Brooks, Paul. Lincoln Center, MA, October 6, 1991.
Brower, David. Pittsburgh, PA, April 9, 1991.
Brower, Stanley. Southport, ME, April 30, 1996.
Capeless, Leona. New York, NY, February 9, 1995.

Cath, Stanwood. Bethesda, MD, November 11, 1991.
Challand, Helen. Shabbona, IL, March 1, 1994.
Christie, Roger A. Cambridge, MA, Southport, ME, June 4, 1991.
Clark, Eugenie. Bethesda, MD, July 1, 1994.
Clement, Roland C. North Branford, CT, June 12, 1992.
Collin, Frances. Wayne, PA, April 7, 1993.
Cook, Phyllis. Boothbay Harbor, ME, July 15, 1992.
Crile, (Mrs. George). See Sandburg, Helga.
Daves, Joan. New York, NY, March 8, 1995.
Davis, Jeanne V. (Mrs. Burnet M.). Chevy Chase, MD, January 10, 1991.
Diamond, Edwin. East Hampton, NY, July 1, 1996.
Dobner, Effie. Springdale, PA, October 10, 1993.
Drury, William L. Bar Harbor, ME, February 29, 1992.
Duff, (Rev.) Bette Haney. Vernona, WI, June 1, 1995.
Egler, Frank E. Norfolk, CT, January 30, 1992.
Ellman, Joanne. Needham, MA, January 6, 1995.
Farr, Marion M. Gaithersburg, MD, June 21, 1994.
Fifer, Margaret. Sewickley, PA, December 15, 1993.
Forbes, Lynn. Woods Hole, MA, March 22, 1994.
Fosberg, F. Raymond. Washington, D.C., October 16, 1991.
Foster, Aurel O. College Park, MD, June 20, 1994.
Frankel, Virginia. New York, NY, January 10, 1995.
Freeman, Stanley, Jr. and Madeleine. Southport, ME, July 21, 1994.
Freeman, Orville S. Washington, D.C., June 6, 1992.
Freeman, Martha. Augusta and Southport, ME, October 5, 1991.
Gardner, Ruth. Southport, ME, July 10, 1994.
George, Evelyn Hirtle. Springdale, PA, October 29, 1993.
George, John L. State College, PA, July 30, 1991.
Gianinni, Claudia (James). Springdale, PA, July 30, 1991.
Goldman, Rachel Bok. Chicago, IL, April 12, 1996.
Goodwin, William. New London, CT, June 30, 1991.
Graham, Frank, Jr. and Ada. Milbridge, ME, July 19, 1992.
Hanley, Wayne. W. Wareham, MA, June 8, 1996.
Hartmann, Erich and Ruth Baines. New York, NY, July 28, 1995.
Hill, Gideon. Washington, D.C., November 4, 1991.
Hines, Bob. Arlington, VA, April 25, 1991.
Hoerner, Frances Carson. Cranberry Twp., PA, August 26, 1993.
Hollister, Sarah. Princeton, NJ, August 13, 1994.
Howell, Mary Frances. Washington, D.C., November 9, 1994.
Howlett, (Rev.) Duncan S. Falls Church, VA, April 21, 1994.
Huettner, Robert and Jane. Woods Hole, MA, March 4, 1994.
Kavaler, Lucy. New York, NY, January 5, 1995.
Kieran, Margaret Ford (Mrs. John). Rockport, MA, April 9, 1994.
Knipling, Edward F. Beltsville, MD, November 26, 1991.
Knox, Helen Myers. Greensburg, PA, February 11, 1992.
Kobrak, Barbara. Kalamazoo, MI, January 6, 1994.
Leiby, Carolyn. Falmouth, ME, October 15, 1993.
Lippy, Grace E. Frederick, MD, March 31, 1994.
Llewelyn, Mary Frye. Pittsburgh, PA, December 9, 1993.
Logan, Jennifer. Boothbay Harbor, ME, June 24, 1992.
McCarthy, John and Klose, Christopher. Washington, D.C., October 28, 1991.

McHarg, Ian. Philadelphia, PA, November 16, 1994.
McMullen, Jay. Greenwich, CT, February 8, 1997.
Moretti, Anne Algire. Dousman, WI, August 28, 1994.
Musser, Dorothy Appleby. Indiana, PA, December 6, 1993.
Neumann, Mary Louise. Evanston, IL, March 2, 1994.
Newton, Page. Silver Spring, MD, May 6, 1993.
Niering, William. New London, CT, April 4, 1994.
Oakley, Walter. New York, NY, June 8, 1995.
Owings, Margaret Wentworth. Cypress Point, CA, June 23, 1994.
Peters, Harold S. Ellenton, FL, May 7, 1992.
Peterson, Roger Tory. Old Lyme, CT, September 28, 1995.
Pough, Richard. Pelham, NY, January 16, 1997.
Rhoades, Geraldine. New York, NY, December 4, 1994.
Ribicoff, Abraham. New York, NY, June 2, 1992.
Roberts, Katherine Howe (Mrs. Sam). Salt Lake City, UT, March 1, 1993.
Rudd, Robert. Davis, CA, November 6, 1991.
Sabrosky, Curt W. Short Hills, NJ, May 26, 1996.
Sandburg, Helga (Mrs. George Crile, Jr.). Cleveland Heights, OH, September 10, 1994.
Scott, Ruth (Mrs. J. Lewis). Pittsburgh, PA, June 5, 1990.
Seif, Dorothy Thompson. Butler, PA, January 31, 1991.
Shaw, Jonathan. Lake Wales, FL, April 23, 1996.
Shaw, Judith (Mrs. James). Silver Spring, MD, June 20, 1994.
Shaw, Marian M. Silver Spring, MD, June 20, 1994.
Shombert, Elizabeth Daugherty (Mrs. George). Cranberry Twp, PA, September 25, 1994.
Skinker, Frances Staley (Mrs. G. Murray). Bethesda, MD, March 7, 1994.
Skinker, Martha. St. Louis, MO, October 14, 1991.
Skinker, Thomas M. Florissant, MO, January 20, 1994.
Skinker, Dr. Thomas M. Tucson, AZ, March 10, 1994.
Smith, Michael Lawler. Washington, D.C., October 25, 1991.
Sonosky, Jerome. Washington, D.C., June 17, 1992.
Spock, Marjorie. E. Gouldsboro, ME, May 26, 1994.
Sprow, Ida. Washington, D.C., October 16, 1991.
Stevens, Christine (Mrs. Roger W.). Washington, D.C., September 13, 1993.
Stiles, Anne and Stephen. Southport, ME, July 21, 1994.
Strom, Else. Goleta, CA, June 1, 1995.
Swetland, George. Alna, ME, July 7, 1994.
Swisshelm, Ruth Hunter. Dunkirk, NY, November 29, 1993.
Totten, Sarah Smith. Manchester-by-the-Sea, MA, September 25, 1993.
Udall, Stewart L. Falls Church, VA, March 8, 1992.
Ulrich, Julia and Robert. Silver Spring, MD, October 27, 1991.
Underwood, Paul C. University Park, MD, May 24, 1994.
Vosburgh, John S. Bethesda, MD, January 18, 1996.
Walford, Christiana. New York, NY, August 12, 1994.
Wilson, Adele "Nicki." Washington, D.C., July 12, 1990.
White, Joseph B. C. Pittsburgh, PA, August 9, 1990.
Wright, Constance (Mrs. J. Richard). Boothbay Harbor, ME, July 17, 1994.
Wyth, M. S., Jr. New York, NY, March 30, 1996.
Yentsch, Clarice. Boothby Harbor, ME, July 10, 1994.
Zahniser, Edward. Harpers Ferry, WV, May 18, 1995.
Zwinger, Ann H. Colorado Springs, CO, March 10, 1994.

SELECT BIBLIOGRAPHY

"The 100 Most Important Americans of the 20th Century." Special Edition. *Life* (September 1990), 19.

Abir-am, Pnina G. "Synergy or Clash: Disciplinary and Marital Strategies in the Career of Mathematical Biologist Dorothy Wrinch." In *Uneasy Careers and Intimate Lives: Women in Science, 1789–1979*, eds. Pnina G. Abir-am and Dorinda Outram. New Brunswick, NJ: Rutgers University Press, 1987.

Abir-am, Pnina G., and Dorinda Outram, eds. *Uneasy Careers and Intimate Lives: Women in Science, 1789–1979*. New Brunswick, NJ: Rutgers University Press, 1987.

Achilladelis, Basil, Albert Schwarzkopf, and Martin Cines. "A Study of Innovation in the Pesticide Industry: Analysis of the Innovation Record of an Industrial Sector." *Research Policy* 16 (1987), 175–212.

After Silent Spring: The Unsolved Problems of Pesticide Use in the United States. Washington, D.C.: Natural Resources Defense Council, June 1993.

Allen, Garland. *Life Science in the Twentieth Century*. Cambridge: Cambridge University Press, 1978.

Alpern, Sara, Joyce Antler, Elizabeth Israels Perry, and Ingrid Winther Scobie, eds. *The Challenge of Feminist Biography: Writing the Lives of Modern American Women*. Urbana: University of Illinois Press, 1992.

Ambrose, Stephen. *Rise to Globalism*. New York: Penguin Books, 1983.

Andrews, John S. *Animal Parasite Research in the Zoological Division, Bureau of Animal Industry, U.S. Department of Agriculture, Washington, D.C., 1923–1938*. Beltsville, MD: Animal Parasite Institute, 1993.

Ascher, Carol, Louise DeSalvo, and Sara Ruddick, eds. *Between Women: Biographers, Novelists, Critics, Teachers, and Artists Write About Their Work on Women*. New York: Routledge, 1993.

Austin, Mary H. *The Land of Little Rain*. Boston: Houghton Mifflin Company, 1903.

Babcock, Franklin L. *Spanning the Atlantic*. New York: Alfred A. Knopf, 1931.

"Baby Tooth Survey Launched in Search of Data on Strontium-90." *Nuclear Information* 24 (December 1958), 1–5.

Bailey, Brooke. *The Remarkable Lives of 100 Women Healers and Scientists*. New York: B. Adams, 1994.

Bailey, Liberty Hyde. *The Nature-Study Idea*. New York: Doubleday, Page & Company, 1903.

Bailey, Ronald. *Eco-Scam: The False Prophets of Ecological Apocalypse*. New York: St. Martin's Press, 1993.

Baldwin, I. L. "Chemicals and Pests." *Science*, 28 September 1962, 1042–1043.

Ball, Howard. *Justice Downwind: America's Atomic Testing Program in the 1950's*. New York: Oxford University Press, 1986.

Balogh, Brian. *Chain Reaction: Expert Debate and Public Participation in American Commercial Nuclear Power, 1945–1975*. Cambridge: Cambridge University Press, 1991.

Barnes, Irston R. "10 Springs Later." *The Washington Post*, 24 September 1972.

Bate, Jonathan. *Romantic Ecology: Wordsworth and the Environmental Tradition*. London: Routledge, 1991.

Bean, William B. "The Noise of *Silent Spring*." *Archives of Internal Medicine* 112, no. 3 (September 1963), 62–65.

Beebe, William. *Half Mile Down*. New York: Harcourt Brace and Co., 1934.

———, ed. *The Book of Naturalists: An Anthology of the Best Natural History*. New York: Alfred A. Knopf, 1944.

Benchloss, Michael. *Mayday: Eisenhower, Krushchev, and the U-2 Affair.* New York: HarperCollins, 1991.

Benson, Keith R. "American Morphology in the Late Nineteenth Century: The Biology Department at Johns Hopkins University." *Journal of the History of Biology* 18, no. 2 (June 1985), 163–206.

Benson, Keith R., Jane Maienschein, and Ronald Rainger, eds. *The Expansion of American Biology.* New Brunswick, NJ: Rutgers University Press, 1991.

Benson, Maxine. *Martha Maxwell: Rocky Mountain Naturalist.* Lincoln: University of Nebraska Press, 1986.

Bercovitch, Sacvan. *The American Jeremiad.* Madison: University of Wisconsin Press, 1978.

Bernstein, Barton J. "The Birth of the U. S. Biological-Warfare Program." *Scientific American* 256 (June 1981), 116–21.

Berrill, N.(orman) J. "The 'Drama-Filled Fringe.' " *Saturday Review of Literature,* 3 December 1955, 30.

———. *The Living Tide.* New York: Dodd Mead & Co., 1951.

Beston, Henry. *Especially Maine: The Natural World of Henry Beston from Cape Cod to the St. Lawrence,* ed. Elizabeth Coatsworth. Brattleboro, VT: The Stephen Greene Press, 1970.

———. "Miss Carson's First." *The Freeman* 3, no. 3 (3 November 1952), 100.

———. *The Outermost House: A Year of Life on the Great Beach of Cape Cod.* New York: Henry Holt and Company, 1949.

Bigelow, Henry B. *Oceanography: Its Scope, Problems, and Economic Importance.* Boston: Houghton Mifflin Company, 1931.

Biskind, Morton S. "On the Alleged Harmlessness of DDT for Man." *Journal of Applied Nutrition* 10, no. 2 (1957).

Black, Allida M. *Casting Her Own Shadow: Eleanor Roosevelt and the Shaping of Postwar Liberalism.* New York: Columbia University Press, 1996.

———. "Perverting the Diagnosis: The Lesbian and the Scientific Basis of Stigma." *Historical Reflections* 20, no. 2 (June 1994), 201–216.

Blend, Benay. "Mary Austin and the Western Conservation Movement: 1900–1927." *Journal of the Southwest* 30 (March 1988), 12–34.

Blodgett, John. "Pesticides: Regulation of an Evolving Technology." In *Legislation of Product Safety,* eds. Samuel S. Epstein and Richard D. Grady. Cambridge, MA: MIT Press, 1974.

Boffey, Philip M. "20 Years After 'Silent Spring': Still a Troubled Landscape." *The New York Times,* 25 May 1982.

———. *The Brain Bank of America: An Inquiry into the Politics of Science.* New York: McGraw-Hill Book Company, 1975.

Bok, Edward W. *America's Taj Mahal.* Lake Wales, FL: Bok Tower Gardens Foundation, 1989.

Bok Tower Gardens. Lake Wales, FL: The American Foundation, 1981.

Bonta, Marcia Myers. *Women in the Field: America's Pioneering Women Naturalists.* College Station, TX: Texas A&M University Press, 1991.

Bookchin, Murray. *Our Synthetic Environment,* rev. ed. New York: Harper Colophon Books, 1974.

———. *Remaking Society: Pathways to a Green Future.* Boston: South End Press, 1990.

Bosso, Christopher J. *Pesticides and Politics: The Life Cycle of a Public Issue.* Pittsburgh: University of Pittsburgh Press, 1987.

Botkin, Daniel B. *Discordant Harmonies: A New Ecology for the Twenty-First Century.* New York: Oxford University Press, 1990.

Boucher, Norman. "The Legacy of 'Silent Spring.'" *The Boston Globe*, 15 March 1987, 17, 37–48.

Boyer, Paul. *By the Bombs Early Light: American Thought and Culture at the Dawn of the Atomic Age*. New York: Pantheon Books, 1985.

———. "Fallout Shelters." *Life*, 15 September 1961, 98–108.

Bradford, Robert Whitmore. "Journey into Nature: American Nature Writing, 1733–1860." Ph.D. diss., Syracuse University, 1957.

Bramwell, Anna. *Ecologists in the 20th Century. A History*. New Haven, CT: Yale University Press, 1989.

Branch, Michael Paul. *The Enlightened Naturalist: Ecological Romanticism in American Literature*. Charlottesville, VA: University of Virginia, 1993.

Branton, Harriet. *Focus on Washington County*, vol. 3. Washington, PA: Observer Publishing Company, August 1982.

Breijer, C. J. "The Growing Insensitivity of Insects to Insecticides." *Mededelingen Directeur van de Tuinbouw*, trans. M. Spock and M. T. Richards. New York: privately published, 1956.

———. "The Growing Insensitivity of Insects to Insecticides." *Atlantic Naturalist* 13, no. 3 (July 1958), 149–155.

Briggs, Shirley A. *Basic Guide to Pesticides: Their Characteristics and Hazards*. Washington D.C.: Taylor and Francis, 1992.

———. "A Decade After 'Silent Spring.'" *Friends Journal*, 1 March 1972, 148–149.

———. "The Edge of the Sea: A Review." *Atlantic Naturalist* 11, no. 2 (November/December 1955), 90.

———. "Island Beach." *Atlantic Naturalist* 6, no. 5 (May/August 1951), 214–219.

———. "The Rachel Carson National Wildlife Refuge." *Atlantic Naturalist* 25, no. 1 (March 1970), 21–24.

———. "Rachel Carson: Her Vision and Her Legacy." In *Silent Spring Revisited*, eds. Gino J. Marco, Robert M. Hollingworth, and William Durham. Washington, D.C.: American Chemical Society, 1987.

———. "The Rachel Carson Legacy." *Pesticides News* 1 (September 1992), 7.

———. *Silent Spring: The View from 1987*. Chevy Chase, MD: Rachel Carson Council, Inc., 1987.

———. "Twenty Years After 'Silent Spring.'" *Garden* (May 1982), 10–15.

Brinkley, David. *Washington Goes to War*. New York: Alfred A. Knopf, 1988.

Brodeur, Paul. "Legacy." *The New Yorker*, 7 June 1993, 114.

———. *Outrageous Conduct: The Asbestos Industry on Trial*. New York: Pantheon Books, 1985.

Brooks, Paul. *The House of Life: Rachel Carson at Work*. Boston: Houghton Mifflin Company, 1972.

———. "Rachel Carson." In *Notable American Women, 1607–1950: A Biographical Dictionary*, ed. Edward T. James. Cambridge, MA: Belknap Press of Harvard University, 1971.

———. *Speaking for Nature: How Literary Naturalists From Henry David Thoreau to Rachel Carson Have Shaped America*. San Francisco: Sierra Club, 1980.

———. *Two Park Street: A Publishing Memoir*. Boston: Houghton Mifflin Company, 1986.

Brower, David. *For Earth's Sake: The Life and Times of David Brower*. Salt Lake City, UT: Gibbs and Smith Publisher, 1990.

Browne, Janet. *Charles Darwin: Voyaging*. New York: Alfred A. Knopf, 1995.

Buck, Solon J., and Elizabeth Hawthorn. *The Planting of Civilization in Western Pennsylvania*. Pittsburgh: University of Pittsburgh Press, 1939.

Buell, Lawrence. *The Environmental Imagination: Thoreau, Nature Writing, and the Formation of American Culture*. Cambridge, MA: Belknap Press of Harvard University, 1995.
Burstyn, Joan N. "Early Women in Education: The Role of the Anderson School of Natural History." *Boston University Journal of Education* 159, no. 3 (August 1977), 50–64.
Carter, Paul A. *Another Part of the Fifties*. New York: Columbia University Press, 1983.
Caufield, Catherine. *Multiple Exposures: Chronicles of the Radiation Age*. New York: Harper & Row, 1989.
Chafe, William H. *The American Woman: Her Changing Social, Economic, and Political Role, 1920–1970*. New York: Oxford University Press, 1972.
———. *Unfinished Journey: America Since World War II*. New York: Oxford University Press, 1986.
Chesler, Ellen. *Woman of Valor: Margaret Sanger and the Birth Control Movement in America*. New York: Simon & Schuster, 1992.
Chodorow, Nancy. *The Reproduction of Mothering, Psychoanalysis and the Sociology of Gender*. Berkeley: University of California Press, 1978.
Clarke, Robert. *Ellen Swallow: The Woman Who Founded Ecology*. Chicago: Follett Publishing Co., 1973.
Clement, Roland C. "From Birds to People: The Politics of the Audubon Movement." Unpublished mss. 1993.
———. "Three Reviews." *Audubon Magazine* 64 (November/December 1962), 356–357.
———. "The Editorial Trail." *Audubon Magazine* 64 (November/December 1962), 306.
———. "The Pesticides Controversy." *Environmental Affairs* 2, no. 3 (winter 1972), 445–468.
Cloos, Hans. *Conversation with the Earth*, trans. E. B. Garside. New York: Alfred A. Knopf, 1953.
Cochrane, Raymond. *The National Academy of Sciences: The First Hundred Years, 1863–1963*. Washington, D.C.: The National Academy of Sciences, 1978.
Codman, R. C. "Prefers DDT Control to Moths, Mosquitoes." *The Boston Herald*, 16 January 1958, sec. 3, 28.
Cohn, Norman. *The Pursuit of the Millennium*, rev. ed. New York: Oxford University Press, 1970.
Colborn, Theo, Dianne Dumanoski, and John Peterson Myers. *Our Stolen Future*. New York: Dutton, 1996.
Cole, LaMont C. "Rachel Carson's Indictment of the Wide Use of Pesticides." *Scientific American* (December 1962), 173–180.
Coleman, William. *Biology in the Nineteenth Century: Problems of Form, Function, and Transformation*. New York: John Wiley & Sons, 1971.
Commoner, Barry. *The Closing Circle: Nature, Man, and Technology*. New York: Alfred A. Knopf, 1971.
———. *Science and Survival*. New York: Viking Press, 1963.
Comstock, Anna Botsford. *The Comstocks of Cornell: John Henry Comstock and Anna Botsford Comstock*, eds. Glenn W. Harrick and Ruby Green Smith. Ithaca, NY: Comstock Publishing Associates, a division of Cornell University Press, 1953.
———. *Handbook of Nature Study*. Ithaca, NY: Cornell University Press, 1911, 1970.
———. "Introduction." In *Nature Study: A Pupil's Text Book*, with Frank Overton and Mary E. Hill. New York: American Book Co., 1905.
Conrad, Joseph. *Sea Stories*. New York: Carroll & Graf, 1985.
———. *Twixt Land and Sea*. Garden City, NY: Doubleday, 1912.
Cook, Blanche Wiesen. *Eleanor Roosevelt*, vol. 1. New York: Viking Penguin Press, 1992.

———. "Female Support Networks and Political Activism: Lillian Wald, Crystal Eastman, Emma Goldman." *A Heritage of Their Own*, eds. Nancy F. Cott and Elizabeth Pleck. New York: Simon & Schuster, 1979.

———. " 'Women Alone Stir My Imagination': Lesbianism and the Cultural Tradition." *Signs* 4, no. 4 (Summer 1979), 718–739.

Cottam, Clarence. "A Noisy Reaction to *Silent Spring*." *Sierra Club Bulletin* (January 1963), reprint.

———. "*Silent Spring:* An Appraisal." *National Parks Magazine* 36, no. 182 (November 1962), reprint.

Cottam, Clarence, and Elmer Higgins. "DDT and Its Effect on Fish and Wildlife." *Journal of Economic Entomology* 39 (February 1946), 44–52.

Cottam, Clarence, and Thomas G. Scott. "A Commentary on *Silent Spring*." *Journal of Wildlife Management* 27, no. 1 (January 1963), 151–155.

Cremin, Lawrence A., David A. Shannon, and Mary Evelyn Townsend. *A History of Teachers College, Columbia University*. New York: Columbia University Press, 1954.

Crile, George, Jr. *The Way It Was: Sex, Surgery, Treasure & Travel, 1907–1987*. Kent, OH: Kent State University Press, 1992.

Crisler, Lois. *Arctic Wild*. New York: Harper & Bros., 1958.

———. *Captive Wild*. New York: Harper & Bros., 1968.

Crone, Hugh D. *Chemicals and Society*. Cambridge: Cambridge University Press, 1986.

Cronon, William, ed. *Uncommon Ground: Toward Reinventing Nature*. New York: W. W. Norton and Company, 1995.

Crosby, Mrs Robert R. *Fifty Years of Service: National Council of State Garden Clubs, 1929–1979*. St. Louis, MO: National Council of State Garden Clubs, 1979.

D'Innocenzo, Michael. "A Literature of Warning." *Port Washington Library Survey*. Port Washington, NY: Port Washington Public Library, 1992.

Daly, Herman E., and John B. Cobb, Jr. *For the Common Good: Redirecting the Economy Toward Community, the Environment, and a Sustainable Future*. Boston: Beacon Press, 1989.

"Danger—Strontium 90." *Newsweek*, 12 November 1956, 88–90.

Daniel, Pete. "A Rogue Bureaucracy: The USDA Fire Ant Campaign of the Late 1950s." *Agricultural History* 64 (spring 1990), 99–121.

Darby, William J. "A Scientist Looks at *Silent Spring*." *Chemical and Engineering News*, 1 October 1962, 60–61.

———. *Safe Use of Pesticides in Food Products: A Report of the Food Protection Committee*. Washington, D.C.: NAS-NRC, 1956.

Darling, Louis, and Lois Darling. *Bird*. Boston: Houghton Mifflin Company, 1962.

Davidson, Cathy N., ed. *Reading in America: Literature and Social History*. Baltimore: Johns Hopkins University Press, 1989.

Davis, Kenneth S. "The Deadly Dust: The Unhappy History of DDT." *American Heritage* 22 (February 1971), 44–47, 92–93.

Davis, Lee Niedringhaus. *The Corporate Alchemists: Profit Takers and Problem Makers in the Chemical Industry*. New York: William Morrow and Co., 1984.

Day, Sherman. *Historical Sketches of the State of Pennsylvania*. Port Washington, NY: Ira J. Friedman, Inc., 1969.

"DDT Dangers." *Time* 45, 16 April 1945, 91–92.

"DDT." *The New Yorker*, 26 May 1946, 18.

de Steiguer, J. Edward. *Age of Environmentalism*. New York: McGraw-Hill Book Co., 1997.

DeGregori, Thomas R. "Apocalypse Yesterday." In *The Apocalyptic Vision in America: Interdisciplinary Essays on Myth and Culture*, ed. Lois Parkinson Zamora. Bowling Green, OH: Bowling Green University Popular Press, 1982.

Desmond, Adrian, and James Moore. *Darwin*. New York: Warner Books, 1992.
"The Desolate Year." *Monsanto Magazine* (October 1962), 4–9.
DeVoto, Bernard. "Shall We Let Them Ruin Our National Parks?" *Saturday Evening Post*, 22 July 1950, 17–18, 42–48.
DeWitt, James B. "Effects of Chlorinated Hydrocarbon Insecticides upon Quail and Pheasants." *Agricultural Food and Chemicals* 3 (August 1955), 672.
Diamond, Edwin. "The Myth of the 'Pesticide Menace.' " *Saturday Evening Post*, 28 September 1963, 16, 18.
Dillard, Annie. *The Writing Life*. New York: HarperCollins, 1989.
Divine, Robert A. *Blowing on the Wind: The Nuclear Test Ban Debate, 1954–1960*, New York: Oxford University Press, 1978.
Doughty, Robin. *Feather Fashions and Bird Preservation*. Berkeley: University of California Press, 1975.
Douglas, Helen Gahagan. *A Full Life*. Garden City, NY: Doubleday, 1982.
Douglas, William O. *My Wilderness: East to Katahdin*. Garden City, NY: Doubleday, 1961.
Dowie, Mark. *Losing Ground: American Environmentalism at the Close of the Twentieth Century*. Cambridge, MA: MIT Press, 1995.
Downs, Robert B. *Books That Changed America*. New York: Macmillan & Company, 1970.
Duggan, Lisa. "The Trials of Alice Mitchell: Sensationalism, Sexology, and the Lesbian Subject in Turn-of-the-Century America." *Signs* 18 (June 1993), 791–814.
Dunlap, Thomas R. " 'The Coyote Itself'—Ecologists and the Value of Predators." *Environmental Review* 7 (spring 1983), 54–70.
———. *DDT: Scientists, Citizens, and Public Policy*. Princeton, NJ: Princeton University Press, 1981.
———. "Nature Literature and Modern Science." *Environmental History Review* 14, no. 1–2 (spring/summer 1990), 33–44.
———. *Saving America's Wildlife*. Princeton, NJ: Princeton University Press, 1988.
Dupree, A. Hunter. *Science in the Federal Government*. Cambridge, MA: Belknap Press of Harvard University, 1957.
Durgin, Cyrus. "Overnight Miss Carson Has Become Famous." *The Boston Globe*, 20 July 1951, 1, 4.
"Dynamite in DDT." *New Republic*, 25 March 1946, 415–416.
Dysart, Laberta. *Chatham College: The First Ninety Years*. Pittsburgh, PA: Chatham College, 1959.
Earle, Sylvia A. *Sea Change: A Message of the Oceans*. New York: G. P. Putnam's Sons, 1995.
Easterbrook, Gregg. *A Moment on the Earth: The Coming Age of Environmental Optimism*. New York: Viking Press, 1995.
Egler, Frank E. "Pesticides and The National Academy of Sciences: A Review of Pest Control and Wildlife Relationships, Evaluation of Pesticide-Wildlife Problems, and Policy and Procedures for Pest Control, National Academy of Sciences National Research Publications 920-A, 920-B, and 920-C, Washington, D.C., 1962." *Audubon Naturalist* 17, no. 4 (October 1962), 23.
———. "Pesticides—in Our Ecosystem." *American Scientist* 52, no. 1 (March 1964), 110–136.
———. "Pesticides in Our Ecosystem: Communication II." *Bioscience* (November 1964), 29–36.
———. "Science, Industry, and the Abuse of Rightsofway." *Science* 127, no. 3298, (1958), 573–580.
———. *60 Questions and Answers Concerning Roadside Rightofway Vegetation Management*. Litchfield, CT: Litchfield Hills Audubon Society, 1961.

———. *The Way of Science: A Philosophy of Ecology for the Layman.* New York: Hafner Publishing Company, 1970.

Eherhart, Sylvia. "How the American People Feel About the Atomic Bomb." *Bulletin of the Atomic Scientists* 3 (June 1947), 146.

Ehrlich, Paul R. "Paul R. Ehrlich Reconsiders *Silent Spring*." *Bulletin of Atomic Scientists* 35 (October 1979), 34, 36.

Eiseley, Loren. *Darwin's Century: Evolution and the Men Who Discovered It.* Garden City, NJ: Doubleday, 1958.

———. "Using a Plague to Fight a Plague." *Saturday Review of Literature,* 29 September 1962, 18–19, 34.

Eisler, Benita. *Private Lives: Men and Women of the Fifties.* New York: Franklin Watts, 1986.

Elder, John. *Imagining the Earth.* Urbana: University of Illinois Press, 1985.

Elton, Charles S. *The Ecology of Invasions by Animals and Plants.* London: Metheun, 1958.

Epstein, Samuel S. "Corporate Crime: Can One Trust Industry's Safety Data." *The Ecologist* 19, no. 1 (January 1989), 23–30.

Evernden, Neil. *The Social Creation of Nature.* Baltimore: Johns Hopkins University Press, 1992.

Exman, Eugene. *The House of Harper: One Hundred and Fifty Years of Publishing.* New York: Harper & Row, 1967.

Faderman, Lillian. *Odd Girls and Twilight Lovers: A History of Lesbian Life in Twentieth Century America.* New York: Columbia University Press, 1991.

———. *Surpassing the Love of Men: Romantic Friendship and Love Between Women From the Renaissance to the Present.* New York: William Morrow and Co., 1981.

Fee, Elizabeth. *Disease and Discovery: A History of Johns Hopkins University School of Hygiene.* Baltimore: Johns Hopkins University Press, 1987.

Finch, Robert, and John Elder, eds. *The Norton Book of Nature Writing.* New York: W. W. Norton and Company, 1990.

"The First Atomic Blast." *Time,* 27 August 1945, 65.

Fleming, Donald. "Roots of the New Conservation Movement." In *Perspectives in American History,* vol. 6. Cambridge, MA: Belknap Press of Harvard University, 1972.

Flippen, John Brooks. "The Nixon Administration, Politics, and the Environment." Ph.D. diss., University of Maryland, 1994.

Fosberg, F. R. "The Community Ecologist." *American Institute of Biological Sciences Bulletin* (April 1957).

Fowler, John M. *Fallout.* New York: Basic Books, 1960.

Fox, Stephen. *The American Conservation Movement: John Muir and His Legacy.* Madison: University of Wisconsin Press, 1985.

Fradkin, Philip L. *Fallout: An American Nuclear Tragedy.* Tuscon: University of Arizona Press, 1989.

Free, Ann Cottrell, ed. *Animals, Nature, and Albert Schweitzer.* Washington, D.C.: The Flying Fox Press, 1988.

———. *Since Silent Spring: Our Debt to Albert Schweitzer and Rachel Carson.* Washington, D.C.: The Flying Fox Press, 1992.

Freeman, Martha, ed. *Always, Rachel: The Letters of Rachel Carson and Dorothy Freeman, 1952–1964.* Boston: Beacon Press, 1995.

French, John C. *A History of the University Founded by Johns Hopkins.* Baltimore: Johns Hopkins University Press, 1946.

"A Frightening Message for a Thanksgiving Issue." *Good Housekeeping* (November 1958), 61.

Fulford, Robert. "When Jane Jacobs Took on the World." *New York Times Book Review,* 16 February 1991, 1, 28–29.

Galbraith, John Kenneth. *The Affluent Society*. Boston: Houghton Mifflin Company, 1958.

Galtsoff, Paul S. *The Story of the Bureau of Commercial Fisheries Biological Laboratory, Woods Hole, Massachusetts*. Washington D.C.: U.S. Department of Interior Circular 145, 1962.

Garb, Yaakov. "Change and Continuity in Environmental World-View: The Politics of Nature in Rachel Carson's *Silent Spring*." In *Minding Nature: The Philosophers of Ecology*, ed. David Macauley. New York: The Guilford Press, 1996.

Gartner, Carol B. *Rachel Carson*. New York: Frederick Ungar Publishing Co., 1983.

Gay, Peter. *The Tender Passion: The Bourgeois Experience from Victoria to Freud*. New York: Oxford University Press, 1986.

Genelly, Richard E., and Robert L. Rudd. "Chronic Toxicity of DDT, Toxaphene, and Dieldrin to Ring-Necked Pheasants." *California Fish and Game* 42, no. 1 (January 1956), 5–14.

George, John L. *The Pesticide Problem*. New York: The Conservative Foundation, 1957.

George, John L. et al. "Pesticide-Wildlife Studies." *Circular 167*. Washington D.C.: U. S. Fish and Wildlife Service, 1963.

———. "Pesticides and Wildlife: The Need for More Knowledge." *New Scientist*, 6 July 1961, 15–17.

Gilbert, Sandra M., and Susan Gubar. *Madwoman in the Attic: The Woman Writer and Nineteenth Century Literary Imagination*. New Haven, CT: Yale University Press, 1979.

Gill, Brendan. *Here at the New Yorker*. New York: Random House, 1975.

Glazer, Penina Migdal, and Miriam Slater. *Unequal Colleagues: The Entrance of Women into the Professions, 1890–1940*. New Brunswick, NJ: Rutgers University Press, 1987.

Glotfelty, Cheryll. "Rachel Carson." In *American Nature Writers*, ed. John Elder. New York: Charles Scribner's Sons, 1996, 151–171.

Glotfelty, Cheryll, and Harold Fromm, eds. *The Ecocriticism Reader: Landmarks in Literary Ecology*. Athens, GA: University of Georgia Press, 1995.

Goldman, Eric. *The Crucial Decade and After, America 1945–1960*. New York: Vintage Books, 1960.

Goldsmith, Edward J. "Towards a Biospheric Ethic." *The Ecologist* 19, no. 2 (March 1989), 53–62.

Gornick, Vivian. *Women in Science: Portrait From a World in Transition*. New York: Touchstone Books, 1983.

Gottlieb, Robert. *Forcing the Spring: The Transformation of the American Environmental Movement*. Washington D.C.: Island Press, 1993.

Gould, Stephen J. "The Invisible Woman." *Natural History Magazine* 102, no. 6 (June 1993), 14–23.

Govan, Ada Clapham. *Wings at My Window*. New York: Macmillan Co., 1940.

Graham, Frank, Jr. *The Adirondack Park: A Political History*. New York: Alfred A. Knopf, 1978.

———. *The Audubon Ark*. New York: Alfred A. Knopf, 1990.

———. *Disaster by Default*. New York: M. Evans, 1966.

———. "Rachel Carson." *EPA Journal* (November 1978), 6, 7, 38.

———. *Since Silent Spring*. Boston: Houghton Mifflin Company, 1970.

Green, Constance McLaughlin. *Washington: A History of the Capital, 1800–1950*. Princeton, NJ: Princeton University Press, 1976.

Greenacre, Phyllis. "The Childhood of the Artist: Libidinal Phase Development and

Giftedness." In *Emotional Growth: Psychoanalytic Studies of the Gifted and a Great Variety of Other Individuals* by Phyllis Greenacre. New York: International Universities Press, 1971. (Reprinted from 1957.)

Guth, Dorothy Lobrano, ed. *Letters of E. B. White.* New York: Harper & Row, 1976.

Hagen, Joel. *Nature's Entangled Bank. The Origins of Ecosystem Ecology.* New Brunswick, NJ: Rutger's University Press, 1992.

Halberstam, David. *The Fifties.* New York: Villard Books, 1993.

Halle, Louis J. *Spring in Washington.* New York: Harper & Row, 1947.

Halsey, Francis W. "The Rise of the Nature Writers." *American Monthly Review of Reviews* 26 (1902), 571.

Hanley, Wayne. *Natural History in America: From Mark Catesby to Rachel Carson.* New York: Quadrangle/New York Times Books Co., 1977.

Hardin, Garrett. "The Lesson of Rachel Carson: You Can't Do Just One Thing." *The Minneapolis Star*, 14 January 1970.

Harding, Sandra. *Whose Science? Whose Knowledge? Thinking From Women's Lives.* Ithaca, NY: Cornell University Press, 1989.

Harding, Sandra G., and Jean F. O'Barr. *Sex and Scientific Inquiry.* Chicago: University of Chicago Press, 1987.

Harvey, Mark T. W. A *Symbol of Wilderness: Echo Park and the American Conservation Movement.* Albuquerque, NM: University of New Mexico Press, 1994.

Hawkes, Jacquetta. "The World Under Water." *The New Republic*, 23 January 1956, 17–18.

Hays, Samuel P. *Beauty, Health, and Permanence: Environmental Politics in the United States, 1955–1985.* Cambridge: Cambridge University Press, 1987.

Heidenry, John. *Theirs Was the Kingdom: Lila and Dewitt Wallace and the Story of Reader's Digest.* New York: W. W. Norton, 1993.

Heilbrun, Carolyn. *Writing a Woman's Life.* New York: W. W. Norton, 1988.

Henson, Pamela M. "The Comstocks of Cornell: A Marriage of Interests." In *Creative Couples in Science*, eds. Pnina Abir-Am, Helena Pycior, and Nancy Slack. Brunswick, NJ: Rutgers University Press, 1996.

———. "The Smithsonian Goes to War: The Increase and Diffusion of Scientific Knowledge in the Pacific." In *Pacific Science in World War II*, ed. Roy MacLeod. (forthcoming)

———. " 'Through Books to Nature': Anna Botsford Comstock and the Nature Study Movement." In *Using Nature's Language: Women Engendering Science, 1690–1990*, eds. Barbara T. Gates, and Ann B. Shteir. Madison: University of Wisconsin Press, 1997.

Herber, Lewis [Murray Bookchin]. *Our Synthetic Environment.* New York: Alfred A. Knopf, 1962.

Herrscher, Walter John. "Some Ideas in Modern American Nature Writing." Ph.D. diss., University of Wisconsin, 1969.

Hicks, Philip Marshall. "The Development of the Natural History Essay in American Literature." Ph.D. diss., University of Pennsylvania, 1924.

Hines, Bob. "The Woman Who Started a Revolution: Remembering Rachel Carson." *Yankee Magazine* (June 1991), 62–67.

Hint, Paul W. A *Conspiracy of Optimism. Management of the National Forests Since World War Two.* Lincoln, NE: University of Nebraska Press, 1994.

Hodge, Clifton F. *Nature Study and Life.* Boston: Ginn & Co., 1902.

Hodgson, Godfrey. *America in Our Time.* Garden City, NY: Doubleday, 1976.

Holtz, Frederick L. *Nature-Study: A Manual for Teachers and Students.* New York: Charles Scribner's Sons, 1908.

Hounshell, David A., and John Kenly Smith. *Science and Corporate Strategy: Du Pont R&D, 1902–1980.* Cambridge: Cambridge University Press, 1988.

Horowitz, Helen Lefkowitz. *Alma Mater: Design and Experience in Women's Colleges from Their Nineteenth-Century Beginnings to the 1930s*. New York: Alfred A. Knopf, 1984.

———. "*Nous Autres:* Reading, Passion, and the Creation of M. Carey Thomas." *Journal of American History* 79 (1992), 68–95.

———. *The Power and Passion of* M. *Carey Thomas*. New York: Alfred A. Knopf, 1994.

Howard, Jane. *Margaret Mead: A Life*. New York: Ballantine Books, 1984.

Howard, Leland O. *The Insect Menace*. New York: Century Publishing, 1931.

Huckins, Olga Owens. "Evidence of Havoc by DDT Air Spraying." *The Boston Herald*, 29 January 1958, sec. 3, 14.

Hueper, Wilhelm C. "Adventures of a Physician in Occupational Cancer: A Medical Cassandra's Tale." Wilhelm C. Hueper Papers, National Library of Medicine, Bethesda, MD. Unpublished autobiography.

———. "The Cigarette Theory of Lung Cancer." *Current Medical Digest* (October 1954), 35–39.

———. *Occupational Tumors and Allied Diseases*. Springfield, IL: Thomas, 1942.

———. "Recent Developments in Environmental Cancer." *AMA Archives of Pathology* 58 (1954), 475–523.

———. "Significance of Industrial Cancer in the Problem of Cancer." *Occupational Medicine* 2 (1946), 190–200.

Hull, Helen S. "*Silent Spring* Becomes an Uproar." *Flower Grower Magazine* (December 1962), 18–19.

Hunter, Beatrice Trum. "Aerial Spray Program Imperils Wildlife." *The Boston Sunday Herald*, 12 January 1958, sec. 3, 2.

Hunter-Cox, Jane. *The Golden Age of Transatlantic Travel*. Exeter, England: Webb and Bower, 1989.

Huth, Hans. *Nature and the American: Three Centuries of Changing Attitudes*. Lincoln: University of Nebraska Press, 1957.

Huxley, Julian, A. C. Hardy, and E. B. Ford, eds. *Evolution as Process*. New York: Collier Books, 1954.

Huxley, Julian, and W. Suschitky. *The Kingdom of Beasts*. London: Thames and Hudson, 1956.

Hyde, Francis E. *Cunard and the North Atlantic, 1840–1973: A History of Shipping and Financial Management*. Atlantic Highlands, NJ: Humanities Press, 1975.

Hynes, H. Patricia. "Ellen Swallow, Lois Gibbs, and Rachel Carson: Catalysts of the American Environmental Movement." *Women of Power* 9 (March 1988), 37–41.

———. *The Recurring Silent Spring*. New York: Pergamon Press, 1989.

Insect Control Committee, U.S. Department of Agriculture. "DDT and Other Insecticides and Repellents Developed for the Armed Forces." Prepared by the Orlando, Florida, Laboratory of the Bureau of Entomology and Plant Quarantine *Interim Report*. Washington, D.C.: Government Printing Office, August 1946.

Jeffries, Richard. *The Pageant of Summer*. Portland, ME: Thomas B. Mosher, 1905.

Jennings, H. S. "Raymond Pearl, 1879–1940." *Proceedings, National Academy of Science, USA*, (1940) 2925–2347.

Jukes, Thomas H. "People and Pesticides." *American Scientist* 51, no. 3 (September 1963), 355–361.

Kass-Simon, G. "Biology Is Destiny." In *Women of Science: Righting the Record*, eds. G. Kass-Simon and Patricia Farnes. Bloomington: Indiana University Press, 1990.

Keeney, Elizabeth Barnaby. "The Botanizers: Amateur Scientists in Nineteenth-Century America." Ph.D. diss., University of Wisconsin, 1985.

Keller, Evelyn Fox. *A Feeling for the Organism*. New York: W. H. Freeman and Co., 1983.

———. "Gender and Science." In *Discovering Reality*, eds. Sandra Harding and Merrill B. Hintikka. Boston: D. Reidel Publishing Company, 1983.

———. *Reflections on Gender and Science*. New Haven, CT: Yale University Press, 1985.

Kenfield, Warren G. [Frank E. Egler]. *The Wild Garden in the Wild Landscape: The Art of Naturalistic Landscape*. New York: Hafner Publishing Company, 1966.

Kennan, George. *American Diplomacy*. Chicago: University of Chicago Press, 1984.

Kevles, Daniel J. "The American Greens." *The New York Review of Books*, 6 October 1994, 35–39.

Kieran, John, ed. *John Kieran's Treasury of Great Nature Writing*. Garden City, NY: Hanover House, 1957.

Killingsworth, M. Jimmie, and Jacqueline S. Palmer. *Ecospeak: Rhetoric and Environmental Politics in America*. Cardondale: Southern Illinois University Press, 1992.

———. "Millennial Ecology: The Apocalyptic Narrative from *Silent Spring* to Global Warming." In *Green Culture: Environmental Rhetoric in Contemporary America*, eds. Carl G. Herndl and Stuart C. Brown. Madison, WI: University of Wisconsin Press, 1996, 21–45.

Kingsland, Sharon E. "A Man Out of Place: Herbert Spencer Jennings at Johns Hopkins 1906–1938." *American Zoologist* 27, no. 3 (1987), 807–817.

———. *Modeling Nature*. Chicago: University of Chicago Press, 1985.

———. "Raymond Pearl: On the Frontier in the 1920s." *Human Biology* 56 (1984), 1–18.

Knight, Paul. "Case Study on Environmental Contamination." Chevy Chase, MD: Rachel Carson Council, Inc. [1964].

Knipling, E. F. "Insect Control Investigations of the Orlando, Florida, Laboratory During World War II." *Annual Report of the Board of Regents of the Smithsonian Institution*. Washington, D.C.: Smithsonian Institution, 30 June 1948, 331–348.

Knipling, E. F. et al. "DDT and Other Insecticides and Repellents Developed for the Armed Forces." USDA Bulletin #606 (August 1946).

Kofalk, Harriet. *No Woman Tenderfoot: Florence Merriam Bailey, Pioneer Naturalist*. College Station, TX: Texas A&M Press, 1989.

Kohlstedt, Sally Gregory. "In From the Periphery: American Women in Science, 1830–1880." *Signs* 4, no. 1 (1978), 81–96.

———. "Maria Mitchell and the Advancement of Women in Science." In *Uneasy Careers and Intimate Lives: Women in Science, 1789–1979*, eds. Pnina G. Abir-am and Dorinda Outram. New Brunswick, NJ: Rutgers University Press, 1987.

Kopp, Carolyn. "The Origins of the American Scientific Debate Over Fallout Hazards." *Social Studies of Science* 9 (1979), 405–413.

Krabbendam, Johannes Leendert. *The Model Man: A Life of Edward Bok, 1863–1930*. Utrecht, The Netherlands: privately published, 1964.

Krasner, James. *The Entangled Eye: Visual Perception and the Representation of Nature in Post-Darwinian Narrative*. New York: Oxford University Press, 1992.

Kruth, Jerry. "Silent Spring—Thirty Years Later." *Carnegie Magazine* (March 1992), 24–29.

Kuhn, Thomas S. *The Structure of Scientific Revolutions*. Chicago: University of Chicago Press, 1970.

Kulp, J. Lawrence et al. "Strontium-90." *Science* 125 (1957), 219.

Kumin, Maxine. *In Deep Country: Essays*. Boston: Beacon Press, 1987.

LaFeber, Walter. *America, Russia, and the Cold War*. New York: Alfred A. Knopf, 1985.

Lapp, Ralph. *The Voyage of the Lucky Dragon*. New York: Harper & Row, 1958.

Laslet, Barbara, Sally Gregory Kohlstedt, Helen Longino, and Evelyn Hammonds, eds. *Gender and Scientific Authority*. Chicago: University of Chicago Press, 1996.

Le Guin, Ursula K. "Introducing Myself." *Left Bank* 3 (December 1993), 12–15.

Lear, Linda J. "Bombshell in Beltsville: The USDA and the Challenge of 'Silent Spring.' " *Agricultural History* 66, no. 2 (spring 1992), 151–170.

———. "Rachel Carson's *Silent Spring.* " *Environmental History Review* 17, no. 2 (summer 1993), 23–48.

———. " 'War in the Garden?' Rachel Carson, Gender, and Pesticides." Unpublished mss, American Society of Environmental History, Pittsburgh, PA, 1993.

Lee, Gary. "EPA Study Links Dioxin to Cancer." *The Washington Post,* 12 September 1994.

Leonard, Jonathan Norton. "And His Wonders in the Deep: A Scientist Draws an Intimate Portrait of the Winding Sea and Its Churning Life." *New York Times Book Review,* 1 July 1951, 1.

———. "The Public and 'Silent Spring.' " *NAC News and Pesticide Review* (October 1964), 5.

———. "Review of 'Silent Spring.' " *Time,* 28 September 1962, 45–49.

Lillie, Frank R. *The Woods Hole Marine Biological Laboratory.* Chicago: University of Chicago Press, 1944.

Lindbergh, Anne Morrow. A *Gift from the Sea.* New York: Random House, Inc., 1955.

Linduska, Joseph P., and Eugene W. Surber. *Effects of DDT and Other Insecticides on Fish and Wildlife, Summary of Investigations During 1947.* Washington, D.C.: Government Printing Office, 1947.

Logan, Jennifer Wilder. "A Scientist's Reverence for Life." *Chrysalis* 7, no. 1 (1992), 65–70.

Longgood, William F. *The Poisons in Your Food.* New York: Simon & Schuster, 1960.

Ludmerer, Kenneth M. *Genetics and American Society: A Historical Appraisal.* Baltimore: Johns Hopkins University Press, 1972.

Lutts, Ralph H. "Chemical Fallout: Rachel Carson's *Silent Spring,* Radioactive Fallout and the Environmental Movement." *Environmental Review* 9 (fall 1985), 214–225.

———. *The Nature Fakers: Wildlife, Science & Sentiment.* Golden, CO: Fulcrum Publishing, 1990.

Lyon, Thomas J., ed. *This Incomperable Lande: A Book for American Nature Writing.* Boston: Houghton Mifflin Company, 1989.

MacIntryre, Angus. "Administrative Initiative and Theories of Implementation: Federal Pesticide Policy, 1970–1976." In *Public Policy and the Natural Environment,* eds. Helen M. Ingram and R. Kenneth Goodwin. Greenwich, CT: JAI Press, 1985.

———. "Why Pesticides Received Extensive Use in America: A Political Economy of Agricultural Pest Management to 1970." *Natural Resources Journal* 27, no. 3 (1987), 533–578.

Maienschein, Jane. *Defining Biology: Lectures From the 1890s.* Cambridge, MA: Harvard University Press, 1986.

———. *100 Years Exploring Life, 1888–1988: Marine Biological Laboratory at Woods Hole.* Boston: Jones and Bartlett Publishers, 1989.

———. *Transforming Traditions in American Biology.* Baltimore: Johns Hopkins University Press, 1991.

Manes, Christopher. *Green Rage: Radical Environmentalism and the Unmaking of Civilization.* Boston: Little, Brown & Company, 1990.

Marco, Gino J., Robert M. Hollingworth, and William Durham, eds. *Silent Spring Revisited.* Washington, D.C.: American Chemical Society, 1987.

Marx, Leo. *The Machine in the Garden: Technology and the Pastoral Ideal in America.* New York: Oxford University Press, 1964.

"Mary Mapes Dodge." *Folio: The Magazine for Magazine Management* 20 (March 1991), 106–108.

Matthiessen, Peter. *Wildlife in America*, rev. ed. New York: Viking, 1987.
Maxtone-Graham, John. *Crossing & Cruising: From the Golden Era of Ocean Liners to the Luxury Cruise Ships of Today*. New York: Scribners, 1992.
———. *Liners to the Sun*. New York: Macmillan Co., 1985.
Maxwell, Gavin. *Ring of Bright Water*. London: Longmans Green, 1960.
May, Elaine Taylor. *Homeward Bound: American Families in the Cold War*. New York: Basic Books, 1988.
Mayr, Ernest. *The Growth of Biological Thought: Diversity, Evolution, and Inheritance*, Cambridge, MA: Harvard University Press, 1982.
Mayr, Ernst, and William B. Provine, eds. *The Evolutionary Synthesis: Perspectives on the Unification of Biology*. Cambridge, MA: Harvard University Press, 1980.
McCay, Mary A. *Rachel Carson*. New York: Twayne Publishers, 1993.
McDougall, Walter A. *The Heavens and the Earth*. New York: Basic Books, 1985.
McGehee, Judson. "The Nature Essay as Literary Genre: An Intrinsic Study of the Works of Six English and American Nature Writers." Ph.D. diss., University of Michigan, 1958.
McIntosh, Robert. *The Background of Ecology: Concept and Theory*. New York: Cambridge University Press, 1985.
Mead, Margaret. "The Legacy of Rachel Carson." *Redbook Magazine* (August 1972).
Meine, Curt. *Aldo Leopold: His Life and Work*. Madison: University of Wisconsin Press, 1988.
Mellanby, Kenneth. *Pesticides and Pollution*. London: Collins, 1967.
Merchant, Carolyn. *Death of Nature: Women, Ecology, and the Scientific Revolution*. San Francisco: Harper & Row, 1980.
———. "Earthcare: Women and the Environment." *Environment* 23 (June 1981), 6–13, 38–40.
———. *Earthcare: Women and the Environment*. New York: Routledge, 1996.
———. "Ecofeminism and Feminist Theory." In *Reweaving the World*, eds. Irene Diamond and Gloria Feman Orenstein. San Francisco: Sierra Club Books, 1990.
———. "Gender and Environmental History." *Journal of American History* 76, no. 4 (March 1990), 1117–1121.
———. "Women of the Progressive Conservation Movement, 1900–1916." *Environmental Review* 8 (March 1984), 57–86.
Meyer, Agnes E. *Out of These Roots: The Autobiography of an American Woman*. Boston: Little, Brown and Company, 1953.
Mies, Maria, and Vandana Shiva. *Ecofeminism*. London: Zed Books, 1993.
Mighetto, Lisa. *Wild Animals and American Environmental Ethics*. Tuscon: University of Arizona Press, 1991.
"The Milk All of Us Drink—and Fallout." *Consumer Reports* 24 (March 1959), 102–103.
Mills, Eric. L. *Biological Oceanography: An Early History, 1870–1960*, Ithaca, NY: Cornell University Press, 1989.
———. "The Oceanography of the Pacific: George F. McEwen, H. U. Sverdrup and the Origin of Physical Oceanography on the West Coast of North America." *Annals of Science* 48 (1991), 241–266.
Milne, Lorus, and Margery Milne. "There's Poison All Around Us Now." *The New York Times Book Review*, 23 September 1962, 1, 26.
Minton, Tyree G. "The History of the Nature-Study Movement and Its Role in the Development of Environmental Education." Ph.D. diss., University of Massachusetts, 1980.
Mintz, Morton. "Heroine of the FDA Keeps Bad Drug Off Market." *The Washington Post*, 15 July 1962.

Mittman, Greg. *State of Nature*. Chicago: University of Chicago Press, 1992.
Moore, Ernest G. *The Agricultural Research Service*. New York: Frederick A. Praeger, 1967.
Moore, Lillian. "Rachel Carson's 'Silent Spring'—Its Truth Goes Marching On." *Smithsonian Magazine* 1, no. 4 (July 1970), 4–9.
Mott, Frank Luther. *A History of American Magazines*, vol. 4. Cambridge, MA: Belknap Press, 1957.
Mozans, H. J. *Women in Science*. Cambridge, MA: MIT Press, 1974.
Murie, Olaus J. "Wild Country as a National Asset." *The Living Wilderness* 45 (June 1953), 11–12.
Murphy et al. v. *Benson et al. U.S. Supreme Court Reports, Memorandum Cases*, no. 662, 28 March 1960.
Nash, Roderick Frazier, ed. *The American Environment: Readings in the History of Conservation*, 2nd ed. Reading, MA: Addison-Wesley Publishing Company, 1976.
———. *The Rights of Nature: A History of Environmental Ethics*. Madison: University of Wisconsin Press, 1989.
———. *Wilderness and the American Mind*. New Haven, CT: Yale University Press, 1982.
"Nature Lovers." *New York Times Saturday Review of Books*, 9 May 1903, 320.
Noble, David F. *A World Without Women: The Christian Clerical Culture of Western Science*. New York: Alfred A. Knopf, 1992.
Norman, Geoffrey. "The Flight of Rachel Carson." *The Recorder* 54, no. 2 (March 1985), 9.
Norton, Bryan. *Toward Unity Among Environmentalists*. New York: Oxford University Press, 1991.
Norwood, Vera. "Heroines of Nature: Four Women Respond to the American Landscape." *Environmental Review* 8 (March 1984), 343–357.
———. *Made From This Earth: American Women and Nature*. Chapel Hill, NC: University of North Carolina Press, 1993.
———. "The Nature of Knowing: Rachel Carson and the American Environment." *Signs* 12 (June 1987), 740–760.
———. "Rachel Carson." In *The American Radical*, eds. Mary Jo Buhle, Paul Buhle, and Harvey J. Kay. New York: Routledge, 1994.
O'Brien, Sharon. "My Willa Cather: How Writing Her Story Shaped My Own." *New York Times Book Review*, 20 February 1994, 24–25.
———. *Willa Cather: An Emerging Voice*. New York: Oxford University Press, 1987.
Oelschlaeger, Max. *The Idea of Wilderness*. New Haven, CT: Yale University Press, 1991.
"Olga Owens Huckins." (Obituary) *The Boston Herald Traveler*, 10 July 1968, 12.
"Olga Owens Huckins." (Obituary) *The Boston Globe*, 10 July 1968, 39.
Olmsted, Richard R. "The Nature Study Movement in American Education." Ed.D. diss., Indiana University, 1967.
"On Controlling Pests." *The Washington Post*, 13 July 1962, 17.
Oravec, Christine. "An Inventional Archaeology of Rachel Carson's 'A Fable for Tomorrow,' " in *Proceedings of The Conference on Communication and the Environment*, ed. Kandice Salomone. Chattanooga, TN: University of Tennessee School of Journalism, 1997.
———. "Rachel Louise Carson." *Women Public Speakers in the United States, 1925–1993, A Biocritical Source Book*, ed. Karlyn Kohrs Campbell. Westport, CT: Greenwood Press, 1994.
Orlando Florida Laboratory of the Bureau of Entomology and Plant Quarantine. *DDT and Other Insecticides and Repellents Developed for the Armed Forces*, USDA #606 ed. Washington, D.C.: Government Printing Office, August 1946.
Ortner, Sherry B. "Is Female to Male as Nature Is to Culture?" *Women, Culture, and*

Society, eds. Michelle Rosaldo and Louise Lamphere. Stanford, CA: Stanford University Press, 1974.

Osborn, Fairfield. *Our Plundered Planet*. Boston: Little, Brown & Company, 1948.

"Our Next World War—Against Insects." *Popular Mechanics* 81 (April 1944), 66–70.

Pachter, Marc, ed. *Telling Lives: The Biographer's Art*. Washington, D.C.: New Republic Books, National Portrait Gallery, 1979.

Paehlke, Robert C. *Environmentalism and the Future of Progressive Politics*. New Haven, CT: Yale University Press, 1989.

Parry, Albert. *Russia's Rockets and Missiles*. New York: Doubleday & Co., 1960.

Paul, Sherman. *For Love of the World: Essays on Nature Writers*. Iowa City: University of Iowa Press, 1992.

Pauly, Philip J. "Summer Resort and Scientific Discipline: Woods Hole and the Structure of American Biology, 1882–1925." In *The American Development of Biology*, eds. Ronald Rainger, Keith R. Benson, and Jane Maienschein. Philadelphia: University of Pennsylvania Press, 1988.

Payne, Daniel G. *Voices in the Wilderness: American Nature Writing and Environmental Politics*. Hanover, NH: University Press of New England, 1996.

Penn, Irving. "Famous in Washington." *Vogue*, 15 August 1951.

Perkins, John H. *Insects, Experts, and the Insecticide Crisis: The Quest for New Pest Management Strategies*. New York: Plenum Press, 1982.

———. "Insects, Food, and Hunger: The Paradox of Plenty for U.S. Entomology, 1920–1970." *Environmental Review* 7 (spring 1983), 71–96.

———. "The Quest for Innovation in Agricultural Entomology, 1945–1978." In *Pest Control: Cultural and Environmental Aspects*, eds. David Pimentel and John H. Perkins. Boulder, CO: Westview Press, 1980.

———. "Reshaping Technology in Wartime: The Effect of Military Goals on Entomological Research and Insect-Control Practices." *Technology and Culture* 19, no. 2 (April 1978), 169–186.

"Pest Control and Wildlife Relationships." NAS-NRC, Reprint 920A, B&C. Washington, D.C.: National Academy of Sciences, 1962.

Petulla, Joseph M. *American Environmental History*. Columbus, OH: Merrill Publishing Company, 1988.

Pimentel, David, et al. "Environmental and Economic Effects of Reducing Pesticide Use." *BioScience* 41, no. 6 (June 1991), 402–409.

Pimentel, David, ed. *Handbook of Pest Management in Agriculture*. Boca Raton, FL: CRC Press, 1991.

Pimentel, David, and Hugh Lehman, eds. *The Pesticide Question, Environment, Economics, and Ethics*. New York: Chapman and Hall, 1993.

Plumwood, Val. *Feminism & Mastery of Nature*. London: Routledge, 1993.

Poore, Charles. "Books of the Times." *The New York Times*, 26 October 1955, 17.

Porter, Gene Stratton. *A Girl of the Limberlost*. New York: Gramercy Books, 1991.

Proctor, Robert N. *Cancer Wars*. New York: Basic Books, 1995.

"The Rachel Carson Explosion." *The Boston Globe*, 17 March 1970.

Rainger, Ronald, Keith R. Benson, and Jane Maienschein, eds. *The American Development of Biology*. Philadelphia: University of Pennsylvania Press, 1988.

Raymond, Janice G. *A Passion for Friends: Toward a Philosophy of Female Affection*. Boston: Beacon Press, 1986.

Reed, Nathaniel P., and Dennis Drabelle. *The United States Fish and Wildlife Service*. Boulder, CO: Westview Press, 1984.

Rehbock, Philip F. "Organizing Pacific Science: Local and International Origins of the Pacific Science Association." In *Nature in Its Greatest Extent: Western Science in the*

Pacific, eds. Roy MacLeod and Philip F. Rehbock. Honolulu: University of Hawaii Press, 1988.

Rhodes, Richard. *Dark Sun: The Making of the Hydrogen Bomb*. New York: Simon & Schuster, 1995.

Rich, Adrienne. *Of Woman Born: Motherhood as Experience and Institution*. New York: W. W. Norton and Company, 1976.

———. "Toward a Woman-Centered University." In *Women and the Power to Change*, ed. Florence Howe. New York: McGraw-Hill Book Company, 1975.

Rossiter, Margaret W. *Women Scientists in America: Struggles and Strategies to 1940*. Baltimore: Johns Hopkins University Press, 1982.

Rosta, Paul. "The Magazine that Taught Faulkner, Fitzgerald, and Millay How to Write." *American Heritage* 37 (December 1985), 40–47.

Rubin, Charles T. *The Green Crusade: Rethinking the Roots of Environmentalism*. New York: Free Press, 1994.

Rudd, Robert L. "The Chemical Countryside: A Review of Rachel Carson's 'Silent Spring.' " *Pacific Discovery* 15, no. 6 (November 1962), 10–11.

———. "Chemicals in the Environment." *California Medicine* 113, no. 5 (November 1970), 27–32.

———. *The Ecological Consequences of Chemicals in Pest Control, Particularly as Regards Their Effects on Mammals*. International Union for Conservation for Nature, Symposium. Leiden: E. J. Brill, 1961.

———. "The Irresponsible Poisoners." *The Nation*, 30 May 1959, 496–497.

———. "Pesticides: The Real Peril." *The Nation*, 28 November 1959, 399–401.

———. *Pesticides and the Living Landscape*. Madison: University of Wisconsin Press, 1964.

Rudd, Robert L., and Richard E. Genelly. "Pesticides: Their Use and Toxicity in Relation to Wildlife." *California Department of Fish and Game Bulletin*, no. 7 (1956).

Russell, Edmund P. III. "Lost Among the Parts Per Billion: Ecological Protection at the United States Environmental Protection Agency, 1970–1993." *Environmental History* 2, no. 1 (January 1997), 29–51.

———. "Safe for Whom? Safe for What? Testing Insecticides and Repellents in World War II." Unpublished mss., American Society for Environmental History, Pittsburgh, PA, March 1993.

———. " 'Speaking of Annihilation': Mobilizing for War Against Human and Insect Enemies, 1914–1945." *Journal of American History* 82 (March 1996), 1505–1529.

———. "War on Insects: Warfare, Insecticides, and Environmental Change in the United States, 1879–1945." Ph.D. diss., University of Michigan, 1993.

Sale, Kirkpatrick. *The Green Revolution: The American Environmental Movement, 1962–1992*. New York: Hill and Wang, 1993.

Scharff, Virginia. "Are Earth Girls Easy?" *Journal of Women's History* 7, no. 2 (June 1995), 164–175.

Scheffer, Victor B. *The Shaping of Environmentalism in America*. Seattle: University of Washington, 1991.

Schiebinger, Linda. *Nature's Body: Gender in the Making of Modern Science*. Boston: Beacon Press, 1993.

———. *The Mind Has No Sex?: Women and the Origins of Modern Science*. Cambridge, MA: Harvard University Press, 1989.

Schlee, Susan. *The Edge of an Unfamiliar World: A History of Oceanography*. New York: E. P. Dutton & Co., 1973.

Schmitt, Peter J. *Back to Nature: The Arcadian Myth in Urban America*. New York: Oxford University Press, 1969.

Schweitzer, Albert. *Out of My Life and Thought*. New York: Henry Holt & Company, 1933.

Sears, M., and D. Merriman, eds. *Oceanography: The Past*. New York: Springer-Verlag, 1980.

Seif, Dorothy Thompson. "How I Remember Rachel Carson." *The Recorder: The Chatham Alumnae Magazine*, 54, no. 2 (March 1985), 9.

———. "Letters from Rachel Carson: A Young Scientist Sets Her Course." Chevy Chase, MD: Rachel Carson History Project/Rachel Carson Council, Inc., ca. 1986.

Sellers, Christopher Clare. "Manufacturing Disease: Experts and the Ailing American Worker." Ph.D. diss., Yale University, 1992.

Seton-Thompson, Grace Gallatin. *A Woman Tenderfoot*. New York: Doubleday Page & Co., 1900.

Shabecoff, Philip. *A Fierce Green Fire: The American Environmental Movement, 1962–1992*. New York: Hill and Wang, 1993.

———. " 'Silent Spring' Led to Safer Pesticides, but Use Is Up." *The New York Times*, 21 April 1986.

Shepherd, Linda Jean. *Lifting the Veil: The Feminine Face of Science*. Boston: Shambhala Press, 1993.

Shephard, Paul, and Daniel McKinley, eds. *The Subversive Science: Essays Toward an Ecology of Man*. Boston: Houghton Mifflin Company, 1900.

Shi, David E. *The Simple Life: Plain Living and High Thinking in American Culture*. New York: Oxford University Press, 1985.

Shteir, Ann B. "Botany in the Breakfast Room: Women and Early Nineteenth Century British Plant Study." In *Uneasy Careers and Intimate Lives, Women in Science, 1789–1979*, eds. Pnina G. Abir-am and Dorinda Outram. New Brunswick, NJ: Rutgers University Press, 1987.

Sicherman, Barbara. "Reading and Ambition: M. Carey Thomas and Female Heroism." *American Quarterly* 45 (1993), 73–103.

Siry, Joseph V. *Marshes of the Ocean Shore: Development of an Ecological Ethic*. College Station, TX: Texas A&M University Press, 1984.

Slack, Nancy G. "Nineteenth-Century American Women Botanists: Wives, Widows, and Work." In *Uneasy Careers and Intimate Lives: Women in Science, 1789–1979*, eds. Pnina G. Abir-am and Dorinda Outram. New Brunswick, NJ: Rutgers University Press, 1987.

Smith-Rosenberg, Carroll. *Disorderly Conduct: Visions of Gender in Victorian America*. New York: Alfred A. Knopf, 1985.

———. "The Female World of Love and Ritual: Relations Between Women in the Nineteenth Century." In *A Heritage of Her Own*, eds. Nancy F. Cott and Elizabeth H. Pleck. New York: Simon & Schuster, 1979.

Sonneborn, T. M. "Herbert Spencer Jennings, 1868–1947." 47, *Biographical Memoirs*, 182–206; Washington, D.C.: National Academy of Sciences.

Soule, Michael E. and Gary Lease. *Reinventing Nature: Responses to Postmodern Deconstruction*. Washington, D.C.: Island Press, 1995.

"A Spare Room Fallout Shelter," *Life*, 25 January 1960, 46.

Spectorsky, A. C., ed. *The Book of the Sea*. New York: Grosset & Dunlap, 1954.

Spencer, Steven M. "Fallout: The Silent Killer, Part One." *The Saturday Evening Post*, 29 August 1959, 26, 89; 5 September 1959, 86.

Springdale: From Indian Village to Power City: Seventy-Five Years (commemorative publication). Springdale, PA: 1981.

Stare, Frederick J. "Some Comments on *Silent Spring*." *Nutrition Reviews*, (January 1963). Reprinted by The Nutrition Foundation, Inc.

Stegner, Wallace E. *This Is Dinosaur*. New York: Alfred A. Knopf, 1955.

Steingraber, Sandra. "If I Live to Be 90 Still Wanting to Say Something: My Search for

Rachel Carson." In *Confronting Cancer, Constructing Change*, ed. Midge Stocker. Chicago: Third Side Press, 1993.
———. *Living Downstream: An Ecologist Looks at Cancer and the Environment.* Reading, MA: Addison-Wesley Publishing Co., Inc. 1997.
Sterling, Philip. *Sea and Earth: The Life of Rachel Carson.* New York: Thomas Y. Crowell Co., 1970.
Stewart, Frank. *A Natural History of Nature Writing.* Washington, D.C.: Island Press, 1995.
Stineman, Esther Lanigan. *Mary Austin: Song of a Maverick.* New Haven, CT: Yale University Press, 1989.
Stinnett, Caskie. "The Legacy of Rachel Carson." *Down East* (June 1992), 38–43.
The Story of Silent Spring. Boston: Houghton Mifflin, 1963.
Strong, Douglas H. *Dreamers and Defenders: American Conservationists.* Lincoln: University of Nebraska Press, 1988.
Stroud, Richard H., ed. *National Leaders of American Conservation.* Washington, D.C.: Smithsonian Institution Press, 1985.
"Survival: Are Shelters the Answer?" *Newsweek*, 6 November 1961, 19.
Sverdrup, H. U., Martin W. Johnson, and Richard H. Fleming. *The Oceans: Their Physics, Chemistry, and General Biology.* Englewood Cliffs, NJ: Prentice-Hall, 1942.
Swanson, C. P. "A History of Biology at the Johns Hopkins University." *Bios* 22 (December 1951), 223–262.
Takacs, David. *The Idea of Biodiversity: Philosophies of Paradise.* Baltimore: Johns Hopkins University Press, 1996.
Taussig, Helen B. "The Thalidomide Syndrome." *Scientific American* 207, no. 2 (August 1962), 29–35.
Taylor, Bob Pepperman. *Our Limits Transgressed: Environmental Political Thought in America.* Lawrence: University of Kansas Press, 1992.
Teale, Edwin Way, "DDT." *Nature Magazine* 38, no. 3 (March 1945), 121–124, 162–163.
Teale, Edwin Way, ed. *Green Treasury: A Journey Through the World's Great Nature Writing.* New York: Dodd, Mead & Company, 1952.
Terres, John K. "Dynamite in DDT." *The New Republic* 114 (March 25, 1946), 415–416.
Thomas, Keith. *Man and the Natural World.* New York: Pantheon Books, 1983.
Thompson, Paul B. *The Spirit of the Soil: Agricultural and Environmental Ethics.* London: Routledge, 1995.
Tidball, M. Elizabeth, and Vera Kistiakowsky. "Baccalaureate Origins of American Scientists and Scholars." *Science*, 20 August 1976, 646–652.
Tjossem, Sara F. "Preservation of Nature and Academic Respectability: Tensions in the Ecological Society of America, 1915–1979." Ph.D. diss., Cornell University, 1994.
Tobey, Ronald C. *Saving the Prairies.* Berkeley: University of California Press, 1981.
Tomlinson, H. M. *Out of Soundings.* London: Heinemann Ltd., 1931.
———. *Sea and Jungle.* New York: E. P. Dutton & Co., 1921.
Turner, James Crewdon. *Reckoning With the Beast: Animals, Pain, and Humanity in the Victorian Mind.* Baltimore: Johns Hopkins University Press, 1980.
Turner, James S. *The Chemical Feast: The Nadar Report.* New York: Grossman Publisher, 1970.
Turner, Thomas B. *Heritage of Excellence: The Johns Hopkins Medical Institutions, 1914–1947.* Baltimore: Johns Hopkins University Press, 1974.
Tuveson, Ernest Lee. *Millennium and Utopia: A Study in the Background of the Idea of Progress.* Berkeley: University of California Press, 1949.
Udall, Stewart L. *The Quiet Crisis.* New York: Holt, Rinehart and Winston, 1963.
———. *The Quiet Crisis and the Next Generation.* Salt Lake City, UT: Gibbs and Smith Publisher, 1988.

U.S. Congress, Senate Subcommittee on Reorganization and International Organizations of the Committee on Government Operations. "Interagency Coordination in Environmental Hazards (Pesticides)." 88th Congress, 1st Session, Part I, 16, 22, 23 May & 4, 25 June 1963. Washington, D.C.: Government Printing Office, 1964. Hearings. "Statement by Rachel Carson," 4 June 1963, 206–248.

U.S. Environmental Protection Agency. *The Guardian: Origins of the EPA*. Washington, D.C.: U.S. Environmental Protection Agency, 1992.

"The Uses of Pesticides: A Report of the President's Scientific Advisory Committee." The White House. Washington, D.C.: Government Printing Office, 15 May 1963.

Van den Bosch, Robert. *The Pesticide Conspiracy*. New York: Doubleday and Co., 1978.

van der Post, Laurens. *Venture to the Interior*. New York: William Morrow and Co., 1951.

van Loon, Hendrik Villem. *Ships and How They Sailed*. New York: Simon & Schuster, 1935.

———. *The Story of the Pacific*. New York: Harcourt, Brace, and Company, 1940.

———. *The Story of Mankind*. New York: Liveright, 1951.

———. *Van Loon's Lives with Illustrations by the Author*. New York: Simon & Schuster, 1942.

Veglahn, Nancy. *Women Scientists*. New York: Facts On File, Inc., 1991.

Vogt, William. *Road to Survival*. New York: William Sloane Associates, Inc., 1948.

Wagner-Martin, Linda. *Telling Women's Lives: The New Biography*. New Brunswick, NJ: Rutgers University Press, 1994.

Walker, J. Samuel. "The Controversy Over Radiation Safety: A Historical Overview." *Journal of the American Medical Association*, 4 August 1989, 664–668.

"War on Insects." *Time*, 27 August 1945, 65.

Wareham, Wendy. "Rachel Carson's Early Years." *Carnegie Magazine* 58, no. 6 (November/December1986), 20–23, 27.

Warner, Deborah Jean. *Graceanna Lewis*. Washington, D.C.: Smithsonian Institution Press, 1979.

———. "Science Education for Women in Antebellum America." *ISIS* 246 (1979), 58–67.

Watkins, T. H. *Righteous Pilgrim: The Life and Times of Harold L. Ickes, 1874–1952*. New York: Henry Holt and Company, Inc., 1990.

Weart, Spencer. *Nuclear Fear: A History of Images*. Cambridge, MA: Harvard University Press, 1988.

Webster, Bayard. "The Lasting But Partial Influence of *Silent Spring*." *The New York Times*, 9 January 1997.

Weeks, Edward. *Writers and Friends*. Boston: Atlantic–Little Brown, 1981.

Weinberg, Arthur, and Lila Weinberg. "Where Are Today's Muckrakers?" *Saturday Review*, 9 July 1966, 54–55.

Weiner, Douglas R. "Demythologizing Environmentalism." *Journal of the History of Biology* 25, no. 3 (September 1992), 385–412.

Weir, Gary. "Up and Running: A History of Naval Oceanography." Washington, D.C.: Naval Historical Center, mss.

Weisgall, Jonathan M. *Operation Crossroads: The Atomic Tests at Bikini Atoll*. Annapolis, MD: Naval Institute Press, 1994.

Weiskel, Timothy. "The Ecological Lessons of the Past: An Anthropology of Environmental Decline." *The Ecologist* 19, no. 3 (May 1989), 98–103.

Wentzell, Greg Webster. "Wilderness and the American Mind: The Social Construction of Nature in Environmental Romanticism from Thoreau to Dillard." Ph.D. diss., Miami University, 1993.

Westcott, Cynthia. "Experts Review Pesticide Progress." *The New York Times*, 17 January 1965.
———. "Half Truths or Whole Story? A Review of *Silent Spring*." Manufacturing Chemists Association, 1962.
———. *Plant Doctoring Is Fun*. Princeton, NJ: D. Van Nostrand Company, Inc., 1957.
———. "The Question Has Two Sides." *The National Gardener* (September/October 1962), 30–31.
———. "Spray Chemicals: Are They Really Dangerous?" *American Home* 12 (March 1963), 86–88.
[White, E. B.]. "DDT" in "Talk of the Town." *The New Yorker*, 26 May 1945, 18.
White, Joseph B. C. "Rachel Carson." In *Famous Men and Women of Pittsburgh*, ed. Lenore R. Elkus. Pittsburgh: Pittsburgh History and Landmark Foundation, 1981.
Whitfield, Stephen J. *The Culture of the Cold War*. Baltimore: Johns Hopkins University Press, 1991.
Whitten, Jamie L. *That We May Live*. Princeton, NJ: D. Van Nostrand, 1966.
Whorton, James. *Before Silent Spring: Pesticides and Public Health in Pre-DDT America*. Princeton, NJ: Princeton University Press, 1974.
Wiesner, Jerome B. *Where Science and Politics Meet*. New York: McGraw-Hill Book Company, 1961.
Wild, Peter. *Pioneer Conservationists of Eastern America*. Missoula, MO: Mountain Press Publishing, 1986.
Wilkinson, Ruth Mary. "Fifty Years Ago When I Was a College Girl." *Tradition* 1 (1979), 5–6.
Williams, Dennis C. *The Guardian: EPA's Formative Years, 1970–1973. EPA 202-K-93-002*. Washington, D.C.: U.S. Environmental Protection Agency, April 1993.
Williams, Terry Tempest. "The Spirit of Rachel Carson." *Audubon* 94, no 4 (July/August 1992), 104–107.
Williamson, Henry. *Salar the Salmon*. Boston: Little, Brown and Co., 1935.
———. *Tarka the Otter*. New York: E. P. Dutton Co., Inc., 1928.
Winkler, Allan M. "A 40-Year History of Civil Defense." *Bulletin of the Atomic Scientists* 40 (June 1984), 16–22.
———. *Life Under a Cloud: American Anxiety About the Atom*. New York: Oxford University Press, 1993.
Wood, James P. *Of Lasting Interest: The Story of Reader's Digest*. New York: Doubleday, 1967.
Woody, Thomas. *A History of Women's Education in the United States*, vol. 2. New York: Science Press, 1929.
Worster, Donald. "Ecology of Order and Chaos." *Environmental History Review* 14, nos. 1–2 (March 1990), 1–18.
———. *Nature's Economy: A History of Ecological Ideas*. New York: Cambridge University Press, 1977.
———. *The Wealth of Nature*. New York: Oxford University Press, 1993.
Worster, Donald, ed. *The Ends of the Earth: Perspectives on Modern Environmental History*. New York: Cambridge University Press, 1988.
Worzel, J. Lamar, Chaim L. Perkeris, and Maurice Ewing. *Propagation of Sound in the Ocean: Explosion Sounds in Shallow Water*. New York: Geological Society of America, 1948.
Zakin, Susan. *Coyotes and Town Dogs: Earth First! and the Environmental Movement*. New York: Viking Press, 1993.

Index